ULTIMATE
FOOD JOURNEYS

ULTIMATE
FOOD JOURNEYS

THE WORLD'S BEST DISHES & WHERE TO EAT THEM

LONDON, NEW YORK, MELBOURNE,
MUNICH AND DELHI

LIST MANAGER Christine Stroyan
MANAGING EDITOR Julie Oughton
SENIOR EDITOR Sadie Smith
DESIGN MANAGER Mabel Chan
DESIGNER Tracy Smith
SENIOR DTP DESIGNER Jason Little

SENIOR CARTOGRAPHER Casper Morris
PRODUCTION CONTROLLER Sophie Argyris

PUBLISHER Vivien Antwi

Produced for Dorling Kindersley by

cobaltid

The Stables, Wood Farm, Deopham Road,
Attleborough, Norfolk NR17 1AJ
www.cobaltid.co.uk

EDITORS Louise Abbott, Sarah Tomley,
Marek Walisiewicz

DESIGN AND PICTURE RESEARCH Paul Reid, Darren Bland

First Published in Great Britain in 2011
by Dorling Kindersley Limited
80 Strand, London WC2R 0RL

11 12 13 10 9 8 7 6 5 4 3 2 1

Printed and bound in Singapore by Tien Wah Press

We're trying to be cleaner and greener:

• we recycle waste and switch things off
• we use paper from responsibly
managed forests whenever possible
• we ask our printers to actively reduce
water and energy consumption
• we check out our suppliers' working
conditions – they never use child labour

Find out more about our values and
best practices at www.dk.com

Every effort has been made to ensure that this book is as up-to-date as
possible at the time of going to press. Some details, however, such as
telephone numbers, opening hours, prices, and travel information are liable
to change. The publishers cannot accept responsibility for any consequences
arising from the use of this book, nor for any material on third-party websites,
and cannot guarantee that any website address in this book will be a suitable
source of travel information. We value the views and suggestions of our readers
very highly. Please write to: Publisher, DK Travel Guides, Dorling Kindersley,
80 Strand, London, WC2R 0RL, or email travelguides@uk.dk.com.

www.traveldk.com

MAIN COVER IMAGE: Dusk over Santorini, Greece
HALF TITLE PAGE IMAGE: Grilling sardines, Algarve, Portugal
TITLE PAGE IMAGE: Outdoor market, Kota Bharu, Malaysia

Contents

Left to right A colourful fruit stall at a Mexican market; fresh-caught mackerel, Maine, USA; South African white wine on the Cape Town waterfront; a dim sum window menu in Hong Kong

Introduction

Somewhere in the world, it is always time for dinner. That happy fact is one of the joys of travel, as much a part of the holiday experience as visiting a destination's top sights. Rome offers the thrill of walking in the footsteps of the Caesars inside the Roman Forum and gazing heavenwards at the Biblical tales that Michelangelo splashed across the ceiling of the Sistine Chapel. Yet the cuisine of the Eternal City is equally unforgettable. After a day of sightseeing, earthy fried artichokes – *carciofi alla giudia* – await in a neighbourhood trattoria where the white-shirted waiter balances plates over his head as he weaves between tightly packed tables. There is no better way of finding out what makes a nation tick than through its culinary traditions.

> *Food does more than satisfy hunger – it awakens the senses and becomes the touchstone of memory.*

Food does so much more than satisfy hunger – it awakens the senses and becomes the touchstone of memory. Anyone who has ever visited Marrakech associates the lemony tang of a Moroccan chicken tagine with the phantasmagorical scene of evening dining on Jemaa el-Fna, the medina's central square. One nibble and it all floods back: the scent of wood smoke, calls to prayer rising from surrounding mosques, the nasal flutes of snake charmers, the deepening colour of the sky as it arches from dusky rose to inky blue. Even months later, a single bite can summon up happy memories of an entire holiday.

But food is more than memory's trigger: it also recalls the deep history of a place. Long after people change their language, their dress, and even their religion, they continue cooking like their ancestors. Fresh food markets, many of which are featured in these pages, are tangible links between past and present. Winding mountainside streets and elaborate Spanish Baroque churches make Ecuador's Quito the best-preserved colonial city in the Americas. Yet its market stalls brimming with potatoes speak of an era when Andean peasants first domesticated the humble spud, centuries before the conquistadors or even the Incas. Hungry travellers who tuck into a hearty bowl of the Ecuadoran potato stew, *locro de papa*, savour history one bite at a time.

In contrast to the epic sweep of the centuries, family traditions are often inextricably tied to the simple act of dining. A traveller in the right place at the right time might feel like a member of the extended clan. For many families in Rio de Janeiro, Sunday would be incomplete without a swim in the gentle surf and a romp on the sands of Ipanema Beach, immortalized in the bossa nova tune *The Girl from Ipanema*. Equally important is the afternoon gathering at an Ipanema restaurant to share a large casserole

Below (left and centre) A luxury chocolate shop in Brussels, Belgium; women selling vegetables at a street market in Jaisalmer, Rajasthan, India

of the black-bean-and-sausage stew called *feijoada*. Food sets the rhythm of the day in the land of the samba – and around the world.

This book explores more than 125 destinations around the globe, with itineraries that pinpoint must-see attractions, from the dimly lit tango halls of Buenos Aires to the mirrored walls of the Jain Temple on Mumbai's Malabar Hill. Because taste and place are often inseparable, the book also identifies signature dishes and dining experiences for each destination. Riding the Star Ferry across Victoria Harbour and haggling over carvings in the Jade Market are don't-miss experiences for every traveller to Hong Kong. So is eating dim sum in a crowded restaurant – summoning the rolling carts of steamed delights until finally tasting the perfect *har gau* (shrimp dumpling).

The hundreds of restaurant recommendations have been hand picked by the authors for unsurpassed versions of a destination's signature dish. They also identify other places to find the dishes in the region (where you can sometimes try interesting regional variations) and even around the world. The dining spots range from cosy one-room *bouchons* in Lyon to a theatrical 900-seat duck restaurant in Beijing, from brightly lit 24-hour taco stands in Mexico City to lobster shacks on floating docks along the craggy Maine coast. They share a single characteristic: authenticity.

Encountering a familiar food in its birthplace is one pleasure of any journey. From a hillside vista, a traveller can drink in the sweep of Naples: its red-tile rooftops cascading down to the crescent harbour, the ominous volcanic peak of Vesuvius on the horizon, the garden isles of Capri and Ischia bobbing in the bay. Down in the pulsing heart of the city, a tangle of Vespas stands outside every pizzeria as their riders wait for bubbling pies to emerge from wood-fired beehive ovens.

Travel can also unveil surprising culinary experiences and new flavours. Mozambique's capital Maputo, for example, fuses African heart and Mediterranean style. At every turn it is as spicy and exotic as the piquant chilli-based piri-piri sauce ladled over barbecued chicken and prawns at the city's finest

Encountering a familiar food in its birthplace is one pleasure of any journey.

restaurants and casual roadside stands. Whatever your destination, this book offers the promise of a good meal and convivial surroundings at the end of the day.

Nearly two centuries ago, French epicure Jean Anthelme Brillat-Savarin wrote, "Tell me what you eat, and I will tell you who you are." The food experiences presented in this book will certainly leave you fulfilled, both in body and in spirit.

Below right Open-air food stall vendor serving spicy tea and snacks in Jemaa el-Fna, Marrakech, Morocco

Above A traditional neighbourhood restaurant in Paris, France, offering bistro fare, patisserie and ice creams

POM'CANNELLE

RESTAURANT
SALON DE THE
PATISSERIES
GLACES

DEGUSTATION
DE GLACES
ET SORBETS
DE LA MAISON
BERTHILLON

Europe

The Flavours of
Europe

From the Silk Road gateway of Tbilisi, Georgia, and the rolling plains of Portugal's Alentejo to the volcanic islands of Sicily and the chill highlands of Scotland, the European continent is a complex patchwork of landscapes, cultures and cuisines. The tale of its tables is a celebration of local products augmented by the spoils of empire, the fruits of trade and the enthusiastic embrace of meats, vegetables and cooking techniques from North Africa, Asia Minor and the Americas.

Certain flavours pale when uprooted. The rich-tasting Greek fava bean becomes a plain-Jane pulse in other soils. Shavings of Italian black truffles lend an earthy musk to pastas and risottos wherever they're used, but never with such piquancy as in the dishes of Umbria. The exquisite Roman artichoke anywhere else is just another globe thistle, while the distinctive basil and olive oil of Genoa combine to make Ligurian pesto the green queen of pasta cuisines.

Warm water or cold, sweet or salt – the oceans, lakes and rivers of Europe are the starting point for many iconic dishes, from steamed mussels in Brussels to fried fish on Whitby's North Sea strand. The crystalline Adriatic waters of Croatia teem with succulent scampi – all the better cooked with tomato, garlic and white wine. In the Caspian Sea, armour-plated sturgeon produce delicious, rich caviar, while the pink-fleshed salmon from the mouths of icy Norwegian rivers are salt-cured to create the pungent delicacy, gravadlax.

> *Salmon from the mouths of icy Norwegian rivers are salt-cured to create the pungent delicacy, gravadlax.*

Across Europe, cooks make fish stews that are virtual census counts of their harbours. Marseille bubbles with bouillabaisse spiked with a garlicky *rouille*, while Barcelona sings the light opera of fish known as *zarzuela*. Far to the north, the white fish of Belgian rivers form the toothy basis of Ghent's creamy *waterzooi*. All three fish stews rely on the ethereal but haunting overtones of saffron, the crocus spice brought to Europe in the North African conquest of Iberia. The Moors left an even more indelible stamp on European cuisine by introducing the short-grained rices essential to Valencia's seafood-studded paellas and Italy's unctuous, saffron-scented *risotto milanese*. Masters of metallurgy, the Moors also introduced the clamshell-shaped steaming vessel that became the Portuguese *cataplana*, though it took the Portuguese Christians to concoct the nation's signature dish of pork and clams.

New World Ingredients

Iberian seafarers revolutionized European cuisine with their New World culinary finds. Potatoes swiftly took hold in central Europe, forming the basis of the Swiss rösti, the *Reiberknödel* dumpling of

Right The vineyards of Burgundy, France, play an important role in the area's cuisine
Below Alfresco dining in Istanbul, Turkey, opposite the 17th-century Blue Mosque

Munich, and the *patatnik* pie of Bulgaria's Rhodope mountains. Seville's refreshing cold salad soup, gazpacho, was born with the landing of New World capsicum peppers and sweet tomatoes. Few New World plants had the transformative impact of the tomato, so perfectly matched to mozzarella cheese, fragrant basil and fulsome olive oil in Capri's *insalata caprese*. Mount the same ingredients on a thin bread crust – but with the tomato strained and lightly cooked – and the combination becomes Naples' pizza Margherita, a dish that now graces tables across the globe.

Changing Traditions

Many culinary traditions of Europe embrace the same informality as pizza. Spanish tapas are often eaten with the fingers or skewered with a toothpick. The bite-sized meze of Istanbul reprise the old Ottoman empire, from the stuffed vine leaves called dolmades (shared with the cuisine of Greece) to the aubergine salads, little meatballs, white cheese and sliced melons of the far reaches of Asia Minor. The twin themes of bounty and hospitality underpin such a feast – concepts echoed far to the north with the Swedish smorgasbord buffet and its dishes of herring, eel, meatballs, potato casseroles, sliced meats and fat sausages.

Traditionally, Europeans are the world's great meat-eaters. Feasts can be as rustic as a Toulouse cassoulet of pork, sausages and beans, or Burgundy's braised beef stew, or as ceremonial as the roast haunch of beef with all the trimmings that's key to the identity of the English. Similarly, few Greeks would give up their roast Easter lamb – nor the *Madrileños* their mixed *cocido* hotpot, the Berliners their hearty braised pork knuckle, or the Alsatians the tangy pickled vegetables and rich sausages of their *choucroute garnie*. No German worth his or her salt would pass up the spicy pot roast known as sauerbraten, while any Scot worth a tartan feasts on haggis every Burns Night.

But Europeans also love to turn tradition on its head. English pub cooks have transformed the leaden repasts of yesteryear into the bright, fresh-ingredient cooking of the gastropubs. The master chefs of Spain's San Sebastián married inventive genius with Basque traditions to revolutionize fine dining in Spain – and, by example, across Europe and the Americas.

The master chefs of Spain's San Sebastián married inventive genius with Basque traditions.

Creative genius applies to European sweets as well, from pistachio and honey confections like Anatolian baklava to the elaborate torten of Salzburg, from the simple cream-filled *pasteis de nata* of Lisbon to the textural perfection and simple grace of a Parisian *macaron* delicately filled with a chocolate ganache. In Europe, the French say it best: *Bon appétit!*

Left Cakes and pastries were raised to the level of an art form in the patisseries of France
Below A restaurant terrace in Vernazza on the Cinque Terre coastline of Italy

LISBON PORTUGAL

Creamy Custard Tarts in Lisbon

The Tagus river meets the sea at Lisbon, and it was from the city's historic riverside district, Belém, that Portuguese explorers set sail, their discoveries creating an empire for Portugal. The most famous of all, Vasco da Gama, set his course for India here, and his fame is perhaps matched by a pastry first produced in Belém in 1837, and now the country's favourite treat.

Belém is an essential visit on any trip to Lisbon; its great monuments and buildings still shimmer with the wealth and glory of Portugal's Golden Age in the 16th century. Riches poured into the country through the discoveries of bold Portuguese explorers, who can be seen commemorated in the famous Monument to the Discoveries. The period gave birth to a magnificent architectural style known as Manueline (after the king, Dom Manuel I), and two defining examples are the highlights of any visit to Belém – the Torre de Belém and the Mosteiro dos Jerónimos, the stupendously decorated monastery that graces the riverside here. Elaborate sculpted detail virtually drips from its columns, vaults and window frames, with naturalistic and maritime motifs to the fore, from twisted ropes and seashells to entwined leaves and branches.

The monastery, museums, cultural centre, royal palace and botanic gardens at Belém add up to a great day out from the Portuguese capital. But for many visitors, the first stop is a pastry shop, to sample a small *pastel de nata* served warm from the oven, its flaky pastry slightly crunchy to the bite, the creamy custard blistered by the heat. Three or four bites and it's gone, but it's a fleeting taste that will conjure fond memories of Portugal long after you've returned home.

The Portuguese take on the custard tart is actually one of its more restrained confections — other pastry and pudding recipes commonly use a dozen eggs, mounds of sugar and lashings of cream, but the *pastel de nata* is simple and rather elegant, calling for nothing more than well-made puff pastry and a modest, if rich, cream-custard filling. Like many traditional Portuguese tarts and desserts it owes its origins to an unsung pastry chef in a religious order, in this case from Belém's Jerónimos monastery. Selling pastries to supplement church income was once a common sideline, and since 1837 the custard tarts have been inextricably linked with one particular pastry shop and café near the monastery, the Antiga Confeitaria de Belém, which remains in business today. This is why in Lisbon the tart is known as a *pastel de Belém* — but everywhere else in the country, you need only ask for a *pastel de nata*, or even simply a *nata*, to sample this sweet favourite.

Above The Torre de Belém *(far right in picture)* was built as a defence and ceremonial gateway to Lisbon by Portugal's king João II, sponsor of great explorers

---

What Else to Eat

Fish and shellfish are Lisbon specialities, and there's an entire central street – **Rua das Portas de Santo Antão** – devoted to seafood restaurants. The painted Portuguese tiles known as *azulejos* are another typical feature of the city, and the two come together in Lisbon's traditional *cervejarias*, or beer halls, which are often elaborately tiled and serve great seafood. **Cervejaria Trindade** *(www.cervejariatrindade.pt)* is the oldest in the city and magnificently decorated with Masonic imagery. Lisbon is also home to populations of immigrants from Portugal's former colonies of Brazil, Angola, Mozambique and Goa, and they have endowed the city with some great ethnic eateries — try **Comida de Santo** *(www.comidadesanto.pt)* for spicy Brazilian dishes and punchy cocktails.

A Day in Belém

Central Lisbon spreads across various distinct neighbourhoods, from the medieval castle area to the 18th-century centre known as the Baixa. Belém is a small district lying around 7 km (4 miles) from Lisbon city centre, and its historic sights and monuments make a visit here a must.

MORNING If you're staying in Lisbon, take the tram along the **Rio Tejo** (Tagus river) to **Belém** (around 20 minutes), getting off near the **Mosteiro dos Jerónimos**. Explore the grandiose monastery and its exquisite cloister before strolling along the landscaped riverfront, past the striking **Monument to the Discoveries** to the fanciful **Torre de Belém** (Belém Tower).

AFTERNOON Visit the engaging **Museu dos Coches** (carriage museum), then walk through the leafy pathways of the **Jardins do Ultramar** to reach the **Palácio Nacional da Ajuda**, an opulent 19th-century royal residence.

EVENING For drinks with a river view, and to sample something from a rich cultural programme spanning jazz to opera, visit the striking **Centro Cultural de Belém** (Belém Cultural Centre), situated opposite the monastery.

Essentials

GETTING THERE
Fly to Lisbon's international **airport**, Aeroporto de Lisboa, then take the **bus**, **train** or a **taxi** into the city centre. The **tram** to Belém departs from Praça do Comércio in Lisbon's Baixa neighbourhood.

WHERE TO STAY
Oasis (inexpensive) is a stylish city-centre backpackers' hostel. www.hostelsoasis.com
As Janelas Verdes (moderate) has lovely rooms in an intimate 18th-century town house. www.heritage.pt
Solar dos Mouros (expensive) is a boutique hotel five minutes from the city centre with wonderful views. www.solardosmouros.com

TOURIST INFORMATION
Rua do Arsenal 15, Lisbon; www.visitlisboa.com

The Best Places to Eat Pasteis de Nata

Antiga Confeitaria de Belém
moderate

Despite the charms of the riverside in Belém, it's hard not to make a beeline for the Antiga Confeitaria, the "old pastry shop", but you can reassure yourself that it's just as much a cultural highlight as the nearby monastery and other attractions. The busy, traffic-choked street outside gives way to a typically Portuguese tiled and polished interior, the vaulted rooms lined with antique *azulejo* tiles. There's a bustling takeaway counter and café tables inside, and while a score of different cakes and pastries vie for attention, there's only one real choice for aficionados — a *pastel de Belém* (ask for *pasteis de Belém* if you want several), made to the same recipe since the shop first opened in 1837. They're sprinkled with ground cinnamon in the traditional manner (not all cafés serve them this way), and while most Portuguese people would take one with an espresso coffee (known here as a *bica*), it's also perfectly in order to have a pot of tea.

Rua de Belém 84–92, Belém, Lisbon; open Jun–Sep: 8am–midnight daily; Oct–May: 8am–11pm daily; www.pasteisdebelem.pt

Also in Lisbon

To enjoy a custard tart with a view, try the elegant if slightly touristy cafés on central Lisbon's main square, the Rossio, or the stately **Confeitaria Nacional** *(www.confeitarianacional.com; moderate)* on the adjacent Praça da Figueira. Other famous cafés in the capital, each with tantalizing cakes and pastries, include **Martinho da Arcada** *(+351 218 879 259; moderate)*, an old literary haunt under the arches on Praça do Comércio, and the uptown and very ornate **Café Versailles** *(+351 213 546 340; moderate)*.

Also in Portugal

There are traditional cafés in every town and city that serve an excellent *pastel de nata*. In Porto, try the beautifully decorated **Café Majestic** *(+351 22 200 3887; moderate)*. In the medieval university city of Coimbra, the **Café Santa Cruz** *(www.cafesantacruz.com; inexpensive)* serves delicious *pasteis de nata* in the vaulted rooms of a former monastery.

Around the World

In any city with a large Portuguese population you can be guaranteed to find a *pastel de nata*, from London to Luanda. It's a different matter just across the border in Spain, however, which has its own, very different, pastry-making heritage. But in Barcelona's excellent **A Casa Portuguesa** *(www.acasaportuguesa.com; moderate)*, a deli-cum-café in the hip suburb of Gràcia, they serve a *pastel de nata* every bit as good as those made in Portugal.

Above *Pasteis de nata* are traditionally served warm, often with a generous sprinkling of cinnamon

Right Home of the *pastel de nata*, the Mosteiro dos Jerónimos in Belém is a much more elaborate confection, in Portuguese late-Gothic style

BEAUNE FRANCE

Tender Beef in Wine Country

Almost every French province has its own version of a beef stew, but vine-rich Burgundy's boeuf bourguignon has to be the most famous, and nowhere is it better made than in its birthplace. Perched in the centre of the Côte d'Or wine region, the pretty town of Beaune is the perfect base for exploring the vineyards and cuisine of this exceptional part of France.

Burgundy has more than its share of legendary, grape-related names: Pommard, Romanée-Conti, Nuits-Saint-George, Montrachet. The red wines of this region are made from Pinot Noir grapes, the whites from Chardonnay. The greatest Burgundies hail from the celebrated Côte d'Or, which is divided into the Côte de Nuits and the Côte de Beaune – and the latter begins just north of the town of Beaune. Each village in the Burgundy region is like a small realm in the empire of wine, and majestic Beaune is its proud capital.

Historic buildings with multicoloured tiled roofs line the cobbled streets of Beaune. Two of the most outstanding are the Hôtel des Ducs, now a wine museum, and the Hôtel Dieu des Hospices de Beaune, a masterpiece of medieval architecture built in 1443 as a hospital for the poor, dubbed the "Palace of the Poor" because of its Gothic grandeur. Now a museum, each November it throws open its doors for a charity wine auction, at which wines from vineyards gifted to the Hospice go under the hammer. The auction dates back to 1859 and a portion of the money raised still goes towards helping the sick, these days via the modern Beaune Hospital.

Beaune's streets are filled with palate-tempting restaurants and shops selling home-made jams, chocolates, cakes, aniseed sweets and fruit liqueurs. The twice-weekly market in the centre of the old town is always a hive of activity, and the place to gather ingredients for a picnic lunch among the vines: *cabrion* (a goat's cheese ripened in grape husks), farm-fresh terrines and pâtés, or a just-roasted Bresse chicken with crispy baby potatoes.

Local cooking is, unsurprisingly, awash with wine. "A la Bourguignon" denotes a dish made with plenty of wine, little white onions, a few mushrooms and bacon – such as boeuf bourguignon, or *oeufs à la bourguignonne* (eggs poached in red wine). Burgundy's boeuf bourguignon isn't just a pot of stewed beef; this perennial wintry favourite must be made with Charolais beef, France's most tender and the region's best, doused in nothing else but a Burgundy red. The meat is braised with the wine, stock, onions, bacon and mushrooms, so that as the sauce reduces, the flavour intensifies. In days gone by, before it morphed into a high-brow classic, boeuf bourguignon was simple farmers' food and the long, slow cooking process evolved to tenderize tough cuts of meat. Even today, this is not a dish in a hurry.

A Day in Beaune

Beaune, an important cultural centre in the Middle Ages, is a medieval city rich in history and tradition as well as a great place for food, wine-tasting and shopping.

MORNING Soak up the past at **Hôtel Dieu des Hospices de Beaune**, pausing at red-curtained cubicles lining the "Room of the Poor" where the sick once languished, before stepping into the courtyard to see the dazzling glazed tile roof. Visit the 12th-century **Basilique Collégiale Notre Dame** for a glimpse of Gothic Beaune.

AFTERNOON Explore food and wine shops in **rue Carnot** and **rue Monge**. Join a mustard-tasting tour at **La Moutarderie Fallot**, a family mustard mill in operation since 1840, or visit a wine cellar in town such as **Bouchard Père & Fils**. This has one of the greatest collections of Burgundy vintages and is housed in the glorious 15th-century **Château de Beaune**; the underground cellars have 7 m- (23 ft-) thick walls.

EVENING Stroll the **old town** to see the antique tiles and façades of buildings lit up against the night sky. Cosy up on a terrace with a velvety Burgundy.

Essentials

GETTING THERE
Aéroport Dijon Bourgogne is 30 km (18 miles) from Beaune. **High-speed trains** operate from Paris, Lyon and Dijon.

WHERE TO STAY
Les Jardins de Loïs (inexpensive) is a serene and smart B&B. *www.jardinsdelois.com*
Via Mokis (moderate) is a modern hotel in the heart of the old town. *www.viamokis.com*
Hôtel de la Poste (expensive) is Beaune's oldest hotel; its stylish rooms feature French fabrics. *www.hoteldelapostebeaune.com*

TOURIST INFORMATION
1 rue de l'Hôtel-Dieu; *www.ot-beaune.fr*

Above The Hôtel Dieu des Hospices de Beaune was built at the end of the Hundred Years War, when Burgundy suffered both poverty and famine

Left The vineyards of the Hautes-Côtes de Beaune spill down the long slopes of the Côte d'Or escarpment, seen here in autumn

Above A great boeuf bourguignon depends on the integrity of its ingredients, specifically Charolais beef and red Burgundy wine

The Best Places to Eat Boeuf Bourguignon

Ma Cuisine inexpensive

Tucked down a side street off the Place Carnot, this cosy restaurant run by husband-and-wife team Pierre and Fabienne has amassed thousands of fans over the years, not just for the well-cooked regional specialities they turn out but equally for the wine list (featuring more than 700 bottles) – this is Burgundy, after all. Ma Cuisine is resolutely, unrepentantly old-fashioned, and that's exactly why people keep coming back. If you crave waistline-friendly, edgy food, give this rustic roost a wide berth. The entreés sound a roll call for old rural France: *jambon persillé* (cubed ham with parsley in aspic), Burgundy's famed *escargots* (snails) served in their shells brimming with parsley butter, and wobbly *oeufs en meurette* (eggs poached in red wine). Main courses run from roasted whole pigeon to soul-warming favourites such as *coq au vin* (chicken in – of course – red wine) and plush, dark, meltingly tender boeuf bourguignon. To finish, try a fresh fruit tart or an eggy *crème brûlée*.

Passage Sainte-Hélène, Beaune; open for lunch and dinner Mon, Tue, Thu & Fri; +33 380 223 022

Also in Beaune

The cool contemporary decor of Bruno Monnoir's **Le Benaton** *(www.lebenaton.com; expensive)* is typified by the tan ostrich-leather chairs. It is advance warning that there are no fusty old classics here; instead you can expect a sophisticated and inventive reworking of Burgundy's culinary traditions. Monnoir's highly refined take on boeuf bourguignon features "nuts" of beef cheek confited in red wine.

Also in France

Those old-world Paris bistros with proper linen tablecloths and food that deserves a return visit seem to be a disappearing breed but **Josephine Chez Dumonet** *(+33 1 4548 5240; moderate)*, in the city's 6th arrondissement, is valiantly fighting the trend – and winning. French classics dominate this menu: steak tartare, crispy-skin *confit de canard*, omelette with truffles (in season, of course) and spoon-tender boeuf bourguignon. This restaurant is reason enough for a Paris stopover.

Around the World

Bustling **Brasserie Les Halles** *(www.leshalles. net/brasserie; inexpensive)* is a typical Parisian restaurant serving up a host of French classics – except it's doing it in New York. The kitchen home of chef, author and straight-talking television host Anthony Bourdain, the restaurant takes its name from Paris's once-thriving, now defunct, market district Les Halles. It's open from noon to midnight, so you can slake a craving for rib-sticking boeuf bourguignon almost any time of day.

Cookery Classes

A cooking class at **The Cook's Atelier** *(www. thecooksatelier.com)* kicks off in style with a glass of chilled *crémant*, Burgundy's bubbly. Marjorie Taylor's menu pays homage to the small artisan producers of the region. **La Terre d'Or** *(www.laterredor.com)* will arrange a session at the stove of a Michelin-starred restaurant with a wine maker on hand to discuss the best partner wines. Learn how to visually recognize, smell and taste regional wines in a three-hour crash course at **Ecole des Vins de Bourgogne** *(www.ecoledesvins-bourgogne.com)*. Longer sessions are also available.

Above The wood-fired ovens of Naples cook the thin, crusty-based pizzas to perfection in around 90 seconds

Above Local San Marzano tomatoes, *mozzarella di bufala* and basil raise the humble Margherita pizza from fast food to gourmet delight

A Day in Naples

Naples has superb and easy-to-reach art galleries, museums and city sights, with plenty for the discerning visitor.

MORNING Start in the lively district of **Spaccanapoli**. Its **Via San Gregorio Armeno** has a concentration of artisans' shops producing painstakingly handcrafted figures, furniture and accessories for the traditional *presepi* – Christmas Nativity scenes. Visit the impressive **Museo Nazionale Archeologico** in the **Piazza** to see the treasures – especially the mosaics and frescoes – unearthed at Pompeii.

AFTERNOON If you go to only one of Naples' numerous churches, make it the ornate **Duomo**. Then visit the impressive **Palazzo Reale**, home to the Spanish, Bourbon and French rulers.

EVENING Take a relaxing ride uphill on one of the famous **funicular railways**, inspiration for the 1880s song, *Funiculì Funiculà*. Essential for transporting hundreds of people on a day-to-day basis, they have all been modernized and now whisk passengers to their homes, and travellers to high spots with great views over the twinkling city lights.

Essentials

GETTING THERE
Naples' **Capodichino International Airport** has frequent **buses** to the city centre. Fast **trains** from many European cities pull in at Napoli Centrale station. The rapid **metro** lines, local **buses** and the historic **funicular railways** are all good ways to get around.

WHERE TO STAY
La Casa della Nonna (inexpensive) is simple and central. *www.lacasadellanonna.it*
Donna Regina B&B (moderate) has charming rooms in a centrally located, converted historic convent. *www.discovernaples.net*
Grand Hotel Parker's (expensive), a sumptuous 1870s hotel, has a superb terrace overlooking the Bay of Naples. *www.grandhotelparkers.it*

TOURIST INFORMATION
Via Santa Lucia 107; *www.inaples.it*

NAPLES ITALY

Perfect Pizza in Buzzing Naples

The bustling, southern-Italian city of Naples may at first seem chaotic, but visitors quickly fall under the spell of this under-appreciated gem and its rich artistic heritage. Naples is quintessential Mediterranean Italy, and as a region it's famous for its delicious tomatoes and outstanding mozzarella cheese, so it's not surprising that it's also the undisputed "home of the pizza".

A sprawling city of dramatic contrasts, Naples displays its regal past in the shape of impressive castles and magnificent palaces erected by Spanish and Bourbon rulers from the 16th to the 19th centuries. But the city is best known for a more ancient event – the eruption of Vesuvius in AD 79. Still visible across the waters of the Bay of Naples, the volcano submerged the neighbouring Roman city of Pompeii in metres of ash and debris, wiping out its entire population.

Amazingly, the narrow streets of the historic heart of modern-day Naples still correspond to an ancient Greek-Roman grid. In this maze, life spills out into the public domain – people call to each other from windows, scooters zoom along doing their best to dodge pedestrians, and minuscule shops, neighbourhood churches and cafés juggle for precious space. Just as in centuries past, a lot of eating takes place outside, bought from open-air stalls and glass-fronted kiosks displaying tempting wares. The vast array of "fast" street food includes sweet and savoury treats, from sugary doughnuts and crispy chunks of potato to fried *arancini* rice balls stuffed with minced meat. There's even fried wrap-over pizza, though this oil-drenched snack is not to everyone's liking.

Originally fare for the poor, pizza has long been the flagship of Italian cuisine across the world. There are countless fanciful international toppings, but the most famous pizza of all is the classic Margherita. Invented by Neapolitan chef Raffaello Esposito in 1889 to honour a visiting Italian queen and the recently unified nation, it features the colours of the nation's flag: white (cheese), red (locally grown San Marzano tomatoes) and green (basil). Today, pizza marinara is a close favourite, its anchovies jostling for attention among black olives, garlic and sometimes capers.

Without a doubt, the best place to enjoy a pizza is at one of the numerous family-run pizzerias in Naples, which fill the air with an irresistible fragrance of sizzling mozzarella and fresh San Marzano tomatoes bubbling under a drizzle of Campania olive oil and a sprinkling of native oregano. Whatever the topping, there is complete agreement on how the pizza is to be consumed – immediately and on the spot.

Above Naples is spread out along the Bay of Naples, overlooked by Vesuvius

What Else to Eat

Naples is also famous for its rich cakes and heavenly desserts, and the city has a mouthwatering choice of *pasticceria*, where freshly baked sweet delights are showcased in glass-topped counters. **Sfogliatelle** are shell-shaped, multi-layered pastries flavoured with vanilla and filled with a delicious mixture of delicate ricotta cheese and morsels of candied orange. The epitome of sugar heaven is a **babà al rhum**, a mushroom-shaped sponge drenched in rum syrup and smothered in whipped cream. Probably introduced to Naples by the French cooks at court, it was created by an 18th-century Polish king, who named it after Ali Baba and the Forty Thieves, stories about whom he adored. Another special treat is a slice of **pastiera napoletana**, a celebratory Easter pie baked with ricotta cheese, candied citrus fruits and spices.

The Best Places to Eat Pizza

Antica Pizzeria Da Michele
inexpensive

The bare marble table tops and stark tiled walls don't put off the constant stream of diners who flock to this highly popular and long-standing Neapolitan establishment. Neither do the long queues. Everyone knows it's well worth the wait and there's a mouthwatering aroma to keep you company in the street. When your number's called, you are given a table amidst jovial groups of families and friends. The choice of liquid refreshment is limited to soft drinks, water or beer, all served in plastic cups. And ordering your meal doesn't take long either, as it's a simple choice between just two pizzas: the marinara or the Margherita. Both are spread with *passato* (puréed) San Marzano tomatoes from the nearby Sarno valley and topped with a fresh, smooth *fior di latte* cow's milk mozzarella from Agerola on the Amalfi coast. The huge, soft pizzas are served steaming straight from the oven, for delicious, immediate consumption.
Via Cesare Sersale, Naples; open 10am–11pm Mon–Sat; www.damichele.net

Also in Naples

Antica Pizzeria de Borgo Orefici (*+39 81 552 0996; moderate*) is a simple, family-run establishment tucked away down a narrow street that was once the heart of the goldsmiths' district. It has many faithful diners and the place can get busy. Toppings are generous and pizzas on offer include *miseria e nobiltà*: a catch-all pizza that's half marinara and half Margherita.

Also in Italy

Muro Frari (*www.murovinoecucina.it; moderate*) at San Polo 2604 in Venice is a modern restaurant offering gourmet pizzas with all manner of treats, such as porcini mushrooms, fresh buffalo mozzarella and smoked swordfish and tuna. Don't miss the delicious apéritifs with seasonal fresh fruit and sparkling Prosecco, which can be enjoyed outside in summer.

Around the World

Long queues form quickly outside **Grimaldi's Pizzeria** (*www.grimaldis.com; inexpensive*) at the foot of Brooklyn Bridge in New York. Regulars rub shoulders with celebrities among the trademark red-and-white check tablecloths. It's the coal-brick oven here that gives the pizzas their sought-after crisp crust and smoky flavour. A long list of toppings allows you to invent your very own pizza with your favourite flavours. In the UK, **Santoré** (*www. santorerestaurant.co.uk; inexpensive*) in London serves outstandingly good, authentic Neapolitan pizzas in lively Exmouth Market.

ALICANTE SPAIN

The Thousand Tastes of Spain

Straining towards the sea as it hunkers beneath a castle-topped mountain, Alicante is fishing port, yacht haven and beach resort in one. Called the "City of Light" for the bright wash of sun on its ancient streets, Alicante – like so many Spanish cities – comes most alive in the evening, when locals and holidaymakers gather around drinks and the savoury delights known as tapas.

Capital of the Costa Blanca, Alicante retains far more of its historic identity than nearby mega-resorts. The romance of its high and lonely Moorish castle contrasts with the elegance of Baroque buildings wedged onto steep medieval streets. Ultimately, Alicante is defined by the sea – trade route to Africa, boundless well of fish and rhythmic source of waves lapping pale, sandy beaches.

Once the holiday-makers have come down from the castle ramparts, or ambled back from Postiguet and Sant Joan beaches, Alicante gets its sea legs for the evening. As a cool ocean breeze stirs, people promenade down palm-lined Explanada de Espanya, the wide esplanade separating ancient city from modern seafront, paved with 6.6 million marble tiles laid in wave-patterns. A sudden urge to drink and snack overwhelms the city. It is time for tapas.

No-one knows when the tapas tradition began, but the practice of placing a small dish atop a glass to keep out the flies has evolved into Spain's most generous act of hospitality. An ingrained part of Spanish culture, tapas sampling lets visitors socialize elbow-to-elbow with fellow drinkers and diners at the bar. Although many tapas – from Jabugo mountain ham to La Mancha's ewe's milk cheeses and the ubiquitous tortilla – can be found across the country, each region also boasts its own specialities. To see what will be on the bars of Alicante at night, one need only visit the Mercado Central by day. The great slabs of red tuna and the clenched blue shells of mussels displayed on ice will become delicate tartares, seared bites or pink morsels in a tangy vinegar sauce. Few drinks better suit these explosively briny titbits than Fondillón, Alicante's unique, long-aged wine, with overtones of almonds, ginger, dates and dark dried fruits.

So superb are the tapas at Alicante's bars that it's tempting to stay put once you have found a rail to lean on. But inertia violates the unwritten rules of a night of tapas-hopping. Each establishment on the esplanade or in the narrow streets of the medieval quarter has a treat it does better than anyone else – so staying in one means missing the others. Eating tapas can be a means to stave off hunger until a typically late Spanish dinner (always after 10pm), or it can become dinner and the evening's entertainment all in one – in which case, it is perhaps wisest not to look down at the swirling, wave-patterned pavement on the way home.

A Day in Alicante

Alicante is one of Spain's major cities on the east coast, so has a much more "Spanish" feel than many of the surrounding Costa Blanca resort areas. The historic port, beautiful beaches, ideal climate and fabulous gastronomy have much to offer visitors.

MORNING Take the lift from Postiguet Beach through Benacantil mountain to the **Castell de Santa Bárbera**, expanded from a 9th-century Moorish castle, for panoramic views of the city and the coast.

AFTERNOON Visit the Baroque **Concatedral de San Nicolás de Bari** with its lovely images of saints painted on wooden panels. Try to decipher the Bible stories on the Baroque façade of **Santa María** church, and don't miss the twisted-barleycorn columns of the **Town Hall**. Leave time to relax on **Sant Joan beach**, easily reached by tram.

EVENING Immerse yourself in one of Spain's best tapas scenes. The splashiest bars are on the **Explanada de Espanya**, but seek out gastronomic heaven on narrow interior streets like Villegas and César Elguezábal.

Essentials

GETTING THERE
European and Spanish carriers fly to **Alicante airport**. Get around the city on foot or by **tram**.

WHERE TO STAY
Hostal Monges Palace (inexpensive) is family-run, with stylish small rooms in the historic centre. www.lesmonges.es
Melia Alicante (moderate) offers resort hotel amenities near the esplanade. www.solmelia.com
Hotel Spa Porta Maris & Suites del Mar (moderate) combines two luxury hotels on a downtown pier. www.hotelspaportamaris.com

TOURIST INFORMATION
www.alicanteturismo.com

Above Super-fresh ingredients of immaculate provenance and an eye for presentation put Alicante's tapas among Spain's finest

Left Fish and seafood such as *gambas* (prawns) and *langostinos* (langoustines) are specialities in this coastal fishing port

Below An extraordinary lift bored through the rock will take you to the Castell de Santa Bárbera, perched high above Alicante

Tapas Around the World

Tapas distil all of Spanish cuisine into perfect little snacks, making the nibbling of small savouries while drinking into a casual feast. The Spanish penchant for two-bite dining and its associated conviviality has swept the world, bringing Iberian dishes along for the ride.

ALICANTE

El Cisne de Oro inexpensive
Calle César Elguezábal 23; www.elcisnedeoro.com
This tile-encrusted traditional bar with hams hanging overhead captures the tastes of both land and sea – slices of mountain ham sit alongside plates of white anchovies in olive oil. The kitchen's own pungent aïoli enlivens both the potato salad and small rolls stuffed with pork and mushrooms.

Nou Manolín Restaurante & Bar moderate
Calle Villegas 3; www.noumanolin.com
One of the quintessential tapas spots, not just in Alicante but in all of Spain, Nou Manolín offers more than 50 different tapas every day in the ground-level bar. All the classics are on offer, as are dishes with a modern twist, from prawns in a spicy garlic sauce to sushi-grade slices of fresh red tuna.

La Taberna del Gourmet expensive
Calle San Fernando 10; www.latabernadelgourmet.com
The owners of this pioneer gastrobar are fanatical about sourcing the best fish, vegetables, fruits and meats and playing up the perfection of the produce. Excellent tapas choices include a fresh tomato salad with tuna belly or tempura-fried baby squid.

GRANADA, SPAIN

Granada's restaurants and bars offer Spain's most generous free tapas, making tapas-hopping an inexpensive way to dine. Dishes might escalate from potato salad to a small dish of stew as customers keep ordering drinks.

Bar Casa Julio inexpensive
Calle Hermosa, just off Plaza Nueva (no telephone)
There's no telling just how old Casa Julio might be, but the jam-packed bar looks little changed from the days before the Spanish Civil War. Speciality tapas here include several variations on octopus and squid – always best with red wine.

Below Bars groaning with tapas dishes welcome workers at the end of the day all over Spain **Bottom left** Air-dried *jamón serrano*, one of Spain's finest delicacies, is often hung from the ceiling **Right (top to bottom)** *Gambas* (prawns) from the grill with, in the background, marinated artichokes; tapas are always best shared, preferably with good red wine; a modern tapas bar in London

On the Menu

Albóndigas Meatballs that combine breadcrumbs with pork, veal, lamb or some combination of meats. They are served in either a brown sauce or a tomato sauce.

Almejas Clams served in the shells, often steamed with wine, herbs and vegetables.

Anchoas The small Spanish white anchovies, usually lightly poached and preserved in olive oil.

Berenjenas rebozadas A dish with North African origins, consisting of aubergine that is salted, breaded and fried in olive oil.

Boquerones Anchovies, either tinned in vinegar or fresh and deep-fried.

Chorizo A distinctive Spanish sausage with many regional variations. It usually contains pieces of cured ham as well as ground pork and is always strongly flavoured with Spanish paprika.

Croquetas These take many forms but most often feature minced cured ham or poached tuna. In both cases, the filling is blended with béchamel sauce, rolled in fine crumbs, and deep-fried in olive oil.

Gambas Shrimp or prawns (species can vary by season): served *a la plancha*, they are grilled whole with the heads on; *gambas al ajillo* are peeled shrimp that are fried in olive oil with copious quantities of fresh garlic.

Jamón serrano The air-dried mountain hams seen hanging from the ceilings of tapas bars, so concentrated and intense that servings are sliced paper-thin.

Morcilla A blood sausage or black pudding. As a tapa, it is usually sliced, fried in olive oil, and served with toothpicks.

In northern Spain, it is filled with pork fat, rice and onions, but in central and southern Spain the filler usually includes breadcrumbs and almonds.

Patatas bravas Named for the Madrid bar that invented them, fried potatoes served with a dip of paprika-laced aïoli (a very garlicky, mayonnaise-like sauce).

Pimientos rellenos Stuffed peppers: there are a number of varieties, the most common being small triangular peppers from the north (either green or red) filled with salt cod and whipped potato.

Queso manchego The famous aged sheep's milk cheese of La Mancha, usually sliced very thin and served in triangles.

Tortilla española Perhaps the most universal dish in Spain, a masterful combination of fried potatoes baked into a thick omelette, sliced and often eaten cold.

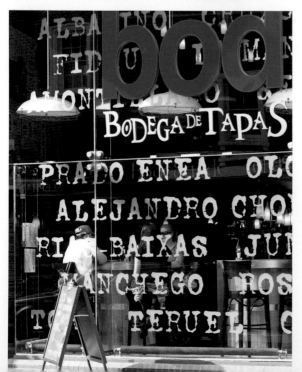

Taberna Salinas inexpensive
Calle de Elvira 13; www.tabernassalinas.com
Widely known for offering high quality at low prices, Salinas proffers tapas that are scaled-down versions of full recipe dishes: scrambled eggs with ham and fried potatoes, broad beans simmered with little pieces of ham or beef braised with sweet peppers.

Cunini Restaurante & Marisquería moderate
Plaza de Pescadería 14; +34 958 250 777
Appropriately for its location on the fishmongers' square, Cunini serves the best seafood tapas in Granada. Salt cod dishes or calamari are common first offerings — it could take three drinks before they bring out the prawns or crisply fried mullet.

NEW YORK, USA
Following the Spanish Civil War, thousands of Spaniards fled to New York and many made their homes in Manhattan's Chelsea neighbourhood. Few restaurants from that era remain, but New York has blossomed with contemporary tapas restaurants.

Boqueria moderate
53 West 19th Street; www.boquerianyc.com
Named for the famous Barcelona market, Boqueria ranges across Spain for its tapas, from the classic potato omelette to bacon-wrapped dates stuffed with almonds and blue cheese and a Catalan sauté of spinach, garbanzos, pine nuts, garlic and raisins.

Txikito moderate
240 Ninth Avenue; www.txikitonyc.com
Serving mostly Basque wines with its *pintxos* (as the Basques call tapas), Txikito pays homage to Spanish Basque cookery with dishes such as blistered peppers with sea salt, or a salad of Basque anchovies and bonito tuna on butter lettuce.

LONDON, UK
The English love affair with holidays in sunny Spain has translated into a boom in Spanish restaurants, especially in Bloomsbury and Soho. Most offer extensive tapas menus and a strong list of Spanish wines.

Navarro's inexpensive
67 Charlotte Street, W1; www.navarros.co.uk
With a menu (and wine list) more redolent of northern than southern Spain, the tapas at Navarro's are rib-sticking and satisfying — like the Galician tuna *empanada* (stuffed pastry), braised oxtail, and lentil stew with chorizo. Its red wine choices are splendid.

Barrafina moderate
54 Frith Street, W1; www.barrafina.co.uk
An intimate room with about two dozen stools around a counter, Barrafina has the crowd density to claim Spanish authenticity and the menu to match, from grilled bread smeared with tomato and olive oil to grilled quail with aïoli.

Tapas Brindisa moderate
18–20 Southwark Street, SE1; www.brindisa.com
The south London tapas bar of a famous Spanish food importer, Brindisa always has just the ingredients on hand for top-notch, authentic tapas like thin slices of *jamón ibérico*, intensely spicy Léon chorizo and the incomparable tinned anchovies of Galicia.

SYDNEY, AUSTRALIA
Although the expansion of Chinatown has nearly absorbed the old Spanish Quarter along Liverpool Street in central Sydney, Spanish tapas restaurants and bars are sprouting up all over the city as dining-by-the-nibble catches on.

Bodega inexpensive
216 Commonwealth Street, Surry Hills; www.bodegatapas.com

With a tapas menu that travels beyond Spain to embrace Latin America, Bodega serves authentic Spanish dishes like salt-cod-stuffed *piquillo* peppers and Argentine plates like beef *empanadas* with *criolla* sauce. The short, sweet dessert list is also a big hit.

Kika moderate
247 Victoria Street, Darlinghurst; www.kika.com.au
The colour splashes of this dynamic tapas bar could have been lifted from an early Pedro Almodóvar film, but dishes like deep-fried aubergine in parsley batter or barbecued pork fillets with blue cheese come straight from rustic Spanish cuisine.

El Toro Loco expensive
49–53 North Steyne, Manly; www.eltoroloco.com.au
The Crazy Bull is as bold as its name, bringing authentic Spanish cooking to Manly Beach with tapas like Jerez-style duck pâté, Madrid-style *cocido*, and Castilian lamb cutlets char-grilled with rosemary. Wines are a great mix of Spanish and Australian.

Above The Dugald Stewart monument on Calton Hill overlooking the city of Edinburgh

A Day in Edinburgh

The Scottish capital runs over seven hills, so there are plenty of places to get a good overview of the city and its glorious surroundings.

MORNING Immerse yourself in 1,500 years of Scottish history at **Edinburgh Castle** on its towering rock above **Princes Street Gardens**. Other high points are **Calton Hill**, with its smattering of monuments, and **Arthur's Seat**, which looks down on Holyrood Palace and the modern architecture of the Scottish Parliament.

AFTERNOON Enjoy modern art in imposing 18th-century surrounds at the **Dean Gallery** and **Scottish National Gallery of Modern Art**, which face each other across sculpture-dotted parkland. Then take a peaceful walk through the **Royal Botanic Garden**. This verdant paradise includes the largest collection of Chinese plants outside Asia, a highland Heath Garden and a towering 19th-century Palm House.

EVENING See Edinburgh's dark past at **The Real Mary King's Close**, a subterranean warren of 17th-century streets where actors bring long-dead former citizens back to life.

Essentials

GETTING THERE
Edinburgh's **international airport** has flights from European cities; Glasgow Airport, 96 km (60 miles away), has flights from long-haul departure points. There are **taxis** and a **bus** shuttle service to the city centre.

WHERE TO STAY
Albyn Town House (inexpensive) is a graceful Victorian house with hearty Scottish breakfasts. *www.albyntownhouse.co.uk*
Hotel Du Vin (moderate) in the Old Town is a former asylum turned into a calm haven, with a whisky snug. *www.hotelduvin.com*
The Witchery (expensive) is a 16th-century gem by Edinburgh Castle with opulently theatrical suites. *www.thewitchery.com*

TOURIST INFORMATION
www.visitscotland.com

Above The Edinburgh International Festival runs alongside its famous younger brother – the Fringe Festival – for three weeks in late summer

EDINBURGH SCOTLAND

Hearty Haggis in Edinburgh

Legendary Scottish bard Robert Burns celebrated his majestic capital Edinburgh as "Scotia's darling seat". The city's evocative history and grand architecture complement a deep love of ideas and culture, epitomized in its world-famous summer arts festival – but the Scots also prize the wild and rugged in life, and it's to this older, less rarified Scotland that haggis belongs.

Set back from the rugged shores of the wide Firth of Forth, Scotland's capital is cradled by hills and crags. The city combines the historic with the chic – grand architecture woven with ancient lanes lined with desirable boutiques. Overseen by its majestic castle, it is a place so old that even the "New Town" is made up of 200-year-old sweeping Georgian crescents.

In the 18th century the Edinburgh edition of Robbie Burns's *Poems* was published, including his ode "Address to a Haggis". Burns saw haggis as a symbol of Scottish life during those harsher times when it was essential to use as much as possible of a slain animal: for food, clothing and even something to write on. While other cuts could be dried for preservation, internal organs were far more perishable. So they were stuffed into the natural casing of the animal's stomach – forming "haggis" – and cooked on the spot.

Traditionally, haggis takes the minced "pluck" of a sheep (heart, liver and lungs), mixes it with onion, oatmeal, suet, spices, salt and stock, then stuffs it into a casing – today usually synthetic – to be simmered for around three hours. Its ingredients may not sound appealing, but the end result is richly meaty, with a nutty texture and delicious spicy savouriness.

On Burns Night, 25 January, the national dish is served with simple accompaniments of neeps (boiled turnips or swede) and tatties (mashed potato) – plus whisky, of course. But the growth of nationalist pride in recent years has led to haggis becoming increasingly popular all year round in Scotland, often with intriguing twists. Scotland's abundance of deer underpins a surge in venison haggis, while the country's significant Indian population has inspired haggis pakora, spiced with ginger, cumin seeds, coriander seeds, turmeric and garam masala.

Haggis was a hearty portable meal for those on the move: whisky-makers transporting their liquid gold across majestic Highland hills; merchants shipping wares across the choppy channels from the dramatically beautiful islands of Orkney and the Hebrides; and drovers taking animals from the heather-clad moors to the hungry cities. Eating haggis is to join the company of these intrepid travellers – an honour indeed.

Above Haggis with "tatties and bashit neeps" – mashed potato and swede or turnip

What Else to Eat

Fish underpins Caledonian classics such as **Arbroath smokies** (salted haddock smoked over beech and oak), which in turn can become part of **cullen skink** (a soup of smoked haddock, potatoes and onion). Other seafood enticements include hand-dived **scallops**, **Loch Etive mussels**, **turbot** and **lobster** from Scrabster, **oysters** from Skye and some of the world's best **salmon**. There's also superb meat, such as **Aberdeen Angus beef**, seaweed-fed **Orkney lamb**, game birds – like **grouse** – and superb **venison** from Scotland's rugged uplands. The sweet-toothed can enjoy **Tipsy Laird** (a Scottish sherry trifle) or **cranachan** (whipped cream, whisky, honey, raspberries and toasted oatmeal). **Scottish cheeses**, such as Arran Brie, whisky-coated Bishop Kennedy, Gruth Dhu (soft crowdie cheese) and Dunsyre Blue are a delight.

The Best Places to Eat Haggis

The Kitchin expensive

Opened in 2006 by husband and wife team Tom and Michaela Kitchin on Edinburgh's hip Leith waterfront, it took just six months for The Kitchin to gain a Michelin star. The restaurant showcases the best of Scotland's superb larder with inventive cooking that nods to fusion without ever over-reaching. When haggis appears here, it is transformed from its humble beginnings to a rare dish indeed, served with accompaniments of pickled turnip, foie gras and crispy potato galette. The range of daily menus provides varied themes and different price levels, from an expansive "Land And Sea Surprise Tasting Menu" or "Celebration Of The Season" to a set lunch hailed by critics as one of the best gourmet deals in Britain.

Seafood temptations might include "spoots" (a Scottish term for razor clams) served with chorizo and lemon *confit*, or perhaps ravioli of Scrabster squid in a langoustine bisque or escabeche of Shetland halibut with fennel, orange and sea buckthorn.

78 Commercial Quay, Leith, Edinburgh; open 12:15–2pm and 6:30–10pm Tue–Sat (closes at 10:30pm Fri–Sat); www.thekitchin.com

Also in Edinburgh

Oloroso (www.oloroso.co.uk; *expensive*) combines a glamorous Edinburgh rooftop setting with unfussy cooking by Tony Singh, who insists on local sourcing. Singh treats the rich earthiness of haggis to a global makeover with dishes such as haggis wonton with plum and whisky sauce, haggis tortellini with spiked salsa verde, and haggis pakora with whisky-tinged *chaat* mayonnaise. The duo serving classic Scottish dishes at the **Urban Angel** (www.urban-angel.co.uk; *inexpensive*) tweak the classic haggis accompaniments by serving theirs with clapshot mash (potatoes, swedes and chives).

Also in Scotland

Their own haggis – venison or vegetarian – is a hearty perennial on the menu at Glasgow's **Ubiquitous Chip** (www.ubiquitouschip.co.uk; *moderate*), in its fifth decade in the city's trendy West End. Other Scottish classics include peat-smoked Finnan haddie (haddock), Rothesay black pudding, Ayrshire halibut and Perthshire wood pigeon.

Also in the UK

London-based haggis-lovers head for **Boisdale** (www.boisdale.co.uk; *expensive*), an upmarket outpost of Caledonian cooking with two spaces: an elegant Regency town house in chic Belgravia and an intimate basement in the heart of the City financial district. The Scottish menu is complemented by a superb whisky list.

RHODOPES

RHODOPES BULGARIA

Patatnik in the Rhodopes

Along the vast green undulations of the Rhodope mountains, shepherds rely on fearsome Karakachan dogs to guard their flocks against wolves, and farmers use oxen to plough the fields. Rural life here is simple, satisfying and healthy, and the cuisine reflects this lifestyle, with a series of delicious, wholesome dishes such as *patatnik*, a golden-crusted potato pie.

Straddling Greece and Bulgaria, the thickly forested Rhodopes spread over more than a million hectares (4,000 square miles), and they are dotted with picturesque villages where life has changed little for centuries. Home to an abundance of wildlife, the mountains are renowned for their stunning limestone gorges, deep caverns and pristine lakes. Hikers can follow a wealth of well-marked trails linked by simple mountain huts, and skiers fill the snow-covered slopes at Pamporovo, one of Bulgaria's premier ski resorts.

A good base for touring is Smolyan, a town near Pamporovo that's also close to the Smolyan Lakes and the towering Orpheus Rocks. The legendary Orpheus is said to have been born in the Rhodope mountains, later entering the underworld to search for his wife at the breathtaking gorge of "The Devil's Throat" near Trigrad. In Zlatograd, a bit further south, there's a chance to see – and stay in – perfectly preserved traditional houses and workshops, now protected as part of an ethnographic complex.

The region has been populated for millennia, but it wasn't until the mid-19th century that potatoes were introduced here. Initially rejected as "devil's apples" by superstitious elders, potatoes eventually proved successful as they thrived at high altitude in the rich Rhodopean soil. Canny villagers were quick to recognize their potential and, having boiled, baked, roasted and fried the hardy new vegetable, began to experiment with a potato version of *banitsa*, a traditional Bulgarian pastry. This ultimately evolved into *patatnik*, a subtle blend of grated potato, white cheese, egg, onion and mint cooked slowly in a pan over a wood-fuelled stove.

During the economic upheaval that followed the collapse of Socialism in the 1990s, the then Prime Minister Ivan Kostov famously exhorted Rhodopeans to profit from their potato expertise and "Make patatnik!" Locals took heed and started to promote the dish as a culinary tourist attraction to be eaten in cosy traditional pubs (*mehanas*). Today *patatnik* is firmly established as the region's classic dish and every *mehana* serves its own version – some add tomatoes and red pepper, while others bake it in an oven rather than cook it on a stove, but all use a few crushed mint leaves to enhance the distinctive *patatnik* flavour. The hour or so's cooking time isn't really a problem, because it's easily spent beside a crackling log fire in a hospitable *mehana*, sampling some freshly baked bread and nursing a fine glass of *rakia*, a spirit distilled from mountain plums.

Above The cheesy onion and potato *patatnik* evolved from the *banitsa*, a Bulgarian savoury filled pastry

Right The village of Shiroka Luka has been declared an Architectural Reserve, with many authentic Rhodopean buildings dating back to the early 19th century

Below Away from the cities, up in the mountains, many people still travel simply with a donkey and cart

Three Days in the Rhodope Mountains

The best way to experience the Rhodopes is to spend weeks walking through them, but if time is short you can easily experience the highlights on a driving tour.

DAY ONE Though blighted by some unappealing Socialist-era buildings, **Smolyan's** mountainous setting is still wondrously dramatic. Visit the **Historical Museum**, then head for the tiny nearby village of **Momchilovtsi**, high in the mountains.

DAY TWO Visit **Zlatograd**, a small ex-mining town 56 km (35 miles) southeast of Smolyan. This has a wonderful **Museum Quarter** where you can watch artisans at work, sip coffee in a 19th-century café, sample Rhodopean delights in a traditional *mehana* and even stay – it offers atmospheric accommodation in period mansions.

DAY THREE Travel northwest past the well-developed ski resort of **Pamporovo** to **Shiroka Luka**, a delightful village of old stone houses tucked away in the mountains. Lunch at the excellent **Pri Slavchev** *mehana* before continuing west to the spectacular **Trigrad Gorge**, where you can visit the **Devil's Throat** cavern.

Essentials

GETTING THERE
Fly to **Sofia Airport**, from which it's a five-hour **bus** journey to Smolyan.

WHERE TO STAY
Trite Eli (inexpensive) in Smolyan has spotless rooms and hiking information. *+359 3018 1028*
Pachilovska Kushta (moderate) in the Museum Quarter at Zlatograd is bursting with period charm. *www.eac-zlatograd.com*
Arena di Serdica (expensive) in Sofia offers five-star comforts. *www.arenadiserdica.com*

TOURIST INFORMATION
Smolyan: Mladeshki Dom; Zlatograd: *www.eac-zlatograd.com*

What Else to Eat

The scrumptious *banitsa* (pastry) known as **klin** is a Rhodopean staple that's cooked slowly on both sides, in a similar way to *patatnik*. The filling is made from rice, eggs, white cheese and butter, and flavoured with nettles or spinach. It's delicious served hot with a dollop of yogurt. Another favourite, **bob chorba**, is a thick, hearty soup that is popular throughout Bulgaria. It contains beans, peppers, tomatoes, celery and carrots, flavoured with mint or parsley. Traditionally prepared in a large earthenware pot, the Rhodopean version is made with white beans from Smolyan. For dessert, try **marudnik**, a kind of pancake with gently cooked wild berries. Buy some strawberry honey to take home.

The Best Places to Eat Patatnik

Alexandrovi Kushti inexpensive

Located in Zlatograd's old Museum Quarter, Alexandrovi Kushti occupies a wonderfully restored 19th-century building with a wood-panelled interior featuring ornate carvings by local craftsmen. As you'd expect from a restaurant that has published its own cookery book of regional delights, the *patatnik* here is superb – cooked slowly over a stove and turned midway through, as the crust develops, according to the traditional recipe.

Bulgarian cuisine is renowned for its broad variety of salads and this is also a great place to sample a classic *shopska* salad of tomatoes, cucumbers, onion and white cheese accompanied by a complimentary glass of *rakia*. Carnivores can choose from a staggering array of meat dishes that range from fried chicken hearts to a whole baked lamb; vegetarians are equally well catered for with enticing options such as *chushky burek* (stuffed peppers) and *sarmi* (vine leaves filled with rice). Save room for a dessert of sticky baklava or sweet *banitsa* filled with Turkish Delight and sit back to enjoy a live performance of Bulgarian folk music.

Museum Quarter, Zlatograd; open for lunch and dinner daily; +359 3071 4166

Also in the Rhodope Mountains

Patatnik, klin, roast lamb and sweet *banitsa* are among the specialities served up at **Mehana Pri Slavchev** *(+359 3030 675; inexpensive)*. This traditional *mehana* is in Shiroka Luka, a pretty village of sturdy stone houses famous for its annual bagpipe festival. In Smolyan, **Trite Eli** *(+359 301 81028; inexpensive)*, also known as Three Fir-tree House, is run by a wonderfully hospitable English-speaking tour guide. This small *pension* has a tiny dining room where guests are served a mind-boggling array of mouthwatering Rhodopean dishes, cooked by the owner using the freshest of ingredients.

Also in Bulgaria

Hidden deep within Sofia's densely forested Borisova Garden, **Veselo Selo** *(www.veseloselo.com; moderate)* is one of the few places that serves *patatnik* in Sofia. The enchanting restaurant complex resembles a country *mehana* – once inside it's easy to forget that you're close to the heart of the capital.

Around the World

One of several Bulgarian restaurants in London, **Arda 2** *(+44 20 7263 5902; moderate)* serves all manner of traditional dishes and, although it doesn't specialize in Rhodopean cuisine, the chef will accept advance orders for *patatnik*. Live folk performances add extra flavour.

BERLIN GERMANY

Prussian Pork in Berlin

Berlin's outward-looking dynamism, non-conformism and hip self-confidence has transformed it into one of Europe's most exciting cities. Many world cuisines flourish here, but in the city's corner pubs, earthy traditional favourites such as *Eisbein* still survive. This tender pork knuckle dish allows a rare taste of the flavours of Berlin in its heyday, as the capital of Prussia.

Berlin had a famously eventful 20th century, to say the least. The Nazi era and the city's subsequent near-obliteration in World War II, followed by its division by opposing ideologies and the Berlin Wall, all left the city deeply scarred. With points of interest that are often sombre and include bombed-out churches, remains of the Wall and dozens of memorials to almost unimaginable horrors, it's not really a place for light-hearted sightseeing, yet exploring its layers of history quickly becomes a compelling activity.

But it's not all gravitas in Berlin. Reunification and an almost constant rebuilding process have fostered a creative atmosphere that encourages the lively and offbeat, evident in the city's many festivals, its thriving arts scene and its intense nightlife. The rebuilding has left the city with a showcase of cutting-edge architecture and its museums have a wealth of treasures to rival any national collection.

Berlin is also inventive in its food and restaurants, which include places where food is served in the dark by blind waiters, or where you pay according to how wealthy you feel. Yet its traditional foods speak of a simpler and earthier time, ruled by calorific dishes like *Eisbein*, which was a particular favourite of both philosopher Immanuel Kant and singer and actress Marlene Dietrich. The enduring popularity of the dish has something to do with Germany's love of pork – the country eats more of it than all other meats and poultry combined. This love affair dates back to Roman times, when wild boar was the meat of choice at feasts. Fresh, pickled or smoked pork became the basis for hundreds of specialities, and there's a recipe in traditional German cuisine for every part of the animal.

Eisbein is a heavily fat-marbled cut of cured pork clinging to a large bone; it frequently takes aback unwary and squeamish visitors, but remains a firm favourite among Berliners. The pork is cured and sometimes smoked before it is soaked overnight in brine or rubbed with salt, pepper, garlic and caraway seeds. Its extreme tenderness comes from hours of slow simmering, after which it is served with simple vegetables, such as sauerkraut, puréed peas and boiled potatoes. First mentioned in a Berlin cookbook in 1638, *Eisbein* is a genuine taste of the past.

Above Berlin embraces the old and the new, from its magnificent cathedral to its high-tech telecoms tower

Cookery Courses

Berliners have developed a healthy interest in world food and most courses at cookery schools reflect this. But you can also find instruction on mastering the basics of German cuisine together with cooking modern and traditional German recipes. **Kochetage** (*www.kochetage.de*) is a highly rated Berlin school whose range of courses include instruction on preparing meat, game dishes and German sauces. **Kochschule Berlin** (*www.kochschule-berlin.de*) offers a huge number of courses, including those on the basics of German cookery and its traditional dishes. **Kochatelier Berlin** (*www.kochatelier-berlin.de*) offers a broad range of courses, including "Oma's Küche" (grandmother's kitchen) and the "Berlin-Brandenburg", lessons on traditional cooking using local ingredients.

A Day in Berlin

Central Berlin gathers around the city's pivotal grand avenue, Unter den Linden, and is compact enough to be explored on foot.

MORNING Begin at the west end of **Unter den Linden**, at the **Brandenburg Gate**. Then ascend the impressive cupola of the neighbouring **Reichstag**, Germany's parliament, for city views. Afterwards visit the giant **Holocaust Memorial** on the other side of the Brandenburg Gate and wander through **Tiergarten Park** to the impressive modern architecture of **Potsdamer Platz**.

AFTERNOON Follow the former course of the **Berlin Wall**, passing a preserved section en route to **Checkpoint Charlie**, the famous former Iron Curtain checkpoint. Then walk north through the **Gendarmenmarkt**, Berlin's most elegant plaza, to **Bebelplatz**, a square surrounded by stately Neo-Classical buildings, before exploring the adjacent **Museum Island**, the location of Berlin's greatest museums.

EVENING Pass through the **Nikolaiviertel**, a rebuilt version of old Berlin, on the way to the distinctive **Fernsehturm Television Tower** for night views of city. Afterwards explore **Hackescher Markt** nightlife area to the northwest.

Essentials

GETTING THERE
Berlin's **Schoenefeld Airport** is being expanded to become Berlin Brandenburg International (BBI) in 2012. The city has an excellent network of **metro trains**, **buses** and **trams**.

WHERE TO STAY
Circus Hotel (inexpensive) is a youthful and central hotel with smart colourful rooms and a beer garden. *www.circus-berlin.de*
Luise Kunsthotel (moderate) is an eccentric and attractive art hotel in an 1820s building near the Brandenburg Gate. *www.luise-berlin.com*
Adlon (expensive) is the *grande dame* of Berlin's hotels, with an elegant 1920s feel and first-class service and amenities. *www.hotel-adlon.de*

TOURIST INFORMATION
www.tourist.visitberlin.de

The Best Places to Eat Eisbein

Zur Letzten Instanz expensive

Berlin's oldest restaurant has a real sense of history. There's been an inn on this spot since 1621, when a schnapps bar opened; it was still going strong when a conquering Napoleon Bonaparte visited in 1806. The present business dates back to 1924 when it was a popular stop on the way to the nearby courthouse. In honour of this, all the dishes here have been given legal-themed names like *Zeugen-Aussage* ("Eyewitness Account"), but it's the wood-clad interior and classic tiled oven that really preserve the historic feel. This, and its superb execution of Berlin's traditional dishes, make the place so authentic and so well known that foreign heads of state have often been brought here, including former Soviet statesman Mikhail Gorbachev and former French president Jacques Chirac. *Eisbein* is the most popular dish, but if you want something lighter, try a *boulette* – a mince and herb burger that's also a Berlin speciality and is done here to perfection.
Waisenstrasse 14–16, Berlin; open noon–11pm Mon–Sat, noon–9pm Sun; www.zurletzteninstanz.de

Also in Berlin

The plastic and Formica decor of **Schusterjunge** *(+49 30 442 7654; inexpensive)* reminds visitors of life in former East Germany, but this old-fashioned Berlin corner pub has built up a cult following for its mountainous portions of no-nonsense Berlin food, including *Eisbein*.

Also in Germany

Outside Berlin, genuine *Eisbein* is hard to find and pork knuckles are more commonly prepared as roasted *Schweinshaxe*, with mustard, horseradish and pickled chillies. However, **Max Walloschke** *(www.max-walloschke.de; inexpensive)*, a friendly 1950s-style urban pub in Hanover, and the lovely old-fashioned **Restaurant Eisbeinhaus** *(+49 20 2251 4670; moderate)* in Wuppertal both serve wonderfully tender *Eisbein*, with giant portions of sauerkraut and mashed potato.

Around the World

Elsewhere in the world, authentic *Eisbein* is almost impossible to come by. However, **Mark's East Side** *(www.markseastside.com; moderate)* in Wisconsin, USA, is extremely competent at cooking German food and will serve *Eisbein* simmered, rather than roasted, if requested. Meanwhile, the slight inauthenticity of *Eisbein* in **Bar do Alemão** *(www. bardoalemaocuritiba.com.br; moderate)* in Curitiba, Brazil, can be forgiven once tasted; the addition of herbs and pickled salads gives this dish some South American flair and colour.

Above Restaurant Zur Letzten Instanz ("To the Last Judgment") has counted Napoleon and Beethoven among its customers

Left The traditional German dish *Eisbein*, a slow-cooked knuckle of pork, is usually served with an accompaniment of sauerkraut

GAZIANTEP TURKEY

Fresh-Baked Baklava in Turkey

Gaziantep, gateway to southeastern Anatolia, claims to be the historic homeland of Turkey's most famous pastry. Among the evocative ruins of past powers, bazaars and museums, nearly 200 pastry shops compete to bake the best version of baklava – and with some excellent restaurants, coffee and tea houses too, Gaziantep has become something of a culinary capital.

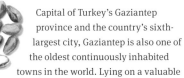

Capital of Turkey's Gaziantep province and the country's sixth-largest city, Gaziantep is also one of the oldest continuously inhabited towns in the world. Lying on a valuable caravan route connecting Mesopotamia, Egypt and Anatolia, the town saw many powers, including the Assyrians, Babylonians, Persians, Greeks and Romans pass through its portals. The ghosts of these transient rulers can sometimes be felt in the evocative and melancholy old ruins that dot the modern city.

Gaziantep is an important centre of traditional and modern industry. Around the town, coppersmiths can be seen, smelled and above all heard as they hammer away at glinting pots and pans. But this is also one of Turkey's most productive agricultural regions, and Gaziantep is the epicentre of the region's famous fıstık (pistachio) cultivation, the fundamental ingredient for the town's famous pastry, baklava. A local saying has it that you are never more than five minutes' walk from one of the town's innumerable pastry shops, and both Turkish and foreign tourists alike flock to the town to satisfy sweet tooths and rumbling tummies.

The baklava, with its countless layers of crisp filo pastry filled with chopped nuts that ooze syrup or honey, is found all over Turkey. The word "baklava" may stem from a Mongolian-Turkic word meaning "to pile up", and local tradition has it that the pastry was developed in the imperial kitchens of the Topkapı Palace in Istanbul as a way of pleasing and placating the Sultan. The sweet later became fashionable throughout the Ottoman empire. Gaziantep's acclaimed version is always made with pistachios and is judged to be the best not just in Turkey, but in the world.

The city's top baklava chefs claim the secret lies in selecting the finest and freshest local ingredients: carefully sourced and organically grown pistachio nuts, olive oil and honey. Gaziantep's soil is believed to infuse the ingredients with a special flavour and aroma, and its top chefs use pastry skills and recipes often closely guarded within a family for generations.

According to local connoisseurs, the perfect pastry should be light in the hand, sweet (but not overly syrupy) in the mouth and, above all, crisp to the bite. A Gaziantep baklava fresh out of the oven, served with a cup of thick, dark Turkish coffee, is an eating experience never forgotten. It's no wonder that so many visitors to Gaziantep come away with a copper Turkish coffee pot tucked under one arm and a box of baklava under the other.

A Day in Gaziantep

Most of the sights, pastry shops, cafés and restaurants can be found within strolling distance of the square still popularly known as **Hükümet Konağı** (Government House).

MORNING Climb up to the Roman-built, Seljuk-restored **Kale** (citadel) for a great view of the city. Then visit the **bazaar**, where you can wander the stalls, alleyways and workshops and shop for pistachios. Stop for coffee and baklava at **Tahmis** *kahvehane* (coffeehouse) or **Tütün Hanı** teahouse, set in an atmospheric former caravanserai – a fortified inn built to protect and house travellers on the Silk Road.

AFTERNOON Head for the **Gaziantep Museum** and the **Zeugma Kültür ve Müze Merkezi** on İstasyon Caddesi, with its stunning collection of Roman mosaics. Picnic in the lovely **100 Yıl Atatürk Kültür Parkı**, then explore the **Hasan Süzer Ethnography Museum** just off Atatürk Caddesi, in a 200-year-old traditional Gaziantep house.

EVENING Take in the 19th-century **Kurtuluş Camii mosque** and the **Alaüddevle Camii**, near the coppersmith market, where you can pick up that copper coffee pot.

Essentials

GETTING THERE
Domestic flights from Istanbul serve **Oguzeli airport**, a short **taxi** or **bus** ride from the centre.

WHERE TO STAY
Has Hotel (inexpensive) is centrally located, with plain but well-furnished, spotless rooms. *email: info@hotelhas.com*
Anadolu Evleri (moderate) is a traditional stone house near the bazaar. *www.anadoluevleri.com*
Dayı Ahmet Ağa Konağı (moderate–expensive) offers central, boutique-style rooms in a *konak* (mansion). *www.dayiahmetagakonagi.com*

TOURIST INFORMATION
100 Yıl Atatürk Kültür Parkı; *+90 342 230 5969*

Above Carefully graded pistachios grown locally fill the bazaars in Gaziantep

Left A pastry counter in Gaziantep, with fresh-baked baklava in the foreground; the sweet may contain up to 70 layers of pastry

The Best Places to Eat Baklava

İmam Çağdaş
moderate–expensive

Family-run İmam Çağdaş is arguably Gaziantep's best *baklavacı* (baklava shop). The eponymous owner, **Burhan Çağdaş**, grandson of **İmam Dede** who founded the pastry shop in 1887, exports his little boxes of baklava daily all across the country and abroad too, including, it is rumoured, to Turkey's premier himself, President Abdullah Gül. Burhan sustains his success and high standards by using only high-quality, organic ingredients hand-selected from carefully sourced, local producers. Though the recently relocated pastry shop itself is unremarkable, decorated in a plain, contemporary style, it is on the excellence of his pastries that Burhan has continued the Çağdaş family reputation. According to Burhan, his baklava should be eaten not with the knife and fork supplied but with the thumb and index finger, placing the baklava in the top of the mouth and then biting down. The *baklavacı* is open all day, serving pastries with coffee and preparing parcels of baklava for its customers to take away.

Eski Hal Civarı, Uzun Çarşı 47, Şahinbey, Gaziantep; **+90 342 231 2678**

Also in Gaziantep

Çavuşoğlu *(+90 342 231 3069; moderate)* has a good reputation as both a *baklavacı* and a *kebapçı* (kebab house) and is a good choice for a complete Turkish meal. Food is fresh, well-prepared and well-priced and the baklava are legendary. Other famous Gaziantep *baklavacıs* well worth visiting include **Baclava Ünlüler** *(+90 342 232 2043; inexpensive–moderate)*, and **Fıstıkzade** *(+90 342 336 0020; inexpensive–moderate)*, both in the centre of town.

Also in Turkey

Karaköy Güllüoğlu *(+90 212 293 0910; moderate–expensive)* opened in Istanbul in 1949, the first in a series of famous *baklavacıs* owned by the Güllü family. From the tantalizing pastry counter, customers can choose a *porsiyon* (portion) of whatever baklava takes their fancy, including *cevizli* (the walnut variety), *fıstıklı* (pistachio) or *sade* (plain).

Around the World

Güllüoğlu *(+1 718 645 1822; expensive)* in Brooklyn, New York, is the first American branch of the famous Turkish chain founded by the Güllü family *(see above)*. The bakers are trained in Istanbul and ingredients are flown in daily from Turkey.

Above The ancient Kale, or walled citadel, was in use as a defensive structure until the end of the Ottoman empire in the early 20th century

Other Sweet Treats

An old and oft-quoted Turkish saying goes "Eat sweet; talk sweet", and **tatlılar** (sweets and puddings) play a vital role in Turkish cultural life, accompanying many of life's major events. At engagements and weddings, **baklava** is the traditional gift; **lokma** (fried doughballs in syrup) and **helva** (halva) are associated with funerals, as well as New Year, and a piece of **Turkish delight** wrapped in muslin is traditionally placed between the lips of a newborn child. Modern Turkish cookbooks list up to 300 sweet recipes, many bearing evocative names including **hoşmerim** (meaning "Something nice for my brave man").

A Day in Milan

Milan has some superb cultural and architectural sights, but leave time for a bout of clothes-shopping at the many fashion outlets.

MORNING Take a tram or the metro to **Piazza del Duomo** and the fantastic Gothic cathedral. Ride the lift or climb the winding stairs to its roof terraces for bird's-eye views over the city and north to the Alps. Then stroll through the grandiose **Galleria Vittorio Emanuele II** shopping arcade to reach the world-famous **La Scala** opera house. Continuing in the same direction you'll reach the **Pinacoteca di Brera**, a cavernous palazzo housing a rich collection of Italian art.

AFTERNOON Head to **Piazza Santa Maria delle Grazie** to gaze on one of the world's masterpieces in a more modest setting – Leonardo da Vinci's *Last Supper* is painted on the walls of the convent's refectory. Relaxing time out can be spent exploring the vast Renaissance brick **Castello Sforzesco** and its adjacent park.

EVENING Wander along the **Navigli canals** and enjoy a drink or meal at the waterside bars and restaurants.

Essentials

GETTING THERE
Milan has two **airports**; Malpensa has frequent **trains** and **buses** to the city, while Linate has only a **bus** link. International and domestic **trains** run into Milano Centrale station, to connect with the **metro**, **tram** and **bus** network.

WHERE TO STAY
Hotel Bernina (inexpensive) is a businesslike hotel that's good value and handy for the railway station. *www.hotelbernina.com*
Antica Locanda Leonardo (moderate) is a charming, 19th-century boutique hotel near Santa Maria delle Grazie. *www.leoloc.com*
Bulgari (expensive) offers stylish modern suites and a relaxing garden. *www.bulgarihotels.com*

TOURIST INFORMATION
Piazza Castello 1; *http://turismo.provincia. milano.it/turismo_en*

Right The rice is stirred as it absorbs ladleful after ladleful of stock until just the right consistency is achieved

Below Milan's Duomo is a 14th-century masterpiece of Gothic architecture, built under the reign of the Visconti family

MILAN ITALY

Risotto in Fashionable Milan

The fashion and finance capital of Italy, Milan is a calm, cool and collected city where traffic flows in an orderly manner and trams rumble along carefully paved streets. Innovation is part of the lifestyle, but thankfully culinary classics such as risotto never change radically. A rich and refined dish, *risotto alla milanese* uses bounty from the fertile plains and hills of Lombardy.

Standing on a street in Milan, you could be forgiven for thinking you're in Switzerland rather than northern Italy, as efficiency and business are obviously paramount. Milan lies at a providential crossroads of transalpine trade routes, and boasts a remarkable heritage of art and architecture from the 14th and 15th centuries, when it was ruled by powerful families such as the Viscontis and Sforzas. Money and art continue to fascinate today, and the city is home to both the Italian stock exchange and many of the world's leading fashion houses.

However, culinary traditions have not been sacrificed for business, and at lunch time a stream of office-dwellers put down their technological tools and head out on to the street in search of sustenance. Rediscovering the healthy custom of a sit-down meal from bygone days when workers went home for a full three courses, Milan's citizens now take a break to dine in eateries that range from glamorous glasshouses to traditional family trattorias.

Milan's long-standing dishes still shine strong. Thanks to the extensive wet fields to the west and south of the city, where the country's best rice varieties, such as *vialone nano* and *carnaroli*, are successfully cultivated, risotto is a constant on city menus – especially *risotto alla milanese*. The cooking process is drawn-out, like the eating. It begins with a slow *soffritto*, where an onion is gently sweated in olive oil. The rice is added and stirred, and then the heat is turned up, and a rich, meaty broth is added, in small ladlefuls – one containing a pinch of saffron – until the rice is just tender. Finally, butter and grated *parmigiano* cheese are beaten in, giving the rice a creamy texture and satin finish. The dish is also known as *risotto giallo* (yellow) for its saffron-bestowed golden sheen.

Saffron is the dried filaments of a type of crocus grown in limited quantities in Abruzzo in southern Italy, as well as in Spain, but it originated in Persia, as did its name. The pretty lilac flowers are painstakingly harvested to produce the most expensive spice in the world, lending Milan's version of this most Italian of dishes the warm yellow of a gentle Italian sun.

What Else to Eat

One of Milan's tasty staples is **osso bucco**, rich and succulent braised veal shank. This is often twinned with *risotto alla milanese* to great effect, as the sauce blends perfectly with the rice. Another meat treat is **cotoletta alla milanese**, a slice of veal layered with ham and cheese, then breaded and fried. Around the beginning of December each year, the windows and counters of the city's leading *pasticceria* (pastry shops) start filling up with huge, festively wrapped packages. **Panettone**, literally "big bread", is a fragrant, soft, yeasty cake baked with dried fruit such as sultanas and candied orange peel. It is traditionally consumed during Christmas celebrations with a glass of sparkling wine, but cooks have begun to play with this age-old recipe, adding fillings or sauces such as ice cream or layers of melted chocolate.

Above The wet fields west of Milan provide the perfect rice for *risotto alla milanese*

The Best Places to Eat Risotto

Trattoria Milanese moderate

Advance booking is highly recommended here, especially for evening dining, as this bustling restaurant is immensely popular with the Milanese for its traditional cuisine. But don't expect a romantic candle-lit atmosphere – this time-tested trattoria has been a serious eating place since 1933 and diners here want to see their meal. Guests are welcomed at the door and ushered into a dining room infused with mouthwatering smells and lined with shelves crammed with precariously balanced bottles and platters of freshly prepared vegetables and sweets. Tables are often shared, encouraging friendly banter and discussion of meal choices. The uniformed waiters never tire of explaining the menu of the day, though most people come here for the signature dish, *risotto alla milanese*. Served piping hot at half-hour intervals, the delicately yellow rice comes out of the kitchen on a flat plate, which allows it to spread to the edges and cool uniformly. On request it can be dished up with osso bucco on top.
Via Santa Marta 11, Milan; open noon–2:45pm and 7pm–12:45am Mon–Fri; +39 2 41 8645 1991

Also in Milan

Going strong since 1921, **Trattoria Masuelli San Marco** (*www.masuelli-trattoria.com; expensive*) has crisp white tablecloths, immaculate service and an affable owner who offers you a personal elucidation of the day's dishes. Here the *risotto alla milanese* is proudly prepared with fresh saffron pistils and is exceptionally fragrant. Meats fresh and cured from the family property include *cotechino*, a flavoursome sausage served with fondue.

Also in Italy

La Risotteria Melotti (*www.melotti.it; moderate*) in Isola della Scala, just outside Verona in the Veneto, has 24 creamy risottos on the menu. Each is masterfully created using the *vialone nano veronese* rice grown locally on the family property. One house speciality, *risotto all'isolana*, is a justifiable favourite for its unusual match of veal and pork with fresh rosemary and cinnamon, while the *risotto con zafferano e finferli* with saffron and wild mushrooms is delicate and heavenly.

Around the World

As its name suggests, **RisOTTO** (*www.ris-otto. de; inexpensive*) in Berlin serves only risotto. Guests can perch on stools and watch the chef at work, creating imaginative variations such as pea and lime or courgette and cinnamon risotto. Open for lunch and early-evening meals, this is a great casual stop.

THESSALONIKI

THESSALONIKI GREECE

Dolmades in Thessaloniki

As a rule, Greek food is for purists and traditionalists, but Thessaloniki, the capital of Macedonia, is an exhilarating exception to the rule. Bridging East and West, Greece's second city has adapted to its cosmopolitan population over the centuries to develop a fusion of Middle Eastern and Balkan cuisine. Its signature dishes – such as dolmades (stuffed vine leaves) – are full of surprises.

Lying on the ancient trade route linking the Adriatic with Istanbul, Thessaloniki has long been a confluence of cultures. Echoes of its former occupants crop up all over the city, in Roman ruins, Ottoman baths, crumbling synagogues and Byzantine chapels. The city's eclectic cuisine also bears the hallmarks of all its past residents. But the most pervasive flavours are those left by the Ottoman empire, whose rule of Macedonia extended to 1913, almost a century after the rest of Greece was liberated.

Centuries of Ottoman occupation are most obvious today in the ramshackle Turkish quarter of Kastra, which is a 19th-century time warp. Minarets poke out among apartment blocks, and former hammams (Turkish baths) are now cultural centres, cinemas or flower stalls. Even the city's most prominent landmark, the White Tower (which isn't white at all), was built by the Ottomans as a fortress, before becoming a notorious prison. The tower is an evocative monument to the city's diversity, and has a fascinating virtual tour of its culinary history on the top floor.

Thessaloniki's thriving meze culture owes much to the influence of Asia Minor (the area that now encompasses most of modern-day Turkey). Convivial meals consist of a succession of small dishes designed to be shared, usually accompanied by a glass of ouzo or *tsipouro*, spirits distilled from the vine. Grape leaves are also used to make one of the city's most popular meze dishes, dolmades, whose name reveals its origin: *dolma* is the Turkish word for "stuffed". These glossy little parcels are also known as *yaprakia*, from the Turkish *yaprak*, or leaf. The cooks of Thessaloniki have access to tender vine leaves from the fertile mountains of Macedonia, the source of northern Greece's robust red wines. The leaves are picked in late spring, blanched and preserved in brine, then rolled by hand.

Eating a dolma is like opening a gift – you never quite know what's inside until the first bite. Tightly wrapped into dainty bundles, they might be filled with minced lamb, currants and pine nuts, spiced with cloves, cumin or cinnamon, speckled with mint, dill or parsley, or bursting at the seams with sardines, fennel and onions. *Yalantzi* (Turkish for "fake") are meatless dolma; *sarmadakia* uses pickled cabbage leaves stuffed with minced lamb and smothered in *avgolemono*, a tangy egg and lemon sauce that is almost as tricky to perfect as mayonnaise. The variations are endless, and always delicious.

A Day in Thessaloniki

Layers of history intersect in Thessaloniki, Greece's most alluring city. With its high density of museums, waterfront bars, restaurants and hip hotels, Thessaloniki also has a vibrant modern identity.

MORNING Visit the **Archaeological Museum**, a thrilling modernist building with an extraordinary collection of artifacts. Then wander along the boardwalk to the **Photography and Cinema museums**, formerly shipping warehouses. Head to the **Teloglion Foundation of Art**, a museum in a hilltop park with a great café, Art 02.

AFTERNOON Get lost in the twisting alleys of the old Turkish Quarter, ringed by Byzantine walls. Old-time *ouzeri* (meze bars) with overgrown courtyards are tucked among the timber-framed houses. Meals here are often accompanied by spontaneous renditions of *rembetika* – the Greek blues.

EVENING The party gets started around midnight; follow the crowds outside the bars on **Valaoritou Street** and around the splendid **Malakopi** arcade.

Essentials

GETTING THERE
Fly to **Macedonia International Airport**, then take **Bus 78** into town. Intercity **trains** from Athens's Larissis station take about 5 hours.

WHERE TO STAY
The Met (inexpensive) is a glossy newcomer with a destination Asian restaurant, spa and rooftop pool. www.themethotel.gr
Excelsior (moderate) is a restored 1920s property with a fun bistro. www.excelsiorhotel.gr
Daios (expensive) offers modern minimalism on the waterfront. www.daioshotels.com

TOURIST INFORMATION
136 Tsimiski Street; www.saloniki.org

Above The streets of Thessaloniki are lined with high-quality restaurants and tempting *ouzeri*

Left Thessaloniki, also known as Salonika, sits around a spacious harbour built by the Romans

Above Dolmades are cigar-shaped, stuffed vine leaves bursting with flavour; a subtle scent of lemon tantalizes the tastebuds

The Modiano Market

The glass-domed Modiano, built in 1922, is Thessaloniki's best and biggest food market. It's a celebration of the city's culinary diversity: stalls are heaped with glistening olives, sticky pastries, delicate rosebuds, pickled peppers, fragrant mounds of saffron and briny buckets of vine leaves. There are several places to sample meze inside the market, which echoes day and night with the banter of bargain-hunters and *bon viveurs*. Gypsy minstrels weave among tightly packed tables, where punters tuck into tiny plates of grilled sardines or smoky aubergine purée. The beauty of these shared feasts is their spontaneity – and the fact that they can go on indefinitely.

The Best Places to Eat Dolmades

Aristotelous moderate

This classic *ouzeri* is a throwback to another era. Situated in a plant-filled arcade decorated with chequerboard tiles and retro posters of Greece, it offers calm respite from the hustle of Aristotelous Square. Writers and artists, lawyers and lovers squeeze around the marble-topped tables while genteel waiters ply them with a parade of little dishes. You must, of course, try the dolmades. But it's also a good place to dip into the vast repertoire of meze dishes – red peppers stuffed with spicy feta, prawns sautéed with garlic and tomato, squid oozing cheese sauce and lightly battered courgettes. With live Greek music most evenings, the experience is as much about the atmosphere as the food. Tourists have discovered its charms, so you often have to queue for a table and prices are a little steep. Yet the appeal of this former Turkish coffeehouse, which miraculously survived the great fire that ravaged Thessaloniki in 1917, is as enduring as ever.

Aristotelous 8, Thessaloniki; open 10am–2am Mon–Sat, 11am–6pm Sun; +30 2310 233 195

Also in Thessaloniki

Aglaia's Kitchen *(+30 2310 280 044; inexpensive)* is a tiny restaurant with a menu straight out of Asia Minor, situated in the heart of the flower market. Dishes of the day depend on what Aglaia finds in nearby Modiano market, but if you're lucky the day's menu will include her legendary *sarmadakia*, smothered in *avgolemono.* The sophisticated bistro **B** *(www.brestaurant.gr; moderate)* is also known as **Vyzantino**, after its location in the Byzantine Museum. It serves tasty dolmades with minted yogurt, and you can enjoy a tour of the museum's frescoes, mosaics and icons as a marvellous *digestif.*

Also in Greece

The far-flung isle of Kasos in the Dodecanese is renowned for its tiny dolmades (or *dourmaes,* as they are called in the local dialect). The best place to try them is **Emborios** *(www.emborios. com; inexpensive)*, a lively, family-run taverna, which serves moreish meze accompanied by fantastically fresh fish and improvised singalongs to a lyre and lute.

Around the World

Melbourne, Australia, has the largest Greek community outside Greece, so it's not surprising that it has several excellent Greek restaurants. **Philhellene** *(www.philhellene.com.au; moderate)* is like eating at home with the garrulous Rerakis family, whose beef and cumin dolmades are wrapped in silverbeet leaves grown in their own garden. Don't miss their wonderful stuffed courgette flowers, only featured when in season.

BRITTANY FRANCE

Crêpes in Cornouaille

Reaching out into the wild Atlantic and dotted with prehistoric megaliths, the granite peninsula of Brittany has an elemental mystery. In the ancient Celtic region of Cornouaille, residents take as much pride in its distinct culture as in its signature dish – the *crêpe*. The Bretons have elevated these simple golden discs, filled with seafood or smeared with honey or lemon, into an art form.

The humble pancake occupies a revered place in Brittany, where delicate, wafer-thin *crêpes* have been a way of life and an essential ingredient of gatherings since medieval times. *Crêpes* certainly rule in Quimper, Brittany's oldest city and the capital of Cornouaille, a historic region that was first settled in the Middle Ages by Welsh and Cornish Celts fleeing from the Anglo-Saxon invasion of Britain. They named this region in the southwest of Brittany "Cornouaille", the same as one of the places they had left – Cornwall.

Brittany became part of France in 1532, but Quimper still has much to show of its Breton history. Cobbled streets lined with 14th-century timber houses still bear the names of the trades that once thrived there: rue Kèrèon was full of shoemakers, rue des Boucheries housed butchers and the Place au Beurre was the place to buy butter. In July every year the town celebrates its Breton culture and heritage in the Festival de Cornouaille, drawing musicians, dancers and visitors from Celtic communities around the world.

Beyond Quimper, Cornouaille's coast of dramatic cliffs, sheltered bays and sandy beaches beckons fans of watersports along with walkers and cyclists. The region has long been a favourite of painters escaping Paris in summer, and in the 1860s a cosmopolitan colony of artists sprang up in Pont Aven, a coastal village southeast of Quimper. It included the celebrated Post-Impressionist artist Paul Gauguin, who immortalized the Bretons in his paintings. The Inn of Marie Henri in neighbouring Le Pouldu still features walls covered in works by the artist and his followers.

Crêpes provide the perfect counterpoint to any activity in Cornouaille, functioning as a snack, meal or dessert according to the size and filling. There are two main varieties: true *crêpes*, which are made from white wheat flour, milk and eggs; and *galettes*, made from buckwheat flour, salt and water. Some insist the batter be beaten with a wooden spoon, while others add local Breton cider and skip the milk, but everyone agrees on the need for a tiny wooden rake (a *rozell*, or *rouable*) to spread the batter on to a piping hotplate, and a spatula (*spanell* or *viroué*) to flip it. Traditionally, *galettes* are savoury – a classic is topped with ham, grated cheese, and a softly fried egg nestling in the middle – while *crêpes* are usually vehicles for sweet treats, such as hazelnut cream or strawberry jam. But the joy of these pancakes is their endless variety, which allows modern tastes to play with a 15th-century classic.

Three Days in Cornouaille

Wild surfing beaches, sandy seaside resorts, lively markets and fishing villages with wonderfully fresh seafood vie for attention with walled towns and the Breton interior with its fascinating Celtic heritage.

DAY ONE Ramble round **Quimper's** charming old town, taking in the twin-spired **St Corentin Cathedral**. Visit the **Breton Museum** to learn how Celtic and Breton folklores intertwine. Anyone with a penchant for pottery will love the **Musée de la Faïence**, with its 2,000-strong collection of centuries-old ceramics.

DAY TWO Drive or catch a bus to **Locronan**, one of France's most beautiful villages. Sacred to the Celts, it was a sail-making hub in the 16th century and its granite houses have inspired many a film director, including Roman Polanski, who filmed *Tess* (based on Thomas Hardy's novel *Tess of the d'Urbervilles*) here in 1979.

DAY THREE Follow the **Painters' Trail** (using guides from the tourist office in Quimper) to see how and where the artists lived and what inspired them.

Essentials

GETTING THERE
Regular **trains** run from Paris to Quimper.
Car hire is essential to explore the region.

WHERE TO STAY
Hôtel Gradlon (inexpensive) offers cosy rooms close to Quimper centre. www.hotel-gradlon.fr
Les Sables Blancs (moderate) is a stylish hotel perched on the Bay of Concarneau. www.hotel-les-sables-blancs.com
Domaine de Kerbastic (expensive) is a boutique hotel in a pretty château 40 minutes from Quimper. www.domaine-de-kerbastic.com

TOURIST INFORMATION
www.quimper-tourisme.com

Above Camembert and chives provide a savoury *crêpe* filling, ideally washed down with some chilled Breton cider

Left Quimper's recently restored granite cathedral, with its distinctive twin spires, towers over the city's half-timbered houses

Above Women wearing traditional headdresses, the strikingly shaped *coiffe bigoudène*, as part of a Breton religious procession

Crêpe Festivals

Fête de la Crêpe On the last weekend in July, the *crêpe* takes pride of place in the village of Gourin, in Morbihan. Breton dancing, pipe bands, Celtic singers, exhibitions by local artists and, of course, fresh *crêpes* provide entertainment for all.
Rennes festival In May and June, *crêperies* in the city of Rennes compete to win the title of best *galette* and best *crêpe*. Pancake eaters are spoiled for choice with everyone vying for accolades.
Fête de la Galette On the last Sunday in September, Pipriac, in Ille-et-Vilaine, hosts its *galette* festival. Expect a *galette*-making competition, buckwheat exhibitions and Celtic concerts.

The Best Places to Eat Crêpes

Crêperie An Diskuiz inexpensive

Billing itself as a *crêperie gourmande*, this establishment is serious about what it puts on a plate – only 100 percent quality buckwheat and wheat *crêpes*. Settle into the tiny stone-walled room with its wooden beams and tables splashed with red, yellow and pale green cloths, order a house cocktail (kir with chestnut cream in winter, or morello cherries and sparkling apple juice in summer) and study the menu. Savoury *crêpe* offerings include *Cabri*, filled with goat's cheese, bacon, walnuts and cream; *La Dahouet*, stuffed with scallops from Saint Brieuc and leek fondue; and *Côte d'Emeraude* – a creamy melange of scallops, mushrooms, bacon and parsley. Dessert *crêpes* feature local products such as jams from Vergers du Cap Coz and de Fouesnant honey, with combinations including orange marmalade with chocolate enveloped in a black wheat *crêpe*, and one bursting with seasonal fruit. Wash it down with farmhouse cider or, better still, apple brandy.
12 rue Elie Fréron, Quimper; open noon–2pm Mon–Sat, 7–10pm Mon–Tue, Thu–Sat; +33 2 9895 5570

Also in Quimper

Sainte Catherine *(+33 2 9853 2824; inexpensive)*, in the shadow of Quimper's cathedral, dishes up *crêpes* bursting with local goodness. Seafood fanciers will fall for the buckwheat pancake with mussels, scallops, prawns and mushrooms in a saffron sauce, while meat-eaters can opt for hearty black pudding and pan-fried apples. Sweet treats include an oozy salted caramel *crêpe*.

Also in France

Crêperies are a common sight in Paris but they're rarely the real Breton deal. For that, you need to head to the rue du Montparnasse in the 14th arrondissement. The reason? Montparnasse station, the hub for trains to and from Brittany, is just nearby. Two popular *crêpe* crusaders in the street are **Crêperie de Josselin** *(+33 1 4320 9350; inexpensive)* at number 67 and **Crêperie Saint-Malo** *(+33 1 4320 8719; inexpensive)* at number 53. The flambéed apple and maple syrup *crêpe* here will crank up lagging sugar levels.

Around the World

French expat Sylvie Lemer is responsible for bringing some Breton flavour to San Francisco's funky Mission district. At **Ti Couz** *(+1 415 252 7373; moderate)*, she cooks up thin buckwheat *galettes* embracing fat scallops in a buttery sauce or classic ham and cheese, and sweet *crêpes* like the decadent white chocolate and Chantilly cream.

SALZBURG AUSTRIA

Creamy Torten in Salzburg

Rich gâteaux, or *torten*, are as much a product of Austria's Baroque era as its classical music or architecture, and all three of these remain wonderfully preserved in today's Salzburg. Deliciously creamy *torten* beckon from gleaming café counters, ready to be served by tuxedoed waiters to diners sitting in the very same chandeliered coffeehouses that Mozart once frequented.

Austria claims to have invented coffeehouses after the 1693 siege of Vienna, when it captured coffee from Turkish troops. Unlike the Ottomans, the drink took the city by storm. The local elite loved it, and cafés soon sprouted up everywhere; fashionable Salzburg opened its first café – the Tomaselli – in 1705. Cake was immediately recognized as coffee's natural partner and before long there were expert pastry chefs in every good café. Their rich and creamy embellishment of traditional cakes created *torten*, a culinary form that has obsessed central Europe ever since.

Most of modern Vienna has tended to move on, but Salzburg's love of tradition has allowed the Tomaselli to thrive, and it is now Austria's oldest café. The main reason for Salzburg's affection for the 18th century is that this was its cultural heyday, as the home town of its most famous son, Wolfgang Amadeus Mozart. Many city attractions still relate to the great composer: the house of his birth and his family residence have both become first-class museums to his life and times, while the city's main square is named after him and dominated by his huge statue. A visit to the medieval Hohensalzburg castle above the city affords a great view on to the square and the city's wonderfully scenic Alpine location, already familiar to those who have watched the classic 1965 film, *The Sound of Music*.

Salzburg's time-warp café culture is so authentic that visitors often find themselves sharing the experience with gossiping elderly ladies tending spoiled dogs on their laps, rumpled writers penning verses over coffee and the occasional Hungarian fiddler pouring out his heart. Aloof waiters usher in coffee on a silver plate, with a glass of water and a small piece of chocolate, or – best of all – a *torte*. Based on eggs, sugar and ground nuts, *torten* are defined by their decorative icing and creamy layers, which routinely contain buttercream, vanilla, cocoa, coffee, fresh or candied fruits, jams, marzipan and even liqueurs. These are the creations of masterly pastry chefs – and Salzburg attracts some of Europe's best.

A Day in Salzburg

Salzburg's compact Old Town centres on several graceful Baroque squares. It straddles the Salzach river and sits below the Hohensalzburg castle.

MORNING Orientate yourself with a trip to the battlements of the medieval **Hohensalzburg** castle, by using Austria's oldest **funicular railway** or walking up its steep cobbled drive. Later, explore the two focal squares near the funicular's base. Elegant Baroque **Mozartplatz** is flanked by the regal living quarters of Salzburg's archbishops and home to a 17th-century Glockenspiel, a musical clock that chimes three times a day. **Domplatz** contains the **Franziskanerkirche**, Salzburg's cavernous Renaissance cathedral, which has dazzling ceiling frescoes.

AFTERNOON Head into the network of atmospheric alleys and streets just north of the cathedral to find the evocative **Mozarts Geburtshaus**, where the composer was born in 1756. Then cross the river to seek out **Mozarts Wohnhaus**, Mozart's home from 1773 to 1787, which is now a first-rate multimedia museum dedicated to his life.

EVENING Seek out the jovial **Augustiner Bräu** beer gardens to discover why the city is regionally famous for its beer.

Essentials

GETTING THERE
Salzburg **airport** has regular flights from large European cities, and is a half-hour **bus** ride from the city centre. Austria's **fast-train**, Railjet, runs between Munich, Salzburg and Vienna.

WHERE TO STAY
Sandwirt (inexpensive) is a basic but clean and friendly *pension* near the station. +43 662 874 351
Haus Wartenberg (moderate) is a relaxed, family-run B&B in a 350-year-old city-centre house. www.hauswartenberg.com
Hotel Goldener Hirsch (expensive) offers elegant, traditional Austrian comforts in the centre of Salzburg's Old Town. www.goldenerhirschsalzburg.com

TOURIST INFORMATION
www.salzburg.info/en

Left Café Tomaselli, the oldest café in Austria, serves a wide range of luscious *torten*

Above The Baroque buildings of Salzburg's Old Town are dominated by Hohensalzburg castle

Below The busy, upmarket shopping street of Getreidegasse, where Mozart was born

Patisserie Around the World

Throughout German-speaking lands, afternoon *Kaffee und Kuchen* (coffee and cake) has become a sophisticated social ritual that demands lavish surroundings and ornate *torten*.

SALZBURG

Café Tomaselli

Alter Markt 9; www.tomaselli.at

Austria's oldest coffeehouse, founded in 1705, was once the haunt of Mozart and prides itself on barely having changed since then. The *torten* are outstanding, but the place prides itself on its *Guglhupf*, a simple marble cake.

Café Fürst

Brodgasse 13; www.original-mozartkugel.com

The upmarket coffeehouse opposite Café Tomaselli invented the ubiquitous marzipan "Mozart Ball" in 1890. It has many delicious *torten* and some lovely outdoor seating on the square outside.

Fingerlos

Franz Josef Strasse 9; +43 662 874 213

This is the locals' choice for coffee and cake: a little off the beaten path, but well worth the effort for its broad selection of freshly made, high-quality *torten* and the lively and contemporary atmosphere.

Konditorei Zauner

Pfarrgasse 7, Bad Ischl; www.zauner.at

Located in Salzburg's hinterland spa town of Bad Ischl, the glittering chandeliers, marble floors and fantastical confectionery of this patisserie are a draw for the entire region. It began life in the early 19th century as a supplier to the Austrian royal family.

VIENNA, AUSTRIA

The Viennese claim that they invented the notion of afternoon coffee and cake, and they certainly have enough venerable cafés and patisseries, or *Konditoreien*, to help prove it.

Hotel Sacher

Schwarzstrasse 5–7 and Philharmonikerstrasse 4; www.sacher.com

The Sacher hotel chain is a legacy of the pastry chef who invented the Sacher Torte, and it has branches in Salzburg and Vienna. Both have slightly snooty cafés with deep-red upholstery, liveried tableware and arguably the best Sacher Torte in the world.

Café Central

Corner of Strauchgasse/Herrengasse; www.cafecentral-wien.at

The favourite coffeehouse of Sigmund Freud and Leon Trotsky (in exile) is still steeped in Viennese tradition with tuxedoed waiters, extravagant chandeliers and locals poring over newspapers. The setting, ambience and unique *torten* often make it very busy, but it's spacious enough to cope.

Demel

Kohlmarkt 14; www.demel.at

A fine, long-standing Viennese coffee house that opened as an aristocrats' playground in 1786. It is best known for its Sacher Torte, which was first made here by Eduard Sacher (son of Franz, its inventor), sparking a legal contest within the family. The café today is more exceptional for its many coffees and extraordinary multicoloured *torten*, which have included waxwork-style recreations of celebrities. It also has branches in Salzburg and New York.

Konditorei Heiner

Wollzeile 9; www.heiner.co.at

A popular local café chain with several Viennese branches, including this cosy wood-panelled one on Wollzeile. Reasonable prices belie the superb quality and the pedigree of this bakery, which once supplied the Austrian court. The succulent poppy-seed *torte* is in a league of its own.

BLACK FOREST, GERMANY

The namesake of that famous gâteau, Black Forest cake, this region of southwest Germany loves to celebrate fine foods and its heritage, be it in the form of cuckoo clocks, traditional dress, wooden farmhouses or delicious *torten*.

Café König

Lichtentaler Strasse 12, Baden-Baden; www.chocolatier.de

This is a stylish throwback to Baden-Baden's 18th-century heyday, as depicted in the black-and-white prints that line the café walls. Elderly ladies in extravagant hats adore its famously delicate Black Forest gâteau; the fruit *torten* are also superb.

Left (top to bottom) Café Tomaselli, Austria's oldest "Viennese coffee house"; Schwarzwälder Kirschtorte, or Black Forest gâteau; coffee and the classic Sacher Torte.

Below (top to bottom) A tempting display of *torten* in a Viennese café with, far right, the tall, ring-shaped *Guglhupf*; afternoon coffee and cake in Café Gerbeaud in Budapest

Café Adler

Hauptstrasse 52, Triberg; www.hotel-cafe-adler.de
An understated café and patisserie with some of the best cakes in the region, which can be enjoyed in its twee pastel interiors or outside in a lovely little courtyard. They have a tremendous line in decorative confectionery items that make perfect gifts.

Café Decker

Hauptstrasse 70, Staufen; www.cafe-decker.de
The star café of the southwestern Black Forest region has a lovely riverside outdoor terrace and around 40 stunning fresh *torten* every day. It is also a first-class chocolatier and ice-cream maker, but beware: it gets packed at peak times.

ZURICH, SWITZERLAND

Chocolate and confectionery are a major export for the Swiss, so it's no surprise that they take great pride in their cakes too. There is a touch of the French *pâtissier* in their smaller and more delicate confections.

Confiserie Sprüngli

Bahnhofstrasse 21; www.spruengli.ch
This is run by a world-famous confectioner who's famed for *Luxemburgerli*, a sugar-based biscuit much like a French *macaron*. But there are plenty of *torten* to choose from too and everything is lovingly handmade using the best ingredients – though some might gripe about the high prices.

Café Bauer

Badenerstrasse 355; www.cafe-bauer.ch
This has been a local institution since the 1920s, thanks to its great selection of freshly made *torten* as well as a fine range of French-style patisserie. It also has delicious versions of everyday bakery products, such as pretzels and croissants.

BUDAPEST, HUNGARY

As the joint capital of the Austro-Hungarian empire, Budapest shared much of Vienna's culture, and the "coffee and cake" tradition took root here at about the same time. The results are almost as venerable.

Café Gerbeaud

Vörösmarty tér 7–8; www.gerbeaud.hu
A large and noble coffeehouse where hanging drapes and extraordinary chandeliers dominate interiors that have barely changed since its foundation in 1858. Despite seating over 300 people, a relaxed atmosphere prevails and the *torten* are impeccable.

Konditorei Ruszwurm

Szentháromság utca. 7; www.ruszwurm.hu
This tiny and charmingly well-preserved 1820s coffeehouse sits on Budapest's Castle Hill and has a superb cake selection, including traditional Hungarian favourites such as the *Dobos* and the walnut *Esterházy* with its succulent marbled icing.

On the Menu

Torten are rarely labelled and it's often simply a case of picking something that catches the eye. Even so, it's worth bearing the classics in mind and seeking them out.

Dobos Torte Simple but elegant five-layered Hungarian chocolate buttercream sponge cake from the 1880s. Often coated with ground nuts and topped with an angled wedge of caramel.
Frankfurter Kranz (Frankfurt wreath) Classic rum-flavoured cake with layers of buttercream filling and a single layer of jam.
Herrentorte (Gentlemen's cake) A term used for a range of cakes made with large amounts of dark chocolate, particularly in their icing.
Linzer Torte A Christmas favourite from the 17th century with a latticework top and chopped almonds around the edge. The pastry is a crumbly combination of lemon, cinnamon and ground nuts, and its most common filling is redcurrant jam.

Obsttorte (Fruit *torte*) Usually the simplest-looking *torte*, this fruit tart generally uses glazed fruits (often strawberries) and is sometimes decorated with toasted nuts.
Prinzregententorte (Prince Regent Cake) A layered *torte* with chocolate buttercream and apricot preserve, often dubbed the "Sacher Torte of Bavaria", where it's particularly popular.
Sacher Torte This classic, dark chocolate cake with a layer of apricot jam was invented by 16-year-old apprentice pastry chef Franz Sacher in 1832; the recipe remains a closely guarded secret.
Schwarzwälder Kirschtorte (Black Forest cherry cake) This is probably the most famous gâteau. Layers of whipped cream and Kirsch-flavoured chocolate cake studded with maraschino cherries are topped with dark chocolate curls.
Zuger Kirschtorte (Zug cherry cake) Swiss *torte* made from ground almonds and hazelnuts, filled with Kirsch and buttercream and topped with a dusting of icing sugar.

TBILISI GEORGIA

Satsivi in Medieval Tbilisi

Perched on the slopes above the Kura river, and scattered with medieval churches and old wooden houses, the capital of Georgia is one of the most atmospheric cities you could hope to visit. It is also one of the few places in Georgia where you are likely to find *satsivi*, one of the most famous and memorable dishes in a country renowned for its cuisine.

The Georgian capital, Tbilisi, has an almost kaleidoscopic range of architecture, from ancient stone churches to grand Soviet constructions, and traditional wooden houses to modern high-rise buildings. The city is around ten times the size of any other city in Georgia, yet it is small enough to get around the main sites on foot. It was founded in the 5th century by the Georgian king Vakhtang Gorgasali, whose fortress stood on the site of the present Metekhi church above the Kura river; there is a statue of the ruler next to the church.

Among the city's narrow lanes and along its broad avenues you'll stumble upon everything from cafés to carpet shops and thermal baths, and some first-rate theatres and museums, together with a wider choice of restaurants than anywhere else in the country. *Satsivi* is one of Georgia's most luxurious dishes, and this classic concoction is often served on festive occasions. Appearing deceptively simple, *satsivi* is essentially a whole portioned turkey, or sometimes chicken, bathed in a thick walnut sauce – and herein lies the secret. The sauce is a mix of ground walnuts and a distinctive blend of spices that incorporates coriander, cinnamon, cloves, paprika, a small sprinkling of chilli flakes and

a touch of saffron or ground marigold petals. A similar, ready-made spice mix called *khmeli-suneli* is sometimes used. The turkey (or chicken) is poached, then roasted, and finally combined with a sauce made from the poaching liquid and the ground walnuts, onions, garlic and spices. The *satsivi* is not served piping hot – the dish is allowed to "sit" for a period before serving, its sauce thickening as it cools to room temperature. Any extra sauce is eagerly scooped up with bread or *gomi* (polenta-like cornmeal porridge). The Georgians even have a summer version of *satsivi* called *bazhe*, another nut-based sauce dish that uses chicken or turkey, but fewer spices.

Georgian feasts are legendary, and eating out in Georgia is a genuinely memorable experience. As well as dishes such as *satsivi* and *chakapuli* (lamb with fresh tarragon and other herbs), there is a wide range of delicious starters, including more unusual ones such as *khachapuri*, a delicious cheese-filled bread. No self-respecting Georgian table would be complete without a plate of *khinkali* – fig-shaped, meat-filled dumplings eaten with lashings of freshly ground black pepper. The challenge lies in holding these by the "stem" and catching the flood of juice that runs out with the first bite.

A Day in Tbilisi

A walking tour of Tbilisi is the best way to see its historic churches and explore the warren of streets that run through the old town and up to the hilltop fort.

MORNING Start at **Rustaveli Avenue**, then head downhill past the State and Rustaveli Theatres and the **Kashveti church**, to **Freedom Square** and the historic **Sioni Cathedral**. Continue to the Kura river, crossing the Metekhi bridge to the **Metekhi church** and the statue of the founder of Tbilisi, Vakhtang Gorgasali.

AFTERNOON Return to the southern side of the river and head up through the warren of old streets of the old town (with their bathhouses) to the **Narikala fortress** and the **botanical gardens**. From here walk west to the huge statue of **Kartlis Deda**, Mother of Kartli (the central region of Georgia), who – in true Georgian fashion – wields an enormous sword with one hand while the other holds a bowl of wine.

EVENING Wander back down through the old town for dinner – and wine – on the terrace at Hotel Kopala.

Essentials

GETTING THERE
Tbilisi's **international airport,** around 15 km (9 miles) outside town, is connected to the city by **bus, train** and **taxi.**

WHERE TO STAY
Irine's Place (inexpensive) is a hugely popular guesthouse. *www.irinesplace.com*
Hotel Villa Mtiebi (moderate) has stylish, Art-Nouveau-decorated rooms, set round a plant-filled atrium. *www.hotelmtiebi.ge*
The British House (moderate) has sumptuous old-style rooms. *www.british-house.ge*

TOURIST INFORMATION
www.info-tbilisi.com

Above The walnut sauce of *satsivi* is a favourite at winter festivities in Tbilisi, along with the juicy dumplings known as *khinkali* (top left)

Left Tbilisi has been the capital of Georgia almost continuously since its founding in the 5th century

Above Georgia's thriving wine industry can draw on more than 500 varieties of grape, and most – 90 per cent – are Georgian varieties

Georgian Wines

Relatively little-known outside the Caucasus and Russia, Georgian wine is superb, and Georgia may be the oldest area of wine production in the world – dating back to around 4000 BC, when locals buried it in the ground in clay jars to ferment. The main area for wine production is the **Kakheti region** in the east, in particular **Telavi**. Among the most distinctive of Georgian wines are semi-sweet reds such as **Pirosmani** or **Khvanchkara**. The country has an elaborate wine toasting tradition, which includes a *tamada* or toast-master whose duty it is to propose suitable toasts throughout the course of a feast, and ensure no guest runs short of *gvino* (wine).

The Best Places to Eat Satsivi

Hotel Kopala moderate

With a terrace overlooking the old town, the Hotel Kopala is a great place to stay, and its restaurant – one of the finest in Tbilisi – has an excellent range of traditional Georgian dishes. Starched white tablecloths indoors give way to pretty, wrought-iron tables and chairs on the lovely open terrace, where customers dine at a relaxed pace. This vantage point has unbeatable views of the Metekhi church and across the river to the Narikala fort, rising above the atmospheric streets and houses of the old town. Inside the restaurant, large floor-to-ceiling windows share the same view (as do most of the rooms in the hotel). The menu includes either *satsivi* or *bazhe*, together with other favourites such as juicy *shashlik* (kebabs) and various specials, such as stuffed mushrooms. Both *satsivi* and *bazhe* are served with warming, homely *gomi* – the preferred earthy accompaniment to these thick, fragrant sauces. Pick a wine from the extensive Georgian wine list, and enjoy a delicious dining experience with an unforgettable view.

8–10 Chekhov Street, Tbilisi; open noon–11pm daily; www.kopala.ge

Also in Tbilisi

The large **Kolkheti** restaurant *(+995 32 357153; moderate)*, on the bank of the Kura river, has long tables with comfortable wood and leather chairs, and a wide range of traditional dishes including *satsivi* made – unusually – with sturgeon and other fish. **Ortachala** *(+995 32 788050; moderate)* is another good choice in the Georgian capital. For an indulgence in *khinkali*, head for **Khinklis Sakhli** *(www.khinklissakhli.info-tbilisi.com; inexpensive)* on Rustaveli Avenue, which specializes in *khinkali* in all their guises, along with other Georgian dishes.

Also in Georgia

There is no guarantee of finding *satsivi* on the menu in restaurants outside the Georgian capital, but one of the better bets if you're in Telavi is the **Hotel Rcheuli Marani** *(www. rcheuli.ge; moderate)*, which has its own cellar restaurant, the Old Marani.

Around the World

The excellent (and appropriately named) **Tbilisi** *(+44 20 7607 2536; moderate)* restaurant in London's Holloway Road serves a delicious *satsivi* among other Georgian dishes, including some mouthwateringly good entrée platters and super *khinkali*. They also serve Georgian wines such as the heady Pirosmani. **Little Georgia** *(+44 20 7739 8154; moderate)* and **Mimino** *(www.mimino.co.uk; moderate)* are two more excellent choices in London, which both have regularly changing specials.

Right The regular queue outside the famous Magpie Café fish-and-chip restaurant in Whitby, North Yorkshire

Below Crisply battered cod and piping-hot chips are accompanied by the traditional northern garnish, mushy peas

A Day in Whitby

Most visits to Whitby are divided between the cobbled old town and the beach. It's only a small place (population around 15,000), but makes a great base for exploring the nearby smugglers' villages and coastal cliff-top paths and also the North York Moors National Park.

MORNING Make an early visit (by 7am) to the **fish market**, and then stroll along the harbour for a view of town from the long, curving pier. Cross the river by the swing bridge to explore the **old town** on the east side – including the **Captain Cook Memorial Museum** – before climbing the 199 steps to the dramatic ruins of **Whitby Abbey**.

AFTERNOON Even if the beach beckons, don't miss **Whitby Museum** and its amazing collection of Jurassic period fossils. Fang-fans can also follow the **Dracula trail** around town – Bram Stoker set his famous novel here.

EVENING Walk up to the **Captain Cook Monument** to join an early evening guided "ghost walk" around the town's hidden alleys and lanes, before choosing a fish and seafood restaurant for dinner.

Essentials

GETTING THERE
Whitby is on England's northeastern coast, an hour's **drive** (or **bus ride**) from York. York lies on the East Coast **railway** line between London and Edinburgh; there are also direct **trains** to York from **Manchester International Airport**. A **steam railway** runs to nearby Pickering.

WHERE TO STAY
Dillons (inexpensive) has classy, contemporary B&B rooms. *www.dillonsofwhitby.co.uk*
White Horse & Griffin (moderate) is a stylishly updated coaching inn and restaurant. *www.whitehorseandgriffin.co.uk*
La Rosa (expensive) offers quirky, vintage Victorian surroundings. *www.larosa.co.uk*

TOURIST INFORMATION
Whitby Tourist Information Centre, Langborne Road; *www.discoveryorkshirecoast.com*

WHITBY ENGLAND

The Great British Seaside Dish

It's hard to think of a more atmospheric coastal resort than Whitby in North Yorkshire, its red-roofed houses hugging the River Esk below the striking ruins of an ancient abbey. Generations of holiday-makers have wiggled their toes in Whitby's golden sands and strolled along the bustling harbour, building up an appetite for that greatest of seaside pleasures: deep-fried fish and chips.

The sea is embedded in Whitby's history — from humble medieval herring port to booming 18th-century whaling town — while its shipyards built the vessels that took England's greatest explorer, Captain James Cook, on his remarkable voyages of discovery. Even today, there's a real air of romance and excitement on any visit, from the steam trains that chug into the harbourside station to the higgledy-piggledy cottages of the Georgian old town.

While Whitby and its glorious sandy beach remains at heart a traditional bucket-and-spade resort, there are boutique stirrings among the town's hotels and B&Bs, and a new wave of café-bars and restaurants doing great things with shellfish, sea bass, oysters and lobster along with other locally sourced produce. But there's still only one must-have dish on a day trip to Whitby — good old-fashioned fish and chips.

For such a well-known dish, its origins are obscure. The fried-fish dishes of immigrant Portuguese and Spanish Jews were already popular in London during Victorian times, while contemporary northern mill workers were enthusiastic consumers of fried "chips" made from potatoes dug from the rich Lancashire soils. When the two came together, a cheap, nutritious working-class delicacy was born. It quickly took hold across the nation – nowhere in England is more than 110 km (70 miles) from the coast – but for the quintessential fish-and-chip experience, there's still no beating the beguiling marriage of sand, sun and sea air.

In Whitby, chunky cod and haddock fillets are the mainstays of takeaways and upmarket restaurants alike, deep-fried in golden batter, sprinkled with salt and malt vinegar and served with a mountain of chips. Batter recipes are zealously guarded, and the best places are proud to say they fry their fish and potatoes in traditional beef dripping or lard. For purists, the only accompaniment is mushy peas (marrowfat peas, cooked down to a purée), and if the whole lot is eaten out of paper on the beach, so much the better. The harbourside cafés and restaurants of Whitby are selling more than just a dish – those heady salt-and-vinegar tones evoke nothing less than a collective national memory of seaside jaunts and happy holidays.

What Else to Eat

Fortune's (*www.fortuneskippers.co.uk*) is Whitby's only traditional smokehouse, tucked up a cobbled lane in the old town, just beyond the bottom of the 199 Steps. It's been a Fortune family concern since 1872, producing what many argue are England's best oak- and beech-smoked kippers — locals, visitors and TV chefs alike all make the pilgrimage to the unassuming smokehouse and shop that lies sheltered under the east-side cliffs. Kippers are smoked Atlantic herrings, still prepared by hand at Fortune's, alongside a delicious kipper pâté and smoked salmon, haddock and bacon. A pair of Fortune's kippers is a true taste of Whitby to take home, while many local hotels and restaurants serve Fortune's kippers to their guests.

Left Whitby viewed from the end of West Pier

The Best Places to Eat Fish and Chips

Magpie Café moderate

The venerable Magpie Café – run by three generations of the same family over several decades – is synonymous with fish and chips, both in Whitby and far beyond. It's a traditional-looking black-and-white building on the harbourside, right by the fish market, unremarkable from the outside save for the queue snaking down the steps and along the street, in any weather, at any time of the year (reservations aren't usually accepted). The lure is simply spectacular fish and chips – and not just cod and haddock, but plaice, skate, monkfish, lemon sole or halibut, sourced wherever possible directly from Whitby fishing boats or fish merchants and perfectly fried in their own-recipe batter. The same fish also comes grilled or poached, while a very long menu also offers time-honoured Magpie favourites from Whitby crab and kippers to seafood chowder and lobster thermidor. Portions are "Yorkshire-sized" (ie big), and the long-serving staff are helpful and motherly.
14 Pier Road, Whitby; open 11·30am–9pm daily; www.magpiecafe.co.uk

Also in Whitby

The queues aren't so long, but the fish and chips are still excellent at **Trenchers** (*www. trenchersrestaurant.co.uk; moderate*), where you can also watch the fryers at work. For posh fish and chips, and a more upmarket fish and seafood experience all round, **Green's** (*www. greensofwhitby.com; expensive*) sets the local standard – the boat skippers who land their fish are name-checked on the menu.

Also in England

Every town and city in England has a favourite local "chippy" (fish and chip restaurant or takeaway), and annual competitions and awards anoint the best, often in otherwise unsung places. **Colmans** in South Shields, also in the northeast (*www.colmansfishandchips.com; inexpensive*) is a classic of its kind, in business since 1926, and while **Harry Ramsdens** (*www.harryramsdens.co.uk*) is now a well-known national chain, the original restaurant in Guiseley, outside Leeds, still draws pilgrims.

Around the World

The dish has followed the English around the world, from New York to New Zealand. In Hong Kong, there's classic cod and chips at **Dot Cod** (*www.dotcod.com; expensive*), an upmarket seafood restaurant and oyster bar, while Sydney in Australia is renowned for quality beachside fish and chips, like those from **Mongers** (*www.mongers.com.au; inexpensive*), found at Manly and Bondi beaches.

Three Days in Gruyères

Gruyères – a château-crowned, hill-top medieval town surrounded by snow-capped peaks – is in La Gruyère: rolling, cow-studded countryside in western Switzerland's French-speaking canton of Fribourg. It is the home of Gruyère, the most popular fondue cheese.

DAY ONE Head to **La Maison du Gruyère** (opposite the train station) to see Gruyère being made, then visit the 13th-century castle. On your way back down, see some exceptional Himalayan art at the **Musée Tibétain**, and then call in at the **H R Giger Museum**, which displays work by an Oscar-winning, Surrealist artist and designer.

DAY TWO Drive to **Bulle**, where folk art at the **Musée Gruérien** charmingly demonstrates the traditional life of dairy farmers. Take a tour of **Maison Cailler** chocolate factory in Broc. Wind down with a soak in the warm baths at **Les Bains de la Gruyère** in Charmey.

DAY THREE From May to September, high up in **Moléson-Village**, you can see cheese-making the old-fashioned way. After lunch, walk the two-hour **Cheese Trail** down to Gruyères–Gare.

Essentials

GETTING THERE
Fly to Geneva or Zurich **airports** and then either take a **train** to Gruyères via Palézieux (one change); or take a **train** to Bulle and then catch a **bus** to "Gruyères-Ville".

WHERE TO STAY
La Ferme du Bourgoz (inexpensive), outside the town walls, has three cosy guest rooms. Breakfast includes the farm's own cheese. *www.lafermedubourgoz.ch*
Hostellerie St Georges (moderate) is a charming hotel in the town with a good restaurant. *www.st-georges-gruyeres.ch*
Romantik Hôtel Broc'aulit (expensive) in nearby Broc-en-Gruyère offers stylish rooms in a renovated 1830s building. *www.brocaulit.ch*

TOURIST INFORMATION
1 rue du Bourg; +41 848 424 424

Right A cheesemaker carries a wheel of Gruyère cheese to a cool cellar, where it will mature over 6–10 months

Below Diners enjoy spectacular views while eating alfresco on Gruyères' cobbled main street

GRUYERES SWITZERLAND

Cheese Fondue in Switzerland

Ensconced in fleecy falls of snow, or lit up by the clear spring sunshine, the walled and castle-topped town of Gruyères has a fairy-tale aura. It sits on a hill amid Alpine peaks, gently tinkling with the sound of cowbells as the animals graze on surrounding slopes. This is dairy paradise and the cradle of Gruyère cheese – one of the staples of a luscious, bubbling pot of fondue.

The tiny town of Gruyères sits high on a hill in the Fribourg pre-Alps, dominated by its medieval castle. Its name is said to come from the French word for crane, *grue*, because the bird adorned the heraldry of the counts of Gruyères, who lived here from the 11th to the 16th centuries. The town consists of little more than one pedestrianized, cobblestoned street, lined with beautifully maintained, centuries-old shopfronts, many bearing ornate wrought-iron signs. This is fairy-tale country, where geraniums tumble from every window box in summer, and twinkling lights shine on the cobbles at Christmas. Visitors come for two reasons: to see the chocolate-box town and to sample its more famous ware – Gruyère cheese – especially in the form of fondue, a pot of hot, melted cheese made for communal dipping.

Cheese has been made in the Gruyère region for centuries, and the apocryphal tale of fondue is that it was created by cowherds who had nothing to eat but stale bread and cheese, and discovered that the combination was better if the cheese was melted. Sadly, Swiss food historians dispute this, pointing out that cheese was too expensive for cowherds. They claim that fondue was a bourgeois dish invented just a few hundred years ago in Neuchâtel – once ruled by the French Dukes of Burgundy, but now part of Switzerland – and its fame later spread into Vaud, Fribourg and beyond.

Fondue is simple to make: the cook rubs a heavy casserole dish (a *caquelon*) with garlic, adds and heats either white wine or water, then stirs in lots of cheese, sometimes with a little cornstarch, nutmeg and Kirsch. The fondue is carried to the table and eaten communally from its pot, by diners who dip in small cubes of crusty bread held on long forks. The most popular fondue cheeses are Gruyère and the slightly softer Vacherin Fribourgeois. Sometimes Vacherin is used alone (as in *fondue Fribourgeoise*), but the most common form in Gruyères is the Swiss favourite, *moitié-moitié*: half-and-half Gruyère and Vacherin. Fondue is traditionally a winter dish, but in Gruyères its sheer popularity is such that it is served all year round.

Swiss Food Festivals

In late September the cowherds of Charmey don traditional jackets embroidered with edelweiss for **Désalpe**, a traditional festival when cows are led through the streets wearing headdresses of flowers. There are lots of food and craft stalls too (www.desalpe.ch). Every village in the region holds a kind of Thanksgiving festival in September or October known as **Bénichon**, a feast that includes saffron-flavoured *cuchaule* bread and *moutarde de Bénichon*, a jam-like sweet-and-sour spread (www.fribourgregion.ch). Also in October, the town of Bulle holds a huge event known as the **Salon Suisse des Goûts et Terroirs** – a veritable tumble of sausages, cheeses, baked goods, pickles, honeys, sweets, wines and spirits, together with demonstrations by top-starred chefs – and you get to taste the results (www.gouts-et-terroirs.ch).

Above Cheese fondue is kept hot on the table so diners can dip their bread chunks

The Best Places to Eat Cheese Fondue

Café-Restaurant des Remparts
inexpensive–moderate

Locals and tourists blend at the no-frills Remparts as cosily as a good pot of fondue. Two types of fondue are served here: *moitié-moitié* ("half-and-half"), combining Gruyère and Vacherin Fribourgeois, garlic and white wine; and *fondue au Vacherin* – a fondue of Vacherin Fribourgeois with garlic and water. Spear a piece of crusty bread or potato on your fondue fork and dip it into the cheese. As the pot begins to empty, ask the waitress to explain how best to get a good crust of cheese at the bottom that you can chip off and eat – it's delicious. The perfect accompaniments to fondue are *viande séchée* (air-dried beef, cut sliver-thin), pickles and a cool glass of white Chasselas wine.

Berries are ideal for dessert, but you'll probably feel overwhelmingly tempted to have them with Gruyère double cream, so you might as well add in some good meringues too.
19 rue du Bourg, Gruyères; open 9am–9:30pm daily; www.remparts-resto.com

Also in Gruyères

Try *moitié-moitié* at **Auberge de la Halle** (www.la-halle.ch) or **Hôtel de Ville** (www.hoteldeville.ch). **Le Chalet** (www.chalet-gruyeres.ch) has both good *moitié-moitié* and *fondue au Vacherin*, as does **La Fleur de Lys** (www.hotelfleurdelys.ch), which also serves fondue with boletus mushrooms (*aux bolets*). Prices at these restaurants are inexpensive to moderate, varying only marginally.

Also in Switzerland

Many eateries around Switzerland offer their own takes on cheese fondue. In Geneva, try *fondue au Crémant* (made with sparkling wine), a winter-only, dinner speciality at the **Buvette des Bains** (www.buvettedesbains.ch; inexpensive). Zurich's **Le Dézaley** (www.le-dezaley.ch; moderate) makes fondue using a good but secret "grandma's recipe". In the Swiss capital of Bern, **Restaurant Harmonie** (www.harmonie.ch; expensive) is renowned far and wide for its cheese fondue, which is served with morels, or truffles and Champagne.

Around the World

The **St Moritz** (www.stmoritz-restaurant.co.uk; moderate) in London offers several kinds of fondue besides that perennial favourite, *moitié-moitié*. They also serve cheese fondue Valais-style (with tomatoes); Neuchâtel-style (Gruyère and Emmenthal); and *forestière* (with wild mushrooms). In New York, **Trestle on Tenth** (www.trestleontenth.com; moderate) has Fondue Sundays, when a trio of Gruyère, Emmenthal and Vacherin go into the pot.

PORTO PORTUGAL

Bacalhau in the Port Capital

In Portugal's second city, Porto – famous for its port-wine lodges – the revitalized riverside Ribeira district is now a UNESCO World Heritage site and provides a magnificent backdrop for sampling that most Portuguese of foodstuffs: *bacalhau*, or dried, salted codfish. In skilled hands, this defies its unpromising beginnings to become no less than the country's national dish.

Arriving in Porto by rail or road, there's a first, dramatic view of the broad Douro river, which — more than any monument or museum, more than its stunning Baroque architecture — gives the city centre its distinct character. From the elevated medieval cathedral, an intricate jumble of stepped alleys tumbles down to the river's north bank and to the sparkling waterfront known as the Ribeira. Fish restaurants line the arcaded quayside, some tucked into former warehouses, while above looms the iconic Ponte Dom Luís I, the 19th-century double-decker bridge whose graceful profile frames both river and city. A meal here on the quayside, looking across the river to the port-wine lodges with their names emblazoned across their roofs, is an absolute must on a trip to Porto.

For all the Ribeira's alfresco restaurants and riverside promenades, Porto remains at heart a straightforward working city, something that is reflected in its down-to-earth cuisine. The locals, for example, are known as *tripeiros* — tripe-eaters — due to their penchant for tripe dishes, but there's another classic dish on the menu in every Porto establishment that's more palatable to most visitors.

In the 15th and early 16th centuries, the Portuguese were the world's greatest maritime explorers, opening up trading routes to Africa and India. Long sea journeys were made possible in part by the preservation of food, notably dried, salted codfish *(bacalhau)*, which became one of the first truly global dishes — eaten from Portugal to Scandinavia, and in far-flung Portuguese colonies from Brazil to Macau.

After centuries of experimentation, the number of Portuguese *bacalhau* recipes is famously large — some say 365, one for every day of the year, others say a thousand. Every region has its own speciality, and so does every chef. In Porto, the favoured preparation is named after the 19th-century cod merchant who invented it, *bacalhau à Gomes de Sá* – baked with potato and onion, and garnished with olives and hard-boiled eggs — but it also comes boiled, roasted or fried, poached in olive oil, and cooked with everything from cream to chilli sauce. It's a popular festive meal, with Portuguese families sitting down on Christmas Eve to *bacalhau com todos* ("with everything"), served with boiled potatoes, chickpeas, cabbage and carrots. It may seem strange to anyone brought up on the idea of a Christmas turkey or goose, but the *bacalhau*-loving Portuguese wouldn't have it any other way.

A Day in Porto

Porto regards itself as the capital of northern Portugal, and it's a vibrant, cultural university city with a strong Baroque heritage and a fascinating riverside district.

MORNING Start with coffee and fresh bread in the **Mercado do Bolhão** market, then walk to the **Torre dos Clérigos** (Clérigos Tower) for an eagle-eye city view. Visit the medieval **Sé** (cathedral), after which you can descend the stepped alleys to the **Ribeira district**, where former merchant wealth is evident in buildings like the stunning Baroque **São Francisco church** and the **Palácio da Bolsa** (Stock Exchange).

AFTERNOON The Douro river has been at the heart of Porto's life and trade for centuries and taking a **river cruise** under the city's famous bridges brings much of the history to life. Afterwards, take the bus out to the **Fundação Serralves**, Porto's stunning contemporary art museum and sculpture park.

EVENING Drink an apéritif in the **Solar do Vinho do Porto**, the bar of the Port Wine Institute, before returning to the quayside restaurants of the **Ribeira**.

Essentials

GETTING THERE
Porto airport is the main airport for northern Portugal. Fast, reliable **intercity trains** connect Porto and Lisbon (around three hours).

WHERE TO STAY
Grande Hotel de Paris (inexpensive) is a charming city-centre mansion. *www.ghparis.pt*
Guest House Douro (moderate) has stylish B&B riverside rooms. *www.guesthousedouro.com*
Pestana Porto (expensive) is a classy boutique hotel on the quayside. *www.pestana.com*

TOURIST INFORMATION
Posto de Turismo Centro, Rua Clube dos Fenianos 25; *www.portoturismo.pt*

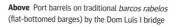

Above Port barrels on traditional *barcos rabelos* (flat-bottomed barges) by the Dom Luís I bridge

Left Stiff as a board and almost as weatherproof, the split and dried salt cod can be seen hanging from shopfronts all over Portugal

Above *Bacalhau a espanhola* – "in the Spanish way" – cooked with peppers, potatoes, fresh tomatoes, white wine, garlic and green olives

On the Port Wine Trail

Since the 18th century, port wine has been shipped downriver from the Douro vineyards to large quayside warehouses – lodges – in Porto, with historic company names that resonate through the ages. All offer fascinating tours (often free) of their premises, and at lodges like Sandeman (*www.sandeman.eu*), Cálem (*www.calem.pt*) and Ramos Pinto (*www.ramospinto.pt*), you can get to grips with the difference between a ruby, tawny or vintage port before a tasting or two of their wines. There's more information on the Port Wine Institute website (*www.ivdp.pt*), while the Rota do Vinho do Porto (*www.rvp.pt*) guides visitors on the Douro river "Port Wine Route".

The Best Places to Eat Bacalhau

Dom Tonho expensive

Dom Tonho occupies a favoured position on the Ribeira quayside, its dining room windows and outdoor terrace looking directly on to the Douro river and Dom Luís I bridge. It has a sleek look that marries stylish design with the building's ancient, slabbed granite walls and arches, and visiting celebrities are very much on its radar, but for all its undoubted star attraction it's what comes out of the Dom Tonho kitchen that seals the deal. The exciting menu puts a contemporary twist on traditional Portuguese dishes, not least its own take on salt cod, *bacalhau à Dom Tonho*, in which the fish is fried with potatoes and egg and served with garlic-sautéed onion, bacon and cabbage. This or another *bacalhau* dish is always on the menu, while for an appetizer try the tantalizingly named *peixinhos da horta* (little garden fish), which are actually deep-fried green beans – nothing less than Portuguese-style tempura.
Cais da Ribeira 13–15, Porto; open 12:30–3pm & 7:30–11.30pm daily; www.dtonho.com

Also in Porto

Filha da Mãe Preta *(+351 222 055 515; inexpensive)* is one of the best-known traditional Portuguese restaurants on the Porto quayside, its tiled arches and river views forming a charming backdrop for local dishes, including a daily *bacalhau* choice. **Café Majestic** *(www.cafemajestic.com; moderate)*, a gloriously decorated Art Nouveau café, also has *bacalhau* on its lunch menu, while a 30-minute metro ride from the centre takes you to the in-the-know suburb of Matosinhos for the city's finest fish and seafood restaurants.

Also in Portugal

Virtually every restaurant in Portugal serves a *bacalhau* dish – favourites to look out for include *bacalhau à brás* (fried, with egg, onion and potatoes), *com natas* (baked with cream) and *com piri-piri* (cooked in chilli sauce). At Lisbon's fashionable dockside **Bica do Sapato** *(www.bicadosapato.com; expensive)* they serve an unusual *bacalhau* risotto accompanied by deep-fried *bacalhau* fillets.

Around the World

Portuguese salt-cod preparations are rare outside the Portuguese-speaking countries, though *bacalhau* itself has travelled the world (as it was intended to) and turns up on menus as *bacalao* (Spain), *baccalà* (Italy), *klippfisk* (Norway), saltfish (Jamaica) and *morue* (France). In the Spanish capital, Madrid, one of the signature tapas dishes at the famous bullfighting tavern, **La Taberna de Antonio Sánchez** *(+34 915 397 826; inexpensive)*, is *tortilla de San Isidro*, a classic *madrileño* salt-cod omelette.

Right The *bouchons* of Lyon promise an old-fashioned warmth along with unpretentious, hearty regional food

Below *Saucisson chaud à la lyonnaise* is a simple dish of poached pork sausage and warm, dressed potato salad

A Day in Lyon

Old Lyon is a UNESCO World Heritage site, full of medieval churches and Renaissance buildings, and its narrow streets are full of surprises.

MORNING Explore the city's *traboules* (hidden passageways linking ancient streets). Map in hand, set out from **Place St Paul** in Old Lyon to explore the cobbled lanes. Visit **Cathédrale St-Jean** to admire the stained glass and the astronomical clock.

AFTERNOON Look out for the giant modern murals that are splashed across Lyon, sometimes covering whole buildings. The architecture-rich **Presqu'île** area has some of the best, including **Fresque des Lyonnais**, picturing Lyonnais celebrities, and the nearby **Bibliothèque de la Cité**, where huge books decorate the building.

EVENING Take the funicular up to the gilt-rich basilica of **Nôtre Dame de Fourvière**, built in the 1870s on the site of a Roman temple. Alongside are two 12th-century chapels, and there's a sweeping view of the whole city from the terrace.

Essentials

GETTING THERE
There are **flights** (Lyon-Saint Exupéry Airport) and **high-speed trains** to Lyon from many European cities. The city has an efficient **tram**, **train** and **bus** network, and free **bicycle** hire.

WHERE TO STAY
Collège Hotel (inexpensive) is a quirky school-themed hotel with all-white decor. *www.college-hotel.com*
Artelit Chambres d'Hôtes (moderate) has romantic rooms in a 16th-century building with a pink tower in Old Lyon. *www.dormiralyon.com*
Villa Florentine (expensive) is a restored 17th-century convent with a city panorama that's hard to top. *www.villaflorentine.com*

TOURIST INFORMATION
Place Bellecour; *www.lyon-france.com*

The Best Places to Eat Lyonnais Cooking

La Meunière moderate

Bouchon purists agree that they don't come much more atmospheric and traditionally French than La Meunière. The patron, Jean-Louis, has the spherical stomach, handlebar moustache and cheeky, welcoming smile of those long-disappeared bistro owners you might have glimpsed in sepia photos, but he's no phantom. And like Jean-Louis, the food is hearty, so prepare by running a triathlon, swimming the Channel or walking up and down Lyon's Fourvière Hill at least twice. Start the meal with a traditional apéritif known as a "communard" – a heady mix of red wine and red fruit syrup handed out with slices of cured sausage. Then launch into a range of robust salads (brains, tripe, lentils, herrings, sheep's feet or the ever popular *salade lyonnaise* of bacon, croutons, *frisée* lettuce and a poached egg). One of the city's oldest *bouchons*, La Meunière dishes up the classics with gusto: black pudding with apples, gratin of tripe sausage, chicken braised in vinegar, pistachio sausage and veal kidneys with mustard. For dessert, pears cooked in red wine or a plum tart are irresistible.

11 rue Neuve, Lyon; open noon–1:45pm and 8:15–9:30pm Tue–Sat; closed mid-Jul–mid-Aug and last week Dec; http://la.meuniere.free.fr

LYON FRANCE

The Lyonnais Bouchon

Travellers have passed through Lyon for thousands of years, en route from Italy to Flanders, or more recently from grey northern skies to southern sunshine. These days, it is a destination in its own right, luring visitors with its architecture, history and homely *bouchons* – cosy traditional inns that specialize in the city's very own style of hearty cuisine.

"In the kingdom of good taste, Lyon's cuisine reigns above all others", or so says a popular adage in Lyon. There's certainly no shortage of wonderful ingredients – Lyon is surrounded by fine food, from Bresse chickens, Charolais beef and Jura pork to the fish of the alpine Savoie lakes and the gleaming fruit of the Rhône Valley. Sitting at the crossroads between north and south, the city has cemented its gastronomic supremacy.

Once the capital of the Gauls, and still sometimes referred to in this way, Lyon has been a magnet for trade through the ages. During the Renaissance its four annual fairs drew traders from all over Europe, and wealthy families soon began to ensconce themselves in the old town around St Jean, taking care to be close to both church and state (the governor's house, the cathedral and the archbishop's house). The regal former home of the Gadagne family, influential Italian bankers, is now the Lyon history museum.

But the bourgeoisie did not make up the clientele at the local *bouchons*, which were the haunt of the workers, such as coachmen, who knew they could always count on a fresh, hearty meal and a pot of Beaujolais at a price to suit their meagre wages. Pork was a menu constant, from *andouillette* (tripe sausage) and *petit salé* (pork belly) to fried crackling. It was not until the early 1900s that the *Mères Lyonnaises* (the mothers of Lyon) made Lyon a cuisine capital with their simple, subtle cooking. Mère Guy, Mère Fillioux, Mère Brazier and Mère Bourgeois turned *bouchon* cooking into an art, and brought a new type of clientele to the table. Mère Brazier went on to become the first woman to win three Michelin stars, but it is often the modest Lyonnais cooking that draws the contented sighs: the pork and salty lentils, boiled pink sausages studded with pistachios, black pudding with melting apples, chicken softly braised in vinegar, salads of frizzy endive, egg and chunks of smoky bacon, the cheesy potato gratin and butter-soaked apple tarts. Look out for an authentic *bouchon* by spotting the *Authentiques Bouchons Lyonnais* label, a guarantee of traditional warmth and astonishingly good food.

Also in Lyon

With its turned-wood and tiled street façade, **Chez Hugon** (*+33 4 7828 1094; inexpensive*) looks just like the convivial *bouchon* it is. Expect authentic Lyonnais food served up in plentiful quantities – potato and herring salad, pike quenelles in a creamy crayfish sauce, black pudding and apples, and for insatiable carnivores, *tête de veau* (calf's head).

Also in France

In Paris, **Aux Lyonnais** (*www.auxlyonnais. com; moderate*) is a delicious looking place, from its extravagant mirrors and mouldings down to its flowery *belle époque* tiles and period apéritif posters. As part of super-chef Alain Ducasse's L'Esprit Bistro group, Aux Lyonnais is more refined than rustic *bouchon*, but the cooking is definitely *bouchon*-inspired: calf's liver with parsley and garlic, farm-raised chicken in cream, pig's head sausage and black pudding with potato purée arrive on the table in cast-iron pots and frying pans. All the cured meats and sausages are shipped up from Lyon.

Around the World

If you're in Los Angeles searching for French food with a hint of Lyon, slip into Thomas Keller's **Bouchon** (*www.bouchonbistro.com; moderate*). It has the casual, chattery vibe of a *bouchon* with the panache of a Paris bistro, and serves chunky country pâté, foie gras terrine and blood sausage with caramelized apples.

Cookery Classes

Veteran super-chef Paul Bocuse is a local treasure, known for his Michelin three-star restaurant and more pocket-friendly bistros, but he also runs the **Institut Paul Bocuse** (*www. institutpaulbocuse.com*), just outside Lyon in the Château du Vivier, which has been teaching cooking skills – from one- to three-day courses for amateurs to degree courses – for more than 20 years. Aurélie Chauvin is another passionate cook, who worked beside Michelin-starred chef Mathieu Vianney at Les Oliviers before deciding to open her own cooking school in Lyon, **Délicieusement Votre** (*www.delicieusementvotre.com*). You can learn to make an entrée, main course and dessert in three hours or take a themed class, for example in patisserie.

Left The Cathédrale St-Jean and Notre Dame de Fourvière on the banks of the Saône river, which joins the Rhône at Lyon

BURSA TURKEY

Choice Kebabs in Anatolia

Despite its prestigious past and proximity to Istanbul, the ancient city of Bursa is often overlooked by visitors. It thrived under the Romans and was the birthplace of the Ottoman empire, which enriched the city as it experimented with new forms of architecture. Bursa today has much to offer visitors in its historic buildings and its cuisine, including the original form of the doner kebab.

The intriguing city of Bursa boasts a distinguished history dating back to 200 BC, when King Prusia of Bithynia established a kingdom on the remains of an ancient civilization here. The fertile plains, brisk trade and healing thermal springs later made it a favourite of the Romans, but it was not until the Ottomans conquered the city in 1326 that the economic prosperity of the region was translated into art and architecture. Bursa was the Ottoman empire's first capital, and it became a kind of architectural laboratory – the city's 14th- and 15th-century buildings are uniquely important early examples of the developing Ottoman style.

Today's cosmopolitan city is littered with the majestic ghosts of its august past, with vast and magnificent mosques, exquisitely carved royal tombs, ornate medieval *medresesi* (seminaries) and elegant *hammams* (baths) seemingly haunting every corner. Bursa's spectacular setting beneath Mount Uludağ on the edge of a national park, its green spaces, café culture and lack of touts pressing for business also add to the town's attractions. As does the Iskender kebab, invented here by Iskender Usta in 1867 when he first experimented with roasting lamb on a vertical spit.

Although the word "kebab" (or *kebap*) is thought to be Persian in origin, the dish is thought to have developed from the nomadic lifestyle of the early Turkic tribes as they swept in from Central Asia in the 6th century. The world's first shish kebabs are said to have been hunks of meat skewered on the swords of marauding warriors as they sat around their camp fires. Today, the kebab is one of the most recognized and popular prepared foods in the world, but often serves as a cheap, easy stomach-filler after a night out. In fact, kebabs are a far more sophisticated and varied food form than the ubiquitous doner or shish commonly suggest.

In Turkey, where lamb and chicken most commonly fill kebabs, the meat is either compressed to form a giant cone for spit-roasting (*döner* means "rotating" in Turkish) and slicing, or cut into cubes and grilled on skewers (*şiş*), ground into meatballs (*köfte*), or steamed (*buğu*) and prepared as a casserole. The İskender *kebap* is quite an experience. In restaurants, waiters serve diamond-shaped slivers of spit-roasted lamb on warm *pide* (pitta) bread, topped with fresh, fragrant tomato sauce and accompanied by grilled chilli and tangy yogurt, before drizzling the entire dish in lightly browned butter. Washed down with fresh grape juice, it's a veritable feast in the first city of the Sultans.

A Day in Bursa

Bursa is now a sizable and frenetic modern city, but its long and prodigious history is evident in its impressive mosques, tombs, houses and pretty tea gardens.

MORNING Start the day admiring the 20 domes of Bursa's largest mosque, the 14th-century **Ulu Cami** (Grand Mosque). Just east of the square known locally as "Heykel" lies the exquisite 15th-century **Yeşil Cami** (Green Mosque) and the tiled **Yeşil Türbe** (Green Tomb). Then head for the covered market behind the mosque, where you can eat the town's famous candied chestnuts and drink Turkish coffee.

AFTERNOON West of the mosques are the 14th-century **tombs of Osman and Orhan**, the first sultans of the Ottoman empire, and just beyond them, the beautiful **Muradiye Complex**. Picnic in the adjacent **Kültür Parkı** then take a cable-car ride up **Uludağ** for views over the national park and Turkey's largest ski centre.

EVENING Head for the spa suburb of **Çekirge** or a city **hammam** for a revitalizing hot mineral bath, then enjoy a juicy Iskender kebab in one of the city's fine restaurants.

Essentials

GETTING THERE
Bursa's small international **Yenişehir Airport** is 53 km (33 miles) from the city centre. Istanbul is within easy reach by fast **ferries** and **buses**.

WHERE TO STAY
Hotel Güneş (inexpensive) is a family-run, centrally located hotel. *+90 224 222 1404*
Safran Otel (moderate) is a restored Ottoman house near the Osman tomb. *+90 224 224 7216*
Hotel Gönlüferah (expensive) offers historic charm with modern comforts, including a spa. *www.gonluferah.com*

TOURIST INFORMATION
Just off Atatürk Caddesi; *+90 224 220 1848*

Above The Bursa İskender restaurant is the original home of the İskender *kebap*, the original form of the now-ubiquitous doner kebab

Left The serene interior of the 14th-century Ulu Cami mosque with its three-tiered ablution fountain and walls adorned with Koranic calligraphy

Below The delicately flavoured *kebaps* of Bursa are served with various savoury pastries, often topped with yogurt and chillies

Kebabs Around the World

Some sources claim that the Near East's shortage of cooking fuel led to the development and rapid spread of the quick-cooking kebab. Today, kebabs are found across the Near and Middle East, stretching as far as Central and South Asia.

TURKEY

Meşhur Köfteci Ali Usta inexpensive
Yali Caddesi, Tekirdağ; +90 282 261 1621
This popular kebab house has been serving up the regional speciality, *bugu kebabı*, along with the town's celebrated *Tekirdağ köftesi* spicy meatballs, in its promenade-facing restaurant since 1966. The food is authentic and competitively priced.

Dibek moderate
Hakkı Paşa Meydanı 1, Göreme; www.dibektraditionalcook.com
The Cappadocian town of Göreme is famous for its *köfte* and *testı kebap*, and Dibek serves both along with other enticing Cappadocian dishes in a cosy, atmospheric 16th-century building.

Kebapçi İskender expensive
Ünlü Caddesi 7, Bursa; +90 224 221 4615
Founded in 1867, and something of an institution, this kebab house takes its name from the inventor of the İskender kebab, from whom the current owners claim descent. It serves the İskender along with Bursa's other famous dish, the *inegöl köftesi*.

IRAN

Akin to a kind of national dish, kebabs dominate most Iranian menus. They are served principally in the form of shish kebabs, on bread or with steamed rice, or as *kubide* (like *köfte*). Grilled tomatoes, sliced raw onion and sumac spice are typical accompaniments.

Ferdosi Sonnati inexpensive
Ferdosi St, Tehran; +98 21 6671 4503
With a firm local following, the Ferdosi prepares fresh, seasonal and carefully cooked classic Persian dishes (including kebabs) at excellent prices. Try the homemade *dugh*, a refreshing sour yogurt drink that's the traditional kebab accompaniment.

The Khayyam Traditional Restaurant moderate
Khayyam St, Tehran; +98 21 5580 0760
After a trip around the Tehran bazaar, there's no better escape than to the Khayyam, lying on the bazaar's western periphery. Set in an early 18th-century building, this Oriental-style oasis is atmospheric, cool and relaxed and offers classic Iranian food and drink from a menu that's more eclectic than most in Tehran *(see also pp178–9)*.

Sofre Khane Sonnati Sangalag moderate
Park-e Shahr, Tehran; +98 21 6673 1075
Conveniently situated close to Tehran's Golestan Palace and city museums, the Sangalag makes a perfect pit stop while sightseeing. Set in the Park-e Shahr, it's tranquil and verdant and serves good home-prepared traditional fare, including kebabs and salads, at decent prices.

INDIA

Despite the significant rate of vegetarianism in India, meat kebabs (mainly chicken, lamb and sometimes goat) have long featured in Indian cuisine, particularly in tandoori cooking and the meat-dominated Mughlai cuisine of northern India. The famous Arab traveller Ibn Battuta recorded a description of kebabs when he visited India in the 14th century.

Karim's inexpensive
168/2 Jha House Basti, Nizamuddin West, Delhi
Karim's may seem simple and unremarkable, but it's been serving first-rate Mughlai cuisine for nigh-on a century and is much loved locally for its succulent and subtly spiced kebabs. It's located down a side street opposite the south gate of the Jama Masjid (Great Mosque). Try the *burrah* (marinated lamb kebab) and finish with a creamy *firni* – a sweet rice pudding with cardamom, almonds and pistachios.

Tunday Kababi moderate
Aminabad Rd, Lucknow; +91 522 552 4046
Although Lucknow is famous for its sophisticated Mughlai cuisine and its variety and quality of kebabs, the Tunday has established a near-iconic status both at home and abroad. Its mutton kebab, made of ground or minced lamb, is legendary. The *kathi kebab*, cooked on skewers in a tandoor oven, is also great.

Left (top to bottom) Carving a spit-roasted *döner kebap* in Istanbul; Greek lamb koftas served with mint yogurt; restaurant-sized souvlaki cooked outdoors in Greece

Below (top to bottom) India's *kakori* kebabs are spicy minced lamb or goat rolls, grilled on skewers; the classic shish kebabs take their name from the Turkish word for "skewer"

Khyber expensive

145 Mahatma Gandhi Road, Fort, Mumbai; www.khyberrestaurant.com

Counted among Mumbai's top tables, the Khyber specializes in the meat-dominated Punjabi cuisine, including expertly flavoured and cooked kebabs and *köfte*. With its reputation for fine dining, impeccable service and hip decor, the Khyber boasts a fervent following among local celebrities, diplomats and the business community.

PAKISTAN

In contrast to India, Pakistan's cuisine is firmly rooted in the carnivore camp and kebabs feature frequently on menus, including *seekh* or *tikka* kebabs (shish kebabs), *shawarma* (doner kebab) and a few Pakistani variations such as *chapli* kebabs – spicy, minced mutton or beef patties shaped like a slipper *(chapli)* served with yogurt, rice, salad and naan bread.

Gowal Mandi inexpensive

Off Railway Road, Lahore

The network of lanes just south of Railway Road in Lahore is known locally as "Food Street" for its rows of stalls, selling simple but fresh and skilfully cooked Pakistani fare. At sunset, the roads close and all the locals congregate. It's a great place to try Pakistani dishes at rock-bottom prices in a great atmosphere.

Village Garden Restaurant moderate

Palace Cinema Bldg, Karachi; +92 21 521 2880

Karachi's oldest surviving restaurant also boasts one of the capital's best locations: an attractive and breezy garden filled with birdsong and shade where you can watch your *seekh* kebabs spit, sizzle and emit tantalizing smells on the large outdoor grills.

GREECE

Some claim that the kebab originated in Greece in ancient times, alleging that writers such as Homer, Aristophanes and Aristotle made reference to it in their works. The Greek *gyros* is akin to the Turkish *döner kebap*, although pork is often used, and *souvlaki* is akin to shish kebabs. They are as universally popular as their Turkish counterparts.

To Etsi inexpensive

Nikoforos Fokas 2, near the White Tower, Thessaloniki; +30 2310 222 469

Simple, basic and garishly decorated, the To Etsi in Thessaloniki has won a cult following locally for its succulent *souvlaki* stuffed into freshly baked pitta bread, served with crunchy salad and generous dollops of home-made hot, spicy or garlicky sauces.

Varoulko expensive

Pireos 80, Gazi, Athens; www.varoulko.gr

As famous for its startling views of the Acropolis as for the startling modern-Greek creations of the country's only Michelin-star-rated chef, Lefteris Lazarou, the Varoulko is a must for the foodie. Seafood is the speciality, but the meat dishes don't disappoint. Book a rooftop table.

On the Menu in Turkey

There are dozens of varieties of kebab in Turkey. Many are local adaptations named after the place of origin or their founder.

Adana kebap Minced lamb spiced with chilli peppers, garlic, parsley, paprika, pepper and sumac, moulded into a sausage and grilled over coals on a special long, flat skewer. The meat is served on top of warm strips of pitta bread with a salad of tomatoes, peppers and sliced onions tossed in sumac.

Buğu kebap Meat is steamed in a sealed terracotta pot along with pearl onions, garlic, thyme, sumac and cumin.

Çiğ kebap Raw, ground lamb pounded with bulgur wheat and onions, spiced with cinnamon, cloves, paprika and pepper.

Döner kebap Compressed meat (chicken or lamb) grilled on an upright and rotating skewer and sliced on to pitta bread.

Erciyes kebap Lamb served on a bed of thinly sliced sautéed potatoes with garlic and yogurt.

Fıstıklı kebap Suckling lamb minced and mixed with herbs and pistachios.

İskender (Bursa) kebap Lamb *döner* layered on a bed of pitta bread, topped with tomato sauce and tangy yogurt, then drizzled with lightly browned butter.

Patlıcan kebap Minced or cubed lamb grilled on skewers with aubergine.

Şiş kebap Cubed lamb or chicken marinated in oil, garlic, onion and black pepper grilled on a skewer with onions and peppers.

Tavuk şiş kebap Chicken cubes marinated in olive oil, thyme or rosemary, crushed garlic, black pepper, grated onion and yogurt grilled on a skewer over coals.

Testı kebap Lamb or chicken with vegetables (often onion and mushroom), slow-cooked in a sealed terracotta pot that is broken open at the dining table.

Tokat kebap Cubed lamb grilled on a skewer along with potato, aubergine, tomato and garlic.

Urfa kebap Minced lamb, mildly spiced with chilli, garlic, paprika, pepper and sumac, shaped like a sausage and grilled over coals; served with an onion salad.

Yoğurtlu şiş kebap Grilled skewers of cubed lamb marinated in oil, garlic and onion, along with grilled, skewered ground lamb *köfte*, served on a bed of butter-fried pitta bread, sprinkled with sumac, salt and thyme, and topped with fresh tomato sauce, yogurt and fried strips of aubergine.

ROME ITALY

Jewish Artichokes in Rome

With such a richness of classical sights to savour, it is too easy to miss out on Rome's other fascinating histories. Peoples from all corners of the empire made their home here, and the city's Jewish population traces its presence back two millennia. Their chefs can take credit for one of Rome's culinary highlights – *carciofi alla giudia*, delicious fried artichokes.

Against the backdrop of its imperial Roman past and the Italian Renaissance, the Italian capital is very much alive and moving with the times, ever more international in flavour. It has a vibrant Film Festival, a modern auditorium by Renzo Piano and MAXXI, a spectacular new contemporary art museum designed by Zaha Hadid.

However, the Eternal City's bottom line has changed not one iota. The stereotypes still run true, with scooters zooming along impossibly busy streets, flocks of robed nuns and priests everywhere, noisy neighbourhood markets and the *dolce vita* very much in evidence. The city's host of neighbourhood trattorias could have been plucked straight from Italian films of the 1960s, when a *mezza porzione* (half a helping, and therefore cheaper) was commonplace. Down-to-earth and run by no-nonsense waiters, these trattorias serve exclusively traditional fare, rich, delicious and tomatoey, like *coda alla vaccinara* (braised oxtail) and *spaghetti all'amatriciana,* with tomato, onion, chilli and tangy cured bacon.

One item offered non-stop from October through to June is the typical plump, round Roman (or globe) artichoke. These are usually cooked in one of two ways, each radically different but both avoiding the tiresome ritual of scraping the flesh off the leaves. *Carciofi alla romana* entails slow-braising artichokes in garlic and parsley with a dash of broth. Soft as butter, they are a divine eating experience, as the whole artichoke can be simply sliced and eaten. A different and unusual technique is used for *carciofi alla giudia* ("in the Jewish way"); the artichokes are squashed "face down" to flatten and tenderize them, then fried in olive oil. The magic happens as the outer leaves turn deliciously crisp and golden. These crunchy delights are best eaten sizzling straight out of the pan.

The handsome artichoke is related to the wild thistle and hails from the Middle East. It made its appearance in Italy as an edible vegetable in the 1500s, but its origins can be traced further back to another classical civilization – ancient Greece. Myths hold that mighty Zeus was besotted with the exquisite nymph Cynara, but her capricious behaviour made him mad with jealousy so he turned her into a tough, spiky green plant. However, he did give her a sweet heart, and the "heart" of the artichoke, marinated in oil and herbs and served as antipasto or on pizza, is in fact probably better known throughout the world than the leaves lovingly embraced by the recipes of Rome.

Above Rome's Jewish Ghetto on the banks of the Tiber is now one of the city's most eclectic neighbourhoods

Right The imposing dome of St Peter's Basilica covers a huge and impressive interior – the space can hold 60,000 worshippers

Below *Carciofi alla giudia*, Jewish-style fried artichokes, are a speciality of the ancient Ghetto district of Rome

A Day in Rome

Central Rome, which holds the city's classic sights, is surprisingly compact and walkable, but you need to plan your time carefully to make the best of your day.

MORNING Go to the **Colosseum** and explore the stone tiers where spectators witnessed the ghastly blood sports of ancient Rome. Alongside is the **Forum**, with temples and public buildings, headquarters of the far-reaching Roman empire. Then walk through **Campo de' Fiori** for its lively morning market and cafés.

AFTERNOON Head over to the forbidding **Castel Sant'Angelo** on the banks of the Tiber river. Designed for Emperor Hadrian as his mausoleum, over time it became a prison and even Papal apartments. Follow the broad **Via della Conciliazione** to the vast paved square in front of **St Peter's Basilica**; the **Vatican museums** and the **Sistine Chapel** make a superb conclusion.

EVENING Pick a spot on **Piazza Navona**, resplendent with its gushing Baroque fountains by Bernini, for a magical alfresco dinner.

Essentials

GETTING THERE
Rome has two **airports**: Fiumicino has an express **train** to Termini central railway station; while smaller Ciampino has a direct **coach**.

WHERE TO STAY
Hotel Panda (inexpensive) is a family-run hotel near the Spanish Steps. *www.hotelpanda.it*
Daphne Trevi (moderate) has two locations in the city centre. *www.daphne-rome.com*
Buonanotte Garibaldi (expensive) is a hidden oasis within the Trastevere district. *www.buonanottegaribaldi.com*

TOURIST INFORMATION
Via Parigi 11; *+39 06 488 991*

Artichokes Around Italy

The artichoke is highly prized in regional cuisines around Italy. Varieties of the vegetable are used in Cynar liqueur and even in tantalizing ice cream. Sardinia boasts the yellowish *spinoso sardo*, eaten raw with oil in springtime when fresh and tender. This is also peak time for prized tiny purple *castraure*, a variety jealously cultivated on Sant'Erasmo island in the Venice lagoon. These artichokes have a distinctive bitter tang due to the salt content of the soil. At the end of the artichoke season when the head becomes bristly, market stalls across northeast Italy pare off the top and sell thick *fondi* discs, kept in water and lemon juice to prevent them turning brown.

The Best Places to Eat Carciofi alla Giudia

Da Giggetto moderate

You'd be hard put to find a more pleasant place to have dinner on a balmy summer's evening in Rome than this venerated trattoria in the city's ancient Ghetto district, not far from the banks of the Tiber river. "Giggetto" was the nickname of Luigi Ceccarelli, a returned WWI serviceman who began this well-reputed trattoria back in 1923, and the current manager is his grandson. Dining is alfresco from spring through to autumn, a memorable experience as the tables are set up between shiny stone columns belonging to the Porticus of Octavia, steeped in history. Inside, old brick vaults and arches dangle with plaits of garlic and dried herbs over spacious rooms. A bowl of plump globe artichokes in the entrance informs diners that the traditional Jewish-Roman dish – golden, crisp *carciofi alla giudia* – is available. Another typical offering here is *filetto di baccalà*, fillet of salt cod, battered, fried and served hot with lemon.

Via Portico d'Ottavia 21/22, Rome; open 12:30–2:30pm & 7:30–11pm Tue–Sun; www.giggetto.it

Also in Rome

With long queues outside its otherwise inconspicuous entrance, **Sora Margherita** (+39 06 687 4216; *inexpensive*) is a tiny trattoria in the Ghetto. Once inside, you'll be elbow-to-elbow with other guests. However, it is well worth the wait – nobody ever complains about the food, especially the antipasto, which includes *carciofi alla giudia*, given rave reviews by guests new and old.

Also in Italy

The island of Sant'Erasmo in the Venetian lagoon is a giant vegetable garden, which has supplied Venice with flavoursome fresh produce since ancient Roman times. The menu at **Ristorante Cà Vignotto** (+39 41 24 44 000; *moderate*) on the island is dictated by the seasons, with winter to spring bringing the best *castraure* artichokes. With a bit of luck, their divine gnocchi with crab will be on the day's menu as well.

Around the World

Roman-style crisp-fried artichokes are one of the signature dishes of flamboyant master-chef Sandro Fioriti at his newest restaurant, **Sandro's** (*www.sandrosnyc.com; expensive*), which attracts a cult-like following among New Yorkers. Another house speciality is *spaghettini al limone*, which can be varied with a melon or tomato sauce.

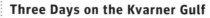

Right Modern seafood restaurants hug the water's edge on Volosko's picturesque harbour

Below Bread or polenta plus a glass of crisp *Vrbnička Žlahtina* are the perfect accompaniments to Kvarner scampi

Three Days on the Kvarner Gulf

The oldest resort on the Gulf, genteel Opatija offers plenty in the way of accommodation, culinary culture and café life. Islands such as Cres and Lošinj, with their stone-built fishing villages and maquis-covered hills, offer more in the way of offbeat relaxed atmosphere.

DAY ONE Stroll **Opatija**'s palm-fringed seaside path, the **Lungomare**, which winds its way round a series of rocky bays and shingle beaches. Strike out to the former fishing village of **Volosko**, and southwards towards **Lovran**, a town filled with picturesque Art Nouveau villas.

DAY TWO Explore **Rijeka**, the Gulf's one real metropolis, enjoying an espresso at one of the cafés lining the central **Korzo**, or browsing the stalls at the bustling market. Take a trip to the hilltop suburb of **Trsat**, site of a ridge-top fortress, for spectacular maritime views.

DAY THREE Take the ferry to the conjoined islands of **Cres** and **Lošinj** (often called "the island of flowers"), where ridges of sheep pasture or Mediterranean maquis loom above sleepy fishing ports.

Essentials

GETTING THERE
International flights arrive at **Zagreb Airport**, a 180-km (112-mile) drive to the Kvarner's main city, Rijeka. **Buses** run from Zagreb's bus station to all of the Gulf's main settlements.

WHERE TO STAY
Pjacal (inexpensive) is a restful family-run B&B in Veli Lošinj. *www.pjacal.eu*
Palace-Bellevue (moderate) is a *belle-époque* hotel with fine high-ceilinged rooms in the centre of Opatija. *www.liburnia.hr*
Draga di Lovrana (moderate) offers creature comforts and superb views in a hillside mansion high above Opatija and Lovran. *www.dragadilovrana.hr*

TOURIST INFORMATION
Nikole Tesle 2, Opatija; *www.kvarner.hr*

KVARNER GULF CROATIA

Scampi on the Adriatic Sea

Framed by grey-green mountains and dotted with arid ochre-coloured islands, the Kvarner Gulf is one of the most starkly beautiful stretches of the Croatian Adriatic coastline. Its gin-clear seas yield an astounding variety of fish and crustaceans, although it is the famously succulent Kvarner scampi that occupy centre stage in the local cuisine.

The Kvarner Gulf has been an essential stop-off for well-heeled visitors since the late 19th century, when Austrian dukes and duchesses descended on the region's coastal towns to enjoy the mild winters.

A sense of the *belle époque* still lives on in resorts like Opatija, where palm-fringed promenades are set against a backdrop of Art Nouveau hotels and holiday villas. A rather different atmosphere, however, prevails on islands such as Cres and Lošinj, where stone-built fishing villages huddle beside rocky coves, the neighbouring scrubby maquis shrubland singing with cicadas. The vibrant city of Rijeka is the fulcrum around which the life of the Gulf revolves: a busy ferry and fishing port whose central market fills daily with the beckoning glisten of fresh fish, octopus and squid. Indeed, it is this diverse array

of seafood that most characterizes the local diet. One culinary treasure particularly associated with the Gulf is the Kvarner scampi, a succulent crustacean that is highly valued on restaurant tables throughout Croatia.

The local scampi are Mediterranean cousins of the large prawn known as the Norway lobster. Blessed with a silty seabed perfect for burrowing, the Kvarner is one of the few parts of the Mediterranean where the scampi flourish in large numbers. In northern European countries the fleshy tails of the scampi are frequently removed and fried in breadcrumbs, although here in Croatia the creature is served whole and unpeeled and is eaten with the fingers – prising open the shells and scooping out the white meat is all part of the ritual. Indeed, locals who have grown up eating scampi will suck the shells dry and then bite open the animal's pincers in the hope of finding a final sliver of succulent flesh.

One recipe on almost every local restaurant menu, a culinary classic here and indeed all down Croatia's Dalmatian coast, is *skampi na buzari* – a simple but sensuous combination of scampi, garlic, tomato and white wine. Eating the sauce-covered scampi is a fantastically messy process – so don't refuse your waiter's offer of a bib, unless you want a Dalmatian-style polka-dot pattern all over your favourite shirt.

Left Boats in harbour on Lošinj Island, Croatia

Croatian Wines

Although not widely known as a wine-producing area, the Kvarner Gulf is home to one of Croatia's most highly regarded dry whites, Vrbnička Žlahtina, from the island of Krk. An indigenous Adriatic grape, Žlahtina (from the Slavic word meaning "noble") is cultivated almost exclusively in a green vale near the port of Vrbnik, one of the few fertile areas on what is otherwise an arid and unforgiving collection of islands. Vrbnik itself is a picturesque town built on a high cliff and is the perfect place to sample the crisp, dry Vrbnička Žlahtina wine; it has a fresh, young bouquet and is the perfect accompaniment to local specialities, such as home-made pasta, lamb, sheep's cheese and prosciutto, as well as the delicious Gulf seafood.

The Best Places to Eat Scampi

Plavi Podrum expensive

Located on the northern fringes of Opatija, the fishing village of Volosko is something of a Croatian gastronomic Shangri-la, featuring several restaurants that regularly make the best-of lists of local food critics. Plavi Podrum, nestling on the curve of Volosko's boat-packed inner harbour, occupies a particular niche, marrying the best of local seafood with a modern European sense of culinary invention. Kvarner-caught fish and crustaceans form the backbone of the menu: seafood risottos, grilled squid and scampi in all its varieties keep the locals coming back in droves. Other main courses are more experimental, mixing fish and meat flavours or making subtle use of oriental spices. Local ingredients, however, reign supreme, with wild asparagus and pungent Istrian truffles featuring heavily in season and a variety of Croatian olive oils arranged on the tables. The owner is one of Croatia's leading sommeliers, so if advice on the country's most intriguing wines is what you're after, this is emphatically the right place. The smart, starched-napkin interior is ideal for a formal meal, while the outdoor terrace, with its views of stone houses and fishing boats, has an altogether more romantic appeal.

Ulica Frana Supila 12, Volosko; open noon–midnight daily; www.plavipodrum.com

Also in the Kvarner Gulf

The road southwest from Opatija passes through the quaint seaside town of Lovran, where the **Najade Restaurant** *(+385 51 291 866; expensive)* serves up fresh scampi, squid and fish dishes on a large sea-facing terrace. It's well worth venturing across the water to Lošinj, too, where the **Bora Bar** *(www.borabar.com; expensive)*, overlooking Rovenska harbour, offers local scampi either *na buzari* or in a Grand Marnier sauce, alongside a range of home-made pastas.

Also in Croatia

Of the many seafood restaurants in the capital, Zagreb, **Gašpar** *(www.restoran-baltazar.hr; expensive)* offers an across-the-board selection of Adriatic treats, including a particularly good *buzari*. Gašpar's sister-restaurant **Baltazar**, in the same courtyard, is the place to sample the central Croatian repertoire of hearty grilled meats.

Around the World

Skampi na buzari is known all over the Adriatic, but is more difficult to find further afield. In Slovenia's capital, Ljubljana, there is seafood aplenty: **Most** *(www.restavracija-most.si; expensive)* serves up scampi and other fresh crustaceans in a riverside setting right opposite the city's colonnaded fish market.

Above The iconic Eiffel Tower, built in 1889, towers over the pretty Parisian buildings in the 7th arrondissement

Above *Macarons* on display at Ladurée on rue Royale in Paris, where the family has been selling luxury cakes and pastries since 1871

A Day in Paris

Paris, the ultimate walking city, is teeming with sights. Skip your hotel breakfast and instead wander the neighbourhood, taking in the scene, and grab your coffee and croissants at a café packed with locals.

MORNING Make your way to the chic **Marais** district and **Les Enfants Rouges**, Paris's oldest covered market, dating back to 1615. The evocative name recalls the children of a nearby orphanage, which closed in 1534, who uniformly wore red. Follow up with a *coup sur le zinc* (a pick-me-up – coffee or something stronger) at a local café.

AFTERNOON Ramble the *quais* of the Seine to the **Ile de la Cité**, stopping at the **Square du Vert Galant** to take in the grandeur of the **Louvre**. At the other end of the island, enjoy the view of **Notre Dame's** flying buttresses. Scour the art galleries of **St Germain**.

EVENING Head for **Place de la Concorde** to parade up the **Champs Elysées**. Look out over the city from the top of the **Arc de Triomphe**, tracing the 12 radiating avenues to arches and obelisks in the east and the contemporary **La Grande Arche de la Défense** to the west.

Essentials

GETTING THERE
Paris has two **airports**: Paris-Charles de Gaulle and Paris-Orly. The former has its own RER **metro** station; at Orly a **shuttle bus** links to the metro line.

WHERE TO STAY
Hôtel Jeanne d'Arc (inexpensive) is a cosy, family-run hotel in the history-soaked Marais district. *www.hoteljeannedarc.com*
Hôtels Paris Rive Gauche (moderate) boasts five bijou properties on the Left Bank. *www.hotels-paris-rive-gauche.com*
Paris institution **Le Meurice** (expensive) has public spaces by Philippe Starck (those chairs sporting ladies' shoes), while rooms channel luxurious Louis XVI. *www.lemeurice.com*

TOURIST INFORMATION
www.parisinfo.com

PARIS FRANCE

Marvellous Macarons in Paris

There's a lot to love about the French capital: temples of high art, sophisticated music haunts, cool *quartiers* and lofty landmarks that span the centuries. But beyond the Louvre's masterpieces, Notre Dame's gargoyles and the towering lights of the Eiffel Tower lies another tiny gem that never fails to draw crowds of Parisians and tourists: the perfect *macaron*.

An artistic city *par excellence*, Paris proffers an astonishing array of tempting pastimes. Culture-vultures can swoop on highbrow opera and orchestral performances, or more bohemian attractions such as art-house cinema and circuses. Myriad museums satisfy cravings for any and all types of painting, photography, installations and sculpture, while city parks and gardens – such as the 17th-century Jardin du Luxembourg – provide the tranquillity in which to reflect on it.

Visitors can soak up the ambience of centuries past through the city's astonishing architecture, from the 12th-century Gothic masterpiece of Notre Dame to the Renaissance buildings of the Marais or the high-tech Pompidou Centre. The shopping is just as extraordinary; Paris is arguably the fashion capital of the world, and an afternoon's shopping can easily encompass both the *haute couture* of rue du Faubourg Saint-Honoré and the flea-market finds of Saint-Ouen. And then there's the food – reason enough for a visit on its own. Not simply fuel, food is more fine art here,

and nowhere is that better illustrated than in Paris patisseries. The most French of fancies – the *macaron* – is a byword for pastry perfection.

Henri II's Italian wife, Catherine de Medici, is credited with bringing the meringue to France in 1533, but it was a Frenchman, Pierre Desfontaines – cousin of Paris tea-salon owner Louis Ernest Ladurée (*see right*) – who first hit upon the idea, in the early 20th century, of joining two *macarons* together with a blob of chocolate ganache. Like all things painfully delicious, this ensemble requires real finesse. The ingredients are simple: egg whites, ground almonds, sugar and flavouring. But it's the sifting, folding in, piping, letting them sit (or not) and baking at just the right temperature that determines whether they achieve that perfect crust and glossy dome. And it's the combination of chewy meringue and velvety centre that causes people to sigh as they bite into ivory buttons oozing salted caramel, baby pink discs encasing rose petal or snowy puffs cloaking hazelnut and white truffle. Some connoisseurs insist they taste better the day after they're made, but who has the steely nerve to wait that long?

Above An alfresco café in the formal gardens of the Jardin du Luxembourg

Cookery Classes

There's no better place to learn the art of patisserie than in Paris. There are half-day, full-day and multi-day courses, usually for 3–6 people. All the courses here need to be booked ahead. At **Promenades Gourmandes** (www.promenadesgourmandes.com), pastry and *macaron* master Joël Morgeat imparts an infallible technique for turning out perfect little meringue domes of chocolate, raspberry or grapefruit, under the watchful eye of Parisian gourmet Paule Caillat. **Ecole Ritz Escoffier**, in the Ritz Hotel (www.ritzparis.com), runs classes showing how to whip up *macarons* in many flavours; expect to learn one flavour in 2 hours, or several in a 4-hour class. **La Cuisine Paris** (www.lacuisineparis.com) runs afternoon *macaron*-making classes in both French and English in the centre of Paris.

The Best Places to Eat Macarons

Pierre Hermé expensive

Fourth-generation pastry-maker Pierre Hermé is the resident *macaron* magician, conjuring up creations that people cross town for. Hermé claims he only makes "what feels right" when it comes to these jewel-box discs, and there's no denying his surefire instincts. That crunchy shell and those creamy flavours: vanilla and olive oil, crème brûlée, wasabi and strawberry, and quince and rose are all life-enhancing combinations. Hermé started his career at the age of 14, when he was apprenticed to the famed *pâtissier* Gaston Lenôtre, and was head of the pastry kitchen at esteemed patisserie Fauchon by the time he was 24. Hermé now has his own sweet empire with four boutiques in Paris: those in rue Bonaparte and rue de Vaugiraud showcase his complete range of pastry pleasures, while those in rue Cambon and Avenue Paul Doumer concentrate solely on *macarons* and chocolates. It's worth making a pilgrimage to one of his two pastry shops in summer, when raspberries are in season, just to try "Ispahan" – two large rose-flavoured *macarons* sandwiching rose petal cream, whole raspberries and lychees. Ladurée may have invented the *macaron* but Pierre Hermé, dubbed "the Picasso of Pastry", perfected it.

4 rue Cambon and 58 Avenue Paul Doumer, Paris; open 10am–7pm daily; www.pierreherme.com

Also in Paris

Ladurée, on rue Royale (www.laduree.fr; *expensive*), draws a constant stream of customers, lured by the unchanged, old-world interior and the delicious, ever-changing window displays: *croquembouche* made of rainbow *macarons*, *macaron* stacks anointed with papery butterflies and tiers of pastel-coloured *macaron* boxes lashed with ribbons. While Pierre Hermé (*see above*) opts for daring pairings, Ladurée turns out timeless classics: chocolate, vanilla, pistachio, orange blossom, lemon and seasonal specials. There are other Paris branches, but this one is precious.

Also in France

Gastronomic Lyon has its own *macaron* masters. **Sève** (www.chocolatseve.com; *expensive*) dishes up to-die-for apple *tatin macarons* and savoury domes filled with sesame and Gorgonzola, while **Sébastian Bouillet** (www. chocolatier-bouillet.com; *moderate*) dreams up fairy-floss *macarons* and salted caramel in a chocolate shell flaked with gold leaf.

Around the World

Pierre Hermé's **Aoyama** boutique (*+81 3 5485 7766; expensive*) in Tokyo was his first shop. The first floor is devoted to display, while upstairs in the Bar Chocolat, you can nibble on chocolates, pastries and *macarons*.

A Day in San Sebastián

In July and September the beautiful people flock to San Sebastián for respectively, the annual jazz and film festivals, but the decorous city and beachside promenade are just as delightful when the paparazzi and their targets have left town. Be sure to arrive hungry.

MORNING Explore the narrow streets of the **Parte Vieja**, or old quarter, which was rebuilt on the medieval street plan after Napoleon burned the city. At the harbour, explore the fishermen's docks and visit the **Palacio del Mar**, San Sebastián's intriguing aquarium, focused on the marine life of the Bay of Biscay.

AFTERNOON Walk up the circular road around **Monte Urgull** to see the 12th-century ruins of the **Castillo de Santa Cruz de la Mota**. Then catch some sun on **Playa de la Concha**.

EVENING Ride the funicular to the summit of **Monte Igueldo** to survey the city from this western headland. Then return to town for an evening of bar-hopping to sample the city's inventive *pintxos* (Basque tapas) before winding up at a fine restaurant for dinner.

Essentials

GETTING THERE

San Sebastián Airport has domestic flights; the **international airports** of Bilbao and Biarritz are relatively close. The city can also be reached by **train** on the **TGV Paris–Madrid** route, and by **bus** from many European cities.

WHERE TO STAY

Hotel Niza (inexpensive) offers airy rooms with Playa de la Concha views. *www.hotelniza.com*
Hotel de Londres y de Inglaterra (moderate) is a restored *belle époque* resort hotel with traditional furnishings. *www.hlondres.com*
Hotel María Cristina (expensive) is San Sebastián's most palatial hotel, with luxurious appointments in even the simplest rooms. *www.luxurycollection.com/MariaCristina*

TOURIST INFORMATION

Boulevard 8; *www.sansebastianturismo.com*

Right Monkfish and minted beans with Iberian tomato ravioli and Jerez vinegar by Basque chef Juan Mari Arzak

Below The uninhabited island of Santa Clara lies just off the scallop-shaped coastline of San Sebastian

SAN SEBASTIAN SPAIN

Basque Coast Innovation

Napoleon sacked and burned San Sebastián in 1813, but the resort that rose from the ashes is the epitome of refined hedonism. Royalty and movie stars bask in the sizzle of the Spanish sun, while San Sebastián's Basque chefs demonstrate the innovative Modern Spanish cuisine that has raised the bar for European gastronomy, much as Picasso rewrote the rules for modern art.

Playa de la Concha, San Sebastián's main beach, nestles between the twin headlands of Monte Urgull and Monte Igueldo. Its 6-km (4-mile) swathe of white sand makes the city the pearl of the Basque coast. Once the sun goes down, beach-goers wash off their tanning lotion, dress for dinner, and prepare for an evening at the tables of San Sebastián's world-class restaurants. The city has more Michelin three-star establishments per capita than Paris or Tokyo, and a host of wonderful cafés, taverns and bars where the quality of the food belies the humble surroundings.

San Sebastián is an intriguing mix of the old and the new. The broad avenues of the sophisticated modern town, lined with upmarket shops and restaurants, give way to the atmospheric streets of the old town beneath the base of Monte Urgull. Centring around the ancient Plaza de la Constitución, these narrow lanes hide treats such as the church of Santa Maria del Coro, a masterly example of Basque Baroque. The old town's sheltered harbour curls around a series of stone embankments, where a small fishing fleet unloads its rich daily catch of bream, sardines, anchovies, prawns, spider crab, mullet, monkfish and hake. The Basques are legendary fishermen and inventive cooks – Basque cuisine was a culinary revolution waiting to happen. With its emphasis on perfect ingredients artfully presented, Basque cooking proved the perfect foil to French nouvelle cuisine.

When San Sebastián's chefs began bringing theatre to the plate in the 1970s, they championed local produce, fish and meat, and jettisoned the elaborate, time-intensive preparations of traditional *haute cuisine*. They had fired the opening salvo of Modern Spanish cuisine – and have wowed diners ever since. They experiment with flavours like an artist expanding his palette, endowing each plate with an element of surprise. But the emphasis here is on flavour rather than culinary pyrotechnics: parsley foam brings out the sweetness of spider crab steeped in spicy tomato sauce; a sprinkling of crispy garlic wafers provides a crunchy counterpoint to pan-fried codfish with clams. Every dish is a sublime medley of texture and tastes.

Basque Wines

There are two distinctive wine regions in the Basque lands of Spain: the **Rioja Alavesa**, where the famous bodega of Marqués de Riscal is based; and the **Basque coast**, where the Txakolí wines are produced. The red Tempranillo and Cabernet Sauvignon blends of **Rioja** are justly famous as bold accompaniments to roasted meats and hearty stews. The mostly white, often slightly fizzy **Txakolí** wines are characterized by a bracing acidity that makes them the perfect foil for Basque seafood. Although Txakolí has been cultivated for at least 1,200 years, it has been the Basques' carefully guarded secret, and did not enter the export market until the 21st century. Three Txakolí districts are recognized, but the pale yellow to green wines from **Getaria** and **Zarautz** on the coast between Bilbao and San Sebastián are considered the best.

Above Basque Michelin three-star chef Juan Mari Arzak and his daughter Elena

The Best Places to Eat Modern Spanish Cuisine

Restaurante Arzak expensive

One could say that Juan Mari Arzak got his revenge on Napoleon by launching Modern Spanish cuisine – a revolution that toppled French *haute cuisine* from its gastronomic throne. This was Spain's first restaurant to be awarded three Michelin stars, and eating at Arzak remains as exciting today as it was in the 1970s, when the unknown provincial chef first applied the principles of French nouvelle cuisine to the traditions of Basque cookery. Arzak reduces dishes to their essential flavours, then plates them with unfussy but witty theatre. Now working with his daughter Elena, Arzak continues to experiment with new twists on familiar foods – his "perfect egg" dishes are legendary among Spanish chefs – without sacrificing the integrity of the ingredients or the surprise of the presentation. Most diners opt for the astonishing tasting menu, which allows the broadest experience of Arzak's creative and experimental approach. It begins with a half-dozen or so small dishes, explodes into three to four "main" dishes built around meat or fish, and then segues into a series of sweet and delicious surprises.

Avenida Alcalde José Elosegui 273, San Sebastián; open for lunch Tue–Fri, dinner Tue–Sat; www.arzak.es

Also in San Sebastián

Pedro Subijana is the master magician of **Akelare** (www.relaischateaux.com; *expensive*), where mountainside views of the Bay of Biscay match his culinary sleight of hand. Martín Berasategui crafts a roller coaster of flavour surprises at his flagship **Berasategui** (www.martinberasategui.com; *expensive*) while offering an affordable sampling of his free-form imagination at **Restaurante Kursaal** (+34 943 003 162; *moderate*).

Also in Spain

In Madrid, diners greet dishes at **Villa Magna by Eneko Atxa** (www.villamagna.es; *moderate*) with either a hearty laugh or an exclamation of delight. At **Sergi Arola Gastro** (www.sergiarola.es; *expensive*), also in Madrid, Catalan star chef Sergi Arola composes just a few strong flavours per plate, cooking much like fellow Catalan Joan Miró painted. Innovator Ferran Adrià's greatest hits form the menu at **Hacienda Benazuza** (www.elbullihotel.com; *expensive*), in Sanlúcar la Mayor, near Seville.

Around the World

Spanish-born and trained, José Andrés launched a craze for Modern Spanish cuisine in the USA. His most theatrical and magical restaurant, **The Bazaar** (www.thebazaar.com; *moderate*), in Beverly Hills, California, won *Esquire* magazine's Restaurant of the Year award in 2009.

SANTORINI GREECE

Golden Fava on Santorini

A magnet for honeymooners, Santorini has more five-star hotels and fancy restaurants than any other Greek island. Yet its signature dish, fava, is a humble staple food. This golden bean purée owes its rich, nutty flavour to Santorini's volcanic terrain. An eruption blew out the heart of the island 3,500 years ago, and this natural disaster proved an unexpected blessing for fava farmers.

Its red cliffs frosted with whitewashed hamlets and fringed with black sand beaches, Santorini has a savage beauty. The volcanic eruption that created the flooded caldera, or basin, in 1500 BC also buried the island's biggest settlement at Akrotiri. This Bronze Age city was discovered barely 30 years ago, buried beneath 10 m (33 ft) of ash. Recreations of the stunning frescoes unearthed at Akrotiri are on display in the island's capital, Fira, which can be reached by a thrilling cable-car ride from the port of Gialos.

The dramatic landscape makes for wondrous sunsets, but made it difficult for locals to eke out a living until the advent of tourism. Only a few crops can be coaxed from the island's arid soil – succulent grapes, sweet white aubergines, cherry tomatoes bursting with flavour, piquant capers, and the resilient fava bean. More prized (and much pricier) than fava grown elsewhere in Greece, this plain little bean has been cultivated on Santorini since the Bronze Age, its flat plants able to absorb moisture from the porous pumice stone. After harvesting, the beans are left to dry then stripped of their brown husks to reveal yellow grains, bright as jewels.

Primarily a Lenten food in much of Greece, fava is eaten year-round on Santorini and always served warm. Simmered gently until it dissolves into a smooth paste, fava remains a popular foil for seafood – it forms a pillowy bed for octopus stewed in sweet wine, salty sardines or crunchy calamari rings. Amazingly versatile, it might be topped with raw onions, doused in lemon or flecked with dill. *Fava pandremeni* ("married fava") is a lyrical euphemism for leftover fava jazzed up with fried onions, capers and a swirl of tomato paste. The less evocative *fava tis grias* ("crone's fava") is a winter variation with smoked pork. As it cools, a well is made in the fava and filled with olive oil; hence the Greek expression "there's a hole in the fava", which loosely translates as "there's something fishy going on".

Once a peasant food, fava is now an expensive gourmet product cultivated by fewer than 200 farmers. Most producers focus instead on the island's wines, following a tradition as old as Akrotiri. Vaulted wine cellars and humble cave dwellings have been converted into glamorous hotels teetering on the brink of the volcano, with infinity pools suspended between sky and sea. They make ideal vantage points from which to ponder whether the flooded crater does indeed conceal the lost city of Atlantis.

Three Days on Santorini

For all its black-sand beaches and wealth of antiquities, Santorini's main attraction is the spellbinding volcanic caldera. Boat trips to and around the islets are a must.

DAY ONE Sailing into the caldera is like floating into an open-air geological museum. Sizzling in the centre is the crater of **Nea Kameni**, which you can climb if you dare. Wallow in the hot springs of **Palea Kameni**, then shin up the **Islet of Thirassia** to **Manolas**, a clifftop time-warp with astonishing views of the archipelago.

DAY TWO Hike the daredevil path running along the rim of the caldera from **Fira** to **Oia**, the quintessential Cycladic village. Zigzag down the red cliffs for just-caught fish and iced ouzo at **Ammoudi**, a fishing port with half a dozen good tavernas.

DAY THREE Admire reproductions of the frescoes unearthed at Akrotiri at the Petros Nomikos Foundation in **Fira**. Travel south from Fira to **Vothonos**, where you can buy top-quality fava beans to take home at the **Yiannis Nomikos Estate**. Continue onwards to **Pyrgos**, a beautifully preserved village built around a medieval castle.

Essentials

GETTING THERE
There are direct flights to **Santorini Airport** from Europe, and regular domestic flights from Athens. The high-speed **ferry** from Athens takes about five hours.

WHERE TO STAY
Zannos Melathron (moderate) is a grand manor house in Pyrgos. *www.zannos.gr*
Kapari (moderate) has spectacular caldera views and snug rooms. *www.kaparisantorini.gr*
Perivolas (expensive) offers laidback luxury on the outskirts of Oia. *www.perivolas.gr*

FURTHER INFORMATION
www.santorini.net

Above Selene restaurant in Pyrgos is world-renowned for its authentic Greek cuisine and imaginative use of local ingredients

Left The whitewashed church of Agios Gerasimos in Firostefani ("The Crown of Thira") is dramatically perched on the cliffs of the volcanic caldera

Above The much-prized fava beans of Santorini are simmered until they dissolve into a delicious paste, then eaten with fresh fish or octopus

Santorini Wines

Santorini's mineral-rich *terroir* yields some of the most delicate and distinctive wines in Greece. Around 40 indigenous grape varieties have been cultivated on the island for centuries. The bone-dry Assyrtiko and potent Vinsanto (unique to Santorini) are world-class. Wineries all over Santorini offer tours and tastings. Savour the sunset with oaky Oia Vareli and stuffed vine leaves straight from the surrounding vineyards at the peaceful **Sigalas Winery** (*www.sigalas-wine.com*) in Baxedes. Or drink in the 360° views with a glass of crisp Nyxteri from the **Santo Cooperative's Oenotourism Centre** (*www.santowines.gr*).

The Best Places to Eat Fava

Selene expensive

A mentor to many of Greece's finest chefs, Selene's Yiorgos Hatziyannakis was one of the first restaurateurs to put indigenous dishes such as fava on the menu. But there's nothing rustic about his refined reinterpretation of classic Greek dishes. Since opening Selene in 1986, he has created more than 20 variations of fava: mashed with the crystallized sap of the mastic tree and served with smoked mackerel and almond flakes; fava fritters stuffed with tomato and caper *confit*; fava risotto with grilled sea bass; and even fava ice cream garnished with caper leaves as an intriguing *amuse-bouche*. Other local ingredients are showcased to equally startling effect in dishes such as white aubergine salad with octopus carpaccio and *millefeuille* with cherry tomato marmalade. An informal wine bar below the restaurant serves less experimental but equally sophisticated Greek cuisine at half the price. The restaurant also holds cookery classes once a week.

Pyrgos Village, Santorini; open 7pm–midnight daily, mid-Apr–mid-Oct; www.selene.gr

Also on Santorini

There are also many less expensive places to try fava in Santorini. At **To Psaraki** (The Little Fish) (*www.topsaraki.gr; moderate*), award-winning chef Thanasis Sfougaris has gone back to basics. His *fava pandremeni*, topped with caramelized onions, is divine, and phenomenally good value. **Ta Dichtia** (*www.tadichtia.gr; moderate*) sits on a pretty terrace on Perivolos beach, serving lemony fava, cuttlefish and bulgur pilaf, and baked grouper. **Kyra Roza** (*+30 22860 24378; inexpensive*) is off the beaten track at Vourvoulos, but attracts off-duty chefs with its creamy fava, crispy red mullet, and mint-flecked *domatokeftedes* (tomato fritters).

Also in Greece

Santorini locals mourned when Chrysanthos Karamolegos, one of Greece's most inventive chefs, moved from the island to Halkidiki. His restaurant **Tomata** (*www.sani-resort.com; expensive*) features fava in unusual ways, such as paired with sea bass in ouzo vinaigrette, or with feta croquettes and watermelon coulis.

Around the World

Greek-American chef Michael Psilakis has single-handedly elevated Greek cuisine several notches. He has moved on from the Michelin-starred Anthos in New York, but you can sample his innovative fava with sea urchin sashimi as part of the post-modern meze at **Eos** at the Viceroy Hotel, Miami (*www.viceroymiami.com; expensive*).

A Day in Munich

Munich's focal Marienplatz square, bustling with street musicians and artists, is the perfect place to start a day's tour.

MORNING Catch the Rathaus carillon (chiming bells) in **Marienplatz** at 11am; pop into the **toy museum** in the Altes Rathaus, then climb the **Peterskirche tower** for fantastic views. Stop at the **Viktualienmarkt** (food market) to eat a *Weisswurst*, Munich's famous white sausage, en route to the Renaissance **Residenz palace**.

AFTERNOON Walk to the **Pinakothek** museums, Munich's clutch of excellent art museums, and view either old masters or modern and contemporary art. Or take a bus to Munich's grandest museum: the **Deutsches Museum**, with its science and technology collection.

EVENING Choose between high culture — perhaps one of Munich's three first-rate **symphony orchestras** — or head to **Hofbräuhaus**, to while away the evening in the classic Bavarian way.

Essentials

GETTING THERE
Trains link Munich's **airport**, 30 km (18 miles) from the city, to its main **train** station, west of Marienplatz. Central Munich is easily walkable, but the **public transport** system is excellent.

WHERE TO STAY
Pension Seibel (inexpensive) is simple, central and very Bavarian. *www.seibel-hotels-munich.de*
Torbräu (moderate) is a dependable, family-run four-star choice close to the Viktualienmarkt. *www.torbraeu.de*
Charles Hotel (expensive) is a top-class hotel with huge rooms. *www.thecharleshotel.com*

TOURIST INFORMATION
Neuen Rathaus, Marienplatz; *+49 89 23 39 65 00*

Right Bacon and herb dumplings in a rich broth of mushrooms and cream is Bavarian comfort food at its finest

Below Munich's Hofbräuhaus, once the royal brewery, is one of the oldest beer halls in Germany

MUNICH GERMANY

Dumplings in Munich

As jolly and hearty as Bavaria itself, dumplings, or *Knödel*, have been a cornerstone of this region's cuisine since records began. Local legends even talk of dumplings being thrown at an enemy to end a 13th-century siege of the town of Deggendorf. With dumplings on the menu of most of its inns and beer halls, Bavaria's largest city, Munich, is the perfect place to sample them.

At least as old as their first mentions on 11th-century parchments, *Knödel* (or *Klöse* to north Germans) are one of Germany's most enduring and adaptable dishes. In the Middle Ages, meat dumplings, or *Fleischknödel*, were popular among the wealthy, who commonly used bread to bind them; the peasant version, reversing the proportions, was the *Semmelknödel* – a bread dumpling incorporating scraps of meat. The potato, arriving from Latin America in 1565, hardly challenged the *Knödel* at all, simply inspiring the potato dumpling. By the 19th century, Bavarians considered and declared the *Knödel* a national dish.

Like the *Knödel*, Munich is a Bavarian icon and has been its capital since 1503. Its remarkably compact medieval core boasts a glorious Renaissance palace, atmospheric squares, venerable churches and museums that can keep art-lovers occupied for days. Yet much of Munich's charm today lies in its vibrancy, as the energetic, modern capital of Germany's high-tech industry. This energy shines in the summer when beer gardens, street cafés and bars are in full swing, or during the world-famous Oktoberfest beer festival, when the city loses its head. Fortunately, if you need to escape the madness, these are also great times to visit the Alpine lakes and mountains that are only an hour's drive or train ride from the city.

Such a journey will take you through traditional Bavarian countryside, from which the ingredients of Munich's *Knödel* still come. Of the three main types of dumpling – meat, bread and potato – the most popular is the *Semmelknödel*, based on stale rolls soaked in milk and broken down into doughy crumbs, mixed with onion, parsley and lemon peel, though countless variations exist: *Speckknödel* have bacon bits in the mix, and *Leberknödel* are made with liver.

Dumplings can be served in soups or as a side order, but come into their own in classic main dishes, smothered with tangy beef or venison goulash or a rich and creamy mushroom sauce – one of Germany's few traditional vegetarian meals. But it doesn't stop there – only by ordering dessert *Knödel*, either served cold or sliced and fried and accompanied by stewed fruit, will you prove yourself a dedicated dumpling diner.

German Beer

Bavaria's extensive high plateaus are particularly well suited to growing the wheat and barley required by Germany's 1,300 or so breweries to make the country's favourite drink. Only the Czechs drink more per capita than the Germans, whose variety of beers is astonishing – all the way from summery golden lagers and cloudy wheat beers to dark brown Bock, traditionally brewed in winter and drunk in spring. Beers also vary tremendously in strength, up to a staggering 28 percent alcohol. Bavaria's classic beer is its Märzenbier, the mid-brown brew of its most famous annual celebration, the Oktoberfest. But even when it's not on, drinking in a jovial summer beer garden or hunkering down in a high-arched beer cellar, to lock arms with neighbours, sing and stomp, remains a quintessential part of enjoying German beer.

Above An Oktoberfest waitress in traditional Bavarian costume

The Best Places to Eat Dumplings

Wirtshaus in der Au moderate

This lovely old Bavarian inn lies just far enough from Munich's centre to put it off the beaten track, yet it's still an easy walk from the Deutsches Museum. It has been serving beer and dumplings since 1901, and its simple, airy interiors with high vaulted ceilings, tiled floor and rustic wooden furniture still speak of that time. But this is not a restaurant hamstrung by tradition; it likes to innovate by offering dishes such as spinach or beetroot dumplings and organic cheeses. All are executed with great success, as you might expect from a restaurant that has published its own dumpling cookbook (in English, too) and runs dumpling cookery courses. Dedicated to serving nothing but dumplings, and with waitresses that bustle in their traditional dirndl dresses, this is a cultural and gastronomic experience not to be missed. **Lilienstrasse 51, Munich; open 5pm–1am Mon–Fri, 10am–1am Sat & Sun (kitchen closes at 11pm); www.wirtshausinderau.de**

Also in Munich

Dumplings combine with a jolly beer hall experience amid the long benches at the **Augustiner Bräustuben** (www.braeustuben.de; moderate) on Landsberger Strasse, perhaps less the complete tourist experience than the Hofbräuhaus, but just as good. The dumplings are served with duck or pork knuckle, smothered in mushroom sauce, or as liver dumpling soup.

Also in Germany

Knödel are thinner on the ground in northern Germany, but you can find potato dumplings. In Frankfurt, **Klabunt** (www.klabunt-frankfurt.de; moderate), a simple pub, is fussy about using the finest ingredients; the speciality is half-and-half dumplings, made from equal measures of cooked and raw potatoes.

Further north in Berlin, only southern German restaurants serve dumplings, such as **Spätzle & Knödel** on Wühlischstrasse (+49 30 2757 1151; moderate). They even offer *Marillenknödel*, delicious apricot dessert dumplings.

Around the World

Austrians, particularly Tyroleans, are every bit as keen on dumplings as Bavarians, so excellent Austrian versions, such as those served in Innsbruck at **Lewisch** (+43 51 258 6043; moderate), are fairly easy to find. Their menu includes *Serviettenknödel*, a large dumpling that is sliced like bread before serving.

It's an Austrian, too, that has opened one of the best dumpling restaurants in the New World: **Kinski** (www.kinski-nyc.com; inexpensive), a modern eatery in New York's diverse and hip Lower East Side. Its savoury goulash-smothered dumpling and the many different sweet *Knödel*, served with nougat, raspberry or apricot, are as good as they are far from home.

Above Astonishing Baroque stonework supports the balconies of the Palazzo Nicolaci di Villadorata in Noto

Above Glorious Sicilian lemons are used to make sorbet, a palate-cleansing contrast to the wealth of creamy, rich *gelati* flavours

Three Days in the Val di Noto

The old cities of the Val di Noto boast an exceptional artistic and cultural heritage. But this small corner of the island is also known for its dramatic, fertile interior landscape and stunning coastal scenery.

DAY ONE Visit the Baroque cathedral of **San Nicolò** in Noto and explore the nearby **palazzi** (palaces). After lunch, head inland to **Noto Antico** (old Noto) and wander around this atmospheric "ghost town".

DAY TWO Jump in a car or taxi and head south out of town, through the agricultural and wine-producing centre of **Pachino** and onwards towards **Capo Passero** – Sicily's southernmost headland. Here you can spend time in the charming seaside town of **Portopalo**, and enjoy the view of the lighthouse from **Capo delle Correnti**.

DAY THREE To the north of Noto in the **Monti Iblei**, deep river valleys have shaped the plateau housing the wonderful ancient site of **Pantalica**, where a scattering of tombs are smothered by wild flowers in spring. Below, the shady **Anapo river** can be followed on foot along the track of the former railway.

Essentials

GETTING THERE
Sicily's main **airport** is Catania Fontanarossa. There are **buses** to Noto from the airport and there is a single-track **railway** from Noto to Ragusa, Modica and Scicli. A **hire car** is useful for exploring the area and the island.

WHERE TO STAY
Agriturismo Calamosche (inexpensive) is a simple place with rooms and a campsite, 10 km (6 miles) outside Noto. +39 347 858 7319
La Fontanella (moderate) is Noto's only central hotel, located in a 19th-century palazzo. *www.albergolafontanella.it*
Terre di Vendicari (expensive), a stylish country house, lies in a nature reserve south of Noto. *www.terredivendicari.it*

TOURIST INFORMATION
Piazza XXVI Maggio; +39 931 573 779

NOTO ITALY

Gorgeous Gelati in Baroque Sicily

Built on a hill a few miles from the sea, Noto is the apogee of Sicilian Baroque. Much of its charm lies in its limestone buildings, their colours changing from gold to apricot depending on the light. Sicily has been defined as a place where "doing nothing is not seen as a waste of time, where people still eat jasmine ice cream" – and Noto, on a summer evening, is a fine place to do both.

In the wake of the terrible earthquake of 1693 that devastated Sicily, the ruined hill town of Noto was completely reconstructed, building by building, on a flatter location closer to the sea. Through the 18th century this became an enormous construction site run by the prominent architects of the day. Today, the town's Baroque architecture is unique in Sicily and, after substantial restoration, its long-decaying buildings are being revealed in all their glory. The steps that lead up to the cathedral from Largo Landolina are a good place to start a tour of the town's voluptuous *palazzi* and grandiose churches, replete with ornamental detail.

Designed specifically to include vistas of the surrounding countryside, Noto's urban plan was people-friendly and still works well today. Steps lead to the upper part of town, and breathtaking views. One of the most popular tourist activities in Noto is just to wander the picturesque streets, taking in golden stone buildings with their handsome façades and elegant balconies, and enjoying spectacular vistas. The other favourite pastime for visitors – and locals – is simply to savour the delicious *gelato* (ice cream) and almond sweetmeats for which the town has become famous.

Noto's reputation for ice-cream making originated 1,000 years ago, when Sicily was under the rule of the Arabs. They planted citrus and almond groves across the island, and brought with them the technique of making sherbet, or *sharbat*, from fruit syrups, flower essences and snow from the slopes of Mount Etna. It seems probable that it was a resourceful Sicilian who first had the idea of making a good thing even better, freezing a mixture of milk, sugar or honey, and fruit, and giving the world one of its favourite foods.

By the 18th century, ices were so popular in Italy that almost the entire revenue of Sicily's Bishop of Catania came from selling the snow from Mount Etna. Not far from Noto you can still see *neviere*, limestone pits roofed with domes of stone, where snow was buried in winter, remaining frozen for months. Warm winters provoked national crises: in 1777 a boat thought to be carrying snow was attacked and its precious cargo seized – by Syracusans, desperate for ice cream.

What Else to Eat

Sicily and sweet things go together. The superb offerings from local *pasticcerias* feature locally grown **almonds,** and the pastries have a divine melt-in-the-mouth quality. Try Pasticceria Mandolfiore (*www.pasticceriamandolfiore.com*) or Caffè Sicilia (*see right*), whose nougat and home-made jams make perfect takeaways. Look out too for **biancomangiare** – blancmange as you've never tasted it, not unlike the *panna cotta* of northern Italy. The **chocolate** of nearby Modica is still made using the Aztec technique, with pure cocoa and sugar, so that it has a crunchy texture. You may be able to peep at the Iacono family making it in the kitchen behind the bar at Caffè dell' Arte, on Modica's Corso Umberto (*+39 932 943 257*) – or cross the road to the more famous Bonajuto (*+39 932 941 225*), founded in 1880, for free chocolate tastings.

Above Farmers harvesting almonds with poles and nets in southern Sicily

The Best Places to Eat Gelati

Corrado Costanzo inexpensive

Tucked into a narrow lane below Noto's luscious central piazza, Largo Landolina, is a café that looks like any other in Sicily. But the ice cream created in *gelateria* Corrado Costanzo is judged by connoisseurs from all over the world to be the best on the planet. Eating a Costanzo ice cream is one of the world's most voluptuous gastronomic experiences, melting neither too slowly nor too fast on the tongue, suffusing the mouth with the unadulterated essence of mandarin, almond, rose, pistachio, mulberry, jasmine or whichever locally grown fruit, nut or flower is in season.

The death of Costanzo himself in 2003 has changed nothing – his daughter and son continue to produce ice creams and granitas like no-one else. In spring, opt for rose, jasmine or wild strawberry, and in summer pistachio, ricotta with cinnamon or dark chocolate with orange. Unlike most, Costanzo's *gelati* contain no gums, using only egg white as a thickener.
Via Spaventa 7 (behind the Palazzo Ducezio), Noto; closed Mon; +39 931 835 243

Also in Noto

Noto is blessed with another great dessert-creating family, the Assenza brothers, Carlo and Corrado, who own the popular and authentic **Caffè Sicilia** (*+39 931 835 013; inexpensive*), which has been operating since 1892. The cakes, pastries and home-made jams here are as superb as the innovative *gelati* – people come from far and wide to sample the flavours, which include almond blended with cinnamon, lemon, saffron, mulberry, wild strawberry and a radical basil-scented ice.

Also in Italy

When in Rome, eat *gelato*. The Italian capital's favourite place to do so is **San Crispino** (*www.ilgelatodisancrispino.it; moderate*), a short walk from Rome's own Baroque masterpiece, the Trevi fountain. It is famous for subtle flavours, including cream with honey or figs. Venice boasts **Alaska** (*+39 41 715 211; inexpensive*), beloved of *gelato* gourmets who appreciate Carlo Pistacchi's fresh ingredients and experimental flavours such as celery and peach, and liquorice and artichoke.

Around the World

Americans eat more ice cream than any other nation in the world, and one of their most famous ice-cream producers, **Ben & Jerry's** (*www.benjerry.com; moderate*), offers tours of its factory in Vermont – on snowshoes in winter. Arguably even tastier ice cream can be found in Buenos Aires, Argentina, at family-owned **Persicco** (*+54 11 3339 7377; expensive*), which has several branches.

MADRID SPAIN

Sweet Surrender in Madrid

Spain's traditional capital reveals its playful side in the early hours, when office-bound bankers cross paths with hungry clubbers in the *churrerías*. These small shops work round the clock crafting *churros* – deep-fried strips of dough that are Madrid's classic breakfast or afternoon snack and a powerful late-night restorative, especially when dipped in thick hot chocolate.

From its formal old world plazas and medieval lanes to its modernist offices and galleries, Madrid comes alive each day to the smell of *churros*. This essential breakfast fuels office-workers and labourers alike, and it also provides a morning power-start for museum-goers making their pilgrimages to the treasure houses on the city's Golden Triangle of art: the eclectic Museo Thyssen-Bornamisza, the legendary Museo del Prado with its works by Goya and Velázquez *(see also pp136–7)* and the thought-provoking, sometimes controversial Museo Nacional Centro de Arte Reina Sofía, Spain's national museum of 20th- and 21st-century art.

By mid-afternoon, there are shopping bags at every table in the *churrerías*, as intrepid boutique warriors pause for the *merienda*, or afternoon snack, whether in the cluster of designer shops and bespoke cobblers of the Salamanca neighbourhood or along the bustling streets in the vibrant barrio of Chueca. *Churros* are often hard to find after dark in other Spanish cities,

but not in Madrid, where the tasty fritters imbue *Madrileños* with the stamina to keep going until they drop. When the flamenco show ends at 1am or the sky shows dawn's early streaks as the dance clubs close, the *churrerías* beckon.

Thought to have been created as an easy breakfast for mountain shepherds (*churra* is an ancient breed of Iberian sheep), *churros* are among the simplest of sweets – a basic batter of flour, salt and water piped into bubbling vats of oil. Fried into finger-sized sticks that are soft on the inside but brown and crisp on the outside, they must be eaten before they cool – ideally dusted with sugar and dipped into coffee or a cup of mud-thick Spanish hot chocolate – for an explosion of warmth that radiates from mouth to fingertips.

So central is the shepherd's breakfast to *Madrileños* that no festival in the city is complete without *churro* carts. As the street music rises to a proper Spanish din, vendors fire up their gas heaters to bring their oil to a bubbling sizzle, squirt in the dough and transform a simple batter into a sweet celebratory treat.

A Day in Madrid

Madrid remains as vibrant at night as during the day. The monumental fountains of Neptuno and Cibeles along the Paseo del Prado are most dramatic when illuminated. The complex rhythms and mournful song of flamenco only begin after dinner (that is, midnight), and the trance beat of the dance clubs starts throbbing in the *madrugada*, or early morning.

MORNING Picasso's masterpiece, *Guernica,* is reason enough to visit the **Museo Nacional Centro de Arte Reina Sofía**, but don't miss the extensive collection of paintings and sculptures by Madrid-born Juan Gris and the ever-cryptic and mercurial Joan Miró.

AFTERNOON Seek out fashions by many of Spain's young, avant-garde designers in the trendy **Chueca** neighbourhood, also known for its gay-friendly nightlife. For the best in Spanish footwear at bargain prices, peruse the shops on **Calle Augusto Figueroa**.

EVENING Begin with drinks in the upmarket culinary centre of **Mercado San Miguel**. Eat dinner and watch Madrid's best flamenco at **Casa Patas**. After the show, dance until dawn at **Disco-Teatro Joy Eslava** and end the evening's revelries with the obligatory *churros* and chocolate.

Essentials

GETTING THERE
Madrid lies near the geographical centre of Spain. Most international airlines fly into **Madrid-Barajas Airport**, 12 km (7 miles) from the city centre. The best way to get around the city is by **metro**.

WHERE TO STAY
Hotel Plaza Mayor (inexpensive) is a welcoming option in a 200-year-old church building. www.h-plazamayor.com
Room Mate Oscar Hotel (moderate) is a playful designer hotel in hip Chueca. www.room-matehotels.com
Catalonia Las Cortes (moderate) offers rooms in a converted 18th-century palace. www.hoteles-catalonia.com

TOURIST INFORMATION
Plaza Mayor 27; www.esmadrid.com

Left The chocolate for *chocolate con churros* should be rich, dark and thick, perfect for dipping

Above The long, curled form of the Madrid *churro* is cut into small pieces for serving

Below A modern addition to the Museo Reina Sofía has enhanced the display space for 20th-century art

Doughnuts Around the World

Madrileños eat *churros* around the clock, but many cultures have their own love affairs with sizzling deep-fried dough. Whether they are called doughnuts, fritters, *beignets* or *sopapillas*, they are often eaten as breakfast food or sweet treats at street fairs and markets.

MADRID

Chocolatería San Ginés inexpensive
Pasadizo de San Ginés 5; +34 913 656 546

Neat rows of cups and saucers on a marble bar greet customers at this institution beloved by generations of *Madrileños*. At midnight, dawn and noon, San Ginés serves the thick chocolate and lightly crisp *churros* against which all others are judged.

Chocolatería Valor inexpensive
Calle Postigo de San Martín 7; www.valor.es

Founded in 1881, Valor is one of Spain's most famous makers of premium chocolate, used for baking, cooking and confectionery. The company's signature *bonbonería* (sweets and bakery store), just a few steps from Puerta del Sol, serves rich hot chocolate with unusually large, unfluted *churros*.

Maestro Churrero inexpensive
Calle Atocha 19; www.maestrochurrero.com

This popular *churrería* traces its roots to a rolling cart from 1902 that allowed a *Madrileño* named Don Florencio to cater to theatre-goers. Five generations down the line, his successors continue to warm hungry breakfast patrons and revellers needing a sweet bite after hours of tapas and drinks.

VALENCIA, SPAIN

Deep-fried pastries are as integral to Valencian cuisine as paella. Street vendors even sell hot chocolate and pumpkin *buñuelos* (a small bun similar to a *churro*) during the March carnival of Las Fallas (the Fires).

Estación del Norte inexpensive
Calle Xàtiva 24

Whether travellers are arriving or departing, they can always count on a quick pick-me-up of toasty *churros* and hot chocolate from the gleaming stainless steel outdoor kiosks that operate from dawn to midnight in front of Valencia's Art Nouveau train station in the heart of the city.

Horchatería El Siglo inexpensive
Plaza Santa Catalina 11, +34 963 918 466

Founded in 1836, this venerable café is celebrated for its milky *horchata* drink made from *chufa*, or tiger nuts. Cool and refreshing, it is usually served with *churros* or *buñuelos* (cheese doughnuts) – which staff often cook outdoors to attract customers, as the aromas are virtually irresistible.

Horchatería Santa Catalina inexpensive
Plaza Santa Catalina 6;
www.horchateriasantacatalina.com

Decorated in classic Valencian painted tiles, this rival to El Siglo is acclaimed for its hot chocolate, often ordered with *churros*. A larger sweet bread called a *farton*, which lacks the fluting of a *churro* and is sometimes glazed, usually accompanies *horchata*.

USA

The United States spawned the sweetened fried dough known as the doughnut – a spherical or ring-shaped variation on the *churro*. But the country's many immigrant groups have not forgotten their own ethnic variations on deep-fried sweet fritters.

Doughnut Plant inexpensive
379 Grand Street, New York, New York;
www.doughnutplant.com

This artisanal doughnut shop in the Lower East Side of Manhattan has become a confectionery cult, in part because it incorporates fresh seasonal fruits such as strawberries and blueberries into the glazes. Weekend queues literally stretch out the door.

Dunkin' Donuts inexpensive
543 Southern Artery, Quincy, Massachusetts;
www.dunkindonuts.com

Dunkin' Donuts opened its first shop in Quincy, Massachusetts, in 1950, featuring fresh coffee and a doughnut with a small handle, enabling it to be dunked. The chain has since spread the American doughnut – in 52 varieties, including the perennially favourite plain, glazed and jam-filled types – to 31 countries around the world.

Left (top to bottom) A *chocolateria* stall serving hot chocolate at the carnival of Las Fallas in Valencia, Spain; coffee and doughnuts provide on-the-go urban fuel on Times Square, New York

Below (top to bottom) Sugar-coated ring doughnuts; a mariachi band performing near Churrería El Moro in Mexico City; *churros* dipped in chocolate in Oaxaca, Mexico

Morro Castle inexpensive
2500 Northwest Seventh Street, Miami, Florida; +1 305 642 4747

This classic 1950s drive-in is known for its Cuban sandwiches and *fritas* (burgers) made with a mixture of ground beef and chorizo sausage. But many locals also believe that Morro Castle serves the best traditional Spanish-style *churros* and hot chocolate in Miami.

Spudnut Shop inexpensive
228 Williams Boulevard, Richland, Washington; www.richland.tri-cityshopping.com/spudnuts

A family-run bakery in the same location for more than 60 years, Spudnut uses a combination of potato flour and wheat flour to produce unusually airy yeast-raised and cake doughnuts. The family also bakes a line of spudnut muffins and cakes.

Café du Monde moderate
1039 Decatur Street, New Orleans, Louisiana; www.cafedumonde.com

A stalwart of the city's French Quarter, this marketplace café creates legendary *beignets* – high and puffy squares of fried dough covered in powdered sugar. They are served in orders of three to accompany coffee given a nutty, slightly acrid taste by roasted chicory.

Maria's New Mexican Kitchen moderate
555 West Cordova Road, Santa Fe, New Mexico; www.marias-santafe.com

This restaurant is justly famed for its authentic northern New Mexican cooking, based on fresh and dried chilli peppers. The perfect conclusion to the hot and spicy courses comes in the form of soothing, honey-drizzled *sopapillas* – small, hollow, triangular "pillows" of sweet, fried dough.

Sra. Martinez moderate
4000 Northeast Second Avenue, Miami, Florida; www.sramartinez.com

Diners at this stylish bistro in a former post office in the Design District understand that *churros* are no longer just street food. For dessert, chef Michelle Bernstein serves *churros* with a chocolate dipping sauce that she spikes with cayenne pepper.

MEXICO

It is said that when the Spanish explorer Hernán Cortés arrived in Mexico in 1519, the Aztecs mistook him for an incarnation of their god Quetzalcoatl, and served him up a feast including *xocoatl*, a cocoa-bean drink. The Spanish kept the popular drink's ingredients a secret for 100 years, and eventually returned the favour by introducing Mexicans to the pleasures of *churros* dipped in thickened hot chocolate.

Cafe San Agustín inexpensive
Calle San Francisco 21, San Miguel de Allende; +52 5154 9102

Both *churros* and chocolate at this popular café come in three degrees of sweetness: Spanish, French and Mexican. The sweetest is Mexican, and it is spiced with the brassy, bright flavour of the papery Mexican *canela*, or cinnamon.

Churrería El Moro inexpensive
Calle Lázaro Cárdenas 42, Mexico City; +52 5512 0896

Even the bespangled mariachi musicians from nearby Plaza Garibaldi patronize this 1935 landmark *churrería* for bags of *churros* doused with grainy sugar and the speciality hot chocolate, which is frothed with carved wooden *molinillos* (whisks) and served up in earthenware jugs.

ARGENTINA

Café culture is central to the Argentine capital, and *Porteños* (the inhabitants of Buenos Aires) often treat their favourite cafés as second living-rooms – places to entertain friends and even conduct business over plates of *churros* and cups of hot chocolate.

La Giralda inexpensive
1453 Avenida Corrientes, Buenos Aires; +54 11 4371 3846

This erstwhile hangout for Argentine intellectuals and theatre-goers is the most famous of the cluster on Avenida Corrientes. It caters to the *Porteño* sweet tooth by filling its *churros* with chocolate cream or with *dulce de leche*, the city's signature milk caramel. Early risers and clubbers on the way home compete for morning tables.

Café Tortoni moderate
825 Avenida de Mayo, Buenos Aires; www.cafetortoni.com.ar

Possibly the oldest café in Argentina, the historic and atmospheric Tortoni has been an integral part of *Porteño* life since 1858. A long-time favourite of politicians, intellectuals and artists, its cigar-shaped, thick and somewhat crunchy *churros* are best enjoyed with a *submarino* – a cup of hot milk served with a bar of dark chocolate (the "submarine") which melts when dipped.

A Day in Colmar

Colmar is one of the most captivating towns in Alsace, with intriguing medieval and Renaissance buildings, winding canals and pretty gardens.

MORNING Head for the huddle of pedestrianized streets of the old town. Wander past the **Maison des Têtes** (House of Heads), with its façade of 111 faces, to the wooden **Pfister House**, which has glorious Renaissance balconies. Then visit the **Bartholdi Museum**, the former home of Frédéric Auguste Bartholdi, creator of the Statue of Liberty.

AFTERNOON Start with the **Unterlinden Museum**, an ex-Dominican convent full of Alsatian treasures, including the striking Isenheim Altarpiece, created in around 1515 – a riot of grisly monsters and demons. There's a fine batch of gargoyles, too, at the Gothic marvel on Place de la Cathédrale: **St Martin's Collegiate Church**.

EVENING Walk down to the **Quai de la Poissonnerie** in Petite Venise. Cross the flower-draped bridges, and look down the canals along the rows of houses teetering drunkenly on the water's edge. Stop in a waterside café to sample some *tarte flambée*.

Essentials

GETTING THERE
Fly to either **Basel-Mulhouse** or **Strasbourg airports**; Colmar lies between the two, with good rail links. There are also fast **trains** three times a day from Paris.

WHERE TO STAY
L'Hôtel Beausejour (inexpensive) is a charming hotel in a restored early-20th-century building with family rooms. *www.beausejour.fr*
La Maison des Têtes (moderate), built in 1609, is chock-full of history and Alsatian appeal. *www.maisondestetes.com*
L'Hôtel Quatorze (expensive) is an ancient pharmacy turned into a designer hotel with hip paintings by Spanish artist Alfonso Vallès. *www.hotelquatorze.com*

TOURIST INFORMATION
www.ot-colmar.fr

Right *Tarte flambée* with the classic white cheese, bacon and onion topping
Below Half-timbered houses sit alongside the canal in Petite Venise, Colmar

The Best Places to Eat Tarte Flambée

La Maison Rouge inexpensive

A Colmar gem known for its warm welcome and well-priced food, La Maison Rouge has been serving up Alsatian favourites for more than 30 years. In keeping with its name, there's a lot of red splashed about, from lamps and red-trimmed tablecloths to the blazing *rouge* walls of the cellar dining room. It's whispered, however, that the name dates back to a less cheery time, when the executioners from the guillotine stayed here and the red was a reference to the blood on their hands. There's nothing to fear these days, though, and the delicious food runs from *bibalakas* – a rib-sticking mix of *fromage blanc* (soft white cheese), chives and garlic served with sautéed potatoes, cheese and ham – to the house favourite of ham spit-roasted on the bone (*jambon à l'os braisé à la broche*). But locals flock for the four kinds of *tarte flambée*, including one garnished with goat's cheese and basil, and a de luxe Upper Rhine version made with Munster, a high-fat, full-cream-milk cheese.

9 rue des Ecoles, Colmar; open noon–2pm and 6:30–10pm Tue–Sat; www.maison-rouge.net

Also in Colmar

Aux Clefs de Colmar *(+33 3 8923 9215, inexpensive)* serves up traditional regional food, from pork knuckle baked with a Munster-cheese crust to a host of *flammekueche*, or as they're known here, "flams". There's a basic flam of bacon, onion and *fromage blanc*, several cheese versions (with Emmental, Munster and goat's cheese), plus one with smoked salmon and another with mushrooms.

Also in France

La Strasbourgeoise *(+33 1 4205 2002; moderate)* in Paris sits appropriately opposite the Gare de l'Est, for trains to and from Alsace. In place since 1950, this is a little corner of Alsace in the French capital, from the choucroute piled high with pork to the traditional *tarte flambée*, a crispy thin crust painted with cream and specked with bacon and finely sliced onion. Wash it down with a mug of Alsatian beer or a pitcher of Riesling.

Around the World

Alsatian specialities litter the menu at Boston's **Brasserie Jo** *(www.brasseriejo.com; inexpensive)*, including *tarte flambée*. They serve the classic – with fresh white cheese, bacon and onions – plus two new versions that might earn the disdain of traditionalists but please the locals, with spinach, Gruyère cheese and garlic chips, or blue cheese and walnut.

COLMAR FRANCE

Fiery Tarte Flambée in Alsace

Colmar's old town reflects a time when half-timbered houses were all the rage and you could never have enough gables, balconies or spires. Delightfully Alsatian in look and attitude, the town is a little more German than French, and so is the food: pretzel, sausage, cabbage and *tarte flambée*, a satisfyingly crispy crust anointed with a rich cream and bacon topping.

Colmar has both French and Germanic traits in its cooking, its architecture and its festivals. Full of Alsatian atmosphere, from its half-timbered houses to its medieval alleyways, the town is a vivid reminder not just of the proximity of the German border, but of the many disputes over its allegiance; it has been alternately part of France and Germany many times in its history. In the Middle Ages, Colmar was the region's port, and farmers were still using the canals to deliver their produce to the central covered market right up until the 1950s. The farmers are long gone, and the area – now known as Petite Venise – features tourist boats, a tootling train and quayside cafés, but still something of the old-world charm remains, as the canals gently weave among the tall, ornately carved, 16th-century buildings.

It was not until the 19th century that the Alsatians invented their famous tart – *tarte flambée* – and it was more by accident than intention. The canny farm women of the Kochersberg region used to roll out their left-over bread dough and pop it in among the wood-stoked flames to check the readiness of their oven for bread-baking. Its place in the oven flames explains its name, although some like to think it's also because the edges are always singed black, or flamed.

Larder staples began to grace the rectangular, ultra-thin crust: a slather of home-made cream, some thinly sliced onions picked from the field and chunks of home-cured bacon. In the fierce oven heat, it took a matter of minutes to cook – the ultimate fast food. At first the lunch of choice for just a small clutch of farmers in the Lower Rhine, it soon became emblematic of all Alsace. Towns both high and low on the Rhine now serve up "flame tart", or *flammekueche*. There's even a *Confrérie de la Veritable Tarte Flambée d'Alsace* (Brotherhood of the Real Alsatian Flamed Tart) who ensure the quality of the crust dished up in Alsatian restaurants. They insist on a certain recipe, cooked in a wood-fired oven, but they are open to variations on ingredient ratios, and even sanction a sweet version with sliced apple. In keeping with all things Alsatian, a happy blend is finally what counts.

The Alsatian Wine Route

Colmar is the "capital of Alsatian wine" and part of the 170-km (106-mile) *Route des Vins* (Wine Route). Threading through vast vineyards dotted with cobblestone villages and castles, it's easy to follow and a great way to explore the region. The route runs from Marlenheim to Thann, along the eastern foothills of the Vosges mountains, and there are more than 40 vineyards with wines to try along the way. Around 90 per cent of Alsatian wine is white – Riesling, Sylvaner, Gewürztraminer and Pinot Gris. If you'd like to do some wine tasting but don't want to drive the wine trail, try cellars in Colmar that are open for tastings, such as **Domaine Viticole de la Ville de Colmar** *(www. domaineviticolecolmar.fr)*, **Domaine Robert Karcher et Fils** *(www.vins-karcher.com)* or organic wine grower **Martin Jund** *(www.vin-bio-jund. com)*, who also offers accommodation.

Above Dining alfresco in the Place de l'Ancienne Douane, Colmar

ST PETERSBURG RUSSIA

Blinis and Caviar on the Baltic

Russia's hauntingly beautiful former imperial capital has been justly described as the Venice of the North. Since Tsarist times, its cuisine has combined the simplicity of peasant cooking with the epicurean delights of this vast nation's rivers. Blinis with caviar are cherished by every Russian as their culinary birthright, whether eaten in a humble café or a fancy restaurant.

Founded by Tsar Peter the Great to be a "window on the West" that exposed backward Holy Russia to the European Enlightenment, St Petersburg is said to have been "built on bones" by forced labour, on a desolate swamp where the Neva river flows into the Baltic Sea. It supplanted Moscow as Russia's capital and remained so until Lenin returned the seat of power to the Kremlin. As the second city of the Soviet Union – renamed Leningrad – it withstood the epic 900 Days of Nazi siege, when 670,000 citizens perished from starvation, cold or shelling.

Although the last Tsar, Nicholas II, once remarked that "St Petersburg is Russian – but it is not Russia", the city is associated with a host of renowned figures. Here, Tchaikovsky, Stravinsky and Shostakovich composed; Pushkin, Gogol and Dostoevsky wrote; Rasputin, Lenin and Trotsky made political history; and Catherine the Great defined decadent living. The city's historical associations abound, from unbridled autocrats to suicidal poets and ruthless revolutionaries.

The city's layout was determined by Peter the Great, who regulated the size of dwellings for each social class and plotted the great avenues that converge on the golden-spired Admiralty. Nevsky Prospekt, the city's main street, has examples of every style of architecture, from Baroque and Neo-Classical to Art Nouveau and Constructivism. The façades of this harmonious ensemble are painted in cool greys and blues or warm tawny hues, producing luminous reflections in the dark waters of the Neva river, its tributaries and the numerous canals.

Ever since pagan times – before Russians adopted Christianity – the winter festival of Maslenitsa has been celebrated by gorging on blinis oozing melted butter, symbolizing the sun and hopes of fertile crops for the year ahead. The pancakes are traditionally prepared from buckwheat or wheat flour, mixed with butter, eggs, milk and yeast; they can be topped with anything, but the classic accompaniment is caviar.

Red caviar (*krasnaya ikra*) is the plump orange eggs of salmon roe; it is far cheaper than black caviar (*chornaya ikra*), harvested from four varieties of Caspian sturgeon. The most treasured is the pea-sized, black-to-silvery-grey Beluga, followed by the smaller, golden Sterlet, the brownish Osetra and lastly the grey Sevruga. Canapé-sized blinis are the perfect foil to their oily saltiness, garnished with lemon slices, a dollop of sour cream and a sprig of dill. Each one is a delicious testament to the decadence of the Tsars.

A Day in St Petersburg

The Neva river defines the city; its majestic bridges link the city centre (on the mainland) to Petrograd Side and Vasilevsky Island. During the mid-summer White Nights, crowds gather to watch the bridges being raised; in winter the Neva freezes over, with spectacular ice floes during the spring thaw.

MORNING Tour the **State Hermitage Museum**, an architectural ensemble that includes the magnificent **Winter Palace** and houses a collection of artworks that rivals the Louvre's. Then stroll along the **Moyka** canal to the **Church of the Saviour on the Spilled Blood**, marking the spot where Alexander II was assassinated.

AFTERNOON Visit the **Peter and Paul Fortress**, where the Romanovs (now buried in the Peter and Paul Cathedral) imprisoned generations of revolutionaries. Walk on the cruiser **Aurora**, whose guns heralded the October Revolution in 1917.

EVENING Explore the **Haymarket** district (the setting of Dostoevsky's *Crime and Punishment*), before attending a performance at the **Mariinsky Theatre**.

Essentials

GETTING THERE
St Petersburg's international **airport**, Pulkovo, has **buses** and **taxis** to the city centre, 17 km (11 miles) away. It's easy to get around by **metro**, **bus**, *marshrutka* (**minibus**) or on foot.

WHERE TO STAY
Randhouse (inexpensive) is a hip B&B chain with good locations. *www.randhouse.ru*
Casa Leto (moderate) is an elegant mini-hotel near the Hermitage. *www.casaleto.com*
Grand Hotel Europe (expensive) is true old-style decadence. *www.grandhoteleurope.com*

TOURIST INFORMATION
www.visitrussia.org.uk

Above Mounds of caviar with soured cream and a sprig of dill constitutes the classic blini topping

Left The Church of the Resurrection of Christ, also known as the "Church of the Saviour on the Spilled Blood", was built in 1883 in the style of 16th- and 17th-century Russian churches

Above Once the food of poor villagers living by the Caspian Sea, caviar became the choice of the elite before becoming widely available across Russia

Zakuski

On restaurant menus, blinis with caviar (or mushrooms or puréed herring) come under the heading of *zakuski*, or hors d'oeuvres. Salted sprats or herrings, gherkins, pickled garlic, spiced feta, cold meats, gelatines and salads are also popular, together with the oddly named *selyodka pod-shuby* – herring "in a fur coat" of beetroot, carrot, egg and mayonnaise. *Zakuski* form the basis of the *Russky stol*, or "Russian table", which among the Tsarist upper classes was merely the prelude to the main meal of the day. The *Russky stol* can be enjoyed at restaurants or private parties celebrating New Year, Orthodox Christmas (6–7 January) or "Old New Year" (13–14 January).

The Best Places to Eat Blinis

Caviar Bar & Restaurant
expensive

If money's no object, reserve a table at the Caviar Bar & Restaurant in the Grand Hotel Europe, where Tchaikovsky spent his honeymoon. Founded in the 1870s, the Yevropeyskaya (as locals call the hotel) became an orphanage after the 1920s Civil War and was only restored to its previous splendour six decades later. Though there's no formal dress code, you'll feel underdressed in casual wear amidst the Caviar Bar's Art Nouveau marble decor, damask upholstery and tinkling fountain.

Its menu offers such delights as Kamchatka crab, Siberian *pelmeni* (ravioli) in Champagne sauce, sturgeon and salmon mousse – and blinis with caviar. Their blinis are cooked to perfection – thin and crispy – and caviar is mouthwatering, from the finest Beluga and Sterlet to unsalted (*malossol*) red caviar (which elsewhere tends to be over-salted). Served with panache, they are best washed down with shots of ice-cold vodka, of which there's a vast range of different flavoured brands available.

Mikhailovskaya ul. 1–7, St Petersburg; open 5pm–midnight daily; www.grandhoteleurope.com

Also in St Petersburg

You needn't spend a fortune to enjoy blinis with caviar. Providing they're freshly made, they can be delicious in cafés or as takeaways from street kiosks serving Russian-style fast food. Some chains serve deep-frozen blinis, defrosted in a microwave, which are truly revolting. If in doubt ask, "*Oni svyezhi?*" ("Are they fresh?"). One sure-fire option – that also offers an all-you-can-eat *zakuski* buffet – is **Yolki Palki** (*inexpensive*), a rustic-style chain of Russian tavernas with 24-hour branches at Malaya Konyushennaya 9 and Nevsky Prospekt 88. Besides a selection of vodkas, they also serve *kvas*, a delicious beverage made from fermented rye bread. Neither branch takes bookings.

Also in Russia

Yolki Palki *(see above)* is ubiquitous in Moscow, but **Teremok** (www.teremok.ru; *inexpensive*), a chain with kiosks near metro stations, is a good alternative for a takeaway. For a sit-down meal in Moscow, try the funky **Café Margarita** *(www. cafe-margarita.ru; inexpensive)*, named after the heroine of Mikhail Bulgakov's classic novel, *The Master and Margarita*.

Around the World

Blinis are also a feature of Polish, Yiddish, Lithuanian and Ukrainian cuisine, and feature on the menu in restaurants from Vilnius to Berlin and beyond. In the USA, there are many Russian restaurants in Brooklyn; the **Baku Palace** *(www.bakupalace.com; moderate)* also has Azerbaijani dishes on its menu.

A Day in Ulm

Central Ulm is easily explored on foot: most places of interest lie between the Danube and Ulm Minster, which are just minutes apart.

MORNING Climb the 768 tight stairs of the **minster spire** while you are fresh, then admire the church's 15th-century choir stalls and its fine stained glass. Head downhill to the **Fishermen's Quarter** on the banks of the Danube and the 1443 **Schiefes Haus**, or crooked house, which leans worryingly over a stream.

AFTERNOON Walk along the medieval riverside **city wall** to the equally crooked **Metzgerturm**, a 14th-century defensive tower uphill of which lies the **Rathaus**. It contains a replica of the world's first hang-glider and is decorated with frescoes of Ulm's medieval heyday. Cross the square to enter the striking modern **Kunsthalle Weishaupt** and enjoy its contemporary and modern art, then visit the adjoining **Ulmer Museum** for an overview of city history.

EVENING When there's no festival in town, travel 1 km (1½ miles) south of the centre to the **Roxy**, a huge, happening cultural venue.

Essentials

GETTING THERE
Stuttgart International Airport lies an hour's **train** journey from Ulm. The rail station is within walking distance of all central attractions.

WHERE TO STAY
Pension Rösch (inexpensive) offers basic but clean and quiet rooms in the riverside Fishermen's Quarter. +49 7316 5718
Hotel Bäumle (moderate) is a welcoming hotel with good-value standard rooms in a 500-year-old building by the minster. www.hotel-baeumle.de
Hotel Schiefes Haus (expensive) is an eccentric Ulm landmark – a half-timbered 1443 house that is "the most crooked hotel in the world". www.hotelschiefeshausulm.de

TOURIST INFORMATION
www.tourismus.ulm.de

Left The multi-shaped pieces of handmade *Spätzle* are often stirred through with cheese and herbs for a simple meal
Below The soaring spire of Ulm Minster rises above the city to an astonishing height of 161 m (530 ft)

ULM GERMANY

Swabian Noodles in Ulm

Most visitors to the pretty city of Ulm are drawn there to see the world's tallest church spire, a staggering piece of Gothic architecture that demonstrates the city's prosperity in medieval times. But this city – the birthplace of Albert Einstein – is full of surprises, not least the fine cuisine of the Swabian Alp region and its Italianate little egg noodles known as *Spätzle*.

Ulm sits on the banks of the Danube river, a sleepy, old city that was first mentioned as a royal domain in 854 and became rich in the Middle Ages through the linen trade. Its magnificent church dates back to 1377, though its ambitious spire wasn't completed for another 500 years. On clear days even the Alps are visible from the top, making it well worth the long climb. The streets leading downhill from the minster to the Danube are scattered with fascinating buildings, from the attractive jumble of half-timbered 15th-century houses in the Fishermen's Quarter to the Rathaus (town hall), with its historic frescoes. The Eagle's Bastion, a nondescript 17th-century building by the river, is worthy of a visit in memory of the "tailor of Ulm", who attempted the first recorded (unsuccessful) flight from here in 1811.

The city's symbol is the sparrow. The legendary tale relates that while building the church, workmen were unable to get one of the huge wooden beams through the city gates, until they were inspired by the sight of a sparrow carrying a twig vertically in its beak.

The legend of the *Ulmer Spätze* (sparrow of Ulm) was born. Interestingly, the city's best-loved dish, *Spätzle*, means "little sparrow", although no-one is quite sure why; it may refer to the legend or to the *Spätzle*'s original hand-pressed shapes, evident in medieval drawings.

Spätzle are served at most of Ulm's restaurants and at all of its many, boisterous festivals. Shaped like tiny dumplings or thin ragged fingers of pasta, *Spätzle* are made from white wheat flour, egg and milk dough, to which minced pork liver is sometimes added to make *Leberspätzle*. This dough is then either finely chopped, forced through holes in a strainer, or grated into boiling salted water where it is cooked until it surfaces.

As a stand-alone dish, *Spätzle* most commonly appear as *Käsespätzle* (in a cheese sauce) or as *Krautspätzle*, which includes sauerkraut, onion, butter, marjoram and caraway. *Spätzle* also make an important appearance in the regional beef stew *Gaisburger Marsch*, along with chopped potatoes and butter-fried onions, but most often they simply take the place of potatoes or dumplings in traditional German meat dishes such as sauerbraten (*see pp92–3*).

Ulm Bread Museum

Bread had religious importance in Germany for many centuries as an offering in pagan rites. This explains the many shapes still available today: round flat loaves once represented the sun, while braided loaves symbolized shorn hair. A tradition also developed of shaping bread into nature's creations, such as horses, birds, deer, fish or sheaves of wheat for special occasions. Ulm's **Museum der Brotkultur** (bread museum) confirms bread's historical importance with its staggering 25,000 related objects and books. Most Ulm bakeries offer a wonderful range of breads to admire and buy, spanning from coarse, dark and slightly sweet rye pumpernickel to multigrain loaves sprinkled with poppy or sunflower seeds. Many end up in a simple evening meal; the German word for dinner, *Abendbrot*, literally means "evening bread".

Above The elaborately painted walls of the 14th-century Rathaus

The Best Places to Eat Spätzle

Zunfthaus der Schiffleute
moderate

Once the local guild headquarters for fishermen, this 15th-century half-timbered house is home to one of Ulm's oldest restaurants. Inside, stone floors with timeless, heavy wooden furniture set the perfect scene for traditional Swabian foods, many of which involve outstanding home-made *Spätzle*. Virtually the whole range of possibilities are here; among them the standard *Käsespätzle*, in its rich cheese sauce, and the fairly common *Linsen* (lentils) *mit Spätzle* and *Krautspätzle*. More unusual meal options include the *Zunfthaustöpfle*, with its creamy herb heavy mushroom sauce; and the robust *Ulmer Pfännle*, in which pork kebabs are smothered in fiery pepper sauce. Often the most interesting choices are on the restaurant's seasonal menu, where delicious ingredients such as asparagus, chanterelle mushrooms and venison are served with *Spätzle*. A good selection of local beers is on hand to provide the perfect accompaniment to this rustic fare. But be sure not to overindulge on the main courses, as the vanilla ice cream with hot figs is well worth leaving a space for.

Fischergasse 31, Ulm; open 11am–midnight Mon–Sat; www.zunfthaus-ulm.de

Also in Ulm

If you'd rather have your *Spätzle* served with a gourmet twist, try charming **Zur Forelle** (*www.zurforelle.com; expensive*), which is also based in a 15th-century Fishermen's Quarter house. Its *Gaisburger Marsch* (Swabian beef stew) is particularly wonderful.

Also in Germany

Elsewhere in Swabia, in the venerable university town of Thübingen, the **Hotel am Schloss** (*www.hotelamschloss.de; moderate*) is largely famous for its *Maultaschen* (Swabian ravioli) and fine views of the city, but it always serves great *Spätzle* too and isn't afraid to experiment with dishes such as venison pot roast with hazelnut *Spätzle*. While it's easy to find good *Spätzle* in Swabia, it's much harder elsewhere in Germany, particularly in the north, which makes Berlin's **s'Brätle** (*+49 30 8862 7138; moderate*) all the more valuable. Its range of southern German specialities include superb *Spätzle*.

Around the World

With many Swabians emigrating to North America, it's also possible to find good *Spätzle* there too. In Alameda, California, the **Speisekammer** (*www.speisekammer.com; moderate*) provides San Francisco's Bay Area with a *Käsespätzle* to be proud of. On the east coast, **Cafe Steinhof** (*www.cafesteinhof.com; inexpensive*) does a first rate job of the same dish, even though it classifies itself as an Austrian restaurant.

Above The main square in Brussels – the Grand Place – dates back to the Middle Ages

Above Steamed *moules marinière* cooked with garlic, white wine, parsley and shallots are eaten using an empty shell as a pincer

Three Days in Brussels

Brussels is full of wonderful sights, food and drink, and its attractions can easily be sampled by walking or taking the hop-on, hop-off buses.

DAY ONE Begin at the magnificent **Grand Place**, and take a short detour to the city mascot, the little bronze figure of the **Manneken-Pis** ("Peeing Boy"). Walk back through the elegant **Galéries St-Hubert** arcade to the Gothic **Cathédrale des Saints Michel et Gudule**. End the day at the **Musée des Instruments de Musique**.

DAY TWO Start the day at the **flea market** in the **Place du Jeu de Balle**. Then walk through the **Place du Grand Sablon**, with its upmarket antique and chocolate shops, to reach the **Musées Royaux des Beaux-Arts**, a monument to Belgian art.

DAY THREE Visit the **Horta Museum**, a shrine to Art Nouveau set in the home of its pioneer, Victor Horta. Then head for the wonderfully quirky **Musée Wiertz**, a 19th-century art studio. Continue to the **Parc du Cinquantenaire**, with its three museums: military, historic automobiles and world-class antique treasures.

Essentials

GETTING THERE
Brussels has an international **airport** at Zaventem, three major **railway stations**, and an extensive city network of **trams** and **buses**.

WHERE TO STAY
Sleep Well Youth Hostel (inexpensive) is more of a budget hotel than a hostel, with a good choice of accommodation close to the city centre. *www.sleepwell.be*
Noga (moderate) is a neat, elegant and well-run hotel in a tranquil location, close to the Place Sainte-Catherine. *www.nogahotel.com*
Le Dixseptième (expensive) is a stylish boutique hotel in the 17th-century residence of the Spanish ambassador, close to the Grand Place. *www.ledixseptieme.be*

TOURIST INFORMATION
Grand Place; *www.visitbrussels.be*

BRUSSELS BELGIUM

Mussels in Brussels

Brussels is an hour's drive from the Belgian coast but, as a great medieval trading city, it has a historic connection with the sea. It's no surprise, then, that the classic Belgian dish of *moules-frites* – mussels and chips – is the mainstay of many of the capital's restaurants. It's a simple and nutritious dish that depends crucially on fresh, quality ingredients being cooked to perfection.

In 1561, an ambitious new waterway – the Willebroek Canal – was completed, leading to the heart of Brussels and giving the city a direct link to the sea. The canal terminated at Place Sainte-Catherine, a stone's throw from the city's splendid centrepiece, the Grand Place. In the late 19th century, when the canal's course was diverted and the basins at the city centre filled in, the area became the site of a huge fish market, the Marché aux Poissons. The fish market has since disappeared, but the connection with the sea remains in the wonderful fish restaurants of Place Sainte-Catherine.

Belgium has acquired a dizzying reputation for its food in recent decades, and its capital is also the effective capital of the European Union, attracting a cosmopolitan crowd that demands high standards. In the Belgians themselves a culture of good food is instilled from an early age: they like to eat well, but have little tolerance of pretension. *Moules-frites* (mussels and chips) falls into this tradition. The high-end restaurants here are too grand to serve such a simple dish, and you're more likely to find it in bistros and family restaurants, but *moules-frites* is not to be sniffed at. It's a simple enough dish: the mussels are usually cooked *marinière* (steamed with chopped shallots, celery, parsley, thyme, bay leaves and a glass of white wine), then served in large casseroles accompanied by copious *frites* (chips). But its creation en masse in lively restaurants creates glorious scenes reminiscent of the festive village celebrations painted by Pieter Brueghel the Elder, a resident of Brussels in the mid-16th century.

There is plenty for the visitor to see and admire in Brussels, including a fine cathedral and excellent art museums. But the real joy of visiting the city lies in glimpsing something of its individual character, which nurtured the Surrealist vision of René Magritte, and gave birth to Art Nouveau architecture and Tintin, the famous cartoon reporter. In the same spirit, the Belgian artist Marcel Broodthaers produced his most famous sculptural work in 1964–6 in several versions. His *Grande Casserole de Moules* is just what it says – real mussel shells filling a blackened casserole.

Above The old district of Les Marolles is renowned for its comic-strip murals

Les Frites Belges

Belgian *frites* (chips) set the gold standard: when properly prepared, there are simply no better chips in the world. There are several factors involved. First, the choice of potato: only certain varieties (such as Bintje) are sufficiently sweet and floury to produce the optimum flavour and crispness. Second, the chips must be cut into just the right shape – about the size of a woman's little finger. Third, the oil (traditionally beef dripping) must be clean and piping hot. Lastly – and crucially – the *frites* are cooked twice: once to a pale softness; then, after cooling and resting, to a crispy, golden finish. The traditional Belgian accompaniment is mayonnaise. In Brussels, perfection is achieved not just in restaurants, but also in humble roadside chip stands (called *friteries* or *frietkoten*). A cornet of hot *frites* and dollop of mayonnaise can be a meal in itself.

The Best Places to Eat Moules-Frites

La Marée moderate

Portuguese-born Mario and Teresa Alves have been building a solid reputation for delicious fish cookery for over 30 years. Their restaurant's name means "The Tide", and this pretty 17th-century red-brick building is full of seafaring memorabilia, alongside old photos of the Marché aux Poissons. But essentially an unfussy simplicity prevails, so clients can concentrate on the food concocted by Teresa and her team in a kitchen open to view. It is a perfect setting for *moules-frites*: hospitable, unpretentious, yet with careful attention to detail. Prepared in four different ways (*marinière, au vin blanc, à la provençale and maison*), the mussels come to the table in large, cast-iron casseroles. You can dig them out of their shells with a fork or by using an empty pair of shells as pincers; then drink the cooking juices with a spoon. Simple, beautifully done and classically Belgian.
Rue de Flandre 99, Brussels; open 12–2pm and 6:30–10pm Tue–Sat; www.lamaree-sa.com

Also in Brussels

In't Spinnekopke (*www.spinnekopke.be; moderate*) is a delightfully atmospheric *estaminet* (traditional tavern) dating back to 1762 that specializes in Belgian beers and dishes, including *moules-frites*. **Chez Patrick** (*www.chezpatrick.be; moderate*) is another splendidly traditional eatery close to the Grand Place that has been serving *Bruxellois* favourites including *moules-frites* for over 70 years.

Also in Belgium

Go to the coast to sample really delicious mussels and other seafoods. **Oesterput** (*www.oesterput.com; moderate*) stands right by the harbour at Blankenberge, and this workmanlike warehouse with a canteen-style restaurant serves first-class seafood of all kinds. **A l'Improviste** (*www.a-l-improviste.be; moderate*) is a stylish, modern seafood restaurant with a terrace overlooking the sea at Knokke-Heist that serves classic dishes such as *moules-frites* with great flair.

Around the World

The high international reputation of Belgian cooking has spawned outposts abroad in numerous formats. London has the **Belgo** chain (*www.belgo-restaurants.co.uk; moderate*) – brasserie-style restaurants specializing in Belgian dishes and beer. There are two **Belgian Beer Cafés** (*www.belgianbeercafemelbourne.com; moderate*) with a similar mission in Melbourne, Australia. Elsewhere, look for restaurants specializing in authentic Belgian cuisine. **Jeannine's Bistro** (*www.jeanninesbistro.com; moderate*) in Houston, Texas, is a fine example.

UMBRIA ITALY

Buried Treasure in Umbria

The dramatic, mountainous landscapes of Umbria in central Italy have inspired some of the world's greatest artists, including Michelangelo, Giotto and Fra Angelico. Medieval and Renaissance towns tumble down its mountainsides like living history, many hiding exquisite art. In the fertile soil, hunters look for another Italian treasure: the knobbly tubers known as truffles.

Beautiful enough to make painters of us all, Umbria seems to hide a masterpiece in every little church and chapel. It produced more saints than any other part of Italy, including St Francis of Assisi, whose kind friendliness seems to live on in the spirit of Umbrians today. This landlocked region of Italy has witnessed the passage of tramping armies, pilgrims and traders over the centuries, but remains supremely hospitable to those wishing to admire its landscape, art and rare, regional produce.

The culture and economy here are based on farming and hunting. In southeastern Umbria, the splendid towns of Spoleto and Norcia are surrounded by countryside, some carefully cultivated, some still wild and wooded as of old. From December to March, when dawn mists cloak the hills and valleys, a curious but well-rehearsed pas de deux performance takes place in this wondrous landscape. A solitary hunter sets out with his dog across a field of stubble lined with pale, pencil-thin birch trees. The animal sniffs the clay earth, its olfactory senses trained to pick up the scent from the prized *Tuber melanosporum*: the black truffle. Unearthed and cleaned, these deeply aromatic rhizomes become a transformational ingredient.

The sophisticated Romans and ancient Greeks revered truffles for their therapeutic and aphrodisiacal properties, and believed they were created as a result of the sacred thunderbolts that Jupiter periodically hurled to Earth. In reality the Umbrian *tartufo nero* (black truffle) is a rather dull, woody fungus that needs a light brushing to remove the dirt clinging to it. Its otherworldly qualities are not evident until it is cut and tasted – at which point the all-pervading aroma of the freshly cut tuber translates into a fleeting moment of gustatory heaven that is rarely matched.

Less prized than the white truffles of Piedmont, which have sold in the past for prices exceeding €100,000 per kilo, the aromatic black truffle is still a rarity with the capacity to amaze. Though never cooked, the raw truffle is occasionally warmed, and in Umbria it is popularly grated sparingly over simple, hot pasta, such as *stringozzi*, an Umbrian form of pasta that's akin to spaghetti. The only other ingredient is a drizzle of olive oil, and Umbria boasts the best in Italy – all of its olive oils have DOP ("*denominazione origine protetta*") status. Black truffle is also used sparingly in the region's almost indefinably good meat and fish dishes, and in risotto – whose simplicity belies the glorious taste that awaits, courtesy of Umbria's "black diamonds".

Three Days in Umbria

Umbria is an Italian Renaissance painting come to life. Its medieval hilltop towns and stunning countryside provide many opportunities for great sightseeing and dining.

DAY ONE Spend the morning in the lovely walled town of **Norcia**, birthplace of St Benedict. Try the delis – the butchers here are so renowned they gave Italy its word for butcher: "*norcino*". Take an afternoon bus to **Preci**, where pastel houses dot the steep hillside, and walk on to the splendid nearby abbey of **Sant'Eutizio**.

DAY TWO Magnificent **Spoleto** is dense with captivating buildings where the Roman, medieval and Renaissance periods are pieced together. Unmissable sights are the open-air **Teatro Romano** and the **Ponte delle Torri**, a spectacular stone bridge.

DAY THREE Drive up to the breathtaking spread of the **Piano Grande**, the basin of an ancient subsided lake. It is crowned by the rugged peaks of the **Sibillini mountain range** in one of Italy's newest National Parks, and pans out below the iconic village of **Castelluccio di Norcia**, the perfect starting point for a walk in the park.

Essentials

GETTING THERE
There are **trains** and **buses** to the area from Perugia, the closest international **airport**.

WHERE TO STAY
Fonte Antica (inexpensive) offers B&B within a 700-year-old farmhouse in the National Park of Monti Sibillini. www.fonteantica.com
Hotel agli Scacchi (moderate) in Preci has home comforts and a swimming pool. www.hotelagliscacchi.com
Hotel Gattapone (expensive) is a boutique hotel in Spoleto. www.hotelgattapone.it

TOURIST INFORMATION
www.english.regioneumbria.eu

Above Freshly made ribbon pasta with shavings of black truffle and slices of ceps, or *funghi porcini*, which also grow in the Umbrian valleys

Left The enchanting village of Castelluccio di Norcia is famous for its lentils, traditionally cooked in Italy as part of New Year's Eve celebrations

Above Truffle hunting in the valleys here is a painstaking business, using specially trained dogs to sniff out the precious truffles

What Else to Eat

Norcineria roughly translates as "pork sausages". These are a serious business in Norcia, as testified by the abundance of shops crammed with rows of weird and wonderfully shaped dried and cured **salamis** tied up in string bundles. The *cremoso* variety is soft and perfect for spreading on bread for your picnic lunch, while the richer *cinghiale*, made with wild boar, is more often used in cooked dishes. The tiny, sweet, nutty **lentils** from the vast grassed plain that surrounds Castelluccio di Norcia are famous throughout Italy. At other times of year sheep graze there, and their milk is lovingly transformed into the tangy and instantly recognizable **pecorino cheese**.

The Best Places to Eat Truffles

La Locanda di Cacio Re
moderate

The delights begin even before you reach the doors of this well-reputed restaurant, as the Locanda is set in the beautiful medieval village of Vallo di Nera, still ringed by old stone walls. The restaurant itself is a refurbished 16th-century farmhouse; in summertime, guests can relax over their meal on a spacious terrace overlooking the wild wooded valleys, and there's a light-filled dining room for cooler weather. Three wonderful varieties of truffle are served – the black summer truffle, the winter "special black" and the white. Keen chef Paolo Brunclli has put together a choice of four-course menus, one entirely devoted to the truffle. As well as being shaved over fresh *tagliolini* pasta, it accompanies smoked beef carpaccio, stars in truffled lamb and flavours local cheeses such as *caciotta*. The signature dish is *stringozzi* pasta with sage, *guanciale* cured pork and flakes of pecorino sheep's cheese. Cooking courses, local products and guest rooms are also on offer.

I Casali di Vallo di Nera, Vallo di Nera; open for lunch and dinner Tue–Sun; www.caciore.com/locanda

Also in Umbria

The **Taverna Castelluccio** in Castelluccio di Norcia *(www.tavernacastelluccio.it; moderate)* is a wonderful institution, run by a welcoming host who is an expert on all matters local. As well as classics such as *tagliolini al tartufo nero di Norcia* (tagliatelle with Norcia black truffles), he serves *violatri* – wild spinach and hearty sausage stewed with organic lentils grown on the plain below the taverna.

Also in Italy

In a lovingly renovated Piedmont farmhouse in Madonna di Como, Alba, **Locanda del Pilone** *(www.locandadelpilone.com; expensive)* is a superb place to savour the white Alba truffles, as well as other Piedmont specialities. Desserts such as *millefoglie* with cocoa, chestnuts and vanilla sauce are superb.

Around the World

In California's Bay Area, **Poggio** in Sausalito *(www.poggiotrattoria.com moderate)* regularly gets rave reviews. The menu changes on a daily basis, but throughout autumn diners are guaranteed delicate white truffles imported from Alba, which on request are shaved over pasta dishes such as gnocchi fashioned from Yukon Gold potatoes smothered with ultra-creamy Valle d'Aosta fondue. Organic vegetables are grown on site and the mozzarella is made in-house.

VALENCIA SPAIN

The Original Paella in Valencia

The pearl of eastern Iberia, Valencia was contested between Christians and Moors in medieval times, and the old town echoes with these ancient cultures. In stark contrast, the City of Arts and Sciences may be the world's most futuristic complex. Old or new, every quarter of the city cherishes paella, a dish that perfectly captures the salty, earthy essence of Valencia.

Valencia's medieval centre, its exceptional white-sand beaches, and its gleaming modern yacht harbour should be enough to satisfy anyone. But after the Turia river flooded catastrophically in 1957, Valencia remade itself by re-routing the river and creating a parkland in the dry riverbed. The capstone of civic reinvention was the astonishing City of Arts and Sciences, a "city within a city" designed by native son and avant-garde architectural superstar Santiago Calatrava. So marvellous is this paean to artistic and scientific discovery that visitors are torn between just wandering among the buildings, which function as giant-scale outdoor sculpture, and going inside to wander among first-class exhibitions and performances.

No such transformation has ever been necessary to Valencian cuisine, where paella is king. When the Moors introduced rice to Europe through Valencia in the 8th century, the dish became all but inevitable. The original *paella valenciana* uses the bounty of the garden patch to create a dish that is simultaneously light and earthy, as crisp green beans combine with sweet tomatoes and peppers and the chewy, meaty

morsels of land snails and hare. The more famous *paella de mariscos* bristles with the sweet crunchy prawns and other shellfish of the Valencian coast. But in every form of paella, the rice is key.

Valencian rice can absorb up to four times its volume in liquid while still remaining firm, swelling prodigiously as it soaks up wine, fish broth, chicken stock, squid ink or vegetable juices. Cooked in a *paellera* – the shallow, wide iron pan that gives paella its name – the dish forms a definitive nutty, caramelized golden crust, or *socarrat*, at the base of the pan. The best paellas also absorb a smoky flavour from cooking over a wood fire.

Some of the city's leading paella restaurants are found on Playa Malvarossa, the broad beach where locals and visitors swim and bask in the Mediterranean sun. Diners patiently await tables, knowing that the rituals of paella cannot be rushed. First comes the difficult choice over the type of paella, then the wait, as the dish is prepared to order, before – finally – the waiter presents a *paellera* big enough to serve the entire table for admiration. It is a celebration of centuries of gastronomic fusion in a single dish.

Above The futuristic buildings of the City of Arts and Sciences include a science museum (pictured), opera house, planetarium and the largest aquarium in Europe

---

The Mercado Central

More than 400 vendors fill Valencia's central food market, and many more spill out on to the adjoining sidewalks and streets. The 1928 Modernista building is often cited as one of the largest covered markets in Europe. With its soaring ceilings and ornate central dome, it is a modern cathedral of gastronomy. Yet the fanciful architecture is upstaged by the bounty and beauty of the food stalls – pyramids of sweet oranges, glistening clear-eyed fish splayed out on crushed ice, thick green pods of fresh fava beans. The rich choices perhaps explain why Valencia's cooks have invented so many variations of paella. Stall-hopping yields the essentials – large cloth bags of heirloom Bomba rice, heaping mounds of bright paprika, small tins of precious saffron and an iron *paellera*.

A Day in Valencia

The ages of Valencia's long history are evident everywhere. The Cathedral alone incorporates Roman relics and a Moorish minaret as its bell tower. As the city radiates outwards it becomes ever more modern, culminating in the futuristic fantasies of the architecture at the City of Arts and Sciences.

MORNING Marvel at the restored Renaissance-era frescoes in the stately **Cathedral**, then climb the minaret-turned-bell tower for a panorama of the old city. Across **Plaza de la Reina** in an extravagant Baroque palace, the **Museo Nacional de Cerámica** features a charming tiled Valencian kitchen.

AFTERNOON After photographing the interplay of forms in the **City of Arts and Sciences**, visit the planetarium at **L'Hemisfèric** or catch the graceful play of beluga whales and bottlenose dolphins at **L'Oceanogràfic**.

EVENING Stroll the narrow streets of the old fishermen's quarter, **El Cabanyal**, until you reach the broad strand of **Playa Malvarossa**. Catch the last rays of the sun at this urban beach or join the Valencians as they promenade along the shore before an evening of socializing and dining.

Essentials

GETTING THERE
Many European and Spanish airlines fly into **Valencia Airport**, and the city is well-served by **train** services from points all over Spain.

WHERE TO STAY
Hostal Venecia (inexpensive) has modest but cheerful rooms in a landmark building in the city centre. *www.hotelvenecia.com*
Hotel Meliá Valencia (moderate) offers stylish, modern rooms near the City of Arts and Sciences. *www.melia-hotels.com*
Hotel Neptuno (expensive) makes the most of its beachfront location on Playa Malvarossa with a rooftop solarium. *www.hotelneptunovalencia.com*

TOURIST INFORMATION
Calle Paz; *www.comunitatvalenciana.com*

The Best Places to Eat Paella

La Pepica moderate

Ernest Hemingway, Orson Welles and their matador friends all heaped praises on La Pepica, where the menu features a modest eight rice dishes. These encompass all that is great about Valencian rice cookery, from the classic *paella valenciana* and the shellfish-topped *paella marinera* to the squid-and-its-ink *arroz negro*. The formality of the waiting staff, smartly clad in white shirts and black waistcoats, heightens the sense of ceremony, especially when the paella is presented with a slight bow. The restaurant was established in 1898 on Playa Malvarossa and remains the principal temple of paella in the city that invented the dish. The front door is on the beach, but entering through the back from Paseo Neptuno gives customers a look backstage at the voluminous kitchen of blue-and-white tiles and stainless-steel appliances where *paelleras* of every size dangle overhead like hams in a bar.

2, 6, 8 Paseo Neptuno, Playa de la Malvarossa, Valencia; open for lunch Mon–Sun, dinner Mon–Sat; www.lapepica.com

Also in Valencia

At the edge of the old city, **Restaurante de Ana** *(www.restaurantedeana.com; moderate)* is a stickler about using exquisite fresh snails in its *paella valenciana*. Its *arroz estilo Albufera* is a paella with succulent duck. Traditional paella at the chic eatery of superchef Vicente Chust, **Restaurante Chust Godoy** *(www.chustgodoy.com; expensive)*, is well worth the one-hour wait for its preparation.

Also in the Valencia Region

Literally across the road from rice fields in the Albufera, **La Matandeta** in Alfafar *(www.lamatandeta.com; moderate; open Easter–Sep only)* often prepares its sublime paellas in the outdoor courtyard during the summer months. The casual **El Pescador** *(+34 965 842 571; inexpensive)* in Altea creates excellent seafood paellas as well as grilled local fish. In Elche, **Els Capellans** *(+34 966 610 011; moderate)* is famed for its Alicante-style paella studded with meatballs and topped with fluffy egg.

Around the World

Many restaurants in the great Mexican fishing port of **Veracruz** (try **La Choca**) make a delicious New World seafood paella called *arroz a la tumbada*, seasoned with hot peppers and usually topped with clams, prawns, conch, squid and red snapper. In New York, USA, **Socarrat Paella Bar** *(www.socarratpaellabar.com; moderate)* serves five different kinds of paella, including the traditional *paella valenciana* and a vegetarian version, and waiters offer to help you scrape up the crunchy *socarrat* at the bottom of the *paellera*.

Above Many cooks today add smoked paprika to give their paella the earthy, smoky taste traditionally imparted by cooking over a wood fire

Left The secret to a great paella lies in the *sofrito*, a slow browning of meat and vegetables, before the rice is added to the *paellera*

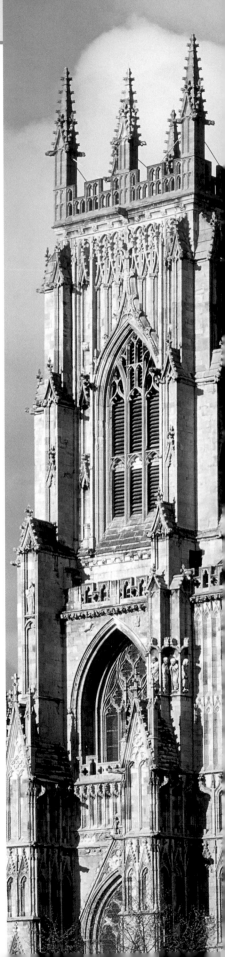

YORK ENGLAND

Afternoon Tea in Historic York

To the English, tea is more than a drink – it is the universal pick-me-up, the "cup that cheers". Combined with scones, sandwiches and cakes, the English afternoon tea – served with near-ceremonial reverence – approaches an art form. There's nowhere better to indulge in this tradition than in heritage-drenched York, one of northern England's most alluring cities.

York has a central place in English history that makes it one of the country's most popular visitor destinations. It's a picturesque, riverside city of pale stone buildings, with a central old-town area that's entirely concealed within a great fortified wall. Unsurpassed as a touring base for northern England, it's within easy reach of genteel Harrogate, stately Castle Howard and the bluff North Yorkshire coast.

A day in historic York will find you walking around the stunning medieval walls or exploring York Minster, Britain's biggest and most impressive Gothic building. Getting lost in the tangle of cobbled streets is half the fun, happening upon fascinating timber-framed houses and grand Georgian buildings, while a score of innovative museums, hands-on history centres and restored churches reveal the city's Roman, Viking, industrial and religious heritage. Worn-out visitors need no persuasion to fall gratefully into a welcoming café for a restorative "cuppa" and something to eat.

The English have had a taste for tea since the 17th century. King Charles II's Portuguese queen, Catherine of Braganza, is usually credited with popularizing the drink, first brought back from India

and China by Portuguese traders. By the 19th century, taking afternoon tea — a light meal between lunch and dinner — had become a social occasion in upper-class circles, and it's a tradition that survives today in the grand salons of fancy hotels, where pristine-jacketed waiters serve tiered platters of wafer-thin sandwiches and dainty cakes.

Away from the starred hotels, there's a more rustic tradition of cheery, old-fashioned tearooms serving generous slabs of home-made cake or, most typically of all, warm scones with clotted cream and strawberry jam — the so-called "cream tea". Whether this originated in Devon or Cornwall, both in England's rural southwest, is a hotly contested point — wars have been started over less, as is the correct method for eating the scones. A true Devonshire cream tea, for example, requires that the cream should be spread first, followed by the jam second, and there's even a campaign to seek for the cream tea the same European protected status afforded to Champagne or Gorgonzola cheese. That an afternoon snack could arouse such passions might appear strange, but as with the perennial question about the beverage itself — milk or tea in the cup first? — the vexed social habits of the English are a window on to their very soul.

A Day in York

Exploring York on foot is easy as most of its attractions lie within the city walls. This compact area is a treasure trove of architecture and heritage.

MORNING Start at **York Minster** to see England's finest stained-glass windows, and then walk down the former main road in Roman times, now called **Stonegate**, lined with shops, boutiques and historic buildings. The nearby **Shambles** – the site of York's medieval butchers' shops – is equally photogenic.

AFTERNOON Simply choose a historical period and pursue your interest, either at **Jorvik** (the Viking-era attraction), **Fairfax House** (Georgian period), the **Castle Museum** (Victorian and Edwardian times) or the fantastic **National Railway Museum** (railway history and working steam engines).

EVENING Evening **ghost walks** are a York speciality, following guides around the walls and alleys and hearing tales of royal villains, treasonous nobles, Civil War battles and dastardly highwaymen (Dick Turpin was hanged in York).

Essentials

GETTING THERE
There are direct trains to York from **Manchester International Airport**. York is just under two hours from London by **train**.

WHERE TO STAY
Bar Convent (inexpensive) has simple but comfortable guest rooms in a working Georgian-era convent. *www.bar-convent.org.uk*
The Blue Rooms (moderate) are contemporary studio-style apartments. *www.thebluebicycle.com*
Hotel du Vin (expensive) is in boutique style, with a classy bistro. *www.hotelduvin.com*

TOURIST INFORMATION
1 Museum Street; *www.visityork.org*

Above Afternoon tea is served all afternoon and may include dainty sandwiches with their crusts cut off as well as cakes

Left A church has occupied the site of York Minster since the 7th century; the present building was completed in 1472

Below Little Bettys is a smaller, cosier branch of York's famous Bettys tearoom; it sells provisions downstairs and delicious teas upstairs

Afternoon Tea Around the World

The gentle tinkling of china teacups announces the civilized interlude between 3 and 5pm when the world stops for tea in both cosy English tearooms and fancy Far Eastern hotels. This is the time to sit back and savour a longstanding and treasured ritual.

YORKSHIRE

Bettys moderate

6–8 St Helen's Square, York; www.bettys.co.uk
Established in 1919, Bettys has six tearooms scattered around Yorkshire. The York establishment must be the most glamorous tearoom in England, an Art Deco gem whose elegant interior was inspired by the famous *Queen Mary* ocean-going liner. From the craft bakery issue extraordinary breads, cakes and confections, including the speciality cherry-and-almond "Fat Rascals", while Bettys' house-blend Yorkshire Tea is an English classic.

The Black Swan Tearoom moderate

Market Place, Helmsley; www.blackswan-helmsley.co.uk
Yorkshire's market towns are full of traditional, honest-to-goodness cafés, but there's far more style in evidence in this boutique tearoom and patisserie (a Tea Guild award-winner) attached to a classy country hotel. A rare and exotic tea menu ranges far and wide, or order afternoon tea with Champagne for a real indulgence.

Swinton Park moderate

Masham, Ripon; www.swintonpark.com
For a taste of the noble life, take tea in Swinton Park castle hotel, which is set in 200 acres of private parkland on the eastern fringes of the Yorkshire Dales. The local choice here is a "Wensleydale Tea", served with the crumbly, eponymous cheese from the Dales and Yorkshire fruitcake.

ALSO IN ENGLAND

London offers a stylish introduction to afternoon tea in a score or more famous hotels and glitzy stores, while in every region of England there's a seductive café or tearoom devoted to serving the perfect cream tea.

Otterton Mill inexpensive

Otterton, Budleigh Salterton, Devon; www.ottertonmill.com
Of the many contenders for the best Devonshire cream tea, they go the extra mile at Otterton Mill, which is set in a glorious riverside location in the wildlife-rich Otter Valley. The scones are made daily using their own milled flour, both clotted cream and jam are supplied by nearby artisan producers, and the tea is organic and Fairtrade.

Cavendish Rooms moderate

Chatsworth House, Bakewell, Derbyshire; www.chatsworth.org
Enjoy a gracious afternoon tea that's entirely in keeping with the surroundings at Chatsworth House, Britain's finest Baroque stately home, the ancestral digs of the Dukes of Devonshire. Dainty cakes and pastries made by Chatsworth's own bakers are served in what is surely the most elegant stable block in the land, a glorious 18th-century space given a contemporary makeover.

De Grey's Tea Rooms moderate

Broad Street, Ludlow, Shropshire; www.degreys.co.uk
In central England's foodie capital, Ludlow, afternoon tea is at its traditional best at De Grey's, a half-timbered Tudor town house with an atmospheric oak-beamed interior and smart, black-and-white clad staff. An in-house bakery produces wonderful cakes and pastries, and if you eat more than is wise you may be grateful to learn that there's also very cosy guest accommodation.

The Secret Garden moderate

Mersham-le-Hatch, Hythe Road, Ashford, Kent; www.secretgardenkent.co.uk
In the county of Kent – the so-called "garden of England" – afternoon tea and handsome locations go hand in hand, as in this restored coachhouse and impressive Victorian walled garden. The strawberry cream tea served here incorporates locally sourced jam and clotted cream, while seasonal variations add a glass of Kentish sparkling wine or even mince pies and mulled wine at Christmas.

The Tea Cosy moderate

3 George Street, Kemptown, Brighton, East Sussex; www.theteacosy.co.uk
In the south coast's most flamboyant resort, this charming tearoom is dedicated, with its tongue

Below (top to bottom) Cakes await service at Bettys, purveyor of exquisite afternoon teas since 1919; the Piccadilly frontage of Fortnum & Mason in London, grocer to the English gentry

Right (top to bottom) A staunchly colonial tea in Hong Kong, with scones, clotted cream and strawberry jam; afternoon tea at Raffles, Singapore; taking tea English-style in Jaipur, India

firmly in its cheek, to the gracious art of taking tea. Etiquette and manners are explained for beginners and visitors alike, from the use of the sugar tongs to the allowable volume of conversation at the tea table, while on Sunday afternoons everyone rises for a rendition of "God Save the Queen".

Fortnum & Mason expensive

181 Piccadilly, London W1; www.fortnumandmason.com

Few places can offer as wide a range of teas as Fortnum's, the fashionable London grocery store *par excellence* founded in 1707. Their tea department offers over 70 blends and single-estate teas, available as part of afternoon tea or a grander High Tea in the store's elegant St James's restaurant.

The Ritz expensive

150 Piccadilly, London W1; www.theritzhotel.co.uk

For many, there is simply no better place to experience the quintessential afternoon tea in all its pomp and glory than the Ritz Hotel's magnificent, gilded Palm Court. This is tradition poured straight from the pot and, as befits the surroundings, you are expected to dress up; no jeans or trainers, and gentlemen require a jacket and tie.

NORTH AMERICA

Coffee has long been the more popular drink in North America, but across the USA and in Canada there are Anglophiles and tea fanatics who keep alive the genteel traditions of a bygone age.

Crown & Crumpet Tea Salon moderate

207 Ghirardelli Square, 900 North Point, San Francisco, USA; www.crownandcrumpet.com

The Crown & Crumpet presents a mix of English wit and San Francisco style in a bright and breezy tearoom that offers a playful take on traditional afternoon tea. All the right ingredients are in place — well-sourced teas, home-made scones and cakes, toasted crumpets — but this creative Californian café is never in danger of taking itself too seriously.

Tea & Sympathy moderate

108 Greenwich Avenue, New York, USA; www.teaandsympathynewyork.com

Greenwich Village, original heart of New York's counter-culture, is a melting pot of ideas and influences, including this self-styled "corner of

England", known for its home-from-home food. Scones and jam are always on the menu, alongside other tea-time favourites like rarebit or sardines on toast, and the teas include both English-style house blends and speciality brews.

Fairmont Empress Hotel expensive

721 Government Street, Victoria, British Columbia, Canada; www.fairmont.com

For over a century, Victoria's dashing, *grande-dame* hotel has been serving afternoon tea with a harbour view in its glorious, imperial lobby. There's every attention to detail, from tea tasting notes to the signature raisin scones that form the centrepiece of this most elegant of experiences.

ASIA

As the British Empire touched every corner of the world, so did the taste for a reviving mid-afternoon break. The English took tea back to its Eastern roots, and in Singapore, Hong Kong and India the ceremony lingers on in upmarket hotels.

Mandarin Oriental expensive

5 Connaught Road, Central, Hong Kong; www.mandarinoriental.com

Even on the most hot and humid of days there's an air of calm in the Mandarin Oriental's legendary Clipper Lounge, where the great and good of Hong Kong come to see and be seen. Here, in one of the world's most renowned luxury hotels, afternoon tea is a truly magnificent repast, including artistic creations from the hotel's own patisserie.

Raffles Hotel expensive

1 Beach Road, Singapore; www.raffles.com

White-jacketed waiters glide effortlessly around the period-piece "Tiffin Room" in one of Southeast Asia's most emblematic hotels. Much like having a Singapore Sling (the iconic cocktail invented in the hotel), taking High Tea at Raffles is part of the whole colonial-revival experience and not to be missed.

Rambagh Palace expensive

Bhawani Singh Road, Jaipur, Rajasthan, India; www.tajhotels.com

This former royal guest house and hunting lodge, later a Maharajah's palace and now a sumptuous hotel, makes for a wonderfully extravagant backdrop for afternoon tea. Pots of tea and dainty bites, impeccably presented, are served overlooking the stunning palace gardens.

NICE FRANCE

Flavours of the Southern Sun

In Nice's Bay of Angels, the limpid blue water laps the shore, but when the summer sun is pulsing like a furnace it's the old town that beckons. Shade is offered by the pedestrian-friendly alleys with their pale façades and myriad galleries, while bars and bistros provide refreshment. A freshly made salade niçoise, a taste of sea and land, perfectly captures the essence of the city.

Nice has long lured artists and the idly affluent escaping a wintry north, attracted by the pastel-coloured old town, the glitzy marina lifestyle, the palm-trimmed seafront and the gloriously fresh food dished up in bistros, seaside cafés and de luxe hotels. The city is a delicious culinary and cultural combination, proudly flaunting the influence of successive waves of outsiders. The Greeks were here, the Romans, too, and the northern Italians via the powerful Counts of Savoy. Nice finally passed into French hands in 1860 but the strong Italian influence, especially table-side, remains. This is, after all, the birthplace of ravioli and of Garibaldi.

The British, who have been visiting since the 1730s, also left their mark. Nice became the sundrenched sandpit of choice for aristocrats in the 19th century, even entertaining Queen Victoria. Luxury hotels sprang up to accommodate them while they built villas and raised a subscription to erect a walkway by the sea, the aptly named Promenade des Anglais.

When it comes to living and cooking, the Niçois keep it simple. You won't find rich sauces blanketing food; instead it's subtle seasoning with an emphasis on newly picked, freshly caught, just made, and preferably enjoyed alfresco. There's no mistaking, then, that salade niçoise is a dish born of Nice. Each ingredient evokes the sun-soaked Mediterranean city, from the fragrant summer tomatoes to the salty, sea-kissed anchovies.

Some argue that a true niçoise contains only tomatoes, artichoke hearts, bell peppers, tiny, black niçoise olives and anchovy fillets, dressed with rich local olive oil and fresh herbs: no vinegar – and certainly no tuna or lettuce. Others insist on tuna – canned, not fresh – but counsel against hard-boiled eggs. An infamous ex-city mayor turned cookbook author was adamant that potatoes, or any kind of cooked vegetables (those pesky green beans, for example), had no place in his niçoise salad bowl; and it's either tuna or anchovies, never the two together.

Today's innovative chefs insist, however, that the humble niçoise is at its best when it takes its lead from the seasons. Thus rocket, radishes, ruby-ringed onions, broad beans and even thinly sliced cucumber may stake their claim among the flavour-infused tomatoes, olives, tuna, anchovies and just-cooked eggs. And therein lies the key. The supremely generous Côte d'Azur climate enriches both the cuisine and the city so that, whatever its makeup, the signature dish of this southern city tastes like summer on a plate.

A Day in Nice

This historic seaside resort, nicknamed *Nice la Belle* (Nice the Beautiful), has buzz and beauty in spades, and there's plenty to see when the beach doesn't beckon.

MORNING Opt for a lazy café breakfast in **cours Saleya** and watch market vendors spin their spiel. Take to the cobbled alleyways, stopping at **Palais Lascaris** to glimpse how the very well-heeled once lived. Catch the lift to **Castle Hill** for a Nice panorama, via **Tour Bellanda**, where Berlioz composed his *King Lear* overture.

AFTERNOON Hike up to **Cimiez** to pore over Henri Matisse's paintings, drawings and sculptures in the **Musée Matisse**, the 17th-century villa in which the artist spent his last 34 years. Wander the nearby **Franciscan monastery** and its gardens, and on to the cemetery where Matisse and his fellow artist Raoul Dufy are buried.

EVENING Come sunset, walk or cycle the **Promenade des Anglais** along the cherubic **Bay of Angels**, past the swaying palms, pausing for a sundowner in the Relais bar of the flamboyant **Hotel Negresco**.

Essentials

GETTING THERE
Buses run from **Nice airport** to the central railway station, with trains to Monaco, Cannes, Marseille and Paris. Get around the city on **foot**, by **bus**, **taxi** or free *vélo bleu* **bicycles**.

WHERE TO STAY
Villa la Tour (inexpensive) is a family-run gem in the heart of the old town. *www.villa-la-tour.com*
The Hotel Windsor (moderate) is full of contemporary art. *www.hotelwindsornice.com*
La Perouse (expensive) is a chic oasis looking over the Bay. *www.hotel-la-perouse.com*

TOURIST INFORMATION
5 Prom des Anglais; *www.nicetourisme.com*

Above In the old town, traditionally colour-washed walls glow in the southern sunshine

Left The crescent-shaped city hugs the curve of the Baie des Anges – the Bay of Angels – backed by the soft contours of the Alpes-Maritimes

Above Today's chefs embellish the core niçoise ingredients with fresh herbs and blanched young vegetables such as green beans and baby leeks

Cookery Schools

Food writer and Cordon Bleu-trained cook Rosa Jackson runs **Les Petits Farcis** *(www. petitsfarcis.com)* from her restored 17th-century apartment in Nice's old town. Passionate about locally grown, organic food, Rosa dishes out cooking hints, recipes and city tips during a class. Join her for a market tour, then learn to cook, then enjoy, a four-course niçoise lunch. Alternatively, stay in a farmhouse looking over the Côte d'Azur and learn to make tarts, tapenades, fragrant roast lamb and other authentic Provençal goodies, or take a Nice food tour, with Tricia Robinson from **A Taste of Provence** *(www.tasteofprovence.com)*. Programmes run Apr–Jun, Sep and Oct.

The Best Places to Eat Salade Niçoise

Bistro d'Antoine moderate

The outside terrace sheltering beneath a cheery red awning and the snug upstairs dining room of Bistro d'Antoine are unfailingly loaded with patrons, so chef Armand Crespo is definitely doing something right. Since he and his wife took over the bistro a few years ago, it has rapidly gained a loyal following, with locals and Nice blow-ins seduced by its breezy ambience and uncompromisingly seasonal, and suave, menu. It's the kind of place you wish was in every French town. Scallop carpaccio with slivers of turnip, lightly fried calamari with mixed wild leaves, lentils with plump sausages, and gravadlax with shaved fennel fresh from the morning market showcase the chef's technique and imagination. The salade niçoise is another winner. Naturally, there are the tiny black niçoise olives, tuna, anchovies and at the height of summer, tomatoes that taste of the Mediterranean sun. Depending on the market, fine slices of sweet red onion or tiny violet artichoke might make a guest appearance on the plate. The wine list also draws applause.
27 rue de la Prefecture, Nice; open noon–2pm & 7:15–10pm Mon–Sat; +33 4 93 85 29 57

Also in Nice

Acchiardo *(+33 44 93 85 51 16; moderate)* on rue Droite is one of those homely family-run concerns that seem so perfectly in tune with old-town surrounds. From its elbow-to-elbow tables to the blackboard menu touting *"cuisine nissarde"* (that's "niçoise" in the local dialect), it's honest and unassuming. The Acchiardo salade niçoise has the obligatory tuna, tiny black olives, eggs, tomatoes and anchovies, often with a surprise from the morning's market – maybe small red radishes or artichoke hearts.

Also in France

From April to October, **Plage 45** in the impeccably slick Grand Hotel at Cannes *(www.grand-hotel-cannes.com; expensive)* serves up salade niçoise with the works, all raw – not counting the hard-boiled eggs, tuna and anchovies. That means cucumber, tomato, celery, red peppers, radishes, broad beans, black niçoise olives and *cébette* (similar to leek but eaten raw), tossed through with fresh basil.

Around the World

While French pastry great François Payard parades his favourite sweet treats at **François Payard Bakery** in New York's Soho *(www. fpbnyc.com; inexpensive)*, he also finds room for savouries, including a snap-fresh salade niçoise. It's tweaked according to the season and dressed with a mustard vinaigrette, not olive oil, but tuna, hard-boiled eggs, plum tomatoes and anchovies feature.

TREVISO ITALY

Luscious Tiramisu in the Veneto

The deliciously creamy coffee and chocolate taste of tiramisu puts it high on any list of sweet indulgences. Yet this rich and regal dessert had its origins not in a Renaissance court, but in a family-run restaurant in Italy's Veneto region, an often overlooked part of the country that delivers exquisite food, wine and cultural experience in equal measures.

While many hurry through the Veneto on their way to Venice, few stop to sample the delights of this historic region. The relative lack of visitors only adds to the appeal of its small towns and cities, such as Verona, the setting for *Romeo and Juliet*, Vicenza, a UNESCO World Heritage site for its outstanding Palladian buildings, and Treviso, which makes a charming base for exploration.

Pretty and prosperous, Treviso has authentic Italian charm within its impressive city walls and gateways. Its porticoed main square, Piazza dei Signori, comes to life every evening when locals meet to exchange news and indulge in the ritual of apéritif-taking in the shade of an elegant medieval *palazzo* with a majestic external flight of stairs.

The peaceful heart of the old town is a maze of narrow alleyways crammed with tiny wine bars serving sparkling local Prosecco. As in Venice, albeit on a smaller scale, water is a big theme. Pretty shaded canals, lined with willow trees and parks, thread through the town – artificial offshoots of the Sile river that rises at a spring on the outskirts before flowing

southeast through to the Venice lagoon. Despite its apparent charms, Treviso is no chocolate-box town; it has moved with the times, becoming one of Italy's leading fashion centres – labels such as Benetton and Sisley are based here – making it a great place to refresh your wardrobe.

Treviso's famous tiramisu is also a recent innovation. It was developed in the kitchens of the town's Ristorante Beccherie *(see facing page)* in 1962 from *sbatudin* – a pick-me-up for nursing mothers that comprised egg beaten with sugar accompanied by coffee and *savoiardi* – light-as-air sponge finger biscuits. With the addition of creamy mascarpone and powdered cocoa the dish gradually evolved into the tiramisu we all know and love today, complementing the bountiful cuisine of the Trevigiano countryside.

The area's trademark *radicchio rosso* (red chicory) is also a constant on most restaurant menus, as a delicious wine-red salad, as pâté or braised and bottled. Fresh salad leaves are also served with the traditional *pasta e fagioli* (bean and pasta) soup, an effective twinning of bitter flavour and soft texture that makes for a classic lunch in the Veneto.

Above Grapes are grown for the Veneto's celebratory drink, Prosecco, in vineyards north of Treviso, where the gentle hills provide a perfect microclimate

Prosecco Wine

Grown in the Veneto, in the gentle sun-blessed hills around Treviso, Prosecco grapes are used to make the eponymous light white wine. The wine continues to ferment when bottled, producing tiny bubbles that give Prosecco its characteristic sparkle, giggling their way to the surface when the wine is poured. Unlike *spumante* dessert wines, Prosecco is invariably dry and has been dubbed "Italian champagne". It can be enjoyed on its own, to accompany a dessert, or mixed with fresh peach purée to make a refreshing Bellini cocktail. It is also widely found in the hugely popular Spritz apéritif consumed of an evening in every piazza of the Veneto. Here it is combined with a bright orange or red mixer – either Campari, Select or Aperol – and soda, lemon and a juicy fat green olive.

Three Days in the Veneto

Treviso itself is well worth exploring and is a fine base for trips to Venice and other towns of the Veneto, and for touring the gentle surrounding countryside.

DAY ONE Stroll through the heart of **Treviso** starting at the cobbled **Piazza dei Signori**, passing inviting delicatessens on Via Trevisi, to the **Pescheria**, the town's fish market in the middle of a canal. Adjacent is the atmospheric porticoed walkway, the **Buranelli**. Walk over to the other side of town for the **Cattedrale di San Nicolò** to admire its frescoes, which date back to 1352.

DAY TWO Drive northwest through cultivated countryside to the **Montello hills**, famous for their porcini mushrooms and vineyards around **Venegazzu**. Trattorias scattered through the woods and clearings serve the local specialities.

DAY THREE Take the train to **Venice** to wander the car-less streets, and treat yourself to a cappuccino at a canalside café. Don't miss the mornings-only fresh produce market at **Rialto**, close to the vast stone arch of the eponymous bridge. Afterwards take a relaxing ride on a vaporetto along the **Grand Canal** to admire the magnificent line-up of *palazzos*.

Essentials

GETTING THERE
Treviso's **Canova Airport**, with flights to and from many European cities, is 5 km (3 miles) from the town; Venice's international **Marco Polo Airport** is 30 km (18 miles) away, and is well connected to Treviso by rail and bus.

WHERE TO STAY
B&B Dolce Vita (inexpensive) provides cheery lodgings a short hop from Treviso's centre. www.dolcevitatreviso.com
Albergo Il Focolare (moderate) is good value in the heart of the town. www.albergoilfocolare.net
Relais Monaco (expensive) is a laid-back country villa with swimming pool and extensive parkland, a short drive out of town. www.relaismonaco.it

TOURIST INFORMATION
Via Sant'Andrea 3; +39 04 2254 7632

The Best Places to Eat Tiramisu

Ristorante Beccherie moderate

A gastronomic institution, this historic restaurant opened its elegant doors to diners in 1939 and the founder's grandson and his wife are continuing the tradition as ideal hosts. Unless you have some knowledge of the local dialect, you'd never guess that these lovely premises were a butcher's shop back in the 1700s. Alfresco dining is delightful in summer when the tables spill out into the traffic-free square, whereas in winter they're moved back inside under dark timber beams. The service is both impeccable and friendly, with attention to details like warm plates and tasting portions of extra dishes. Tiramisu is just one dish that has made this restaurant so well known. Flat slices of the delicate dessert, its thin layers of mascarpone cream and sponge imbued with coffee and cocoa, are served all year round. The rest of the menu respects seasonal produce. Autumn brings *faraona al forno* in *salsa péarada* – baked guinea fowl in a delicious sauce of liver and herbs. Flavoursome red radicchio stars in winter in delights such as a warming soup or crepes, then at warmer times of year there's *risi e bisi* – risotto with fresh peas.

Piazza Ancilotto, Treviso; open for lunch and dinner Tue–Sat, lunch only Sun; www.anticoristorantebeccherie.it

Also in Treviso

Run by a celebrated pastry chef, **Pasticceria Andrea Zanin** *(+39 04 2254 0437; moderate)* is a cake shop-cum-café tucked down a narrow street near the main square. It is an ultra-modern haven for professionals and residents who pop in for a quick espresso and something sweet. Heavenly tiramisu is but one of the irresistible mini-portions lined up on the glass counter, a feast for the eyes as well as for the waistline.

Also in Italy

One of the oldest and most venerable cake shops in Venice, **Pasticceria Rizzardini** *(+39 04 1522 3835; moderate)* is a tiny standing-room-only establishment. It offers a tough choice: should you opt for an individual slice of luscious tiramisu, a freshly baked fruit tart or a mini *beignet* with *zabaglione* with your cappuccino? The crunchy *croccantini* (peanut toffee) makes a perfect takeaway gift.

Around the World

Run by a non-Italian brother and sister team, Sydney's **Alio** *(www.alio.com.au; expensive)* serves Italian-inspired food made with the freshest produce and immaculate attention to detail. The almost classic tiramisu is enhanced by the addition of Marsala wine to the fluffy mascarpone mixture, giving a more pungent flavour, while scrumptious albeit bitterish grated chocolate is the finishing touch.

Above Tiramisu – literally "pick-me-up" – is certainly an uplifting dish, with a kick of coffee and sometimes liqueur

Left Treviso's centre is a maze of streets lined with arcaded walkways and dotted with tiny *osterias*

Right Aachen cathedral was built in AD 800 to symbolize the unification and political revival of the West; it is a UNESCO World Heritage site

Below The marinated beef of sauerbraten is served in a rich gravy, sometimes thickened with gingerbread

A Day in Aachen

Aachen's medieval Old Town is easily navigable on foot, but to explore its best museums and spa you'll need to take a bus.

MORNING Head straight to Aachen's highlight, the **Dom**, which contains Charlemagne's remains in a gilded shrine and a treasury of extraordinary relics. Afterwards amble around the relaxed **Old Town**, visiting the **Rathaus**, whose façade is lined by the figures of 50 Holy Roman Emperors and whose top floor – the **Kaisersaal** (emperor hall) – has 19th-century frescoes and reproduction crown jewels.

AFTERNOON Take a 10-minute bus ride to the **Suermondt-Ludwig-Museum**, an art museum renowned for its stained glass collection and Old Masters such as Albrecht Dürer and Rembrandt. Or head around the corner to the **Ludwig Forum für Internationale Kunst**, a contemporary art museum in an elegant old Bauhaus-style factory.

EVENING Soak in the healing waters Charlemagne once enjoyed at the luxurious **Carolus Thermen** spa.

Essentials

GETTING THERE
Cologne/Bonn **airport** lies 73 km (45 miles) and 50 minutes by train from Aachen. High-speed **trains** connect Aachen to Brussels and Paris. There's a good **bus** service around the town.

WHERE TO STAY
Da Salvatore (inexpensive) has simple rooms above an Italian restaurant by the train station. *www.zimmer-in-aachen.de*
Drei Könige (moderate) is a boutique hotel with brightly coloured rooms and apartments in a great central location. *www.h3k-aachen.de*
Pullman Aachen Quellenhof (expensive) is a grand old hotel with top facilities that backs on to the Carolus spa. *www.pullmanhotels.com*

TOURIST INFORMATION
www.aachen.de

AACHEN GERMANY

Gingery Sauerbraten in Aachen

Emperor Charlemagne's Frankish empire once covered most of modern-day Germany, France and northern Italy. His capital was Aachen, on the border of Belgium and the Netherlands, which still has many impressive reminders of his rule, not least of which is an unusual dish he invented: sauerbraten. This slow-cooked, sour-sweet stew is commonly regarded as Germany's national dish.

Historical accounts suggest that the Emperor Charlemagne was a foodie. He loved Roquefort cheese, introduced peacocks as a dish at court and took efforts to improve people's diets throughout his lands. He obviously liked the good life, because his main reason for choosing Aachen as his capital was its natural hot springs; relaxing in them was a favourite imperial pastime and they remain a major draw for visitors today.

Charlemagne was also a devout Christian and his wonderful palace chapel, now incorporated into Aachen's Dom (cathedral), has been a destination for pilgrims for hundreds of years. The structure remains a highlight of any visit to the town today, thanks to the sense of history and devotion that seems fused into its brickwork and magnificent stained-glass windows.

Aachen's attractive Old Town is lovely to explore on foot. At its heart lies an expansive market square, encircled by some of the city's finest medieval houses and the 14th-century Rathaus (town hall), where around 30 of the Holy Roman Emperors that followed Charlemagne feasted after their coronations.

Much of this feasting almost certainly involved sauerbraten, the local delicacy. The dish is said to have been Charlemagne's clever idea for leftovers, and although it takes a long time to prepare, its practical and versatile nature has made it an enduring German favourite. The name means "sour roast" and much of its flavour comes from its marinade; the meat is marinated in strong vinegar for three days prior to its hours of roasting. This helps tenderize the meat – traditionally horsemeat, but today most often beef. The marinade also contains other ingredients, and it is these that bestow a uniquely delicious flavour on the dish. Marinades vary from region to region, and even between restaurants, but the key ingredients – wine, cloves, bay leaves and juniper berries – are always part of the mix. The meat is then browned and put back into the marinade to cook for several hours before the sauce is thickened, often with ground gingerbread to give it a real zing. Eaten with noodles or potato dumplings, it's a food fit for emperors.

Aachen's Christmas Market

As a city with an impressive history and a love of tradition, it's not surprising that Aachen has one of Germany's most atmospheric and popular Christmas markets, which attracts some 1.8 million visitors every year. Aachen's large medieval square provides the perfect backdrop for carousels, Nativity scenes and a myriad stalls selling traditional handicrafts. But the serious temptation lies in the seductive foods on sale. Roasted chestnuts and sausages sizzle on charcoal grills, their aromas mingling deliciously with the scent of waffles, potato cakes and warming *Glühwein* (mulled wine). The Christmas cakes and biscuits, including the favourite, *Printen* – a crunchy spiced gingerbread-style cookie – make ideal Christmas gifts.

Left Aachen was the principal coronation site of the Holy Roman Emperors

The Best Places to Eat Sauerbraten

Sauerbraten-Palast inexpensive

The priorities of this restaurant are obvious from its name, which translates as the "palace of sauerbraten". Certainly the quality of its sauerbraten would be fit for Charlemagne, though he might not appreciate rubbing shoulders with the complete cross-section of society that has made this restaurant a local institution for more than 20 years. The rather workaday, wood-clad pub interior is hardly a palace, although antiques and old prints of pre-war Aachen provide an atmospheric early 20th-century feel and time-honoured authenticity. The unpretentious atmosphere rightly keeps the sauerbraten centre stage and it is served here in giant portions, its meat so tender that it feels almost buttery in the mouth. Yet the real secret of the dish's success here is the sweet-and-sour gravy that uses the excellent local *Printen* form of gingerbread as an ingredient. The accompaniments – sweet-sour red cabbage and thick-cut Benelux-style chips – are also delicious. The only drawback is that improbably low prices ensure a popularity that frequently translates into a wait at the bar, as reservations are not accepted.

Vaalser Strasse 316, Aachen; open noon–3pm & 5–11pm Thu–Tue (closing at 10pm Sat and Sun); +49 241 837 73

Also in Germany

Most traditional pubs and restaurants in Germany have sauerbraten on the menu, so there's often somewhere good for the dish, yet in Aachen nowhere comes close to the Sauerbraten-Palast. So if you're in Aachen and want to try it elsewhere, hop on a train for the short journey to Cologne, where the **Brauhaus Ohne Namen** (*+49 221 81 26 80; moderate*) on Mathildenstrasse has a region-wide reputation for the dish. Here it's served with dumplings, apple compote and the fine local beer, Kölsch. It's rare to find sauerbraten on the menus of finer restaurants, so it's a welcome speciality of **Lutter & Wegner** (*www.l-w-berlin.de; expensive*) in Berlin, who have won national gastronomic awards for a dish that they have served in elegant surroundings since 1881.

Around the World

Outside Germany it's common to find good sauerbraten wherever Germans have settled. This particularly includes the American Midwest, where **Karl Ratzsch** (*www. karlratzsch.com; expensive*) does a superb rendition of Aachen-style sauerbraten in Milwaukee using a ginger-snap gravy. In South Africa, in the former German colony of Namibia, one of several places with good sauerbraten is the **Swakopmund Brauhaus** (*www. swakopmund brauhaus.com; moderate*), a jolly German beer hall in an unusual setting.

MOSCOW RUSSIA

Russia's Superpowered Soup

Moscow is a city where fusion isn't just a style of cuisine, but the leitmotif of local gastronomy. Even fast-food chains sell a range of sushi, Thai, Chinese and Italian dishes to tempt Muscovites. This "mix and match" approach might seem new, but it goes back centuries – as does the Russian love of soup – and the two combine in *solyanka*, a soup that can feature almost anything.

Conspicuous consumption is the credo of this city, which revolves around power and money, and sees excess as a virtue. The global recession may have halted the construction of the world's tallest skyscraper, but menus still feature dubious exotica such as endangered species smuggled out of African war zones. From historic Red Square to the fashionable malls of the Garden Ring road, this febrile city has re-created and re-imagined itself to become "the new New York". Radiating in concentric circles from its medieval hilltop citadel, or Kremlin, Moscow exemplifies the best and worst of Russia. Its beauty and ugliness are inseparable, its sentimentality the obverse of a brutality rooted in centuries of despotism and fear of anarchy. Private and cultural life is as passionate as business and politics are cynical.

Eating well has always been not only an affirmation of success but also a way of fortifying oneself for the hardships that may befall even the richest. As illustrated by the fate of Bolshevik leaders in Stalin's day, even the greatest can end up in Siberia – so it's important to enjoy it while you can. Traditionally, the main meal of the day has been *obyed* (lunch), with supper limited to leftover *zakuski* – Russian hors d'oeuvres *(see p75)*. Even today, when slimmed-down business lunches are widely available, many Muscovites expect to eat a hearty four-course lunch of *zakuski*, soup, a main dish and a dessert, washed down with beer or vodka.

Soup has always been the mainstay of Russian cuisine; spoons appeared on Russian tables over 400 years before forks did. Peasants subsisted on cabbage soup and buckwheat porridge, with flavourings limited to sour cream, garlic, honey, vinegar, dill and a few other fresh herbs. These tastes – salty, sweet, sour and pickled – remained the norm even among the nobility until Peter the Great introduced French chefs to his court. *Solyanka* is a rich jumble of a soup that combines indigenous with foreign ingredients. Its name derives from the Russian word for salt *(sol)*, but it also means "mixed" due to the wide variety of possible ingredients. The soup is prepared by cooking salted cucumbers, before adding the main ingredient: meat, mushrooms or fish. The core ingredient dictates what else goes in, from allspice and dill to cabbage and breadcrumbs. Like a Dostoevskian fictional hero, cast aside any doubts and throw yourself wholeheartedly into the dish and into Moscow itself – you're sure to leave poorer but wiser.

A Day in Moscow

Be sure to travel between sights on Moscow's metro, deservedly famous for the lavish decor of its stations. Ploshchad Revolyutsii, Komsomolskaya, Park Kultury and Mayakovskaya are among the best examples of the grandiose, High Stalinist style.

MORNING Visit **Red Square**, whose iconic **St Basil's Cathedral** and **Lenin Mausoleum** symbolize Russia's tumultuous past, as does the **Kremlin**. See the crown jewels in the **Armoury Museum**, the colossal **Tsar Cannon** and the world's largest bell before lunch at the nearby Shield and Sword restaurant *(see facing page)*.

AFTERNOON Take a cruise on the **Moskva river**, past the fairy-tale **Cathedral of Christ the Saviour** and the 91-m (300-ft) high **Monument to Peter the Great**, bestriding a galleon. Disembark at the **Novodevichy Convent** to visit the cemetery where Gogol, Shostakovich and other luminaries are buried beneath quirky effigies.

EVENING See what's happening on the scene at **Garage**, a wonderful Constructivist bus depot turned art space, like the Tate Modern's Turbine Hall in London.

Essentials

GETTING THERE
Domodedovo international **airport** is 34 km (22 miles) from the city centre; there are regular Aeroexpress **trains** to the city centre.

WHERE TO STAY
Alfa (inexpensive) is a 3-star giant 20 minutes from the centre. *www.hotelizmailovo-alfa.ru/eng*
Akvarel (moderate) is very central, located off chic Tverskaya Ulitsa. *www.hotelakvarel.ru*
Savoy (expensive) is a historic 4-star hotel with an Art Nouveau restaurant and a sauna, extensively restored in 2005. *www.savoy.ru*

FURTHER INFORMATION
www.visitrussia.com; www.moscowcity.com

Above *Solyanka* is a rich mix of vegetables and meat or fish, enriched with a dash of sour cream

Left Legend has it that St Basil's Cathedral, completed in 1561, was so beautiful that Ivan the Terrible ordered the architect to be killed, so he could not build its equal elsewhere

Above *Worker and Collective Farmer* (1937) is an iconic Soviet-era sculpture that is now located at an entrance to the All-Russian Exhibition Centre

Russian Vodka

"Drinking is the joy of the Russians. We cannot live without it." So said the 10th-century Prince Vladimir, rejecting Islam as the state religion in favour of Christianity, which allowed the drinking of vodka. Over a millennium later, vodka remains central to Russian life – as much a curse as a joy, being the prime cause of falling life expectancy in Russian males. Russians seldom go for mixers, but never drink vodka without eating (if only bread). Vodka may be infused with lemon (*limonnaya*), hot peppers (*pertsovka*), bison-grass (*zubrovka*), juniper berries, cloves (*okhotnitchaya*) or other flavourings. Russians adore elaborate toasts, but you can get by with "*Za zdrovyie!*" ("To health!").

The Best Places to Eat Solyanka

Café Pushkin expensive

Named after the Romantic poet, whose ill-starred wedding occurred in the vicinity, this establishment would have delighted him. People gape as they enter the building, a former pharmacy with huge windows and rich, Biedermeier-style fittings; its upper floors formed part of an aristocrat's home in the 1820s. The apothecary prepared drugs in the cellar, which is now furnished like a mad scientist's laboratory, with Bunsen burners, a Morse telegraph and other retro gadgetry. The first floor is grander, with a sumptuously panelled library of rare editions and a ballroom built for an ancestor of the composer Rimsky-Korsakov, which now serves as the VIP dining room. During summer, there's also a rooftop terrace café. Each floor has a different menu – though all feature a rich meat *solyanka* that leaves just enough room for a main course. You can choose between medieval specialities such as baked sterlet (a small sturgeon) in caviar sauce or pike head stuffed with fish and apple *confit*, or Frenchified dishes such as crab salad with quails' eggs and basil-and-raspberry mayonnaise. As befits the clientele of oligarchs, film stars and politicians, the wine list is princely.
Tverskoy bulvar 26A, Moscow; open 24 hours daily; www.cafe-pushkin.ru/en

Also in Moscow

Solyanka can be found in the humblest cafés, but visitors to Moscow usually prefer somewhere with a touch of style or sheer oddity. **Shield and Sword** *(+7 495 222 4446; inexpensive)* is a KGB-themed place whose dining room contains a replica of the statue of "Iron Felix" Dzerzhinsky that once stood outside the Lubyanka headquarters of the secret police, which he founded. Its Soviet-style menu includes *solyanka*, *pelmeni* (Russian ravioli) and chicken Kiev. Many dishes come with a shot of vodka. Alternatively, check out **Solyanka** *(http://s-11.ru/english; moderate)*, a hip restaurant, bar, club and boutique, named after the street on which it stands (which once led to the Royal Salt Yard) rather than the dish (which only features on its lunch-time menu on Wednesdays). Solyanka offers plenty of alternatives to Russian food, from *tom yam* soup and chicken curry to Mediterranean salads and pasta dishes. There are queues outside at the weekend, when DJs play hip-hop until 6am.

Also in Russia

In St Petersburg, you can enjoy *solyanka* at the **Café Sunduk** *(www.cafesunduk.ru; inexpensive)*, a funky art-café that has live Spanish, blues or jazz music.

Right The "old town" quarter of Patershol offers some of the best options for eating and drinking in Ghent

Below Creamy-white *waterzooi* fish stew includes delicate spices traded in Ghent since the Middle Ages

A Day in Ghent

All the main sights are within easy walking distance of the historic city centre, but the main art museums are in the Citadelpark in the south of the city, a tram-ride away.

MORNING Start with **St-Baafskathedraal** and a pilgrimage to Jan van Eyck's glorious painting, *The Adoration of the Mystic Lamb*. A short walk past the **Belfort** (belfry) and Gothic **St-Niklaaskerk** will lead you to the **Graslei** and **Korenlei**, where medieval and Renaissance guildhouses line the old river port. The **Groot Vleeshuis**, a medieval butcher's hall, showcases regional food specialities.

AFTERNOON Head for the cutting-edge museum of contemporary art, **SMAK**, or the nearby **Museum voor Schone Kunsten**, which has an impressive collection of pre-20th-century art.

EVENING For tickets at the **Vlaamse Opera** in the evening you have to book well in advance; if this is impossible, head back to the old centre for a stroll in **Patershol** district and a supper of *waterzooi*.

Essentials

GETTING THERE
The nearest **international airport** is Brussels (Zaventem), 60 km (37 miles) away. Ghent's main **train** station, Sint-Pieters, is near the Citadelpark, a tram-ride from the city centre. The city has an excellent **tram** and **bus** network.

WHERE TO STAY
Flandria (inexpensive) is a small, family-oriented and central hotel. *www.hotelflandria-gent.be*
Erasmus (moderate) is a delightful small hotel in a 16th-century house filled with antiques. *www.erasmushotel.be*
NH Gent Belfort (expensive) offers elegant, international-style comfort in the city centre. *www.nh-hotels.com*

TOURIST INFORMATION
www.visitgent.be

GHENT BELGIUM

Waterzooi in Ghent

On a clear winter's day, the tips of the medieval spires and gables of Ghent glint under the sun's low rays and the gilded skyline is freeze-framed in the mirror-still waters of the canals and rivers. Shoppers bustle about among the busy streets and market squares, pausing at lunch time for a warming dish of *waterzooi*, a creamy white stew that's Belgium's comfort food *par excellence*.

The Leie river forms a picturesque mini-port at the heart of medieval Ghent, surrounded by grand buildings that demonstrate the city's historic importance as a centre of craft and manufacturing. The soaring town belfry, muscular Gravensteen castle and grave Gothic churches give way at the riverside to the imposing guildhouses, magnificent examples of Renaissance architecture. Tucked away in the 14th-century St-Baafskathedraal lies one of the great masterpieces of northern European art – *The Adoration of the Mystic Lamb*, a huge, multi-panelled altarpiece painted in around 1432 by Jan van Eyck and his brother Hubrecht.

But Ghent also has a newer face. It was the first Belgian city to industrialize, initially around the textile trade. The beguiling Patershol district was the old weavers' quarter, but once industrialization got under way, Ghent began to acquire the grander adornments of a successful European city, with theatres, a fine opera house and a respected university.

River links to the North Sea made Ghent into a prosperous trading city during the Middle Ages and the Renaissance, and the ingredients of its signature dish, *waterzooi*, reflect this history. This creamy stew uses the produce of the surrounding rural landscape, but its spices and wine were classic trading goods of the Middle Ages. Pieces of fish or chicken are poached gently in a cream-laden broth flavoured with julienned leeks, shallots, carrots, celery and white wine, and scented with parsley, saffron, pepper and bay leaves. *Waterzooi* was originally cooked with river fish, but today it is usually made with fish from the North Sea, such as cod, turbot, monkfish, halibut, scallops or prawns.

Waterzooi is essentially simple and unpretentious; the name itself brings together the word "water" and a derivative of *kooksel*, "something cooked". But quality ingredients and the deft skills of the cook can also bring to it a smooth elegance. Said to have been the favourite dish of Charles V, the Holy Roman Emperor born here in 1500, it is – like the city itself – both down-to-earth and sophisticated; a heartwarming dish that has long been a favourite of peasants and kings.

What to Drink

Belgium is famous for the quality of its beer, with dozens of small, traditional breweries, numerous brands and labels and a huge range of flavours and alcoholic strengths. The most celebrated beers are made by five Trappist monasteries, including Chimay and Westmalle. One good place to sample the range is the pub called **Dulle Griet** (*www.dullegriet.be*), which is packed with character and beer memorabilia, and serves over 250 kinds of Belgian beer. Less well-known is Belgian *jenever*, a traditional and well-crafted form of gin, drunk neat or in its many flavoured versions – lemon, apple, vanilla, hazelnut and more. Try this at **'t Dreupelkot** (*www.dreupelkot. be*), a cherished institution that offers 200 different flavours.

Left Historic guildhouses of Graslei Street, on the banks of the Leie

The Best Places to Eat Waterzooi

Bij den Wijzen en den Zot
moderate

Waterzooi is treasured as a home-cooked dish, often made to grandmother's cherished recipe, so it is not easy to find in restaurants, even in Ghent. You have to seek out the kind of welcoming, unpretentious restaurants that take pride in specializing in traditional Flemish dishes, such as Bij den Wijzen en den Zot. As suggested by its curious name – "At the House of the Wise Man and the Fool" – this is a restaurant full of character. It is set in the folksy Patershol area and occupies a beautiful 16th-century, step-gabled building that was formerly the guildhouse of the leatherworkers. The food is traditional Flemish cuisine, with dishes such as *gentse stoverij* (Ghent beef stew) made with Westmalle beer. They serve an award-winning *waterzooi* here, embellished with other seafood such as mussels and Dublin Bay prawns.
Hertogstraat 42, Ghent; open noon–1:30pm and 6:30–9:30pm Tue–Sat; www.bijdenwijzenendenzot.be

Also in Ghent

Two other restaurants in Ghent regularly have *waterzooi* on the menu. **'t Klokhuys** (*www. klokhuys.com; inexpensive*), also in the Patershol district, is a charming, brasserie-style restaurant with wooden tables set out beneath exposed beams. **Brasserie 't Stropke** (*www. brasserietstropke.be; inexpensive*), lying close to the Gravensteen castle, is in a similar mould.

Also in Belgium

To find *waterzooi* elsewhere in Belgium, you need to look out for restaurants that are not ashamed of presenting "home-cooking" style dishes. In Brussels, **Aux Armes de Bruxelles** (*www.auxarmesdebruxelles.be; expensive*) is unusual for being a first-class, traditional Belgian restaurant in the Rue des Bouchers, where most restaurants are touristy and to be avoided. In Bruges, try the **Gran Kaffee de Passage** (*www.passagebruges.com; inexpensive*), a wonderfully atmospheric, candlelit restaurant that serves well-priced traditional Belgian dishes.

Around the World

The **Belga Café** (*www.belgacafe.com; moderate*) in Washington DC prides itself on its authentic Belgian flavours and atmosphere. In New York, **Waterzooi Belgian Bistro** (*www. waterzooi.com; moderate*) enriches its signature dish with lobster, mussels and clams. It's a similar seafood bonanza at the **Leuven Belgian Beer Café** (*www.leuven.co.nz; moderate*) in Wellington, New Zealand.

SAVOIE FRANCE

Say Cheese in the French Alps

The French Alps are renowned for valleys sprinkled with story-book chalets and swish ski resorts, and impossibly pretty scenery. They are also famous for their food: sturdy stews and soups, *diots* (little sausages), mushrooms and game from the forests, and dairy produce from the rich alpine pasture: the Haute Savoie alone has more than 30 different varieties of cheese.

The snowy summits and ice-dipped peaks of the French Alps have long lured skiers chasing powder thrills and downhill speed, nourished in their conquest of the slopes by honest, robust French mountain food.

The Savoie, vestige of a kingdom that ruled this corner of Europe for eight centuries, sits at the heart of the French Alps. Divided into Savoie and Haute Savoie, it is home to many of France's most stylish ski resorts – Chamonix, Courchevel, and Val d'Isère – and some of its finest cheeses. These came long before the folks in chunky boots and salopettes. The first skis – simple wooden planks – made their debut in 1878, while local farmers were making cheese in the Middle Ages.

Thus, cheese has always been a mountain staple. Reblochon de Savoie, Abondance and Beaufort are acclaimed local cheese celebs, while the region's most legendary dish is the dippy *fondue Savoyarde* (Beaufort cheese melted with local dry white wine and Kirsch).

Cheese is intrinsically linked to the gloriously scenic landscape. Beaufort, named after the pretty Beaufontain region, trumpets the flavours of the Savoie. In summer, the Tarentaise cows graze on alpine grasses high up on the mountains around the town of Beaufort, infusing the cheese with flowery-herb flavours. In winter, they remain in the barns on a diet of hay. Thus, the colour and aroma of the poetically named Beaufort d'Alpage (literally "Beaufort from the high mountain pasture") is completely different from the ghostly winter Beaufort.

The region's next most famous *fromage* is the delicate-tasting Reblochon, from the eastern slopes of the Haute-Savoie; almost two-thirds is produced in the magical Aravis Massif, a stone's throw from Lake Geneva. In winter, the snow-covered slopes around the villages of La Clusaz and Le Grand-Bornand are the domain of skiers, but come spring, the dairy godmothers trot out to reclaim the grassy slopes. Again, the local diet bestows a unique taste to the cheese.

Lake Annecy, with its lofty backdrop and blue, blue water – dubbed "the purest in all of Europe" – is proof that lakes and mountains are inspiring cohorts. At its northern tip, the town of Annecy itself, former seat of the Comtes de Genève, makes a good base for exploring the country roads and *fromageries* of the Haute-Savoie. A trip to Chamonix will give skiers and mountain-climbers the wide open slopes they crave: this was, after all, the birthplace of mountaineering, as well as the site of the first Winter Olympics, in 1924.

Three Days in the French Alps

Annecy makes an excellent base: its public transport links around the region are good, but taxis are also plentiful and car hire is available.

DAY ONE Explore Annecy's **medieval quarter** with its atmospheric canals and arcades. Visit the turreted **Château d'Annecy** to see traditional arts and crafts. In fine weather, opt for a three-hour guided bicycle tour of the town. Bird-fanciers can explore the **Sentier de découvertes des Roselières** around the lake to spy water fowl.

DAY TWO Visit a traditional **fromagerie** *(see overleaf)* to see how cheese is made. Farms around the village of **Grand-Bornand** make Reblochon, and **Beaufort** is charming. In summer, listen out for the clang of cowbells on the mountains.

DAY THREE Head for **Chamonix** and take a cable car up to **Aguille du Midi**, 3842 m (12,300 ft) high, for sweeping views. Take a train up to France's longest glacier, the 7-km (4.3-mile) **Mer de Glace** (Sea of Ice). Spoon down *tartiflette* – potato, bacon, onion and cream topped with melted cheese – at **La Bergerie** to ward off the chills.

Essentials

GETTING THERE

Trains run frequently from Lyon and Paris to Annecy. **Coaches** serve the closest major airport, Geneva, with daily flights also from Paris to Annecy's **Meythet airport**.

WHERE TO STAY

Hôtel Les Cimes (inexpensive) in Annecy has a warm, chalet feel. *www.hotel-les-cimes.com*

Hameau Albert 1er (moderate) offers old-style comfort in Annecy. *www.hameaualbert.fr*

Auberge du Père Bise (expensive) has views over glorious Lake Annecy. *www.perebise.com*

FURTHER INFORMATION

www.lac-annecy.com; www.chamonix.com

Above Reblochon is a key ingredient in fondues and in the local dish *tartiflette*, a comforting baked potato and cheese concoction

Left The unmistakeable peak of Mont Blanc, highest mountain in western Europe, rises up behind the railway station at Chamonix

Below Moving at an imperceptible pace, the mighty Mer de Glace ("Sea of Ice") glacier travels down the valley it has carved in the rock

Cheese Around the World

While milk might taste the same throughout the world, cheese is the consummate individual. Climate, history, tradition, landscape, the eating habits and the breed of the animal, and the dexterity of the cheesemaker all help ensure that the slice is right, from the lofty French Alps to the flatlands of Holland and the heart-shaped island of Tasmania.

THE FRENCH ALPS

Coopérative Laitière de Haut Tarentaise

www.fromagebeaufort.com

The Dairy Cooperative of the High Tarentaise has shops in Bourg St-Maurice, Val d'Isère, Les Arcs, La Rosière and Tignes selling Beaufort cheese, dubbed "the prince of Gruyères". A hard, cooked cheese, it is pressed into beechwood moulds to shape it, then drained, turned and rubbed with salt daily, and aged for six months.

La Laiterie des Halles

2 place de Genève, Chambéry; www.fromager-denis-provent.com

Denis Provent, who runs La Laiterie des Halles, is a master of Savoie cheeses; his family has been in the *fromage* business for three generations. His shop in Chambéry brims with Savoie cheeses, including Reblochon Fermier, Abondance, Beaufort, Tome de Bauges (semi-soft cow's milk cheese), Tomette de Brebis de Savoie (ewe's milk cheese), and Tarentais (farmhouse goat's cheese). Provent ages many of the cheeses in his own cellars. He has a second cheese "boutique", Les Délices Savoyardes, on rue de Genève in Aix-les-Bains.

Le Grand-Bornand

www.legrandbornand.com

Farms in and around this pretty winter-sports village near Annecy welcome visitors during the summer months to see Reblochon Fermier (farmhouse Reblochon) cheese being made, from the milking of the cows to a tasting of the final creamy product. Le Grand-Bornand, with some 55 farms in operation, boasts as many cows (2,000) as people! Le Grand-Bornand Tourist Office organizes tours.

NORMANDY, FRANCE

The land of cows, apple trees and thatched roofs produces one of France's most famous cheeses – the fruity Camembert – as well as Pont l'Evêque, Livarot and Brillat-Savarin.

La Foire aux Fromages de Livarot

A festival featuring all the finest local cheeses is held in Livarot, in the heart of Camembert country, every August. Bravehearts can attempt to win the title of fastest Livarot cheese-scoffer; the current record is 750 g (26 oz) in 1 minute 51 seconds.

La Fromagerie François Olivier

40 rue de l'Hôpital, Rouen; http://fromagerieolivier.free.fr

Possibly the best cheese shop in France, with a huge choice of French and Normandy cheeses, including exquisite artisan-made Camembert.

La Route du Fromage

Livarot; www.paysdelivarot.fr

A selection of farms in the picturesque Pays d'Auge region – which includes big-cheese villages such as Livarot, Pont l'Evêque and Camembert – offer tastings as well as cheese for sale. Pick up a map of the touring route at a local tourist office.

FRANCHE-COMTE, FRANCE

This unspoiled region on the eastern edge of France produces tangy, traditionally made Comté, the country's biggest selling hard cheese. Other popular local picks for the cheeseboard include Mont d'Or and Morbier.

Fromagerie Marcel Petite

22 rue Bernard Palissy, Granges Narboz; www.comte-petite.com

Here you can see how impressive 65,000 wheels of Comté look stored in a converted fort, and follow up the adventure with a tasting in these atmospheric surroundings.

La Fromagerie du Mont d'Or

2 rue du Moulin, Métabief; +33 3 81 490 236

A cheese shop specializing in the rich, runny Mont d'Or cheese, a firm Christmas favourite in France, which is only available from September to March. Morbier cheese is also on sale. The fromagerie uses the milk from 13 regional producers.

Left (top to bottom) Silky Camembert, one of the world's most-copied cheeses; dairy cows in Normandy, France; turning Comté in the Fort Saint Antoine cellars, home of Fromagerie Marcel Petite

Below (top to bottom) Traditionally dressed cheese porters load up at the Alkmaar cheese market in the Netherlands; artisanal cheeses on display on an Italian market stall

Les Routes du Comté
www.lesroutesducomte.com
Follow suggested itineraries or tailor your own driving tour along this route, and let local farmers demonstrate the care with which Comté is made and how good it is. Dairyman Jean François Marmier runs a herd of Montbeliarde cows, the ones most closely aligned with Comté, which visitors can help milk or feed for a more hands-on Alpine experience.

LOMBARDY, ITALY
Plump with natural beauty – rivers, lakes, mountains – as well as cities brimming with art and history, the kingdom of Lombardy is also rich in *formaggio*, with big hitters such as Gorgonzola, Grana Padano and Taleggio.

Formaggi Galli
Piazza Wagner, Milan
Marco Galli's stall in Milan's huge Piazza Wagner food market specializes in Lombardy cheeses. Slow Food supporter Galli is known for sourcing exceptional Gorgonzola, some aged to mind-blowing maturity.

La Baita del Formaggio
Via Italia 42, Milan; www.labaitadelformaggio.it
This traditional cheese shop offers up a host of artisanal Italian cheeses. The Lariano Speziato, a soft cheese from the mountains surrounding Lake Como, is exclusive to the shop.

Rossi y Grassi
Via Ponte Vetero 4, Milan; www.rg.mi.it
In the classy Brera district, this top-quality gourmet food shop displays a tempting selection of Italian cheeses, including fruity Grana Padano and soft Taleggio, plus wines from Italy's greatest producers. There is another branch close by on Via Solferino.

THE NETHERLANDS
The Dutch have been making cheese since at least the 4th century, with Gouda and Edam now global favourites. Both towns are within easy striking distance of Amsterdam. Don't miss the legendary cheese carriers at the weekly summer markets.

Abraham Kef
Marnixstraat 192, Amsterdam; www.abrahamkef.nl
A little piece of France in central Amsterdam, this shop specializes in French as well as Dutch cheeses. Their philosophy is that good cheese is inseparable from good wine, and you can enjoy both in the shop's small dining area.

De Kaaskamer
Runstraat 7, Amsterdam; http://kaaskamer.nl
In the newly fashionable "Nine Streets" shopping area, this shop, with its floor-to-ceiling selection of cheeses – including organic Dutch offerings – is sure to keep cheese fans both happy and busy.

Kaashuis Tromp
Utrechtsestraat 90, Amsterdam; www.kaashuistromp.nl
Henk van Kol's "House of Cheese" has expanded into a small universe, with another three branches in Amsterdam and 10 more throughout the Netherlands. The flagship store, noted for its friendly service, is packed with Dutch cheeses of all kinds, including many from small-scale producers, along with 250 foreign cheeses.

TASMANIA, AUSTRALIA
With its pristine environment, clean, clear waters, lush green pastures and fertile soil, Tasmania is home to many boutique dairy farms and artisan cheesemakers turning out creamy brie styles, full-bodied cheddar and artisanal cow and goat cheeses.

Bruny Island Cheese Company
1807 Main Road, Great Bay, Bruny Island; www.brunyislandcheese.com.au
On this small island off Tasmania, famed for its fairy penguins and other wildlife, Nick Haddow churns out handmade cow, sheep and goat's milk cheeses, ranging from "Barney", a blue cheese, and the mild, Gruyère-like "C2" to specialities such as prosciutto-wrapped and olive oil-marinated cheeses. See and taste the cheeses being made, and don't miss their home-baked bread and home-made ice cream too.

King Island Diary
Currie, King Island; www.kidairy.com.au
Situated on another tranquil little island, Australia's best-known speciality cheese and dairy producer makes a range of creamy bries, pungent blues and sharp aged cheddars, and has a tasting room in which they can be discovered.

Pyengana Cheese Factory
St Columba Falls Road, Pyengana; +61 3 6373 6157
Australia's oldest cheddar is made following a method developed in the local cooperative in the 1890s by cheesemaker Jon Healey's grandfather. There are dairy and cheese factory tours by appointment, plus cheese sales in The Factory Sho

Right Gaudí worked on the still-unfinished La Sagrada Familia for more than 40 years, famously declaring that "my client is not in a hurry"

BARCELONA SPAIN

Zarzuela in Stylish Barcelona

The cuisine of Barcelona can be as phantasmagorical as its architecture by Gaudí and his fellow Modernistas. Just as La Sagrada Familia makes the viewer wonder how the architect could possibly pile on so many ornamental encrustations, Barcelona's signature fish stew, zarzuela, makes the diner wonder if there is no end to the seafood delicacies hidden in a single bowl.

It seems perfectly natural that Barcelona, a city graced with free-flowing, fanciful architecture and a lively street life, would have developed a fish stew as studded with textures, shapes, colours and flavours as the *zarzuela de mariscos a la catalana*. How this Catalonian cousin of Marseille's bouillabaisse (*see pp128–9*) and Provençal *soupe aux poissons* got its name is something of a mystery, but "zarzuela" is also a form of Spanish light opera that includes rustic dances, spoken dialogue and songs. It is perhaps the similarly surprising and delightful mixture that has earned this fish stew – a veritable seafood operetta – the same name.

Spruced up for the 1992 Olympics, Barcelona nonetheless retains its character as a colourful beachfront town first settled by fishermen in 1754. The formerly disreputable shoreline district of working wharves and sailors' enticements is now an area of flourishing seafood restaurants, where Barcelonans and visitors alike go to promenade alongside a sandy beach that flows from the Olympic sports harbour to the Old Port. Here the statue of the explorer Columbus marks the foot of the city's most famous pedestrian boulevard, La Rambla.

Barcelona springs to life along the broad, car-free expanse of La Rambla, with flower vendors, living statues, bird-sellers, newspaper kiosks and cafés as still points in the flowing human river. Side streets branch off into the Barri Gòtic (Gothic quarter), where folk-dancers tread the *sardana* every Sunday in front of the cathedral. At the head of La Rambla, the 19th-century district of L'Eixample contains much of the city's famous Modernista architecture, including two buildings by Gaudí that are now World Heritage sites: the undulating, organic Casa Mila ("La Pedrera") and his most famous building, the uncompleted cathedral of the Holy Family – La Sagrada Familia.

No place looks like Barcelona, and likewise Barcelona's zarzuela stands apart from other fish stews. The easy-going Catalans improvise endlessly, and cooks can add any firm fish to the garlicky broth tinged sunset-golden with saffron, as long as they also include bright prawns, earthy small clams, pink mussels in their blue shells, a king prawn and half a lobster. This rich dish is served in wide, shallow bowls so diners can admire the jumble of colours, inhale the rising aromas and sop up the ocean-salty broth with garlic-rubbed toast. Like Barcelona itself, zarzuela is a feast for all the senses.

Above The Plaça Reial, a large square in the Barri Gòtic, provides an atmospheric setting for its many renowned restaurants, cafés and bars

Below The distinctive, saffron-rich fish stew called zarzuela is a riot of warm colour, as red pepper curls among the gently poached pink and white seafood

A Day in Barcelona

As the capital of Catalan culture – neither precisely Spanish nor French – Barcelona is a city of rich artistic ferment. Joan Miró was born here, Pablo Picasso spent his formative years here and Antoní Gaudí became the city's most famous architect, bequeathing it the iconic Sagrada Familia and a range of other Modernista masterpieces.

MORNING See a masterpiece nearing completion as the morning light strikes the spires of **La Sagrada Familia**. Then visit **Casa Mila**, Gaudí's finished crowning glory.

AFTERNOON Stroll through the circus-like scene of **La Rambla**, veering into the quieter **Barri Gòtic** to visit the **Museu Picasso**, repository of the artist's earliest works. Take the cable car up to **Montjuïc** where the organic building designed by architect Josep Lluís Sert showcases the surrealism of Miró's paintings and sculptures.

EVENING As evening falls, stroll the **waterfront promenade** and enjoy tapas then dinner at the bars and restaurants of Barceloneta, the 18th-century waterfront district.

Essentials

GETTING THERE
Barcelona's **international airport**, El Prat de Llobregat, lies 13 km (8 miles) from the city centre, and has connecting **trains** and **buses**.

WHERE TO STAY
El Jardí Hotel (inexpensive) has bright rooms in the old town. *www.hoteljardi-barcelona.com*
Hotel Casa Fuster (moderate) is an historic Modernista building. *www.hotelcasafuster.com*
Hotel Arts Barcelona (expensive) provides luxurious comfort on Barcelona's revitalized waterfront. *www.ritzcarlton.com*

TOURIST INFORMATION
Plaza de Catalunya; *www.barcelonaturisme.com*

La Boqueria Food Market

There has been a fresh food market on La Rambla since 1701, although the current incarnation of the Mercat de la Boqueria – which resembles a Modernista train shed with its soaring steel roof – dates from 1914. If La Sagrada Familia expresses Barcelona's faith, La Boqueria expresses the city's obsession with good food. More than 300 stalls and dozens of mini-restaurants, cafés and bars make up the market, which is among the largest in Europe. The fishmongers, their catch heaped on ice, fill the centre, and butchers, fruit and vegetable sellers and preserved-food dealers radiate outwards. From wild mushrooms to baby squid, if Cata[l] eat it, someone in La Boqueria sells it.

The Best Places to Eat Zarzuela

Restaurante Set Portes expensive

Everyone from Che Guevara to Errol Flynn, and from the King of Spain to Yoko Ono, has dined at Set Portes, and commemorative plaques even mark their favoured seats. Founded in 1836, the restaurant famously has seven entrances, and shares the building where Picasso and his parents first lived when they came to Barcelona in 1895. After the Spanish Civil War, Set Portes emerged as the most elegant restaurant in Barcelona and has tenaciously clung to its crown by serving only brilliant preparations of the best ingredients. The restaurant's version of zarzuela always features a generous half (the one with the large claw) of an Atlantic lobster, as well as cuts of fish that other restaurants would reserve for grilling. The wine list is optimally paired with the menu and is particularly robust, with Priorat reds and Penedés whites from Catalonia.

Passeig Isabel II 14, Barcelona; open 1pm–1am daily; www.7portes.com

Also in Barcelona

As the son of a fisherman, the proprietor of the Barcelona tavern **Can Majó** *(www.canmajo.es; moderate)* knows how to make a brilliant zarzuela. Book ahead for an outdoor table overlooking the harbour. **Can Culleretes** *(www.culleretes.com; inexpensive)* is a marvellously old-fashioned restaurant (founded in 1786) that often caters for large groups, and serves a good zarzuela among its many Catalan specialities.

Also in Catalonia

Few zarzuelas are so loaded with amazing crustaceans as the version served at **Restaurant Sa Gambina** *(www.restaurantsagambina.com; moderate)* in Cadaqués. Their "Gala-Dalí zarzuela" was named for painter Salvador Dalí and his wife Gaia, who ordered it frequently when living in Cadaqués. Considered by many to be perhaps Spain's greatest seafood restaurant, **Joan Gatell Restaurant** *(www.joangatell.com; expensive)* in Cambrils makes a transporting zarzuela as well as *suquet*, a humbler but similar soup without the crustaceans.

Around the World

Any seafood stew with crustaceans, clams and mussels could technically be called a zarzuela, but in the resorts of coastal Colombia and Venezuela, cooks prepare a *mariscada* that traces its roots to the Spanish zarzuela. An excellent version is available daily at **Restaurante de Albahaca** *(+58 295 263 7552; inexpensive)* on Venezuela's Isla de Margarita. A *mariscada* made with dark beer and seasoned with coriander is the house special of **Juan del Mar Restaurante** *(+57 5 664 5862; moderate)* in Cartagena, Colombia.

ALGARVE PORTUGAL

Cataplana in the Algarve

The Moors' conquest of the Iberian peninsula in the 8th century still resonates in Portugal. In the southern coastal province that they named "al-Gharb"– today's Algarve – the new settlers built walled towns and castles, planted rice and citrus trees, and influenced the native cuisine in the shape of the *cataplana*, a cooking utensil still used today to prepare Portugal's finest seafood dishes.

Like the brimming paella pan or clay tagine pot, the sight of a waiter bearing the burnished, domed, copper *cataplana* immediately signals the arrival of a dish that's firmly rooted in place, in this case the long, alluring coastline of the Portuguese Algarve. The iconic shape of the *cataplana* — like a hinged, lidded wok — is as recognizable as the golden sands and rocky coves of the region itself, and, as the clasps are released, the steam within rises like wisps of cloud into the azure Algarve skies. It's a fanciful image, but there's a real majesty in both the dish and its presentation that goes far beyond a simple seafood meal.

The word "cataplana" refers to both the cooking vessel and the dish, and to add to the confusion, there is no single dish represented by the name. The most typical — and some would say, most authentic — preparation is an *amêijoas na cataplana (cataplana* of clams), where clams are steamed in their shells along with chopped onion, tomato, garlic, paprika, a little piri-piri seasoning and strips of *presunto* (smoked ham) and garlicky *chouriço* sausage. It's a wonderful combination, with the melded flavours and juices retained during cooking within the sealed *cataplana*. But it's by no means the only *cataplana* dish available, as many restaurants offer versions using other shellfish and fish, particularly *lagosta (*lobster), *gambas* (prawns), *pescada (*hake) and *tamboril (*monkfish).

Common to all good *cataplanas* are the quality and freshness of the prime ingredients, and that's where the sunny, sea-facing Algarve comes into its own. It's one of Europe's finest resort regions, more relaxed than the heavily developed Spanish costas and featuring an undulating, 200-km (125-mile) coastline that's synonymous both with fantastic beaches and terrific seafood. Away from the well-known resorts, on the wilder, far western stretches beyond Lagos or the idyllic eastern sandbank islands between Faro and Tavira, you'll find hidden grottoes, isolated beaches and charming whitewashed villages that still retain echoes of their Moorish past, and small fishing ports with lively local fish markets that are centuries old but still play a central part in daily life. Rather like the *cataplana* itself, you only need to lift the lid to discover all that's best about the Algarve.

Above The Algarve is dotted with small coves and beaches, such as Praia do Carvalho in Lagoa, which offers sheltered sands and crystal-clear water

---

What Else to Eat

The classic sight – and smell – of the Portuguese coast is smoke rising off rows of salt-flecked sardines being cooked on an outdoor charcoal grill. Fresh fish, notably **robalo** (seabass) and **dourada** (bream), get the same treatment, while **atum** (tuna) — a significant Algarve catch — is often baked in an earthenware dish with a caramelized onion sauce *(atum de cebolada)*. It's also well worth trying the delicious fish stew called **caldeirada**, but for a thoroughly Portuguese experience there's no beating **arroz de marisco** served with an Algarve seaside view. This is a spicy, soup-like combination of rice and shellfish (clams certainly, and perhaps also mussels, crab and prawns), garnished with coriander and served with a simple salad.

Three Days on the Algarve

Don't spend all your time on the beach, however tempting. It pays to explore the less-visited inland areas too, particularly the pretty Serra de Monchique (Monchique mountains) in the west and the shores of the Rio Guadiana, the river that forms the border with Spain, in the east.

DAY ONE From Faro airport head east to the lovely riverside town of **Tavira**, which has a fish market, some fine boutique accommodation and a line of simple riverside restaurants. Then catch the ferry across to the sandy beaches of the **Ilha de Tavira** (Tavira island).

DAY TWO Make attractive **Albufeira** your next base. Its magnificent cove beaches are within easy reach of town. Take a side trip by car up to the old hillside village of **Alte** for lunch, and return via the medieval walled town of **Silves**.

DAY THREE Visit the western headland of **Sagres**, with its historic fort and dramatic beaches. North of here along the western, Atlantic coast, as far as **Odeceixe**, lies a series of remote beaches and youth-oriented surf resorts, backed by the mountains of the **Serra de Monchique**.

Essentials

GETTING THERE
Faro **international airport** is used by many holiday operators and budget airlines. A **car** is the best way to get around, though there is a useful **train** service between Lagos in the west and Vila Real de Santo António in the east.

WHERE TO STAY
Hotel Lagosmar (inexpensive) is a traditional, family-run guesthouse in the centre of the busy resort of Lagos. www.lagosmar.com
Pousada de Sagres (moderate) is a quiet retreat in the far western Algarve. www.pousadas.pt
Casa Três Palmeiras (expensive) is a wonderfully sited cliff-top villa above the beach near Praia da Rocha. www.casatrespalmeiras.com

TOURIST INFORMATION
www.visitalgarve.pt

The Best Places to Eat Cataplana

Don Sebastião expensive

Don Sebastião is a welcoming restaurant on a central cobbled street in the western resort of Lagos, whose owner believes that for *cataplana*, simple is best. His enduringly popular *amêijoas na cataplana* (clam *cataplana*) is presented in the traditional copper vessel and sticks firmly to the basics: small local clams cooked with tomato, onion, garlic, peppers and a splash of white wine, with *presunto* (smoked ham) and *chouriço* (garlic sausage) added for body and flavour. The *chouriço*, incidentally, makes an early appearance in any meal at Don Sebastião, served as a hot, sliced and flaming appetizer, doused in *medronho*, a local firewater made from the fruits of the strawberry tree (which taste rather like lychees). You can eat outside on the cobbles, which is the best way to get a flavour of lively Lagos, though there's a warm, rustic interior too, as well as a rather fine underground *adega* (wine cellar), which the waiters can usually be persuaded to show off at the end of a meal.

Rua 25 de Abril 20–22, Lagos; open noon–10pm daily; www.restaurantedonsebastiao.com

Also on the Algarve

In Lagos, dine on the rooftop terrace of the **Estrêla do Mar** *(+351 282 769 250; moderate)* — the restaurant couldn't be better placed for the ingredients for a *cataplana* as it's right on top of the fish market. In Tavira, the stunning **Pousada de Tavira** *(www.pousadas.pt; expensive)*, a boutique hotel fashioned from a 16th-century convent, has an excellent restaurant that puts a contemporary twist on regional dishes like the *cataplana*.

Also in Portugal

Many of Lisbon's inhabitants escape to the nearby coast at the small fishing port and resort of Ericeira, where the unpretentious **Mar à Vista** *(+351 261 862 928; moderate)* is the best place for *cataplana*. Further north, the Atlantic-facing resorts of Nazaré and Figueira da Foz are both traditional summer bolt holes for Portuguese families, with lots of great seafood restaurants. Try Figueira's renowned shellfish specialist, **Caçarola II** *(www.cacaroladois.com; expensive)*, which serves a fish, prawn and clam *cataplana*.

Around the World

Outside Portugal it's rare to find a genuine *cataplana*, cooked in the traditional copper utensil, but London's oldest Portuguese restaurant, **O Fado** *(www.ofado.co.uk; expensive)*, prepares a monkfish-and-mussels version in the correct manner.

Above Charcoal-grilled seafood, from sardines to lobsters, is a feature of life in the Algarve, and its tempting smell wafts along the coast

Left The two-handled copper *cataplana* has a hinged lid and seals completely, retaining all the flavoursome juices of the ingredients

Right Pedestrians rule in Højbro Plads, a lively square in the central, car-free Strøget shopping district

Below Careful attention to the aesthetics of presentation turns a simple sandwich into an elegant dish

A Day in Copenhagen

Central Copenhagen lends itself to easy strolling and many parts are pedestrianized. Royal parks and gardens further add to the charm.

MORNING Take a stroll around the **harbour** area, starting at the **Kastellet** fortification for good views of the city. Nearby is the world-famous statue of Hans Christian Andersen's **Little Mermaid**, sitting on a rock in the harbour. From here it's only a short walk to the so-called **Marble Church**, with the largest dome in Scandinavia, and, almost opposite, the somewhat unassuming royal palace, **Amalienborg**.

AFTERNOON AND EVENING Continue your walking tour to **Nyhavn**; this colourfully painted waterfront quarter, dating from the 17th century, is full of restaurants, bars and cafés popular with locals and visitors alike. Squeeze in a visit to **Rosenborg castle** with its splendid gardens before hitting the shops. **Strøget** is the longest car-free shopping area in Europe, with all the big names, quirky designer shops and eateries; many stay open late in summer and for Christmas.

Essentials

GETTING THERE
Copenhagen is located on Zealand and Amager in eastern Denmark. Flights arrive into **Kastrup international airport**, 8 km (5 miles) from the centre. There are **metro**, local **buses** and **bike rental** options to get around the city.

WHERE TO STAY
Cabinn City (inexpensive) is a centrally located, comfortable budget hotel. *www.cabinn.com*
Hotel Alexandra (moderate) is a retro hotel with modern Danish art, not far from the shopping district. *www.hotelalexandra.dk*
First Hotel Skt Petri (expensive) is the city's latest übercool hotel, and the birthplace of the Copenhagen cocktail. *www.sktpetri.dk*

TOURIST INFORMATION
Vesterbrogade 4A; *+45 7022 2442*

COPENHAGEN DENMARK

Denmark's De Luxe Sandwiches

Danes know how to turn a humble snack into a lavish feast, for the eye as well as the palate, with their traditional *smørrebrød* open sandwiches. In Copenhagen, entire restaurants are dedicated to this wonderfully versatile dish, and there are many other delights to sample, from shopping paradise Strøget to royal palaces and the colourful Nyhavn harbour area.

The Danish capital – "Wonderful, wonderful Copenhagen" as the old movie tune goes – has a long history as a centre for trade and commerce, growing into one of Scandinavia's most diverse and cosmopolitan cities. Southern Sweden and all of Norway were ruled from here for several none-too-peaceful centuries, making Copenhagen the main hub of Scandinavia, a role it still lays claim to today. Warmongering among neighbours is now thankfully past; old enemies Denmark and Sweden are connected via Europe's longest bridge and the bartering in the harbour has been replaced by shopping in the fabulous pedestrianized district of Strøget.

Despite its size, Copenhagen has a nicely compact centre, where most of the main sights can be visited on foot. A busy day's sightseeing can take in several royal palaces, the Little Mermaid of children's story fame, the old harbour area of Nyhavn and much more – all fuelled by *smørrebrød*, the most Danish of snacks.

Originally called *smør og brød*, literally meaning "butter and bread", the Danish open sandwich today has developed from a simple worker's packed lunch – perhaps a couple of slices of rye bread with cheese – into quite possibly the most varied dish in Denmark. While Swedes make their smorgasbord a feast of small dishes, Danes simply heap goodies on to slices of bread, piled high and beautifully arranged. Making these open sandwiches has become an art form, with the stylishly arranged toppings a perfect match of flavours, textures and colours, all splendidly coordinated.

Traditionally, dark rye bread is used, setting off the other colourful ingredients, although it's not at all uncommon for *smørrebrød* toppings to be so heavily piled that you are left guessing as to whether there is actually a slice of bread hiding underneath. Popular toppings include pink slices of roast beef with pickled gherkins and golden roasted onions, roast pork with red cabbage and orange, smoked salmon with dill, cucumber and lemon, or indeed whatever the chef has to hand. Find a cosy restaurant, pick your favourite(s) and tuck in. *Smørrebrød* makes the "wonderful" in Copenhagen even more well-deserved.

What Else to Eat

Danes eat more **pork** than any other nationality, and not a single part of their most beloved of meats goes to waste. Roasted, salted, smoked, cured, even pickled pork is popular, and fabulous-tasting sausages, hams and salamis abound. **Frikadelle**, pork meatballs or rissoles, is one of the best-known and loved national dishes, often accompanied by boiled potatoes, bright red beetroot, deep green pickled gherkins and a warming, thick brown sauce. **Beef** is almost as popular, and a dish managing to fit in both meats is **biksemad**, a hash of cubed beef and pork, along with potatoes, carrots and onions, all topped off with a fried egg, sunny side up: hearty food to keep the cold at bay in winter and energize you in summer.

Left Brightly painted canalside buildings in Nyhavn

The Best Places to Eat Smørrebrød

Ida Davidsen moderate

Five generations of Davidsens can't be wrong. Boasting the proudest *smørrebrød* tradition in Copenhagen, this family has been making open sandwiches since 1888. Today Ida Davidsen is queen of the kitchen, with her son Oscar running the cosy cellar establishment right in the heart of central Copenhagen. The original Oskar, the current proprietor's great-great-grandfather, was a wine merchant, aiming to quench thirsts, not fill bellies, when he first set up business. But customers weren't used to simply sipping without nibbling, and so the bar began selling *smørrebrød* to go with the wines. Today the restaurant has a selection of 250 different *smørrebrød* to choose from – the largest in Denmark. The humble sandwich has never looked so good, and the only problem is actually choosing what to have. Whatever your heart's desire, you can probably find it as a sandwich topping here, from the traditional to the more adventurous. Leg of lamb on a *smørrebrød*? Not a problem! Bacon, pâté, herrings, meatballs, smoked cheese – anything goes, and usually very nicely too.

Store Kongensgade 70, Copenhagen (with another outlet at Ketchup in Tivoli Gardens); open 10:30am–4pm Mon–Fri; www.idadavidsen.dk

Also in Copenhagen

Slotskælderen hos Gitte Kik on Fortunstræde **(+45 33 11 15 37; moderate)** is another long-runner in the *smørrebrød* stakes, celebrating over a century in business. Housed in what's known as the Castle Cellar, the restaurant lies directly opposite the Danish Parliament building, making this a busy spot at lunch time. Traditional recipes are used and they even pickle their own herring and make their own schnapps.

Also in Denmark

Brøndums Hotel (+45 98 44 15 55; inexpensive) is beautifully located in Skagen, on the tip of Jutland – former home to Scandinavia's most famous colony of painters. It's perfect for old-fashioned *smørrebrød* in a scenic setting. The building oozes old-world charm and has picturesque terrace seating in summer overlooking the sea.

Around the World

At **Madsen Scandinavian Restaurant** *(www. madsenrestaurant.com; moderate)* in London's fashionable South Kensington district you can sample traditional *smørrebrød* in a trendy setting. They've even made up their own, slightly smaller lunch-snack version, called "Smushi", on either dark rye or sourdough bread. Toppings include well-known favourites such as roast beef with remoulade, roast pork with crackling and red cabbage, and several tasty vegetarian options.

BUDAPEST HUNGARY

On Budapest's Paprika Trail

One of Europe's great capitals, Budapest combines the drama of its Danube-spanning location with the mystique of a city that has witnessed great events in history. Ottoman conquerors, Habsburg monarchs and Communist planners have all left their mark, but it is in Budapest's markets, coffeehouses and restaurants that you will find the ebb and flow of Hungarian life.

The name Budapest literally links a city of two halves: tranquil, hilly Buda on the west bank of the Danube, and bustling Pest, with its shops, cafés and museums, on the eastern bank. The castle district on Buda hill recalls the glory days of Hungary's medieval monarchs and their Habsburg successors, while over the river in Pest, boulevards heavy with 19th-century buildings convey a palpable sense of national pride. Elsewhere, downtown façades are studded with decorative motifs, constituting a three-dimensional pattern-book of early Hungarian (Magyar) folk art. Modern buildings such as the wonderful Ludwig Museum of Modern Art on the banks of the Danube river reveal that Budapest is a restlessly contemporary city too.

Hungarians take their food very seriously. Bakery counters groan under the weight of speckled loaves and rolls, café windows contain displays of delicate pastries and cakes, while the chalked-up boards outside restaurants deliver the rich promise of roast breast of duck or fried liver of goose. However, no dish sums up Hungarian culinary culture more than goulash, the ubiquitous paprika-flavoured stew whose origins are as old as the Hungarian nation.

For many, the word "goulash" is a catch-all term, but in Hungary itself the word *gulyás* usually refers to a rather thin stew that is served as a soup; the full-blooded stew that most non-Hungarians would consider to be goulash goes by the name of *pörkölt*. This is most often made with chunks of veal *(borjúpörkölt)*, although there are many variations – *pörkölt* featuring huge, scaly chunks of freshwater fish is a favourite in the south. There is also a silkier version of goulash known as *paprikás*, thickened with lashings of cream. All of these dishes originated in the simple stews prepared by Hungarian cattle-drovers over campfires, and you'll still see them served in traditional metal dishes, or *bogrács*, with a huge ladle protruding from the rim.

In Budapest you'll find goulash on menus everywhere, from bus station buffets to high-class restaurants. The one essential ingredient is paprika, the frequently fiery spice grown on a huge scale throughout southern Hungary. Strings of dried paprikas are a colourful feature of Budapest's markets where they are labelled according to their heat and flavour – there are eight grades, ranging from the sweet and mild *különleges* to the maroon-coloured, tongue-blisteringly hot *erős*.

A Day in Budapest

Bisected by the mighty Danube, Budapest has been destroyed and rebuilt over the centuries, giving it an eclectic appearance and elegant feel. The banks of the river have UNESCO World Heritage status, justifying the city's name, the "Pearl of the Danube".

MORNING Start off by visiting **Buda**, a historical quarter of 18th-century mansions and cobbled squares. The parapets of the **Fishermen's Bastion** provide sumptuous views across the Danube river.

AFTERNOON Cross the river to **Pest** and its animated main shopping street, **Váci utca**, pausing for coffee and cakes in one of the many fine café-patisseries. Afterwards take a trip on the 100-year-old M1 metro line to leafy **Városliget Park**, where both a zoo and a reconstructed Transylvanian castle await. If you have time for a gallery, the **Museum of Applied Arts** is the ideal introduction to Hungarian visual style.

EVENING Promenade along Pest's Danube shore and admire the illuminated bridges before heading for **Ráday utca**, an up-and-coming area of cafés and restaurants.

Essentials

GETTING THERE
Flights arrive at **Ferihegy Airport**; buses travel the 16 km (10 miles) to the city centre.

WHERE TO STAY
Anna (inexpensive) is a small, homely B&B in a central Pest location. www.annahotel.hu
Ibis Centrum (moderate) is in a lively part of Pest. www.ibis-centrum.hu
Danubius Hotel Gellért (expensive) combines Art Nouveau elegance with proximity to the world-famous Gellért thermal baths complex. www.danubiushotels.com/gellert

TOURIST INFORMATION
Sütő u. 2, Deák tér; www.budapestinfo.hu

Above The 19th-century basilica of St Stephen overlooks the Chain Bridge, which spans the Danube connecting Buda and Pest

Left Wrought-iron work and vaulting give the Great Market its spacious character

Above Paprika-hued *gulyás* (goulash) served in a metal *bogrács* cooking pot is considered an important part of Hungary's national heritage

The Great Market

Dating from the 1890s, Budapest's Great Market Hall or *Nagycsarnok* is one of the landmarks of the city, with steep-roofed corner towers giving it the air of a Transylvanian castle. Inside, cast-iron pillars preside over row upon row of stalls, selling everything from fruit and veg to embroidered blouses. Rows of salamis hang curtain-like above tins of goose-liver pâté arranged in pyramids. Many stalls feature dried paprikas strung together into chains – ideal decorations for a rustic kitchen. If you're a keen user of paprika in cooking, a couple of chains will be enough to keep you going for a year or more.

The Best Places to Eat Goulash

Bock Bisztró expensive

With a bright creamy interior lined with cookbooks and wine magazines, Bock Bisztró doesn't at first sight look like the average Hungarian tavern. However, once you receive your "pre-starter" (a pot of spicy pork lard with plenty of crusty bread to smear it on), you quickly realize that there is more in the way of Magyar tradition here than at first meets the eye. By putting traditional national recipes and modern Mediterranean dishes on the same menu, Bock has done a great deal to make old-school Hungarian cooking fashionable again. Head chef Lajos Bíró is something of a national culinary celebrity, with several TV shows and coffee-table books to his name. Mains like veal paprikash (*borjúpaprikás*) delight with their velvety texture and delicate paprika tones – extra spice is provided on the side if you feel the need to increase the temperature. Bock is also a wine shop, so you can get good advice on which Hungarian red to drink with your meal and the chance to buy a bottle as you leave.

Erzsebet korut 43–49, Budapest; open noon– midnight Mon–Sat; www.bockbisztro.hu

Also in Budapest

Ostentatiously decorated with Transylvanian folk motifs, 19th-century relic **Kárpátia (www.karpatia.hu; expensive)** is a long-established favourite with both locals and tourists, and its goulashes remain of unimpeachably high quality. Away from the tourist trail, **Régi Sipos (www.regisipos.hu; moderate)** serves up homely southern Hungarian delights such as carp goulash (*pontypörkölt*) or the much-prized catfish stew (*harcsapaprikás*), accompanied by lasagne-like sheets of delicious cheesy noodles.

Also in Hungary

Gulyás and *pörkölt* can be found throughout the country, but are at their best in the rural south and east. Located in Kecskemét, close to the paprika-growing plains of the south, **Kecskeméti Csárda és Borház (+36 76 417 640; moderate)** excels in spicy traditional cooking. The southern town of Baja is famous for its paprika-meets-fish cuisine, with riverside restaurants like **Vendio (www.vendio.hu; moderate)** drawing in customers with catfish stew with cheesy noodles.

Around the World

One Hungarian restaurant that is the absolute equal of any establishment in Budapest is the **Gay Hussar (www.gayhussar.co.uk; expensive)** in London's Soho, famous not just for its fine goulashes and duck roasts but also for a clientele that has included media folk and many a leading politician over the years.

ISTANBUL TURKEY

Meze by the Bosphorus

East meets West quite literally in Istanbul, the only city in the world that bestrides two continents. Set on the shores of the Bosphorus and Golden Horn, its majestic domes, elegant minarets and towers float above the hubbub of 13 million people in motion. At meal times, a momentary lull sees locals and visitors settle into spreads of meze, one of the great joys of travel in Turkey.

Istanbul, the meeting point of two worlds, is one of the most vibrant, colourful and heritage-rich cities on Earth. Capital of the Byzantine and Ottoman empires, it boasts the evocative remains of its Genoese, Roman and Greek overlords. Its people live among some of the world's finest Byzantine and Ottoman architecture, including the Blue Mosque, Topkapı Palace and the Roman emperor Justinian's famous church, Haghia Sophia. There's plenty to keep Orientalists happy too: medieval-era bazaars, markets selling pyramids of exotic produce, 14th-century hammams that still steam and stalls where master craftsmen still ply their ancient trades.

There's an almost overwhelming amount of choice, but there's one way in which Istanbul can be digested on even a short break – in its cuisine, and the platters of little bite-sized dishes known as meze. There are dozens of types of meze to try, all dressed with fresh herbs and spices and rich with intriguing flavours such as sesame, pomegranate and walnuts. Plump olives and yogurty, garlicky dips; white beans and cheeses, salted fresh tuna, stuffed mussels, crisp little savoury pastries and rissoles, stuffed courgette flowers and, everywhere, Turkey's glorious aubergines, braised with tomatoes,

roasted, grilled, or mashed into dips: this is a terrific way to sample the sophisticated and eclectic cuisine and flavours of Turkey's different regions.

The word "meze" is believed to derive from the Persian, meaning "pleasurable taste". According to Turkish tradition, meze have their roots in the opulent era of the great 16th-century sultan, Süleyman the Magnificent. Fond of throwing extravagant feasts, the Sultan nonetheless needed to ensure against intrigue and poisoning by keeping food-taster slaves in his court. Ordering the palace kitchen to prepare taster portions before he sat down to table, he inadvertently started a trend among Istanbul's courtiers and aristocracy.

Today meze are served both as starters and as a complete meal in themselves. Sample them in Istanbul's atmospheric *meyhanes* (traditional Turkish taverns) found in the Beyoğlu, Nevizade and Sofyalı areas, where crammed tables of chattering locals pick from the large trays of meze wheeled around by waiters. Raki is the traditional accompaniment, an aniseed-flavoured firewater with the kick of a Seljuk pony. To follow, relax with a thick, fragrant Turkish coffee, accompanied perhaps by the soothing bubble of a *nargileh* (water pipe), and feel blissfully satiated in the capital once justly dubbed "The City of the World's Desire".

Three Days in Istanbul

Istanbul contains enough to keep the visitor occupied for a month. Three days will give you a chance to take in the main sights, and plenty of opportunities to feast on meze.

DAY ONE Start in the historic **Sultanahmet** district with the iconic **Blue Mosque** and its famous, ethereal neighbour, **Haghia Sophia**, then visit the **Basilica Cistern**. Spend the afternoon shopping at the **Grand Bazaar**, and later the **Spice Bazaar** in Tahtakale.

DAY TWO Spend the morning taking in the magnificent **Topkapı Palace**, and after lunch, the collection of the **Istanbul Archaeological Museums**. Take a refreshing tea and a bath at an old Ottoman **hammam** (Turkish bath) before dinner.

DAY THREE Board a **ferry at Eminönü** and sail along the **Bosphorus** and **Golden Horn**. After a reviving coffee and baklava, head for the **western districts** of old Istanbul to admire the beautiful Byzantine mosaics and frescoes of the **Chora Church**. After lunch, head for Sultanahmet and the **Museum of Turkish & Islamic Arts**, before ambling via the Arasta Bazaar to the **Great Palace Mosaic Museum**.

Essentials

GETTING THERE
The **LRT** (Light Rail Transport) and **taxis** connect the **international airport** to central Istanbul.

WHERE TO STAY
Hotel Empress Zoe (inexpensive–moderate) is charming, in boutique style, with a garden and rooftop terrace. *www.emzoe.com*
Sirkeci Konak (moderate): central, comfortable, with a pool and hammam. *www.sirkecikonak.com*
Four Seasons Hotel Istanbul (expensive) is famous for its central location, sumptuous service and comfort. *www.fourseasons.com*

TOURIST INFORMATION
Divan Yolu, Sultanahmet; +90 212 518 8754

Above A meze buffet in Istanbul, with olives, tomatoes, cucumber, cheeses and anchovies laid out in traditionally decorated bowls

Left The Blue Mosque dominates the skyline in Istanbul; beneath it, in the old city, diners tuck into traditional Turkish cuisine alfresco

Below Istanbul's Grand Bazaar is one of the largest covered markets in the world, with 58 streets contained within its gated walls

Meze Around the World

Meze are found throughout the Middle East and Mediterranean, albeit under different names or forms. The fashion is believed to have spread from the Sultan's court in Istanbul at the height of the Ottoman empire.

ISTANBUL

Sofyalı 9 inexpensive
Sofyalı Sokak 9, Tünel; +90 212 245 0362

In an area famous for its *meyhanes* (taverns), this is one of Istanbul's best, serving superb meze and traditional Anatolian cooking in attractive surrounds and a warm, vibrant and buzzing atmosphere. Try the speciality, *arnavut ciğeri* (fried lamb's liver).

Asitane expensive
Kariye Camii Sokak 6, Edirnekapı; www.asitanerestaurant.com

Just south of the Chora Church, upmarket Asitane has established a speciality in and a reputation for fine Ottoman cuisine. Its dedicated chefs source original recipes from the kitchens of the old Ottoman palaces and employ original methods of preparation and cooking for all their dishes, including their sumptuous meze.

Mikla expensive
Marmara Pera Hotel, Meşrutiyet Caddesi 15, Tepebaşı; www.miklarestaurant.com

Considered the city's top table, Mikla is overseen by local "celebrity chef" Mehmet Gürs, who creates stunning modern Mediterranean dishes with Turkish ingredients, cooking methods and flavours. Spectacular views, impeccable service and sumptuous decor complement the food.

SYRIA

Syrian cuisine is one of the oldest, richest and most sophisticated in the world, and the range of meze found in its restaurants reflects this, combining a wide range of raw ingredients with centuries-old culinary know-how.

Bab Al-Hara inexpensive
Sharia Al-Qaimariyya, Damascus; +963 11 541 8644

Set deep in the old city close to the Umayyad Mosque, Al-Hara boasts a fervent local following for its fresh, flavoursome and authentic cooking, at excellent prices, served in an old courtyard house. The meze and grills are a particular speciality.

Bazaar Al-Charq moderate
Between Sharia Al-Mutanabi and Sharia Hammam Al-Tat, Aleppo; +963 21 224 9120

The cellar-like Charq is cosy, atmospheric and welcoming. The kitchen offers an impressive variety of Damascene and Aleppine specialities, including a wide range of meze; the heavenly, smoky baba ghanoush (aubergine purée) is a must-try. There's usually live traditional music in the evening.

Al-Khawali expensive
Maazanet al-Shahim, Damascus; +963 11 222 5808

Considered one of Syria's best restaurants and counting its president among its customers, Al-Khawali is a great choice for sampling meze Syrian-style. Set in a restored Damascene courtyard house dating to 1368, it combines beautiful surrounds with first-class cooking and service.

Sissi House expensive
Just off Saahat Al-Hattab, Jdeideh, Aleppo; www.sissihouse.com

Considered a cut above in decor, ambience and cooking, Sissi House attracts a well-heeled and glamorous local following. It specializes in Aleppine cuisine, beautifully prepared, cooked and served, including a selection of over 50 meze. Classical Arab music is often played live.

LEBANON

For many people, Lebanese cuisine forms their main experience of meze, aided undoubtedly by the large Lebanese communities and their eateries found in many Western cities. In Lebanon itself, eating out is an important part of social interaction.

Abdel Wahab moderate
Rue Abdel Wahab El-Inglizi, Achrafiye, Beirut; +961 1 200 552

With tables spread around the pretty garden and high-ceilinged rooms of an old Ottoman villa, the Abdel Wahab is an atmospheric and romantic place for dinner *à deux*. The lavish buffets are famous and include a wide range of meze, among them several varieties of heavenly hummus.

Left (top to bottom) The beautiful courtyard setting of the Al-Khawali restaurant in Damascus, Syria; alfresco dining in Istanbul, overlooking the Bosphorus; meze in Egypt

Below (top to bottom) Greek meze, with olives, fava beans (foreground), octopus and (centre left) char-grilled halloumi cheese; arranging cold meze dishes at a Lebanese restaurant

La Tabkha moderate

Rue Gouraud, Gemmayzeh, Beirut; +961 1 579 000

Modern, minimalist and contemporary, La Tabkha serves a terrific array of modern Lebanese dishes with a touch of French influence, including an excellent lunch-time meze buffet that changes daily.

Shahrazad moderate

6th Floor, Centre Commercial de Yaghi & Simbole, off Rue Abdel Halim Hajjar, Baalbek; +961 8 371 851

The location may lack style or atmosphere, but it's the spectacular views over Baalbek's Roman ruins that draw a loyal following, along with the simple but hearty and well-prepared home cooking, including a good selection of delicious, freshly prepared meze.

EGYPT

At one time part and parcel of the Ottoman empire and today part of the Middle East, Egypt has long been influenced by both regions' cooking. It has also developed its own distinct versions of meze, using local ingredients and cooking traditions.

Samakmak moderate

42 Qar Ras At Tin, Alexandria; +20 3 481 1560

Established by a former belly dancer, the Samakmak is a cosy, intimate and atmospheric restaurant. It is best known for its excellent, imaginatively prepared fish and seafood dishes, which include an unusual and very good meze selection.

Abou El Sid expensive

157 Sharia 26 July, Zamalek, Cairo; +20 2 2735 9640

Styled like an Orientalist boudoir-cum-restaurant-bar, the Abou El Sid is one of Cairo's eating hot spots. Diners recline on cushions pasha-style around low brass tables while tucking into well-prepared traditional Egyptian cooking, including mouthwatering meze. Reservations are essential.

CYPRUS

Though unquestionably influenced by Turkey and Greece as well as the Middle East, Cyprus nonetheless proudly possesses its own culinary traditions. The Cypriots love and value their food and keep up a vigorous tradition of meze.

Fetta's inexpensive

Ioanni Agroti 33, Pafos; +357 2693 7822

One of Cyprus's top traditional restaurants, Fetta's bases its reputation on enduring culinary values: quality ingredients, locally sourced, and simple but sound home cooking passed down the generations. The meze platter of grilled meats is a speciality.

Zanettos Taverna inexpensive

Trikoupi 65, Lefkosia; +357 2276 5501

One of the oldest surviving tavernas in the Old City, Zanettos is a bit of an institution and retains a loyal local following. Though located in a rather lugubrious part of town, it's worth the journey: the meze are superb and the atmosphere convivial and fun.

On the Menu in Turkey

Acı domates ezmesi Spicy tomato dip.
Ançüz Pickled anchovies.
Arnavut ciğeri Diced, fried lamb's liver with raw onion, sumac, chilli and chopped parsley.
Barbunya pilaki Salad of red beans.
Beyaz peynir White sheep's or goat's cheese.
Cacık Yogurt with grated cucumber and mint, served either as a kind of soup or as a dip.
Çerkez tavuğu Literally, "Circassian chicken" – chicken, walnuts and bread flavoured with garlic.
Deniz börülcesi Samphire dressed with olive oil, garlic and lemon and traditionally served with fish and seafood meze.
Enginar Boiled artichoke.
Ezme salatası Tomato, pepper and chilli dip.
Fasulye piyazı Salad of haricot beans.
Fava or **fava salatası** A puréed broad bean dip.
Haydari Yogurt dip made with garlic and mint.

Kabak çiçeği dolması Stuffed courgette flowers.
Kısır Salad made of spiced bulgur wheat.
Lakerda Tuna fish, sliced and salted.
Mercimek köftesi Spicy balls made of red lentils and bulgur wheat traditionally served at weddings and family feasts.
Midye dolması Stuffed mussels.
Patates köftesi Cheese and potato croquettes.
Patlıcan biber tava Fried aubergine and sweet green peppers with tomato sauce and chilli.
Patlıcan ezmesi Roast aubergine with yogurt.
Patlıcan kızartması or **salatası** Fried aubergine and tomato, served warm or as a salad.
Sarımsaklı havuç Grated carrot in a garlicky yogurt.
Semizotu salatası Salad of purslane in a yogurt and garlic dressing.
Sigara böreği Cigar-shaped pastries deep-fried and stuffed with cheese.
Yaprak dolması Vine leaves stuffed with pine nuts, rice and herbs.

LOIRE VALLEY FRANCE

Tarte Tatin in the Regal Loire

The upside-down apple tart is quintessentially French – but one village in particular lays claim to its invention, saying that it was born in the tiny village of Lamotte-Beuvron when the Tatin sisters pulled it from their oven. Their name still clings to the dish, but every bakery and bistro throughout the château-strewn Loire Valley has a version of the apple and sugar-soaked *tarte Tatin*.

The year 1889 was a significant one for France: the Eiffel Tower was completed, and an upturned apple tart blazed its way into the culinary chronicles. Stéphanie and Caroline Tatin, two sisters who ran a hotel in the little village of Lamotte-Beuvron, created their tart *tour de force* purely by accident, or so the story goes. While racing to get through a busy lunch service, Stéphanie threw a pan of apples, sugar and butter into the oven, thinking there was pastry on the bottom. The apples caramelized, turning a luminous bronze, and she then attempted to "save" the dessert by adding a pastry lid and putting it back into the oven. Rather than admit a mistake, the sisters flipped over their "tart nouveau", carved it up immediately and served it just so. That's the official story, at least, recounted by *La Confrérie des Lichonneux de Tarte Tatin* (The Brotherhood of the *Tarte Tatin*), its vigilant protectors and promoters.

Sticklers for tradition, the Brotherhood insists the butter goes in first, followed by the sugar, with the apple quarters layered on top – then it's into the oven to bake, just as in the sisters' day. Not everyone follows this code; some cooks prefer to caramelize the butter and sugar separately before adding the apples to bake.

The tart has a formidable fan base, which grew from that first bunch of hunters at the sisters' hotel, who lined up again the following week for a taste of the new apple dessert. More than 120 years later, hunters still flock to the Sologne region in autumn, hot on the trail of wild boar, deer, duck, pheasants and mushrooms.

Tourists, however, stalk different prey: the châteaux of the Loire, which materialize at every curve and corner. In the 16th century the French court moved between these pleasure palaces for days of hunting and nights of feasting. The vast Château de Chambord was the brainchild of François I, who at 25 vowed to show the world just how passionate he was about architecture and hunting; his extravagant white stone Renaissance palace is in the midst of a forest teeming with game. In October it rings with the sound of stags rutting, as they clash antlers and bellow to establish their superiority and claim to the best of the hinds.

Towards the north lies Orléans, once the capital of France and now the capital of the Loire Valley. It was here that Joan of Arc famously liberated the city of Orléans from the English in 1429, aged only 17. From castles and grand gardens, to deeds of great bravery and accidental culinary creation, the Loire is full of astonishing sights, tales and tastes.

Three Days in the Loire Valley

Loved by kings and blessed by nature, the Loire Valley is an all-round crowd-pleaser.

DAY ONE **Lamotte-Beuvron** sits deep in the Sologne, a region rich in nature and known for hiking, hunting and horse-riding. Wander the tree-flanked **Canal de la Sauldre** just outside the town, or take to one of the many hiking tracks on foot or horseback – they're the ideal antidote to *tarte Tatin* over indulgence.

DAY TWO Visit **Orléans** and immerse yourself in history, specifically that of the Maid of Orléans, Joan of Arc. Her former home is now a museum – **Centre Jeanne d'Arc** – devoted to telling her story. The stained-glass windows of **Sainte Croix Cathedral** also pay tribute. There's even a Joan of Arc festival in May, complete with medieval fair.

DAY THREE Head for **Chambord**, to explore **Château de Chambord**, Renaissance status symbol *par excellence*. There's a magnificent interlocking double staircase, false windows, turrets galore and an expansive roof terrace on to which the king used to ascend in order to watch the commencement of the hunt, tournaments and festivals.

Essentials

GETTING THERE
Fly to **Tours airport**, or take a **high-speed train** from Paris to the Loire Valley region.

WHERE TO STAY
Auberge du Cheval Blanc (inexpensive) in Yvoy le Marron has comfortable rooms in an old coaching inn. *www.aubergeduchevalblanc.com*
Château de Beauharnais (moderate) is grand, and just 12 km (7 miles) from Lamotte-Beuvron. *www.châteaudebeauharnais.com*
Grand Hôtel du Lion d'Or (expensive) (*see facing page*). *www.hotel-liondor.fr*

TOURIST INFORMATION
www.loirevalleytourism.com

Above *Tarte Tatin* is an "upside-down" apple pie, where the golden-brown caramelized apples sit atop a layer of flaky, buttery pastry

Left The extravagant Château de Chambord, a hunting lodge for François I, is the largest of the Loire châteaux, boasting 440 rooms

Above Lamotte-Beuvron's Hôtel Tatin, where the Tatin sisters cooked up their famous tart, is still going strong today as a hotel and restaurant

Tarte Tatin Festival

The annual *Foire au Pays des la Tarte Tatin* (*tarte Tatin* festival) takes place in mid-September in Lamotte-Beuvron. There are tart-making demonstrations, often by a renowned, Loire-based chef employing only the ingredients used by the revered Tatin sisters. Baking aficionados can enter the *tarte Tatin* contest, and the winner walks away with a handsome trophy. This is, after all, a festival designed for people "wishing to taste, evaluate and defend the *tarte Tatin*". It's a serious, if delicious, business. But individualists beware – any attempts to improve on the original recipe will be treated with the appropriate disdain.

The Best Places to Eat Tarte Tatin

Grand Hôtel du Lion d'Or
expensive

Didier Clément, chef at the Michelin-starred Lion d'Or in Romorantin-Lanthenay, is inspired by the produce of the Sologne and driven by the seasons. He's also a fan of long-forgotten varieties of herbs, spices and heritage vegetables and fruits, such as *reine de reinettes* ("king of the pippins") apples, and he works with gardeners and farmers in the region to grow them for his table. In autumn and winter he showcases his version of "*la tarte des demoiselles Tatin*", cooking up perfectly caramelized apples on a puff-pastry base that would have the sisters beaming. He admits, however, that he actually prefers to serve his "lighter version" of the apple classic: a millefeuille of *reinette* apples crowned with quince ice cream (an old-fashioned favourite that Clément champions) and frothy caramel. In summer, diners can eat in the flower-filled courtyard of the 16th-century hotel, and in winter they're ensconced in high-end country comfort in the formal dining room, with its chandeliers and starched white cloths.
69 rue Georges Clemenceau, Romorantin-Lanthenay; open for lunch and dinner Wed–Mon, closed 1–13 Aug, 19–29 Dec and 16 Feb–10 Mar; www.hotel-liondor.fr

Also in the Loire

A visit to sleepy little Lamotte-Beuvron wouldn't be complete without a pit stop at the **Hôtel Tatin** (*www.hotel-Tatin.fr; moderate*), the alleged birthplace of the tart. It still has the same coal- and wood-burning tiled stove in which the famed sisters baked their tarts. *Reine de reinettes* remains the apple of choice, cut into slices, quarters or chunks, layered in a special pan, cooked to golden perfection and served comfortably warm.

Also in France

Philippe Conticini is an artist when it comes to cakes, tarts and all the finer, sweeter things in life. His Paris bakery, **La Pâtisserie des Rêves** (*www.lapatisseriedesreves.com; inexpensive*), is chock-full of his creations, including an irresistible *tarte Tatin*. His rendition has slivers of apple piled high on a square of crispy puff pastry; the pale, almost translucent apple sheets on the bottom rise up the colour scale to the caramel-coloured beauties on top. The *tarte* is served with a pot of lime-flavoured mascarpone.

Around the World

London's much-lauded **Le Gavroche** (*www.le-gavroche.co.uk; expensive*), founded in 1967 by the Roux brothers, dishes up a delicious *tarte Tatin* that perfectly finishes a top-end French meal. Individual-sized tarts brimming with caramelized apples come with a dollop of Madagascan-vanilla-flavoured ice cream.

Above Klädesholmen is one of 3,000 islands off Sweden's west coast, connected by bridge to the island of Bockholmen

Above Smorgasbord in Bohuslän's restaurants includes deliciously large helpings of fish and shellfish, such as lobster, crayfish and prawns

Three Days in Bohuslän

Bohuslän's coastline, featuring islands, skerries, Sweden's only fjord and its only marine national park, can be explored in just a few days.

DAY ONE Drive north from **Gothenburg** following the archipelago, passing the two largest islands, **Orust** and **Tjörn**. After an hour's drive you reach the charming settlement of **Lysekil**, on Sweden's only fjord, **Gullmaren**. In the afternoon, continue to nearby **Smögen**, one of the most scenic fishing villages on the coast, now a popular holiday spot.

DAY TWO Follow the main coastal road north towards the unusual Bronze Age rock carvings at **Tanum**, a UNESCO World Heritage site. Reach the hub of **Strömstad**, near Norway, in the evening and treat yourself to some pampering at its renowned spa, before dinner at **Rökeriet**, a traditional smokehouse in the harbour.

DAY THREE Take the morning ferry to the **Koster Islands** and explore the car-free north island, hiking between the purple heather, yellow gorse and pink-tinged cliffs before cycling or canoeing around the south island. Return to **Strömstad** by ferry in the evening.

Essentials

GETTING THERE
The coastal region of Bohuslän lies between Gothenburg and the Norwegian border. Flights arrive at **Gothenburg-Landvetter international airport,** 20 km (13 miles) from the city centre. There are good local **buses** and car hire.

WHERE TO STAY
Strandflickorna (inexpensive) is an old-fashioned, peaceful hotel near the sea in the coastal town of Lysekil. *www.strandflickorna.se*
Salt & Sill (moderate), Sweden's first floating hotel, has 23 stylish rooms in two buildings off the island of Klädesholmen. *www.saltosill.se*
Quality Spa & Resort Strömstad (expensive) is a world-class hotel and traditional health spa. *www.stromstadspa.se*

TOURIST INFORMATION
www.westsweden.com; www.vastsverige.com

BOHUSLAN SWEDEN

Smorgasbord in Sweden

The coastline between Gothenburg and the Norwegian border on the west coast of Sweden is teeming with islands, islets and skerries, where small fishing communities still make a living from the sea. In the province of Bohuslän, they've given a twist to the traditional smorgasbord – a feast of buffet-style dishes – by adding the bounty of the sea to the luxurious spread.

The province of Bohuslän has a distinctive fishing culture, full of tall tales of hardy fishermen and howling storms. The area can have fierce winters, but is blessed with sizzling summers. Running the length of the west coast north of Gothenburg, right up to the Norwegian border, the province is replete with quietly picturesque fishing villages. Some 3,000 islands and 5,000 islets follow the line of the Bohuslän archipelago, and in summer many of the cosy settlements turn into lively seaside resorts. Pleasure boats line the harbours, and the cafés and restaurants open up their terraces along the seafront, serving the freshest of west coast cuisine. Many of the tiny islands just off the coast have old-fashioned fishermen's huts, some of which are now summer houses, perching on the gently sloping, pink-tinted granite cliffs. The air tingles with the smell of seaweed, smoked fish and pickled herrings.

The humble herring has been fished along the coastline of Bohuslän for centuries and no local smorgasbord would be complete without this little fish.

The smorgasbord – a buffet-style spread of mostly cold dishes – is said to date back to the mid-14th century, when the upper classes began offering guests a small side table of hors d'oeuvres to accompany the alcoholic schnapps, or *brännvin*, for which they had a penchant. Over the centuries these little appetizers, initially just bread, butter, some cheese and of course the occasional herring, went from plain and simple to increasingly lavish and elegant, moving from side table to main table, with all manner of dishes.

Today these colourful, abundant lunch buffets tend to have seasonal and regional twists, such as the emphasis on fresh fish and seafood in Bohuslän, where they often include "the Big Five" – lobster, oysters, prawns, crayfish and mussels. Most spreads include a variety of breads, from dark rye and crispbreads to flatbreads and seeded rolls, and plenty of pickled herrings in various sauces, from strong mustard to a subtle onion. Add a mix of salads, cold cuts, eggs, pies, potatoes and cheese, and the smorgasbord becomes a feast for the eye as well as the stomach, a rainbow of colours like the pretty painted houses of the wharves.

The Good Food Trail

Making all the difference to the culinary scene in the region, Taste of West Sweden has been highlighting the best of West Swedish food and produce for just over a decade. Member restaurants, food producers and farm shops all focus on locally sourced produce and fresh ingredients, from seafood and fish to game and dairy products, including many of the ingredients of a good smorgasbord. The 25 restaurants, traditional inns and old manor houses featured in the programme (*www.vastsverige.com*) offer the finest in dining experiences and many include a smorgasbord with Bohuslän's "Big Five". You can visit cheese-makers, dairies and even a brewery as part of the scheme. Kosters Trädgårdar (*www.kosterstradgardar.se*) on Sydkoster Island is a particular highlight in summer, when their herb garden and café are open.

Above The quayside restaurants of Fjallbacka, on the Bohuslän coast

The Best Places to Eat Smorgasbord

Salt & Sill moderate

Hotel and restaurant Salt & Sill sits prettily on the tiny island of Klädesholmen, one of the west coast's most scenic locations and famed for its herring trade – they even celebrate a "Day of the Herring". The chef serves up one of the best classic smorgasbords in the region and as the name – "Salt & Herring" – might suggest, there are a few delights of the sea included in the spread. On Sunday lunchtimes guests can pick and choose from the many nibbles lined up, with a particularly fine selection of herrings – there are 40 different types of preparation. In December, the smorgasbord turns into a *julbord*, a Christmas version that features traditional festive dishes such as Christmas ham and salted-cod *lutefisk*, as well as the year-round favourites – different types of bread, cold cuts, cheeses, pickled gherkins, beetroot salad, sausages, roe, mackerel and so much more. It's all traditionally washed down with strong spirits, such as aquavit, schnapps or *brännvin* (literally "firewine"), which certainly lives up to its name.

471 51 Klädesholmen, Tjörn; open from 5pm Fri, from 1pm Sat, & 1–5pm Sun for classical smorgasbord; www.saltosill.se

Also in Bohuslän

Lökeberga (*www.lokeberga.se; moderate*) is a family-run hotel and restaurant right by the sea, half an hour north of Gothenburg. It is renowned for its smorgasbord, which uses typical ingredients from Bohuslän, including seafood and goat's cheese. There is even a cake and dessert smorgasbord to sample if the main dishes don't fill you up.

Also in Sweden

Operakällaren's smorgasbord was legendary in its day and, after a 15-year break, it's back (*www.operakallaren.se; expensive*). Served in what is perhaps the best restaurant in Sweden, under cut-glass chandeliers in a listed Stockholm building, the lavish spread here rivals the finest of culinary experiences. Expect plump soused herring, gravadlax, smoked reindeer, meatballs and delicious side dishes from cheeses to pâtés. A true feast.

Around the World

Miss Maud (*www.missmaud.com.au; inexpensive*) opened as a Swedish hotel and restaurant in Perth, Australia, in 1971, offering a sumptuous smorgasbord at breakfast, lunch and dinner. Open 365 days a year, Miss Maud boasts Australia's only authentic Swedish smorgasbord, with a few Aussie favourites snuck in for good measure, such as Princess Cake and the eternal favourite: "pavlova downunder".

A Day in Seville

Capital of Andalusia for more than 800 years, Seville is southern Spain's seat of power and glory, and boasts magnificent palaces and churches. The city's grace and joy are expressed in sweet gardens, tiled patios and the catharsis of its signature flamenco, the *Sevillana*.

MORNING Begin with the wondrous **Real Alcázar** before touring the **Cathedral**, which holds the tomb of Columbus. Climb the ramps of **La Giralda** to survey the medieval maze of **Barrio Santa Cruz**, where whitewashed houses line narrow, cobbled streets and are interspersed with quaint tapas bars and centuries-old gardens.

AFTERNOON Visit the exquisite palace and gardens of **La Casa de Pilatos**. Don't miss the haunting paintings of saints by Zubarán in the **Museo de Bellas Artes**. Founded by a famous dancer, the **Museo del Baile Flamenco** charts the flowering of the art form.

EVENING Return to the **Museo del Baile Flamenco** if a dance performance is scheduled, or catch equally authentic flamenco music and dance at **Los Gallos**.

Essentials

GETTING THERE
Flights arrive into **Seville Airport**, 10 km (6 miles) from the city centre. **Buses** from the airport take 25 minutes and run every half-hour; **car rental** and **taxis** are available.

WHERE TO STAY
YH Giralda (inexpensive) squeezes intimate but cheerful rooms on three levels around a central courtyard in a former abbots' residence. *www.yh-hoteles.com*

La Hostería del Laurel (moderate) is a romantic and atmospheric old inn where *Don Juan* was written. *www.hosteriadellaurel.com*

Hotel EME Fusion (expensive) brings luxurious avant-garde designer sensibility to the plaza next to the cathedral. *www.emehotel.com*

TOURIST INFORMATION
Plaza de San Francisco; *www.turismo.sevilla.org*

Right Like a raw vegetable smoothie, gazpacho is often served chilled in glasses as a thirst-quenching starter

Below The Salon de los Embajadores (Hall of the Ambassadors) in the Real Alcázar

SEVILLE SPAIN

Cool Gazpacho in Sultry Seville

Seville became the most ornate city in Europe in the 16th century, when New World gold and silver sailed up the Guadalquivir river. The ships also brought culinary riches – tomatoes and bell peppers – which *Sevillanos* added to the ancient Roman soup of bread, garlic, salt, vinegar and olive oil to create gazpacho, the refreshing chilled soup often called "salad in a bowl".

Like its signature dish, the city of Seville melds layers of history and styles into a single unified masterpiece. The ceremonial tomb of the explorer Christopher Columbus, whose discoveries forever altered Seville, holds a place of honour inside the massive cathedral, where New World gold on the altars sends glints of light into the soaring darkness overhead. The cathedral was built on the site of the city's Arabic mosque; its glorious bell tower – the Giralda – was originally the minaret of Seville's great mosque, and the muezzin would ride on horseback up the ramped passage to its top to call the faithful to prayer.

Moorish and Christian pasts intermingle with ease in the city. The Muslim ruling family of the Almohads built the Torre de Oro on the Guadalquivir river in 1220, and three centuries later the Spaniards turned it into the custom house to count New World riches. Treasure barges no longer ply the river; these days cruise boats motor from the Arenal shipyards to the artful, harp-shaped bridge of Puente del Alamillo.

Gazpacho is also history in a bowl. When the Moors conquered Andalusia, they took the basic stale-bread soup introduced by the Roman legions and dressed it up with ground almonds and fresh grapes to create a white gazpacho still favoured in the coastal city of Málaga. But it was not until the conquistadors brought home the curious fruits of the Aztec and Inca empires — tomatoes and both sweet and piquant capsicum peppers — that something like modern gazpacho became the city's signature-bowl of cold-soup refreshment. The sharp snap of green bell peppers, raw garlic and onion brightens the unctuous blend of sweet tomatoes with faintly astringent but melon-like cucumbers and yeasty dried bread.

Contemporary chefs make gazpacho a blank canvas for painting with the flavours of fresh fruit, exotic nutmeats and a world of spices. Yet cool, red gazpacho remains the pride of Seville, best showcased in clear glass bowls. Each diner can season to taste with garnishes of toasted croutons, slivers of green onion, diced tomatoes, peppers and cucumber. Few dishes so quickly relieve a fevered brow.

Gazpacho Variants

Gazpacho has many traditional variants throughout Spain, most of which add either chopped ham or chopped hard-boiled egg as garnishes. But the Andalusian coastal region near Málaga clings to its Moorish dishes, including the white gazpacho that is a relic of an era before tomatoes and peppers entered the Spanish diet. **Ajo blanco con uvas** is based on ground almonds, garlic, bread and peeled grapes, and is served with croutons and grapes. The white gazpacho of Extremadura, known as **gazpacho Extremeño**, is a complex dish of egg, bread, garlic, bell pepper and cucumber that is then blended with a strained broth of simmered onion, parsnips, carrots, turnips and celery and liberally laced with vinegar and a dash of hot paprika. This richer version of gazpacho, served very cold, really soothes and nourishes.

Above Sara Baras demonstrates the traditional Andalusian dance of flamenco

The Best Places to Eat Gazpacho

Restaurante Sabina moderate

Long before the Slow Food movement made "local" the mantra of modern gastronomy, Sabina championed Andalusian products and culinary traditions. Many restaurants in Seville serve Andalusian fare, but Sabina specializes in the dishes of the countryside.

A classic gazpacho, almost sweet from the inclusion of extremely ripe tomatoes, makes the perfect starter, especially when accompanied by a glass of one of the acidic Macabeo white wines from the mountains northwest of the city. The restaurant is set in a former shipyard building about halfway between the cathedral and the bullring, and impresses with its high vaulted ceilings. Hearty main dishes kissed by the heat of its ovens excel; try braised pig's trotters, roasted leg of lamb larded with rosemary, stewed partridge, or a fulsome rendition of the Spanish standard, *rabo de toro* (oxtail stew). The wine list abounds with sturdy Rioja and Ribera del Duero reds, which are able to stand up to such rich fare, but if you're feeling curious, try a more unusual Tempranillo from the Sierras de Málaga.

Calle Dos de Mayo 4, Seville; open 1:30–4pm and 9pm–midnight Mon–Sat; +34 954 562 547

Also in Seville

The elegant Triana restaurant **Rio Grande** *(www.riogrande-sevilla.com; expensive)* is known mainly for its simply grilled fish, but the kitchen also makes a quintet of gazpachos in season, each tinted a different colour by their dominant vegetables. The venerable tavern of **El Rinconcillo** *(www.elrinconcillo.es; inexpensive)*, with its decoration of Feria and bullfight posters, is one of the oldest bars in Seville; celebrated as a tapas bar, it also serves a purely authentic *gazpacho Sevillano*.

Also in Spain

In Marbella, superchef Dani García plays with seasonal fruits and vegetables to make gazpachos based on everything from spring vegetables to wine grapes at **Calima** *(www.restaurantecalima.com; expensive)*. **Café de Paris** in Málaga *(www.rcafedeparis.com; inexpensive)* garnishes its *ajo blanco con uvas* with red wine granita. In Cácares, **El Figón de Eustaquio** *(+34 927 248 194; moderate)* showcases Extremaduran classics, including the white gazpacho.

Around the World

Centuries after Spain got tomatoes and peppers, gazpacho has returned to the Spanish-inflected American Southwest. In Santa Fe, New Mexico, **Inn at Loretto** *(www.innatloretto.com; moderate)* serves its chilled gazpacho with unusual but delicious avocado sorbet and lump crab meat.

Three Days in and around Capri

Stunningly beautiful views and spectacular sights are everywhere here, demanding to be admired from land, sea and mountaintop.

DAY ONE Take a morning **boat trip** around the island to see the cliffs and fantastic rock formations such as the **Faraglioni rock stacks**. If the tide is right, boatmen will row you into the splendid recesses of the **Blue Grotto**. An easy afternoon walk from Capri town leads to **Villa Jovis**, former holiday home of the Roman emperor Tiberius.

DAY TWO From **Anacapri** take the dizzying chairlift up **Monte Solaro** to the brilliant belvedere and café. Afterwards take the bus to the landmark **Faro lighthouse** and enjoy a swim at the small beach.

DAY THREE Make a full-day boat trip to the mainland, to **Sorrento** and around the peninsula to the spectacular **Amalfi Coast**. Here the pastel-coloured houses of **Positano** cascade down the mountainside to a beautiful bay. Surrounded by terraced lemon groves, **Amalfi** nestles at sea level, its majestic black-and-white chequered *duomo* dominating narrow alleyways dating back to Norman and Arab times.

Essentials

GETTING THERE
Fast **hydrofoils** and **ferries** from Naples and Sorrento run many times a day all year round. Once there, a **funicular** climbs to the town itself, and orange **buses** make the trip to Anacapri and around the island.

WHERE TO STAY
Pensione La Tosca (moderate) is a peaceful, welcoming little hotel with a beautiful terrace. *www.latoscahotel.com*
Villa Eva (moderate), just out of Anacapri, has a pretty garden, swimming pool and panoramic views from the terraces. *www.villaeva.com*
Hotel Tragara (expensive) is luxurious, with breathtaking views over the Faraglioni rock stacks. *www.hoteltragara.com*

TOURIST INFORMATION
Capri Harbour; *+39 81 837 0686*

Right The tempting *tricolore* of *insalata caprese*: ripe red tomatoes, pearly white mozzarella and fresh green basil

Below The town of Anacapri is watched over by a statue of Caesar Augustus, first of the Roman emperors

CAPRI ITALY

The Colours of Italy on Capri

Capri, the divinely picturesque island getaway in the Gulf of Naples in southern Italy, sums up *la dolce vita*. Well known to the ancient Romans, who built sumptuous imperial villas on its spectacular headlands, Capri also spells meal after memorable meal. Its simple but delicious summertime signature dish, *insalata caprese*, is now prepared the world over.

A surprisingly rugged mountainous island with sheer limestone cliffs rearing out of the crystal-clear Mediterranean, Capri has a remarkably temperate climate. Its pleasant winters suit the cultivation of citrus fruits, both lemons and sweet oranges. Hot summers tempered by sea breezes encourage grape vines that produce superb red and white wines. In the island's villages, charming houses are surrounded by gorgeous gardens that overflow with all manner of exotic plants, from palm trees to vividly coloured bougainvillea.

Picture-postcard Capri has attracted huge numbers of visitors for centuries, from fleets of day-trippers and cruise ship passengers to the international jet set and royalty. It was probably for the latter that the island's signature salad, with its three colours – red, white and green – of the Italian flag, was invented.

Insalata caprese is a simple spread of thick slices of fresh tomato alternated with mozzarella cheese. It is important that both the main ingredients be at room temperature, not straight from the fridge, so that their individual flavours are brought out. A little salt may be added to the tomato, but only just before serving to ensure it stays firm. Aromatic fresh basil with its strong oily perfume is a crucial addition, either as whole leaves or torn or chopped, depending on the school of thought, and the whole is given a light drizzle of extra-virgin olive oil. Sometimes oregano and olives are added for extra fragrance and flavour.

The dish was eulogized by the Italian Futurist movement of the early 20th century for its lightness and flavour, in contrast to the ubiquitous stodgy pasta they rejected as far too heavy for a modern diet in the industrial age. (Legend has it that Egypt's King Farouk, while holidaying on the island, managed to buck this healthy trend by having his *insalata caprese* served as the filling in his toasted sandwiches.) For a dish this light, fresh and simple to succeed, the ingredients must be of superb quality – especially the cheese. The finest mozzarella, made from buffalo milk, has to travel from the mainland region of Campania, just across the water. But few would disagree that *insalata caprese* tastes best of all on the lovely island on which it was invented.

What Else to Eat

With a bounty of fresh seasonal produce from land and sea, Capri and the Amalfi Coast have plenty for gourmet visitors. Order **ravioli alla caprese,** luscious rounds of pasta filled with moist *caciotta* cheese blended with egg, and dressed with a light sauce of tomato and herbs. Otherwise go for **gnocchi alla sorrentina,** tiny potato dumplings smothered in a smooth cheesy sauce with a hint of tomato. **Totani** are tender squid, which are stewed slowly and deliciously with potatoes. This part of Italy is famed for its lemons, which grow to gargantuan size, and on the dessert front, one landmark is **delizia al limone,** a heavenly frothy cream of lemon with egg white. A superb conclusion to any meal is a slender frosted glass of cold **Limoncello** liqueur, a delicious, tingly after-dinner drink made with lemon rind steeped in alcohol.

Above Water buffalo, whose milk is used to produce the finest mozzarella cheese

The Best Places to Eat Insalata Caprese

Ristorante Villa Verde expensive

Discreetly tucked out of the way down a quiet alleyway a short stroll from Capri's central Piazzetta, this smart restaurant has its fair share of suntanned VIP guests, whose photos adorn the walls of the entrance. A courtyard garden fringed by trees enables alfresco dining in candlelight. The *insalata caprese* comes on a vast white platter, with overlapping layers of luscious mozzarella, thickly cut, alongside piles of rich red tomato rounds. Giant dark green olives, whole basil leaves, a sprinkling of oregano and a splash of olive oil are the finishing touches. Similar high-quality ingredients are used for the restaurant's pizzas, baked in a wood-fired oven to guarantee that authentic smoky tang. Seafood also ranks high on the menu, with daily specials depending on availability. The fried *moscardini*, tender baby octopus, melt in your mouth. The bulging wine cellar is well stocked with bottles from the key regions of Italy as well as Spain and Australia.
Vico Sella Orto 6, Capri town; open noon–4pm & 7pm–1am daily; www.villaverde-capri.com

Also on Capri

Down narrow Via Lo Palazzo in Capri town centre, down-to-earth **Verginiello (+39 81 8370944; inexpensive)** bustles non-stop as laden waiters dash from the animated kitchen to the spacious, panoramic dining room. Excellent-value Neapolitan dishes include *linguine malafemmina*, with tomato, anchovies, capers and black olives, while fresh ingredients are showcased in salads such as the *caprese*.

Also in Italy

In Alberobello in Puglia, snug beneath the ancient stone arches and vaults of a 1700s olive press, **Ristorante Casanova (www. casanovailristorante.it; inexpensive)** makes good use of fresh mozzarella and its twin *burrata*, a similar but richer cheese. Both are served alongside salamis as antipasti. The typical local dishes feature fava beans and broccoli.

Rest of the World

Buffalo mozzarella sourced from an organic farm in the UK goes into the *insalata caprese* served at the **Ristorante Carpaccio** in London **(www.carpacciorestaurant.co.uk; moderate)**. The mouthwatering menu also offers a unique range of carpaccio, with ultra-thin slices of ox tongue, smoked duck and octopus, among others. The cuisine is basically Italian but with a creative twist, so the *frittura mista di pesce* (a platter of mixed, fried fish) comes with a sweet and sour condiment.

AMSTERDAM

AMSTERDAM NETHERLANDS

Rijsttafel Feasts in Amsterdam

Vast riches have flowed between Asia and Holland for hundreds of years, from the 17th-century heyday of the Dutch East India Company to 20th-century plantation wealth. As well as funding the canal-threaded elegance of cities like Amsterdam, this historic link has left a delicious edible legacy, *rijsttafel* – an assemblage of classic dishes inspired by traditional Indonesian feasts.

Holland is home to over 170 nationalities, but the most intriguing food influence is Indonesian. The Dutch dominated this vast Asian archipelago – home to evocative locations like Java, Bali and Sumatra – from the early 17th century, taking full political control of the "Dutch East Indies" from 1800 until its independence in 1945. Politics and palates were intimately linked, however, and Holland was forced to joust with rival nations for commercial control of spice treasures such as nutmeg and cloves.

Colonial leaders met – and ate – amid the ornate courtyards of opulent venues such as the long-gone Hotel des Indes in Batavia (now Jakarta). It was in places such as these that a new type of feast gained popularity in the early 20th century, bringing together favourite local dishes in a dazzling showcase of Indonesia's exotic flavours. Christened *rijsttafel* ("rice table"), it took inspiration from traditional Indonesian feasts such as *tumpeng*, where a mound of rice was flanked by dishes forming a taste symphony of spicy, sweet, sour and salty. Classics included in the Dutch feast were *teri kacang* (tiny dried fish fried with peanuts), *telur pindang* (marbled boiled eggs), sweet dry-fried *tempeh* (a tofu-like soybean cake) and *sambal goreng ati* (liver in chilli sauce). The dishes were Indonesian but the combination was Dutch, and today's *rijsttafel* – consisting of 12 to 30 little dishes – is found mainly in Amsterdam and The Hague. Restaurants offering this delicious feast range from small, unadorned backstreet hangouts to upmarket foodie shrines that still nod to the ambitions of the old Indonesian chefs, who were renowned for trying to out-do one another with the quality and inventiveness of their dishes.

Amsterdam's Tropenmuseum is a fascinating place to visit for a colourful overview of Indonesia's influence on Holland over the past 350 years. Nearby, the Eastern Docklands showcase the city's contemporary style – old, run-down quays have been transformed with 21st-century modernism to provide a striking contrast to the cobbled lanes and historic façades of the more traditional old town centre. The old docks also offer another island called Java, though this one is home to modern design shops and cutting-edge architecture rather than exotic food and valuable spices.

Above Amsterdam is a wonderful place to walk or cycle around; its colourful streets hide a plenitude of laid-back cafés and multicultural restaurants

What Else to Eat

Cheese is Dutch gold. **Edam**, a low-fat delight, is named after a beautiful 12th-century town on the shores of the Ijsselmeer inland sea. Another charming medieval town gave its name to Holland's other famous cheese – **Gouda** – which is still sold in giant wheels on the cobbled main square; choose between sweeter *jong* ("young") or more pungent *oud* ("old"). Salty **raw herring** is a unique Dutch classic. Try it on its own (dangle by the tail and slip it into your mouth) or stuffed with onions in a roll. The perfect way to wash down the herring is with **genever**, a Dutch predecessor to gin. Also good on its own, you can enjoy a lip-smacking blast of this Netherlands gem in one of Amsterdam's cosy vintage genever bars, such as De Drie Fleschjes on Gravenstraat or Oloofspoort on Nieuwebrugsteeg.

Three Days in and around Amsterdam

Short distances and fast trains make it easy to discover how much more there is to Holland beyond Amsterdam's atmospheric canal-laced beauty.

DAY ONE In Amsterdam, reflect on artistic genius at the **Van Gogh Museum** and the **Rijksmuseum**, which houses works by Rembrandt. You can then visit his former home, the **Rembrandt House Museum**, or that of another much-loved Amsterdam inhabitant, **Anne Frank**. Then dive into the galleries, boutiques and bars of the charming **Jordaan** area, or its neighbour, the multicultural **De Pijp**.

DAY TWO Combine culture and coast in Holland's capital, **The Hague**, where you can see Old Masters at the 17th-century **Mauritshuis**, discover Mondrian at the **Gemeentemuseum**, then sniff sea air amid the dunes at **Scheveningen** or hop on tram 1 for a 20-minute ride to lovely **Delft** for an afternoon on its historic tiles.

DAY THREE Visit **Utrecht** to climb **Domtoren**, Holland's tallest and oldest church tower, and visit **De Haar**, a restored medieval castle. The city also has Europe's only **Aboriginal Art Museum** and is home to the iconic Rietveld–Schröder House, a modernist home designed by Gerhardt Rietveld and Truus Schröder in the 1920s.

ESSENTIALS

GETTING THERE
Amsterdam's large international **airport**, Schipol, is 15 minutes by **train** from central Amsterdam. There are also **shuttle buses** from the airport to around 100 of the city's hotels.

WHERE TO STAY
Citizen M (inexpensive) is an exciting modern hotel with great facilities at an affordable price. www.citizenmamsterdamcity.com
The Convent Hotel (moderate) is a central, 4-star hotel carved from two medieval monasteries. www.accorhotels.com
Hotel Pulitzer (expensive) offers canalside luxury in a row of 17th- and 18th-century houses in the Old Quarter. www.pulitzeramsterdam.com

TOURIST INFORMATION
www.iamsterdam.com/en

The Best Places to Eat Rijsttafel

Blue Pepper expensive

Amsterdam's Blue Pepper adds *haute* modern touches to the abundance of *rijsttafel*. Executive chef Sonja Pereira's interpretation of classic *rijsttafel* keeps the number of dishes down while adding flavours to maintain diversity of taste. Zesty additions to the traditional array include salads such as *salada asinan segar* (crab, mango and pineapple with tamarind) and *salada bebek* (roasted duck with green turmeric leaves), while clever reinventions include grilled fish pâté in place of dried fish, or lime and soy replacing peanuts in a lamb satay sauce. Dutch shrimps add a local presence to spicy green beans.

A more contemporary influence permeates the alternative Indonesian menu overseen by Pereira's colleague Tani Morabe. Shaped by modern Indonesia's vibrant culinary interactions with its Southeastern Asian neighbours, spicy chicken soup mingles with glass noodles and floating quail eggs, while grated coconut gives an East Indies tinge to wok-fried vegetables. "Indonesian cooking at its summit" raved one Dutch critic, and many would agree.

Nassaukade 366, Amsterdam; open 6–10pm Wed–Mon; www.restaurantbluepepper.com

Also in Amsterdam

In the Eastern Canal district, restaurants line Utrechtsestraat, including the **Tempo Doeloe** *(www.tempodoeloerestaurant.nl; moderate)*, a well-regarded eatery that offers an air of restrained privacy along with attention to detail. It serves three different sizes of *rijsttafel*, from 15 to 25 dishes. Those on a budget should head for **Bojo** *(www.bojo.nl; inexpensive)* on Lange Leidsedwarsstraat, where huge portions don't mean compromising on quality and its late hours make it a boon for night owls.

Also in the Netherlands

In The Hague, two places stand out: **Garoeda** *(www.garoeda.nl; moderate)*, which was opened by Indonesians resettling after independence in 1949; and **Raffles** *(www. restaurantraffles.com; expensive)*, which sits amid Archipel's beautiful streets and boasts an interior based on the Javan house of the owner's grandparents.

Around the World

The opulent **Oasis Restaurant** *(www.oasis-restaurant.co.id; expensive)* in Jakarta is one of the few places in Indonesia that now serves *rijsttafel*. This two-storey mansion was built in 1928 as the private home of Dutch millionaire F Brandenburg van Oltsende – who, in true colonial style, made his fortune from plantations of tea, rubber and cinchona (a quinine-rich tree). Enjoy your "rice feast" here in grand style, served by up to 15 waiting staff.

Above Modern Dutch restaurants, such as Amsterdam's Blue Pepper (pictured), offer innovative versions of classic Indonesian dishes

Left *Rijsttafel* today consists of 12–30 dishes; in the 1920s the Hotel des Indes in Batavia (now northern Jakarta) served 60 different dishes

A Day in Evora

Evora is the single most interesting destination in the Alentejo and it's also convenient for the nearby carpet-making town of Arraiolos and the elegant "marble towns" of Estremoz, Borba and Vila Viçosa.

MORNING Visit the daily **Mercado Municipal** (municipal market) for Alentejan produce, but if possible, also go to the even more impressive open-air market held in Rossio square on the first Tuesday of the month. In the old town, don't miss the majestic **Sé** – the largest medieval cathedral in Portugal – or the Corinthian **Templo Romano** just a short walk away.

AFTERNOON Cafés line the central square, **Praça do Giraldo**, and after coffee and cakes, you can stroll to **São Francisco** church to see its macabre **Capela dos Ossos**, a chapel lined with the skulls and bones of former monks. The pretty public gardens lie beyond.

EVENING Watch the sun set from the outdoor café by the **Templo Romano** before investigating the traditional taverns and local restaurants hidden in the city's medieval alleys.

Essentials

GETTING THERE
From **Lisbon international airport** it's a 90-minute drive east to **Evora**. If you don't want to hire a car, there are direct **buses** and **trains** from Lisbon city centre.

WHERE TO STAY
Residencial Policarpo (inexpensive) is a charming if modest *pension* in a 16th-century manor house. *www.pensaopolicarpo.com*
Albergaria do Calvário (moderate) has boutique-style rooms in a former olive-oil mill. *www.albergariadocalvario.com*
Pousada de Evora – Lóios (expensive) is an elegant hotel in an ancient convent building, situated next to the Templo Romano in the centre of town. *www.pousadas.pt*

TOURIST INFORMATION
Praça do Giraldo 73; +351 266 777 071

Right The black pigs of the Alentejo wander the region's oak forests, grazing freely on acorns

Below The view from Estremoz – the largest of the "marble towns" – over the plains of Upper Alentejo

Porco à Alentejana in Portugal

The Alentejo region, a vast area between Lisbon, the Tagus river and the Algarve coast, is Portugal's agricultural heart – a giant patchwork of olive and wine estates, wheat and corn fields, rooting pigs and grazing cattle. The regional cuisine is typically rustic, and boasts one of Portugal's best-loved dishes, the unusual meat-and-shellfish combination of *porco à alentejana*.

Any journey from Lisbon to the Algarve cuts right through the dramatic rural landscapes of the Alentejo, which has been the "bread-basket" of Portugal since Roman times. It's a land of burning summers and freezing winters, where a string of walled, medieval hill towns in the north gives way to endless, rolling plains that characterize much of the region.

In Baixo (Lower) Alentejo, quiet country roads run past shady stands of cork trees, isolated farmsteads, storks nesting on posts, and mile after sprawling mile of olive groves and vineyards. Among the few towns there's occasionally a magnificent surprise, like the so-called "marble towns" of Alto (Upper) Alentejo, whose buildings, roads and monuments are all constructed from the same locally quarried pale stone. But there's only really one must-see historic destination in the region: the northern city of Evora, which boasts a stunning Roman and Moorish legacy, a fascinating tangle of late-medieval alleys, and a famous monthly open-air market showcasing local crafts and produce.

In such a rural area, it's hardly surprising that the local cuisine relies heavily on hearty peasant produce. Corn bread is used in many traditional recipes, crumbled into thick soups with fresh, aromatic coriander (these dishes are known as *açordas*) or soaked, mashed and fried with spicy sausage and paprika *(migas)*. Sheep's cheese from the walled market town of Serpa is highly prized, while pork from the acorn-fed Alentejo *porco preto* (black pig) is fêted for its rich flavour.

It's loin of Alentejo pork that's at the heart of the one truly outstanding regional dish, *porco à alentejana*, which uses cubes of this fine meat marinated in a mix of white wine, garlic, paprika and bay leaves. The twist in the recipe comes with the addition of clams, a surprising ingredient in a largely landlocked region, but explained by the ease with which (in pre-refrigeration times) shellfish could be transported from the coast and kept alive in buckets or trays until needed. Add coriander, fried potatoes and sometimes a helping of pickled vegetables, and you have a distinctive taste combination that has seduced the entire country.

Above *Porco à alentejana* is a favourite in both cafés and high-end restaurants

---

Alentejo Wines

The Alentejo is one of Portugal's best-regarded wine-producing regions, especially for reds. There is a long history of wine making here, especially around the towns of **Borba, Reguengos, Redondo** and **Evora**, but it's only since the 1980s that Alentejo wine has gained an international reputation — in particular since many Alentejo vineyards started producing gutsy modern wines in a "New World" style (some even have Australian wine makers on board). **Herdade do Esporão** (*www.esporao.com*) produces the Esporão Reserva, Monte Velho and Alandra wines you'll find in restaurants and shops across the country, and offers tastings and wine courses. In Evora, there's a visitor centre that provides information about all the winery tours along the Alentejo wine route (Rota dos Vinhos do Alentejo; *www.vinhosdoalentejo.pt*).

The Best Places to Eat
Porco à Alentejana

O Fialho (expensive)

O Fialho is the best place to sample Alentejan *cozinha típica* (regional cuisine) in Evora. Loved by locals for its easygoing charm, and considered a find by in-the-know visitors, the restaurant has been in the safe hands of the Fialho family since the late 1940s. It's a cosy and comfortable place to dine, with locally sourced ingredients and produce – cheese, olives, cured meats, seasonal vegetables, Alentejo pork and game – at the heart of a typically rustic menu that demands a large appetite. While you might choose a hearty meal-in-itself soup, an unusual rice dish (with shredded hare, for example) or roast mountain lamb, this is undoubtedly the place to find out what *porco à alentejana* is all about. O Fialho serves a classy version of this classic dish, but even this more refined serving proves too large for many people — much to the disappointment of the restaurant staff, who offer an array of rich and creamy Portuguese desserts to follow.

Travessa das Mascarenhas 16, Evora; open 12:30–3:30pm and 7:30pm–midnight Tue–Sun; www.restaurantefialho.com

Also in the Alentejo Region

The road east from Evora to Spain passes through the attractive border town of Elvas, where **Restaurante O Lagar** (*www.restauranteolagar.com.sapo.pt; inexpensive*), sited in a former olive-oil mill, is an excellent choice for *porco à alentejana* and other local dishes. In historic Beja, the capital of Baixo Alentejo, there's fine regional dining in the garden restaurant of the **Pousada de Beja** (*www.pousadas.pt; expensive*), a splendid hotel fashioned from the former São Francisco convent.

Also in Portugal

The best place for Alentejan dishes in Lisbon, the Portuguese capital, is **Casa do Alentejo** (*www.casadoalentejo.pt; moderate*), an Alentejan cultural centre and restaurant with a palatial courtyard and impressive tiled dining room. *Borrego* (lamb) is also an Alentejan speciality, and the menu offers grilled *costeletas* (chops) served with rice as well as a typical lamb *ensopado*, a soupy, stew-like dish.

Around the World

It's rare to find the specific combination of pork and clams anywhere other than in a Portuguese restaurant, although the northeastern Catalonia region of neighbouring Spain has a chicken-and-shrimp dish that mixes meat and shellfish in a similar fashion. To sample a true *porco à alentejana* in unexpected surroundings, visit the former Portuguese colony of Macau (now in China), where a score or more restaurants offer authentic Portuguese dishes. **Restaurante Litoral** (*www.restaurante-litoral.com; moderate)* has a loyal local following.

MARSEILLE FRANCE

Fishy Feast in the South of France

Marseille may not be pretty in a traditional Provençal way, but France's oldest city is not short of appeal. Marseille's charm lies in its multicultural, Mediterranean vibe, charismatic scruffiness and that most famous of all Marseille dishes, bouillabaisse – a rich, briny boil-up of the morning's catch fresh from the port, fragrant, silky and golden-glistening in the luminous sunshine.

Bouillabaisse was originally a fishermen's stew – the unsold catch of, usually, the smallest and most unprepossessing fish, cooked up in a pot of bubbling water on the beach. Today it is a more sumptuous dish, enriched with butter and saffron, much more in keeping with the recipe's origins in legend – concocted by Venus to lull her husband Vulcan to sleep so she could have some fun with Mars. Lots of variations exist in Provence, but Marseille lays claim to the best: a jamboree of local fish and shellfish, olive oil, onions, garlic, fennel, tomatoes, potatoes, parsley and the golden ingredient, saffron. The city even has an official Charter of Bouillabaisse listing the ingredients that "must" be used in the dish, including a minimum of four fish from a choice of red mullet, John Dory, *rascasse* (scorpion fish), monkfish and conger eel.

Small, bony rockfish and *rascasse* provide the base for the broth, which is reduced and concentrated – the word bouillabaisse probably derives from *bouille abaisse*, or "boil and reduce" – until it's as pungent as Davy Jones's locker. The soup is served first, bobbing with, traditionally, a single large crouton daubed with lip-smacking, garlicky *rouille* – a ruddy mayonnaise

spiked with chilli – followed separately by a heaped platter of fish that have been simmered in the broth.

The fish is landed daily at the Vieux Port (old port), where fishermen have been selling their catch for 350 years. Marseille today may be a huge, modern city – multi-ethnic, football-crazy, and with one of the most hair-raising traffic systems in France – but it's rich in history, as vibrant and eclectic as its signature dish. Not for nothing was it voted European Capital of Culture 2013. Painted by Cézanne, Renoir and Dufy, it is the home of the Château d'If, where Alexandre Dumas's *Count of Monte Cristo* was imprisoned, and of architect Le Corbusier's seminal Unité d'Habitation.

Rising up behind the Vieux Port, Le Panier is the oldest part of the city, a hub of narrow streets and steps with pale candy-coloured houses and a cosmopolitan mood thanks to decades of immigration. Nearby is the souk-like Marché des Capucins, a North African-flavoured market piled with exotic produce and pastries. On the other side of the harbour, surveying the designer hotels, lounge bars, cool galleries and boutiques that have sprung up below, sits Marseille's "Good Mother" – the magnificent, Byzantine church of Notre Dame de la Garde, keeping watch over a city that gave France one of its most classic recipes.

A Day in Marseille

A modern city with 26 centuries of cultural heritage and, at its heart, a fishing village atmosphere, come together to make Marseille a compelling destination.

MORNING Set off from **Fort St Jean** and meander the winding streets of **Le Panier**, stopping to check out local archaeological finds at **La Vielle Charité**. Once a poorhouse, it's now crammed with priceless ancient artifacts. Drop into Marseille's answer to Istanbul's Haghia Sophia, the huge **Cathédrale de la Major**.

AFTERNOON Contrast old and new at **La Joliette** docks, where the Euroméditerranée Project is making bold architectural statements, including the shimmering, 148-m (485-ft) **CMA-CGM Tower** designed by Zaha Hadid. If fashion is more your passion, peruse the collection of 20th-century clothes and accessories in the **Musée de la Mode**.

EVENING Climb up to **Notre Dame de la Garde** to take in a sweeping, 360° city view. Meander back to the **Vieux Port**, grab a seat on the terrace of a quayside bar, order a tall pastis and watch the sun fade before dinner.

Essentials

GETTING THERE
Shuttle buses and taxis run from Marseille's **international airport** to the city. **Trains** link to most of France and beyond, with **bus** services to Provençal towns, including Nice.

WHERE TO STAY
Hôtel Le Corbusier (inexpensive): perfect for 1950s design fans. *www.hotellecorbusier.com*
Casa Honoré (moderate): a tiny boutique hotel steps from the Old Port. *www.casahonore.com*
Le Petit-Nice Passédat (expensive): a fabulous family-run villa. *www.petitnice-passedat.com*

TOURIST INFORMATION
www.marseille-tourisme.com

The Best Places to Eat Bouillabaisse

Le Petit Nice expensive

Gérald Passédat's three-star Michelin eatery sits on an idyllic rocky point surveying the blue, blue Mediterranean. The chef is so attached to his surroundings and Marseille's culinary heritage that he's devoted an entire tasting menu to bouillabaisse. It's an extravagantly poetic, and expensive, version of the original, inspired by Passédat's childhood memories – he was born on this very spot. His dedication to achieving the most intense, authentic flavours begins with the fish stock, boiling down live rock crabs and an assembly of small rockfish (it takes some 3 kg of fresh fish to make a litre of stock) to fashion the fragrant base of the dish. The bouillabaisse menu is then served in three courses, kicking off with a mussel and clam carpaccio with fried strips of *girelle* (rainbow wrasse), followed by the catch of the day, perfectly cooked in a sea-spiked artichoke broth. Then comes the soup: red scorpion fish, sea bream and potatoes in a saffron-rich broth, with *rouille*, of course.

Anse de Maldormé, Corniche JF Kennedy; open for lunch and dinner Tue–Sat (open Mon evening in July and August); www.petitnice-passedat.com

Also in Marseille

The lovely setting of **L'Epuisette** *(www.l-epuisette.com; expensive)* alone makes it worth a visit. Luckily, the bouillabaisse cooked up by Guillaume Sourrieu is just as impressive. Perched on the jetty in the tiny cove of Vallon des Auffes, this is an impossibly perfect spot for a plate of de luxe fish soup and a platter of squeaky fresh monkfish, red scorpion fish, John Dory, conger eel (all Bouillabaisse Charter-sanctioned) and waxy yellow potatoes, infused with the perkiest saffron broth around.

Also in France

Fittingly, it's a former fisherman's hut that's home to St Tropez's top seafood soup. **Chez Camille** *(www.chezcamille.fr; moderate)*, perched at one end of the bay of Pampelonne, has been dishing up simple seafood since it was mistaken for a beach bistro back in the '50s by director Roger Vadim and his then wife, Brigitte Bardot. Locals claim it serves up one of the best bouillabaisses on the Riviera.

Around the World

Whatever the weather in London, you can get a taste of sunshine at **Bistro Bruno Loubet** at the Zetter Hotel *(www.bistrotbrunoloubet.com; moderate)*. Ex-Michelin-star chef Bruno Loubet cooks up affordable French food, from rustic favourites like the bouillabaisse with *rouille* and croutons to classics with a modern bent, such as duck *confit* with honey and North African spice.

Above A classic bouillabaisse in the Marseille style, with the broth and the fish, garnished with lemon and herbs, served separately

Left Seagulls wheel hopefully above a fisherman selling his catch on the Quai des Belges, Marseille's exuberant fish market

Above Boats moored in the Vieux Port, with the basilica of Notre Dame de la Garde reaching into the sky in the background

What Else to Eat

Pizza is big in Marseille, and even the pizza vans that dot the city dish up a mean crust. Best of all are the thin-crusted, wood-fired pizzas from Le Panier restaurant **Chez Etienne** *(43 rue de Lorette, no telephone)*. For North African delights, find delicious couscous, tagines and pastries from boisterous Algerian canteen **Sur le Pouce** *(+33 4 9156 1328)*, near the Marché des Capucins. The weird and wonderful chocolates made by the Le Ray family at their shop, **La Chocolatière du Panier** *(+33 4 9155 7041)*, are also unmissable: try black cherry, ginger, lavender, basil, lime and coriander, and even onion paired with chocolate.

NUREMBERG GERMANY

Franconia's Mini-Bratwurst

Nuremberg is a small city with a big history. The unofficial capital of the Holy Roman Empire, it was a powerful trade centre in the Middle Ages and the cultural heart of the German Renaissance in the 15th century. The modern city is no less energetic; it heads up the pretty Franconian region, where wine competes with beer and the local sausages are delicious little bratwurst.

Probably invented by Chinese butchers in the 6th century BC, sausages began as an efficient way of using edible meat scraps. With the addition of herbs and spices they quickly became popular enough for the idea to spread west, giving the ancient Greeks and Romans the chance to really popularize them. In medieval times the Germans made them into a culinary art form, inventing around 1,200 different types, most of which were smoked, dried or pre-cooked. But in the early 15th century cooks in the Nuremberg region invented the most popular German sausage, bratwurst – a fresh sausage that was designed to be cooked.

Central Nuremberg looks like a city frozen in time, from much the same era. It lost most of its medieval glories in the bombing of World War II, but some survive in the old town, where crooked half-timbered houses and surviving city walls hug twisting alleys and tight cobbled streets. A large part of enjoying the town is simply strolling around and soaking in the atmosphere. The Hauptmarkt, its bustling focal square, is often filled with colourful market stalls and is overlooked by the Frauenkirch, a beautiful Gothic church. The next square to the north, the Rathausplatz, is equally attractive, thanks partly to the presence of the town hall and the 13th-century St Sebald church, with its impressive bronze Gothic shrine. But the city's most magnificent single sight is its Kaiserburg (known locally as "The Burg"), the city's huge medieval castle, which took 400 years to complete and whose position above the old town provides impressive views over its red-roofed core.

Eating out in Nuremberg is a treat. Franconian fare is hearty and filling, and often served with the very good local wines. But beer goes best with wurst, and the wurst here is some of the finest in Germany. The *Nürnberger Rostbratwurst* was standardized by town council decree in 1497; each sausage must be 7–9 cm (3 inches) long and 25 g (0.8 oz) in weight. This was probably due to the high prices of meat at the time, but it turned out to be as important to the sausage as its ingredients. It makes for a large surface area around the marjoram-and-caraway-flavoured pork, and the crispy outer skin readily absorbs the traditional beech-wood fire aromas. The tangy flavours beg for mouthwateringly sharp German mustards, so the other natural accompaniment is something mild and forgiving, such as potato salad or sauerkraut. But the little sausages seem to taste best served three abreast on a warm bun, as comfort food on a cold day.

A Day in Nuremberg

Bombs obliterated Nuremberg's heart in World War II, but meticulous rebuilding since has reproduced the original, charming medieval core, ideal for enjoyable wandering.

MORNING Get a feel for the lively city centre at the **Hauptmarkt**, the focal market square, before taking in the attractive venerable buildings around the neighbouring square of **Rathausplatz**. Then climb steadily on narrow cobbled streets north to the **Kaiserburg** to view its imperial living quarters and the old town from above.

AFTERNOON Cross Nuremberg's walled core to explore the city's two best museums on its southern side. Choose from stimulating your mind with the contemporary art of the **Neues Museum** or getting a better grip on German history in the **Germanisches Nationalmuseum**, which has many intriguing artifacts, including the world's first globe.

EVENING Head to a **beer hall** such as the Barfüsser Hausbrauerei (Hallplatz 2) to absorb the traditional atmosphere of a vast cellar where you can enjoy handcrafted blond and dark German beers and *Bierbrand*, a schnapps made of beer.

Essentials

GETTING THERE
Nuremberg's international **airport** is 7 km (4 miles) from the city and has an underground train to the centre. There are **buses** and direct **rail** connections to many European cities.

WHERE TO STAY
Elch (inexpensive) offers simple lodgings in a 14th-century house. *www.hotel-elch.de*
Dürer Haus (moderate) has bright and airy rooms near the castle. *www.duerer-hotel.de*
Le Méridien Grand (expensive) is a premier hotel with sleek styling. *www.lemeridien.com*

TOURIST INFORMATION
www.nuernberg.de

Above *Nürnberger Rostbratwürste* are a favourite from the market stalls in the city, where they're sold *Drei im Weckla* ("three in a bun")

Left Most visitors choose to stay in the Altstadt ("Old Town"), close to the main square of the Hauptmarkt and the Frauenkirche.

Below The mini-bratwurst are often served with tangy sauerkraut and pretzel or rye bread and hot mustard

Sausages Around the World

The Nurembergers of Germany's Franconia region may lay claim to having invented the bratwurst, but a love of grilled sausage has long-since spread throughout much of the Western world. Over time, many nations have developed unique and delicious twists that rival even the age-old recipes of Germany.

NUREMBERG

Bratwurst Herzle inexpensive
Brunnengasse 11; www.bratwurstherzle.de
This old-fashioned and down-to-earth little place, tucked away in a central old town alley, has served the perfect Nuremberg mini-sausages and sauerkraut since 1529. It's always so busy that most diners have to share a table.

Nassauer Keller inexpensive
Karolinenstrasse 2; +49 911 225 967
Worth visiting for the atmospheric medieval cellar dining experience alone, this restaurant is based in one of the only surviving medieval tower houses. It specializes in Franconian cuisine, such as *Schweineschäufele* (roast pork shoulder) and serves several types of sausages, including "original Nuremberg sausages".

Bratwurst-Häusle moderate
Rathausplatz 1, 90403; +49 911 227 695
This tiny historic restaurant in the shadows of St Sebald church is so well known and touristy that it's often too packed for its own good. Yet it remains a great place to pick up bratwurst to go along with jars of cured or smoked sausages as gifts.

Bratwurstglöcklein expensive
Waffenhof 5; +49 911 227 625
This is the oldest bratwurst restaurant in Nuremberg, dating back to 1313, and its half-dozen set menus strive to create an interesting Franconian meal. They include dishes such as dumpling soup, pork knuckle, Nuremberg sausages that have been simmered with onions and vinegar before grilling, wine sauerkraut, home-made potato salad with a creamy horseradish sauce, and *O´batzder,* a rich local cheese dip made with Camembert and served with pretzels.

ERFURT, GERMANY

The German state of Thüringia also claims to have invented bratwurst. The city is certainly sausage-mad: every adult here consumes an average of two 15–20 cm (6–7 inch) bratwursts every day, and Thüringian sausage has become the German standard.

Faustfood inexpensive
Waagegasse 1; www.faustfood.de
A minimalist grilled meat and sausage eatery with modern interiors; you can sit at chunky wooden tables or perch at the busy counter to enjoy a quick barbecued *Thüringer Rostbratwurst.*

Wirtshaus Christoffel inexpensive
Michaelisstrasse 41; +49 361 2626 943
This medieval-themed restaurant has been serving its speciality sausage with bread and broth continuously since 1477.

Zum Wenigemarkt moderate
Wenigemarkt 13; www.wenigemarkt-13.de
Popular for alfresco eating in summer, this cosy restaurant excels at traditional Thüringian cuisine. It serves an especially crispy *Rostbratwurst* with fried potatoes and sauerkraut laced with bacon flakes.

BERLIN, GERMANY

A city that is always on the go is reliant on a good supply of snacks, and in Berlin this means sausages, especially "currywurst"– chopped sausage smothered in tomato sauce mixed with curry powder.

Curry 195 inexpensive
Kurfürstendamm 195, Berlin; +49 030 881 8942
A neon-lit sausage eatery known as much for its excellent juicy currywurst sausages as its popularity with German celebrities – which explains the Champagne on the menu.

Konnopke's Imbiss inexpensive
Schönhauser Allee 44a; www.konnopke-imbiss.de
Berlin's most famous sausage kiosk sits beneath noisy elevated train tracks. It has survived the Nazis, World War II and the privations of East Germany to continue to dole out some of the city's best currywurst: marvellously juicy, served with crispy chips and sprinkled with paprika.

Left (top to bottom) An alfresco lunch at Zum Wenigemarkt in Erfurt; a Thuringian sausage hot from a charcoal grill; traditional Berlin currywurst from the famous Konnopke's kiosk

Below (top to bottom) *Boerewors* cooking on the barbecue at Lyhala Game Reserve, South Africa; coiled English Cumberland sausage, one of the Lake District's meaty treats

Fleischerei moderate
Torstrasse 116–118; www.fleischerei-berlin.com
A place to actually sit and eat currywurst is a rarity in Berlin, which would give this central restaurant with its simple and functional decor an edge even if its wurst wasn't so good.

THE LAKE DISTRICT, UK
Cumbria's contribution to sausage culture is peppery and made of chopped meat, rather than minced, giving it a real chunkiness. Its greatest characteristic is its huge length, forming a great wheel on the plate.

Mason's Arms moderate
Cartmel Fell, Grange-over-Sands, Cumbria; www.masonsarmsstrawberrybank.co.uk
High-quality local food and a great selection of local ales make this fellside inn stand out. Its Cumberland sausage embarks on a successful European adventure on a toasted ciabatta, with caramelized onions, damson chutney and thin chips.

The Yanwath Gate Inn moderate
Yanwath, Cumbria; www.yanwathgate.com
A quintessential northern English country pub, this old inn dates back to 1683. Its chunky and peppery Cumberland sausage comes with home-made black pudding, mashed potato, broccoli, carrots and gravy.

SOUTH AFRICA
The South African *boerewors*, or "farmer's sausage", is a spicy national signature dish. It's made largely from beef seasoned with coriander and is always barbecued on a braai.

Wandie's Place inexpensive
618 Makhalemele St, Dube, Soweto, Johannesburg; www.wandies.co.za
An unpretentious eatery with long tables, colourful tablecloths, bustle and sociable chatter that started life as a *shebeen*, or illicit bar. It now specializes in a Soweto-style festive buffet including dishes such as mutton curry, beef *potjie* (a stew), *pap* (a porridge), *umqushu* (corn and bean stew), *ting* (soft porridge) and of course *boerewors*, served both fresh from the barbecue and dried as *wors*.

Karoo Cattle and Land moderate
Irene Village Mall, Irene, Pretoria; www.karoocattleandland.com
A great South African steakhouse that claims its *boerewors* would be the pride of any *karoo tannie* (local elderly aunt), which seems at odds with the

cosmopolitan black leather, chrome and glass decor. But the mix is so successful that the restaurant has opened half a dozen branches.

Karibu expensive
Shop 156, The Wharf Centre, V&A Waterfront, Cape Town; www.kariburestaurant.co.za
Views of Table Mountain and the tranquil blue Atlantic prepare the palate perfectly for the restaurant's vibrant South African flavours. The chefs here are experts in barbecuing *boerewors* over open coals, then serving them with local breads such as *Kaapse broodjie*, or with *putu* and *chakalaka* (porridge and relish).

WISCONSIN, USA
Wisconsin's many German immigrants have developed old recipes to create their own signature "brats", such as poaching them in beer before grilling, part-filling them with cheddar or lacing them with chilli, Cajun style.

Charcoal Inn South inexpensive
1313 South 8th Street, Sheboygan; +1 920 458 6988
South Sheboygan's annual bratwurst festival is the big Wisconsin draw for sausage lovers, but when it's not on, the Charcoal Inn is the place to head to. The must-order meal here is a double brat with the works: two sausages in a bun with pickles, mustard and raw onions, with butter oozing out on every side. As in Germany, the key to its great taste is the flavour of heavy spices unlocked by a smoky charcoal fire and superb traditional bread rolls with thin, crispy crusts and soft centres.

Milwaukee Brat House moderate
1013 3rd Street Milwaukee; www.milwaukeebrathouse.com
Though it only opened in 2008, this sausage specialist already has a cult following. Its late-19th-century brick town-house home, with stained glass, long dark-wood bar and historic photos of Milwaukee, is the perfect backdrop for great brats from Fred Usinger's excellent butcher's shop opposite the bar.

Water Street Brewery moderate
1101 N Water St, Milwaukee; www.waterstreetbrewery.com
Milwaukee has the only baseball stadium in the USA where bratwurst outsells hot dogs; many of its pubs and bars are mad keen on it too. This microbrewery, with its brick warehouse interiors, adds its own signature by simmering its bratwurst in beer and mixed spices prior to grilling.

Above Plaza Mayor, Madrid's principal square, abounds in historic buildings and pavement restaurants

A Day in Madrid

When Madrid became the capital in 1561, Spain's monarchs went to work transforming the sleepy regional city into the gleaming seat of the crown. From monumental plazas to broad boulevards, and masterpieces of Spanish art to elegant garden parks, their legacies remain some of the most engaging sights of the city.

MORNING View wondrous renditions of the royal family by Diego Velázquez in the **Museo del Prado** – created when the crown transferred much of its collection to this public museum. Then stroll the gardens of the **Parque del Buen Retiro**, once a royal retreat.

AFTERNOON Rimmed with cafés and restaurants, **Plaza Mayor** has been Madrid's central gathering spot since it was completed in 1619. Leave this bustling realm of the people to spend hours getting a glimpse of the royal lifestyle in the **Palacio Real**.

EVENING Dress for the red carpet to attend a concert, recital, opera or ballet in the **Teatro Real**, the 19th-century jewel-box concert hall ordered by Spain's queen, Isabel II.

Essentials

GETTING THERE
Most international airlines fly into **Madrid-Barajas Airport**, 12 km (7 miles) from the city centre. There are **buses**, **metro trains** and shared and standard **taxis** to the city centre. Use the fantastic metro to get around the city.

WHERE TO STAY
Hostal Macarena (inexpensive) has spacious but simple rooms near Plaza Mayor. *www.silserranos.com*
Hotel Moderno (moderate) is a gracious family-run property. *www.hotel-moderno.com*
Husa Hotel Paseo del Arte (expensive) is a sleek, stylish hotel near the Reina Sofía art museum. *www.hotelhusapaseodelarte.com*

TOURIST INFORMATION
Plaza Mayor 27; +34 915 881 636; *www.esmadrid.com*

Above *Cocido madrileño* traditionally includes a mixture of salt meat, fresh meat and smoked sausages, made tender by slow cooking

MADRID SPAIN

Hearty Cocido in Old Madrid

Behind its gloss of 21st-century chic, Madrid reveals itself as an imperial capital of dazzling Baroque monuments and atmospheric warrens of narrow streets. No dish is more emblematic of this old Madrid than *cocido madrileño* – a comfort meal of delicate soup, earthy vegetables, chickpeas, smoky meats and sausages, perfectly suited to the measured pace of a family lunch.

Few dishes stir such primal nostalgia in the hearts of *Madrileños* as *cocido*. This is the soul food of the Madrid de las Asturias – the old city that sprawled out from the Puerta del Sol under Habsburg rule between 1561 and 1665. The dish can be sampled at its traditional best in the ancient taverns below Plaza Mayor, so little changed that it is easy to imagine Velázquez tipping a lunch-time glass during a break from painting royal portraits.

Tradition and ritual not only define Spanish dining but infuse every interaction that Spaniards at leisure have with their capital city. To fully understand Madrid, follow suit, perhaps by capping a morning in the Velázquez and Goya galleries in the Museo del Prado with people-watching from a café table in Plaza Mayor. In a similar vein, no visit to the lavish rooms of the Palacio Real is complete without pausing to admire the statues and fountains in the Jardines de Sabatini surrounding the royal residence. On Sunday, Parque del Buen Retiro is full of families watching puppet shows or rowing on the lake and Madrid's restaurants come alive with diners enjoying the social and gastronomic pleasures of *cocido* – the dish that everyone's grandmother used to make. This hearty stew is a winter favourite, though it can be sampled in many of the city's restaurants throughout the year.

Some of Madrid's *cocido* restaurants are old-fashioned folksy establishments where the stew simmers in earthenware jugs. Others are fine-dining icons where this working-man's hotpot – itself derived from a stew devised by Spain's Sephardic Jews that could be cooked slowly and without human intervention on the Sabbath – achieves an elegance and formality that belies its origins.

Cocido is served in three courses of increasingly intense flavour: first, the savoury broth with slender noodles, then, a plate of toothsome chickpeas and boiled vegetables, and a final plate of hearty meats – heaps of sausages, pork, roast beef, chicken, slabs of bacon and chunks of ham. The result is a taste of old Madrid and one of the most bounteous and filling dishes in Iberian cuisine.

A Celebratory Dish

Spain was one of the first countries in Europe to grow sugar cane, and there is no denying the Spanish penchant for devouring a special sweet themed to each holiday. The biggest celebration in the city honours Madrid's patron saint **San Isidro** with a nine-day fiesta centered on his feast day, 15 May. Pastry shops fill their windows with the special *buñuelos de San Isidro*, an intensely sweet pastry deep-fried until crisp and injected with a creamy custard that spurts out on first bite. Celebrations include parades, concerts and traditional dance performances, as well as the *corridas* (bullfights) at Madrid's Moorish-influenced **Las Ventas** bullring – a huge red-brick edifice decorated with ceramic tiles. Impromptu bars spring up along the main streets at night to sell what the Spanish call "minis" – big plastic cups of beer, wine and mixed drinks.

Above Older restaurants advertise *cocido madrileño* on their wall tiles

The Best Places to Eat Cocido Madrileño

La Bola Taberna moderate

Cocido has been a menu centrepiece since this beloved tavern opened in 1870. In the early days, the Verdasco family (who still operate La Bola) served three versions: a noon stew for labourers, a 1pm version with stewed chicken popular with students and the full-on *cocido* with mixed meats and pork fat at 2pm – a favourite of politicians and journalists, according to newspaper reports of the era. The restaurant still prepares *cocido* by letting it bubble slowly in colourful ceramic casseroles over oak charcoal in ancient stoves. As a nod to modernity, service for small tables is in two courses – soup followed by vegetables and meat together. However, it is common for at least half of the *taberna* to be occupied by groups of a dozen or more, enjoying the complete three-course presentation on white tablecloths in the wood-panelled rooms. La Bola also serves a celebrated version of *callos*, Madrid's signature tripe dish.

Calle Bola 5, Madrid; open for lunch daily, dinner Mon–Sat; www.labola.es

Also in Madrid

For a refined *cocido* experience, try the glittering upstairs dining room at **Lhardy** *(www.lhardy. com; expensive)*, which first opened its doors to diners in 1839. A less daunting meal can be had at **Taberna de Antonio Sanchez** at Calle Mesón de Paredes 13 *(+34 915 397 826; moderate)*, which offers miniature *cocido* servings as a tapa.

Also in Spain

A regional variety of *cocido* found throughout Andalusia, *cocido andaluz* uses Arabic spices (mostly cumin and saffron), fresh beans, soft squashes and spicy sausages. One of the best is served in the city of Jaén at the **Parador de Jaén** *(www.parador.es; moderate)*. In Galicia, *cocido gallego* pairs the region's famous pork and veal with turnips, potatoes and white beans.

Around the World

In **Portugal**, a variant of the stew, *cozido à portuguesa*, can be found in most restaurants in the city of Coimbra, such as **Zé Manel Dos Ossos** *(+351 239 823 790; inexpensive)*. It differs from Spanish *cocido* by including Braganza cabbage and several varieties of smoked sausages, and using rice and beans instead of chickpeas. In **Brazil**, the national dish, *feijoada (see pp320–1)*, is a South American adaptation of Portuguese *cozido*, made with black beans, pork ribs and dried beef.

ZURICH SWITZERLAND

Striking Gold in Zurich

Big money is never far away in the small city of Zurich – it is in the gleaming façades of its financial institutions, historic guild halls and churches, abundant cultural offerings and opulent shops. The city's classic dishes – liver with herbs, or veal in cream sauce – also have a soul-satisfying richness, especially when served with the delicious potato pancakes known as rösti.

Zurich is a city of commerce. The clink of coin has accompanied trade, manufacturing and not least – from 1755, with the creation of Bank Leu & Cie – the banking sector, which has made this city of around 400,000 inhabitants one of the world's leading financial centres. Nestled on the shores of Lake Zurich and straddling both banks of the Limmat river, Zurich saw the passage of Celts and Romans before settling into its solidly Teutonic mould, which has shaped the diet of the city's burghers. *Zürcher Geschnetzeltes*, strips of tender veal cooked in a cream sauce, and *Leberli*, calf's liver pan-fried with garden herbs, are two favourites, especially when accompanied by rösti. These buttery potato cakes are made by boiling unpeeled potatoes until semi-soft; they are then peeled and grated, and shaped in the frying pan into a round pancake. The taste of butter and a little salt permeates the cake, which is soft within and a crusty golden brown without.

Rösti may be a local star, but Zurich has much more to offer the taste buds. From *Kaffee und Kuchen* (coffee and cake) in a bakery tearoom to bistro food,

ethnic restaurants and temples of Michelin-starred refinement, there's much to savour. Very much part of the mix is the street market held twice weekly at Bürkliplatz near the lake – a riot of seasonal fruit, vegetables and flowers and wild mushrooms in autumn.

Despite its wealth, Zurich remains a small city – and its manageable size is what makes getting around downtown on foot, or via Zurich's clean and efficient tram system, the preferred option. Leading straight down towards the lake from the Hauptbahnhof, or main railway station, is Bahnhofstrasse, Zurich's answer to Bond Street and Fifth Avenue. Some of the largest banks mingle along this stretch with a lush spread of retail havens. Off to the left is part of Zurich's Old Town, linked by several foot bridges to the rest of the Old Town on the other side of the river. Aside from its medieval guild halls, crowning Old Town glories include the Chagall-windowed Fraumünster church and the Grossmünster (cathedral), surrounded by art galleries, antiques stores, chic boutiques, eateries and food shops. Mixing art, café culture and shopping is Cabaret Voltaire, a reminder that the Dada movement began in Zurich in 1916.

Above Surrounded by snow-clad peaks, Zurich's Old Town straddles the Limmat river, which flows out from the northern end of Lake Zurich

---

What Else to Eat

Savoury Swiss cuisine can be rich, but be sure to leave room for Zurich's many sweet treats. **Confiserie Sprüngli** (www.confiserie-spruengli. ch) on Paradeplatz is not only a favourite meeting point but also the place to buy sinfully good macaroons called *Luxemburgerli*. **Café Schober** (http://peclard-zurich.ch) on Napfgasse in Zurich's Old Town is deservedly popular. Its decor is as Baroque-extravagant as its pastries, cakes and biscuits; the hot chocolate is not to be missed. **Teuscher** (www.teuscher.com) on Storchengasse is one of the world's finest chocolatiers; don't miss their superlative Champagne truffles, made with Dom Perignon. There's no café here, but visitors enjoy the extravagant decorations that change with each season. There's a smaller branch on Bahnhofstrasse.

A Day in Zurich

Switzerland's largest city is not just for shopping and eating, but also for culture, as a considerable amount of Zurich's wealth – private and public – goes into art and performance. The Old Town bears witness to a rich history, and the lake, particularly in summer, lends the waterfront an almost Riviera-like quality: walk along the promenade parallel to Utoquai to soak up that vibe.

MORNING Visit the **Kunsthaus**, a world-class fine art museum with an extraordinary collection of work by Swiss artist Alberto Giacometti, as well as significant works by Edvard Munch, Van Gogh, Picasso and leading Expressionists. Leave some time for shopping in the **Old Town** and **Bahnhofstrasse**.

AFTERNOON Check whether the **E G Bührle Collection** is having a public viewing, or visit the **Museum Rietberg**, a Mecca of non-Western art housed in part in the villa where German composer Richard Wagner wrote the *Wesendonck Lieder*. Families may prefer the **Swiss National Museum** or **Zurich Zoo**.

EVENING Enjoy chic wine bars, trendy dining and clubbing, or book for a concert at the **Tonhalle**, or a performance of opera or ballet at Zurich's **Opera House**.

Essentials

GETTING THERE
Flights from around the globe land at **Zurich Airport**. Trains leave every 10 minutes for the 10-minute ride to Zurich's main **train station**. Zurich's **tram** system covers the city.

WHERE TO STAY
Hotel Leoneck (inexpensive) uses Swiss icons such as dairy cows to create a fun, friendly space. www.leoneck.ch
Romantik Hotel Florhof (moderate) is a charmingly converted patrician home. www.florhof.ch
Hotel Widder (expensive), in imaginatively converted Old Town buildings, is pure luxury. www.widder.ch

TOURIST INFORMATION
Zurich main train station; +41 44 215 40 00

The Best Places to Eat Rösti

Kronenhalle expensive

In Switzerland, many fashionable city eateries either don't serve rösti or re-interpret them into dainty patties. However, at Kronenhalle there's no fooling around with the rösti; it's the real thing – a large, rich, buttery potato cake that's eaten with the restaurant's Châteaubriand steak, Wiener schnitzel or veal bratwurst.

This establishment has been home to Zurich's *crème de la crème* for generations and has a collection of art by masters such as Miró and Chagall. Whether you're in the front room or one of the two dining rooms, the buzzy atmosphere is that of a chock-a-block brasserie rather than a hallowed hall of gastronomic distinction (although the food is very savvily done). With so much history – it opened its doors in 1862 – to go with the art and the beautiful people, the Kronenhalle is quintessential Zurich.

Rämistrasse 4, Zurich; open noon–midnight daily; www.kronenhalle.ch

Also in Zurich

Once the home of the city's mayor, the building housing **Restaurant Bierhalle Kropf** *(www.zumkropf.ch; moderate)* is a magnificent piece of heritage, dating back to the Middle Ages; try their house speciality of *Würstplatte* – a selection of sausages – *mit Rösti*. At the **Rössli** *(www.roessli-zollikon.ch; moderate)* in Zollikon, an upmarket area just outside the city centre, try your rösti with calf's liver, garlic, onions and herbs. **Zunfthaus zur Haue** *(www. zunfthaus-zur-haue.ch; moderate)* serves its *Geschnetzeltes mit Rösti* with added calf kidney for that extra zing.

Also in Switzerland

Lucerne's iconic **Wirtshaus Galliker** *(+41 41 240 10 02; moderate)* is a bastion of homely Swiss cooking, with rösti galore. **Café du Grütli** *(www.cafedugruetli.ch; inexpensive)* in Lausanne serves up Swiss classics with rösti including local *saucisse à rotir* (roast sausage). **Restaurant Schnabel** *(www.restaurant-schnabel.ch; moderate)* in Basel has a whole selection of rösti dishes as main courses as well as accompaniments to liver dishes such as the Basel speciality *Suuri Läberli* (sour beef liver).

Around the World

In Canada, order rösti as a side dish with the Swiss classic *eminc de veau à la Zurichoise* (strips of veal cooked in a cream sauce) at Montreal's **La Raclette** *(www.laraclette.ca; moderate)*. In Hong Kong, **Chesa** *(www. peninsula.com; moderate)*, at the Peninsula Hotel, serves rösti (which they pronounce "roastee") with both *Geschnetzeltes* (listed on the menu by its French name, *eminc de veau)* and bratwurst (see pp130–1).

Above Zurich is a city of sober efficiency and clean streets, served by a smooth-running network of trams and trolleybuses

Left Classic Swiss rösti may be served with a fried egg on top as a weekday meal, or as an accompaniment to veal or liver dishes

TINOS GREECE

An Easter Feast on Tinos

Easter is the biggest event of the year in Greece – and nowhere is it celebrated with greater aplomb than on the island of Tinos in the Cyclades. The solemnity of the midnight mass is finally broken by firecrackers; congregations embrace and depart in candlelit processions that shimmer through the villages, descending on the tavernas to break the 40-day Lenten fast with 24 hours of feasting.

Every year, thousands of Greeks in search of salvation flock to the miracle-working church of Panagia Evangelistria, on a hill above Tinos town (also known as Chora), the island's capital. But Tinos is also a Mecca for epicures and artists seeking solace in the whitewashed villages lodged in the folds of thyme-scented hills. Ancient footpaths crisscross the terraced valleys, and a rambler's sole companions are inquisitive goats and indifferent sheep.

Traditions run deep on Tinos, an island saved from overdevelopment by the all-powerful Greek Orthodox church. Apprentices still chip away at the marble sculpture school in Pyrgos. Old men thread baskets by hand in Volax, a hamlet built around a mysterious cluster of boulders like giant bowling balls. Kids play hopscotch among the flowerpots on the main street of Agapi – a village endearingly called "Love".

Easter is the main event on the island, and the centrepiece of the Orthodox Easter feast is spring lamb, naturally flavoured with the wild herbs on which the animals graze. None of the sacrificial lamb goes to waste. Once mass is over, the midnight feast begins with a bowl of *magiritsa* soup, made from lamb's liver, lungs, head and intestines, *avgolemono* (egg and lemon) sauce, and seasoned with spring onions and dill. This pungent broth prepares the stomach for the meat spree to follow – a kind of digestive purgatory after 40 days of Lenten fasting. The ordeal is sweetened with slices of *tsoureki*, a braided brioche flavoured with the resinous sap of the mastic tree, and *lychnarakia*, sweet cheese pies shaped like miniature toques.

Traditionally, the Easter lamb is marinated in olive oil, lemon and oregano, then roasted whole on a spit. This laborious process is an essential part of the culinary ritual: a pit must be dug, a fire built, then everyone must take a turn at the spit (secretly tearing off bits of crispy skin). It takes several hours for the lamb to cook; meanwhile, hard-boiled eggs, dyed red to represent the blood of Christ, are cracked open, wine is drunk, songs are sung and cigarettes are smoked. Squeamish cooks and lazy restaurateurs often slow-roast a leg of lamb in the oven instead – but the result is almost as good. Potato wedges drenched in lemon and garlic are tucked into the cooking dish, and a simple green salad with a zingy lemon dressing is all that's required on the side. It would be almost sacrilegious to serve anything else.

Three Days on Tinos

The travel writer Lawrence Durrell dubbed Tinos "the Lourdes of modern Greece". But with spectacular vernacular architecture, a thriving crafts industry and scores of sandy beaches, there's much more than churches to explore.

DAY ONE There are around 50 villages on Tinos – each one lovelier than the last. Buy baskets in **Volax**, where cottages crouch beneath colossal boulders. Visit the Museum of Marble Crafts in **Pyrgos**, where every doorway bristles with sculpted marble birds, boats and hearts; the village is also famous for *galaktoboureko*, sticky custard pie.

DAY TWO Admire some of the island's 800 carved, decorated dovecotes, found everywhere. Visit the Venetian fortress at craggy **Exobourgo**; return to Tinos town and light a candle at **Panagia Evangelistria** before visiting the neighbouring bazaar.

DAY THREE Aeolos, god of the winds, allegedly resides on **Mount Tsiknias**, the island's highest peak. Make the most of winds at the surf school on **Kolimbithra beach**, or head for a sandy cove such as **Livada**, **Apigania** or **Pachia Ammos**.

Essentials

GETTING THERE
There is no airport; **ferries** from Athens take 3–5 hours. You'll need to hire a **car** to explore.

WHERE TO STAY
Tinion (inexpensive) in Tinos town is a basic but charming *pension*. www.tinionhotel.gr
Vega Apartments (moderate) in Agios Markos offer self-catering in sleek Cycladic style. www.vegaapartments.gr
Anthia (expensive) is a family-friendly hotel with a pool and restaurant, close to Agios Fokas beach. www.anthia.gr

FURTHER INFORMATION
www.tinos.gr

Above On Easter Sunday, lamb marinated in lemon juice, olive oil and oregano is spit-roasted over coals as the centrepiece of the Easter feast

Left The small, medieval village of Triantaros lies 6 km (4 miles) northeast of Tinos town, and is home to the picturesque Church of the Holy Apostles

Above A Greek Orthodox priest prays over the *epitaphios*, a sacred cloth carrying an image of Christ, taken into the sea at Tinos on Good Friday

What Else to Eat

Lamb is often stewed with **artichokes** here: it's one of the few crops that thrive on the wind-whipped island. Locals battle it out for the best recipe at the Artichoke Festival in the village of Komi in May. Buy marinated artichoke hearts *(aginares)* and other Tinian delicacies straight from the source at the daily farmers' market by Tinos port: **thyme honey** thick as treacle, slabs of **louza** (cured pork), **graviera** cheese and necklaces of **sun-dried tomatoes.** Many of these find their way into **fourtalia,** the delicious frittata of the Cyclades. The ultimate comfort food is *fourtalia* with **fennel-seed sausage** at To Agnandi *(+30 22830 21095)*, a quaint *ouzeri*-cum-grocery in Ktikados.

The Best Places to Eat Greek Lamb

Ta Isternia inexpensive

It's extremely hard to have a bad meal on Tinos, but some tavernas are quietly but consistently sensational. This unassuming local haunt is one of them. While two (admittedly excellent) rival restaurants – Thalassaki and Naftilos – battle it out on the waterfront at Isternia bay, those in the know escape the crowds and head up the treacherous, winding road to the village of Isternia proper. Tucked away on a back street near the parking lot, this is the only taverna in town. Despite the lack of competition, its owners Nikos and Anna maintain very high standards. They serve traditional Greek food with a Tinian twist: caper croquettes, garlic and potato dip, black-eyed beans with sun-dried tomatoes. The traditional Easter feast is cooked exactly as it should be: tender lamb that falls off the bone, lemony potatoes that fall apart in your mouth and crisp lettuce salad. The small terrace has a handful of tables with ravishing views of the Aegean.

Isternia, Tinos; open 1pm–midnight Easter–Sep; +30 22830 31005

Also on Tinos

Douar *(+30 22830 41231; inexpensive)* in the village of Steni is a *hasapotaverna* (a butcher and no-frills restaurant) that is strictly for carnivores. Gruff service and cramped tables don't deter the regulars, who come from miles away to gnaw on the addictive lamb chops.

Also in Greece

The tradition of roasting whole lambs on a spit comes from **Roumeli**, a region in central Greece. On Easter Sunday, residents in its towns of **Livadia**, **Amfiklia** and **Amfissa** set up makeshift barbecues on the streets and offer hunks of roast lamb and *kokoretsi* (skewered innards encased in intestines) to all passers-by.

Around the World

George Calombaris is one of Australia's most influential chefs. **The Press Club** *(www.thepressclub.com.au; expensive)*, his flash but accessible flagship restaurant in Melbourne, is an exemplary showcase for modern Greek food. Dramatically presented, deceptively simple dishes include roast loin of lamb with beetroot *horiatiki* (a salad with feta cheese) and almond *skordalia* (a thick, garlicky purée). Greeks eat leftover lamb sandwiches for days after Easter, and you can recreate the experience in Palo Alto, California, at **Evvia Estiatorio** *(www.evvia.net; moderate)*. This upmarket Greek restaurant in Silicon Valley serves roasted-lamb pitta bread sandwiches with tzatziki, tomato and seasonal greens.

A Day in Toulouse

Toulouse is pretty, prosperous and rich in culture. Known as *La Ville Rose* (the Pink City), the Place du Capitole lies at its heart; head here for a relaxing coffee and people-watching between visiting sights.

MORNING Visit the **Théâtre du Capitole** to marvel at its painted ceilings. From there walk the **rue du Taur** to Europe's largest Romanesque church, **St Sernin Basilica**.

AFTERNOON Explore the fortress-like **Jacobins Convent**, with its soaring "palm tree" pillars and vaults. Call into the **Musée des Augustins**, a 14th-century convent, for Gothic statuary. Contrast the old with the new at **Les Abbatoirs**, where more than 2,000 pieces of modern art are housed in what was a 19th-century slaughterhouse.

EVENING Come sunset, take up a seat on the terrace in **Place du Capitole** and watch the 18th-century red-brick buildings that cast a rosy tint by day begin to blush and glow lilac as dusk falls. Wander along the banks of the **Garonne river** to see the vaults of the old **New Bridge** lit up at night.

Essentials

GETTING THERE
Aéroport Toulouse Blagnac is an 11-km (7-mile) **drive** or **bus** ride from the city, and has flights to most major European cities. There are also **high-speed trains** from Paris and Lille.

WHERE TO STAY
Le Clos des Potiers (inexpensive) is a refined retreat with bags of (Empire) style and atmosphere. *www.hotel-closdespotiers.com*
Hôtel Le Grand Balcon (moderate) is a 1930s hotel much loved by French author Antoine de Saint-Exupéry, now completely renovated. *www.grandbalconhotel.com*
Grand Hôtel de l'Opéra (expensive) is a former 17th-century convent-turned-plush hotel on the Place du Capitole. www.*grand-hotel-opera.com*

TOURIST INFORMATION
Donjon du Capitole; *www.toulouse-tourisme.com*

Right The Toulouse version of cassoulet always includes garlicky sausage and either goose or duck

Below Dining alfresco in the Place du Capitole, which hosts a market on Saturdays

TOULOUSE FRANCE

Full of Beans in Toulouse

Several towns in the southwest of France claim the earthy pork and bean cassoulet as their own, and Toulouse stands tall and proud among them. Cassoulet is as emblematic to the city as its rugby-loving locals, rowdy bistros and dusky red bricks. Slow-cooked, smoky, thick with handmade sausage and goose, this classic French stew is a byword for warmth and country comfort.

Toulouse's links with the past are omnipresent, from its medieval spires to its rich peasant food. The city's streets are lined with mansions built on the wealth of the *pastel* (woad plant) dyeing industry, and they open up on to cascading fountains, quiet squares and the banks of the Canal du Midi, a waterway to the Mediterranean constructed in the 17th century for the burgeoning grain trade. But this is a city that's also firmly fixed in the present; it's a flourishing student town with an enviable nightlife, and an enclave for sharp-minded scientists toiling for the airline and space industries. Ancient and modern rub shoulders comfortably in Toulouse.

Toulousains often claim to have more in common with Barcelona, a two-hour drive away, than Paris. There is a definite laid-back, Latin ambience here, and the view, like the stone of the city buildings, is generally rose-coloured. But things were quite different during the Hundred Years War of the 14th and 15th centuries, during which the nearby town of Castelnaudary came under siege. It's said that desperate citizens created a collective dish – the heart-warming cassoulet – so full-bodied that it perked up everyone sufficiently to fight the good fight. The Académie Universelle du Cassoulet, however, begs to differ, maintaining that cassoulet evolved around the family hearth as simple peasant fare, not combat cuisine. As time passed and rural folk left the farms to seek work as cooks or domestics in the city, their recipes went with them and on to bourgeois tables.

Whatever the truth of the matter, this hearty casserole of white beans and meat is steeped as much in history and legend as in flavour. Castelnaudary, Carcassonne and Toulouse have been dubbed cassoulet's "holy trinity" with each boasting their own variation of it. In Toulouse, chefs add garlicky *Toulousain* sausage, pork rind and goose or duck *confit* to enrich the bean mixture. Experts insist that the secret to a great cassoulet lies in the beans: they must be cooked just long enough and lie in a stock that's smooth and thickened by the pork rind. Then follows hours of patient slow-baking in a traditional earthenware pot – the *cassole* – that gives the dish its name.

Food Shopping in Toulouse

The covered market in **Place Victor Hugo** has 100 stalls open for business from Tuesday to Sunday. Pick up *confit de canard* (preserved duck) and local *saucisse* (pork sausage) for your cassoulet, and a slab of foie gras for a starter. The **Saint Aubin** Sunday market offers the best of the season, such as wild mushrooms and oysters from Arcachon, and live pigeons and geese fresh from local farms, while **Place du Capitole**'s Saturday's market is organically themed. If you prefer not to jostle for your food, **Maison Busquets** on rue Rémusat has a vast array of regional goodies, including wine and pre-made cassoulet. **Violettes et Pastelles** on rue St Pantaléon is the place to visit for everything violet, from bonbons to syrup. The violet, supposedly brought back from Italy by Napoleon's soldiers, is the city's symbol.

Above Toulouse lies on the banks of the Garonne river in southwest France

The Best Places to Eat Cassoulet

Le Cantou moderate

With its leafy garden, interspersed with flowery colour bursts, Le Cantou feels more like a country house than an elegant city restaurant just 10 minutes from the centre of Toulouse. That may be because it reflects the cooking style of chef Philippe Puel, who grew up watching his grandmother cooking cassoulet in her farmhouse kitchen – her passion for the dish and the region still infuses his doggedly seasonal cooking. While an ardent fan of her original dish, which took days to prepare, Puel believes old recipes can be made new. So, in as much as it's possible with a dish this hearty, Puel's version is light! There's the requisite Toulouse sausage, some thinly sliced pork rind and the essential duck *confit*, which he trims of excess fat. (*Confit*, meaning "cooked in its own fat", developed as a way of preserving meat before refrigeration. It renders the meat tender.) Puel adds thin-skinned, sweet white beans from Tarbes, then puts everything into the oven for several hours to emerge bubbling, browned and begging for a spoon.
98, rue de Velasquez, St-Martin-du-Touch; open for lunch and dinner Mon–Fri; www.cantou.fr

Also in Toulouse

Die-hard cassoulet fans can follow one of two cassoulet trails: the Route de Cassoulet or the Route Gourmand du Cassoulet. Chef Claude Taffarello's **Auberge du Poids Public** (www.auberge-du-poids-public.fr; moderate) in pretty Saint-Félix-Lauragais is on the latter. His cassoulet, served in a traditional *cassole*, is a rich mix of beans, duck and goose *confit*, and sausage, bobbing in a thick, plentiful sauce – good, sustaining stuff, all sourced locally, including the earthenware *cassole* in which the the dish is cooked. The restaurant also has a wonderful view across the surrounding countryside.

Also in France

If you can't make it to the south, upmarket **Au Trou Gascon** (www.autrougascon.fr; expensive) in Paris will transport you there with its cassoulet. The chef's favourite just happens to be this famous dish, and here it's a marvellous melding of lamb, pork, duck and incomparable Tarbais beans.

Around the World

Toulouse-style cassoulet is always on the menu at Anthony Bourdain's New York temple to everyday French cooking, **Les Halles** (www.leshalles.net/brasserie; inexpensive). Close your eyes, take a spoonful and, just for a minute, you could almost be in the pink city itself.

BOLOGNA ITALY

Tortellini in Italy's Gourmet Heart

The down-to-earth city of Bologna is renowned for the world's oldest university, a lively central district and long, elegantly porticoed streets. But the majority of visitors from Italy and beyond flock here for food, either eaten in the excellent trattorias or bought to take home from the mouthwatering gourmet shops. The simple, fresh *tortellini in brodo* is a firm favourite.

Bologna hums with activity. A stroll through the compact city centre in the company of fleets of bicycles reveals innovative bookshops, cafés blending chocolate and spices packed to the rafters, and time-tested restaurants that are crowded with diners every day of the week. Resting on a foundation of ancient Roman buildings, the city has grown up in a compact layout, with delightful architectural gems such as Romanesque chapels slotted between butcher's shops or apartment blocks. This is a city that can easily be explored on foot, and most tourists start in the oldest part of town, the Quadrilateral, which is dominated by Bologna's favourite church, the vast, 14th-century San Petronio.

Bologna is nicknamed *La Grassa* (meaning "the fat one"), and it is widely regarded as the gastronomic capital of Italy. The city is located in Emilia-Romagna, a region synonymous with good food; it is home to the aromatic balsamic vinegar from Modena, *parmigiano* (Parmesan) cheese and prosciutto from Parma, Felino

salami, Bologna's own enormous, pistachio-studded mortadella sausage and, last but not least, fresh egg pasta. A perfect combination of nearly all of these regional delights comes in the shape of tortellini, tiny knotted parcels of thinly rolled pasta filled with a finely minced, delicate blend of *prosciutto crudo*, mortadella, *parmigiano* cheese and a hint of nutmeg. Tradition dictates that tortellini be both cooked and dished up in *brodo*, a delicate consommé made from beef and capon or chicken. They should be served sprinkled with more *parmigiano* and very much *al dente* – almost disconcertingly undercooked. This is because the pasta continues to cook in the hot liquid in the bowl.

There are two stories about the invention of tortellini. The first is practical yet poignant – it was a way for locals departing for the Crusades to take the tastes of home with them. The second seems somehow more Italian: during a convention of the Gods that took place in mythical times, an innkeeper inadvertently glimpsed Venus naked, and was inspired by the beautiful sight to create these golden "belly buttons".

Three Days in and around Bologna

This fascinating region is packed with historic churches and monuments, and fantastic food markets that spell heaven for gourmet travellers.

DAY ONE Start in Bologna's **Piazza Maggiore**, the vast square edged by brick palaces and the imposing medieval church of **San Petronio**. Take narrow-flagged **Via Orefici** into the old district lined with mouthwatering gourmet delicatessens, pork butchers and greengrocers.

DAY TWO Make the 20-minute train trip to **Modena** for its priceless Romanesque art and architecture, recognized on the World Heritage list by UNESCO. The **Duomo** and **Torre Ghirlandina** are outstanding. Then head for the town's **covered market** to sample the famous balsamic vinegar and sparkling Lambrusco wine.

DAY THREE One hour away by train is prosperous **Parma**, where the sights are all within walking distance. Visit the graceful 11th-century **cathedral** and baptistry with their art treasures, then move on to **Palazzo Pilotta** and its gallery of works by **Correggio**. Don't miss the magnificent opera house, **Teatro Regia**, or the birthplace of the great conductor Arturo Toscanini, but leave plenty of time for the speciality gourmet shops and restaurants.

Essentials

GETTING THERE
Bologna's **international airport** is a 20-minute **bus** ride from the city, which is well served by **trains**. Take an orange **city bus** to get around; the best way to explore the historic centre is on **foot**.

WHERE TO STAY
B&B Centrale (inexpensive) offers good-value, light-filled accommodation handy for the station. www.bbcentrale.com
Hotel Metropolitan (moderate) is a smart, modern, Eastern-inspired hotel. *www.hotelmetropolitan.com*
Casa Sant'Angelo (expensive) is a small, beautifully renovated 15th-century palace with a roof terrace and spa. *www.casasantangelo.com*

TOURIST INFORMATION
http://iat.comune.bologna.it

Left *Tortellini in brodo* are dished up with nothing but their cooking broth for a classic, simple Italian dish

Above Bologna is the capital city of Emilia-Romagna, and conforms to a medieval street plan

Below Bologna has one of Italy's largest food markets, which sells a huge variety of fresh pasta

A Day in Bergen

You can easily explore Bergen in a day; walk around the centre and use the funicular for the surrounding peaks.

MORNING Start the morning with a stroll around the harbour area and the **Bryggen UNESCO site** – a walk among these old wooden buildings is a step back in time. The Quarter has existed since the mid-14th century, but most of the wooden houses still standing date from 1704, after the great fire of 1702. Visit the **Hanseatic Museum and Schøtstuene**, the old Assembly Rooms.

AFTERNOON Walk to the **fish market** and wander around it to admire the stalls of fish and seafood. Choose one of the great places on offer for lunch. Then take the **Fløibanen Funicular Railway** for a swift ride up to **Mount Fløyen** with gorgeous views over the city.

EVENING In summer the funicular is open until midnight so you can stay late in the mountains enjoying the extraordinary light. Beware that Bergen is "blessed" with abundant rainfall and if the day starts off sunny, reverse the itinerary, starting with the funicular railway.

Essentials

GETTING THERE
Bergen lies on the coast of western Norway. Flights arrive at **Flesland International Airport** and there are **shuttle buses** and **taxis** to the city centre, 20 km (12 miles) away.

WHERE TO STAY
Hanseatic Hotel Bergen (inexpensive) has 16 unique rooms within the Bryggen UNESCO site. *www.dethanseatiskehotell.no*
Augustin Hotel (moderate) is the oldest family-run hotel in Bergen, with a cosy restaurant and bar. *www.augustin.no*
Clarion Collection Hotel Havnekontoret (expensive) is Bergen's most luxurious hotel. *www.clarionhotel.com*

TOURIST INFORMATION
Fresco Hall, Vågsallmenning Square (opposite the fish market); *+47 55 552 000*

Left The beautiful Lofoten Islands can be reached by plane or coastal liner from Bergen
Below Colourful merchant buildings line the wharf at the World Heritage site of Bryggen

The Best Places to Eat Gravadlax

Enhjørningen Fish Restaurant
expensive

Enhjørningen Fish Restaurant, Bergen's oldest fish restaurant, is steeped in the city's history, housed as it is in an old Hanseatic wharf house in the Bryggen quarter near the harbour. Parts of the building date from the 14th century and the enchanting decor gives you the feeling of having stepped into the living room of an old merchant's house, complete with antique furniture and paintings.

The menu ranges from the traditional to the more adventurous, with an emphasis on fresh local fish and seafood. Top choice must be their gravadlax, which is cured in aquavit – a caraway-flavoured schnapps – and served with mustard sauce. For those with a hearty appetite there are plenty of other unusual dishes to sample, including *rakørret* (cured trout – another traditional Norwegian dish) and vendace roe, a speciality. The three-course set menus, one of which includes the gravadlax dish, are particularly good value.

Enhjørningsgården 29, Bergen; open 4–11pm daily, closed Sun Sep–mid-May; www.enhjorningen.no

Also in Bergen

To taste some exquisite homemade gravadlax, try newly opened **Cornelia Seafood Restaurant** *(+47 55 011 885; moderate)*, somewhat ironically located in the old meat market area. Alf Roald Sætre and Odd Einar Tufteland, the men behind the establishment, really know their seafood. In 2004 they opened one of the city's most popular seafood and fish restaurants, **Cornelius Restaurant** *(www.cornelius-restauranter.no; moderate)*, reached only by boat from central Bergen. Both restaurants are worth a visit for the sheer variety of fresh fish and seafood they offer; they also have no less than five different recipes for home-cured gravadlax, which is available to buy in the fishmonger's next door to the Cornelia Restaurant.

Also in Norway

In Stavanger, **Sjøhuset Skagen** *(www.sjohusetskagen.no; expensive)*, housed in a brightly red-painted, old, timbered building, serves home-cured gravadlax with the traditional accompaniments of salad, mustard dressing and dark rye bread.

Around the World

The Smörgås Chef *(www.smorgas.com; inexpensive)* has no less than three prime locations across New York, offering the very best of Scandinavian cuisine, including their own home-cured gravadlax. A special treat is their aquavit-cured salmon with traditional cucumber-dill salad and mustard sauce.

BERGEN NORWAY

"Buried" Salmon in Bergen

When the rays are glittering across Bergen harbour on a sunny summer's day, the fish market, or *fisketorget*, seems literally to sparkle as visitors and locals gather to shop, browse and eat. The hub of this bustling port city for several hundred years, this famous market is full of stalls heaped high with delights of the sea and that Scandinavian favourite: deep-hued gravadlax.

Bergen's history stretches back as far as the 11th century and in its heyday it was a headquarters for the Hanseatic League – northern Europe's dominating trade alliance in the late Middle Ages. The league was made up of German and Scandinavian seafaring merchants, and the legacy of the German merchants can still be experienced in the oldest, most charming of the city's neighbourhoods, known as Bryggen. A UNESCO World Heritage site since 1979, the 62 gently leaning wooden merchants' houses here have been lovingly restored to their former glory and wandering among these rickety antique houses is like entering a wooden maze. Several have been opened up as museums, while others sell typical Norwegian handicrafts, from fluffy knitwear to ornate Sami reindeer-bone knives.

Fish has always played a vital role in Bergen – it was responsible for drawing the Hanseatic League to the town's shores in the 13th century, at around the same time that one of Norway's national dishes *par excellence*, gravadlax, appeared on the culinary scene.

This signature dish, today most often served as an appetizer, was invented by fishermen, who would salt and then bury their freshly caught salmon, leaving it to ferment in the sand at high tide. "*Grav*" literally means "grave", and "burying" the salmon gave it a very distinctive flavour. These days you won't see any Norwegians digging up their dish of the day from the beaches, but gravadlax remains just as tasty, having been "buried" and cured in a marinade of salt, sugar, dill and often a dash of aquavit or gin.

Much has changed in Bergen since the fish-trading of the Middle Ages, but the scene at the fish market is every bit as lively, as gregarious stallholders vie for customers against the backdrop of the Hanseatic houses. Stalls are piled high with bright orange or pink gravadlax, smoked salmon, rosy prawns, purple lobsters, red crayfish and apricot-coloured mussels. Open sandwiches stacked with fish and seafood call out to be eaten from improvised cafés with rustic wooden benches. It's not hard to imagine a merchant in the Middle Ages tucking into the same dishes on the same spot some 600 years ago.

Food with a View

Bergen is surrounded by *de syv fjell* ("the seven peaks"), mountains with stunning views of Bergen and the nearby islands and fjords. Several offer foodie experiences with a view. **Fløien Folkerestaurang** *(www.bellevue-restauranter.no)*, one of the Historic Restaurants of Norway, is reached by the Fløibanen Funicular Railway, one of Bergen's main sights. Its old, atmospheric building is open daily in summer for traditional Norwegian cooking. Mount Ulriken, reached by bus and gondola from central Bergen, has the city's highest restaurant, **Sky:skraperen** *(www.ulriken643.no)*. It serves gravadlax and other traditional dishes. **Jacob Aall Bar & Brasserie** *(www.jacobaall.no)* offers good views without the need to climb a peak first. Located on top of a tall city-centre building, you can admire the views from the bar on the premises.

Above Gravadlax with fresh dill and black peppercorns

STRASBOURG FRANCE

Choucroute Garnie in Strasbourg

Strasbourg's outstanding historic architecture is now protected as a UNESCO World Heritage site; its medieval churches, grand public buildings and tangle of narrow streets offer a unique insight into a bygone age. Long contested by both Germany and France, its shifting borders have also given it a distinctive cuisine, exemplified by a deliciously heaped platter of *choucroute garnie*.

The capital of Alsace, Strasbourg lies on the French/German border, and has habitually scuttled back and forth between France and Germany. In fact, from 1870 to 1945, it was alternately French and German no less than four times. Its chequered nationality is evident everywhere, from the medieval neighbourhood of La Petite France to the grand Neo-Gothic German Quarter, both of which carry street signs written in French and the Germanic Alsatian dialect.

La Petite France is impossibly charming, with a web of waterways, half-timbered houses and wooden bridges, but its hospital and noisy canal-boat workshops led the Germans to skirt the area when they annexed the city in 1870. They struck out instead past the old town, throwing up grandiose public buildings, private homes and graceful gardens, spawning the German or Imperial Quarter. The buildings still sparkle today and the German influence on local culinary habits remains as palpable. It's sometimes striking, in fact, just how "unFrench" an Alsatian menu can seem. Thanks to Jewish immigration in the 1100s, foie gras is a firm favourite, but German influence on local culinary habits is everywhere in evidence – sauerkraut (*choucroute*), wursts, pretzels, braised meats, gingerbread and *kougelhopf* still loom large on an Alsatian plate.

Choucroute garnie is the Alsatian dish *par excellence*: salt-pickled cabbage braised with salted and smoked pork, and seasoned with juniper berries. The dish seems encoded in Alsatian genes, and everyone has a favourite way of making sure the *choucroute* is silky, the sausages perfectly simmered and the pork moreish. Most recipes also include bay leaves, garlic, onions, potatoes, white Alsatian Riesling wine and a dollop of duck or goose fat to get it started. Above all, the flavour should be delicate, not tart, so the pickled cabbage is rinsed twice before it is added to the pot. Some like to go the whole hog and add a titanic ham hock, smoked pork chops or even liver quenelles (dumplings). When it is brought to the table, a glistening hillock of *choucroute* crested with slices of smoked and salted pork, fat sausages and steamed potatoes, it should provoke a gasp of delight.

A Day in Strasbourg

With its picture-postcard houses and lapping canals, Strasbourg is full of charm. A good way to get your bearings in this city is to take a canal cruise.

MORNING Visit **Notre Dame Cathedral** with its pink-hued sandstone façade and soaring spire (at 142 m/465 ft, it was the tallest monument in the world from 1647 to 1874). Its elaborate astronomical clock parades the 12 apostles at 12:30pm. Sidle into a *winstub* (wine room) such as the one in the marvellously medieval **Maison Kammerzell** for a glass of Sylvaner wine.

AFTERNOON Spend the afternoon at the **Musée d'Art Moderne et Contemporain (MAMCO)** appreciating the works of Kandinsky, Arp and the German Symbolists, and admiring the museum's impressive collection of *belle époque* posters. Take tea (and cake) in the light-filled **Art Café**.

EVENING Wander the cobbled, illuminated streets of **La Petite France**, with their geranium-festooned Hansel and Gretel-like houses. Follow the canals to the **Ponts Couverts** and survey old Strasbourg from the **Barrage de Vauban**, a dam designed to protect the city. If you have time, walk through the grandiose **German Quarter** and ponder the historical to-ing and fro-ing of this fine city.

Essentials

GETTING THERE
Aéroport Strasbourg International is 10 km (6 miles) from the city; there's a **shuttle train**. Strasbourg has **high-speed train** connections across France and Europe, and a good network of **trams** and **buses** around the city.

WHERE TO STAY
Hotel 21 Siècle (inexpensive) is a minimalist, modern hotel that also offers apartments with kitchenette. *www.hotel-cyber-21.com*
The **Cour du Corbeau** (moderate) is housed in a 16th-century building. *www.cour-corbeau.com*
The **Régent Petite France** (expensive) is a contemporary riverside hotel in a former ice factory. *www.regent-petite-france.com*

TOURIST INFORMATION
17 place de la Cathédrale; *www.otstrasbourg.fr*

Above The canal-side restaurants of La Petite France allow diners to sample authentic Alsatian food in a time-honoured setting

Left The Gothic towers of Strasbourg Cathedral form a stunning backdrop to the Christmas market, held here since 1570

Above *Choucroute garnie* is nostalgia on a plate for many Alsatians, evoking precious memories of childhood and home

The Best Places to Eat Choucroute Garnie

Chez Yvonne inexpensive

Chez Yvonne is something of an institution in Strasbourg. Sandwiched between 16th-century timber-fronted houses in a street just a step or two from the mighty cathedral, this woody *winstub* oozes old Strasbourg. Rustic and down-to-earth, it has a menu that includes all of Alsace's tried and tested, true and timeless dishes: goose foie gras, *presskopt*, *coq au Riesling*, *jambonneau* and, of course, *choucroute garnie*. *Winstub* cooking is, above all, familial, and Alsatian families tend to have a favourite one that they like to call their own. Chez Yvonne is that kind of place. "Winstub" translates as "wine room", and the room ("stub") refers to a cosy one in someone's house where everyone relaxes. Yvonne herself may have retired long ago but the *kelsch* (gingham) curtains, warm wood panelling and pottery live on, along with the generous plate of *choucroute garnie*, a happy confluence of pork liver quenelles, pork knuckle, blood sausage, Strasbourg and Monbéliard sausages, salted pork loin, smoked pork belly and fermented cabbage. It's perfect with the restaurant's dry white Sylvaner wine.

10 rue du Sanglier, Strasbourg; open noon–2:15pm & 6pm–midnight daily; www.chez-yvonne.net

Also in Strasbourg

Captivating **Le Clou** *(www.le-clou.com; inexpensive)* is everything you could wish for in a *winstub*: welcoming, warm, woody and full of delicious smells. Tables are shared, so you'll be rubbing shoulders with strangers, but somehow that doesn't seem inappropriate when you're eating this kind of food. People dream of the consommé with bone-marrow quenelles and the *choucroute royale avec wädele*, a regal version of *choucroute garnie* that substitutes champagne for wine and adds a hefty pork knuckle to the meat contingent.

Also in France

Drouant *(www.drouant.com; expensive)* in Paris started out as a humble tobacco-bar in 1880, but today it's a first-class restaurant owned by three-star Michelin chef and Alsatian Antoine Westermann. Its founder Charles Drouant also hailed from Alsace, and his former customers included the artists Renoir, Rodin and Pissarro. Westermann champions French products and traditions and has a particular penchant for his childhood home of Alsace. Come winter, *choucroute* pops up on the menu.

Around the World

The *choucroute Alsacienne* at **Brasserie Jo** *(www.brasseriejo.com; moderate)* in Boston, USA, is the real thing; founder and owner Jean Joho hails from Alsace and cooked for many years in Strasbourg and the award-winning Auberge d'Ill before decamping to Boston.

What Else to Eat

Centuries of shifting borders between Germany and France have imbued the city and its cuisine with a unique style. Try **baeckeoffe**, a hearty stew of potatoes, pork, beef, lamb and white wine, which is always on the menu at **Le Baeckeoffe d'Alsace** *(www.baeckeoffe.com)*. **Fleischschneke**, minced beef rolled in noodle dough then sliced and cooked in a meaty broth, is good at **Le Clou** *(see right)*. For a quick snack, grab a **bretzel** (pretzel) from any bakery – they've been cooking them here since the 14th century. If you prefer something sweeter, try a **kougelhopf**, a brioche studded with raisins.

Above Manarola, one of the five picturesque Cinque Terre villages on the Ligurian coast

Above The elegant town of Portofino is part of the Riviera di Levante

Three Days in Liguria

The Italian Riviera is an easy place to spend time, whether you want to sightsee, hike or relax in a spectacularly beautiful setting.

DAY ONE Genoa's spectacular **aquarium**, designed by architect Renzo Piano, is a brilliant start to any visit. Then take a short stroll to the city centre to explore the medieval streets and visit the **Duomo**.

DAY TWO Pack your swimming costume and set out along the spectacular 12-km (7-mile) **Sentiero Azzurro** path that links the picture-postcard villages of the **Cinque Terre**. Begin at **Monterosso al Mare** and go southeast along the cliffs dotted with medieval watchtowers and through the fishing settlements, all the way to **Riomaggiore**. If you get tired, jump on a train or a ferry.

DAY THREE A rocky wooded peninsula east of Genoa is the stunning setting for "impossibly beautiful" **Portofino**, with its pastel houses and luxury yachts. From there, catch a ferry to the exquisite abbey of **San Fruttuoso**, which sits on the beachfront in a secluded bay. Continue on to hospitable **Camogli** either on foot or by ferry.

Essentials

GETTING THERE
Genoa's Cristoforo Colombo **airport** has flights from most European cities. There are **buses** every half-hour to the city centre, 6 km (4 miles) away. Extensive **bus** and **train** networks link the towns of the Italian Riviera.

WHERE TO STAY
Hotel Agnello D'Oro (inexpensive) is a quiet converted monastery close to the railway station in Genoa. *www.hotelagnellodoro.it*
Hotel Cenobio dei Dogi (moderate) in Camogli is a beautiful seafront hotel in a refurbished 17th-century villa. *www.cenobio.it*
Hotel Splendido Mare (expensive) provides unabashed luxury in the heart of fabulous Portofino. *www.hotelsplendido.com*

TOURIST INFORMATION
www.turismoinliguria.it

LIGURIA ITALY

Pesto on the Italian Riviera

Renowned for its mild Mediterranean winters, the Italian Riviera runs all along the rocky Ligurian coastline. It represents old-fashioned glamour, and its romantic resorts – such as Portofino and San Remo – have long attracted the world's elite. But from the palaces of Genoa to the tumbling fishermen's houses of Cinque Terre, one simple sauce reigns supreme: *pesto alla genovese*.

The marvellous region of Liguria, in northwest Italy, is remarkably varied. It boasts landscapes stretching from the snowbound Alps to the dramatic coastline of the Mediterranean, where soaring cliffs rise from secluded bays and long beaches of yellow sand. At its heart stands the sprawling capital city of Genoa, a strategic port for more than 2,000 years and a supreme example of old-world capitalism from its heyday in the 16th century. The region retains much of its old appeal, easily enchanting visitors who wander the charming fishing settlements or medieval city streets. Elegant resorts dot the coast in both directions from Genoa: to the west the Riviera di Ponente runs quickly to the star of the 1900s, San Remo; while to the east the Riviera di Levante glories in upmarket Portofino and the pretty clifftop villages of Cinque Terre.

Genoa has produced many extraordinary people, from the 15th-century explorer Christopher Columbus to the 20th century's wondrous architect, Renzo Piano, and the countryside around it produces equally famous

food. Olives – such as the tiny, flavoursome Taggiasco variety – grow everywhere, flourishing on the sun-soaked terraced hillsides. They are pressed to make a superb, delicate extra-virgin oil, which then forms the basis of the area's best-known pasta sauce, *pesto alla genovese*. "*Pesto*" simply means "crushed", referring to the way that the basic raw ingredient, fresh basil, is traditionally pounded by hand using a mortar and pestle, along with pine nuts and (sometimes) garlic. Many cooks today crush the ingredients in an electric blender, before adding the finishing touches – olive oil and grated Parmesan cheese. A little water may be added if the paste is too thick, and then it is carried triumphantly to the table, where it silkily coats pasta or gnocchi with rich Ligurian flavours.

Pesto has spawned a huge number of variations, from the common Ligurian version with runner beans and potatoes to an exotic Sicilian one enriched with tomatoes and almonds. Chefs in other countries play with it freely, even trying other herbs and vegetables in place of basil. It seems that the basic mix – of leaf, oil and nuts – is so fine that nothing is able to spoil it.

The Best Places to Eat Pesto

Ristorante Da Genio moderate

Having reliably served up delicious traditional Ligurian cuisine for over 50 years, this restaurant has a devoted following of diners from both Genoa and further afield. It is well worth the baffling wander through a warren of old streets to find the place. The decor is 1950s Italian, and the walls are lined with paintings by local artists. The signature dish is a classic pesto, freshly made in-house using a special variety of small-leaved Genoa basil blended with pine nuts and Parmesan. The resulting bright green, oily cream is tossed with hot *troffiette* – squiggles of pale tender pasta – and sprinkled with grated Parmesan. They also serve pesto on *trenette*, a type of flat spaghetti, and as *corzetti con sugo di pinoli*, an ancient dish and a rarity these days in Liguria – flat pasta medallions in a pine nut dressing. Second courses focus on fish, notably a stew of *stoccafisso* (cod) with black olives and pine nuts. There's a great selection of Ligurian wines, too.
Salita San Leonardo 61r, Genoa; open 12:30–3pm & 7:30–10pm Mon–Sat, Sept–July; www.mangiareinliguria.it/dagenio

Also in Liguria

The tiny, friendly eatery of **Il Portico Spaghetteria** (*www.ilporticodicamogli.it; inexpensive*) in Camogli is tucked under the archways facing the beachfront. Aromatic pesto is served with ricotta on a *crostino* for antipasto, then with *trenette* as a first course. Try the good *intingolo di mare* dip of mussels and bread too.

Also in Italy

Trattoria Cantina Siciliana (*www.cantinasiciliana.it; moderate*) is a friendly Slow Food restaurant in Trapani, Sicily, that serves some memorable Sicilian food. One of the stand-out dishes is *busiate*, strips of fresh pasta curled into spirals around a knitting needle. They are dished up with delicious *pesto trapanese*, which translates as a superlative blend of finely chopped tomato, basil, garlic and almonds with pecorino cheese.

Around the World

In New York, the "food temple" that is **Eataly** (*www.eatalyny.com; inexpensive*) consists of several restaurants and small food stores; it resembles a giant food exhibition. This is the first member of the chain outside northern Italy, and they do a great *pasta al forno al pesto*, Ligurian-style pesto spread on top of lasagna pasta sheets that have been layered with a cheesy béchamel sauce. The final touch is a sprinkling of toasted pine nuts and cracked black peppercorns.

Ligurian Food Festivals

The pretty Cinque Terre village of **Monterosso al Mare** is the place to go if you love lemons; every spring it holds the Sagra del Limone, a fair celebrating lemons and everything made from them. The whole village is adorned in yellow and a myriad products – from marmalade and lemon cakes to the alcoholic Limoncello – can be tasted and bought. Every May the village of **Camogli** hosts a unique Sagra del Pesce, a fish fair first held by local fishermen in 1952. A truly gigantic frying pan, rated as the world's biggest, is set up in the seafront square and plates of fried fish are handed out to all and sundry during festivities for the patron saint San Fortunato. Also in May, neighbouring **Recco** celebrates another Ligurian speciality, the delicious *focaccia con formaggio*, a thin, fragrant bread spread with soft fresh cheese and baked quickly in a very hot oven.

Above Fragrant *pesto alla genovese* may be utterly smooth or deliciously grainy

Above Perfect cones of ground spices fill the air with aromas in the Mellah, the old Jewish quarter of Marrakech, Morocco

The Middle East and Africa

The Flavours of
The Middle East and Africa

Mention the Middle East in a culinary context and most people think of kebabs and kofte. In fact, the region's cuisine is as rich, colourful and ancient as its history. The region is also renowned for its hospitality, where "a guest is a gift from God"; travellers often find themselves invited to sample dishes where they taste best: in the home. In contrast to the Middle East's homogenous approach, Africa's 61 territories have enormously varied cuisines, offering surprising delights.

Mesopotamia, as it was known in ancient times, is called the "Cradle of Civilization" and it was here, around 7,000 years ago, that man first turned from nomadic hunter-gatherer into settled farmer. Part of a wider region known as the "Fertile Crescent", which stretched sickle-like from North Africa's Nile along the Mediterranean coast all the way to the Persian Gulf, this was the home of the Biblical Garden of Eden, and long was known as the "land of milk and honey".

It was the region's abundance of food and, in particular, wheat that first caught the covetous eye of the Romans, who occupied the area in the 2nd century AD. Hot on the heels of the Romans came other powers who introduced their own culinary traditions but also adopted the local ones. Later, they carried this culinary combination with them as they swept east or west, bequeathing the whole region an unusual culinary homogeneity. Like the magnificent ancient monuments of the Middle East, its foods are a legacy of the powers that passed through it. With the Arabs in the 7th century came dates and nuts as well as exotic spices from seafaring merchants, bringing turmeric, cardamon and cumin, peppercorns, cloves and allspice from India and Southeast Asia. With the Mongols came dumplings

> *This was the home of the Biblical Garden of Eden, and long was known as the "land of milk and honey".*

and the roasting of meat on fires – the world's first kebabs. The Persians brought rice and poultry, sometimes combining both into such sumptuous dishes as *khoresh-e fesejan* and *polo*. The Ottomans introduced the fine art of sweet and savoury pastry, conspiring to make such delectable delicacies as baklava, as well as the tradition of meze – dining on little dishes such as falafel and *kibbeh nayyeh* – and the fashion for drinking coffee.

The Phenomenon of the Souk

Nowhere are the region's riches more evident than in the souks, each one a labyrinthine warren of stalls selling the finest local goods and produce. There's rice and waxy saffron from the Caspian Sea, honey-sweet soft fruits including translucent apricots from Lebanon, plump cherries, quinces and melons from Iran, fragrant figs from Turkey, and beautiful artichokes, peppers, okra,

Right Pomegranate on sale in Iran, where it has long played a key role in the cuisine
Below Women selling the daily catch of sardines on a beach in Maputo, Mozambique

courgettes and aubergines from all over. The souk is a unique phenomenon of the Middle East, found in almost every town of the region; some are virtually unchanged since medieval times.

Africa's Ever-Evolving Cuisine

The second largest landmass on Earth, Africa comprises over a billion people inhabiting environments that range from hot deserts and snow-capped mountains to tropical forests and coastal wetlands. The continent's diversity of both peoples and geography is reflected in the contrast of its cuisines.

In East Africa, cattle are kept as a form of currency and wealth, so beef is generally reserved for special occasions; lamb, goat, poultry and game are all eaten too. Arabs who settled the coastal areas of East Africa over a millennium ago introduced rice and spices such as cinnamon and cloves, together with golden saffron from Persia. Later, Indian settlers introduced their own cuisines, including spices and curry dishes as well as pulses such as lentils, pickled vegetables, and breads such as chapatis. European colonization saw the introduction of citrus fruit and yet more spices from their Asian colonies; chillies, peanuts, peppers, maize and tomatoes from the New World; and tropical fruits from Brazil. Almost the only country in Africa to escape colonization – bar a brief, fiercely resisted seven-year period – was Ethiopia, which to this day retains much of its indigenous culture and cuisine, including its distinctive sourdough bread, *injera*.

North Africa, culturally part of the Middle East, shares that region's culinary traditions and influences, as well as boasting its own, particularly in regions close to the Atlantic and Mediterranean. South Africa's cooking is sometimes described as a "rainbow cuisine" because of the many influences that have shaped it. The indigenous Bantu-speaking people lived on wind-dried meat and wild game roasted over fires – traditions still seen today in the form of biltong and the South African love of braai, or barbecues. Other influences included the Dutch and

> *The continent's diversity of both peoples and geography is reflected in the contrast of its cuisines.*

British colonizers and Asian immigrants, who introduced pulses, soups and curries. The resulting culinary synthesis of Asian and Dutch influence can be seen in dishes such as *bobotie*.

West African cuisine is best known for its starchy staples made from the locally grown yams, cassava, cocoyams, maize and plantain that accompany spicy stews and soups. Outside Muslim Africa, alcoholic drinks are widely brewed, from the wines of Tunisia and South Africa and the honey wine – *tej* – of Ethiopia to the widely consumed palm wine and millet beer. The Middle East and Africa are brimming with exciting tastes and sights.

Left Seafood vendor in Forodhani Gardens, by the beach in Zanzibar, Tanzania
Below Spices for sale at the crowded Bzouriyah market in Old Damascus, Syria

A Day in Cairo

After a traditional breakfast of *fuul* (cooked, mashed fava beans), head first for the monumental 10th-century gateway, Bab Zowaylah.

MORNING Just outside the gate, take a look at the **Mosque of Salih Talay** and the **Souk Al Khayyameyyah**, which once furnished the Fatimid armies with tents and saddles. Climb the ramparts for spectacular views over the old city. After a visit to the **Mosque-Madrasah of Sultan Mu'ayyad Shaykh**, continue along Shari' Al Mu'ez Li Dinillah until you reach the 16th-century **Al Ghuri** complex.

AFTERNOON Visit the famous 10th-century mosque of **Al Azhar**, one of the oldest educational institutions in the world. Have Arabic coffee at Suliman Café and then shop for perfume, spice and gold in the famous **Khan al-Khalili bazaar**. If you have time, visit the **Fatimid** and **Mamluk** complexes, containing the world's densest collection of mosques, madrasahs, mausoleums and *khanqahs* (Sufi "monasteries").

EVENING See Sufi whirling dervishes at the **Wikala Al Ghuri**, then retire to a restaurant for falafel meze and delicious fresh seafood.

Essentials

GETTING THERE
Buses, minibuses and **taxis** connect Cairo's international **airport** with the city centre, 20 km (12 miles) away. Around town, the **metro** and **taxis** are the simplest ways of getting about.

WHERE TO STAY
Carlton Hotel (inexpensive) is centrally located in a 1930s building with simple but spotless rooms. www.carltonhotelcairo.com

Grand Hotel (moderate) is less grand than it once was but the former five-storey palace still offers large and comfortable rooms at good prices. www.grandhotelcairo.com

Mena House Oberoi (expensive) is a stunning 19th-century hunting lodge with breathtaking pyramid views. www.menahouseoberoi.com

TOURIST INFORMATION
www.egypt.travel

Left Fast food Egyptian-style: crunchy falafel in pitta bread with cucumber, lettuce, mint leaves and yogurt
Below One of the many glorious food and spice stalls in the legendary Khan al-Khalili bazaar, Cairo

CAIRO EGYPT

Fast Falafel in Old Cairo

A world away from the tourist-thronged pyramids and the commotion of central Cairo lies the quarter known as "Medieval Cairo". This small area has 850 listed monuments, making it one of the most heritage-rich enclaves on Earth. Evocative, atmospheric and little changed, the fascinating quarter is also believed to be the home of Egypt's version of fast food: the falafel.

For many, Egypt's capital Cairo is synonymous with pharaohs, pyramids and sphinxes. But Cairo was never in fact a Pharaonic city, despite being situated close to the ancient capital of Memphis, and was only formally founded in the 10th century under the Fatimids, who marched in from modern-day Tunisia. Al Qahira ("the victorious"), as Cairo is still known in Arabic today, soon grew into a great and prosperous city ruled by a series of wealthy, tyrannical and sometimes capricious sultans.

The magnificent monuments erected during this time made the city a legend in its own day and many still survive. Extending from the old Fatimid gate of Bab Zowaylah in the south to Bab Al Futuh in the north, Al Qahira is as well preserved architecturally as it is atmospherically; it is quite simply one of the finest, most evocative medieval cities in the world.

Market-goers for centuries have had to dodge the donkey carts that still clatter down the alleyways. In the souks, the piles of pungent spices and the earthy aromas emanating from the food stalls are a heady mix; and the competing cries of the *gallabiyya*-clad market vendors echo around the city walls.

From the 4th to the 6th centuries the Copts, a very early Christian community, were the largest religious group in Egypt. They were keen to create a vegetarian alternative to meat for days of fasting and are credited with the invention of falafel (or *ta'amiya* as it's better known in Cairo) for this purpose. The popular fritter caught on throughout Egypt, then across the Middle East and beyond. It is usually made from uncooked, ground fava beans in Egypt (or from chickpeas or a combination of both elsewhere), which are mixed with garlic, parsley, sesame seeds, onions, pepper, cumin and coriander, then deep-fried until golden brown.

Falafel is served as meze (*see also pp110–13*), and sometimes as part of *iftar*, the meal that breaks the daily fast after sunset during Ramadan. But it's usually eaten as a kind of fast food, in pitta bread or *lafa* (another flatbread), with salad, pickled vegetables, hot chilli sauce and tahini (a sesame seed paste). Hot, crisp and freshly made falafel is the perfect thing to eat while drifting among the beautiful buildings of old Cairo.

Egyptian Eating Etiquette

In the Arab world, the right hand only is used for eating. The left, reserved for toilet ablutions, is kept firmly tucked away. If eating from a communal plate, it's considered bad manners to tuck in with too much relish – including reaching for dishes not placed near you, overfilling your mouth or eating too fast. The refusal of at least some second helpings is equally frowned upon. Once full, locals sometimes place their right hand over their stomach or heart to show repletion and gratitude. During the Muslim month of Ramadan, it shows sensitivity and respect to avoid eating, drinking or smoking in public. If invited to an Egyptian household, it's considered good manners to bring a small gift such as flowers, chocolates or pastries. Shoes are left at the door, hands are washed, and guests are seated next to a person of the same sex.

Above The Al Azhar mosque was completed in 972 for the new city of Al Qahira

The Best Places to Eat Falafel

Naguib Mahfouz Café expensive

Naguib Mahfouz is like an oasis amid the swirling motion and commotion of the Khan al-Khalili bazaar. Named after Egypt's 1988 winner of the Nobel Prize for Literature, who regularly came here, the café-cum-restaurant provides a cool, serene and civilized escape from Cairo's chaos. The elegant, marbled café is a great place for a fresh falafel snack, reviving cup of Arabic coffee or *sheesha* pipe – or better still, all three. Deeper inside, the lavish decor *à l'Oriental* of the formal restaurant provides an atmospheric and moody setting for a quiet lunch or dinner, particularly inside the private niches off the corridor. Specializing in classic Egyptian dishes that are well prepared, cooked and served, the Naguib is an excellent choice for a first foray into Egyptian cooking or for a last-night splurge. The Naguib's *ta'amiya* (falafel) are prepared with finely diced green onion and garlic, subtly spiced with coriander and cumin and topped with sesame seeds.

5 Sikket Al Baddistan, Khan al-Khalili, Cairo; open 10am–11pm daily; +20 2 2590 3788

Also in Cairo

Run by the same family for 50 years, the **Felfella Restaurant** *(+20 2 2392 2833; moderate)* on Shari' Hoda Shaarawi has carved a niche and reputation for itself by offering fresh, wholesome and good-quality Egyptian cooking at competitive prices in clean, convivial surroundings. *Ta'amiya* is the speciality: the crisp and carefully fried exterior hides a bright green fava interior which shouts of freshness and attentive cooking. For a good inexpensive pit stop when you're sightseeing, try **Al Halwagy** *(inexpensive)*, located 150 m (165 yards) east of Shari' Al Mu'ez Li Dinillah. Over a century old, this tiny, modest little place has survived through force of reputation: its *ta'amiya* and *fuul* are legendary.

Also in Egypt

Mohammed Ahmed *(+20 3 487 3576; inexpensive)* in Alexandria is an unassuming restaurant with a fanatical local following. Two staples have made it famous: *ta'amiya* and *fuul*. The menu (available in English) offers a good choice of salads, sauces and condiments to accompany the little golden beauties, which can be eaten in or taken away.

Around the World

In central London, the **Ali Baba** *(+44 20 7723 7474; inexpensive)* near Regent's Park has developed something of a cult following for both nostalgic Egyptians and Londoners seeking fresh, decent Middle Eastern food at attractive prices, including the crunchy and flavoursome *ta'amiya*.

ISFAHAN IRAN

Khoresh-e Fesenjan in Isfahan

As the call to prayer rises from its minarets, Isfahan's famous mosque, Masjid-e Emam, glitters in the late afternoon sun. In the nearby bazaar, the air is filled with the scent of spices, and towards the city's edge an ancient fire temple is silhouetted against low, jagged hills. There is no more atmospheric place to sample *khoresh-e fesenjan*, one of the most opulent dishes in Persian cuisine.

Isfahan is an unforgettable place. Imagine a square – originally a polo ground – surrounded by some of the most exquisitely beautiful architecture to be found anywhere in the Islamic world. The Persian capital during the 16th and 17th centuries, Isfahan is for many synonymous with the art and architecture of Iran – refined palaces, elegant gardens and mosques lavishly decorated with dazzling blue and turquoise tiles.

Iran (Persia) has an exceptionally long history. It was already a formidable empire some 2,500 years ago, against which first the Greeks and then the Romans measured themselves. Though there are plenty of signs of this long history in Isfahan, the city is most closely associated with the Safavid period, when the great ruler Shah Abbas turned it into his capital in the late 16th century. He laid out the Meydan-e Emam (a huge square) together with the Masjid-e Emam (the famous royal mosque on the south side of the square) and the smaller Masjid-e Lotfallah mosque. These buildings still constitute one of the greatest architectural ensembles on the planet, and along with the Meydan-e Emam are inscribed on the UNESCO World Heritage list.

The cuisine of the Persian empire also developed over the course of many centuries, and is equally refined. *Khoresh* is the Persian word for a stew or sauce, and it comes in many guises, of which *fesenjan* is one of the best known and certainly one of the richest. This dish – also called the king of stews – is often prepared at home for special occasions. Chicken, or more traditionally duck, is simmered with onion, ground toasted walnuts and pomegranate syrup until literally falling off the bone. The resulting sauce is a rich, dark brown, with an exquisite sweet-bitter flavour from the walnuts, pomegranate, lemon and cinnamon. Some say the dish originates in northern Iran, though it can be found across the country – at least, in restaurants serving a range of dishes rather than just kebabs, the nation's favourite fast food.

Khoresh-e fesenjan is served with rice, cooked slowly to perfection and topped with melting butter, a serving of tasty yogurt and a wedge of the golden crust (called *tah-dig* in Persian) that forms at the bottom of the rice pan. This is the best part of the dish, as far as many Iranians are concerned. Of course, this being Iran, you won't be drinking wine with your meal – think more in terms of a glass of cool mineral water.

A Day in Isfahan

Most of Isfahan's main sights, including the Meydan-e Emam and the bazaar, are north of the Zayandeh river, while the Armenian quarter and a few other places lie south.

MORNING Start with the **Masjid-e Jame**, a 12th-century masterpiece that has an amazing carved stucco prayer niche from the Mongol period. Then walk through the streets of the **bazaar** to the **Meydan-e Emam**, the vast square laid out at the close of the 16th century, and visit the magnificent **Masjid-e Emam**.

AFTERNOON Visit other buildings on the Meydan-e Emam, including the breathtaking **Masjid-e Lotfallah** and **Ali Qapu Palace**, then take a short walk to the **Hasht Behesht Palace** in the gardens nearby. Share a taxi to the old Armenian quarter of **New Julfa**, with its fascinating churches.

EVENING Return to the river, ducking under one end of the **Si-o Se** bridge to stop at the atmospheric teahouse beneath the arches. Walk to **Restoran-e Shahrzad** in the centre of the city for *khoresh-e fesenjan*.

Essentials

GETTING THERE
Iranian Air and other Gulf states airlines fly into Isfahan's airport. There are **shared taxis** to the city 25 km (15 miles) away. **Trains** run from Tehran.

WHERE TO STAY
Amir Kabir Hostel (inexpensive) is the most popular low budget option. *+98 311 222 7273*
Hotel Julfa (moderate) in the Armenian quarter is another good choice. *+98 311 624 4441*
Hasht Behesht Apartment Hotel (moderate) is modern and just five minutes from the Meydan-e Emam. *www.ehbhotel.webs.com*

FURTHER INFORMATION
www.isfahan.ir

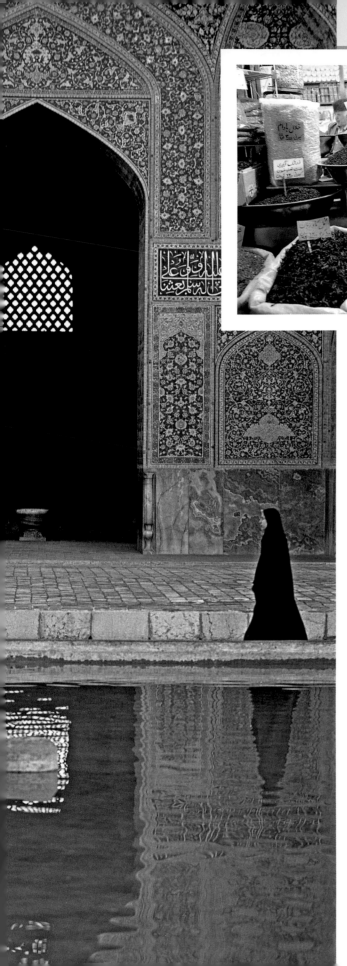

Above The Bazaar-e Bozorg is a 400-year-old market selling an astonishing array of goods, including a vast range of spices

Left It is said that nearly half a million tiles make up the exquisite mosaic patterning and calligraphy decorating the Masjid-e Emam, or Imam Mosque

Above The thick, dark sauce of *khoresh-e fesenjan* surprises the taste buds with its unique sweet-bitter flavour from pomegranates and walnuts

What Else to Eat

Khoresh-e fesenjan is a great example of a *khoresh* or sauce-based dish, but there are many others, such as **khoresh-e bademjan** (aubergines with chicken, lamb or duck), **khoresh-e ghormeh sabzi** (lamb cooked in a sauce of fresh green herbs) and **khoresh torsh** (lamb with dried fruit). Along with plenty of fresh herbs and spices such as cinnamon and nutmeg, another popular ingredient you may encounter in these dishes is whole dried lime, which imparts a wonderful flavour. The accompaniment to *khoresh* is a mountain of perfectly cooked rice. Iranians generally eat their main meal in the middle of the day – so look for *khoresh* then, rather than in the evening.

The Best Places to Eat Khoresh-e Fesenjan

Restoran-e Shahrzad moderate

In the centre of Isfahan and only a short walk from the Meydan-e Emam, Restoran-e Shahrzad serves some of the finest Persian cuisine in Isfahan – including a delicious *khoresh-e fesenjan*. There is a good range of dishes on the menu, from golden *tachin (see p179)* and other rice dishes to fish and sizzling kebabs. Portions are generous, the staff polite and efficient and the interior decor suitably lavish, complete with wood panelling, colourful stained glass windows and paintings in the style of Persian miniatures. Prices are slightly higher than average for Isfahan, but still very reasonable. As with most restaurants, the *fesenjan* here is made with chicken rather than duck – but it is nevertheless incredibly rich and fragrant, deep-coloured and bursting with sweet and sour flavours. The buttery rice is, as always, a perfect partner to this heady stew. The long-established Shahrzad is understandably popular with locals as well as foreign visitors, and is both a great place to eat out in Isfahan and a wonderful introduction to the delicious Persian *fesenjan*.
Abbas Abad Street, Isfahan; open 11:30am– 10:30pm daily; +98 311 220 4490

Also in Isfahan

The **Khan Gostar** restaurant (*+98 311 627 8989; moderate*) in the Hotel Julfa is one of the best places to eat in town – perhaps as good as Shahrzad – and a good place to try a range of Persian dishes. Popular with Isfahanis, this restaurant is further from the city centre, but an obvious choice if you're spending time in Isfahan's historic Armenian quarter. By far the most atmospheric place to sip tea in town is in the **teahouse** (*inexpensive*) under the Si-o Se bridge – you may even find *abgusht*, a thick meat and potato stew that's a speciality of Tabriz in northwest Iran, rather than *khoresh*.

Also in Iran

Ferdosi Sonnati (*+98 21 6671 4503; inexpensive*) is a busy place at the southern end of Ferdosi Street in Tehran, which serves plenty of traditional Persian dishes including several types of *khoresh*.

Around the World

One of the best Persian restaurants in London is **Shandi's** (*www.shandispersianrestaurant. co.uk; moderate*). Smaller and less well-known than some others, this gem of a restaurant has excellent food, reasonable prices and offers a genuinely warm welcome. The *khoresh-e fesenjan* is delicious.

CAPE TOWN SOUTH AFRICA

Bobotie Beneath Table Mountain

Situated near Africa's southern tip, cosmopolitan Cape Town is a city of singular natural beauty. Rising from a gorgeous natural harbour to the footslopes of iconic Table Mountain, it is also the home of *bobotie*, the definitive dish of the Cape Malay community, whose fusion of Indonesian, Dutch and indigenous elements has created a unique cuisine emblematic of the city itself.

Boasting world-class restaurants that represent every conceivable global cuisine, Cape Town is Africa's culinary answer to London or New York – but with the added advantages of a warm climate, a tourist-friendly exchange rate and one of the world's top winelands on the doorstep. It's ironic, then, that you could spend quite some time in Cape Town without realizing that it boasts its own distinctive cuisine; but possible, because Cape Malay cuisine, like the community, stands slightly outside the South African mainstream.

The Cape Malay are an anomaly. In a land whose history is dominated by the clash between indigenous Africans and European settlers, this tightly knit community is descended from Indonesian slaves and religious dissidents brought here by the earliest Dutch settlers. The community retains a strong Islamic identity, despite South Africa being predominantly Christian, yet its mother tongue is the Dutch derivative called Afrikaans, while the famously sentimental songs performed by its choirs are called *Nederlandsliede* (Dutch Songs).

Unsurprisingly, Cape Malay cuisine is a curious mixture. The curries are sweeter and milder than their Indonesian forerunners due to the use of fruit preserves. *Sosaties* – kebabs soaked in a sweet, spicy marinade – are a linguistic fusion of the Dutch *saus* (sauce) and Indonesian satay (skewered meat). And the inclusion of Cape pondweed in a lamb dish called *waterblommetjiebredie* (water-flower stew) is borrowed from the indigenous Khoikhoi. The national dish of South Africa, *bobotie*, was probably introduced to the Cape by early Dutch settlers before being re-adopted by their Indonesian slaves. Rather like a spicy moussaka, it comprises a fruity, curried minced meat base, topped with an eggy sauce that forms a crust when baked.

Cape Malay culture still thrives in the Bo-Kaap (Upper Cape), a residential district of brightly painted houses that offers superb views across the city bowl to the unmistakeable flat top of Table Mountain – accessed from the city centre by a thrilling revolving cable car. Further afield, Cape Town offers limitless opportunities for memorable expeditions, including whale-watching in False Bay, a hike to the clifftop Cape Point Lighthouse or a boat trip to Robben Island.

Above Cape Town sits at the foot of the spectacular Table Mountain, which dominates the city skyline; the summit can be reached in minutes by cable car

Cape Wines

Viniculture in the Cape dates back to 1659, when the colony's founder Jan van Riebeeck produced a small amount of doubtless rather rough wine. The subsequent arrival of French Huguenots prompted the fledgling industry to spread inland to **Stellenbosch, Franschhoek** and **Paarl,** the site of historic vineyards such as Blaauwklippen, Boschendal and Vergelegen. Today, South Africa is the world's seventh-largest wine producer, with about a dozen different grape varieties. **Cabernet Sauvignon,** the most widely planted red, produces heavy wines that complement red meats. **Pinotage,** a uniquely South African cultivar, makes a fruity, purple wine that often represents the best value among the reds. Of the whites, **Sauvignon Blanc** provides a crisp zesty complement to Cape Malay dishes and seafood.

Three Days in and around Cape Town

Cape Town and its immediate environs could easily keep you busy for a fortnight. It boasts iconic mountains, rustic wine estates, colourful botanical gardens, modern shopping malls, windswept oceanic cliffs and superb swimming beaches, all set against the craggy spine of Table Mountain National Park (TMNP).

DAY ONE Head to the summit of **Table Mountain,** which is most easily reached by cable car. It has interesting wildlife and offers breathtaking views in all directions. After lunching at **Noon Gun,** head to the **Company's Gardens,** founded by van Riebeeck and encircled by historic landmarks such as the **Old Slave Lodge, National Museum, St George's Cathedral** and **House of Parliament.**

DAY TWO Take off for the **Western Cape Peninsula** and the **Constantia Winelands,** taking in the spectacular Cape of Good Hope sector of **TMNP** and the penguin colony at **Boulders.** Lunch at Groot Constantia's **Jonkershuis Restaurant,** then enjoy an afternoon stroll around **Kirstenbosch Botanical Garden.**

DAY THREE Visit sedate old **Stellenbosch,** famed for its wealth of Cape Dutch architecture, then go wine-tasting in the surrounding **Cape Winelands.**

Essentials

GETTING THERE
Most international flights land at **Johannesburg,** two hours by air from Cape Town; **trains** and **buses** connect the cities. There are also direct flights from Europe to **Cape Town International Airport,** 30 minutes from the city centre.

WHERE TO STAY
For cosy good value, the **Lord Nelson Inn** (inexpensive) in historic Simonstown is hard to beat. www.lordnelsoninn.co.za
Cape Town Hollow (moderate) is a conveniently central hotel situated opposite the Company's Gardens. www.capetownhollow.co.za
The Cape Grace (expensive) is the epitome of contemporary five-star chic. www.capegrace.com

TOURIST INFORMATION
www.tourismcapetown.co.za

The Best Places to Eat Bobotie

Jonkershuis Restaurant moderate

A historic setting in suburban Groot Constantia, South Africa's oldest wine estate, is just one of many reasons why a relaxed lunch at the Jonkershuis ranks among the Cape Peninsula's most iconic dining experiences. The setting here really is lovely, with long leafy rows of vines sloping up to the base of the ragged peaks of the Constantia Mountain, and the option of dining alfresco in the oak-shaded gardens. If this doesn't appeal, you can eat inside the period-furnished main building, a thatched and whitewashed Cape Dutch edifice dating to the 18th century. Owned and managed by a team of the Cape's most experienced restaurateurs, Jonkershuis prides itself on its Cape Malay menu, which includes *bobotie* – here served with an accompaniment of *sambals* (chilli sauces) and almond-flavoured yellow rice. For those seeking a one-stop introduction to the local cuisine, the restaurant produces a sumptuous Cape Malay "tasting plate", a kind of mini-buffet featuring *bobotie* alongside a rich lamb curry, a lighter chicken curry and cinnamon-flavoured roast butternut. There's a great choice of Cape whites, including the estate's own oaked Chardonnay and Sauvignon Blanc, and the dessert menu includes Cape specialities such as *melktert* (milk tart) and *malva* pudding, a spongy, apricot-flavoured dish of Dutch origin.

Off Constantia Main Road, Cape Town; open 9am–10pm Mon–Sat; 9am–5pm Sun; www.jonkershuisconstantia.co.za

Also in Cape Town

The **Noon Gun Tea Room & Restaurant** *(www.noonguntearoom.co.za; inexpensive)* dishes up excellent *bobotie* along with the likes of *deningvleis* (a hearty sweet-sour lamb stew), chicken *breyeni* (a spicy rice-based risotto-like dish) and a good selection of characteristically sweet desserts to finish. Set in the world-famous Kirstenbosch Botanical Garden on the eastern slopes of Table Mountain, the **Silver Tree Restaurant** *(www.kirstenboschrestaurant.com; moderate)* is famous for its picnic hampers, but it also serves a good *bobotie* – made with super-lean ostrich meat in a traditional *potjie* (black pot) – and tasty Cape Malay curry.

Also in South Africa

Gramadoelas *(www.gramadoelas.co.za; expensive)* in Johannesburg has played host to luminaries as diverse as Queen Elizabeth II and the actor Danny Glover. *Bobotie* is a firm favourite on the menu, alongside other Cape dishes such as *waterblommetjiebredie* (water-flower stew) and piping hot, grilled *sosaties*.

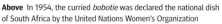

Above In 1954, the curried *bobotie* was declared the national dish of South Africa by the United Nations Women's Organization

Left The lines of colourful houses in the Bo Kaap Malay quarter are occasionally broken by *kramats* (Muslim saint shrines) and mosques

MARRAKECH MOROCCO

Spicy Tagine in the City of Souks

The sunset tinges the distant Atlas mountains a deep rose-red, and the call to prayer echoes from the turret of the Koutoubia Mosque. This is the time for the snake-charmers and henna artists of Jemaa el-Fna square to make way for the food-laden stalls of Marrakech's night food market. Take a stroll around the spectacle before tucking into a traditional Moroccan tagine.

An oasis in every sense of the word, Marrakech was once a beacon for trading caravans that had travelled north through the desert and navigated over the often snow-capped Atlas Mountains. The fabulous palaces and lush palms of the city have always been where sub-Saharan Africa meets Arab North Africa, and even today this market town on the edge of nowhere remains a compellingly exotic port of call.

Life in the medina – the old walled city – revolves around the towering medieval minaret of the Koutoubia Mosque. For many visitors, though, this is eclipsed by the atmospheric Jemaa el-Fna, the nerve centre of Marrakech, with its weird and wonderful cast of artists and performers – from water-sellers to fortune-tellers – and spectacular, frenetic food market.

Next head for the ancient souk – a vast area of higgledy-piggledy, cupboard-sized shops and stalls filling dozens of narrow alleyways. Delicious smells draw you further into the endless maze of lanes, where stalls are laden with bundles of fresh mint, jars of plump olives infused with lemon and garlic, and bright pyramids of spice. Intricately made leather goods, metalwork, inlaid boxes, brass lanterns, carpets and jewellery overflow the little stallholders' tables and floor. Slightly less overwhelming are the food and spice markets of the Mellah, the old Jewish quarter; the Place des Ferblantiers, where tinsmiths make and sell their wares, is a relative haven from the hustle and bustle. Find a rooftop café terrace for a refreshing mint tea – and look out for white storks, soaring to their nests on top of the old royal tombs and palaces.

After a day's sightseeing, shopping or wandering the souk, there is nothing better than sitting down to enjoy a rich, fragrant tagine – the signature dish of Morocco. This aromatic dish combines meat – usually lamb, sometimes chicken – with fruit (often dried), vegetables and a heady mix of herbs and spices, including saffron, cumin, coriander and nutmeg.

The concoction is then braised slowly over a bed of charcoal in its distinctive and eponymous clay pot. The traditional conical-lidded dish synonymous with tagine – effectively a robust, portable cooking pot and serving dish all in one – originated with the Berber and Tuareg tribes of the Sahara. The use of dried fruits and the emphasis on aromatic spices also stem from this nomadic culture. Marrakech may have smartened itself up a little in recent years for the tourist trade, but its ancient, desert heart still beats strong.

A Day in Marrakech

The rich history of Marrakech is reflected in its various quarters. The medina corresponds to the old town, with Jemaa el-Fna, the hub of all activity, at its heart. Within the ramparts are the souks, the kasbah and the Mellah.

MORNING Start at **Jemaa el-Fna**, the vast square at the heart of the medina, which is as old as Marrakech itself. Just off the square, and dominating Marrakech's skyline, is the tower of the **Koutoubia Mosque**. Like most mosques in Morocco, it is closed to non-Muslims, but is an impressive sight nonetheless.

AFTERNOON Laid out in the narrow streets north of Jemaa el-Fna are a spectacular array of **souks**, or bazaars, selling everything from carpets and slippers to magic spells, in which you can while away whole mornings or afternoons. Continue to the **city walls** that enclose the medina, studded with 20 ornamental gates.

EVENING Return to **Jemaa el-Fna**, which transforms itself at night into a circus, theatre and restaurant, with itinerant musicians and entertainers drawing crowds.

Essentials

GETTING THERE
Menara International Airport is 4 km (2 miles) from the city centre. **Taxis** are readily available.

WHERE TO STAY
Hôtel Sherazade (inexpensive) has simple rooms within a *riad* (traditional Moorish town house). *www.hotelsherazade.com*
Tchaikana (moderate) is a beautiful *riad* within the medina. *www.tchaikana.com*
La Maison Arabe (expensive) was the first boutique hotel in Marrakech, and offers luxury and comfort. *www.lamaisonarabe.com*

TOURIST INFORMATION
Place Abdelmoumen Ben Ali (Av Mohammed V).

Above Richly coloured and scented mounds of saffron, paprika and cumin for sale in the souk

Left The Jemaa el-Fna at night becomes a noisy mass of food stalls, suffused with the aromas of kebabs grilling on charcoal braziers

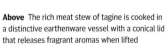

Above The rich meat stew of tagine is cooked in a distinctive earthenware vessel with a conical lid that releases fragrant aromas when lifted

Cookery Schools

Take more than just a tagine dish home from your trip to Marrakech – there are several great cookery schools in and around the city offering workshops and courses in Moroccan cuisine and tagine is always on the syllabus. **Kasbah Agafy** (*www.kasbahagafay.com*) offers outdoor cookery courses in the organic herb and vegetable garden of a beautifully renovated 150-year-old fort, 20 minutes from Marrakech. **La Maison Arabe** (*see Where to Stay*) holds half-day cookery workshops for residents and guests. **Rhodes School of Cuisine** (*www. rhodeschoolofcuisine.com*) runs week-long courses with luxury *riad* accommodation.

The Best Places to Eat Tagine

Restaurant Al Fassia moderate

Restaurant Al Fassia faces on to a tiny but leafy courtyard and is decorated in warm, earthy colours in a modern Moroccan style. Here, chef Halima Chab and her all-woman team prepare and serve a repertoire of tagines, with up to 13 on the menu at any one time – and all of them supreme examples of the art. They might include tender lamb with caramelized onions and pumpkin, or dates and roasted almonds; chicken with olives and preserved lemons; or *kefta* (spicy meatballs) with eggs.

Begin your meal with a selection from Al Fassia's stunning range of meze, which includes a delicious honey- and cinnamon-scented squash purée, and finish with Halima Chab's signature dessert of *b'stilla* (a filo pastry) with almonds and milk.

Founded over 20 years ago, Al Fassia was once legendary – and loved – for its no-nonsense service. Since its move to a more upmarket venue in the residential Guéliz district, the atmosphere has become more refined – but the standard of cooking undoubtedly remains one of the high points of any visit to Marrakech.
55 Boulevard Zerktouni, Guéliz, Marrakech; open noon–2:30pm and 7:30–11pm daily, except Tue; www.alfassia.com

Also in Marrakech

To sample a tagine as part of a fine-dining experience, try the elegant and atmospheric **La Maison Arabe** (*www.lamaisonarabe.com; expensive*) or the historic **La Mamounia** hotel (*www.mamounia.com; moderate*), with its magnificent terrace on the ground floor and bar and tearoom on the top floor. And for a simple but authentic tagine, as well as a jaw-dropping view over the city, opt for the rooftop tables of popular **Chez Chegrouni** at 4–6 Jemaa el-Fna (*no telephone; inexpensive*).

Also in Morocco

Interesting regional variations on the tagine are on offer around Morocco. In Fès, try **Al Firdaouss** (*+212 535 634 343; moderate*). This is one of Fès's most enchanting restaurants and serves a delicious tagine. A short walk away is the traditional **Palais Tariana** (*+212 535 636 604; expensive*).

Around the World

London's Moroccan community first started to arrive in the 1960s. Since then Moroccan food has become increasingly available and fashionable. **Momo**, just off Regent Street (*www.momoresto.com; expensive*), is London's most famous and glam Moroccan restaurant, serving high-quality food. Also in central London, **Original Tagines** (*www.original-tagines.com; inexpensive*) serves excellent tagines in contemporary Moroccan surrounds.

Three Days on Zanzibar

Though Stone Town boasts several striking architectural landmarks to head for, it is also conducive to whimsical exploration, routinely throwing up fantastic sights, sounds and smells – and it's not so large that you could truly get lost.

DAY ONE Dedicate the day to Stone Town. Start at the **Palace Museum** then follow the waterfront south to the **House of Wonders**, **Forodhani Gardens** and lastly the **Old Arab Fort**, a great spot for lunch. In the afternoon, browse the shops on **Kenyatta**, **Gizenga** and **Hurumzi Streets**, or venture north into the tangle of alleys at the heart of Stone Town. Have a drink at the historic **Africa House Hotel**.

DAY TWO An organized **Spice Tour** will combine a visit to a local *shamba* (subsistence farm) with stops at several ruined 19th-century palaces and baths north of town.

DAY THREE Drive south to **Kizimkani** for a dhow trip and swimming with dolphins. Return via **Jozani Forest** to seek out the Zanzibar red colobus, a spectacularly coiffed monkey unique to this island.

Essentials

GETTING THERE
Zanzibar International Airport has flights from Ethiopia and Kenya; there's a larger airport at Dar es Salaam, a short trip away by **plane** or **ferry**. The town is easily explored on **foot**.

WHERE TO STAY
Hotel Kiponda (inexpensive) is a long-serving budget favourite that's centrally located with some period character. *www.kiponda.com*
236 Hurumzi (moderate–expensive) has an unbeatable atmosphere; it's a three-storey, 19th-century mansion lavishly furnished in period style. *www.236hurumzi.com*
Zanzibar Serena Inn (expensive) is a more conventional and overtly luxurious hotel on the waterfront. *www.serenahotels.com*

TOURIST INFORMATION
www.zanzibartourism.net

Right *Mnazi wa kamba* (prawn curry), bathed in the golden-brown sauce made from masala and coconut milk

Below The legendary food stalls of Forodhani Gardens fire up their grills at sunset

ZANZIBAR TANZANIA

Swahili Curry on Zanzibar

For over 1,000 years, Zanzibar has been a cultural melting pot. Its historic centre, Stone Town, has a captivating blend of African, Arabic, Asian and European architecture, and there's a rich mix of languages and cultures among its inhabitants. Zanzibari dishes are equally cosmopolitan, such as *mnazi*, a tangy, coconut-milk curry that seamlessly blends Indian, Arabic and homegrown elements.

The very name "Zanzibar" drips with exoticism; most visitors agree that the Spice Island, which lies in the Indian Ocean off Tanzania's Swahili coast, is one of those travel destinations that truly matches expectations. Around the coast, mysterious ruins recall a millennium of maritime trade with Arabia. The pristine swathes of palm-lined white sand give way to a sea that offers magical diving and snorkelling, and the opportunity to swim with dolphins.

Zanzibar's cultural heart is historic Stone Town: a labyrinthine knot of narrow alleys, ostentatious Omani palaces and multistorey Swahili homesteads emanating from a medieval harbour with an imposing 17th-century Omani fort. The town's prosperity peaked in the mid-19th century, when it served as a capital for the Sultan of Oman and formed the main trade conduit for slaves captured on the African mainland. One of the most symbolically resonant landmarks on the island is the Anglican Cathedral, built on the site of the town's notorious slave market.

Today, the giddying smell of spiced Swahili *kahawa* (coffee) permeates Stone Town, punctuated by tantalizing wafts of home cooking. There are stalls piled with aromatic foodstuffs; fresh and dried spices vie with the heady scents of juicy fresh fruits.

Zanzibari cuisine has been influenced by centuries of trade with Arabia and Asia, and its most popular dish is Swahili coconut curry. Made with chicken, fish or seafood – and sometimes even beef – it incorporates the golden-brown Zanzibari masala, a superb mix of ground cinnamon, roasted coriander, cumin and fennel seeds, fresh chilli and coriander. This imparts a spicy tang that blends with fresh coconut milk to produce a curry with a deep, creamy texture and rich aftertaste. Accompanied by *wali na nazi* (rice boiled in coconut milk), chapatis and spinach-like *sukuma wiki*, Swahili curry – *mnazi* –is the culinary embodiment of the glorious Spice Island and its cosmospolitan past. It's arguably best eaten from the overflowing dinner stalls of the waterfront Forodhani Gardens, which emerge mysteriously by the shore as the sun sets over the Indian Ocean, offering a unique sensory treat.

What Else to Eat

Seafood features strongly on Zanzibari menus, with a particular favourite being marinated and grilled **prawns**. These are served at a cluster of food stalls in Forodhani Gardens, alongside other East African favourites such as **nyama choma** (grilled meat), **chapatis** (flatbreads) and **sugar cane juice**. Fresh fruit is also prominent, including outsized and super-tasty coconuts and pineapples, but the adventurous might want to try **embe keri** (unripe mango sprinkled with chilli flakes) or the delicious but foul-smelling, spiky-coated durian fruit. Other popular Swahili dishes on the island include **boko-boko**, an aromatic porridge-type dish made of shredded meat and bulgur wheat, and **urojo** (literally "mixed") soup, in which cubes of grilled beef are placed with potatoes, chickpea fritters and whatever-else-is-going in a fruity stock.

Above Zanzibar's uncrowded beaches are interspersed by small fishing villages

The Best Places to Eat Swahili Curry

Monsoon Restaurant moderate

The ultimate Zanzibari night out is provided by this well-established traditional restaurant, especially if you time your visit to coincide with the live *taarab* (classical Swahili music) performances on Wednesday and Friday nights. The terrace is ideal for an early evening drink, allowing you to watch the sun set over Forodhani Gardens while sailing dhows billow romantically across the Indian Ocean. Inside, the restaurant is divided into two areas. The homely bar is the place to relax over a fresh cocktail or ginger-spiced coffee, accompanied perhaps by a sweet *kashata* (nutty biscuit). The main culinary action takes place next door, in a large open area decorated in the Swahili way, with *mikeka* matting spread across the floor and ground-level seating on brightly coloured cushions set around knee-high tables, their tops scattered with fragrant fresh jasmine. An imaginative à la carte menu combines traditional Zanzibari favourites – Swahili chicken curry, kingfish in coconut sauce, prawns marinated in garlic, ginger and lime – with fusion fare that incorporates influences from all corners of the Mediterranean. There's a four-course dinner for diners with adventurous palates.

Hurumzi St, Stone Town, Zanzibar; open 10am–midnight daily; www.monsoon-zanzibar.com

Also on Zanzibar

Situated on the ground floor of the historic "House of Tea" hotel on Kelele Square, **Beyt al Chai Restaurant** (*www.bluebayzanzibar.com; expensive*) might not look anything special in daylight, but the food is arguably the finest on Zanzibar, and it's complemented by a lovely candle-lit ambience at dinner. The cuisine can be categorized broadly as Swahili fusion, with keynote dishes including a Zanzibar casserole of seafood poached in coconut and lemongrass broth, and there is an excellent wine list.

Also in Africa

Traditional Swahili cuisine is poorly represented at restaurants in Dar es Salaam, the largest city in Tanzania and former capital, but **Sweet Eazy Restaurant & Lounge** (*www.sweeteazy.com; moderate–expensive*) is a notable exception, serving an imaginative menu of traditional and fusion dishes including a superb seafood coconut curry. The arched decor evokes traditional Swahili architecture and there's live music at weekends. On Shela Beach, on the outskirts of the time-warped Kenyan port of Lamu, the stylish "barefoot luxury" **Peponi Hotel** (*www.peponi-lamu.com; expensive*) is renowned for its fresh seafood, whether you like it sushi-style, grilled plain or curried in the traditional Swahili manner.

ALEPPO SYRIA

Cherry Kebabs in Ancient Aleppo

In the shadow of the looming Citadel, the souk of Aleppo teems and bustles with life. It is the beating heart of one of the world's oldest inhabited cities, and shimmers with vivid colours and smells as it has since the days of the Silk Road. It was here that merchants sold Eastern spices alongside fresh local produce, and that most Aleppian of recipes, *kabab bil karaz*, was born.

It is said that the covered souk in Aleppo stretches over 32 km (20 miles), making it the largest in the world. But size matters less than atmosphere in recreating the tumult and excitement of a medieval Arabian marketplace – and Syria's second city has atmosphere in abundance. This is not a touristy souk, although it is perfect for visitors who wish to wander beneath its impressive stone arches and browse without being harassed by traders. Aleppians pride themselves on their hospitality towards travellers, in traditional Bedouin fashion.

During Aleppo's 7,000 years of history, it has been overrun by Hittites, Assyrians, Persians and Romans. Walk around the wonderful Old City, and you'll see architecture left by the Mamluks and Ottomans. Many civilizations helped shape Aleppo, but it was its position on the trade routes that provided its distinct character. As one of the main stops on the Silk Road between China and Europe, Aleppo became a commercial centre that prospered from the flow of goods, wealth, people and ideas. And it was this cultural exchange that helped to shape its proud culinary heritage.

Today Aleppo is heralded as the gastronomic capital of Syria, and a growing destination for food tourism. Surrounded by fertile land, it has always produced fine local ingredients, from fruit and vegetables to meat and poultry. But an influx of exotic spices from the East was to change the way those ingredients were prepared forever. The spice traders in the souks invented delicious recipes to entice customers and encourage trade. And their legacy became the bedrock of a sophisticated, globally recognized cuisine.

Exotic ingredients and local produce come together in *kabab bil karaz*, the cherry kebab. It is made with the sour *wishna* cherries grown in orchards on the outskirts of the city, and tender, locally reared lamb. The minced meat is rolled into small balls, grilled, laid upon thin flatbread and drenched in a thick, dark cherry sauce. A *baharat* spice blend adds cardamom, cloves, cumin and coriander to the mix, and a few spoonfuls of pomegranate molasses rounds it off with a sumptuously balanced sweet and sour quality. A fresh *fattoush* salad, splashed with lemon juice and a sprinkling of sumac, is all you need to complete a dish that's been thousands of years in the making.

Above The Citadel of Aleppo is one of the largest fortresses in the world; its walls sit above a moat that connects to underground passageways and caves

What Else to Eat

There's always a twist to Aleppine food, and **yabrak** is no exception. It's similar to **waraq enab** (cold vine leaves stuffed with rice and minced lamb), but served hot, which changes the flavour and texture of the dish. Aleppo has a large Armenian population, so you should certainly try its **soujouk**, slices of spiced sausage rolled in flatbread. **Basterma** is another Armenian delicacy of cured meat crusted in a peppery herb coating. Both dishes can be found at **Kasr Al-Wali** (www.kasralwali.com), but for one of the city's most traditional and heartwarming experiences, have a breakfast of **ful medames** at **Abu Abdo**'s tiny restaurant in Jdeideh. The old man has been serving the same dish of fava beans, tahini, lemon juice and red pepper paste for around 50 years, and he's a legendary character in the city.

A Day in Aleppo

Few cities in the Middle East can match Aleppo for its mix of historical sites, calming mosques and churches, chaotic streets and atmospheric souks. Wandering through the delightfully haphazard Old City, towards the yellow-taxi-thronged streets of the New City, is the best way to soak it all in.

MORNING Begin by ambling through the streets of the **Old Town** to the huge fortified mound of the **Citadel**. Tour the ruins, from the underground **hammam** to the old **amphitheatre**, and then cool down at the café, with stunning views.

AFTERNOON Explore the famous and sprawling **souk**, for which a stern constitution and a good pair of shoes are essential. Enjoy the tumult of trade along mile after mile of stalls, offering everything from silk and spices to Aleppine olive soap and the entrails of sheep.

EVENING Take refuge in the **Grand Mosque**, then grab a taxi for the **New City**. The shops in the quiet Christian neighbourhood of **Jdeideh** begin to close their shutters by nightfall, which is when you should head to **Hatab Square** and a traditional Syrian courtyard restaurant for delightful Aleppine food and a cold beer.

Essentials

GETTING THERE
Aleppo International Airport is around 15 minutes from the city by **taxi**. There are **trains** from Istanbul to the north and Damascus in the south.

WHERE TO STAY
Baron Hotel (inexpensive) is the oldest hotel in Syria, and once played host to Lawrence of Arabia. A little faded, but full of history. +963 21 210 880
Yasmeen d'Alep (moderate) is a delightful hotel occupying a restored 17th-century mansion in the Jdeideh area. www.yasmeenalep.com
Sheraton Aleppo (expensive) is ideal for when comfort and cleanliness are more important than character. www.starwoodhotels.com

TOURIST INFORMATION
+963 21 21 228

The Best Places to Eat Cherry Kebabs

Zmorod expensive

There's a special ambience at this delightful restaurant, which sits in an elegant courtyard at the centre of a beautifully restored 17th-century house. An ornate wrought-iron staircase climbs up a cool limestone wall, while overhead, intricate lanterns cast a lambent glow on the diners below. The atmosphere intensifies when the dining area is full of families and giggling couples, as fleet-footed waiters bring plate after plate of authentic Syrian delights to each table. The *kabab bil karaz* here is famous across Syria. The cherries and lamb are sourced locally, so both are wonderfully fresh. If you arrive early in the cherry season, the rich, spicy, dark sauce has a sourer edger to it, while later on it's sweeter, as the cherries ripen. Either way, the meat will be cooked to pink and tender perfection, and goes superbly with warm flatbread and fresh salad leaves. Like all Syrian spreads, a variety of dishes should be added, from a spicy *muhammara* red pepper paste with pomegranate molasses to a smoky *baba ghanoush* dip of mashed aubergine.

Raheb Bouhaira Street, Jdeideh, Aleppo; open noon–late daily; www.zmorod.com

Also in Aleppo

Club d'Alep *(+963 21 211 3500; expensive)* is quite possibly the best restaurant in the country, but unfortunately it's a private members club. In Syria however, more than anywhere else on Earth, people are so friendly, warm and welcoming that it shouldn't necessarily stop you from getting in. A friendly word with your hotel manager may be all that's needed. The reward is simply fantastic food, from the cherry kebabs to the desert truffles with lamb. **Bazar Al-Charq** *(www.bazaralcharq.com/aleppoe.htm; moderate)* is a cavernous restaurant in a stone cellar, offering all kinds of kebabs and even some rustic Bedouin dishes.

Also in Syria

Al Halabi *(www.fourseasons.com/damascus; expensive)* is one of the best restaurants in Damascus, but even this grand venue has a distinctly Aleppine bent. "Halab" is the ancient name for Aleppo, and Aleppine (Halabian) chef Mohammed Helal's food bears all the adventurous hallmarks of Aleppo's cuisine. Highlights are the cherry kebab and the *kebbeh saffarjaliyeh* (spiced lamb and bulgur wheat patties with quince, pomegranate and rice).

Around the World

Elsewhere in the Middle East, Dubai has a number of good restaurants offering great, authentic Syrian food, including **Aroos Damascus** *(+971 221 9825; inexpensive)* and **Sarai** *(+971 438 0640; moderate)*.

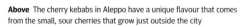

Above The cherry kebabs in Aleppo have a unique flavour that comes from the small, sour cherries that grow just outside the city

Left Fresh, dried, whole, crushed and powdered spices are sold in bins, bags and pyramids in Aleppo's labyrinthine covered souk

TUNIS TUNISIA

A Tricky Treat in Tunis

Africa meets Europe in Tunisia's buzzing capital city, Tunis. Within the ancient medina, shoppers wander the labyrinthine paths of the souks, while in the modern city outside, businessmen sip coffee and read European newspapers. Come lunch time, though, they're all likely to be tucking into the same dish: *brik à l'oeuf*, Tunisia's most delicious – and challenging – treat.

Tunis sits along Tunisia's northern coast, tucked into the innermost corner of the Gulf of Tunis. Its modern outlook and cosmopolitan air make it one of the most accessible North African destinations for visitors. But it exudes plenty of exotic atmosphere too, in the exquisitely tiled mosques and minarets towering above the rooftops, the arched courtyards and decorative doorways, the echoing cry of the muezzin calling the faithful to prayer and the pungent smells of spice and perfume.

The city's impressive Roman history is another of its highlights, from the exquisite mosaics in the Bardo Museum to the outstanding ruins at Dougga, a day trip away. The suburbs contain the remnants of an even more ancient empire, Carthage. From here the seafaring Phoenicians dominated the Mediterranean in the 6th century BC. Since then Arab, Ottoman and French settlers have all influenced Tunisia's culture and cuisine.

Brik à l'oeuf is one such dish that Tunisians have made their own. This delicious triangular parcel of thin pastry, which may be filled with seafood, minced lamb, beef or vegetables and herbs, but always includes an egg yolk, is fried in oil and eaten with the fingers. It has its roots in the deep-fried *börek* of Turkish cuisine and in fact the unusual name, brik, is simply the local variation on the original Turkish word.

But with *brik à l'oeuf*, the Tunisians have made this humble snack food into a work of art. The most impressive briks are more than a hand-span wide, their paper-thin shells shaped like a fan and held daintily upright in a sliced lemon. The brik is often enlivened by fiery harissa, a spicy red mix of hot chilli peppers and olive oil, mashed together into a paste. If you don't like hot sauces, don't even look at harissa; it might make your eyes water. However it's so popular with the locals that many brik recipes include harissa in the filling, so if you can't stomach the heat, make sure to ask for one without. In Tunisia harissa is almost always put on the table at the start of a meal, perhaps with some olives and bread as an hors d'oeuvre. Each chef or household will have their own recipe, and fancier versions might include cumin, coriander and other herbs and spices.

The challenge in eating a *brik à l'oeuf* – especially the large, elaborate ones – is to control the runny egg yolk that explodes with the first bite. Once you can eat one without it running down your chin, then you've mastered the trick of the most Tunisian brik.

A Day in Tunis

The medina, Tunis's walled old town, is a UNESCO World Heritage site harbouring a feast of Islamic architecture. From here, a short (and inexpensive) taxi ride will take you to sights in the surrounding new town and further out along the coast.

MORNING Wander through the streets of the **medina** and soak up the atmosphere, admiring the beautifully carved and tiled decoration on the mosques and minarets. Dodge the carpet-sellers and go shopping in the mesmerizing bazaars of the souks.

AFTERNOON Visit the **Bardo Museum** to see the finest collection of Roman mosaics in the world. Then take a taxi to **Carthage** to see the **Antonine Baths**, the best of the scattered ruins of the once-great Phoenician civilization.

EVENING With its whitewashed, blue-shuttered houses and elaborate painted doors, the hilltop town of **Sidi Bou Saïd** is a favourite stop for visitors, just 20 km (12 miles) from Tunis. Its café terraces are grand spots from which to sip a mint tea and watch the sunset over the sea.

Essentials

GETTING THERE
Buses and **taxis** link Tunis-Carthage **international airport** with the city centre. Explore central Tunis on **foot**, or book **taxis** for further afield.

WHERE TO STAY
Hotel Majestic (inexpensive) is located on the edge of the medina. +216 71 332 666
Hotel Carlton (moderate) is a central, three-star Art Deco hotel. www.hotelcarltontunis.com
The **Oriental Palace** (expensive) is luxurious, and sumptuously decorated. +216 71 348 846

TOURIST INFORMATION
Tunisia National Office of Tourism, 1 Avenue Mohamed V, Tunis; +216 71 341 077

The Best Places to Eat Brik à l'Oeuf

Dar El Jeld expensive

This atmospheric old place in the heart of the medina is one of the finest restaurants in Tunis. It's in a beautiful 18th-century town house, and you might need some help to find it, but once through the flame-lit arched doorway and into the covered tiled courtyard that forms the dining area, you will experience everything that is magical and evocative about North Africa. By Tunisian standards this is an expensive place to eat, but it provides an unforgettable flavour of Tunis. The service is impeccably courteous, and reservations are essential. There is live music on most evenings. Several types of brik are available as appetizers, including a taster selection of mini-briks, and other specialities of the house include lamb couscous, an olive and beef stew, fish couscous, tajines, a North African-style paella and their array of delicious pastry desserts. It is also the place to discover just how good Tunisian wines can be.

5–10 Rue Dar El Jeld, La Kasbah, Tunis; open for lunch and dinner Mon–Sat; closed for lunch in July and during Ramadan, and for all of August; www.dareljeld.tourism.tn

Also in Tunis

A venerable institution in the Souk El Trouk (the Turkish or tailors' souk) in the medina, **M'rabet Café Restaurant** *(+216 71 561 729; inexpensive)* is the perfect place to take a break from the hectic bustle of the souks and relax with a coffee or a mint tea, or something more substantial. It has a café downstairs; upstairs is an inexpensive restaurant that serves brik alongside many other Tunisian specialities, including lamb and chicken couscous. Live music is often on offer.

Also in Tunisia

Restaurant Chargui *(+216 71 740 987; moderate)* is one of the best restaurants in Sidi Bou Saïd, the picturesque little hilltop town close to Tunis. Open daily, it has a lovely blue-and white-washed terrace with great views over the sea, and its menu includes a choice of briks, a range of couscous dishes and locally caught fresh grilled fish.

Around the World

An authentic taste of both Tunisia and Morocco can be found on Sutter Street in the heart of San Francisco at **Cafe Zitouna** *(www.cafezitouna.com; moderate)*, an unpretentious café-takeaway specializing in the flavours of North Africa. Brik is naturally on the menu along with a wide range of tajines, couscous dishes, hot and spicy *merguez* sausages and sticky baklava desserts.

Above Courtyard dining, North African *riadh*-style, at the Dar El Jeld restaurant in Tunis

Left Intricate tiling and stonework at the great mosque complex in Sidi Bou Saïd, a hilltop town a short metro train or taxi ride from the city

Above The crispy pastry of a *brik à l'oeuf* hides a secret: a golden egg yolk at its heart, waiting to burst at the first bite

What Else to Eat

Couscous, simply meaning "food", was originally a staple of the nomadic North African Berber tribes. These granules of semolina are typically layered on herbs and cooked in the top half of a *kiskas*, or double boiler, above a spicy meat, fish or vegetable stew, absorbing the aromas and flavours as it steams. While any ingredients can form the base – camel and octopus are Tunisian specialities – couscous is always enriched by herbs, spices and harissa. One particularly delicious version, known as **burzqan**, is mixed with fresh butter, mutton, saffron and chickpeas, sprinkled with hot milk, and garnished with raisins, almonds, pistachios, hazelnuts and walnuts.

BEIRUT LEBANON

Raw Passion in Beirut

Invigorating and exasperating, vibrant and serene, beautiful and dilapidated – Beirut is all things to all people. Though plagued by strife, it refuses to be beaten. It has emerged from a troubled past as a cosmopolitan crucible of cultures, and from its street life to its nightlife, Beirut's impulses and passions are as raw as can be – just like the city's favourite meat dish, *kibbeh nayyeh*.

Built on a promontory jutting out into the Mediterranean, Beirut is ever the show-off. But as difficult as it might be to imagine today's vivacious capital playing second fiddle to a neighbouring town, it was once deemed less important than the Phoenician trading ports of Sidon and Byblos. It wasn't until the Romans began using Beirut as a military base and commercial hub that it really began to blossom. The ruins of Roman bathhouses can still be seen in the central area, today a buoyant shopping and entertainment district, which itself sprang out of a more recent set of ruins left behind by the devastating 15-year civil war.

Bullet-peppered buildings and army checkpoints serve as a reminder of the city's struggles, but years of conflict and political instability have taught the people to seize life and live it with gusto. This natural energy and *joie de vivre* can be felt on any trip to Beirut, from the daily human tide that flows up and down its sweeping Corniche to the frenetic cafés and bars that line Gemmayze's vivid Rue Gourard. Amble along Hamra Street, and the street food of sizzling *shawarma* grilled meats and falafel will be hard to resist. But

leave space for lunch time, which in Beirut is long, leisurely and all about meze. Guaranteed to be among the array of dishes is *kibbeh nayyeh*, one of Lebanon's most famous delicacies. It's raw lamb, pulverized with cracked bulgur wheat and chopped onion until mousse-soft, often whipped into swirly shapes and served drizzled with olive oil and garnished with fresh mint. Its creamy texture and rich flavour goes perfectly with green olives, pickled chillies and zesty tabbouleh (parsley and bulgur salad).

Like so many Levantine dishes, it may well have its roots in ancient Syria. Some villages, like Ehden in northern Lebanon – considered by some to be the capital of *kibbeh nayyeh* – have claimed it as their own. But for centuries, wherever there were sheep and goats in Lebanon, *kibbeh nayyeh* would be pounded in stone mortars called *jurns*, the sound resonating through the village. The beauty of finding *kibbeh nayyeh* in Beirut lies in discovering regional variations – one recipe might have coarse bulgur, while another might use more olive oil. But as any master of *kibbeh nayyeh* preparation will tell you – the secret ultimately lies in the freshness, quality and leanness of the meat.

Above Much of Beirut's historic central district has required reconstruction, and is now a vibrant shopping, dining and entertainment area

Beirut's Farmers' Market

Souk El Tayeb (*www.soukeltayeb.com*), which meets every Saturday on a site near the Exhibition Centre, is Lebanon's first weekly farmers' market; it brings together over 100 producers and artisans. Founded by Kamal Mouzawak, the souk showcases the seasonal produce of farmers from all over Lebanon, but it's more than just a market. As well as aiming to preserve Lebanon's natural heritage, it also seeks to promote coexistence, social interaction and an environmentally friendly lifestyle. **Tawlet** (*www.tawlet.com*) is the organization's cooperative kitchen, which offers the creations of a different regional cook each day. In addition, the team hold regular **Food & Feast festivals** across Lebanon, from the fruit-growing villages of Mount Lebanon to the herb-growers of the south.

Three Days in Beirut

Lebanon is small and geographically diverse, so it's possible to swim in the morning, ski in the afternoon and go clubbing in the city at night. With a few days to explore, you can revel in Beirut's infectious energy, enjoy the resorts of Mount Lebanon and recover at the beach clubs around the capital.

DAY ONE After a morning stroll along the **Corniche**, have an espresso in a **Hamra café** among the students from the American University. Head east to the beautiful **Mohammed al-Amin mosque** on the site of the Green Line that divided Beirut during the civil war. Then check out the cafés and bars in the Christian neighbourhoods of **Achrefiyeh** and **Gemmayze**.

DAY TWO Drive or take a taxi to the **Jeita Grotto** to see the impressive stalactites and stalagmites in the subterranean caverns. Then head on to the slopes of **Faraya Mzaar**, where the après-ski culture is every bit as lively as the skiing.

DAY THREE If the weather's fine, kick back at one of Beirut's beach clubs. **AUB Beach** has a wonderful ambience, while the **St George Yacht Motor Club** is where the beautiful people go to hang out.

Essentials

GETTING THERE
From **Rafic Hariri International Airport** it's just a 10-minute **taxi** ride to the city centre; if you dislike haggling, choose a logo-ed, registered white cab.

WHERE TO STAY
Port View Hotel (inexpensive) in the Mar Mikhael area is within walking distance of the bars and restaurants of Gemmayze. *www.portviewhotel. blogspot.com*
Marble Tower (moderate) is a comfortable and recently renovated hotel in the lively Hamra district. *www.marbletowerhotel.com*
Le Gray (expensive) is a modern luxury hotel in the revamped Central district.
www.campbellgrayhotels.com

TOURIST INFORMATION
I Rue Banque du Liban, Hamra; +961 1 343 073

Above With an almost dip-like texture, creamy *kibbeh nayyeh* should be scooped up with Lebanese flatbread

Right The stunning new Mohammed al-Amin mosque is modelled on the Sultan Ahmed Mosque in Istanbul

The Best Places to Eat Kibbeh Nayyeh

Abdel Wahab moderate

A bastion of tradition in one of Beirut's most fashionable districts, Abdel Wahab is a sure-fire bet for authentic *kibbeh nayyeh* in a charming setting. Occupying an attractive Ottoman house in a Monot side street, the dining area is an enclosed courtyard, which is suitably untainted by 21st-century trappings. The waiters are used to serving vast meze spreads, which they deliver with speed and efficiency.

From the olives and pickled vegetables to hummus and tabbouleh, the dishes begin arriving thick and fast. Abdel Wahab has a reputation for using only the best butchers, some of whom are from the famous meat markets of Sabra, so the *kibbeh nayyeh* here is one of the freshest in the city. Beautifully presented in pink swirls, it has a richness that will flood your palate with flavour, and a texture as smooth as paste. Those of a sterner constitution might enjoy *sauda nayyeh*, or raw lamb's liver and fat cubes, served with little mounds of pepper and ground spices for dipping. Meze is all about contrasts, so have a mix of hot and cold dishes, from barbecued chicken livers to stuffed vine leaves. When a long meze lunch in the mountains is just out of reach, Abdel Wahab is the next best thing.

El Inglizi Street, Monot, Achrefiyeh, Beirut; open noon–midnight daily; +961 1 200 550/1

Also in Beirut

You'll find a refreshingly contemporary take on Lebanese cuisine in **Babel** (*+961 70 425 777; moderate*), a breathtaking new restaurant on the Dbayeh Highway on the outskirts of town. The cavernous dining room is high and wide, built of huge blocks of sandstone. It's like dining at a palace in ancient Baalbek, but the *kibbeh nayyeh* has a thoroughly modern twist – served in individual, bite-size portions, rolled and dotted with black sesame seeds like sushi.

Also in Lebanon

Twenty minutes' drive from Beirut is the mountain retreat of Brummana, where **Kasr Fakhreddine** (*www.fakhreddine.com; expensive*) has sweeping valley views of the Chouf Mountains and great *kibbeh nayyeh*. For a distinctly northern Lebanese version of the dish, **Le Mortier** (*+961 3870 507; inexpensive*) in the town of Ehden near Tripoli has a beautiful setting and *kibbeh* in all of its wondrous forms, both raw and cooked.

Around the World

There are more people of Lebanese extraction living outside Lebanon than within. Brazil has one of the largest migrant communities, and São Paulo's **Almanara** (*www.almanara. com.br; inexpensive*) has been preparing and serving authentic meze, including *kibbeh nayyeh*, since the 1950s.

Above The Church of St George, Lalibela, is carved in the form of a Greek cross, from an excavation 12 m (40 ft) deep

A Day in Lalibela

Lalibela's lovely churches can be split into three main groups: the first two, the Northern and Eastern Groups (conveniently containing some of the town's most impressive and important) lie with a short distance of the town centre; the third group lies scattered outside town. For a tour of the churches, visit the tiny Tourist Office, where you can find a guide and the informative pamphlet, *Lalibela: World Heritage*.

MORNING Visit the Northern and Eastern Groups of churches. The two most impressive are **Bet Giyorgis** (The Church of St George), considered the most perfect of all the churches, and **Bet Medhane Alem**, which measures 33.5 m by 23.5 m, and is believed to be the largest rock-hewn church in the world. Other highlights of the Northern Group include **Bet Golgotha** and **Bet Mikael**. In the Eastern Group, don't miss **Bet Amanuel** and **Bet Abba Libanos**.

AFTERNOON Consider a trip to one of the churches outside the town. Particularly recommended are **Yemrehanna Kristos**, **Ashetan Maryam** and **Na'akuto La'ab**.

Essentials

GETTING THERE
Lalibela has a domestic **airport** 23 km (14 miles) south of town and there are **minibus taxis** to the town centre. There is a daily **bus** from Addis-Ababa, which takes two days to reach Lalibela.

WHERE TO STAY
Seven Olives Hotel (inexpensive) has simple but peaceful rooms with views across lovely gardens. *+251 3 3336 0020*
Tukol Village (moderate) offers the option of staying overnight in a *tukul* (traditional Ethiopian hut). *+251 3 3336 0564*
Yemereha Hotel (moderate) has comfortable rooms furnished with traditional Ethiopian crafts. *www.greenlandethiopia.com*

TOURIST INFORMATION
Main Lalibela road (near St Lalibela Secondary School); *+251 3 3336 0167*

Above *Injera* forms the base for *seg wat*, a spicy meat stew that traditionally uses *beri-beri*, a very hot Ethiopian chilli pepper

The Best Places to Eat Injera

Blue Lal Hotel Restaurant
inexpensive

Although Lalibela and its extraordinary churches are becoming better known and visitor numbers are increasing, the range and quality of the town's restaurants (and hotels) remain rather limited. One of the better options for sampling Ethiopian food is the Blue Lal Hotel Restaurant. Designed like a *tukul* (traditional Ethiopian hut), complete with freshly cut grass strewn on the floor and multicoloured *mesobs* (traditional, mushroom-shaped dining tables woven like baskets) dotting the dining floor, the Blue Lal Restaurant serves fresh, authentic and good-quality Ethiopian dishes, including a well-prepared *injera*, at excellent prices. Try the unctuous *doro wat*: chicken drumsticks or wings accompanied by hard-boiled egg served in a hot sauce of butter, onion and cardamon and a good sprinkling of *berbere* (a spice mixture of up to 16 ingredients, including the fiery *beri-beri*). If you don't fancy stew, try *kitfo*, minced beef or lamb traditionally served warm but not cooked — like a form of steak tartare — and flavoured with the even hotter *mitmita* spice mixture.

Town centre, Lalibela; +251 3 3336 0380

Also in Lalibela

The **Seven Olives Hotel** *(+251 3 3336 0020; inexpensive)* is furnished with Ethiopian arts and crafts and offers the classic range of *injera*-plus-*wats*, as well as *injera* and *ye som megeb* (vegetarian dishes traditionally served on Friday, the day of fasting). If you're keen to taste multiple Ethiopian dishes, request the *beyanatu* — you'll receive small portions of different meat and vegetable dishes.

Also in Ethiopia

Habesha Restaurant *(+251 3 3351 8358; moderate)* in Addis-Ababa is traditionally decorated and known for its good-quality, more eclectic menu, including *injera*-accompanied dishes such as *dulet* (minced tripe, liver and beef fried in butter, onions, chilli and cardamon) and *kwanta* (strips of beef rubbed in chilli, butter, salt and *berbere*). In the evening, there's live Ethiopian music, singing or dancing.

Around the World

London has a sizeable Ethiopian community and **Wabe Shebele Restaurant** *(+44 20 7378 9009; moderate)* serves authentic Ethiopian food in a traditionally decorated dining room. Regulars include *gored gored* (warmed cubes of raw beef served with spiced Ethiopian butter) and *goden tibs* (lamb ribs sautéed with *berbere* and rosemary). At the weekends, there is traditional Ethiopian dancing.

LALIBELA ETHIOPIA

Injera in Holy Lalibela

Dubbed "Africa's Petra" for its astonishing rock-hewn churches, Lalibela has drawn Western visitors since the 16th century. It is hidden high in the Ethiopian highlands, and the journey is long and arduous for the thousands of pilgrims who travel there on foot. Many seek replenishment in its famous, pancake-like flatbread, *injera*, topped by a hot, steaming and revitalizing stew.

Cradle of the Zagwe dynasty in the 12th and 13th centuries, Lalibela was once the country's capital and the home of kings. According to local tradition, the town's ruler and namesake, King Lalibela, was briefly forced into exile to Jerusalem by his evil, usurping brother. Amazed by the churches there, Lalibela vowed to build a holy city on African soil upon his return to his homeland.

Lalibela's churches are exceptional for three main reasons: their artistic refinement, their sophisticated construction (many are not just carved into the rock, but freed entirely from it) and their number – so many are found within such a small area. For the visitor, Lalibela's unique appeal also lies in its timeless continuity. Monks and deacons, traditionally robed, glide along the candle-lit passageways and tunnels that connect the medieval churches, and the sound of chanting still rises from the hidden crypts and grottoes. The deep, cool recesses of the extraordinary church interiors are filled with the heady fragrance of incense and burning beeswax candles.

The taverns and restaurants of Lalibela have also been serving the pilgrims for centuries. They offer up an often quite sophisticated and eclectic cuisine that includes piquant meat *wats* (stews) and mild, smooth curries of vegetables and pulses. Underpinning all – literally – is the country's staple, *injera*, a kind of large, round flatbread upon which the cooks heap one or more meat and vegetable dishes. Used as a base and also as a tool (small pieces are torn off with the right hand and used to pick at the dishes), *injera* famously serves as foodstuff, plate and cutlery.

Injera is traditionally made from the flour of *teff*, a small-grained indigenous Ethiopian cereal that is found throughout the Ethiopian highlands. This distinguishes the higher-quality *injera*, which is lighter, smoother, thinner and springier than non-*teff* varieties. After a day's exploration of Lalibela's wondrous churches, there's no better way to end the day than by tucking into *injera* and a large, communal plate of steaming, slightly spicy stew with some newly found friends. Ethiopians believe that sharing a meal in this way cements a friendship forever.

What to Drink in Lalibela

Once the drink of Ethiopian emperors and kings, *tej* – a kind of mead – is now the popular local tipple. Made from locally produced honey and an Ethiopian shrub called *gesho*, it is found today in the *tej beats* (a kind of Ethiopian equivalent of pubs) in most Ethiopian towns, as well as in higher-end restaurants. Served in delightful little flasks known as *birille*, *tej* comes in varying degrees of sweetness. Ask for *derek* if you want it dry and strong (the drier it is the more alcoholic the content), *mahakalenya* for medium-sweet and *laslasa* or *bers* for a sweeter and less alcoholic version. Local men congregate at *tej beats* to gossip, cogitate and commiserate. As in Western pubs, most men tend to gather during a weekend afternoon, while women traditionally drink *tej* from glasses during market days as they work and exchange news.

Above *Injera* dough is fermented overnight then cooked like a pancake

Right Fresh produce, seafood and curios can be found in the covered Central Market

Below The chicken takes its colour and heat from the small but feisty piri-piri pepper, also known as the bird's eye chilli or African red devil

A Day in Maputo

Easily and safely explored on foot, central Maputo is a compact grid of shady avenues filled with unexpected architectural curiosities.

MORNING Start at Praça dos Trabalhadores and **Maputo Railway Station**, the palatial 1910 creation of Gustave Eiffel. From here, the bar-lined **Rua de Bagamoio** (once known as the "Street of Trouble" by visiting sailors) leads through the old town to the 18th-century **Fortalezada Nossa Senhora da Conceição**, the city's oldest extant building and home to interesting artworks. Take a short ferry ride to rustic **Catembe** for fabulous views and an inexpensive seafood lunch at the redoubtable **Restaurant Diogo** on the beach.

AFTERNOON Take the ferry back and follow Av Patrice Lumumba uphill to the prestigious **Polana District** and shady **Av Friedrich Engels** for clifftop views over the harbour.

EVENING Dive into the fantastic **Barracas de Museu** for a drink or two before or after dinner.

Essentials

GETTING THERE
Maputo is Mozambique's main **port** of entry, and the **international airport** is only 10 minutes from the city centre, traffic permitting.

WHERE TO STAY
Fatima's Place (inexpensive) is a popular owner-managed hostel with dorms and private rooms. *www.mozambiquebackpackers.com*
Hotel Villa das Mangas (moderate) is a small central boutique hotel set around a pretty garden with pool. *www.hipchichotels.net*
The ocean-facing **Serena Polana** (expensive) has been Maputo's most prestigious address since it opened in 1922. *www.serenahotels.com*

FURTHER INFORMATION
Mike Slater's detailed *www.mozguide.com* is very useful.

MAPUTO MOZAMBIQUE

All Fired Up in Mozambique

Lapped by the balmy Indian Ocean, Maputo is probably the most characterful capital city in sub-equatorial Africa. A seaside port, its wide palm- and jacaranda-shaded *avenidas* are flanked by cosy street cafés and an oddly cohesive cocktail of architectural styles. The city possesses an engaging Afro-Mediterranean mood epitomized by the addictive, fiery zip of chicken piri-piri.

Five centuries ago, the desire to secure control of the spice trade inspired Portugal to establish outposts along the east coast of Africa, one of which grew to become the modern Mozambican capital of Maputo. Today, the most notoriously tongue-searing of these spices – the ferocious chilli known by the Swahili-derived name piri-piri – forms the cornerstone of Mozambique's best-known culinary export.

Mozambique's struggle for independence from Portugal ended as recently as 1974, and the legacy of colonial rule can still be seen in the fascinating architecture of its capital city. Antiquated colonial relics and handsome Art Deco and Bauhaus buildings stand out among bleak Soviet-style apartment blocks, relics of a period of Marxist-oriented government that inspired a bitter civil war. And it is the juxtaposition of the city's contemporary African culture against this time-warped architectural exotica that makes Maputo so compelling. For example, one of Africa's most bizarrely misplaced buildings – a stately palace built in ornate Portuguese Gothic style that now houses the Natural History Museum – sits just around the corner from the utterly African Barracas de Museu. This unpretentious, vast warren of makeshift stalls and bars is inhabited by a bustling cast of guitar-bearing rent-a-crooners, beer-swilling mamas, wild-eyed poolhustlers and after-hours office workers. It is dedicated to the sale and consumption of alcohol and there is no better place to make new friends over a cold Mozambican beer and a sizzling plate of chicken piri-piri.

No other dish is quite so definitely Mozambican as this – spatchcocked chicken, grilled to perfection over hot coals in its mantle of piquant piri-piri sauce. Deep red and viscous, the sauce is dominated by the chilli pepper for which it is named, which is finely chopped and soaked in vegetable oil, garlic, vinegar, lemon juice and coarse salt – and whatever other secret ingredient it is that ensures that, whether you're ordering at a street stall, a hole-in-the-wall takeaway or an upmarket restaurant, no two versions of this unofficial national dish ever taste exactly the same.

What Else to Eat

Maputo, almost uniquely among sub-equatorial African capitals, has long been renowned for its dining-out scene. In the colonial era the city was noted, as it still is now, for its fine **seafood**. Particularly famous are the country's **prawns** (often referred to in southern Africa as LM prawns, after Maputo's old colonial name, Lourenço Marques), which are usually served grilled, with garlic or piri-piri sauce on the side, or baked in a beer-based sauce. The **Costa do Sol** *(see right)* is renowned for its prawns and seafood combos (try the grilled fish and calamari), and there's no finer exponent of sauce-baked prawns than the **1908 Restaurant** *(+258 21 304 428)*, set in a beautiful colonial house on Av Eduardo Mondlane.

Left High-rise buildings give way to beachside homes on the outskirts

---

The Best Places to Eat Chicken Piri-Piri

Restaurante Costa do Sol
moderate–expensive

Boasting a prime seafront location 8 km (5 miles) north of the city centre, the legendary Costa do Sol is the oldest eatery in Maputo, having operated continuously since the 1940s, and throughout the civil war that drove Mozambique to an economic standstill in the 1980s. Fittingly, this family-run institution has a somewhat time-warped Mediterranean ambience, with its Art Deco façade, wide terrace overlooking a palm-lined beach and gentle rolling breakers, reasonably priced daily specials chalked up on a board, white-starched tablecloths and famously erratic (but invariably friendly) service. As with most restaurants in Maputo, seafood features heavily on the menu, but the Costa do Sol also arguably serves the city's finest grilled chicken: marinated in a spicy sauce, sealed and flame-grilled on an open fire and accompanied by a bowl of fiery red sauce whose searing chilli base is, like all the best piri-piri, offset by a delicious tang from the addition of preserved lemons. A chilled Sauvignon Blanc from neighbouring South Africa provides the perfect accompaniment, though the locally brewed 2M lager might be a safer bet for dousing the fiery aftertaste.

Av de Marginal; open 11am–10.30pm Sun–Thu, 11am–midnight Fri & Sat; +258 21 450 115

Also in Maputo

As might be surmised from the restaurant's name, the chef at **Piri-piri** *(+258 21 492 379; moderate)*, an ever-popular eatery in the heart of the upmarket Polana district, isn't afraid of dousing his grilled chicken in antisocial lashings of delicious piri-piri sauce. Aside from the good food, the terrace here, where Av 24 de Julho and Av Julius Nyerere meet, has to be one of the city's top spots for people-watching.

Also in Mozambique

Tucked away on an anonymous dirt road in Vilankulo, one of Mozambique's top resort towns, is **Varanda** *(+258 29 382 412; moderate)*, a family-run restaurant famed for its seafood and superb chicken piri-piri. It overlooks a beach where fishing dhows come to land their catches in the evening.

Around the World

Unsurprisingly, Mozambique's most famous dish long ago made it across two oceans to its former colonizer, Portugal, where it has become a local speciality at the picturesque village of Guia, in the central Algarve. There are several restaurants to choose from here, but none finer than the veteran **Restaurant Ramires** *(+351 289 561 232; inexpensive)*, which has been firing up visitors' taste buds for over 25 years.

Above More than 4,500 years old, the pyramids of Giza are the sole survivors of the original Seven Wonders of the World

Above *Hamam mashi* – Egyptian stuffed pigeon with bulgur wheat

Three Days in Cairo

Cairo has enough to keep sightseers occupied for weeks. The following itinerary takes in all the iconic sites, as well some lesser-known but equally interesting areas, attractions and activities.

DAY ONE Head first for the legendary **Egyptian Museum**. In the afternoon, take a tour of central Cairo including the **Museum of Islamic Art**, interspersed with some coffee-and-cake stops. Later browse the colourful **Khan al-Khalili bazaar**. End the day aboard a felucca (a traditional sailing boat) for a sunset sail on the Nile.

DAY TWO Take an all-day tour of the **Pyramids** and **Sphinx** via **Memphis**, **Saqqara** and **Giza**. Rest and replenish over meze and watch the sun set over the pyramids with a cocktail at Oberoi.

DAY THREE Spend the morning exploring **Coptic Cairo**. Start at the **Coptic Museum** and the **Hanging Church**. After coffee at nearby St George's Café, continue the church tour and visit **St Sergius** and **St Barbara**. Spend the afternoon wandering the **Islamic Quarter**; be sure of visiting the **Mosque of Ibn Tuloan**.

Essentials

GETTING THERE
Buses, minibuses and taxis connect Cairo's international airport with the city centre, 20 km (12 miles) away. Around town, the metro and taxis are the simplest ways of getting about.

WHERE TO STAY
Pension Roma (inexpensive) is a simple but well-run and homely B&B with evening meals available on request. *www.pensionroma.com*
Talisman Hotel (moderate) is a centrally located boutique hotel with attractive rooms decorated in oriental style. *+20 2 2393 9431*
Four Seasons at Nile (expensive) is sumptuous and furnished with original Egyptian art; it overlooks the Nile and is minutes from the Egyptian Museum. *www.fourseasons.com*

TOURIST INFORMATION
www.egypt.travel

CAIRO EGYPT

Stuffed Pigeon in Cairo

Long known locally as *Umm ad-Dunya* ("mother of the world"), Cairo still deserves deference: its museums house some of humanity's greatest historical and artistic treasures, and its old quarters contain some of the world's finest religious architecture. Cairo is also Egypt's culinary capital, and the perfect place to try its unofficial national dish, *hamam mashi*: stuffed pigeon.

Africa's largest city and one of the most densely populated metropolises on Earth, Cairo is also one of the world's most vibrant capitals. Though almost as famous for its overcrowding, congestion and pollution as for its ancient treasures, the city's energy, entrepreneurship and indomitable spirit is nonetheless enthralling. On the roads, camels and donkeys vie for position with the pick-up trucks and clapped-out cars; above the roar of engines the muezzin's age-old call to prayer rises above the cries of the street hawkers. The smog and exhaust fumes mingle with the aromas of street-sold roasted maize and freshly baked bread, along with the unmistakeable waft of fruit infused *sheesha* pipes.

Cairo's world-famous attractions include the astonishing Egyptian Museum and pyramids of Giza, but it has equally interesting, lesser-known sights, such as the Coptic Quarter and Islamic Cairo. Known as the "City of a Thousand Minarets", Cairo has some of the world's greatest Islamic architecture. Its beautiful churches – such as the 7th-century

El Muallaqa (the "Hanging Church") – bear witness to the importance of its early Christian Coptic community.

Like many of its attractions, Cairo's unofficial national dish – *hamam mashi* or stuffed pigeon – is also said to date back to Pharaonic times. The birds were traditionally reared in conical, mud-built pigeon cotes, which can still be seen today lining the Nile Delta, although pigeons are also kept in the towns. For Cairo's millions of rural migrants, old habits die hard: birdcages are placed outside windows and doors and on rooftops and terraces. The dish is usually served during the winter months, when the birds are at their plumpest; only young, tender pigeons are selected.

Traditionally, the birds are served in pairs, stuffed with rice, onion and chopped pigeon or chicken liver, then spiced with cinnamon, cumin and pepper and sometimes nuts. Roasted or grilled on a spit, they are usually accompanied by tabbouleh (a salad of bulgur wheat, parsley, mint, tomatoes and spring onions) and tahini (sesame-seed paste). They are not everyday food, but mark special occasions, made "for those whom you love dearly", as the Cairenes say.

What Else to Eat

A great way to start the day (as Egyptians do) is with filling and sustaining **fuul** (cooked, mashed fava beans). For lunch or dinner, try the much-prized **Nile perch** from the Nile. Other culinary sightseeing might include **molokhiyya**, a popular mallow-based soup with a distinctly slimy texture and earthy flavour, or **koshari** (macaroni, rice, lentils and chickpeas topped with fried onions and a spicy tomato sauce). Drinks worth searching out include the ubiquitous **shay bilnaana** (mint tea) and other herbal infusions such as **helba** (fenugreek), **yansoon** (anis) and **irfa** (cinnamon). **Sahlab**, a hot milky mixture of arrowroot or semolina, nuts and cinnamon, is popular in winter, while **karkadeh** is a hibiscus infusion served as an antidote to the summer's heat. **Zabaady**, a yogurt-based drink, accompanies meat dishes.

Above The busy alleyways of the ancient Khan al-Khalili bazaar in Cairo

The Best Places to Eat Stuffed Pigeon

Citadel View Restaurant
expensive

Aptly named, the Citadel View boasts the best appointment in town. Located in the lovely, landscaped gardens of the Al Azhar Park on a breeze-catching hillock, the Citadel commands panoramic views over the gardens, the Citadel and all of Old Cairo. Housed in a neo-Fatimid palace, the complex comprises a good café and a couple of restaurants, of which the Studio Misr is the highlight. The Studio specializes in traditional Egyptian dishes (particularly grills), including stuffed pigeon, that are artfully prepared. At night, amid the niches, arches and intimate spaces of the lantern-lit interior, the evening can seem like something out of one of Scheherazade's stories of the Arabian Nights. At weekends (Friday and Saturday) there's a fixed-price open buffet, which provides a welcome opportunity to taste a variety of traditional Egyptian and Middle Eastern dishes. The stuffed pigeon (ordered *à la carte* only) is cooked *à point* and is succulent and gamey, with a subtle hint of cinnamon.
Al Azhar Park, Shari' Salah Salem, Cairo; open noon–1am daily; +20 2 2510 9151

Also in Cairo

Old-world through and through, from the dark-panelled dining room to the besuited, taciturn waiters and deep, leather-clad seats, **El Mashrabiah** (*+20 2 3748 2801; moderate–expensive*) prides itself also on its traditional, old-school Egyptian cooking. Specializing in classic meat dishes including stuffed pigeon, grilled rabbit, quail and duck, as well as offering ethereal kofta (spicy meatballs), *tagen* (a slow-cooked stew) and shish kebabs, it attracts a fervent local following among Cairo's well-heeled carnivores.

Also in Egypt

Sofra (*www.sofra.com; moderate*) has rapidly become known as one of Luxor's best eating options. Spread over a series of private dining rooms, a salon and an attractive, atmospheric rooftop terrace, it is a great spot for a pre-prandial or dinner drink. Both decor and dining are traditional and the menu is full of tried-and-tested classics, including a particularly flavoursome roasted stuffed pigeon.

Popular with Aswani families for its simple and traditional menu at excellent prices, the **Al Makka** (*+20 97 230 3232; inexpensive*) in Aswan additionally offers quality and consistency. Specialities include the stuffed pigeon, kofta, shish kebabs and succulent, grilled chicken, all served with tahini, salad and flat bread. No alcohol is served.

Above Rattan panels shade women stallholders and their produce at a busy street market in Bali, Indonesia

Asia and Australasia

The Flavours of
Asia and Australasia

Asia and Australasia contain virtually half the world's population and examples of most of the Earth's geography, so it's perhaps unsurprising that very few culinary opportunities are left unexplored among this melange of interconnected cultures and climates. Spices dominate the foods of Asia, but are used to flavour a huge range of cuisines with distinctive styles. Australasia has combined these with its European heritage to concoct a unique range of Pan-Asian dishes.

In the north of Asia the arid Himalayan plateau descends to a vast swathe of treeless steppes, where wheat is the staple and cooking is kept simple by the limited ingredients. Lower down, humid hills and river plains form the heartland of those two great Asian core crops – tea and rice – that pattern the upland slopes in terracing, colour the landscape a rich green and nourish half of humanity. Rice in particular holds the regional cuisines together, infinitely flexible in its uses: it's eaten steamed, fried, roasted and boiled; made into noodles, cakes and wine; ground into flour and used in desserts. The rice belt extends south into the tropics, where heat, rain and rich soils create an extraordinary fertility in which all manner of spices, fruits and vegetables flourish. Add to this the multitudes of farmed pigs and chickens and an abundance of marine life, and the menu becomes infinite.

Thailand, Malaysia and Indonesia share a southern Indian love of spice pastes, coconut milk and grilled foods.

A Rich Mixture of Cuisines

The story of Asian cuisine is one of cross-fertilization. In terms of variety and influence, India and China completely dominate the region. Migration, trade and conquest spread the philosophies and cuisines of these two behemoths right across Asia, though isolation and distance have preserved local variations: a cuisine might be identifiably "Asian" but there's a world of difference between a Cambodian *amok* fish curry and West Lake fish from China's Hangzhou. However, there are definite cooking "families": Thailand, Malaysia and Indonesia share a southern Indian love of spice pastes, coconut milk and grilled foods; the cooking of Laos, Cambodia and Vietnam has clearer, cleaner flavours built around well-defined ingredients, perhaps closer to the studied simplicity and restrained palette of Japanese and Korean cuisine. India has no qualms about adapting foreign dishes – Mumbai's cosmopolitan *chaat* snacks, for example, embrace even Portuguese influences. Even that inward-looking cultural monolith, China, where alien ideas are absorbed so effectively that they eventually become Chinese, still shows evidence of contact with the outside world – in Peking duck, for instance, which probably owes a debt to Mongol cuisine.

Right Federation Square in Melbourne, Australia, is a major meeting and eating point
Below Chefs preparing sushi in Tokyo, Japan – as much an art form as a dish

Nothing demonstrates the extent of this trade in ideas more than the history of Asian spices, especially ginger, pepper, nutmeg, cloves, cinnamon and cardamom, which are all used extensively in Southeast Asian cooking. Many reached Europe via India in Roman times, and by the Middle Ages had become so valuable (due partly to assumed medicinal properties) that they fired the 16th-century European voyages of global exploration to discover their source, Indonesia's fabled "Spice Islands". These Spanish, Portuguese, Dutch and British explorers (or invaders and colonists) dominated the regional economies of Asia for the next four centuries, and they made one massive contribution to their cuisine too, by importing chilli peppers from South America. So ubiquitous is the chilli today in Asian cooking – it's used in dishes as varied as Sichuanese *gong bao* chicken, Thai green curry, Vietnamese *pho* (noodle soup) and countless relishes and spice pastes – that it's impossible to imagine how local cooks once managed without it.

Food is such an expression of culture in Asia that peoples' lives seem to revolve around it for much of the time. Eating here is always more than simply topping up the body's calories; it is, rather, something to be indulged in or lavished upon others at every opportunity, with special dishes and feasting marking secular and religious festivals. Even the humblest meals can become social events; quiet, romantic restaurants are noticeably rare across much of Asia, where brightly lit, lively venues – the best of which are described in Chinese as being *renao*, or "hot and noisy" – are favoured. That's not to say that there aren't rules; should someone inadvertently touch food with their left hand in Indonesia, onlookers would recoil in disgust at this breach of etiquette. But when wolfing down satay or nasi goreng at a street-side stall, or rubbing elbows with fellow-diners in a south Indian thali house, the sheer enjoyment of eating seems to overwhelm the need to prescribe exactly how this should be done.

Food is such an expression of culture in Asia that peoples' lives seem to revolve around it for much of the time.

Pan-Asian Cooking

The cuisine of Australia and New Zealand is very much that of the mostly European peoples who have colonized these islands in the last 200 years. Not that indigenous methods haven't had an impact: the famous Australian barbecue is only a step away from Aboriginal camp-fire cooking, illustrating a dominant "keep it simple" attitude to food. But the cuisine often self-consciously references European heritage or, in the case of Melbourne's Pan-Asian cuisine, fuses a whole region under one umbrella. Perhaps here, the setting is at least as important to the eating experience as the food; you can't really separate Balmain bugs from their coastal, Sydneyside spot.

Left Farm workers planting rice in a paddy field in Andhra Pradesh, India
Below Street food can be bought from stalls and wandering vendors in Hoi An, Vietnam

HANGZHOU CHINA

The Lucky Fish of Hangzhou

In the Chinese town of Hangzhou in Zhejiang, the blue waters of West Lake slowly darken in the twilight, as couples take an evening stroll beneath the ornamental trees lining the shore. As diners marvel at the view from a waterside restaurant, a plate of fragrant West Lake fish arrives at the table, taking its place amongst a feast of other culinary delights.

A centre of trade and business for over 1,000 years, Hangzhou sprang up during the Tang dynasty on fertile, newly reclaimed plains between eastern China's riverlands and the sea. The Grand Canal brought in merchants, whose money spawned a leisured class that grew fond of the gently poetic scenery of nearby West Lake. The city reached its zenith as China's capital during the 13th-century Southern Song dynasty, but the countryside – and West Lake in particular – has never lost its place in the Chinese mind as the epitome of cultural refinement and natural elegance. Poets, emperors, gastronomes and even Marco Polo have all been drawn here, the latter writing that a cruise around West Lake was one of the most pleasurable experiences in the world.

Today the lakeshore shows off the subtlety of Chinese landscaping, taking nature as its starting point but skilfully tweaking it by adding strategically placed paths, arched bridges, temples and historical monuments to the gently modelled parks and woodlands. A similar vein of artful conceit runs

through the local food, which offers apparently simple dishes with clear flavours, often sweet and rich, whose appearance is refined to the point of pretension – all concealing a huge amount of exacting preparation.

West Lake and its surrounds have always provided a rich assortment of foods, and it has been a place for leisurely fun since its artificial formation from a natural bay in the 8th century. Its high point has long been the Mid-autumn Festival, when families and friends gather to see the full moon over the water. Cruise boats on the lake traditionally served wine and food, and fish – considered auspicious – would naturally be on the menu.

The need to cook quickly in a confined space probably accounts for the simplicity of these dishes, many of which can still be enjoyed today. The West Lake fish itself is in fact a whole carp, which is poached with ginger and then coated with a sticky sweet-and-sour sauce made from its cooking liquor, sugar and the local black vinegar. Served alongside crisply stir-fried prawns, soy-braised pork and a freshly opened parcel of "Beggar's Chicken", this famous fish completes a classic eastern Chinese meal.

Above The vast, tranquil expanse of West Lake *(Xi Hu)* is ringed by stunning tourist attractions, but its serenity is easily enjoyed from a simple walk along its shores

Longjing Tea

The gently undulating hills southwest of Hangzhou are terraced with plantations sprouting the renowned Longjing tea, one of China's most famous brews. Its name, meaning "Dragon Well" comes from the village and water-source of Longjing, near West Lake, but the finest brew is said to be prepared using water from Hupaomeng Quan ("Running-Tiger Dream Spring"), a famous spring in Hangzhou. Longjing is a green tea, whose leaf-buds are picked and dried immediately without allowing them to ferment, creating a pale yellow, delicately aromatic tea. Hangzhou governor and man of letters Su Dongpo (1037–1101) recorded the wonders of this tea, and it was a favourite of the great emperor Qianlong (1711–99), who visited Hangzhou during the 18th century.

A Day around West Lake

There's no reason to linger in humdrum Hangzhou; the main attraction is West Lake itself and the sights scattered around its shore.

MORNING In the north lake area, visit the **tomb of General Yue Fei** (1103–42), a patriotic Song general who defended China against the invading Jurchen armies; the tomb features some extraordinary statuary, including a 4.5-m (15-ft) statue of the general himself. Then delve further into local history at the **Zhejiang Provincial Museum**. From here, cross south over the lake on foot via the **Su Di Causeway**, planted with willow and plum trees. Detour to tiny **Xiaoying Island**, covered in pagodas and reached over a bridge. On the south shore, enjoy a peaceful walk in attractive **Huagang Park**, which was laid out in Song times.

AFTERNOON Catch a cab to **Lingyin Temple**, a famous Zen Buddhist retreat some 3 km (2 miles) west of the lake at **Feilai Hill**. Then take a second cab ride to **Longjing** village to tour the family-run tea factories and plantations.

EVENING Return to **West Lake** and rent a wooden sampan for a short cruise, before finally tucking into local fare at one of the shoreside restaurants.

Essentials

GETTING THERE
Fly to **Hangzhou Xiaoshan International Airport** and take an **airport shuttle bus** or **taxi** to Hangzhou. You can also reach the town by **train** from many other Chinese cities. West Lake is immediately west of Hangzhou.

WHERE TO STAY
West Lake Youth Hostel (inexpensive) has friendly, basic dorms and doubles just south of the lake. www.westlakehostel.com
Crystal Orange Hotel (moderate) has boutique rooms near the shore. +86 571 2887 8988
Ramada Plaza (expensive) is an upmarket chain hotel with attentive service situated on the north shore of the lake. www.ramada.com

TOURIST INFORMATION
Hangzhou Tourist Centre; www.hicenter.cn

The Best Places to Eat West Lake Fish

Lou Wai Lou expensive

If elegant food served in a lakeside setting is what Hangzhou is all about, then Lou Wai Lou – the "Tower Beyond Towers" – is the best restaurant in town. Right on the waterfront, this palatial institution has been in business since the 19th century. It is renowned for its West Lake fish, mooncakes (available during the Mid-Autumn Festival) and *dongpo rou* – fatty cubes of pork belly slow-braised to a butter-like softness, attributed to the ubiquitous Su Dongpo. Other specialities include the banquet classic *bai niao chao feng*, a whole chicken braised in stock, and *xiang xia guoba*, prawn soup poured over sizzling, crispy-fried rice crusts. The decor is a little heavy-handed – sparkling chandeliers, red carpets, gold wallpaper and dark wooden screens and furniture – though you'd expect nothing less of a restaurant that has its own gilded pavilion moored in the lake. This is accessible only by private boat, and provides the ultimate location for a moonlit evening of gastronomic delight and contemplation.

30 Gu Shan Lu, Hangzhou; open 8:30am–8:30pm daily; www.louwailou.com.cn (needs translation)

Also in Hangzhou

Tian Wai Tian *(+86 571 8796 5450; moderate)* is situated in the hills west of Hangzhou, outside the Lingyin Temple. This century-old restaurant features an extensive vegetarian menu alongside local dishes including West Lake fish, Beggar's Chicken (baked in a clay coating, cracked open at the table) and subtly scented freshwater prawns stir-fried with Longjing tea leaves. It is not as refined as some of the lakeside restaurants, but the food is reliably good.

Also in China

In Shanghai, **Xin Kai Yuan** *(+86 21 6439 7999; moderate)* is one of a stylish, city-wide chain of restaurants specializing in Hangzhou cuisine, with all the usual favourites, though you should concentrate on their immaculate *dongpo rou* and duck soup, both indulgently rich dishes without a trace of greasiness. After this, the inevitably oversized restaurant lobby, groaning under an ostentatious dressing of marble and auspicious decorations, is excusable in a city that cherishes conspicuous wealth.

In Hong Kong, **Tien Heung Lau** *(+86 852 2366 2414; moderate)* is a Hangzhou-style restaurant to which elegant furnishings and attentive service are completely alien. But don't be put off – the food is superb and fresh (many of their classic dishes have to be ordered in advance), including the outstandingly fragrant Beggar's Chicken, crispy eel and succulent smoked yellow croaker. If you visit in autumn, try the steamed whole crab or fried shredded crab with noodles.

Above Hangzhou's signature dish is West Lake fish (*Xi Hu cu yu*), whose simple preparation is typical of Zhejiang cuisine

Left Tea has been harvested from the Longjing ("Dragon Well") plantations for more than 2,000 years

A Day in Mumbai

Mumbai's most interesting sights are quite widespread, but with some stamina and the help of an occasional taxi you can cover a remarkable amount of ground in a day.

MORNING The magnificent harbourside **Gateway of India**, built for the visit of King George V in 1911, is the best place to start, though you'll need to keep the hawkers at bay. Then head inland to spend a couple of hours in the **Prince of Wales Museum** (now officially known as Chhatrapati Shivaji), which houses some of India's finest paintings and sculpture.

AFTERNOON Take a taxi up to **Malabar Hill** and stroll along its leafy ridge, passing by the eerie Parsi **Towers of Silence** and visiting the serene **Jain temple**, whose stunning interior is encrusted with mirrors. Further down there is also the famous Hindu **Walukeshwar temple**.

EVENING As dusk falls, wind your way down the hill to the top end of **Chowpatty beach** for some great people-watching while munching a plate of tasty *chaat* by the Arabian Sea.

Essentials

GETTING THERE
Mumbai lies on India's west coast and is a domestic hub for **rail** and **bus** networks. Chhatrapati Shivaji international **airport** lies 30 km (19 miles) north of Mumbai.

WHERE TO STAY
Sea Shore (inexpensive) is a good budget option in Colaba, with some sea-facing rooms, but only shared bathrooms. *+91 22 2287 4237*
City Palace (moderate) is a reliable and conveniently located hotel opposite VT station. *www.hotelcitypalace.net*
Taj Mahal Palace & Tower (expensive), colonial Bombay's oldest hotel, has views of the Arabian Sea and the Gateway of India; it now has a plush modern annexe. *www.tajhotels.com*

TOURIST INFORMATION
www.maharashtratourism.gov.in

Left The puffed rice, noodles and potatoes of *bhel puri* are tumbled with onions, coriander, chilli and tamarind sauce
Below A huge statue of Ganesh is transported through the water off Chowpatty beach during the Ganesh Chaturthi Festival

MUMBAI INDIA

Chaat on a Mumbai Beach

Mumbai is India's economic powerhouse and the cosmopolitan home of Bollywood, the world's most prolific film industry. The city also epitomizes the subcontinent's diversity: it has the worst slums in Asia as well as some of the world's priciest apartments. Frenetically fast-paced, many of its 17 million inhabitants eat on the go – and traditional *chaat* is the snack of choice.

The head-spinning modern city of Mumbai was originally seven islands populated exclusively by fishermen. The islands belonged to several different dynasties over the centuries, but fell under European control when the Portuguese invaded in 1508, renaming the islands *Bom Bahia* (the Good Bay). Some 150 years later, the Portuguese handed the islands to the British, who headquartered the East India Company in "Bombay". They reclaimed vast swathes of land to join the islands together and began a rapid expansion of the port. By the time India gained independence in 1947, Bombay was by far its most prosperous city, boasting a fine collection of Raj-era architecture, including the triumphal arch of the Gateway of India, the Taj Hotel, the VT train station and the Prince of Wales Museum.

The city's reputation as a financial and trade centre was augmented by the booming entertainment business and Mumbai, as it was renamed in 1996, was soon displaying the brash confidence and wealth of the growing middle class. The constant stream of immigrants from other states and foreign lands added to the cosmopolitan atmosphere and to Mumbai's cuisine – so it is fitting that the most popular dish here is not a single item but a collection of snacks that fall under the blanket term *chaat*. They are available at thousands of stalls and roadside *dhabas* (very basic restaurants) throughout the urban sprawl, but the most concentrated and famous string of *chaat* stalls line the back of Chowpatty beach at the end of Marine Drive.

If there is one common ingredient, it is crispy fried dough known as *puri*, which is mixed with a variety of ingredients to produce the different types of *chaat*. It is usually served on a tin plate or in a dried banana-leaf bowl and, of course, eaten with the right hand. Mumbai's favourite version is *bhel puri*, a mixture of *puri*, deep-fried vermicelli, puffed rice, potato, chilli paste, chopped onions, coriander and tamarind sauce. A popular variation, *pani puri*, includes a lentil and potato stuffing with sweet chutney. *Pav bhaji*, found virtually everywhere, is a Portuguese-style bun filled with a spicy vegetable stew. Hot, spicy and nourishing, this is food for fuelling enterprise.

Ganesh Chathurthi

Not actually a food festival in its own right, Mumbai's renowned Ganesh Chaturthi is an excellent occasion to sample the delights of *chaat* at Chowpatty beach. It is a birthday party for the beloved elephant-headed deity Ganesh, and one of the most important and popular Hindu festivals. It falls some time between late August and late September and lasts for up to ten days, culminating in thousands of images of the chubby god being immersed in the soupy waters of the Arabian Sea. Given that the monsoon is often still in full swing during the event, visitors are just as likely to get completely soaked as participants, even if they do not assist in the deity-dunking. Ganesh is said to be fond of sweet puddings, so the *chaat-wallahs* come out in full force, making sure there are plenty of sweet and savoury snacks on offer for his birthday.

Above Mumbai's street stalls are renowned for great *chaat*, especially *bhel puri*

The Best Places to Eat Chaat

Chowpatty Beach Stalls
inexpensive

The whole concept of Indian *chaat* is that it's sold by outlets that are as transient as their customers. Consequently, it is hard to pin down a specific stall amidst the throng of *chaat-wallahs* who wheel their carts up and down the back of Chowpatty beach, advertising their goods with piercing cries or clanging bells. What is indisputable is that locals in Mumbai will all tell you that this is the place to come.

So, let your senses lead you to the most appealing plate of *bhel puri* to suit your own palate. Rest assured that while the stall itself might be dented and grubby, the food will be freshly prepared and the high turnover ensures it remains so.

Chowpatty beach, Mumbai; open all day until late evening

Also in Mumbai

Chaat is available at every turn in Mumbai, but here are two well-known spots. Near the GPO (the main post office), in bustling Crawford Market's 3rd Lane, **Eden's Snacks** *(inexpensive)* is one of central Mumbai's most popular places for grabbing a quick plate of *bhel puri* or *sev puri* (with crispy *papri* wafers) while shopping. On Wodehouse Road in Colaba, where most foreigners stay, **Sunshine Snack Corner** *(+91 22 2215 0646; inexpensive)* is worth trying. If you would rather pass on such unadulterated street food, try **Chaat Lo** *(inexpensive)*, behind Chowpatty beach opposite Bhavan's College, which does many types of *chaat* as well as samosas and *chola bhature*, a Punjabi dish involving spicy chickpeas and fried *puri* bread.

Also in India

Different types of *chaat* are widespread throughout the country. In the capital, Delhi, **Chaat Corner** *(inexpensive)* on Arya Samaj Road does a great range. In Chennai, in the south, you can find local versions of street foods at **Chit Chat** *(inexpensive)* on the city's main thoroughfare, Anna Salai.

Around the World

Apart from well-known snacks like samosas and pakora, Mumbai-style *chaat* can be hard to come by outside India, as most restaurants serve more conventional meals. However, London has quite a few options, such as **Santok Maa's Bhel Poori House** *(+44 20 8665 0626; inexpensive)* in Thornton Heath, which specializes in *bhel puri*, as the name suggests. In Canada, Toronto's **Bombay Bhel** *(www.bombaybhelrestaurant.com; moderate)* offers *pani, bhel, sev* and chickpea-filled *dahi puri* among its appetizers.

Above The restaurant at Vasse Felix has beautiful views over its vineyards, which were the first to be established in Margaret River

Above The fine local venison and wines of Margaret River combine in dishes such as roasted venison with red wine and cranberry coulis

Three Days in Margaret River

The Margaret River region is characterized by its fantastic blend of natural beauty and phenomenal food and wine. Take it all in, but remember distances are long and journeys can take time.

DAY ONE Hop on to the **food and wine trail**: join one of the many guided tours available in the area, or take a **Bushtucker Canoe Tour** along the Margaret River to experience native Australian bush foods.

DAY TWO Head south, exploring the rugged beaches and spectacular caves – the Lake, Mammoth and Jewel show caves – that crop up along the scenic drive to **Augusta**. Have a picnic lunch in the **Boranup Karri Forest**, and finish the day with a visit to the **Cape Leeuwin** lighthouse and have fish and chips on the beach.

DAY THREE Go west to the coast at **Prevelly** for an ocean-view breakfast, then admire the surfing on nearby **Gnarabup Beach**. Head back to town for an afternoon viewing artisan workshops and galleries or get back to nature at the **Wildlife Centre** featuring displays from Australia's largest collection of birds of prey.

Essentials

GETTING THERE
Fly to **Perth international Airport** then **hire a car** for the 3½-hour drive south to Margaret River, or take a **bus** with Southwest Coachlines.

WHERE TO STAY
Adamsons Riverside Apartment and Motel Accommodation (inexpensive) is on beautiful grounds by the river and forest, a short stroll from town. *www.adamsonsriverside.net.au*
Basildene Manor (moderate) offers stately accommodation close to town surrounded by a huge and pretty garden. *www.basildene.com.au*
Merribrook Retreat (expensive) offers every conceivable luxury in a stunning rural setting. *www.merribrook.com.au*

TOURIST INFORMATION
100 Bussell Highway, Margaret River town; *www.margaretriver.com*

MARGARET RIVER AUSTRALIA

Venison Among the Vineyards

South of Perth, on Australia's wild western coastline, Margaret River is a region of natural abundance. Blessed with a maritime Mediterranean climate, its renowned vineyards thrive within the bush landscape, bordered by a river on one side and untamed coastline on the other. Local produce is king here, and the perfect match for the area's fine wines is venison, the meat of kings.

With its rich agricultural soils, life-giving river, dense bush land and isolated situation on one of Australia's wildest stretches of untouched coastline, the commercial development of Margaret River was destined to evolve much more slowly than its natural industry. Alfred and Ellen Bussell built the first homestead here in 1875, but it was another 55 years before a scant collection of three houses allowed the area to declare itself a town.

Little has changed in the last 100 years. Though it now boasts a population of 11,000, the area is still dominated by farming and viticulture. Beef cattle, sheep and deer graze in and around one of the nation's largest wine regions, farmed to feed the appetites of the questing gourmets who flock here each year to devour their favourites among the Margaret River delights.

It's the deer farming that inspires some of the area's greatest culinary experiences. Local couple Graham and Cynthia Morrison established their farm here in 1977, when few people were aware of the combined great taste and health benefits that venison had to offer, but from its humble beginnings the venison farm has gone on to supply its lean and sweet meat to chefs in the local area and right across Australia. Local cooks now serve up tender venison dishes that lend a new richness to old favourites, such as venison spare ribs, slow-cooked in a sticky-sweet barbecue-style sauce, or elegant venison carpaccio teamed with capers and Kalamata olives. Wintry venison osso bucco with chorizo and beans is ideal sustenance after a day spent relaxing on Margaret River's world-renowned surf beaches or trawling the cellars of its many internationally acclaimed wineries.

It is this diversity that propels the region from being a one-day stopover to a multi-dimensional holiday destination. This is a place to indulge every facet of your personality: the wine aficionado, the adventurer, the surfer, the artist, the naturalist and the adventurous gourmand. Because as much as the region is a haven of natural splendour, it is the focus on food and wine that makes it stand out among the nation's coastal hot spots. Margaret River provides a heady change of pace – and tastes – from everyday life.

The Best Places to Eat Venison

Voyager Estate expensive

Just as the glorious natural surroundings of the Margaret River region amaze visitors, so too does the Voyager Estate. The combination of atmospheric grandeur, striking rose gardens and gastronomic excellence – all wrapped up in a pretty Cape Dutch architectural package – is almost too good to be true. And the food is as magnificent as the surroundings. Chef Nigel Harvey does his utmost with the astoundingly good fresh, local produce that comes under his fingertips, including, of course, Margaret River venison, farmed a mere cork pop away. Harvey's deft touch makes the meat shine, in dishes such as his delicately sweet venison carpaccio, matched innovatively with the fresh spiciness of radish and watercress and the bite of Manchego cheese. It is a dish complemented by the blackberry, dark-chocolate and oaky aromatics of the estate's well-regarded Cabernet Sauvignon-Merlot blend. Dishes change with the season, so prepare to be surprised.
Lot 1, Stevens Road, Margaret River; open 10am–4:30pm daily; www.voyagerestate.com.au

Also in Margaret River

Go to the source at **Margaret River Venison** (*www.mrvenison.com; inexpensive*) where you can pick up venison steaks, sausages or marinated kebabs to cook on the barbecue. For something a little more formal there is **Must** (*www.must.com.au; expensive*), a stellar wine bar and restaurant where venison takes on a more sophisticated tone.

Also in Australia

In the small South Australian town of Mount Compass, Judith Phillips is renowned for the venison meat pies she makes and sells at **Mount Compass Venison** (*+61 8 8556 8216; inexpensive*). In Victoria, relish autumnal venison *pithivier* crammed with mushrooms and chestnuts at **Gigi's of Beechworth** (*www.gigisofbeechworth.com; expensive*) in this historic gold-mining town.

Around the World

The reindeer is native to Finland, and there are few better places to experience superbly cooked venison. The top spot in Helsinki is the two-Michelin-starred **Chez Dominique** (*www.chezdominique.fi; expensive*), where venison and oyster tartare is a must. Also in the capital but lower on the price ladder is **Lappi** (*www.lappires.com; moderate*), where traditional sautéed venison comes with mashed potatoes and lingonberries, served in a chic update of the traditional Scandinavian log cabin.

Above The shoreline of Prevelly Park, on the Margaret River Estuary

Margaret River Wines

Wine tasting is a feature of any trip to Margaret River, and most vineyards offer tastings alongside gourmet nibbles or elegant lunches. **Vasse Felix** (*www.vassefelix.com.au*) is the region's oldest vineyard and its wines are some of the most acclaimed. You can enjoy a tasting in its subterranean Cellar Door tasting shop, or try them with food in the winery's elegant restaurant, which has gorgeous views over the vines. **Leeuwin Estate** (*www.leeuwinestate.com.au*) lays claim to one of the region's best Chardonnays – which is no mean feat, given that the region is famed for its Chardonnay grape. Tasting is a must. **Bootleg Brewery** (*www.bootlegbrewery.com.au*) offers a change for those nearing vineyard saturation. Its award-winning ales and lagers can be enjoyed at tables outside in its large and pretty grounds.

KYOTO JAPAN

Fine Dining in Kyoto

The imperial capital for half a millennium until 1869, Kyoto is the cradle of Japanese culture and its historical and spiritual heart. Geishas wander its cherry-tree-lined streets and lanterns are lit at night when the appetizing smell of cooking fills the air. The pinnacle of Kyoto's culinary heritage – the highly refined, multi-course *kaiseki* – lives on in the city's historic *ryotei* restaurants.

Kyoto is such a perfect distillation of Japanese culture that at times it can feel like a theme park.
Spared the destructive might of Allied bombing at the end of World War II, large parts of the city remain well preserved, affording evocative glimpses of life in feudal-era Japan. This is where you will find Japan's most seductive Zen gardens, its most impressive temples and, of course, the fabled geishas, women who are formally trained to entertain men with music, dance and conversation; they are easily distinguished by their formal white makeup, wigs and elaborate kimonos. Costume geishas roam the main tourist district, Gion, for the benefit of the cameras, but you can sometimes spot the real thing on Pontocho, the restaurant and nightlife street.

Kyoto's famous tea ceremony represents the pinnacle of the city's ritual aesthetic, with its impressively controlled and precise choreography. Food-lovers owe it a debt of gratitude, as it led to the creation of a gastronomic treat. Needing some food to counteract all the bitter green tea, the imperial court came up with the similarly ritualized and prolonged multi-course *kaiseki*, Japan's answer to *haute cuisine*.

Perfection, subtlety and above all seasonality are the watchwords of the *kaiseki* chef. *Kaiseki* meals are traditionally served to diners seated on *tatami* (rice-straw mats) in the minimally furnished private rooms of *ryotei* – traditional restaurants housed in old, wooden buildings, usually overlooking immaculate gardens. The menu is fixed and can run to over 20 courses, each with a specific name; the finest *kaiseki* meals cost at least 50,000 Yen (£370) – often much more. The *sakizuke* is the first dish, the all-important overture; ensuing courses draw attention to an aspect of Japan's seasonal bounty, such as spring mountain ferns in May or the fiercely expensive *matsutake* mushroom in autumn. Even the tableware plays a role in reflecting the seasonal narrative of the meal.

For the *kaiseki* novice, there will almost certainly be alien, quite possibly alarming ingredients – sea cucumber roe, salted fish entrails or snapping turtle, for instance – as well as unfamiliar mealy, soft and crunchy textures. There will be little or no meat and some dishes might not even taste of very much, but everything will look exquisite. *Dashi*, a stock made from seaweed and *katsuobushi* (dried bonito flakes), forms the core of any *kaiseki*, but it will invariably end with rice, the foodstuff the Japanese hold most dear.

Above *Kaiseki* is a succession of courses that aim to balance texture, temperature and flavour, while emphasizing the essential character of the season

Right The Golden Pavilion in the Rukuon-ji complex is one of many beautiful temple buildings in Kyoto

Below In Kyoto, geishas and *maiko* (apprentice geishas) dress their hair and bodies in 18th-century style

---

A Day in Kyoto

Kyoto has more than 2,000 temples, shrines and gardens, many of them UNESCO World Heritage sites, so selectivity is the key for sightseeing Kyoto in one day.

MORNING Start at **Nanzen-ji**, which is a good example of the type of temple most common to Kyoto; it is also situated close to many other temples in **Higashiyama**, a wonderful area to wander. For lunch, make for the legendary **Nishiki Market**, a covered corridor filled with dried-fish vendors, grocers selling bewildering indigenous Kyoto vegetables, Japanese sweet shops and ancient knife makers who once fashioned samurai swords and still service the imperial kitchen equipment.

AFTERNOON Visit the **Kyoto International Manga Museum** for a modern take on Japan or explore the **Imperial Palace** for a more historical one. Then stroll around the atmospheric residential area of **Kamigyo ku**; there is a surprise on every street.

EVENING End the day on the outdoor restaurant terraces of **Pontocho**, watching the bats swoop over the Kamo river.

Essentials

GETTING THERE
The **"bullet train"** from Tokyo takes around 2½ hours. The nearest **airport** is Kansai International, 75 minutes away by **train**.

WHERE TO STAY
Ryokan Ishihara (inexpensive) is a traditional Japanese inn that warmly welcomes foreigners. *www.yado-web.com*
APA Hotel (moderate) is a modern hotel close to the main station. *www.apahotel.com*
Tawaraya (expensive) is a superb, 300-year-old traditional Japanese *ryokan*. +81 75 211 5566

TOURIST INFORMATION
www.seejapan.co.uk

What Else to Eat

Kyoto is cradled on three sides by mountains that provide the clear, clean water so essential for its *sake* and tea. The soft, pure water is also important in the manufacture of Kyoto's renowned **tofu**, a key element of the city's cuisine. It used to be delivered fresh to homes every morning, like milk. Kyotoites enjoy tofu simmered in a hot pot, deep-fried (**agedashi tofu**), freeze-dried, or spread with miso and grilled as **dengaku**, among many preparations. They especially value dried tofu skin, or **yuba**. There are several excellent tofu restaurants in Kyoto, many of them located close to the main temples. One of the most famous is **Okutan**, close to the Nanzen-ji temple (*+81 75 771 8709*).

The Best Places to Eat Kaiseki

Kikunoi expensive

Kyoto's finest *kaiseki* restaurants can be rather daunting, impenetrable places – some shun diners they don't know – but there are a few that welcome *kaiseki* novices, offering proper seats instead of a *tatami* mat and explaining the courses to their guests. Of these, the most renowned is Kikunoi ("chrysanthemum well"), awarded three Michelin stars in 2011. It was founded in 1912 and is run by the third-generation chef Yoshihiro Murata in an historic *ryotei* surrounded by immaculate Zen gardens, home to the freshwater spring from which the restaurant gets its name. Courses during a *kaiseki* could include raw baby squid marinated in soy, exquisite sashimi, sumptuous monkfish liver, and, unusually for a *kaiseki*, duck and beef from Hyogo Prefecture's Wagyu cattle. Clients argue over the best time of year to visit – given the seasonal nature of the food – but autumn is probably the most compelling season to dine at Kikunoi. Many of the world's greatest chefs have made a pilgrimage here.

459 Shimokawara-cho, Higashiyama-ku, Kyoto; open noon–2pm and 5–8pm (last entry) daily; www.kikunoi.jp

Also in Kyoto

Kaiseki comes in many forms. Its most perfectly realized expression is usually found in *ryotei*, but the term is just as often used to describe any vaguely traditional, multi-course Japanese meal served *omakase* (orchestrated by the chef). Kikunoi *(above)* has a less formal sister restaurant, **Roan Kikunoi** *(www.kikunoi.jp; moderate)*, but for a more contemporary yet still authentically Kyoto-style *kaiseki* in a restaurant, try **Aunbo** *(+81 525 2900; moderate)*, in the atmospheric Gion district. The meticulously crafted, super-fresh ingredients used by chef Tashima in his cuisine will include tofu, local *kyo-yasai* (Kyoto vegetables) and fish, which you can enjoy gazing thoughtfully out to the restaurant's equally immaculate Zen garden.

Also in Japan

One restaurant that has picked up a great deal of buzz – along with two Michelin stars – in recent years is **Ryugin** *(www.nihonryori-ryugin.com; expensive)* in Tokyo. In this tiny, ornate, windowless dining room in a back street of Roppongi, chef Seiji Yamamoto creates gorgeously elaborate, multi-course meals from super-fresh, seasonal Japanese ingredients.

Around the World

Kaiseki has been hugely influential on the multi-course, fixed menu style of *haute cuisine* dining that has spread throughout the top restaurants of Europe and America. You can see echoes of *kaiseki* in the elaborate cuisine of restaurants such as **The Fat Duck** *(www.thefatduck.co.uk; expensive)* in the UK and Copenhagen's **Noma** *(www.noma.dk)*.

HONG KONG

HONG KONG CHINA

Dim Sum by the South China Sea

"A dream of Manhattan, arising from the South China Sea" – modern travel writer Pico Iyer's description perfectly captures the East–West paradox that is Hong Kong. From imperial stronghold to opium port, Cold War enclave to today's global financial hub, this teeming city still delights in its traditional Cantonese cuisine, especially its bite-sized, delicious dim sum.

Prior to 1997 Hong Kong had been a British colony for 155 years, but this vibrant business centre remains emphatically Chinese under its Western veneer. While you can shop for Armani suits or be serenaded by a string quartet over afternoon tea at an elegant colonial hotel, the dominant language is Cantonese and the city's ultra-modern harbourside has been laid out according to the traditional aesthetic principles of feng shui.

As shops roll up their shutters and the engines of commerce fire up for the day, in the oasis of calm that is Kowloon Park, birds chirp and swoop between dark-green fig trees, and old folk greet each other after their morning tai chi exercises with "*Jousahn, yum cha, yum cha!*" – "Good morning, let's go for dim sum!" When it comes to eating, Hong Kong is the best place in the world to try Cantonese cooking, with its fresh flavours and contrasting textures, and there's no better way to sample its variety than with dim sum, or "little choices" – dainty portions of fried or steamed snacks. In Hong

Kong, dim sum is better known as *yum cha* – "with tea" – and a pot is an essential part of the meal. Favourite is *bo lei*, a dark, strong brew said to help the digestion.

The Hong Kong dim sum experience involves wading into a busy restaurant, finding a free table, then ordering from the trolleys laden with dishes and steamer baskets that constantly cruise by. *Har gau* dumplings, their prawn fillings glowing pink through translucent wrappings; little steamed beef balls, smooth, springy-textured and flavoured with minced celery; fluffy steamed buns filled with scented *char siu* roast pork; aromatic sticky rice steamed in lotus leaves; *cheung fun*, meat wrapped in sheets of paper-thin rice noodles – the main problem is deciding what not to try, so it's no surprise that a dim sum brunch often stretches into the afternoon. It's the perfect way to fortify yourself for sightseeing and, above all in this city built on trade, for shopping, whether browsing in glitzy high-end Central, haggling in hectic Causeway Bay and Nathan Road, or diving into the heady Temple Street night bazaar.

Three Days in Hong Kong

Hong Kong has matchless shopping opportunities, but look beyond them and you'll discover an engaging mix of modern architecture, traditional temples, street markets, island life and even fine beaches.

DAY ONE Explore Hong Kong Island by riding the Peak Tram to the **Peak** for views over the city, then catch a bus to explore traditional Chinese medicine shops and the smoky **Man Mo Temple** at Sheung Wan. After lunch, sunbathe or stroll on the south coast's **Shek O** beach, then mix with expats over a drink at one of **Lan Kwai Fong**'s many bars.

DAY TWO Catch the romantic Star Ferry across the harbour to **Kowloon** and Nathan Road's jewellers' and clothing shops, then work north through the lively jade, goldfish and ladies' markets. Ride the MTR to Diamond Hill's antique-style **Nan Lian Gardens**, before returning to the harbour for the classic night-time view of Hong Kong Island's skyline.

DAY THREE Head to **Lantau Island** and ride the Ngong Ping 360° cable car to the serene, 34-m (110-foot) high **Big Buddha**, then visit the stilt fishing village of **Tai O** for a chance to see pink dolphins, before returning to Hong Kong Island by ferry.

Essentials

GETTING THERE
A major hub, **Hong Kong International Airport** connects directly to much of the globe. The **Airport Express** train has direct links to the city centre and Kowloon. **Buses**, the **MTR subway** and **taxis** are comprehensive and efficient.

WHERE TO STAY
The **Eaton Hotel** (inexpensive) is friendly and functional. *www.eaton-hotel.com*
Hotel LKF (moderate) is smart and in boutique style. *www.hotel-lkf.com.hk*
The Peninsula Hotel (expensive) offers colonial-era luxury. *www.peninsula.com*

TOURIST INFORMATION
Find the helpful Hong Kong Tourism Board at Causeway Bay MTR station and Tsim Sha Tsui Star Ferry Pier (Kowloon); *www.discoverhongkong.com*

Left In the dim sum kitchens, tender dumplings are lifted gently from their traditional bamboo steamers

Above High-speed ferries dart across the harbour against Hong Kong's fabulous illuminated skyline

Below Chefs make their selection from lantern-lit market stalls piled high with artfully displayed produce

Dim Sum Around the World

Naturally, China is the best place to eat dim sum, but cities outside Asia with large Chinese communities come a close second. From London to Sydney and San Francisco, top-class dim sum is increasingly available in gastronomic hubs around the world.

HONG KONG

Tim Ho Wan Shop inexpensive

8 Tai Yuen Mansion, 2–20 Kwong Wa Street, Mong Kok, Kowloon; +86 852 2332 2896

The world's least expensive Michelin-starred restaurant, with queues stretching around the block – take a numbered ticket and go shopping for an hour. Their flaky barbecued pork buns, richly flavoured turnip cake and perfect *har gau* are not to be missed.

Din Tai Fung moderate

3/F Silvercord Centre, 30 Canton Road, Tsim Sha Tsui, Kowloon; +86 852 2730 6928

Courteous service, bright, bustling and everything above average. The specialities are various *xiaolong bao* (dumplings normally stuffed with pork, though one version here comes filled with taro paste), but save room for the crunchy jellyfish and radish salad.

Luk Yu Tea House expensive

24 Stanley Street, Central; +86 852 2523 1970

Perhaps a little overpriced, but it's the ambience that makes this not to be missed: pure 1930s teahouse, with ceiling fans, dark wooden booths and ancient staff wearing crisply starched linen.

GUANGZHOU, CHINA

Sprawling, overcrowded Guangzhou, capital of Guangdong province, shares the same energy, language and cuisine as Hong Kong. But at over 2,000 years old, it has rather more history.

Liwan Mingshijia inexpensive

99 Dishifu Lu; +86 20 8139 1405

This open-fronted canteen on Guangzhou's famous food street is always packed to bursting – sharing tables is inevitable and even Cantonese-speakers have trouble ordering above the din. It is best for exquisitely thin-skinned *cheung fun*, juicy won ton and *shuang pi nai* (custard-like "double-skinned milk").

Chao Hao moderate

6/F World Trade Centre, 371 Huanshi Dong Lu; +86 20 8769 0888

Smart and sophisticated decor makes Chao Hao a favourite place for indulging in crispy-skinned pork, stewed chickens' feet and Hong Kong-style mango pudding, though the speciality dish here is *fun gwor* – dumplings from northeastern Guangdong province.

Tao Tao Ju moderate

20 Dishifu Lu; +86 20 8139 9632

The roast goose – a Cantonese speciality – and the crumbly *char siu* rolls alone justify the reputation of this century-old restaurant, which claims to have more than 200 dim sum dishes on the menu. The greatest variety is on offer after 2pm.

SINGAPORE

This tiny city state sitting at the tip of the Malay Peninsula was, like Hong Kong, founded by the British. With its mix of colonial, Chinese, Malay and Indian heritage, Singapore is one of Southeast Asia's trading hubs.

Yan Ting moderate

The St Regis Hotel, 29 Tangling Road; +65 6506 6866

Probably the finest dim sum in Singapore, served in suave surrounds by attentive staff. The *char siu* roast pork is meltingly soft, the *har gau* dumplings firm and smooth, and their soup stocks awash with complex but subtle flavours.

SYDNEY, AUSTRALIA

Chinese migrants came to Australia during the country's 19th-century gold rushes and stayed on to run market gardens and stores. There are good-sized Chinatowns in all state capitals, but Sydney's is probably the liveliest.

East Ocean Seafood inexpensive

421–9 Sussex Street, Haymarket; www.eastocean.com.au

Come prepared to queue at this authentically busy, hot and noisy dim sum legend, which delivers consistently fine scallop dumplings, steamed black-bean spare ribs and fried vegetable rolls. Hong Kong expats get positively misty-eyed over their *dofu fa* (tofu custard).

Left (top to bottom) Four types of *gao*, or steamed dumplings; the main gateway into Sydney's Chinatown; dim sum dishes with, in the foreground, "phoenix talons" (chickens' feet)

Below (top to bottom) Paper lanterns strung across Gerrard Street, in the heart of London's Chinatown; rolled and skewered steamed pork with chilli and spring onions

LONDON, UK

London's dim sum scene has exploded since the upmarket and innovative Hakkasan opened in the late 1990s, making Chinese food hip, upping the bar for dim sum cooking everywhere, and making London arguably the best city for Chinese food outside Asia.

Phoenix Palace moderate
5 Glentworth Street, NW1; www.phoenixpalace.co.uk
You know where you are with Phoenix Palace's enjoyably familiar dim sum selection – barbecued pork buns, sesame prawn rolls and crunchy fried yam dumplings – all cooked to perfection and served in a polite, bright setting.

Yi-Ban moderate
London Regatta Centre, Dockside Road, Royal Albert Dock, E16; www.yi-ban.com

A converted warehouse serving first-class dim sum with a stylish Docklands view. Their prawn and chive dumplings, pork and preserved egg congee and marinated pork with jellyfish are good enough to make you overlook the occasionally offhand service.

Hakkasan expensive
8 Hanway Place, W1; www.hakkasan.com
Hakkasan's success has brought it a Michelin star. The stylish wooden decor invokes a romanticized image of China, which suits the food – venison puffs and flying fish roe have never appeared on menus in dim sum's homeland. Don't miss the magnificent seafood dumpling consommé.

SAN FRANCISCO, USA

San Francisco's Chinatown is one of the largest outside Asia and the oldest in America. Beneath ornate 19th-century buildings, including a dragon-embossed Bank of America, lie dim sum restaurants that are fairly conservative, but with high-quality food.

Yong Kee inexpensive
732 Jackson Street; +1 415 986 3759
A takeaway bakery that's a favourite with local Chinese, with many dim sum offerings – though it's pretty well mandatory to try their big chicken buns and handmade *char siu* rolls. There's no English sign outside, but it's not hard to find.

Ton Kiang moderate
5821 Geary Boulevard (between 22nd and 23rd Ave); www.tonkiang.net

Though most of the excellent dim sum menu here is mainstream Cantonese, Ton Kiang is unusual in also serving Hakka dishes from northeastern Guangdong province, on the border with Fujian (Hokkien). Shrimp-stuffed aubergine is a Hakka classic.

Yank Sing moderate
One Rincon Center, 101 Spear Street; www.yanksing.com
This family-run institution has been feeding the community since 1958, building up an enviable reputation for fresh tastes and skilful presentation. Must-trys are the *xiaolong bao*, chicken *fan gwor* dumplings and steamed rice packets.

On the Menu

Char siu bao A steamed bun, light and fluffy around its savoury stuffing of barbecued pork.
Cheung fun Thin, light rice noodle sheets folded around prawn or roast meat fillings and flavoured with a soy-oil dressing.
Chun goon "Spring roll", the best-known dim sum outside China though not so popular at home. Usually stuffed with pork shreds and bean sprouts, and served with a sweet-and-sour sauce.
Dan ta Flaky pastry cup filled with egg custard. Macau's Portuguese-influenced version is grilled on top.
Fan gwor Clear-skinned dumplings from Chaozhou (Teochew) in China's eastern Guangdong province. Usually filled with seafood and light-flavoured vegetables.

Foong jow Literally "phoenix talons", actually chickens' feet, prepared in various ways. The skin has a classic, gelatinous crunchiness but they're fiddly things to eat, with dozens of tiny bones.
Har gau Steamed, clear-skinned prawn dumplings; the prawns should be slightly crisp and the wrapping light. A yardstick for a fine dim sum kitchen.
Jook Bland rice porridge, perked up with savoury ingredients; an ideal complement to richer dim sum dishes. Sometimes known by its Indian name, "congee".
Law bak go Fried turnip-paste patty flavoured with dried shrimp and *lap cheung* sausage.
Mong gwor pu deen A refreshing, un-Chinese dessert of Southeast Asian origins, comprising puréed mango pulp set with gelatin.

Nor mai gai Chicken pieces steamed inside a glutinous rice packet, wrapped in a scented lotus leaf. They tend to be rather heavy and filling.
San jook ngau yuk Steamed, springy-textured beef balls, served with a distinctive, aromatic soy sauce.
Siu mai Ubiquitous, open-topped steamed pork-and-prawn dumplings. Inevitably ordered because of their good looks, they can be delightfully firm and juicy, but are often rather stodgy.
Woo gok Crisp and curiously "hairy" fried taro croquettes, filled with minced beef. Surprisingly filling.
Xiaolong bao Addictively tasty steamed pork and shredded cabbage dumplings from Shanghai. They fill with broth during cooking, making eating tricky – bite a hole in the side to drain them first.

PENANG MALAYSIA

Spicy Fish Soup in Penang

Georgetown, capital of the jungly Malaysian island of Penang, is steeped in a fusion of cultures, a legacy of the Malay, Chinese, Indian and Thai traders who settled here after the British set up shop during the 18th century. Colonial architecture aside, Penang's hallmark is its Nonya cooking – a blend of Chinese and Southeast Asian cuisines, typified by pungent, hot-and-sour *laksa*.

Georgetown's old core sits right at Penang's northeastern tip, once defended by the now tropically mouldering Fort Cornwallis, built by the British at the spot where they first landed on the island in 1786. The streets nearby are a cultural mosaic of the peoples that followed them: the waterfront, where the magnificently colonial Eastern & Oriental Hotel stares out to sea; Little India, with its Hindu temples and tandoori chicken shops; the Chinese district, a maze of pastel-coloured, colonnaded shophouses (a cross-cultural product of Chinese and Portuguese influences) and ornate southern Chinese guildhalls; the mosques of modern Malaysia; and a scattering of Thai restaurants. In fact restaurants of all sorts are everywhere, filling the heavy, humid air with competing aromas, though it's off around the markets and on the seafront – where people stroll in the evening, enjoying the cooling ocean breezes – that you'll find true Nonya cooking.

Laksa – spicy Malaysian seafood soup – is a classic Nonya dish, using a Chinese-style noodle soup as a vehicle for Malay flavours and ingredients. It takes several regional forms, but Penang's *asam laksa* stands out for being deliciously hot-and-sour. Scented galangal and lemon grass are used to flavour boiling fish stock, along with tart tamarind pulp – tamarind is called "laksa" in Malay, which also means "sour". The flavoured stock is poured over rice noodles, topped with a healthy sprinkle of fresh and dried chillies, cucumber and pineapple shreds, mint leaves, sliced shallots and pink, finely chopped ginger-flower buds, before pungent prawn sauce is finally drizzled in to link all the flavours together. It's a powerful mix, enough to make any Westerner break a healthy sweat.

Where to cool off? By day it gets pretty hot down on the coast, so heading inland to the heights of Penang Hill makes sense – especially as there's a funicular railway to the forested top, where the climate is a few degrees cooler and everything is shaded. Or, to give hot, tired feet a break, take a driving tour of the island – if you're interested in wildlife, don't miss the chance to see turtles nesting at Penang National Park. The lush Penang Botanic Gardens is another cooling sanctuary, with wonderful tropical trees, orchids and ornamental ponds – and some bold rhesus monkeys. Much of the vegetation here has culinary uses, with helpful signage – from ginger to lychees, mangosteens to tamarind, it's a fascinating way to "meet the cast" of the local cuisine.

Above Penang-style *laksa* omits the coconut milk found in most Malaysian variants of the dish, for a much cleaner, more refreshing taste

Right Boisterous deities welcome you to the Sri Mariamman Temple, the oldest Hindu temple in Penang

Below The Asam Laksa stall at the Ayer Itam market is a legendary Penang food stop *(see facing page)*

Three Days in Penang

Penang is a beautiful island, but for those unused to it, the climate can be punishing. Take it easy, and make plans for the day not too ambitious.

DAY ONE Kick off a walking tour of Georgetown at the site of **Fort Cornwallis**, before plunging southwest into **Chinatown** and its shaded, arcaded shophouses. Stop to admire the riotously decorated Hindu **Sri Mariamman Temple** on the edge of **Little India**, then continue south to a knot of ornate Chinese clan temples – **Khoo Kongsi** on Lebuh Pantai is the most splendid. If you've still got the energy, head west to **Cheong Fatt Tze mansion** for a guided tour of this magnificent Chinese pile.

DAY TWO Catch a bus or taxi to Georgetown's western outskirts and easy, well-marked walking trails at the **Botanic Gardens** and adjacent **Penang Hill**.

DAY THREE Save the third day for touring Penang's **north coast**: aside from slightly overdeveloped beaches around **Batu Ferringhi**, there's the delightful – if tiny – **Penang National Park** at Mukah Head, famed for its turtles and offering short jungle walks.

Essentials

GETTING THERE
Georgetown can be reached via **Penang International Airport**, and by **road** bridge, **rail** and **ferry** from the Malaysian mainland.

WHERE TO STAY
The **Old Penang Guesthouse** (inexpensive) is characterful, and nicely restored. *www.oldpenang.com*
The Cathay (moderate) is a faded but charming Chinese mansion. *+60 4262 6271*
Eastern & Oriental Hotel (expensive): grand, romantic, historic charm. *www.e-o-hotel.com*

TOURIST INFORMATION
10 Pesara King Edward; *+60 4261 6663*

Nonya Cooking

Nonya cooking (also called Straits Chinese cooking) is a blend of Malay and southern Chinese themes, with an occasional nod to Thai and Indian cuisines. The blend is not always even, and both sides adore fish and seafood. The Chinese bring rice dumplings and "cakes", noodle soups and stir-fries to the party, but the Malay influence is clear in the use of chilli-based *sambal* relishes, coconut milk and cooking pastes made from complex blends of fresh and dried spices. The defining Nonya taste is a sharp, sour flavour rich in chillies, tamarind, lime juice and noxious-smelling *belachan* prawn paste (which mellows considerably when cooked) – of which *asam laksa* is the perfect example.

The Best Places to Eat Asam Laksa

Asam Laksa Stall inexpensive

Locals will tell you that this humble stall, west of downtown Georgetown near the foot of Penang Hill, serves the best *asam laksa* in Penang – in which case, it's probably the best *asam laksa* available anywhere. The local family running the show follow the classic recipe and, as everything is laid out at the front of the stall, you can follow the whole process, from chopping and slicing the ingredients through to spooning out the seasoned stock into the bowls of noodles and adding the garnishes. It's all ridiculously cheap but, as portions are generous, you won't need a second bowl. After your meal, be sure to visit the nearby Kek Lok Si, an absurd, pagoda-like temple on an octagonal base dating to 1893, full of brightly painted mouldings and Buddhist statuary. On the hill behind the market is a spectacular, 30-m (100-foot) high bronze statue of Guanyin, the Chinese goddess of mercy, only completed in 2003.

Ayer Itam market, Jalan Ayer Itam; open noon–8pm daily

Also in Penang

While the Asam Laksa Stall *(above)* might have a monopoly on the tastiest *asam laksa*, the **Pesiaran Gurney Night Hawker Centre**, around 3 km (1½ miles) west of central Georgetown – or rather the adjacent waterfront promenade – is definitely the most atmospheric place to eat it. Sit out here with sociable crowds and enjoy the dusk and fresh air, with excellent *laksa* served up fresh at dozens of street stalls – just aim for the busiest one.

Also in Malaysia

In Malaysia's capital, Kuala Lumpur, **Mark's Asam Laksa** in the Weld shopping centre *(+60 2487 0050; inexpensive)* is a central branch of a cheerful restaurant chain serving good-quality *asam laksa* in comfortable, if not exciting, surroundings; try their *hong dou sha* (sweet red bean soup) as an unusual dessert.

Around the World

For a different take on what *laksa* is all about, head to East Coast Road in Singapore, where **328 Katong Laksa** *(+65 9732 8163; inexpensive)* – along with hundreds of other restaurants across the city – serves the richer version with prawns, coconut milk and a heavier, more curry-oriented flavour. Katong's menu stretches to little but *laksa*, but their *otak-otak* (spiced, minced fish steamed in banana-leaf packets) makes a good side dish.

A Day in Chengdu

Though much of Chengdu is modern, there are many places in the city to soak up a more traditional atmosphere.

MORNING Greet the dawn among scores of martial artists in **Renmin Park**, then catch a cab out to Chengdu's **Panda Breeding Research Base** to watch these endangered creatures breakfasting on fresh bamboo shoots. Return to town for tea at the atmospheric **Green Goat Temple**, dedicated to Taoism's mythic founder, Lao Tzu.

AFTERNOON Ride the bus or walk to **Jin Li**, a lane full of antique-style shops and stalls specializing in Sichuan's famous *xiaochi* snacks. Visit the adjacent **Wuhou Memorial Hall**, where emperor Liu Bei of the ancient Shu kingdom is buried, then take a bus to the extraordinary **Jinsha Museum**, packed with cultural relics from the Bronze Age.

EVENING After dark, have supper along **Kuan Xiangzi**, a maze of beautifully restored 19th-century stone lanes and buildings that house some great restaurants. Afterwards, catch a short performance of Sichuan opera at the **Shufeng Yayun** theatre.

Essentials

GETTING THERE
Chengdu has a **train** station and **international airport**. A **metro line** runs south through the city, and **buses** and **taxis** are everywhere.

WHERE TO STAY
Traffic Hotel Chengdu (inexpensive) is a backpacker favourite – clean, friendly, efficient and in a good central location. *www.traffichotelchengdu.cn*
The BuddhaZen Hotel (moderate) is a boutique hotel with a traditional courtyard setting, located in the fascinating "old street" area of Wen Shu Fang. *+86 28 8678 1212*
The Sofitel Wanda (expensive) is Chengdu's best upmarket option. *www.sofitel.com*

FURTHER INFORMATION
194 Qintai Road, Chengdu; or check the listings magazine *GoChengdu: www.gochengdoo.com*

Right Drinking cups *(wan)* have lids *(gai)* to stop the leaves of the tea *(cha)*; together forming the *gaiwan cha* for drinking tea
Below The teahouses of Chengdu vary from grand old buildings to bamboo-pole stalls in temples and markets

CHENGDU CHINA

A Cultural Brew in Chengdu

It's a summer day in Chengdu, the humid capital of Sichuan province, and people are languishing at a riverside teahouse, paralysed by the heat despite shade from overhanging ginkgo and willow trees. In front of each is a thermos of hot water and a steaming cup of tea – which, according to Chinese medicine, is in fact "cooling", making it the perfect thing to drink in this climate.

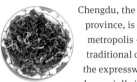

Chengdu, the capital of Sichuan province, is a modern, overcrowded metropolis – but patches of traditional culture survive among the expressways and office blocks, and especially in the people. The city dates back to prehistory, and became known as a base for rebel armies around AD 200, before blossoming as a trading nexus on the "tea-horse roads", which spread out from central China into distant Tibet by the 16th century. Tea has been drunk in China for millennia; there are hundreds of varieties of tea and as many ways of serving it. But teahouse culture – with teahouses serving as hubs of local communities, like a pub or bar in the West – really only survives nowadays in Sichuan, and most obviously in Chengdu.

Sichuanese teahouses take many forms, from a few chairs in the corner of a temple park to grand, antique-style buildings with heavy wooden furniture and a theatre stage for watching Sichuanese opera. Take a seat in either and a waiter will materialize to offer you tea; sometimes there's not much choice – just jasmine or green tea – but other times you may be offered a three-page menu of regional specialities. Tea is normally served in a *gaiwan cha* – a squat, lidded cup and saucer, which is used as a teapot elsewhere in China for pouring the brew into thimble-sized cups, but here it's drunk from directly. Locals pick up the whole assemblage in one hand to take a sip, carefully holding the lid only slightly open to keep back floating leaves. Demanding far less skill, *zhuye qing*, a green tea from the forested foothills of holy Mount Emei, always arrives in a glass tumbler so that you can watch the tiny, spear-shaped buds rise and fall as the drink cools.

The waiter will leave behind a flask of hot water, or periodically return with a metal kettle. Some establishments serve Sichuanese snacks, or at least a plate of dried beans or melon seeds so you can munch on something as you watch your fellow drinkers chat idly in the Sichuanese dialect, or play cards or mah jong. If the teahouse is a theatre, don't expect the audience to devote too much attention to the play; they'll know the story already, and catching up with friends or swapping stories is far more important.

Sichuanese Snacks

Sichuan is famous for the variety of its snacks, or **xiaochi**, which, unlike many Sichuanese main courses, are not always searingly spicy. Savoury **"carrypole noodles"** *(dandan mian)* are named after the way street hawkers of this dish used to cart their wares around, while gruesome-sounding **"husband-wife lung slices"** *(fuqi feipian)* feature slivers of beef in a mild soy-vinegar-chilli dressing. Both *chao shou* (**Sichuanese ravioli** served in plain soup) and *tangyuan* (rice flour **dumplings** stuffed with sweet sesame paste) are chilli-free, though bland *douhua*, **soft beancurd**, is served with hot relish on the side. Upping the chilli stakes considerably, *gege* (rice-coated **spare ribs** cooked in tiny steamers), *liang fen* (**cold bean noodles** in a chilli-vinegar sauce) and *ranmian* (the aptly-named **"incandescent noodles"**) are best avoided unless you have an asbestos mouth.

Above Tea-drinkers watch Sichuan opera at Wuhou temple in Chengdu

The Best Teahouses in Sichuan Province

Heming Teahouse inexpensive

Everyone in Chengdu knows Heming Teahouse. Set underneath a wisteria vine just inside the city's most central park, this open-air teahouse looks out across a large ornamental pond. There's a large bronze kettle at the entrance (actually a water spout for you to wash your hands under on the way in), the regulation bamboo chairs, and some solid, inconveniently shaped stone tables. Cruising hairdressers, shoulder masseurs and even earwax removers move among the locals, some of whom seem to spend the entire day here. There's just the right blend of indifference and attention shown to you by the staff. Weekend crowds sprawl, chew sunflower seeds and slurp their drinks cheerfully, as they gossip, browse their newspapers or stare vacantly at youngsters bumping about in boats on the pond.

A canteen off to one side sells hot and cold snacks, and once a year there's a food fair in the park, where you can buy other local treats such as "three gunshots" — three sticky-rice balls which are bounced off a drum into a tray of toasted flour and served in dark caramel; more performance art than a meal.

North Gate, Renmin Park, Chengdu; open 6am–7pm daily

Also in Eastern Sichuan

For a rural riverside setting, leave Chengdu and head to the village of **Huanglong Xi**, whose rickety antique streets and low-key temples have made it something of a tourist phenomenon. For a similar experience with less raucous crowds, try **Pingle**, about 90 km (55 miles) west of Chengdu. There are wonderfully atmospheric teahouses in **Zigong**, a former industrial town a day's journey from Chengdu; here you can relax over tea in the flagstoned courtyards of Wangye Miao and Huanhou Gong, two splendidly ornate merchants' guildhalls commemorating the town's salt-mining heyday.

Also in Western Sichuan

For a totally different take on what makes a good cup of tea in Sichuan, head to western Sichuan. The teahouses scattered through dusty backlanes in **Songpan** – a Qing dynasty garrison town encircled by stone walls and snowy mountains – make great perches for watching the Muslim, Tibetan and Qiang population go about their business. In the remoter monastery towns of **Litang** and **Langmusi**, pluck up the courage to try Tibetan butter tea: a rare mix of tea, yak butter, salt and water churned into a soup.

HOI AN VIETNAM

Street Food in Happy Hoi An

A powerful trading port for many centuries, Hoi An has a uniquely picturesque Old Quarter, its timeworn wooden buildings a testament to all the cultures that have traded and thrived here. Unscarred by war, the beautiful and easy-going town is also known for its multicultural street food, which blends the best fast-food elements from Vietnam, France, Japan and China.

Hoi An sits roughly midway down Vietnam's coast; its position made it the country's largest and most successful trading port from the 15th to the 19th century. Evidence of the many foreign merchants that were drawn here – from China, Japan, India and Europe in particular – can still be seen in the town's crumbling but beautiful architecture, miraculously untouched by the Vietnam War. It is an extraordinary record of the fusion of different cultures over time and as such has been declared a UNESCO World Heritage site.

The almost entirely wooden architecture of Hoi An, rich in tiling and lacquer, is a fascinating blend of Vietnamese and foreign designs and techniques. The Old Quarter's lanes and alleys are lined with small and grand homes, family cult houses (dedicated to the worship of ancestors), community houses, striking pagodas and even a 17th-century Japanese wooden bridge. Despite the conversion of many interiors into shops, this old area has lost none of its charm.

Visitors able to drag their eyes away from the stunning buildings, with their craft shops, working artisans and tailors, find that there is some fantastic street food on offer. Women in Chinese hats teeter through the cobbled streets, an entire restaurant hanging from a pole across their shoulders. When a suitable spot is found, the mobile restaurateur lays out a collection of plastic chairs and before long customers are tucking into delicate seafood-topped rice pancakes or bowlfuls of sickly sweet desserts, fragrant with ginger and coconut. On the next corner a *banh mi* vendor can be found filling French-style baguettes with pâté and roast meat, before adding pickled daikon radish, chilli and coriander; it's another instance of East meets West.

The pedestrianized Old Quarter is undoubtedly Hoi An's main draw, but the new town offers an interesting, if noisy, glimpse into everyday Vietnamese life. An early-morning visit to the "wet market" is a must; it's here that the street sellers haggle over fish and all the exotic edibles that will go into making some of the freshest, tastiest street food in the world.

A Day in Hoi An

The Old Quarter of Hoi An is pedestrianized and it's a joy simply to wander around its narrow streets, but watch out for motorbikes, which haven't yet been banned from the area. Aim for an early start, along with the locals.

MORNING Head down to the **wet market** before 7am as the locals descend to get their supplies for the day – this is an ideal place to sample some local dishes for breakfast too. While it is still early, take a walk through the **Old Quarter**, so you can appreciate the beautiful buildings and take photographs of the **Japanese Bridge** without interruption. As sites open, visit one of the preserved **old houses** or a **museum**. One special "tourist ticket" buys you entrance to five of the 18 historical sites on offer.

AFTERNOON Leave the mainland behind and head across **Cam Nam Bridge** to **Cam Nam Island** and walk the streets to see glimpses of local life. Then indulge in some thrilling shopping, from artisan goods (such as ceramics and paintings) to bespoke tailoring at a fraction of the normal cost.

EVENING If you're in the town during full moon, you'll be able to witness the monthly **lantern festival** in the Old Quarter: all street and house lights are turned off and the only light comes from glowing silk lanterns.

Essentials

GETTING THERE
Danang International Airport is around 35 km (22 miles) from Hoi An; there are **buses** and **taxis** to the town. All the sights in the town can be reached on foot.

WHERE TO STAY
Cua Dai (inexpensive) is a welcoming, pretty hotel with a large pool, 10 minutes' walk from town. www.cuadai-hotel.com
Long Life Riverside Hotel (moderate) is a modern boutique hotel on An Hoi Islet with views of the river and Old Quarter. www.longlifehotels.com
The Nam Hai (expensive) is located a short trip out of town and provides luxurious beachfront villas, some with their own pools. www.thenamhai.com

TOURIST INFORMATION
www.vietnamtourism.com

Left A blend of Japanese and Vietnamese food, *cao lau* is a pork noodle dish with greens and crispy fried pork skin

Above Impromptu seated "restaurants" spring up around the central market during trading hours

Below The Japanese Bridge, also known as the Pagoda Bridge, doubles as a temple with shrines to several deities

Right Balmain bugs on sale in Sydney Fish Market – the second-largest in the world after Japan's Tsukiji market in Tokyo (see p246)

Below Juicy Balmain bugs, simply and quickly pan-fried with saffron

A Day in Sydney

Sydney is dominated by its iconic harbour and the foreshore abounds with culture and commerce, from the cobbled lanes of the historic Rocks to the celebrated Opera House and the ferry hub of Circular Quay.

MORNING Walk around the forecourt of architect Joern Utzen's **Sydney Opera House** and gaze upon its concrete sails. Saunter around **Circular Quay** and take a guided tour, complete with hard hat and harness, up that other city icon, the **Harbour Bridge**.

AFTERNOON Follow the shoreline through the **Botanic Gardens** to **Mrs Macquarie's Chair** and survey the harbour, then on to the **Andrew (Boy) Charlton**, a glamorous public pool that begs a dip. Drop into the **NSW Art Gallery** and its 11,000 works.

EVENING Hop on a ferry to **Taronga Zoo**, **Balmain** or **Manly Beach**, just to ride it back again to see the sparkling city lights. Head up to **Australia Square** for a cocktail in the **Orbit Lounge Bar** on the 47th floor. It has 360-degree views and revolves – very slowly.

Essentials

GETTING THERE
Sydney Airport, 8 km (5 miles) from the city centre, is served by major international airlines. **Rail** and **bus** services link airport and city.

WHERE TO STAY
The Kirketon (moderate) is an oasis in the lively Darlinghurst area. *http://kirketon.com.au*
Ravesi's (moderate) has a relaxed Bondi beachside vibe with a shot of chic. *www.ravesis.com.au*
Establishment Hotel (expensive) is a sleek place to indulge your rock-star fantasies. *www.merivale.com/#/establishment/hotel*

TOURIST INFORMATION
City Host Kiosks are at the Town Hall, George Street and Circular Quay (corner of Pitt and Alfred Streets); *www.visitnsw.com*

SYDNEY AUSTRALIA

Catching Bugs in Harbour City

Sydney and seafood go together like surf and sand. Few cities do it quite so deliciously: light-as-air fish and chips, oysters with a squirt of lemon, butter-poached scallops and barbecued tiger prawns. This harbourfront city has a passion for all saltwater treasures, including the Balmain bug, a clawless crustacean with stacks of flavour, best eaten in a warm Sydney sea breeze.

Don't flinch when you see Balmain bug on the menu of one of Sydney's stylish seafood restaurants. This creature is in fact a type of lobster; its flat shell, five sets of legs and armour-like body have earned it the "bug" monicker. Shy, retiring types during the day – tending to bury themselves in mud or sand – Balmain bugs emerge only after dark to scoot about. Despite their name, they don't hang around the bay with the other arty residents of Sydney's upmarket suburb of Balmain, but are mostly caught swimming off the coast of New South Wales. This means they're supremely fresh off the boat when they hit the briny Sydney Fish Market. Steamed, poached, pan-fried or char-grilled, they're delicious drizzled with fennel vinaigrette, daubed with aïoli or pesto, or smeared in citrus butter.

If you've a yen to tour a lobster pen, set foot in a sashimi pavilion or scrutinize shellfish shuckers, book in for an early morning tour of the fish market (6:55am), or alternatively, soak up the atmosphere in the harbourside city. Explore the historic Rocks precinct, a cluster of sandstone alleys and courtyards dating back to convict times. It's an easy walk from here past the colonial architecture of Macquarie Street to Hyde Park Barracks, one of 11 Australian Convict Sites on UNESCO's World Heritage list.

Sydney is an outdoors city that begs to be explored on foot. Strike out along the cliffs from Bondi Beach via Tamarama (dubbed "Glamarama" for its fashionable vibe), Bronte and Clovelly to Coogee Beach – the sea views are glorious. Or make the trek from Taronga Zoo to Balmoral Beach, through bushland, past historic buildings, former military bases and spectacular harbour vistas. There's bags of open-air summer entertainment too: catch a movie under the stars, soothed by a sea breeze, at St George Open Air Cinema at Mrs Macquarie's Point, or take in a free concert by the Sydney Symphony at Parramatta Park or the Domain. This huge site on the edge of the city's business district is next door to Sydney's Royal Botanic Gardens – one of the world's best – which itself hosts theatrical and artistic events.

Cooking Classes

With so much local expertise in seafood, Sydney is the perfect place to hone your cooking skills and cook up a fishy feast. **Sydney Seafood School** (*www.sydneyfishmarket.com.au*) at the Sydney Fish Market can show you how best to prepare anything with fins, shells or tentacles. Its classes, which range from evening sessions to weekend workshops, are led by top chefs and take place in an auditorium featuring walls covered in Icelandic fish leather. Down-under food guru Simon Johnson's **Talk, Eat, Drink** classes (*www.simonjohnson.com*) in Alexandria's Providore's Market feature gifted chefs demonstrating their varied skills. You can sample the dishes, quiz the cooks and even take part in the cooking.

Left Downtown Sydney and waterfront with the Opera House

The Best Places to Eat Balmain Bugs

Flying Fish expensive

Peter Kuruvita is a pre-dawn regular at the Sydney Fish Market, and whenever he sees Balmain bugs he swoops on them. They immediately sell out in his slick restaurant, Flying Fish. Head chef and co-owner, Kuruvita grew up in a world permeated with fresh spices and flavours – he was born in Sri Lanka – and his menu perfectly reflects this. He serves the tender, sweet bug tail with a black pepper curry leaf sauce, a sauce of ginger, chilli and shallot, or simply with salt and pepper. Sometimes, too, he boils them up to make a deeply flavoursome bisque. Sri Lankan curries made with kingfish or butternut squash and shellfish from the restaurant's live tank are popular alternatives. Flying Fish, with its old working wharf-meets-designer loft style, might be hard to find but once settled in this harbourside gem, it's hard to drag yourself away.
Jones Bay Wharf, 19–21 Pirrama Road, Pyrmont, Sydney; open noon–2:30pm Tue–Fri, noon–3:30pm Sun, 6–10:30pm Mon–Sat; www.flyingfish.com.au

Also in Sydney

Diminutive and decidedly relaxed, **Fish Face** (*+61 2 9332 4803; moderate*) in Darlinghurst serves the best of Australian seafood, much flown in from around the country. Balmain bugs appear, sometimes in a salad with fennel and watercress, or whipped into a moreish mousse plumping out home-made ravioli in a bisque-like sauce made from the roasted shells, garnished with deep-fried prawns and leek.

Also in New South Wales

Elegant **Zest** (*www.zestrestaurant.net.au; expensive*) on NSW's North Coast is delicious proof that great food isn't restricted to the big cities. Glenn Thompson, head chef and owner, is a master of flavour combinations. His crisp-fried courgette flowers filled with Balmain bugs and sautéed bugs with goat's cheese gnocchi are both to die for.

Other Seafood in Sydney

Slurp Sydney rock oysters and dig into fresh snapper pie with views of the city's skyline at **The Boathouse** (*www.boathouse.net.au; expensive*) as rowers skim the waters of Blackwattle Bay and fishing boats bob in the near distance. Catch a ferry to Watson's Bay to reach **Doyle's on the Wharf** (*www.doyles.com.au; inexpensive*). This family-owned institution has been serving up seafood since 1885; try the takeaway beer-battered fish and chips and eat them on the beach or in the shady local park.

Three Days in Okinawa

Okinawa is made up of over 100 islands spread out over a considerable distance, so if you plan on seeing more than just the main island, you will need at least three or four days. However, many Japanese pop down to the main island simply for a long weekend by the beach.

DAY ONE Spend a day wandering the archipelago's capital, **Naha**. Go shopping (and eat) at the enormous **Makishi Market** and poke among the capital's shops for Ryukyuan lacquerware and glassware.

DAY TWO Head to the north of **Okinawa Honto** to enjoy the beaches or visit the **Ocean Expo Park**, which has a gigantic aquarium and is home to the **Native Okinawan Village**, featuring 20 houses from different eras. Then take a diving trip out to some of Japan's best **coral reefs**, or chill out at a beachside bar and try local delicacies like *goya chanpuru* and *umibudo* (caviar-like seaweed).

DAY THREE Take a short flight to the southernmost island of **Iriomote** and go hiking through the jungle in search of the super-rare Iriomote wild cat (fewer than 100 are thought to remain).

Essentials

GETTING THERE
There are regular flights from mainland Japan to Naha **airport,** which also receives some international flights. There are decent **ferry** and **air** networks between the islands.

WHERE TO STAY
APA Hotel Naha (inexpensive) is a large, business-oriented hotel with reasonable value rooms. *www.apahotel.com*
Okinawa Nahana Hotel (moderate) has large, modern rooms and a spa; it's also handily within walking distance of the market. *www.ishinhotels.com/okinawanahana/en*
Busena Terrace (expensive) is Okinawa's most lavish resort hotel, complete with underwater viewing tower. *www.terrace.co.jp*

TOURIST INFORMATION
www.pref.okinawa.jp/english/tourism

Right The vast Makishi Market in the centre of Naha sells all kinds of foods, including some unique to Okinawa

Below Many of Okinawa's beautiful beaches have coral reefs and are great places for snorkelling

Goya Chanpuru in Okinawa

Mention of the Okinawan archipelago brings a misty-eyed look to many Japanese. These are their holiday islands, more relaxed than the mainland and with their own distinctive culture. The most famous dish of their indigenous cuisine is the stir-fry *goya chanpuru*, one of the super-healthy dishes credited with helping the Okinawans become some of the longest-lived people in the world.

The Okinawan archipelago lies 700 km (435 miles) south of mainland Japan and is made up of over 100 islands. Until the early 17th century, Okinawa was entirely independent from Japan. A few architectural traces of the Ryukyu kingdom from this pre-feudal era still remain, such as Shuri Castle on the main island of Okinawa Honto, and there are glimpses of its culture on the outlying islands of Taketomi and Iriomote.

Until the 17th century, Okinawa's culture and cuisine were more influenced by China, with which it had traded for centuries. The Ryukyus were a famously peaceable people – legend has it that they solved differences with guitars rather than swords – which makes it bitterly ironic that these islands were the scene of some of the bloodiest battles of World War II.

War veterans still make pilgrimages to Okinawa's main battle sites, but far greater numbers come for the diving, watersports and wonderful beaches. Aside from its tourist industry, which is largely made up of Japanese along with Americans from the local US air base, Okinawa is a sleepy kind of place, particularly away from its capital, Naha. However, in recent years there has been a growing interest in the longevity of Okinawans born before 1939. The islands are said to have more centenarians per capita than any other part of the world and the average life span for women is 85 years; it's 78 for men. Gerontologists have ascribed this to a variety of factors, but one of the main ones is thought to be their diet.

Chanpuru is the Okinawan for "stir fry" (it literally means "something mixed" and is also used to refer to the islanders' openness to foreign ideas, as in "*chanpuru* culture"). The most famous kind is *goya chanpuru*, made with *goya*, an indigenous knobbly-looking cucumber that has been proven to reduce blood pressure and has even been used to treat AIDs. Though unbearably bitter when eaten raw, *goya* is transformed when stir-fried with pork, tofu, vegetables, soy sauce, eggs and sake. Word has caught on among the famously health-obsessed Japanese and *goya*'s fast-spreading popularity means *goya chanpuru* is well on the way to becoming a Japanese culinary staple.

The Best Places to Eat Goya Chanpuru

Emi no Mise (Emi's Place)
moderate

The village of Ogimi in northern Okinawa Honto is famous for its large number of elderly residents, including several centenarians, most of whom have become quite used to the attentions of interviewers from international TV channels. The only restaurant in this sleepy town is Emi's, the so-called "longevity restaurant", which is famous for its classic Okinawan cuisine. The eponymous Emi skilfully combines many of the ingredients that are thought to contribute to a long life: plenty of seafood, of course, including squid and octopus, plus lots of tofu – either plain and lightly poached, or the fiery red fermented type known as *tofuyo* (so assertively flavoured that you are supposed to nibble at it using a toothpick). These are accompanied by simply steamed rice, crunchy-tart pickles and, of course, plenty of locally grown fresh vegetables and fruits, including dragon-fruit ice cream made from the fruit that grows outside the restaurant's front door. Some form of *chanpuru* is invariably on the menu, usually with the tell-tale smiling green slices of *goya* cucumber in the mix. Be warned, though – this is no ordinary diet food. Emi's dishes taste terrific and are beautifully presented, but one of the main reasons behind Okinawan longevity is thought to be calorific restriction – in other words, not eating too much. Here, this is tricky indeed.

61 Aza-Oganeku, Ogimi Village; open 10am–4pm Wed–Mon; www.eminomise.com

Also in Okinawa

The largest collection of restaurants in Okinawa is found in its quiet, low-rise capital, Naha. Many serve *goya chanpuru* but by far the best places to eat in town – for atmosphere at least – are the ramshackle restaurants on the first floor of the **Makishi Market**. As well as various *chanpurus*, you can make the most of the astounding selection of tropical seafood on sale in the market downstairs: point at what you fancy, and the stallholders will send it upstairs to your restaurant to be cooked.

Also in Japan

Okinawan restaurants have begun to crop up in the larger cities of Japan. Tokyo has several, of which some are upmarket, but Okinawan food is somehow better eaten in the more rough-and-ready surroundings of an *izakaya*, or Japanese pub, such as **Okinawa** (*+81 3464 2576; moderate*) in the entertainment district of Shibuya. Be sure, too, to try the very special, potent Okinawan spirit *awamori*. It is distilled from rice and often sold with deadly (but dead) poisonous *habu* snakes coiled up in the bottle.

Longevity Food

Okinawa's typhoons make rice-growing tricky, but one crop that flourishes in this rain-washed, mineral-rich earth is the Okinawan purple sweet potato. These **beni imo**, as they are called, are high in flavonoids, which are antioxidant and act as hormone blockers, and they are also rich in carotenoids, vitamin E, fibre and lycopene, which has been shown to help prevent prostate cancer. One of these sweet potatoes contains four times the daily vitamin A and half the vitamin C requirements of an adult. Recent research has also indicated that *beni imo* also help stabilize blood sugar levels and lower insulin resistance. Okinawans eat them in tempura and add them to cakes, but best of all is Okinawan sweet potato ice cream. Of course, this probably undermines a good deal of the health benefits, but the taste is ample compensation.

Above *Goya chanpuru* is a crunchy stir-fry with apparently wondrous health benefits

Right A gateway through the walls of the Forbidden City frames the Hall of Supreme Harmony, the ceremonial centre of imperial power

Below Shredded meat from the roasted duck is wrapped in a wheat-flour pancake with spring onion and cucumber

A Day in Beijing

Beijing's recent modernization hasn't quite managed to obliterate over 700 years of history – and the famous Great Wall is just an hour or so from the centre of the city.

MORNING Organize an early minibus to the **Great Wall** at Mutianyu and spend a couple of hours walking between watchtowers along this incredible structure, then head back to Beijing for a late lunch. Alternatively, start the day at the **Forbidden City**, the mighty imperial palace complex from which generations of emperors ruled China.

AFTERNOON Walk off lunch at the **Temple of Heaven Park**, admiring the splendid exterior of the temple itself, before heading to the *hutongs* for a stroll through the streets of old Beijing.

EVENING Grab a snack at **Dong'anmen Night Market** – you might want to avoid the scorpion kebabs – then decide whether to rub elbows with locals at one of the **Sanlitun** district's many bars, or settle in for a striking, if incomprehensible, performance of **Peking Opera**.

Essentials

GETTING THERE
Beijing is connected to China and the rest of the world by **air** and **rail**. Use a combination of **metro train**, **bus** and **taxi** to negotiate the city's vast, grid-like street plan.

WHERE TO STAY
Beijing Downtown Backpackers (inexpensive) has clean, central rooms. *+86 10 8400 2429*
Bamboo Garden Hotel (moderate), down an old *hutong* alley, is full of character with a splendid landscaped garden. *www.bbgh.com.cn*
Haoyuan (moderate) is a traditionally furnished courtyard house. *www.haoyuanhotel.com*

FURTHER INFORMATION
Go to *www.cityweekend.com.cn/beijing* for English-language news and listings.

BEIJING CHINA

Peking Duck in Old Beijing

Beijing might be the capital of China, but it was founded by the Mongols under Kublai Khan. So it's hardly surprising that the city's signature dish is a marriage of foreign and native cuisine, in the same way that Beijing's palaces and maze of antique laneways reflect a Chinese refinement overlaying four centuries of alien rule, which ended with the last of the emperors in 1911.

On the surface, Beijing is a surprisingly modern metropolis, a somewhat soulless place in which individuals are dwarfed by a grid of enormously wide boulevards lined with glassy office blocks. But a far more traditional side lingers away from the main thoroughfares: the Forbidden City's mighty russet walls and endless puzzle of interlocking palaces, courtyards and gardens, where the imperial families once lived amongst eunuchs and intrigue; the former homes of Manchu princes and officials, hidden among the intricate web of neighbourhood alleys *(hutong)*; and the peerless symmetry of the Temple of Heaven's rotunda, where the emperors used to pray for good harvests. For their part, modern Beijingers are best observed still doing what they enjoy most, shopping in the stores or street markets and, especially, eating – in which case, you'll want to join them in sampling the one dish intimately linked to this city: Peking duck.

Preparation of this classic dish begins with the plucked, cleaned duck – a straw is inserted into the neck and the skin is gently blown away from the body. The ducks are then painted with malt extract and hung on a hook to wind-dry, then roasted in batches over a wood fire, the chefs shifting the birds constantly so that they colour and cook evenly.

Eating Peking duck is a similarly staged process: a three-course study in taste and texture. First comes the skin, roasted to a translucent toffee colour, crispy and succulent. The moist duck meat is then carved from the frame, to be seasoned with salty bean sauce and wrapped in elastic, paper-thin pancakes, with slivers of spring onion and cucumber to add bite. Finally, a palate-cleansing bowl of velvety duck soup arrives, signalling the end of the meal.

Peking duck's origins are obscure, but as roasting only crops up in Chinese cooking where there's been outside influence, it's possibly a distant echo of Mongolian barbecues, where guests would be invited to carve their own portions off whole roasted animals. Only the Chinese taste for refinement could take such a crude cooking method and from it create a work of art.

What Else to Eat

Another classic northern Chinese dish, now enjoyed country-wide, *jiaozi* are China's answer to ravioli. Nobody knows where they originated, but they've been around for a long time – a mummified bowlful was found at a Tang dynasty tomb on China's fabled Silk Road. Wheat dough wrappers stuffed with meat and cabbage and folded into a crescent shape, *jiaozi* are boiled, steamed or fried before being tumbled into a bowl and served with a dipping sauce of your choice – try a mix of soy sauce, black vinegar and crushed garlic. *Jiaozi* are not delicate: you order them by weight and northerners boast of how many they can put away at a single sitting. But as a hearty fuel, they are the ideal defence against Beijing's ferociously icy winters.

Left Studded with towers, the mighty Great Wall winds across China

The Best Places to Eat Peking Duck

Quanjude moderate

Quanjude has been serving up some of the tastiest roast duck in Beijing since first opening its doors during the 1860s. It was one of the capital's first big restaurants to get back on its feet after China's stagnation during the Cultural Revolution, and by the 1980s getting a table here was a mix of luck and hand-to-hand combat, with the restaurant bursting beyond capacity every night and diners being hauled out of their chairs by waiting customers the moment it looked as though they'd finished eating. Nowadays things are far more relaxed, but book in advance or get here early if you don't want a long stint in the lobby. The decor is restaurant red-and-gold, service is flawless and efficient, and the duck – skilfully carved for you at the table – is certainly worth waiting for. Duck is what everyone orders, but the rest of the menu of northern Chinese specialities is extensive, and visiting dignitaries and tour groups are served a multi-course banquet.

14 Qianmen Xi Lu, Beijing; open 10:30am–8pm daily; +86 10 6304 8987

Also in Beijing

Bianyifang *(+86 10 6711 6465; moderate)* can trace its history back to 1416, though the present business is contemporary with Quanjude. Unlike its rival, which cooks its birds over an open flame, Bianyifang slow-roasts its ducks in a closed oven which, according to partisans of this establishment, seals in a richer, juicier flavour. The restaurant lacks Quanjude's splendour, but it is comfortable enough.

Delivering a crisper, leaner duck than the average calorie-packed offering, **Da Dong** *(+86 10 8522 1234; expensive)* is emerging as one of Beijing's most talked-about contemporary restaurants. The menu is huge, the portions artistically small (except for the duck), and the cost somewhere inbetween.

Also in China

Hong Kong's **Dong Lai Shun** at the Royal Garden Hotel, Kowloon *(+852 2733 2020; expensive)* is the local representative of a famous Beijing restaurant chain specializing in Mongolian hotpot – a do-it-yourself meal featuring finely sliced raw lamb, a pot of boiling stock and a host of vegetables and dipping sauces. Their Peking duck is excellent too, cooked to crisp-skinned perfection and served as the traditional three-course meal.

Around the World

Outside China, you'll want to head to Australia's finest Chinese restaurant, the **Flower Drum** in Melbourne *(+61 3 9662 3655; expensive)*. This bills itself as a Cantonese (southern Chinese) institution, but you wouldn't know it from their immaculate Peking duck – though don't expect to be able to fill up on the rather dainty portions.

YOGYAKARTA INDONESIA

Rice and Spice in Java

If the island of Java has dominated modern Indonesian history, the city of Yogyakarta has, thanks to its former sultan, spent the last 50 years at the heart of Javanese culture. To round off a day spent exploring Yogyakarta's palace area and shopping for arts and crafts, head to the night markets to indulge in a simple dish that is equally vital to Indonesian life: fried rice.

In a country where most food is fried and everyone eats rice three times a day, it's perhaps inevitable that nasi goreng – the classic Indonesian snack literally meaning "fried rice" – puts them both together. Pre-boiled rice is stir-fried in smoking-hot oil with chillies, shallots, shredded chicken and dried prawns, and seasoned with *kecap manis* (sweet soy sauce). It's served in a neat dome on a plate, topped with strips of omelette or a fried egg, and garnished with slices of crisp cucumber and crunchy puffed prawn wafers. Add an eye-wateringly spicy blob of chilli *sambal* by way of relish, and you have a meal.

Nobody knows where nasi goreng originated but, while it probably wasn't in Yogyakarta (usually shortened to "Yogya"), few other places provide a more historic setting for such an intrinsically Indonesian dish. The city – centred around the walled Kraton, the sultan's palace area at the heart of the old city – was founded in the 1750s by a disgruntled prince from the declining Mataram empire. His new kingdom endured a stormy few decades of family intrigue and colonial warfare before being pummelled into submission by

the Dutch, and as Yogya's military power declined, the city became instead a cultural oasis, promoting the development of arts and crafts – especially batik work and the several forms of Javanese theatre.

The Kraton is a cultural masterpiece in itself, though – oddly, given Java's ostensibly Muslim beliefs – its design reflects the region's earlier Hindu culture. The interior palace retains the most grandeur, with beautifully proportioned courtyards, pavilions and main buildings still attended by traditionally dressed staff and sometimes hosting Javanese dance and *wayang kulit* shadow-puppet shows. The Taman Sari water palace nearby honours Loro Kidul, the seductive Goddess of the South Seas, with whom Yogya's sultans have always claimed a special relationship. For a return to earth, Jalan Malioboro – the street running north from the Kraton and originally intended as a triumphal route – now hosts Yogya's best-known tourist market, where you can buy endless quantities of local crafts. After dark, the businesses gradually shut up shop, to be replaced by food stalls selling light meals and snacks – and nasi goreng assumes its rightful place, at the heart of life in the old city.

Above Though largely Muslim, Java is an island of many faiths. The serene Borobudur Temple, not far from Yogyakarta, is a relic of an earlier Buddhist kingdom

---

Rice – a Global Staple

Rice is a grass, first cultivated in prehistoric times along China's Yangtze valley – the Chinese still greet each other by asking "have you eaten rice yet?". Today rice is an essential, three-times-a-day fuel for a fifth of the world's population and is a staple throughout Asia, where brilliant green paddy fields and mountainsides terraced for rice cultivation are part of the scenery from India to China, Japan and the Philippines, and south through Vietnam to Indonesia. Its uses are endless: after boiling, rice can be fried, roasted, stewed as a porridge, steamed inside lotus or bamboo-leaf packets, wrapped around seafood and rolled up in seaweed, fermented to produce wine or even puffed and served as breakfast cereal. Raw rice can also be pounded to flour and used for making noodles or cakes.

A Day in Yogyakarta

Yogya's Kraton and shopping alone can easily occupy a leisurely day, but you could alternatively set half the day aside for the 100-km (60-mile) round-trip to the incredible Buddhist complex at Borobodur, which predates the city by an entire millennium and was only fully restored during the 1980s.

MORNING Enter the **Kraton** area via the square where the sultan once settled public disputes and staged fights between buffaloes and tigers (the buffalo symbolized Java, while locals saw the tiger as representing the oppressive Dutch). Go on to browse artworks at the **Sono Budoyo Museum**, the **Taman Sari water palace** and the **Sultan's palace**, where Buddhist, Hindu and Muslim motifs on the Bagsal Kencono pavilion illustrate Indonesia's complex religious relationships.

AFTERNOON After lunch, shop for Yogya's batik, silver, leatherwork and crafts: **Jalan Malioboro** is the most obvious destination, but **Tirtodipuran Road** and **Beringharjo market** are less touristy – check quality and bargain hard.

EVENING Return to the **Kraton** for an evening stroll or take in a performance of Javanese puppetry, theatre or gamelan music.

Essentials

GETTING THERE
Yogya's **Adisucipto airport** has connections across Indonesia, plus Singapore and Malaysia. City transport includes **bus**, **taxi** and **becak** (trishaw).

WHERE TO STAY
Rumah Boedi Pavilion (moderate) is central (near the train station), modern and comfortable, with faux-ethnic chic furnishings. *www.rumahboedi-pavilionyogyakarta.com*
Dusun Jogja Village Inn (moderate) offers mid-range boutique comfort slightly further from the centre. *www.jvidusun.co.id*
The Phoenix (expensive) is a luxury modern revamp of a 1918 mansion. *www.mgallery.com*

FURTHER INFORMATION
Helpful information in English can be found at *www.yogyes.com*

The Best Places to Eat Nasi Goreng

Jalan Malioboro Night Market
inexpensive

The best nasi goreng in Yogya is found in this wonderfully atmospheric market, where small restaurant stalls give you the chance to try *lesehan* dining – sitting on bamboo mats at a low table, rubbing elbows with the locals while mouthwatering food is prepared in front of you. Aside from nasi goreng, try Yogya and Javanese specialities such as *nasi gudeg* (steamed rice with curry made from hefty, heavily scented jackfruit); tempeh (slightly sour, fermented soybean cake, usually sliced and fried); *nasi langgi* (steamed rice served on a banana leaf with a dozen spoonfuls of various curries and *sambals*); Kalasan chicken, stewed, fried and flavoured with copious garlic; and *bakpia pathok* (fried mung bean pastries, similar to Chinese mooncakes). For dessert, *cendol* is a drink of luridly coloured jelly noodles in iced, sweetened coconut milk that – despite being served throughout Southeast Asia – locals insist originated in Java. Otherwise, *wedang ronde*, glutinous rice balls served in ginger syrup, is definitely a Yogya dish.

Jalan Malioboro, Kraton, Yogyakarta; open from dusk daily

Also in Yogyakarta

Also in the Kraton, **Bale Raos** (*+62 274 415 550; moderate*) serves excellent nasi goreng, though it specializes in recipes from the Yogyakartan Sultanate, some of them attributed to former rulers themselves. *Urip urip gulung* is fried catfish stewed in coconut milk flavoured with ginger, *makrut* lime leaves and lemongrass; while *sanggar* is, conversely, previously stewed beef cubes grilled on bamboo sticks like a satay.

Also in Java

In Jakarta, Java's hot, sprawling, chaotic, unwieldy capital, **Seribu Rasa** (*www.seriburasa.com; moderate*) sets the standard for smart, mid-range restaurants dealing in regional Indonesian cooking, with stylish wooden decor. The menu includes several takes on nasi goreng: try *nasi sayur* (fried rice with vegetables) or fried-rice *sundah kelapa*, a seafood variation named after Jakarta's harbour area and fish market (where, incidentally, you can still see fleets of old-style wooden fishing boats pulled up at the wharf).

Around the World

BaliBali (*www.balibalirestaurant.com; moderate*) in London's West End is a relaxed, friendly place in which to try a host of Indonesian staples, including perfect nasi goreng, gado-gado (a salad with boiled eggs, tempeh, bean sprouts and mild peanut sauce), plain Indonesian fried chicken and spicy squid *sambal*.

Above Turning rice at the market: the soil in this region, enriched by volcanic ash, is said to produce wonderfully aromatic grains

Left Nasi goreng knows no social barriers: Indonesians relish their national dish at street stalls, in restaurants and even at banquets

Right Noise, colour and exotic smells characterize Phnom Penh's busy markets

Below Beautifully firm, translucent chunks of fish are suffused with subtle flavours in Cambodian *amok*

A Day in Phnom Penh

In addition to enjoying Khmer food, Phnom Penh is a great place to sample all things delicious and Gallic. Start the day with filtered coffee and fresh croissants or baguettes in one of the French-style eateries in and around Sisowath Quay on the Tonle Sap riverfront.

MORNING After breakfast, cross the road to the river bank and stroll down to the **Central Esplanade** in front of the glittering campus that is the **Royal Palace**. Then walk next door to the **National Museum**. This important storehouse holds artifacts and statuary from every region of Cambodia including much from the glorious era of Angkor.

AFTERNOON Take a cyclo (bicycle rickshaw) ride to **Psar Thmei** (Central Market) – a magnificent, French Art Deco behemoth built in 1937. Head back to the **Tonle Sap** and enjoy a gentle river cruise as the sun sets behind the ochre of the city buildings.

EVENING Finish the day with a display of classical Khmer Apsara dancing at the Bopha Penh Titanic Restaurant on **Sisowath Quay**.

Essentials

GETTING THERE
Phnom Penh International Airport is about half an hour from the centre of town by **taxi**. One can navigate the city by **motorcycle taxi** (risky but fast) or by three-wheeled **"tuk-tuk"**.

WHERE TO STAY
Goldiana (inexpensive) is a spotlessly clean and well-run Chinese hotel popular with visiting journalists and aid workers. *www.goldiana.com*
Villa Langka Hotel (moderate) is a stylish boutique hotel in a quiet and leafy setting. *www.villalangka.com*
Raffles Hotel Le Royal (expensive) is a glorious old French colonial hotel with real history and charm. *www.raffles.com*

TOURIST INFORMATION
www.tourismcambodia.com

PHNOM PENH
PENH

PHNOM PENH CAMBODIA

Running Amok in Phnom Penh

Cambodia was once home to one of the most magnificent civilizations ever seen – the Khmer empire of Angkor, its story one of glorious conquest and savage defeat. The Cambodian dish *amok*, a coconutty fish curry cooked in banana leaves, is a reflection of the myriad influences that have swept over this small but charismatic nation: an echo of the ebb and flow of empire.

Until war and tragedy, in the shape of Pol Pot's genocidal Khmer Rouge, overtook the small kingdom of Cambodia, its modern capital, Phnom Penh, was known as the "Pearl of Asia" and was acknowledged to be one of the most elegant of all the colonial French-built cities in Indochina. Then, it was often called "sleepy" – but no longer. Phnom Penh today is frenetic with bustle. But while the beautiful but decaying French colonial architecture may be battling now with 21st-century sprawl, at the heart of the modern urban jungle still remain magnificent ochre-walled villas and wide, tree-lined boulevards, around which delicate Khmer temple and palace buildings and colourful food markets can be found.

One of the greatest pleasures of being in Phnom Penh is spending time on the riverfront. Lining the river is a series of small cafés and restaurants housed in pretty French colonial buildings. It is a great place to relax and watch people promenade – "*da leng*" as they say in Khmer – and to sample the local fare.

Cambodian cuisine shares much with its neighbour Thailand, but it's less spicy and has its own aromatic and distinctly lemony character. It is defined by two factors – rice in abundance from the fertile plains of the Tonle Sap Basin, and fish from the teeming lakes and rivers that bisect Cambodia and are its lifeblood. *Amok* – a creamy fish curry served with fragrant rice – is close to being the Cambodian national dish. Its base is coconut milk, to which are added galangal, kaffir lime, lemongrass, shallots, garlic and chillies, with a touch of shrimp paste, palm sugar and fish sauce. Egg yolk is also added, to set the sauce during steaming, and then the firm, white fish itself.

The mixture is steamed in a banana leaf "bowl", then served with a touch more coconut cream poured over the top and garnished with shredded lime leaves and a little red chilli. The resulting dish is both rich and sweet while also being spicy, fragrant and salty. It is not only a distillation of the subtle flavours that define Khmer cuisine; it is also, with its bright reds and greens, something of a visual feast, perfectly in tune with the lovely buildings that still grace this busy city.

What Else to Eat

Bok l'hong is a green papaya salad made with string beans, roasted peanuts, cherry tomatoes, tiny, savoury crabs and smoked fish, pounded in a mortar and pestle and flavoured with chilli, lemon juice and Khmer fermented fish paste. **Kralan** is a cake made from steamed rice, beans or peas, grated coconut and coconut milk. **Loc lac** is a popular dish: cubed beef with red onions, served on a bed of salad with a dipping sauce of lemon juice and black pepper. **Pleah** is a grilled beef salad, flavoured with fermented fish paste and tossed with onions and fresh herbs. Khmer meals usually feature at least one soup: **samlor machu** is a sour soup with a tamarind base and includes chicken or fish, tomatoes, lotus roots, water greens and herbs.

The Best Places to Eat Amok

Frizz Restaurant moderate

This unpretentious and airy little restaurant is in the heart of the city's boutique shopping district and not far from the Royal Palace. Many claim it serves the finest *amok* in Phnom Penh, with real care taken over both preparation and presentation. The atmosphere is cool and breezy with plenty of white soft furnishings, ochre floor tiles and rattan furniture. In addition to *amok*, the Frizz offers a huge range of other Khmer dishes, including the hard-to-find *saik ko neung teuk kroch* – thinly sliced beef stir-fried with herbs and spices, served in an orange sauce on a bed of coleslaw. One can also order light Western food such as Mexican burritos, delicious baguette sandwiches and healthy breakfasts. The Frizz runs a small cooking school that inspires respect from chefs both Khmer and foreign. The one-day classes come at a very reasonable price, and are fast becoming a "must-do" for foodies intrigued by the tangy mysteries of Khmer cuisine.
No. 67 Street 240, Phnom Penh; open 10am–10pm daily; www.frizz-restaurant.com

Also in Phnom Penh

Khmer Kitchen (*+855 12 712 541; inexpensive*) is a traditional Cambodian restaurant offering indoor and outdoor seating beneath a grass-and-shingle roof in a wooden house set in leafy garden surrounds. If you prefer to be indoors you can take an upstairs table and dine in comfort while reclining on silk cushions. In addition to the magnificent *amok*, the Khmer Kitchen serves numerous sour soups, including a variety with water spinach and a pleasing balance of sour tamarind with a hint of *prahok* (fermented fish paste).

Also in Cambodia

Any visit to Cambodia usually includes a visit to the spectacular ruins of Angkor Wat. When staying in the nearby town of Siem Reap, **Viroth's Restaurant**, behind La Résidence Hotel on Wat Bo Street (*www.viroth-hotel.com/restaurant.php; moderate*), provides a perfect venue for sampling traditional Cambodian *amok* in a sleek boutique environment.

Around the World

Ties between Cambodia and France remain strong and there is a noticeable Khmer presence in Paris. **La Mousson** (*www.lamousson.fr; moderate*) on Ave Emile Zola, in the 15th arrondissement of the city, specializes in traditional Khmer dishes, with *amok* in its original form or with scallops rather than white fish.

Above The changing of the guard at Gyeongbokgung Palace – the royal Palace of Shining Happiness – in the north of Seoul

Above Night-time bustle in the Myeongdong shopping district

A Day in Seoul

Despite Seoul's size, the city's main sightseeing area is small enough to explore on foot. Here you'll find royal palaces, colossal markets, picturesque temples and countless restaurants, cafés and shops.

MORNING The majestic palace of **Gyeongbokgung** is at its best in the early morning, when its colourful wooden buildings slowly emerge from silhouette. The northern mountains provide the perfect backdrop, glowing pink and orange with the sun's first beams.

AFTERNOON Seoul is a shopper's dream. Hunt down calligraphic brushes, handmade paper and artsy trinkets in the traditional stores of **Insadonggil street**, or head just south to **Myeongdong** for more contemporary offerings. In between runs the gentle stream of Cheonggyecheon, whose quiet banks offer gentle strolls.

EVENING It would be a shame to visit Seoul without hitting **Dongdaemun market**, parts of which are open all night. If you've not booked a banquet, you'll be able to pick up rice wine and mung-bean pancakes at the particularly photogenic Gwangjang stall area.

Essentials

GETTING THERE
Flights arrive at **Incheon International Airport**, around an hour away from the city centre by **express bus**. Seoul has an extensive **subway** network, though taxis are remarkably cheap.

WHERE TO STAY
Doulos (inexpensive) has spick-and-span rooms and is ideally located in the middle of the sightseeing area. *www.douloshotel.com*
Rakkojae (moderate) is a throwback to Joseon times, its wooden buildings set around a beautiful courtyard. *www.rkj.co.kr*
Westin Chosun (expensive) was Korea's first hotel and retains a gentle elegance, though a stylish overhaul has brought its rooms up to date. *www.westinchosun.co.kr*

FURTHER INFORMATION
http://english.visitkorea.or.kr

SEOUL SOUTH KOREA

A Royal Banquet in Seoul

In the sparkling Korean capital of Seoul, it really is possible to eat like a king – the banquets served here replicate those held for the kings of the Joseon dynasty, who ruled from the 14th to the early 20th century. These royal banquets have tables groaning under innumerable exquisite dishes, whose myriad tastes and colours nonetheless blend into a gentle, oriental harmony.

Bustling with commerce, drenched with neon and pierced with innumerable skyscrapers, Seoul is one of the world's most absorbingly modern cities. However, it is also a place of substantial historical merit, having served as the seat of the Joseon dynasty from 1392 until its annexation by Japan in 1910. Joseon's first king, Taejo, was evidently hugely ambitious – the first few years of his rule saw the birth of two mighty palaces, a huge ancestral shrine and a city wall studded with gargantuan gates. Amazingly, despite the passing of half a millennium, the Japanese occupation and the devastating civil war of the 1950s, all of these sites remain, with superb restoration work bringing back their dynastic beauty.

Korea's wonderful cuisine has also emerged unscathed from troubled times, and the food of the Joseon royal court remains at the very top of the tree. Harmony is the key to these banquet-style feasts, with their near-perfect balance of colour, flavour, aromas, texture and shape. This is partly thanks to the Korean concept of *yeobaek*, which dictates that, for example,

fiery-red elements such as spicy *gimchi*, or *kimchee* (preserved vegetables) are counterbalanced by bland soups and delicately seasoned roots.

Traditionally, banquets are made up of 12 main dishes, augmented by smaller side dishes known as *banchan*. Ingredients are always the finest the season can offer, culled from both land and sea. The variety is quite incredible, with offerings as diverse as buckwheat noodles, pumpkin congee, mung-bean pancakes and pheasant-meat dumplings. Many of these dishes can be found in Korean home cooking, but two of the most visually arresting are unique to royal cuisine. The *sinsollo* is a bronze urn used at the table to make a richly aromatic meatball-and-vegetable stew, heated by charcoal embers. Most beautiful of all is the kaleidoscopically colourful *gujeolpan*, an octagonal tray of lacquered wood split into nine sections – the outer eight contain assorted roots, shoots and marinaded leaves, to be wrapped up in paper-thin pancakes stacked in the central ninth segment. The only down-side, it seems, to feasting on royal Korean cuisine is that one must destroy what is effectively a work of art.

What Else to Eat

Royal court food represents the refined epitome of Korean cuisine, but at the other end of the scale – and much-beloved of local students – are homely restaurants, usually decked out with oriental bric-a-brac, serving cheap but filling traditional dishes. Most popular are **jeon**, savoury pancakes made from corn, mung beans or even potato; the fillings are equally diverse, with sesame leaves and seafood being particularly common choices. One other item found on the menu at such places is **dubu-gimchi**, a delicious mix of hot *gimchi* and soft tofu. However, many are not here for the food, for these restaurants also serve milky rice wines known as **makkeolli** and **dongdongju**. Be warned – these taste deceptively weak and many a visitor has been known to "hit the wall" after a night on this uniquely Korean hooch.

Above The colourful *gujeolpan* often forms the centrepiece of a Korean royal banquet

The Best Places for Korean Royal Cuisine

Goongyeon expensive

This deceptively homely restaurant is Korea's only remaining link to the royal court cuisine of old. Its founder, Hwang Hye-seong, learned her trade from one of the last royal chefs of the Joseon dynasty, absorbing the ancient secrets over the course of several decades. These have now been passed on to her daughter Han Bong-nyeo; like her illustrious mother, Han has been designated an official national treasure. After taking your seat, you'll soon find the table blanketed with dishes, almost creaking under the weight of more than 30 individually prepared creations. You'll literally be eating like a king in almost every sense, since both the way in which the meal is laid out and the ingredients in the dishes are as close as possible to what Joseon royalty would have been presented with each evening. Celadon bowls, bronze chopsticks and lacquered wooden trays heighten the air of authenticity, while floor-to-ceiling windows offer views of the pine-studded garden outside.
170–3 Gaheodong, Seoul; open noon–3pm & 5:30–9pm; www.goongyeon.com

Also in Seoul

Set within a clutch of traditional wooden buildings on Pildong Iga, **Korea House** (*www.koreahouse.or.kr; expensive*) serves up mammoth royal banquets – not quite scaling the heights of the cuisine in Goongyeon, but first-time visitors will scarcely be able to tell the difference. For a small extra fee you'll be able to watch colourful performances of traditional folk songs and dancing, which take place after the meal in an on-site theatre. Attendants clad in silken *hanbok* – traditional Korean clothing – contribute further to the courtly air, while just north of the restaurant you'll find Namsangol, a small, re-created Joseon village.

Restaurants serving *yangbansik* – meals served to aristocrats during Joseon times – are cheaper and more numerous than those serving royal cuisine. One recommendation is **Doore** (*www.edoore.co.kr; moderate*), which serves what are essentially smaller versions of the royal feasts in a pleasantly rustic courtyard setting on Insadonggil, a street of teashops, galleries and craft workshops popular with visitors (*see* A Day in Seoul, *facing page*).

Yangbansik was essentially a derivation of royal court food, which was itself a take on Korea's traditional Buddhist temple food. Restaurants serving this meat-free cuisine can also be found around Seoul, the best being **Baru** (*www.baru.or.kr; expensive*), a pine-lined fifth-floor venue on Gyeonjidong in which to enjoy a delectable vegetable banquet overlooking Jogyesa, a major Buddhist temple.

KERALA INDIA

Keralan Coconut Fish Curry

Hugging the tropical Malabar Coast in the southwest of the Indian peninsula, Kerala has a growing reputation as a venue for holistic holidays that include meditation courses or Ayurvedic treatments. Everyone relaxes under the swaying coconut palms and the fruits of these ubiquitous trees deliver the creamy flesh and milk that plays an essential part in *meen moilee*, a delicious fish curry.

Kerala has always relied on fishing, agriculture and, above all, trade. There is evidence of the Sumerians and Phoenicians trading cotton, teak, sandalwood and spices from the Malabar Coast as far back as 3000 BC, when trade ships fuelled by the monsoon winds carried goods to Arabia, and overland caravans ferried those most highly prized westwards towards the Mediterranean and Europe. Merchants continued to ply their trade through the 1st century, when St Thomas arrived in Kerala and introduced Christianity to India, through centuries of Muslim and European domination, reaching new heights of freedom with Indian independence in 1947.

Trade has continued to flourish, but in Kerala it is now augmented by a booming tourist industry. The laid-back, ethnically Dravidian locals have a paradoxical reputation for maintaining a traditional lifestyle while espousing progressive political values – in 1957 they voted in the first democratically elected communist state government in the world. They prize education: this scenically alluring land of brilliant green rice paddies, shady palms, golden beaches, serene waterways and the fertile Western Ghat mountains is home to a population with the highest literacy rate and most equitable division of wealth in the subcontinent. And it runs across religious divides: the bare-chested Brahmin priest you see entering one of the majestic Hindu temples is likely to be a card-carrying member of the same leftist party as a local Muslim fisherman or Christian farmer.

However, it is tradition, not modernity, that holds sway in Kerala's cuisine, and with fishing communities running the entire length of the coast, fish and seafood naturally play a huge role in local recipes. Combine this with the preponderance of coconuts and spices, and it's not surprising that a creamy coconut fish curry, *meen moilee*, is one of the state's signature dishes.

Any number of fish that inhabit the warm waters of the Arabian Sea can be used as the base, though the most common are kingfish, pomfret and, best of all, full-flavoured sear fish. The fish is added along with the coconut milk to a mixture of fried onions, garlic, chillies, ginger, turmeric and cumin, then simmered until more coconut milk and chopped tomato is added, before a final garnish of tomato and fresh herbs. There is something quite wonderful about eating this exotic dish at a beachside restaurant looking out over the sea, where countless old wooden sailing ships once carried the spices you're tasting to other distant lands.

Three Days in Kerala

Even Kerala's state capital, Trivandrum, is laid-back by Indian standards but it is the beaches, backwaters, rural retreats and the colonial splendour of Kochi (Cochin) that have far more appeal to most visitors.

DAY ONE After a filling breakfast of *dosas* (crispy pancakes) or *idlis* (steamed rice cakes), leave **Trivandrum** on an early morning bus or train for **Varkala**, where you can relax down on the golden sands or at one of the beachside cafés and restaurants.

DAY TWO Travel to **Kollam** in time to take a day-long backwaters cruise, passing through peaceful lagoons where fishermen ply their trade. In the early evening you'll arrive in **Allapuzha**. You can alight en route at the fascinating ashram of the "living saint" **Mata Amritanandamayi**, or "Amma" ("Mother"), if you extend your tour by a day.

DAY THREE Take an early bus to **Ernakulam** and then a ferry across the harbour to atmospheric **Kochi**, where highlights include the much-photographed sail-like Chinese fishing nets, **Matancherry Palace** and the **Pardesi Synagogue**.

Essentials

GETTING THERE
Beenapalli (in Trivandrum) and Kochi **airports** are international. Both towns are also hubs for **rail** and **road** connections.

WHERE TO STAY
Johnson's The Nest (inexpensive) in Alleppey is very friendly. www.johnsonskerala.com
Walton's Homestay (moderate) in Fort Cochin is a beautifully renovated Dutch mansion with a lovely garden. www.waltonshomestay.com
Villa Jacaranda (expensive) in Varkala is a boutique guesthouse. www.villa-jacaranda.biz

TOURIST INFORMATION
www.keralatourism.org

Above Awaiting a water-taxi in the Kerala backwaters, a series of connected lakes, rivers and canals that runs half the length of the state

Left The graceful, counterweighted "Chinese" fishing nets of Kochi are raised and lowered into the water from the shore

Below Colourful *meen moilee* combines a taste of Kerala's renowned seafish with locally grown coconuts, tomatoes and spices

Right Hosier Lane is one of Melbourne's many "laneways"; it is well known for its street art

Below Simple Pan-Asian fusion: trout steamed in banana leaf and lemongrass with wild and sticky rice

A Day in Melbourne

The flavour of Melbourne is best experienced by sampling a mixture of the city and some of its inner-city suburban neighbourhoods: St Kilda for beaches and glamorized grit; Fitzroy for eclectic urban cool; and the CBD (Central Business District) for its chic dining and bar scene.

MORNING Start in **St Kilda** with breakfast on the deck of the **St Kilda Sea Baths**. Walk the historic **pier** or drop into **Luna Park** before taking in the buzz of the **Acland Street Precinct**, famous for its continental cake shops and vintage clothing stores.

AFTERNOON Take a tram to **Gertrude Street, Fitzroy**, to experience Melbourne's hipster scene. There's kitsch homeware, intelligent fashion, alluring wine bars and great contemporary art spaces.

EVENING Grab a tram or taxi back to the city bustle and **Federation Square** for a water-view apéritif at **Riverland Bar**. The rest of the night is for Pan-Asian drinks and nibbles: try hawker-style food at **Gingerboy** or a lychee martini at **Longrain**.

Essentials

GETTING THERE
Tullamarine Airport is 23 km (14 miles) from Melbourne's city centre, which can be reached by **shuttle bus** (SkyBus) or **taxi**.

WHERE TO STAY
Bishopsgate B&B (inexpensive) offers good beachside accommodation in quaint St Kilda. www.bishopsgate.com.au
Hotel Causeway (moderate) is a centrally located hotel in one of Melbourne's historic shopping arcades. www.hotelcauseway.com.au
The Olsen Hotel (expensive) is contemporary luxe with an artistic bent. It offers rooms, suites and "residential suites" with kitchenettes. www.artserieshotels.com.au/Olsen

TOURIST INFORMATION
www.melbourneaustralia.org

MELBOURNE AUSTRALIA

Pan-Asian Delights in Melbourne

The fashion pack struts graffiti-adorned "laneways" to enter chic, bolt-hole boutiques, while office workers clink glasses at riverside bars and sports fans cheer at Melbourne Cricket Ground. By nightfall this city of many incarnations is united by a universal passion for food – and a love of Pan-Asian cuisine that owes directly to Melbourne's embrace of its vibrant immigrant culture.

Founded on the Yarra river in 1835, Melbourne's early development was defined by the gold rush: discovery of the precious nugget brought limitless riches and unprecedented development to the city's bluestone-paved streets. Before long this resulted in an animated multicultural mix, as Chinese migrants joined wealth-seekers from as far away as Europe and North America, all packing their gastronomic heritage along with their dreams.

Today this legacy can be seen in vivid Pan-Asian cuisine, which blends Southeast Asian spice with modern cooking techniques to arrive at a culinary crossroads representative of the city itself. Part-artist, part-sports-fan, part-style-seeker, Melbourne is as layered as a Pan-Asian spice mix: the fire of chilli echoes in an electrifying night scene where unmarked doorways lead to dramatic rooftop cocktail bars; the piquancy of lemongrass bristles in the kitsch style of edgy Gertrude and Brunswick Streets; the sweet nuttiness of coconut hovers in the eclectic galleries.

But if the contemporary nerve centre of the city lies in the challenging architectural style of Federation Square, the birth of Pan-Asian cuisine can be found a few blocks over in the historic stretch of Little Bourke Street's Chinatown. The second-longest continuous Chinese settlement in the Western world, it is from here that those once-challenging flavours were disseminated, scattering into Melbourne's modern culinary lexicon. Finding inspiration in the steaming dumplings, spicy soups and textural curries of China and her Southeast Asian neighbours, today's chefs have respectfully turned tradition on its head to create a flavour canon as adventurous as those first émigrés. Within the industrial-chic space of South Melbourne's St Ali, slow-roasted pork belly pairs with sweet fish sauce, *pat chun*, star anise and jellyfish salad, while the glasshouse-style dining room of Verge serves barramundi with Chinese celery and smoked beetroot. But even among such bold, boundary-pushing flavours and the big-ticket cultural and sporting events, Melbourne and its exotic palate provide space for the subtleties – for laneways and lemongrass.

Food Shopping in Melbourne

The gastronomic tourist trail for gourmet junkies will lead you from one end of Melbourne to the other. **Victoria Street**, Richmond, is a short tram ride and a world away from the Central Business District (CBD). Home to an enormous array of Southeast Asian grocers and restaurants, it is a hub for exotic fruits, Peking duck and cheap-but-good Thai and Vietnamese food. The **Queen Victoria** and **South Melbourne Markets** are the city's top open-air food markets, the latter being home to the best steamed dim sum in Melbourne. Not to be missed, the **Abbotsford Convent's Slow Food Farmer's Market** brings together stunning fresh produce and artisanal food producers in the beautifully scenic grounds of a former Catholic convent.

Left The many restaurants and bars of Federation Square, on the banks of the Yarra river, have made it a favourite meeting place

The Best Places to Eat Pan-Asian Food

Ezard expensive

Housed in the chic basement of Melbourne's *über*-hip Adelphi Hotel, Ezard has been setting the pace with its fabulously unobtrusive approach to experimental, Asian-inspired fine dining for more than a decade. The highly successful and well-regarded chef behind the plates, Teage Ezard, calls it "Australian freestyle" dining, but others simply call it unforgettable. Exhilarating dishes will test a diner's limits and still leave them wanting more: from the old Ezard favourites of Japanese-inspired oyster shooters and masterly stock-fried pork hock to seasonal treats such as Chinese-style roast duck with *shaosang* wine dressing, shitake mushrooms and steamed rice noodle roll. Ezard's success lies in combining the finest produce with an inherent talent for knowing when to shout and when to whisper. Dishes will stomp across your palate one moment (think five-spiced Bangalow sweet pork belly with yellow bean and peanut dressing) and tiptoe the next (perhaps steamed crab wonton dumplings with young coconut, mango and crispy shallots). The bill may leave you gasping, but such sorcery will never come cheap.

187 Flinders Lane, Melbourne, Victoria; open noon–3pm Mon–Fri, 6–10:30pm Mon–Sat; www.ezard.com.au

Also in Melbourne

Experience Pan-Asian cuisine at its best with the winning trifecta of **Coda Bar and Restaurant** *(www.codarestaurant.com.au; moderate)*, the hawker-style cuisine of **Gingerboy** *(www.gingerboy.com.au; moderate)* and the upmarket cocktail atmosphere of **Longrain** *(www.longrain.com.au; expensive)*. Or try a more traditional (and cheaper) option at the **Supper Inn** *(+61 3 9663 4759; inexpensive)* on Chinatown's Little Bourke Street.

Also in Australia

In Sydney, internationally lauded chef Tetsuya Wakuda marries the Japanese philosophy of natural and seasonal flavours with French technique at his restaurant, **Tetsuya's** *(www.tetsuyas.com; expensive)*, to riotous acclaim. For a beachside view try **Bistro C** *(www.bistroc.com.au; moderate)* in the holiday town of Noosa, Queensland.

Around the World

San Francisco is home to an enormous Asian community and is renowned for its stellar Pan-Asian cuisine. Enjoy Asian fusion (and amazing mojitos made with rice liquor) at **Lüx** *(+1 415 567 2998; expensive)*, or – for a left-of-centre dining experience – try the Chinese-style savoury buns from the mobile **Chairman Bao Bun Truck** *(twitter: @chairmantruck; inexpensive)*.

Above A reclining Buddha in the eccentric Buddha Park, constructed entirely from concrete by a Laotian mystic in the 1950s

A Day in Vientiane

One of the wonderful things about Vientiane is that the sights can be covered in one day: a pleasure best punctuated along the way with stops for a cup of fresh filtered Lao coffee or a glass of Lao beer.

MORNING Start with the **Ho Phra Kaew Art Museum**, a temple originally built to house the celebrated Emerald Buddha, later appropriated by Siam in 1779. Today it is a museum containing religious art. Then take in **Wat Phra That Luang**: this giant, golden Buddhist stupa is a defining symbol of Vientiane.

AFTERNOON The **National Museum**, in a rambling old colonial structure, is a fascinating collection of artifacts from various eras of Lao history. Then take a taxi 24 km (15 miles) along the river to the **Buddha Park**, a fanciful sculpture garden full of Hindu and Buddhist statuary.

EVENING Sunset over the Mekong is a show in itself. Back in town, if you're not heading for Nang Khambang for dinner, there are many traditional restaurants lining the river to the west of the main **riverfront promenade**. One of the best is Sala Khoun Ta.

Essentials

GETTING THERE
Wattay International Airport is a short **taxi** ride from the centre of town. Alternatively, one can cross the **Mekong** from Thailand. Visa on arrival is available whichever route you choose.

WHERE TO STAY
Mali Namphu Guest House (inexpensive) is an atmospheric ochre-walled building constructed around a shaded courtyard. *www.malinamphu.com*
Hotel Khamvongsa (moderate) is brand-new and is situated in a converted French villa near the river. *www.hotelkhamvongsa.com*
Settha Palace Hotel (expensive) is a renovated French colonial masterpiece with great charm and excellent dining. *www.setthapalace.com*

TOURIST INFORMATION
www.tourismlaos.org

Above Dozens of small, unpretentious restaurants and food stalls hung with lanterns line the banks of the Mekong at night

VIENTIANE LAOS

Laap in Leisurely Laos

Often dubbed the most laid-back nation in Asia, Laos is a country where people live by a very natural rhythm. Vientiane may be its capital city, but it remains as much a series of villages as a true metropolis. Lao cuisine shares much with that of Isan across the Mekong in northeastern Thailand, with a sharp and tangy palette of flavours typified by the dish known as *laap*.

While other Southeast Asian capitals have surged into the 21st century with swift economic development, mushrooming skyscrapers, jammed traffic, cluttered highways and ever-spreading urban sprawl, Vientiane has set itself on a far more sedate path. Its leisurely spread along the northern shores of the Mekong river is still one mostly characterized by sparsely trafficked boulevards and quiet alleys.

The real name for the city is Wieng Chan – "City of Sandalwood". It has endured a torrid history over the last two centuries, being overrun by both Burmese and Chinese marauders. In 1828 it was comprehensively sacked by the Thais, leaving temples smashed and broken, the streets empty and Lao nationhood in tatters. The country rose again as a French protectorate towards the end of the 19th century, and it is their colonial-style buildings, together with magnificent Buddhist stupas and pagodas, that give the city its character, along with the slumberous movement of the mighty Mekong river that runs through it. The streets in the Chanthabuli district in the centre of the city stretch back from the Mekong, intersected by the main boulevards of Samsenthai Road and Setthathirat Road. This is the heart of the city and the place to wander, linger and eat.

Lao cuisine, like that of neighbouring Isan in Thailand – whose inhabitants are ethnically the same people – is defined by fragrant fresh herbs, citrus and pungent fish sauce, and *laap*, the flagship Laotian salad, has them all in spades. It is most often made using beef, chicken, pork or sometimes fish, thinly sliced, chopped or minced, with flavourings that vary from region to region and, indeed, chef to chef.

Typically, the meat or fish is stir-fried quickly over a high heat with chillies, lemongrass and garlic, then mint, lime juice, lime rind, chilli sauce, peanuts, onion and coriander are stirred in. The whole mixture is then spooned on to lettuce leaves. Roughly ground, toasted rice *(khao khua)*, vital to the essential character of the dish, is added as a topping, garnished with mint leaves or heady Thai basil. Even when served with the meat still warm, and with the ubiquitous basket of sticky Lao rice on the side, the result is so delightfully refreshing that you'll soon be ready to stroll the streets once more.

What Else to Eat

Lao cuisine is derived using ingredients mainly from the wild or from the rice field. **Kop yat sai**, or stuffed frog, is something of a delicacy. **Naem khao** (rice-and-sausage ball) is a salad made with deep-fried rice balls, grated coconut, chopped peanuts, Lao fermented pork sausage, sliced shallots, mint, coriander, lemon juice and fish sauce. **Foe** (rice noodle soup) is very similar to Vietnamese *pho (see pp238–9)*, and is the ubiquitous breakfast dish in Laos. **Tam mak hoong** (green papaya salad), literally meaning "pounded papaya", is a sharp and spicy salad made from unripened papaya. Barbecued chicken, or **ping kai**, is a favourite in every street market in Laos. It is marinated in a delicious mixture of fish sauce, garlic, turmeric, coriander and white pepper, then slowly grilled over a low heat on a charcoal burner.

Above *Laap* combines all the sharp and tangy tastes so characteristic of the region

The Best Places to Eat Laap

Nang Khambang inexpensive

For a no-nonsense taste of *laap* at its finest in genuinely authentic, everyday Lao surroundings, Nang Khambang is the place. The name means "Mrs Khambang", and it's a family-run eatery that has been in the same location for three generations. Everything here is of the highest quality, and the *laap* is no exception. The restaurant offers air-conditioned and non-air-conditioned seating and, in a country where service can be slow, the staff are very attentive and efficient. In addition to the *laap*, Nang Khambang offers excellent *paa neua on*, a kind of lightly grilled and seasoned freshwater fish. Also on the menu are Mekong river fish and a sour fish soup, not unlike Thai *tom yam*, called *kaeng som paa*. Their *tam mak hoong* (green papaya salad) is also excellent; here it comes with tiny freshwater shrimps and baby tomatoes. Although Nang Khambang is now well publicized among travellers and tourists, it is still also heavily patronized by a Lao clientele – always a sure sign of quality. Nor have the prices been raised beyond the means of local people.
Khum Bulom, Vientiane; open noon–9pm daily; +856 21 217 198

Also in Vientiane

Amphone *(+856 21 212 489; expensive)* is a gourmet affair where Lao cuisine is given an international "makeover". It is set in beautiful surroundings and the ambience is one defined by chic furnishings, subdued jazz and a fine wine list. The *laap* here is one of many excellent renditions of Lao culinary standards, as is the steamed fish citronella in banana leaves.

Also in Laos

Luang Prabang is the ancient capital of Laos and is an exquisite little town in the mountains now protected as a UNESCO World Heritage site. In addition to the plethora of ancient temples and the beauty of the French-era colonnaded streets, it is home to some very fine restaurants. **Tamnak Lao** *(www.tamnaklao.net; expensive)*, housed in an old French colonial villa, offers an extensive menu of artfully prepared Lao dishes including *laap* with pork, chicken or fish.

Around the World

Given the colonial history of Laos, it is no surprise that the best purely Lao restaurants outside the country itself are found in Paris (although Isan Thai restaurants are found all over the globe and the food is hugely similar). **Lao Lane Xang** *(+66 1 45 85 19 23; moderate)* is to be found in Paris's bustling Chinatown district. It is hugely popular for both lunch and dinner thanks to its low prices, excellent service and the authenticity of the Lao fare served. It is a good idea to book to ensure a table.

A Day in Hanoi

You need to be up early to catch some of the best sights, but no day in Hanoi is complete without a breakfast of *pho*, so buy some on the run.

MORNING Take an early morning trip to **Hoan Kiem Lake** ("Lake of the Returned Sword"), in the heart of the **Old Quarter**, to admire the lake and watch locals exercising before work. Then take a taxi to **Ho Chi Minh's Mausoleum**, which is only open until 11am. The marble building is a place of pilgrimage for many Vietnamese and its grounds contain the **Presidential Palace** and Ho Chi Minh Museum.

AFTERNOON Hop on a local bus (an experience in itself) or take a taxi to the **Vietnam Museum of Ethnology**. Vietnam is home to countless hill tribe minorities and this modern museum gives a fascinating insight into their history and way of life.

EVENING After a day of culture, some relaxation is overdue, so return to the **Old Quarter** and make your way to **Bia Hoi Corner** (Luong Ngoc Quyen/Ta Hien). Sink into one of the tiny plastic chairs on the pavement and drink the cheapest draft beer in town.

Essentials

GETTING THERE
Hanoi's **Noi An International Airport** lies 45 km (28 miles) outside the city. There are **taxis**, **minibuses** and **public buses** to the city centre.

WHERE TO STAY
Make sure you have the address of your hotel, as unscrupulous operators can give their hotels the same names as successful ones.
The Hanoi Fortune Hotel (inexpensive) is close to Hoan Kiem Lake. *www.hanoifortunehotel.com*
Hotel Elegance Ruby (moderate) is a cool, classy retreat from the busy Old Quarter outside. *www.hanoielegancehotel.com*
The Sofitel Metropole (expensive) has long been the choice of diplomats and celebrities. *www.sofitel.com*

TOURIST INFORMATION
www.vietnamtourism.com

Right The many tastes and textures of *pho* come from its great mix of long-braised, freshly steamed and raw ingredients

Below The busy district of Dong Xuan Market at the western end of the Old Quarter

The Best Places to Eat Pho

Pho Gia Truyen inexpensive

Nestled in Hanoi's Old Quarter, a short walk from Hoan Kiem Lake, Pho Gia Truyen (also known as "Pho 49 Bat Dan") is a *pho* restaurant of days gone by. You won't find fancy decor or attentive service, but you will find a version of *pho* that has few rivals. This is one for *pho bac* purists; there is nothing but beef available, although you can choose between *tai* (raw), *chin* (cooked) or *nam* (fatty brisket) by looking at the different cuts that sit tantalizingly behind glass at the service counter. Place your order and then enjoy watching the chef briefly cook the noodles and deftly slice your choice of beef from the display, filling the bowls with a fragrant, cloudy stock. It is then up to you to find a seat among the locals and drink in both the atmosphere and your very fine *pho*.

49 Bat Dan Street, Old Quarter, Hanoi; open 7am–11pm

Also in Hanoi

Northern *pho* doesn't only come with beef: for a fine example of chicken *pho* (*pho ga*) head to **Pho Ga Mai Anh** (*+84 4 3943 8492; inexpensive*). Like all the best *pho* restaurants this is a simple open-fronted affair and its location on Le Van Huu, a short walk from beautiful Hoan Kiem Lake, is perfect for the Old Quarter-based tourist.

Also in Vietnam

In Ho Chi Minh City, **Pho Hua** (*+84 8 3829 7943; inexpensive*) is on Pasteur Street, just a short taxi ride from the main tourist area. It's been in business for over 40 years and caters to both locals and tourists. Spread over two floors, it's one of the best places for *pho* in the city.

Pho has not escaped the restaurant chain industry and **Pho 24** (*www.pho24.com; moderate*) has many franchises that churn out dependable southern-style renditions of the dish and are popular with the younger Vietnamese. Their air-conditioned outlets are all over Vietnam and offer many different varieties of *pho* along with other dishes such as *com tam* (broken rice with pork) and spring rolls.

Around the World

After the fall of the south in the Vietnam War, many Vietnamese settled outside the country and a large community formed in London. Among the host of Vietnamese restaurants on Kingsland Road in the arty Hoxton district, **Song Que** (*+44 20 7613 3222; moderate*) easily stands out. It has the widest selection of *pho* in the city, with beef, beef offal, chicken, seafood and vegetarian options, all bathed in a rich broth.

HANOI VIETNAM

Steaming Hot Pho in Hanoi

Nestled in Vietnam's north, Hanoi harks back to a time before Southeast Asia's recent rapid growth. Its Old Quarter is a labyrinth of ancient, narrow streets, alive with people and a myriad motorcycles, their horns blaring. In the morning, everyone heads for a *pho* stall or restaurant for a bowl of this fresh noodle soup, brimming with crunchy vegetables and tender meat.

Over the centuries Hanoi has been the capital and political centre of Vietnam for many different administrations, from conquering 11th-century Chinese dynasties and French colonialists to those of its own republic under Ho Chi Minh. In 2010 it celebrated its 1,000th anniversary and a long history that has included royalty and revolution along with Taoism, Confucianism, communism and capitalism. Somehow it has managed to both preserve and integrate the past and present in its customs, architecture and food, and visitors can enjoy the pace of modern Vietnam mingled with colonial Indochina.

The colonial period left its mark on the city and beautiful examples of the architecture remain today, such as the stunning Grand Opera House and the many tree-lined boulevards. It is also responsible for the origins of the national dish – *pho* – which is said to have taken its name from the French *pot au feu*, a dish built upon the long, slow simmering of bones and aromatics. *Pho* uses the same initial process, but gains from the addition of noodles, spices and herbs.

Breakfast is the ideal time to experience *pho*, giving you a glimpse into Hanoi life and setting you up for the day's exploring. Choose your restaurant then stand elbow-to-elbow with locals, fighting to place your order at the busy counter. Vats of stock simmer away and the air is fragrant with cinnamon, ginger and star anise. Rice noodles and raw beef are given a quick hot bath before being placed in a bowl, then the diners follow their own routine, carefully squeezing lime juice and a squirt of chilli sauce. A spoonful of sliced chilli makes the finished article unique. There is no talking, but this is a noisy affair, the clash of spoon with bowl and the slurping of noodles adding to the cacophony of service.

The bustle of the *pho* restaurant is a warm-up for the day ahead. Hanoi's Old Quarter is humid and busy and you take your life in your hands each time you dare to cross the road. But walking is still the best way to see this part of the city, as each corner brings a surprise, whether it's a street full of ironmongers or a hawker setting up stall for the day. Where exotic old Vietnam meets the new one head-on, Hanoi is the Asia of your dreams – you're bound to leave wanting more.

North and South

In the middle of the 20th century, during Hanoi's turn to communism, refugees fled from the north taking their recipes with them and *pho* appeared in the south. The dish is many-layered in both flavour and texture: the bite of rice noodles is a base for tender meat and the crunch of bean sprouts. But it is in the broth that the complexity of the dish really shows through. Formed from the slow simmering of beef bones, which gives the stock depth, it gains subtle nuances from charred onion, ginger and the spices of the region – star anise, cinnamon and cloves. No two recipes are the same. The *pho* of the north, *pho bac*, is a simple affair of rice, meat and thinner noodles. In the south, *pho nam* is a more elaborate affair that might be filled with beef, chicken, offal or seafood, and served with a plate of herbs and bean sprouts to add as you like.

Above Fresh *pho* is on sale at most of the roadside cafés in Hanoi

SOUTH ISLAND NEW ZEALAND

Bluff Oysters on South Island

New Zealand's South Island is wild and stunningly beautiful, with coves, fiords and cliffs framing the cool, pristine waters of the Tasman Sea and Foveaux Strait. The cool-climate conditions at the island's southernmost point have produced some fascinating wildlife and delicious foodstuffs, and it's the world-renowned Bluff oysters that attract visitors from around the world.

The town of Bluff runs along the edge of New Zealand's most southerly peninsula, sheltered by the high range of hills that reach a peak in the old volcanic cone of "Old Man Bluff", or Bluff Hill. The South Island's State Highway No. 1 ends just outside town, where the waters of the Foveaux Strait lap around the Bluff Scenic Reserve – or Motupōhue – and its Glory Walking Track. From the summit of Bluff Hill there are panoramic views across the strait to Stewart Island, which offer a rare chance of glimpsing one of the rarest whales in the world, the southern right whale *(tohorā)*, or the charming little blue penguin *(titi)*.

For most of the year Bluff is a sleepy addendum to the livelier nearby city of Invercargill, and it's inhabited by hardy folk who celebrate living at the extremity of a country. But from May to August each year this laid-back town becomes the focus for the world's oyster lovers. *Tiostrea chilensis* oysters have been harvested commercially in New Zealand's deep south since the 1860s, originally off Stewart Island, but closer to Bluff from the 1880s, giving the oysters their name. Today, up to 10 million of the succulent bivalves are gathered annually, and they are considered to be

the finest oysters in the world. The first catches of the year take place in early March, and the boats' return is eagerly awaited. In the restaurants of Auckland, a dozen of these delicious oysters costs upwards of NZ$50, but in Invercargill and Bluff, seafood suppliers sell the same number for less than half the price.

Tourists lucky enough to visit the area in May can attend the annual Bluff Oyster & Food Festival, which is proudly promoted with the line: "Unsophisticated and proud of it!". The day's oyster-opening and -eating competitions are appetizers to heaped plates of local crayfish, *paua* (abalone), scallops and blue cod, and of course more Bluff oysters. Around 20,000 are eaten at the festival, all washed down with the fine wines of the Central Otago vineyards or local beers such as the Pitch Black stout of the Invercargill Brewing Company.

Bluff's easy-going Southern ambience infuses travel throughout the surrounding region. To the west lies the dreamlike scenery of the Fiordland National Park. In a country of astounding landscapes, Fiordland trumps everywhere else, with its jagged mountain peaks, fiords, lakes, vast alpine river valleys and beautiful walking tracks. To the east the isolated coves and clifftop lookouts of the Catlins coast provide the perfect places for impromptu seafood picnics.

Three Days on the Southern Scenic Route

This is a region of astonishing natural beauty – allow plenty of time to be captivated by the views and charmed by some of the southern hemisphere's most engaging wildlife.

DAY ONE From **Dunedin** head south along the rugged **Catlins** coastline. At **Roaring Bay**, *hoiho* (yellow-eyed penguins) waddle from the ocean at dusk. At **Papatowai**, visit Blair Sommerville's quirky **Lost Gypsy** gallery. Detour to the spectacular **Cathedral Caves**, then look for dolphins in the surf along the graceful sweep of **Porpoise Bay**.

DAY TWO Explore **Invercargill**. The **Southland Museum** has a great display of *tuatara*, New Zealand's reptiles, which haven't changed in 220 million years. Catch the ferry from nearby **Bluff** to **Stewart Island** for an opportunity to see kiwis in the wild.

DAY THREE Continue west to the **Fiordland National Park**. Head for **Doubtful Sound** if you fancy kayaking in a beautifully isolated spot – just getting there takes a languid combination of two boats and a bus. Or visit **Milford Sound**, punctuated by the iconic profile of **Mitre Peak**, the spectacular end point for the Milford Track.

Essentials

GETTING THERE
Dunedin has regular **flights** from Auckland, New Zealand's main international airport. The airport has a **bus** shuttle and **car** hire.

WHERE TO STAY
Living Space (inexpensive) has sleek rooms in a restored 1907 warehouse. *www.livingspace.net*
Nugget Lodge (moderate) has two beachfront cabins in the Catlins. *www.nuggetlodge.co.nz*
Te Anau Lodge (expensive) is a luxurious and stately B&B that was originally built as a convent in the 1930s. *www.teanaulodge.com*

TOURIST INFORMATION
www.southernscenicroute.co.nz

Above Freshly shucked oysters are everyone's favourite in Bluff, eaten raw with just a squeeze of lemon

Left The 53-km (40-mile) Milford Track takes walkers past Mitre Peak, in the breathtaking wilderness of Milford Sound

Below The shy kiwi bird is indigenous to New Zealand and is found nowhere else in the world – it is the country's national symbol

Oysters Around the World

Although most food now seems to be available virtually anywhere at any time of year, the only way to sample the finest oysters is to eat them close to their native waters. The exceptional oyster restaurants tend to be close to the best oyster beds.

NEW ZEALAND

Niagara Falls Café moderate

256 Niagara-Waikawa Rd, South Catlins; www.niagarafallscafe.co.nz

Part roadside restaurant and part funky art gallery, the Niagara Falls Café partners Bluff oysters with flinty Central Otago Riesling or zingy Marlborough Sauvignon Blanc. Seafood aficionados should definitely follow up with the blue cod in a herb and Chardonnay sauce.

Redcliff Restaurant & Bar
expensive

12 Mokonui St, Te Anau; +64 3 249 7431

A dozen Bluff oysters or house-smoked salmon at Te Anau's Redcliff Restaurant & Bar is the perfect celebration after completing Fiordland's iconic Milford Track. Redcliff's cosy bar is also the place to catch live music on summer weekends.

On The Menu

Oysters Bienville These are grilled oysters with béchamel sauce and garlic, shrimp, mushrooms, white wine and Tabasco sauce. A New Orleans classic.

Oysters Kilpatrick An Australian and New Zealand dish that combines grilled oysters with Worcestershire sauce, diced bacon and chopped parsley.

Oyster po' boy A traditional Louisiana "poor-boy" sandwich: a baguette filled with breaded, deep-fried oysters.

Oysters Rockefeller Created in 1899, and named after oil magnate John D Rockefeller, these oysters are grilled with finely diced herbs, spinach and butter.

Oyster shooter Fresh oyster served in a shot glass, often in a Bloody Mary cocktail.

TASMANIA, AUSTRALIA

Seafood from Australia's verdant island extension is venerated by mainland chefs in Sydney and Melbourne, especially oysters from Tasmania's pristine, cooler waters. Eating a freshly shucked half-dozen at the source is an essential Down Under experience.

Get Shucked inexpensive

1650 Bruny Island Main Rd, Bruny Island; www.getshucked.com.au

Keep it simple with a splash of Tabasco and a squeeze of lemon at Get Shucked's roadside caravan on rugged and robust Bruny Island. An essential complement is a zingy chilli (non-alcoholic) brew from the Tasmanian Chilli Beer Company.

Freycinet Marine Farm moderate

1784 Coles Bay Rd, Coles Bay; www.freycinetmarinefarm.com

Simple wooden tables belie a sophisticated combo of oysters fresh from nearby Great Oyster Bay and the best of Tasmanian beer and wine. Improbably plump mussels and rock lobsters – from December to May only – are other tasty diversions.

Marque IV expensive

Elizabeth St Pier, Hobart; www.marqueiv.com.au

Hobart's brilliant southern light shimmers on rows of fishing boats as Marque IV's elegant harbourside dining room showcases the best Tasmanian produce. For oyster fans, the most delicious and innovative enhancements include limoncello and chilli or cucumber sorbet and Avruga roe.

SYDNEY, AUSTRALIA

One of the world's great harbour cities is also a brilliant destination for fresh seafood. The oyster experience here stretches from humble market stalls to stylish waterfront bars. Fine Australian wine is usually close at hand.

Sydney Fish Market inexpensive

Bank St, Prymont; www.sydneyfishmarket.com.au

After the fish bazaars of Japan, Sydney Fish Market offers the world's widest variety of seafood. Curious foodie travellers can seek out and sample at least ten different types of oyster, together with only-in-Australia seafood such as leather jackets, yabbies and Moreton Bay bugs.

Left (top to bottom) Pacific oysters on sale in the Sydney Fish Market, Australia; fishing boats and Mures Seafood Restaurant, reflected in Victoria Dock, Hobart, Tasmania; eating fresh oysters at the Swan Oyster Depot, San Francisco **Below (top to bottom)** Preparing oysters at the Galway Oyster Festival, Ireland; oysters on sale in Cancale, France

Doyles on the Beach moderate
11 Marine Parade, Watson's Bay; www.doyles.com.au
With harbour views to downtown Sydney and a beachfront location, Doyles at Watson's Bay is one of Australia's iconic dining experiences. Highlights include creamy oysters mornay and oysters Kilpatrick.

Sydney Cove Oyster Bar expensive
1 East Circular Quay; www.sydneycoveoysterbar.com
With unbeatable views of the cosmopolitan waterborne buzz of Circular Quay, this quintessential Sydney restaurant specializes in seafood – especially oysters – caught off New South Wales.

NEW ORLEANS, USA
From oysters Bienville and Rockefeller to po' boys, New Orleans has inspired more iconic oyster recipes than any other city.

Felix's Restaurant & Oyster Bar moderate
739 Iberville St, French Quarter; www.felixs.com
Felix's stays true to its 100-plus years of French Quarter history, and remains a favourite for New Orleans natives. After a night out in Bourbon St, freshly shucked oysters and a Cajun-style Bloody Mary cocktail make for a reviving brunch.

Drago's Seafood Restaurant expensive
3232 North Arnoult Road, Metairie; www.dragosrestaurant.com

Grilled oysters dot the menus of many New Orleans restaurants, but reputedly Drago's served them first in 1993. Try the locally grown Louisiana bivalves with peanuts and red pepper aïoli, or with sun-dried tomatoes and pine nuts for a Mediterranean spin.

SAN FRANCISCO, USA
The oldest of this city's oyster bars opened in 1912, and San Francisco's love affair with briny bivalves shows no sign of slowing down. North America's best farmers' markets are here too, and keep the local culinary scene buzzing.

Swan Oyster Depot moderate
1517 Polk St (between California St & Sacramento St); +1 415 673 1101
Behind a century-old marble counter in this impossibly narrow restaurant, the wisecracking Sancimino brothers serve up oysters from around North America and the Pacific. Customers usually have to queue, but both the jokes and the oysters are worth waiting for.

Hog Island moderate
Ferry Building Marketplace, One Ferry Building #11; www.hogislandoysters.com

Pacific? Atlantic? West Coast? East Coast? There's a different selection of American oysters every day at this sleek, modern oyster bar in San Francisco's iconic Ferry Building. On Saturday mornings the action flows outside to the weekly farmers' market.

GALWAY, IRELAND
Caressed by brisk Atlantic gusts on Ireland's west coast, Galway's combination of salt water and fresh water produces exceptional oysters. This slice of natural good fortune is celebrated each September at the Galway International Oyster Festival (www.galwayoysterfest.com).

Conlon & Sons moderate
Eglington St, Galway City; +353 91 562 268
Surrounded by Galway's best pubs, a big night in the city often kicks off at Conlon & Sons. From September to April, Galway oysters are served at the granite bar, and salmon, scallops and mussels prove irresistible to seafood buffs.

Moran's Oyster Cottage moderate
The Weir, Kilcolgan; www.moransoystercottage.com
Moran's treats local Clarinbridge oysters simply and with respect; freshly shucked and served with a silky pint of Guinness and some Irish soda bread. A restaurant that's been run by the same family for seven generations really doesn't have a lot to prove.

CANCALE, FRANCE
The Romans, King Louis XIV, Marie Antoinette and Napoleon Bonaparte were all fans of oysters from Cancale, in northwest France. Local *huîtres* include the delicate and nutty Plate Belon, and the robust and rare Pied de Cheval.

Quai Gambetta inexpensive
Just metres from Cancale's oyster beds, several enterprising locals on the quay offer a fresh dozen with a wedge of lemon for around €4. Ad hoc and alfresco dining is enhanced by salty Atlantic breezes.

A Contre Courant moderate
3 Place du Calvaire, 'Le Port', Cancale; www.acontrecourant.net

With modern decor and regular exhibitions from local artists, A Contre Courant resembles a breezy slice of the Med on France's Atlantic coast. Oysters are treated simply, and the wider menu includes scallops with *andouille* sausage and grilled prawn skewers.

Above The Temple of the Emerald Buddha, in the compound of the Grand Palace in Bangkok

A Day in Bangkok

Take advantage of the cool of the morning for a walking tour of the cultural centre, then use the river as an "expressway" to other sights.

MORNING Start the day in **Ko Ratanakosin**, which rests in a bend of the **Chao Phraya** river and contains some of the city's most historic architecture. **Wat Pho** is Bangkok's oldest temple and home to one of the largest reclining Buddha statues in the world. The nearby **Grand Palace** has been superseded by Chitlada Palace as the primary royal residence, but it is still used for ceremonial occasions. Adjacent **Wat Phra Kaew**, home to the "Emerald Buddha" (actually jade), is a gleaming example of Bangkok temple architecture at its most baroque.

AFTERNOON Catch a ferry across the river to **Supatra River House** to sample some great *tom yam*. From Chang pier, hire a long-tailed boat for a two-hour tour through **Thonburi**'s extensive canal network, admiring the old wooden houses and floating vendors.

EVENING Cool off by quaffing a cold beer and sampling more foodie treats at the **Soi 38 Night Market**, off Sukhumvit.

Essentials

GETTING THERE
Suvarnabhumi International Airport is 30 km (18 miles) from Bangkok; there are "Airport Express" **buses** and **taxis** to the city centre.

WHERE TO STAY
Phra-Nakorn Norn-Len (inexpensive) is a trendy hotel with pretty, budget accommodation in a quiet part of Bangkok near the river. *www.phranakorn-nornlen.com*
Conrad Bangkok (moderate) is conveniently located in the city centre near the BTS Sukhumvit line and shopping centres. *http://conradhotels1.hilton.com*
Chakrabongse Villas (expensive) are exquisite riverfront villas in the grounds of a century-old Thai palace. *www.thaivillas.com*

TOURIST INFORMATION
www.bangkoktourist.com

Above Bangkok has many night markets, full of chattering locals and tourists eating, drinking and shopping until late

BANGKOK

BANGKOK THAILAND

Tangy Tom Yam in Bangkok

Bangkok is the archetypal Southeast Asian metropolis. The humid air is thick with the heady scent of jasmine and the oceanic reverberation of distant traffic. Temple spires glitter alongside pounding discotheques, respective temples to the ascetic and the hedonistic. The city's best-loved dish, *tom yam*, explodes with an energy that's perfectly in tune with this whirlwind of a city.

Although intensely urbanized, Bangkok exhibits an uncompromised Thai identity beneath its modern veneer. Glass-and-steel buildings shaped like cartoon robots stand next to terracotta-tiled temples; wreaths of good-luck flowers dangle from the rear-view mirrors of buses and taxis; shaven-headed, orange-robed monks walk barefoot along the street beneath a bank of giant Sony screens carrying images of the latest global pop idol.

Visitors can move across the city on water, via 18th-century canals; through the air, aboard the sleek Skytrain; or below ground, in the high-tech Metropolitan Rapid Transit Authority (MRTA) subway. Cultural highs are both high- and low-brow, from museums, galleries and classical theatre or dance performances to Thai boxing or club outings, to hear international DJs spin the latest house and hip-hop.

Just as the Bangkok Thai dialect has become standard Thai throughout the country, so Bangkok Thai cooking is today considered classic Thai cuisine. *Tom yam*, one of the most quintessential Bangkok Thai

dishes, has an ancient history, making use of the oldest ingredients and techniques known to Thai food historians. It is a spicy, tangy broth with lime and chilli overtones that's almost always made with seafood, though chicken is occasionally substituted.

Lemongrass, kaffir lime peel and lime juice give *tom yam* its characteristic sour taste. Fuelling the fire beneath the broth's often velvety surface are fresh whole bird chillies and sometimes half a teaspoonful of roast chilli paste. Improvisation comes into play with this dish more than most, as Thai cooks try to out-do one another in providing a savoury soup with at least one or two "mystery" ingredients. Many cooks add galangal to give the mix an extra fragrance. For colour and flavour, halved cherry tomatoes will sometimes work their way into the recipe. Aside from the lemongrass and galangal that will remain at the bottom of the serving bowl, solids in this soup are usually limited to prawns and straw mushrooms, jostling beneath a sprinkle of coriander leaf. Like Bangkok itself, the first taste often leaves the uninitiated delighted but gasping for breath.

Cookery Schools

You can amaze your friends back home with deft preparations of *tom yam* and other Thai delights by attending a cooking course in Bangkok. The oldest and most well-known programme in the city is the plush **Oriental Thai Cooking School** (*www.mandarinoriental.com*), opposite the Mandarin Oriental Bangkok, which teaches four dishes a day, Monday to Saturday. At **The Thai House** (*www.thaihouse.co.th*), visitors choose from one- to three-day residential cooking courses held in a traditional Thai teak house about 40 minutes north of Bangkok by boat. The family kitchen lies next to a fruit orchard growing mangoes, bananas, papaya and coconut, and the perfect herb garden. **Baipai Thai Cooking School** (*www.baipai.com*) is one of the newer schools and its popular non-residential programmes are held in a two-storey town house in Bangkok.

Above *Tom yam* is an everyday treat for many people in Thailand

The Best Places to Eat Tom Yam

Taling Pling moderate

One place that scores highly on all counts is Taling Pling, where the cooks make *tom yam* from scratch using ingredients purchased fresh every morning. The restaurant name comes from a venerable taling pling tree (*Averrhoa bilimbi*) that still stands alongside the old Thai house that houses the restaurant. Don't let the trendy mauve walls fool you; this is local food, with a central/southern Thai slant, and you'll get no mercy from the kitchen when it comes to spices. Every dish is prepared with the utmost attention, yet the prices are affordable for middle-class Thais, who make up most of the clientele. Other exemplary dishes that will go well with your *tom yam* include *phanaeng* curry with roast duck and *thawt man plaa* (fried fishcakes with a cucumber-peanut dipping sauce). If you want to try the restaurant's namesake fruit, order *yam plaa salit taling pling*, a fresh salad made with taling pling (a juicy, sour fruit) and small Gulf fish, fried whole. At lunch time, Taling Pling is crowded with local office workers, so it's best to arrive after 1pm or in the early evening to guarantee a table.

60 Pan Road, Bangkok; open 11am–10:30pm; +66 2234 4872

Also in Bangkok

Most locals rate **Supatra River House** (*www. supatrariverhouse.net; moderate*) as the best restaurant on the river; it's an old teak house with wonderful views of the Grand Palace and Wat Arun. Enjoy great *tom yam* either alfresco or indoors with extremely efficient air-conditioning. **Raan Jay Fai** (*+66 2223 9384; inexpensive*) on the Maha Chai Road was once a local secret but is now quite well known among foodies. This open-air café serves a delicious *tom yam haeng*, a dry-fried (rather than soupy) version of the dish, and its *pad khee mao* (drunken noodles) are legendary.

Also in Thailand

If you find yourself on the resort island of Phuket, head to the historic town of the same name and look for **Nai Yao** (*+66 7621 2719; inexpensive*) on Phuket Road. It's one of the oldest seafood restaurants on the island, and uses fish straight from local fishing boats.

Around the World

The world's first Michelin-starred Thai restaurant, **Nahm** (*www.halkin.como.bz; expensive*) is found not in Thailand but in London, where Australian virtuoso chef David Thompson holds court. Try his version of *tom yam* with fresh mussels, or *geng jeut pla meuk yord sai*, another clear soup, made of squid, chicken, samphire and shiitake mushrooms.

Three Days in Tokyo

Tokyo has no centre; think of it instead as several cities that vaguely orbit the Imperial Palace and are connected by the Yamanoto Line railway. The main places visitors gravitate to are Ginza/Marunouchi, Roppongi, Shibuya/Omotesando/Harajuku, Shinjuku, Ikebukuro, Ueno, Akihabara and Odaiba, but there are many more areas to explore.

DAY ONE Visit the **Tsukiji fish market** at the crack of dawn and breakfast at one of its famous sushi bars. From there head to **Ginza** for shopping, before moving on to the vast **Imperial Palace** complex and gardens. End the day amid the liquid crystal lights of **Shinjuku.**

DAY TWO **Shibuya**, **Harajuku** and **Omotesando** are great for watching the best-dressed people in the world go about their business. If all the Gothic Lolita/Hello Kitty craziness gets too much, take a break amid the green spaces of **Yoyogi** park.

DAY THREE If there is a tournament on, head to **Ryugoku** to see some sumo. For a final retail splurge, go to **Tokyo Midtown** in **Roppongi**, a vast and elegant mall with great restaurants, shops and galleries.

Essentials

GETTING THERE

Two international **airports** serve Tokyo: Narita (an hour-and-a-half north of the city by **bus** or **Metro**) and Haneda (40 minutes south of the city by **monorail** or **bus**). Tokyo has a peerless network of under-and overground **trains**.

WHERE TO STAY

The Welcome Inn (inexpensive) has several traditional Japanese *ryokans* (inns) offering great value in an expensive city. *www.itcj.jp/eng*
Citadines Shinjuku (moderate) is reasonably central, modern, spacious and good value. *www.citadines.com*
The Mandarin Oriental (expensive) has stunning views, gorgeous rooms and great restaurants. *www.mandarinoriental.com*

TOURIST INFORMATION

www.seejapan.co.uk

right A sushi bar at breakfast time at Tsukiji fish market, where around 2,700 kg (almost 3 tons) of fish is auctioned every day
Below The busy Shinjuku district boasts Tokyo's largest concentration of skyscrapers

TOKYO JAPAN

Fresh Sushi in Towering Tokyo

During the first decade of the 21st century Tokyo finally edged aside New York, Paris and London to claim the title of the undisputed culinary capital of the world, and its greatest food is sushi. Whether feasted upon at a lavish members-only restaurant or from a cheap and cheerful *kaiten,* where tempting portions roll by on a conveyor belt, the sushi here is invariably delicious.

Tokyo is one of the world's great cities, with cultural, historic and culinary attractions to rival any capital. It is built on a daunting scale and its cityscape changes ceaselessly, but amid the liquid-crystal screens, the nonstop rivers of people and the towering flyovers, there remain pockets of ancient Japan in the form of the city's temples and gardens, which are soothing oases of stillness.

No-one takes food more seriously than the Japanese. Tokyo doesn't just offer every kind of global food and cuisine imaginable; it aims to better the originals. The city has also given the world several great dishes, not least sushi, which dates back to the 7th century when the Japanese acquired the Chinese habit of preserving pieces of fish in rice. The rice was discarded when the fish was eaten, but by the 15th century the Japanese had started to speed up the process using rice wine vinegar, then eating both the fish and the rice. The seasoned rice became known as *sushi*. A further breakthrough occurred in the early 1800s, when a Tokyo inhabitant named Yohei Hanaya came up with the idea of squeezing rice into small blocks and adding toppings. This hand-shaped form of sushi became known as *nigiri* (meaning "to squeeze"); along with *maki* rolls (seaweed-bound rice rolls), it was to become the best known form of sushi around the world.

Now that sushi has become as ubiquitous as sandwiches in the supermarkets of the West, it can seem a little strange to discover that in Tokyo the Japanese don't really think of it as a cheap fast food. You can buy packs of ready-made sushi in supermarkets (and it will be better than any supermarket sushi you've ever tasted), but the Japanese – and Tokyoites in particular – take their sushi much more seriously than that. Here, sushi is a treat, an extravagance. The rice is served at body temperature and very rarely topped with salmon; Tokyo favourites include chilled squid, bream, octopus, sea urchin, turbot, whitebait, shrimp, fish eggs, plaice, sea snails and, of course, various cuts of tuna. Look out too for grilled eel and lightly pickled mackerel. Eating sushi in Tokyo is a ritual to be savoured, from the moment the freshly grated wasabi falls from a sharkskin board on to your colourful, sushi-laden plate.

Japanese Food Halls

For a jaw-dropping glimpse into the Tokyoites' glorious obsession with food, visit one of the city's great *depachika*, or department store food halls. Always to be found in the basement, they are a testament to the Japanese fixation with quality, variety and innovation in food. They sell up to 30,000 different items, including a vast array of local and international ingredients and finished dishes. The *depachikas* of, for example, the **Seibu, Odakyu** or **Takashimaya** department stores in the Tokyo neighbourhoods of Shinjuku, Shibuya, Ginza or Ikebukuro rank among the greatest food halls in the world. You'll find great takeaway tempura, sushi, tofu, noodles, Wagyu beef, fresh fish, *wagashi* (traditional Japanese sweets) and immaculate fruit and vegetables. In general *depachikas* are great places to eat cheaply, or even for free – there are usually dozens of free samples on offer.

Above Sushi is eaten as finger food and each piece should be eaten in one mouthful

The Best Places to Eat Sushi

Tsukiji Fish Market inexpensive

There are sushi restaurants in every Tokyo neighbourhood, ranging from six-seater bars to larger chains and conveyor-belt or *kaiten* sushi places. But the spiritual home of sushi are the restaurants in the heart of the world-famous Tsukiji fish market, the largest fish market in the world. The most famous of these restaurants is Daiwa, but its neighbours, particularly Sushi Dai, are just about as good and they all serve what is perhaps the freshest sushi in the world. Annoyingly, they don't take reservations, so you need to arrive seriously early (around 5am) to avoid the queues. Set some time aside for a walk around the market itself, too, because it is one of the greatest food sights on Earth. Finally, if you want to be guaranteed a sushi meal to remember, there is one word with which you must greet the chef as you take your seat – *"Omakase"*, which means: "I'll leave it up to you". **Tsukiji, Tokyo; open 5am–2pm Mon–Sat (closed on alternate Weds); www.tsukiji-market.or.jp**

Also in Tokyo

The Ginza district in Tokyo is home to fiendishly expensive, exclusive and often impossible-to-get-into sushi restaurants. The most famous of these is **Sukiyabashi Jiro** *(+81 03 3535 3600; expensive),* which was awarded three Michelin stars in 2009 and is run by the eponymous and legendary 84-year old Jiro-san. He has been making sushi for over 60 years and is said to size up each customer's jaw and adjust the size of the *nigiri* to fit their mouth accordingly. Jiro-san's son runs a more accessible branch in the Roppongi Hills mall.

Also in Japan

Though the style of sushi we know best in the West originated in Tokyo, sushi has its historic roots in Kyoto and Osaka, where it was originally made in large portions that were pressed into boxes and typically topped with pickled mackerel. This *zaba-sushi* can still be eaten in Kyoto and Osaka. The most famous restaurant for this surprisingly hearty speciality – which is not served with wasabi or soy sauce – is **Izuu** *(+81 075 561 0751; expensive)* in Higashiyama-ku, Kyoto, which was established in 1781.

Around the World

Sushi's other great spiritual home is the USA, where they have added their own quirks and ingredients to the mix to create wonders such as the inside-out-roll and the California roll. New York's **Sushi of Gari** *(www.sushiofgari.com; moderate)* and LA's **Asanebo** *(+1 818 760 3348; expensive)* are highly recommended.

DUJIANGYAN CHINA

Peanut Chicken in Dujiangyan

Gong bao ji ding is one of the most instantly recognizable Chinese dishes, served up as "spicy chicken with peanuts" in restaurants around the world. History links it to Dujiangyan, a small Sichuanese town just north of the provincial capital, Chengdu, and also to an ancient engineering project that long ago turned this region into one of China's prime agricultural areas.

Gong bao (sometimes *kung po*) chicken is named after Ding Baozhen, the Governor of Sichuan in the 1880s ("Gong Bao" was his official title), whose household is said by some to have invented this dish. Others claim that it is, in fact, an old recipe from neighbouring Guizhou province, where Ding Baozhen was born, or that it was served up to him at a banquet by an obsequious subordinate looking for favours. It doesn't really matter which story is true: this stir-fried assemblage of juicy chicken cubes, crunchy peanuts, chopped dried chillies and aromatic Sichuan peppercorns (called *huajiao*, or "flower pepper" in Chinese), all held together by a malty-sour sauce, is deliciously addictive.

The combination of chillies and *huajiao* is distinctly Sichuanese, though *gong bao* chicken isn't actually a hot dish by local standards. Some Sichuanese food is so fiery that even hardened locals glow crimson when eating it; to watch diners at a back-street night market tucking into innocuously named "boiled beef slices" or a communal, chilli-rich hotpot is to wince in sympathy. After a while, though,

this eye-watering diet becomes a necessity, and the Sichuanese justify their chilli cravings on health grounds, claiming that eating them warms you up in winter and helps you perspire during the summer, ultimately cooling you down.

Ding Baozhen is also famous for restoring Sichuan's agricultural self-sufficiency. Dujiangyan sits where the farmland plains of eastern Sichuan meet the abrupt "foothills" – in reality, steep-sided mountains – of the Tibetan Plateau. Watercourses tumble off these hillsides into the notoriously capricious Min river, which used to cause havoc by alternately drying out or flooding the plains. In 256 BC the Han dynasty governor Li Bing designed a simple-looking collection of dams, dykes and spillways to channel the river into an irrigation system. Ding Baozhen restored his work, and today's vast waterways offer spectacular views over the channels and dams to the mountains and forests beyond. In taming the waters, Li Bing created an area of rich agricultural land, thereby granting the people a livelihood, and his efforts are commemorated in the temples of Erwang Miao and Fulong Guan – "Dragon-Taming Hall".

Above Erwang Miao, the Two Kings Temple, is a tribute to Li Bing and his son, who first irrigated the plains during China's Warring States period, 2,200 years ago

Sichuan Pepper

The characteristic Sichuanese taste is *mala*, literally "hot and numb", created by combining the spicy heat of chillies with the aromatic tingle of Sichuan pepper. Also known as prickly ash, these peppercorn-sized fruits grow on ferociously thorny bushes in western Sichuan – market vendors often hold up scratched hands to prove how fresh their wares are. They contain a volatile oil that creates a weird pins-and-needles sensation in the mouth when eaten. The dried peppercorns are either cooked whole in a dish, as in *gong bao* chicken (be warned, it's a bit of a shock when you bite into one) or ground to a powder and sprinkled over everything at the end. Sadly, the oil's numbing effect doesn't age well and peppercorns bought overseas rarely retain enough volatile oil to surprise an unwary diner.

A Day in Dujiangyan

Dujiangyan town itself is a functional transport hub, so once you've arrived here from Chengdu, there's no reason to delay from heading straight for the riverside parkland surrounding the ancient irrigation scheme.

MORNING Head for **Lidui Park** and admire the main channel from venerable **Fulong Hall**, then catch a cable car over the Min river or cross more adventurously via the narrow **Anlan** suspension bridge. Either way you'll reach **Erwang Miao**, the Two Kings Temple. Seek out the painted bust of Ding Baozhen in an alcove here, then walk through woodland back to town along the flagstoned **Songmao Path**, one of the ancient "tea roads" between Sichuan and Tibet.

AFTERNOON After lunch at one of the many riverside restaurants, head 25 km (15 miles) west to **Qingcheng Mountain**, a small but sacred Taoist peak. Climb the steep flights of steps through thick forest, pausing along the way to admire some small but beautiful temples and shrines.

EVENING Return to **Chengdu** for an evening stroll around the old streets surrounding Kuan Xiangzi, followed by a performance of traditional Sichuan opera.

Essentials

GETTING THERE
Dujiangyan is 30 km (20 miles) north of Shuangliu **international airport** in Chengdu. A **rail** service also runs from Chengdu's north train station.

WHERE TO STAY
Dujianyan is short on foreigner-friendly hotels, so it's best to stay in Chengdu.
Sim's (inexpensive) is centrally located and offers very friendly, helpful service. www.gogosc.com
The Holiday Inn Express (moderate) is business-oriented and very used to dealing with foreigners. www.holidayinnexpress.com.cn
The Jinjiang Hotel (expensive) is a Chinese-style luxury hotel in the centre. www.jjhotel.com

TOURIST INFORMATION
194 Qintai Road, Chengdu; or check the listings magazine *GoChengdu*: www.gochengdoo.com

The Best Places to Eat Gong Bao Chicken

Alfresco restaurants in Dujiangyan inexpensive

For the best *gong bao* chicken experience in Dujiangyan, head to the host of waterside restaurants lining the overflow channel off Fuxing Road, just outside Lidui Park. Places here specialize in river food – including fresh frogs, snails and little crayfish, all kept alive in buckets – but also include a broad range of Sichuanese favourites on the menu. The best way to choose a restaurant is to walk around and pick the busiest. The trick to finding a good plate of *gong bao* chicken (as it lends itself to endless variations, some better than others) is to look for one that includes chicken cubes, peanuts, Sichuan peppercorns and chillies, and is not swamped in chilli oil or sticky sauces. The best variations produce a relatively mild, dry dish with sharp, clear flavours. Whichever establishment you end up in, choose an outdoor table (most have awnings to protect you from the elements) and enjoy the setting, with the water racing roughly past along the broad, stone-lined channel. Make sure you agree prices as you order, or you might get a nasty shock when the bill arrives.

Around Lidui Park, Dujiangyan; open dawn–dusk daily

In Chengdu

The excellent **Manting Fan** *(+86 28 8517 7958; moderate)* serves up first-rate *gong bao* chicken, alongside other Sichuanese favourites such as *mapo tofu* (soft tofu cubes in a hot bean sauce), smoked duck, dry-fried green beans, "fish-flavoured" pork shreds, sweet rabbit threads with steamed buns and sautéed bamboo shoots. **Lao Fangzi** *(+86 28 8509 8822; moderate)* has a similar menu to Manting Fan, and their "mouthwatering chicken" is well worth a try.

Also in China

Baguo Buyi *(+86 10 6400 8888; expensive)* is the Beijing branch of a Chengdu chain, featuring excellent *gong bao* chicken, twice-cooked pork and performances of Sichuan opera to enjoy with your meal. **Chuanguo Yuanyi** *(+86 21 5836 8826; expensive)* does the same job in Shanghai; whilst in Chongqing, **Waipo Qiao** *(+86 23 6383 5998; moderate)* serves some of the best Sichuanese food in town.

Around the World

In London, both the cooking and decor at **Barshu** *(www.bar-shu.co.uk; moderate)* are extraordinarily close to an authentic Chengdu experience. New York's **Grand Sichuan** chain *(www.thegrandsichuan.com; moderate)* is well-regarded for staples including *gong bao* chicken. In Melbourne, aim for **Dainty Sichuan** *(+61 3 9663 8861: inexpensive)*, a crowded, unsophisticated place that likes its spices.

Above Lanterns decorate one of the many small canals that are used to control the Min river levels in Dujiangyan

Left *Gong bao* chicken combines succulent chicken, peanuts, chillies and Sichuan pepper with ginger and garlic in a light sweet-sour sauce

A Day in Old Delhi

Mesmerizing Old Delhi is just a couple of kilometres (a mile or so) north of Connaught Place, the modern hub of New Delhi. Unmistakeably Islamic despite the nation's Hindu background, it is a thoroughly rewarding area in which to explore historic sites and markets.

MORNING From sturdy **Delhi Gate**, at the old city's southern edge, stroll up **Netaji Subhash Marg** until you see the massive ramparts of the **Red Fort** (Lal Qila) on your right. You can spend several hours visiting the exquisite halls, palaces and museum within, including a relaxing stroll in the delightful gardens.

AFTERNOON Head west along crowded **Chandni Chowk**, perhaps dipping into the Hindu **Lal Mandir** temple, then bear south into the jumble of winding lanes that constitute one huge and vibrant market. Getting lost is part of the fun.

EVENING Find your way to **Jama Masjid** mosque, whose minarets tower above the old city. It is at its most magical around the time of evening prayers. Then it's tandoori time.

Essentials

GETTING THERE
Delhi's **Indira Gandhi International Airport**, due to be connected to the new **metro** system, is 15 km (9 miles) southwest of the centre. The metro provides a hassle-free and air-conditioned way of getting around the city.

WHERE TO STAY
Rak International (inexpensive) provides good value in the bustling backpacker area of Paharganj. *www.hotelrakinternational.com*
Godwin Deluxe (moderate) is a bright, modern hotel conveniently located in Ram Nagar, near the old city. *www.godwinhotels.com*
Maidens (expensive) gives you a taste of real Raj-style luxury in a converted colonial mansion in Old Delhi. *www.maidenshotel.com*

TOURIST INFORMATION
88 Janpath, New Delhi; *+91 11 2332 0008*

Right Spices, dried fruits and nuts fill the alleys of Old Delhi's Khari Baoli market

Below Jama Masjid, the largest mosque in India, was commissioned by the Mughal emperor Shah Jahan

DELHI INDIA

Tandoori in the City of Mughals

The sprawling city of Delhi may boast the manicured avenues of the British Raj and be encircled by high-rise suburbs, but at its heart remain the atmospherically chaotic lanes of Old Delhi. This area grew up during the Islamic Mughal empire, and its heritage is reflected in its cuisine. It offers some of the best places in the world to eat tandoori dishes, cooked in a traditional clay oven.

Exploring India's capital is a journey of rich historical discovery, for this is not one but seven successive cities. Predating the New Delhi of the British Raj, settlement began with Rajput-era Lal Kot and culminated in the crowning glory of the Mughal empire: Shah Jahan's eponymous city, Shah-jahanabad, now known as Old Delhi. In between, a succession of Muslim conquerors left behind majestic monuments such as the towering Qutb Minar minaret and the elegant domed tomb of Emperor Humayun, but it is the remains of Shah Jahan's city, founded in 1638, that most captivate the imagination.

Within the space demarcated by the old city's four remaining stone gates and beside the expansive Red Fort and imposing Jama Masjid, India's largest mosque, life goes on in many ways as it did during the Mughal era. Wandering through the web of narrow lanes and bazaars, you will encounter rows of tiny shops selling by turn gleaming metal pots and other household items, sparkling jewellery or colourful spices piled high in bulging sacks.

Old Delhi is a true melting pot of people from all over the Indian subcontinent and beyond. At every turn, restaurants vie for attention with street vendors selling snacks called *chaat (see pp192–3)*, but most distinctive among them – signalled by racks of ruddy-coloured chickens fresh from the oven – are the tandoori restaurants. "Tandoor" is the word for the clay oven in which meat, fish and some vegetables are cooked at temperatures as high as 480°C (750°F). This method of cooking, popular in the Punjab region, was said to be a favourite of the Mughal emperor Jahangir, father of Shah Jahan. However, tandoori cuisine as we know it today is widely credited to the restaurateur Kundan Lal Gujral and his Delhi base, Moti Mahal *(see right)*.

Tandoori dishes are fairly simple, with chicken as the most common ingredient. It is slit and marinaded in a mixture of yogurt, lime juice, garlic and spices such as chilli, garam masala, coriander, cloves and ginger before being baked in the oven. The marinade keeps the meat succulent and moist. It is then served with an onion-based salad and usually eaten with naan flatbread, also fresh from the hot tandoor oven.

The Best Places to Eat Tandoori

Moti Mahal moderate

This restaurant – the epicentre of tandoori cuisine – was established in Delhi by Kundan Lal Gujral over 60 years ago and has since spawned a series of franchises, even beyond the boundaries of India. However, the prototype still has to be the place to sample tandoori cuisine at its best. There is plenty of seating within the relatively plain interior and a large leafy courtyard to dine in for most of the year. Some nights there is live *qawwali*, Islamic devotional music, to accompany your meal.

It is the food, however, that really does the talking. A wide range of tandoori dishes is available, including chicken or fish tikka, lamb kebabs, prawns and a variety of vegetables such as cauliflower, potato and mushroom, as well as some *paneer* (cheese) dishes. Unsurprisingly, tandoori chicken is the most popular main dish on the menu but the traditional butter chicken is another favourite. And, of course, there is a range of freshly baked naan breads to help you mop up any remaining juices.

3704 Netaji Subhash Marg, Daryaganj, Old Delhi; open 11am–11.30pm daily; +91 11 2327 3661

Also in Delhi

The perfect example of how local cuisine has been taken upmarket to suit the lifestyle of Delhi's nouveaux riches, **Punjabi By Nature** *(www.punjabibynature.com; expensive)* has subtle lighting and decor, smart and attentive service and delicious food that preserves its traditional roots. This is a fine spot for a special night out, sampling mouthwatering specialities such as tandoori prawns, fish tikka and *raan-e-punjab* (leg of lamb).

Also in India

Tandoori cuisine has spread to become a staple throughout India. In the city of Jaipur, **Niro's** *(+91 141 221 8520; moderate)* offers a succulent range of dishes from the tandoor as well as Rajasthani specialities. There's no problem finding good tandoori in the south either: Chennai's **Bismillah Biryani Centre** *(+91 98 8464 8345; inexpensive)* is a typical street corner joint that turns tasty items out of its oven, as well as serving biryanis.

Around the World

In London, look no further than the branch of **Moti Mahal** *(www.motimahal-uk.com; expensive)* in Covent Garden. This stylish restaurant offers top tandoori, expertly prepared by chef Anirudh Arora, as well as a variety of other traditional dishes. Over in San Francisco, the place to go is **India Clay Oven** *(www.indiaclayoven.com; inexpensive)*, which offers a wide range of tasty tandoori dishes.

The Spice Market

Khari Baoli, named after its stepped well or *baoli*, once used for bathing and watering livestock, is the largest spice market in Asia. It is a fabulous place to stock up on Indian cooking ingredients and soak up the atmosphere of Old Delhi. Located just beyond the western end of Old Delhi's main street, Chandni Chowk, its crowded stalls, separated by narrow lanes, are still often owned by the same families who began their businesses here ten generations ago. Every kind of spice, seasoning and herb is on display amidst a heady mixture of exotic aromas and a psychedelic palette of varying hues. The constant cries of porters carrying huge sacks and spice merchants advertising their wares adds sound to the sensual overload. You only need to take a pinch of garam masala and touch a little to your tongue to complete a sensory feast.

Above The precise mix of spices used determines the colour of tandoori chicken

Above In midtown Manhattan, New York, a classic diner captures the streamlined, chrome-and-neon dream of 1950s America

North America

The Flavours of
North America

Ask most people around the globe to name the quintessential food of North America and the answer will most probably be "the hamburger". It is true that a good hamburger is available in almost every small town or big city across the USA. But North American cuisine – including its fast food – is far more complex and varied, encompassing everything from home-made pies and perfect barbecue to succulent seafood, southern "soul food" and fiery Mexican dishes.

As Europeans discovered when they began colonizing the New World 500 years ago, the American continent is almost embarrassingly rich in natural food sources and fertile land. The icy waters of the northeast coast yield some of the world's finest shellfish, while much of the world's wheat springs from the black soils of North America's plains. Fruit trees groan with the weight of peaches in Georgia, apples in the Okanagan valley and oranges, lemons and limes in Florida and California. Tomatoes and peppers grow as far as the eye can see in Mexico, and rippling maize stretches to the horizon through the American Midwest.

Nowhere is the taste of North America so celebrated as in northern California, where almost anything will grow.

Nowhere is the taste of North America so celebrated as in northern California, where almost anything will grow. It was here that the farm-to-fork movement took root in the late 1960s, and so-called "California cuisine" – the concept of eating only fresh and local foods – has evolved into the driving force behind fine dining across virtually the whole of North America.

Yet North American cuisine has a distinctly casual streak. The slapdash grill menu – hamburgers included – met the American love affair with automobiles, especially in southern California, to give birth to the roadside diner. Even the streamlined architecture of this icon of American gastronomy reflects the worship of speed. While Americans hardly invented hand-held food, few cities boast such a variety of street food as New York, where the diner on the move can chow down on German wurst in Midtown or Sri Lankan *dosas* in Washington Square Park.

Indigenous Ingredients

Transplanted ethnic cuisines are emblematic of North American gastronomy, yet certain dishes are rooted in their geography. Thanks to air freight, Maine lobster can be tasted all over the world, but never with such resonance as on the dock where it is landed. Clam chowder may trace its ancestry to Breton fish stews, but the clams that define it are limited to New England shores. And few dishes are so location-specific as New Orleans jambalaya, which

Right Cooking up a huge pot of chilli at the Kansas State Fair Chilli Cookoff
Below New York City's love of street food is indulged at its many street fairs

relies on the crayfish and rice of the bayous and the piquant tabasco strain of chilli pepper. In fact, native North American peppers in their hundreds of varieties could be said to be the taste of the continent. The pork rib barbecue of Memphis carries just a hint of chilli heat, while in San Antonio, Texas, spicy stewed-beef chilli contains nearly as much hot pepper as meat. But capsicum peppers have many more qualities than sheer heat: the sweetness of pimentoes, the smokiness of chipotle and the spicy, fruity flavours of the habanero, for example. Further up the Rio Grande, these are wonderfully exploited in the subtle cuisine of New Mexico, where Spanish colonists married Native American corn tortillas and chilli-pepper-based sauces with an old-world taste for meat fillings.

Overseas Influences

A similar collusion between Native American and Spanish cookery took place in Mexico, where the people of Puebla combined their indigenous heritage ingredients of chocolate and chilli with spices introduced by the Spanish to create the rich brown sauce called *mole*. Indeed, it is a rare dish in Mexico that does not contain some

form of chilli pepper; it forms a part of even the *taco al pastor*, or rotisserie taco, so similar to the Middle Eastern doner kebab. The hottest of all the capsicums – the Scotch bonnet pepper found throughout the Caribbean basin – electrifies Jamaican jerk cooking, lending both its heat and citrus notes to the smoky, spicy tang of Jamaican pimento wood, from the shrub that yields allspice. While jerk meat (usually chicken or fish) can be traced back to the original Arawak inhabitants of Jamaica, other Caribbean specialities reflect the islands' cultural overlays. So many East Asians were relocated to the Caribbean islands during colonial times that curries, *aloo* (spicy potato dishes) and the friendship bread of *dosti roti* are standards in the West Indies.

The African diaspora played a profound role in North American cooking as well. African slaves in the cotton and sugar cane regions of the American South cooked with African provender – okra, peanuts, and melons – along with leafy greens and cheap cuts of pork. In time, the hearty fare became known as "soul food", from collard greens cooked in bacon fat to the unctuous sweet potato pie.

Pennsylvania Dutch cooks are wont to encase every berry or tree fruit they grow in a flaky crust.

Americans have always had a sweet tooth, whether for thick cheesecakes made with the cream cheese of Philadelphia or for the sweet pastries of Pennsylvania Dutch country. A farming society with roots in central Europe (where pastry is king), Pennsylvania Dutch cooks are wont to encase every berry or tree fruit they grow in a flaky crust. It is, as the saying goes, as American as apple pie.

Left Local produce for sale at a market in Guadalajara, Mexico
Below A love of cars and fast food came together perfectly in the creation of the diner

Right Lobster-trap marker buoys decorate a shingled Maine lobster pound

Below The sweetest lobster is pulled from icy-cold Maine waters, steamed almost as soon as it is brought ashore, and simply served

Three Days along the Maine Coast

Picturesque fishing villages, lighthouses and yachting harbours dot this meandering coastline, made famous by American painters from Winslow Homer (1836–1910) to Marsden Hartley (1877–1943).

DAY ONE Swim in the surf at **Reid State Park**, the longest sandy beach on this rocky coast, before peninsula-hopping to the yachting centre of **Boothbay Harbor**. Fish for striped bass or tuna, or take a wildlife cruise to search for whales and puffins.

DAY TWO Clamber over the massive boulders of **Pemaquid Point** for a dramatic view of the lighthouse on the headland. Then drive to the fishing hamlet of Port Clyde and take a ferry to **Monhegan Island**, a summer art colony where painters open their studios to visitors.

DAY THREE After stopping at **Tenants Harbor** to visit the lobster-fishing museum, spend the day in the port of **Rockland**, with its world-class Farnsworth Art Museum and Wyeth Center, its child-friendly **Maine Lighthouse Museum** and its excellent restaurants and cafés.

Essentials

GETTING THERE
Air Canada and several domestic US carriers serve **Portland International Jetport**. Hire a **car** to drive north on Route 1.

WHERE TO STAY
Prices vary little across the region.
East Wind Inn (moderate) has lobster boats moored outside its windows in the picturesque fishing village of Tenants Harbor. *www.eastwindinn.com*
Grey Havens Inn (moderate) is a classic shingle-style 1904 hotel on a craggy bluff in Georgetown near Reid State Park. *www.greyhavens.com*
Limerock Inn (moderate) occupies a turreted Rockland manse in a Rockland neighbourhood within walking distance of the Farnsworth Art Museum. *www.limerockinn.com*

MAINE USA

Sweet Lobster on the Maine Coast

From dawn to dusk, wooden boats motor across the tiny harbours of Maine's central coast. Men in rubber bib-overalls toss lobster crates on to floating wooden docks, then abruptly cast off to haul more traps. Cooks hustle the crustaceans from dock to steamer to plates. The feast begins as diners crack shells, dig out the meat and revel in the deep-sea flavour of the sweet-salty flesh.

Early European settlers of what would become the State of Maine wasted little time harvesting the virgin forests to build ships and turning to the sea to build a rich fishery. Maine's maritime heritage remains a way of life on the long, rocky peninsulas that trail off the coast between Casco and Penobscot bays, where briny villages are famous for the quantity and quality of their lobster catch. Drivers who detour down these peninsulas can spend days exploring a coast ruled by summer's long sunlight and the epic rise and fall of the tides. Twisting roads through spruce forest suddenly emerge into open vistas of the swelling green sea. Hidden coves are dotted with lobster boats and craggy headlands are capped with stocky lighthouses that guide the boats to safe refuge through swirling currents and rocky straits.

Down every peninsula lies a harbour, and in every harbour a "lobster pound" – originally a saltwater impound where lobsters were held for market. Most are still no-frills wooden facilities built right at the shore – some even hanging over the water.

Today most "pounds" also serve as casual seafood eateries. Few even have a dining room, serving meals through a takeaway window, but such shortcomings are of no consequence to connoisseurs of Maine's signature crustacean. A burly chaos rules the kitchens of these pounds, where cooks tread a narrow path next to monstrous steam vessels to load bags of lobsters, soft-shell clams and potatoes tumbled with cobs of corn. Twelve to fifteen minutes later, the brownish-green lobsters have become bright red; the order is plated up and at the pickup window, the order number is yelled out loud enough for everyone on the wharf to hear.

The ensuing lobster feast is a messy experience, which is why most aficionados like to eat at picnic tables at the water's edge. Breaking the tail and claws sprays juices all around, and fingers quickly grow sticky picking the meat from the shell and dipping it into melted butter. Bibs, of course, are for sissies. But the sweet, succulent and salty flesh makes all the mess and effort worthwhile.

The Maine Lobster Festival

More lobster comes ashore at the venerable fishing port of Rockland than anywhere else on the Maine coast, and for more than six decades the haul has been celebrated here with the annual Maine Lobster Festival. It takes place from Wednesday to Sunday on the first full weekend of August and draws thousands of visitors. A colourful parade, led by King Neptune and the newly crowned Sea Goddess, is among the highlights. One of the most popular events is the "Great International William Atwood Lobster Crate Race". Contestants vie to avoid falling into the sea as they run across 50 partially submerged lobster crates. Whoever touches the most crates before taking the plunge wins. Lobster, of course, is served daily.

Left A glittering sunrise at Pemaquid Point lighthouse

The Best Places to Eat Lobster

Five Islands Lobster Co. moderate

This quintessential lobster pound offers the perfect synthesis of place and taste, serving classic lobster dinners and other seafood on one of Maine's prettiest harbours, ringed with five spruce-tufted islands. Dining is strictly alfresco, and diners must watch out for brazenly thieving gulls. Lobster is the mainstay. In addition to simply steamed crustaceans, the pound also prepares one of the tastiest lobster rolls on the coast. The kitchen picks the meat daily from steamed lobsters, blends it with just enough mayonnaise to hang together, and serves the lobster salad on a grilled soft bun. Since local lobstermen also haul up many Jonah crabs in their traps, the pound steams and picks their unusually sweet flesh to make crab rolls and crab cakes, which are usually served with a homemade tartare sauce full of chopped dill pickles and capers. Diners who prefer their seafood fried generally rate the restaurant's fried clams as among the best in Maine.

1447 Five Islands Rd, Georgetown, Maine; open 11:30am–8pm daily, mid-May–mid-Oct (may close at 7pm late in the season); www.fiveislandslobster.com

Also in Maine

Coastal Maine is rife with excellent lobster pounds. **Shaw's Fish & Lobster Wharf** in New Harbor *(+1 207 677 2200; moderate)* has the distinction of serving several local beers on draught. In Rockland, chef Melissa Kelly often uses lobster in elegant preparations at **Primo** on Main Street *(www.primorestaurant.com; expensive)*.

Also in New England

Boston chef Jasper White literally wrote the book on ways to cook lobster. His pan-roasted lobster with bourbon and herbs is served at **Jasper White's Summer Shack** on Dalton Street *(www.summershackrestaurant.com; moderate)*. The hot lobster roll – lobster meat reheated in butter and served on a grilled bun – is a speciality of coastal Connecticut. Some of the best are found at **Lobster Landing** in Clinton *(+1 860 669 2005; moderate)* and in Noank, at **Abbott's Lobster in the Rough** *(+1 860 536 7719; moderate)*.

In Quebec

Maine lobsters also frequent the waters of Quebec's Magdalen Islands, where the short season, from May to July, yields superb lobster, much of it shipped to Montreal and Quebec City. To enjoy it at the source, visit **Restaurant La Marée Haute** in Havre-Albert *(+1 418 937 2492; moderate)*, which serves a distinctively local cuisine that features marvellous lobster in season.

A Day in San Antonio

Many of San Antonio's sights lie within walking distance of each other in the city centre, including the Alamo, fashionable River Walk and the bustling Market Square. To the south of the centre, the atmospheric La Villita and King William historic districts are fun to stroll around.

MORNING Visit the **Alamo**, where frontier heroes including Jim Bowie and Davy Crockett were besieged for 13 days by the Mexican army in 1836 and gave their lives for Texan independence. Then make your way via the French-Gothic **San Fernando Cathedral** to Market Square and **El Mercado**, the vivid Mexican marketplace filled with colourful merchandise, crafts, jewellery and lilting mariachi music.

AFTERNOON Drive to the South Side, where four lovely colonial churches lie within the **San Antonio Missions National Historical Park**. On the way back, catch the sunset from the observation deck of the landmark **Tower of the Americas** in Hemisphere Park.

EVENING Stroll along the **River Walk**, where the twinkling lights of its many bars and restaurants make a romantic end to the day.

Essentials

GETTING THERE
San Antonio International Airport is 11 km (7 miles) north of downtown; **shuttles**, a **bus** service and **taxis** run into the city centre. Once there, downtown can be **walked** though a **hire car** is useful for exploring further afield.

WHERE TO STAY
Bonner Garden (inexpensive) is an award-winning B&B in the Monte Vista Historic District. *www.bonnergarden.com*
Crockett Hotel (moderate), a historic building, is just steps from the Alamo and has a friendly atmosphere. *www.crocketthotel.com*
Omni La Mansion del Rio (expensive) is an historic gem offering rustic-style luxury. *www.omnihotels.com*

TOURIST INFORMATION
317 Alamo Plaza; *www.visitsanantonio.com*

Right Chunks of prime beef, not mince, are used in an authentic chilli, with soft beans tempering the fire of the spice

Below An evening river cruise is a perfect way to experience the music, colour and lights of the River Walk

SAN ANTONIO USA

On the Texas Chilli Trail

Street lights cast shadows over the dusky, silent buildings on San Antonio's Military Plaza. It's a far cry from the nights of yore, when this was one of the rowdiest places in Texas. Trail-hardened cowboys rode in from the range and headed straight for the Plaza, where the "Chilli Queens" lit mesquite fires, hung bright lanterns and dished out fiery, ten-cent "bowls o' red" all night long.

Though San Antonio is now one of America's largest cities, its Mexican character and laid-back pace linger at its core. Colonial buildings such as the adobe Spanish Governors' Palace and San Fernando Cathedral resonate with history, and four of its beautiful 18th-century Spanish missions are still active places of worship. The fifth is better known as the Alamo, site of the heroic battle in 1836 for Texan independence. For modern contrast, San Antonio has the delightful downtown River Walk, lined with bustling restaurants, cafés and entertainment, but with quiet stretches too that let you enjoy the city's natural beauty. There are also fine art museums and lovely parks and gardens.

Chilli is the official state dish of Texas, and San Antonio is the city where it was probably invented. Texas chilli remains in a class of its own: the hottest you'll find anywhere, scorching the taste buds, stinging the sinuses and sending chilli-lovers into a state of bliss. In 1828, Houstonian diarist J C Clopper became the first person to describe it, writing of seeing poor families stewing a little meat into "a kind of hash with nearly as many peppers as pieces of meat". This blending of spicy peppers from Mexico with the pioneer love of beef made chilli the earliest Tex-Mex dish. Chilli became a trail food for Texas cowboys, who hammered dried beef, peppers, suet and spices into bricks that could be boiled into stew. While preachers decried the "soup of the Devil, hot as hell's brimstone", writers such as O Henry immortalized the "Chilli Queens", formidable Mexican women who served chilli from their wagons on San Antonio's central Military Plaza. When the "San Antonio Chili Stand" opened at the Chicago World Fair in 1893, chilli went national. By the 1930s, almost every town had a chilli parlour.

When the ornate City Hall was built on Military Plaza, San Antonio's street life moved to nearby Market Square, today lined with the colourful shops and Mexican restaurants of El Mercado. During the many Hispanic festivals held in the square, the Chilli Queens return, and the mouthwatering, piquant aroma of Texas chilli wafts through the heart of San Antonio once more.

True "Texas Red" Chilli

The term *chili con carne* (with meat) is superfluous here, for meat is the key ingredient – usually beef, but anything from bison to armadillo has been known to go into the pot. For real connoisseurs, beans are a travesty, and even tomatoes don't feature in the original dish. In Texas, the Chili Appreciation Society International (CASI) sets the rules for cooking true Texas red. Their biggest event is the World Chili Championship, held east of San Antonio in tiny Terlingua. On the first weekend of November, over 10,000 chilli-hounds flock to this dusty ghost town. Country music plays, barbecues sizzle and beer flows freely from coolers perched on groaning tailgates. Competition is intense, but the cooks and judges take the heat while a good time is had by all. Get yerself a pickup truck and come on down!

Above The Alamo, scene of past conflict but also fierce Texan pride

The Best Places to Eat Chilli

Casa Rio moderate

Casa Rio has been serving food down by the river since 1946 and still sticks to its tried-and-tested recipes. It was the very first business down on the waterfront, and the boats and canoes that would arrive here, bringing hungry diners, helped build up the area to the River Walk that exists today. Colourful umbrellas shelter tables that are right by the water alongside one of the bridges, making it one of the prettiest dining spots around. Casa Rio serves the whole range of Mexican dishes, with starters including a tortilla soup, nachos, *flautas* (wheat-flour tortillas), and a *chili con queso* (with cheese). There's a range of chilli options as main dishes, but if you only eat here once you must have the Regular Plate of chilli with Mexican rice and refried beans, which has been on the menu since opening day in 1946. If you get a second shot, then the slightly grander Deluxe Dinner is the local favourite.

430 E. Commerce Street; open 11am–11pm daily; www.casa-rio.com

Also in San Antonio

Although San Antonio is regarded as the birthplace of chilli, it can be surprisingly hard to find it on restaurant menus, perhaps because it's so strongly associated here with family recipes and festive gatherings. The best place to eat it is in just such an environment, so look for street fairs, festivals and chilli cook offs going on around – and at weekends outside – the city, which are usually open to everyone.

Also in Texas

The **Texas Chili Parlor** (*www.txchiliparlor. com; inexpensive*) only opened in Austin in 1976 but it seems like it's been there forever. It's a popular student and sports bar that has a great chilli section on its menu. You can choose from mild, spicy or hot-hot-hot, have a chilli taster of three different bowls of their best recipes, or try a white chilli made with pork or even a vegetarian chilli. In Grapevine, near Dallas, **Tolbert's** (*www.tolbertsrestaurant. com; moderate*) on Main Street has won all kinds of awards and accolades for its chillis. Founded in 1976 by Texan journalist Frank X Tolbert Sr, it's a lively place with music several days a week and a menu that includes their own Original Texas Red chilli, and a chilli pie too.

Around the World

You can get your chilli fix in London at **Automat**, a chic little American brasserie in the heart of Mayfair (*www.automat-london.com; expensive*). Their *chili con carne*, served as a starter or main course, is made only with premium Nebraskan corn-fed beef.

NEW YORK USA

Deli Delights in Manhattan

If imitation is a form of flattery, then New York's delis receive the highest praise. Even outside New York, many delis add "New York-style" to their name to evoke their rich history, classic ingredients and gargantuan portions. New York's vibrant immigrant heritage, from Jewish to Italian to German, produced the USA's most popular deli cuisines, and today, it's hard to imagine one without the other.

New York's impressive immigrant history is best experienced in Lower Manhattan. Historically, the Lower East Side was the essence of the American "melting pot", with newcomers settling here from around the globe. In the late 1800s, this was one of the most densely populated neighbourhoods in the world, with over half a million Jewish arrivals, followed by working-class Chinese and Puerto Ricans. Its story is told in the superb Ellis Island Immigration Museum, brought to life via historical photographs and voice recordings.

On the Lower East Side, you'll come across vestiges of "old New York" around every corner: the elegant, 1887 Eldridge Street synagogue; the well-known Tenement Museum depicting immigrant life; and perhaps most importantly, a still-lively Jewish food culture, from delicatessens to pickle purveyors. New York's deli history can also be traced back to the Italian immigrants who arrived in droves from 1850 to 1930. Little Italy in Lower Manhattan and, even better,

Arthur Avenue in the Bronx are studded with old-time Italian family delis filled with fat-streaked prosciutto, marinated artichokes and tangy balsamic vinegar. German immigrants also made their mark on New York's deli history. For a taste of Bavaria, explore Yorkville on Manhattan's Upper East Side: the only area left in Manhattan that exhibits the city's German immigrant history, it is home to a couple of hearty delicatessens that peddle wursts of all kinds.

For all its colourful past, these days the Lower East Side seems to define gentrification, with trendy cocktail lounges and sleek boutiques. This is all the more reason to be impressed by the staying power of the deli tradition, which may have its roots in Lower Manhattan, but has since come to symbolize New York cuisine. Hot corned beef slathered with mustard; ruby-red slices of pastrami towering on rye; warm bagels smeared with cream cheese... peruse the menus of New York's quintessential delis, and you'll understand what inspired the classic image of a Jewish grandmother urging you to "eat, eat!".

Three Days in Manhattan

This is one of the top US destinations for visitors, with its world-class museums, iconic skyscrapers, great shopping and lively nightlife.

DAY ONE Start the day with a waterfront walk around the southern tip of Manhattan, from the lively **South Street Seaport** to lush **Battery Park**, where you can catch a boat to visit the **Statue of Liberty** and **Ellis Island**. Afterwards, explore the boutiques and cafés of the **West Village**, and then groove to a jazz show at the famous **Blue Note Jazz Club**.

DAY TWO Immerse yourself in the superb **Museum of Modern Art** (MoMA), which offers a double draw: the world's largest collection of modern art, and a building that's a work of art in itself. Keep an eye out for superstar paintings, from Picasso's *Les Demoiselles d'Avignon* to Vincent van Gogh's *The Starry Night*. A couple of blocks away is the legendary **Radio City Music Hall**; take the Stage Door tour, or check at the box office for evening show tickets.

DAY THREE Explore the lovely **High Line park** in the **Meatpacking District**, with views of the breezy Hudson River. In the afternoon, head north to the **American Museum of Natural History**, which is filled with fossils, skeletons and life-sized models of elephants and dinosaurs.

Essentials

GETTING THERE
New York City is served by three **airports**: JFK and LaGuardia (both in Queens), and Newark (in New Jersey), with **subway** and **shuttle** links to the city. The easiest way to get around Manhattan is by subway and on **foot**.

WHERE TO STAY
The Pod (inexpensive) has mod, thrifty rooms in Midtown. *www.thepodhotel.com*
The Mayfair (moderate) offers mid-range boutique comfort in the Theater District. *www.mayfairnewyork.com*
60 Thompson (expensive) in the SoHo district is elegant yet endearing. *www.60thompson.com*

TOURIST INFORMATION
Times Square Visitor Center, 1560 Broadway; *www.nycvisit.com*

Left The Statue of Liberty, first sight of the United States for generations of European immigrants

Above Classic pastrami sandwiches on the zinc countertop at world-famous Katz's *(see overleaf)*

Below Founded by Russian emigré Max Asnas in 1937, celebrity hangout The Stage is a Broadway landmark

Deli Food Around the World

Delicatessens flourish around the world from New York to Bologna, offering an authentic glimpse into the flavours and ingredients of a country's cuisine. The wonderfully varied choices include bagels heaped with cream cheese in New York; paper-thin slices of pastrami in Montreal; springy rounds of mozzarella in Italy and pickled herring in Denmark.

NEW YORK CITY

2nd Avenue Deli inexpensive

162 East 33rd St; www.2ndavedeli.com

Fill up on triple-decker sandwiches of peppery pastrami and grilled salami with lashings of Russian dressing; mushroom-and-barley soup; broiled chicken livers; and potato pancakes sweetened with warm apple sauce. This time-worn deli may have moved from Second Avenue, but it still offers the same quintessential deli fare, giant portions and no-nonsense service.

Katz's Deli moderate

205 East Houston St; www.katzdeli.com

There are sandwiches, and then there are sandwiches. For the latter, make for Katz's Deli, the renowned Jewish deli established in 1888 on the Lower East Side. Here, pastrami comes towering on rye, and giant, steaming *knoblewurst* (garlic beef sausage) dwarfs the bread it sits on. For dessert, try an egg cream, a uniquely New York concoction of milk, chocolate syrup and carbonated water.

Russ & Daughters moderate

179 East Houston St; www.russanddaughters.com

This shrine to smoked fish dates back to 1914 when Joel Russ began selling salt-cured herring and salmon. Since then, Russ & Daughters has continued to satiate the smoked-fish cravings of New Yorkers with curried herring, smoked Danish salmon and one of the finest caviar selections in Manhattan, from Siberian Osetra to salmon roe.

Eataly expensive

200 Fifth Avenue; www.eatalyny.com

This temple to Italian cuisine, with marble-topped bars and high ceilings, showcases a superb array of Italian specialities: fat-streaked prosciutto from Parma; crumbly *reggiano* Parmesan from Emilia-Romagna; Rome-style pizzas bubbling with mozzarella and pepperoni; and Chianti and Brunello wines from Tuscany. In short: you can skip the trip to Italy – Eataly pretty much has it all.

LOS ANGELES, USA

Los Angeles, with its rich Jewish heritage, features a broad array of historic delis that serve all the traditional favourites, from matzo ball soup, brisket and corned beef to smoked fish, chopped liver and blueberry blintzes.

Factor's Famous Deli inexpensive

9420 West Pico Blvd; www.factorsdeli.com

Slip into a roomy booth at this legendary deli, on Pico Boulevard since 1948, and fill up on rich deli specialities, including hot peppered beef, smoked liverwurst and whitefish salad.

Nate and Al's inexpensive

414 North Beverly Drive; www.natenal.com

Nate and Al's claims to be a "deli with heart" – and chances are you'll agree. It's lively and inviting, and serves home-made specials that might rival those of a Jewish grandmother. Try chicken noodle soup, corned beef and cabbage and bursting frankfurters.

Canter's moderate

419 N Fairfax Ave; www.cantersdeli.com

This historic Jewish deli, long a favourite with the show-business crowd, serves up hearty fare, including matzo ball soup, *challah* (braided bread) and brisket.

Langer's moderate

704 South Alvarado; www.langersdeli.com

Deli-lovers from all over LA make a pilgrimage to Langer's for its famous pastrami sandwich (No.19 on the menu), piled high with thick-cut pastrami and Swiss cheese and served with creamy coleslaw.

MONTREAL, CANADA

Montreal's delicatessens are famous for their smoked meats, often served between huge chunks of rye bread with pickles on the side. The city is also known for its tasty bagels, which Montrealers say are even better than in New York City. You be the judge.

Left (top to bottom) Grab an espresso and panini at New York's Eataly, or sit down for a leisurely Italian feast; deli food Danish-style; Schwartz's in Montreal, famed for its portion sizes

Below (top to bottom) Air-dried hams hang from the ceiling in every Italian neighbourhood grocery store; smoked meats and sausages take centre stage in Bavarian *Delikatessens*

Fairmount Bagel Bakery
inexpensive

74 ave Fairmount ouest; www.fairmountbagel.com

Sink your teeth into one of Fairmount's warm bagels, made with unbleached flour, hand-rolled and – here's the secret – baked in a wood-fired oven, and you'll understand why this is Montreal's best bagelry. There are more than 20 varieties to choose from.

Wilensky's Light Lunch
inexpensive

34 ave Fairmount ouest; +1 514 271 0247

The frozen-in-time decor is as much a draw as the delicious bologna sausage and salami at this deli, which hasn't changed since 1932 – and that includes the grill and drinks machine. The prices, happily, also seem stuck in the past.

Reuben's Deli moderate
1116 rue Ste-Catherine ouest; www.reubensdeli.com

Taste your way through an array of smoked meats at this amiable deli. For variety, Reuben's also serves juicy steaks, Greek salads and even cheesy lasagna. Enjoy a Canadian beer (or three) with your meal.

Schwartz's moderate
3895 boulevard St-Laurent; www.schwartzsdeli.com

This Montreal institution serves colossal smoked-meat sandwiches, with brusque service thrown in as part of the package. Be prepared to wait (and salivate) at the weekend, when the queue stretches out the door and along the pavement.

MUNICH, GERMANY

The word "delicatessen" is derived from the German, although in Germany, delis are more like speciality food halls – emporiums selling delicacies and fine food, from herb-scented sausages and caviar to exquisite tarts.

Feinkost Käfer moderate
Prinzregentenstrasse 73; www.feinkost-kaefer.de

Gourmands flock to this upmarket delicatessen, market and restaurant, which is filled with local and international delicacies, including over 350 types of cheeses, roast ham, smoked meats, walnut-studded bread and their justly famous raspberry tart.

Dallmayr expensive
Dienerstrasse 14–15; www.dallmayr.com

Enjoy everything from smoked sausages and caviar to rich coffees, fragrant teas and flaky pastries at this luxury delicatessen and restaurant that dates back to the 17th century.

BOLOGNA, ITALY

The region of Emilia-Romagna and its capital, Bologna, are celebrated for their rich culinary traditions *(see also pp146–7)*. Bologna's nickname is La Grassa ("the fat one"), and the city's delicatessens feature a bounty of cheeses, olives and especially cured pork meats, from prosciutto to salami to mortadella.

La Salumeria Bruno e Franco
inexpensive

Via Oberdan 16; www.la-salumeria.it

Widely considered one of Bologna's best delis, Bruno e Franco features traditional Italian fare, including superb olive oils, fresh and cured meats, Modena balsamic vinegar, the regional *reggiano* Parmesan cheese, jams and preserves, and also excellent seafood salads, from octopus to shrimp.

A.F. Tamburini moderate
Via Caprarie 1; www.tamburini.com

Ham haunches and fat salami hang from the ceiling and pungent cheeses fill the counter at this venerable delicatessen. Sit in the warm café where you can also order fresh tortellini topped with rich Bolognese sauce, which got its name from the city.

COPENHAGEN, DENMARK

In Copenhagen, traditional delicatessen fare is served in a variety of forms, perhaps most famously as the country's beloved open-face sandwiches, *smørrebrød (see also pp106–7)*, which are heaped with everything from tangy herring and capers to roast pork.

Hansens Gamle Familiehave
moderate

Pile Allé 10; www.hansenshave.dk

Dig in to splendid *smørrebrød* at this historic outdoor eatery (which has a sliding roof so that patrons can stay toasty in winter). Take your pick from thinly sliced roast beef on dark rye, herring topped with a quivering egg, smoked eel, meatballs and more. As for what to drink: Danish beer, of course.

Meyer's Deli moderate
Gammel Kongevej 107; www.meyersdeli.dk

This popular deli and restaurant is helmed by chef and gastronomic entrepreneur Claus Meyer, an enthusiastic proponent of locally sourced Nordic cuisine. Enjoy a wide range of deli fare, including organic bread from the instore bakery, grilled sausage with home-made ketchup and salami with fennel. If you're here at the weekend, don't miss the superb brunch.

SOUTHERN CALIFORNIA USA

Road Food in Southern California

The surf's up and the convertible top's down on Highway 101, southern California's famous coast road. Along with its cross-country counterpart, Route 66, it helped make the road trip a classic American experience. The endless miles soon became dotted with neon beacons, beckoning hungry, weary travellers into a pit stop that became a fast-food icon – the American diner.

Diners have their roots in the horse-drawn lunch wagons that set up on street corners in the late 1880s to feed hungry shift workers, newspapermen and theatre-goers, looking for food after the restaurants closed. They evolved into rolling restaurants with a few seats inside, known as "dining cars" and then simply "diners". By the late 1920s, companies – most famously O'Mahony's of New Jersey – were manufacturing prefabricated diners built to look like railroad dining cars, in Art Deco designs, which were then shipped to their locations. By the 1930s they had acquired all their trademark characteristics: gleaming stainless-steel bodies, shiny chrome counters with swivel stools, tile floors, Formica tables in deep leather booths and flashy jukeboxes full of dance records.

Today, as always, diners serve inexpensive home-made fare. Daily "blue-plate specials" might feature chicken and dumplings or Mom's meatloaf, with a hearty helping of potatoes and veg. All-day breakfasts range from sunny-side-up eggs and biscuits to whopper stacks of buttermilk pancakes with maple syrup. The soda fountain churns out thick, creamy chocolate malts and strawberry milk shakes to accompany juicy burgers, fries and chilli dogs hot off the grill. There's hot fudge sundae or a fat slice of banana cream pie topped with a tower of whipped cream to finish, and all the coffee you can drink.

By the 1950s there were over 6,000 diners across the country, and car culture came into its own. In the balmy nights of southern California, teenagers cruised "the strip" looking for fun (or trouble) and diners became drive-ins, where you placed your order over a speakerphone and ponytailed carhops brought it to your car, often on roller skates. Though the cars and hairstyles have changed, the fascination with the California lifestyle continues. Highway 101 has it all: the surfing hotspots of Oceanside and Huntingdon Beach, the swanky yachts of Newport Beach and the bright lights of Hollywood. And along the way, flashes of neon and gleaming steel that promise bottomless cups of coffee and home-made American pie.

Three Days in Southern California

Southern California offers a great range of sights, activities and environments. You can go from big, bustling theme parks to quiet coves, or small, exotic cactus gardens to huge wetland bird reserves and even old mission churches to modern art galleries, all within a couple of hours' drive of each other. December to March is whale-watching season, with excursion boats leaving from several locations. Whether you're a surfer, a beachcomber or a sunset-watcher, the coast is a highlight all year round.

DAY ONE Spend the day at **SeaWorld San Diego** for a close-up encounter with dolphins, sharks, sealions, penguins and other aquatic creatures. The impressive shows feature performances with dolphins and killer whales.

DAY TWO Visit **Mission San Luis Rey**, the largest of California's 18th-century Spanish missions, at Oceanside. Then head for Oceanside's **Buccaneer Beach** to watch the surfers. In the afternoon, browse the art galleries at **Laguna Beach**, or admire the yachts at **Newport Beach**.

DAY THREE Take a morning stroll along the pier at **Huntington Beach**, another top surf city. Then head into **Los Angeles** and don a pair of roller skates to watch the wilder characters on the boardwalk at **Venice Beach**.

Essentials

GETTING THERE
Fly into an **international airport** at either San Diego or Los Angeles and **rent a car** – this is absolutely essential for exploring.

WHERE TO STAY
The Dana (inexpensive) in Mission Bay is a short walk from SeaWorld and the beach. *www.thedana.com*
Casa Laguna Inn (moderate) in Laguna Beach has charming rooms with ocean views in a mission-style inn. *www.casalaguna.com*
Oceanside Marina Suites (expensive) has spacious rooms with balconies looking over the ocean or harbour. *www.omihotel.com*

TOURIST INFORMATION
California Welcome Center, 928 North Coast Highway, Oceanside; *www.californiawelcomecenter.org*

Left Generous helpings of pancakes, syrup and blueberries are a staple of California's diners

Above Large, comfortable cars and Art Deco-style diners are classic symbols of 1950s America

Below A road trip up the Pacific Coast leads through the magnificent scenery of Big Sur, California

Diners Around the World

Many American diners had closed by the 1970s, victims of the onslaught of fast-food chains. But nostalgia for the simpler postwar lifestyle and a love of '50s kitsch and Art Deco has sparked a new wave of retro-styled diners, in the USA, Europe and beyond.

SOUTHERN CALIFORNIA

101 Cafe inexpensive
631 South Coast Highway, Oceanside; www.101Cafe.net

Built in 1928, the 101 Cafe has gone from diner to drive-in and back again. Painted with bright murals and filled with Highway 101 memorabilia, it serves classic diner meals and sandwiches, from French toast or buttermilk pancakes with bacon to meatloaf or double cheeseburgers with fries. The peanut butter malt is to die for.

Mel's Diner moderate
8585 Sunset Blvd, West Hollywood; www.melsdrive-in.com

The original Mel's opened in 1947, and starred in the film *American Graffiti*, forming the backdrop for teenagers "cruising the strip" in California in 1962. Unfortunately it was demolished shortly after shooting, but this second-generation diner – opened by the original owner's son – has recreated all the best bits, and has an outdoor patio where you can enjoy burgers and diner dinners under the neon lights.

The Nickel Diner moderate
524 South Main Street, Los Angeles; www.nickeldiner.com

Located in an old vaudeville theatre in the newly-gentrified area around Skid Row, the Nickel Diner plays with the classic diner repertoire to create some truly exceptional dishes: try the Big Time Cheddar, maple bacon doughnuts and the red velvet cake.

Ruby's Diner moderate
1128 W Lincoln Ave, Anaheim; www.rubys.com

Nab one of the carhop spaces here and you'll get your chilli fries served on roller skates. Vintage decor and a great menu make it a blast from the past. Also at Laguna Beach, Huntington Beach and other locations around the USA.

REST OF THE USA

From homey neighbourhood hang-outs to slick retro-style restaurants, everyone in America has a favourite diner. Those listed below stand out for their history – some are original O'Mahony pre-war models – and their decor, atmosphere and authenticity, as well as their delicious diner fare.

66 Diner inexpensive
1405 Central Ave NE, Albuquerque, New Mexico; www.66diner.com

Located right on historic Route 66, this fabulous diner has turquoise booths and golden oldies playing on the jukebox, and serves deluxe plates, blue-plate specials and thick, creamy milk shakes from behind its shiny chrome and tiled counter.

Mickey's Dining Car inexpensive
36 West 7th St, St Paul, Minnesota; www.mickeysdiningcar.com

Fresh farm eggs, hand-shredded hash browns, spindle-blended milk shakes and tasty family recipes have been served in this authentic O'Mahony diner since 1939. It's now considered so precious that it's listed on the National Register of Historic Places.

Summit Diner inexpensive
1 Union Place, Summit, New Jersey; +1 908 277 3256

Appropriately located opposite the railway station, this 1938 Art Deco chrome beauty is another of the few remaining O'Mahony diners in the USA. Enjoy Taylor ham (pork roll) and eggs with hash browns at the marble counter or in a red-leather booth.

Ed Debevic's moderate
640 N Wells St, Chicago, Illinois; www.eddebevics.com
Rude waitresses in beehive hair-dos and horn-rimmed glasses who dance on the counter to '50s hits are all part of the experience at this fun, retro diner. Great shakes and burgers.

Rosie's Diner moderate
4500 14 Mile Rd NE, Rockford, Michigan; www.rosiesdiner.com

A long menu of home-cooked favourites, from their signature slow-roasted beef and noodles to sloppy-joe sandwiches and blue-plate specials, are served in this authentic 1946 diner.

Left (top to bottom) A classic diner snack – French fries and a strawberry milk shake; a typical US diner in San Francisco; syrup and butter over waffles, with fresh fruit on the side

Below (top to bottom) Red Formica tables, chequer-patterned plates and jukeboxes help create the retro-diner look; Ed's Easy Diner, in Soho, London is a haven for exhausted shoppers

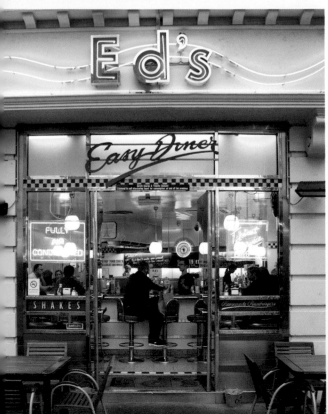

ENGLAND

It's not surprising that London, with its fashionable restaurants and love of quirky style, embraced the retro diner craze, but now shiny silver American-style diners are springing up along the country's A-roads too.

Ed's Easy Diner inexpensive
12 Moor St, London W1; www.edseasydiner.com

The all-day breakfast, juicy burgers and creamy shakes go down a treat at this colourful diner with a prime corner spot in Soho. Chilli addicts will love the "atomic" American fries and onion rings. Grab a red swivel chair at the shiny chrome counter.

Good Life Diner inexpensive
128–130 Curtain Rd, Shoreditch, London EC2; www.goodlifediner.com

Leather booths, lots of neon and a '50s soundtrack form the backdrop to the burgers at this trendy American diner, which has four other London locations, in Camden, Islington, Soho and Kensal Rise.

The 50s American Diner moderate
John St, Church Gresley, Derbyshire; www.the50samericandiner.bravehost.com

Burgers, steaks and hot diggity dogs are served in this authentic, gleaming steel O'Mahony diner, shipped over from Boston to the National Forest in Derbyshire and filled with '50s memorabilia. Friendly waitresses wear vintage dresses to serve up food in four-seater booths and the jukebox plays rock 'n' roll.

IRELAND

With their long connections to America, it's no wonder that the fun-loving Irish have taken classic American burgers, shakes and diner dishes along with 1950s nostalgia into their hearts, and opened some great diners.

Eddie Rocket's inexpensive
7 South Anne St, Dublin; www.eddierockets.ie

Proper fresh-ground burgers, foot-long hot dogs, red basket specials and hand-dipped Shake Shop malts come with a huge helping of '50s attitude. There are 20 Eddie Rocket's diners in greater Dublin and more around the country.

Springsteen's Diner moderate
633 Lisburn Rd, Belfast; www.springsteensdiner.com

With its flashy neon jukebox, all-day breakfasts, Whitehouse burgers (named after US presidents) and big menu of American favourites, this characterful diner could have been born in the USA.

REST OF EUROPE

Retro diners have crossed over to the Continent too. Paris may be the preserve of French culture and cuisine, but even here the stylish appeal of old-style American diners flourishes on the Left Bank.

Breakfast in America inexpensive
17 rue des Ecoles, Paris, France; www.breakfast-in-america.com

An ex-pat American filmmaker, longing for a stack of pancakes and a "bottomless mug o' Joe" (coffee), opened this popular diner serving tasty all-day breakfasts, burgers and blue *plat du jour*.

Happy Days Diner inexpensive
25 rue Francisque Gay, Paris, France; www.happydaysdiner.com

Enjoy mega-burgers, Long Island bagels, milk shakes and more along with rockabilly music and a '50s ambience at this cheery diner sporting turquoise booths and pastel-pink countertops.

Flamme und Feuer moderate
Klein Breitenbach 2, Mörlenbach, near Mannheim, Germany; www.flammeundfeuer.de

Flamme und Feuer ("Flame and Fire") has a long American menu, but it's the all-you-can-eat burger and spare-rib nights and breakfast buffets that draw the Harley- and classic car-loving crowds.

AUSTRALIA

American diners seem completely at home in the land of road trains and beach barbies, especially in the cities, where the 1950s memorabilia, rock 'n roll music and diner fare add up to a really fun place to meet.

Big Rig Diner moderate
231 Oxford St, Darlinghurst, New South Wales; + 61 2 9332 3197

Tasty burgers, home-made chilli and other American favourites come with a big dollop of '50s style amid Elvis posters and great music on the jukebox. Check out the Houndstooth Bar at the back.

Misty's Diner moderate–expensive
103–105 High St, Prahran, Victoria; www.mistysdiner.com.au

Owner Misty hales from Phoenix, Arizona, and her Aussie diner serves fare with a Southern flair, from deep-fried pickles and corn dogs to a bucket of pork ribs or "trailer-trash" fried steak. Misty's motto: "Bring your appetite, it's gonna get messy".

A Day in Macon

This moderately sized city is perfect for strolling, whether admiring the cherry blossom, nibbling on peaches and pecans from the State Farmer's Market, or building up an appetite for the next meal.

MORNING Explore the ancient Indian mounds at the **Ocmulgee National Monument**, with structures and exhibits telling the story of 10,000 years of Southeastern Native American habitation and the distinctive Mississippian culture.

AFTERNOON Visit the **Tubman African American Museum** with its art, artifacts, cultural exhibits and a huge mural depicting the journey from Africa to America. Cross the road to the exhibits of music and memorabilia in the **Georgia Music Hall of Fame**, then wander down to the river where a statue of Otis Redding gleams in the sun.

EVENING Take the self-guided Lights on Macon walking tour of the **Historic District** to see grand antebellum houses, such as magnificent Hay House ("Palace of the South"), and the pretty Lee Alumni House, with its archetypal southern verandas, lit up in all their glory.

Essentials

GETTING THERE
The closest **international airport** is Hartsfield-Jackson Atlanta, 130 km (80 miles) away. There are some commuter flights to **Middle Georgia Regional Airport**, 16 km (10 miles) from Macon. Hiring a **car** is recommended.

WHERE TO STAY
Ramada Plaza (inexpensive) has a pool and is a short walk from the Georgia Music Hall of Fame. *www.ramada.com*
Marriott Macon City Center (moderate) is conveniently located for the downtown historic sites. *www.marriott.com/mcnfs*
1842 Inn (expensive) has romantic rooms in an antebellum mansion. *www.1842inn.com*

TOURIST INFORMATION
Downtown Visitors Center, 450 Martin Luther King, Jr Blvd; *www.maconga.org*

Right Crispy southern-fried chicken uses crushed crackers or even cornflakes for the crunchy coating

Below The thousands of Yoshino cherry trees that line Macon's streets are a froth of white blossom in March

MACON USA

Soul Food in the Deep South

America's Deep South is known for soul music and soul food, and Macon, Georgia, is the place to get a taste of both. Famous in spring for the blossom on the 300,000 cherry trees that line its streets, it's also a city rich in southern and, in particular, African-American heritage. It's a pretty town to explore, and full of places to enjoy old-fashioned home-cooking and hospitality.

 While the term "soul food" denotes a heartwarming style of down-home African-American cooking, it has its roots in sadder days of slavery on southern plantations. African staples such as rice, sorghum, black-eyed peas and okra were brought across the Atlantic on slave ships. Slaves supplemented their meagre diet with greens disdained by their masters: collards, kale and turnip tops. They adopted maize, an ancient staple crop of southern Native Americans, to make sweet cornbread and grits, a coarse porridge. Poor households made do with the cheapest cuts of meat, and nothing was wasted.

The term "soul food" came into use in the 1960s, by southerners both black and white who had migrated north and missed the regional cooking they grew up with. It has evolved into more nourishing, tastier menus of tender baked ham, fried chicken and pork chops, beef stew and barbecue ribs, side dishes of okra, collards, squash or black-eyed peas, and desserts such as sweet bread pudding or potato pie. Greens are cooked with smoked or salted meats, diced onions, vinegar and seasonings in tasty broths and even lowly grits have made it on to fashionable menus today, often mixed with cheese in the manner of Italian polenta.

Deep in the heart of Georgia, Macon is a good place to discover both soul food and southern culture. Its roots go back thousands of years to the ancient Native Americans who built ceremonial mounds here. The city was founded in 1823 and prospered as a market hub for surrounding farms and cotton plantations. Handsome antebellum mansions and Victorian homes grace its historic neighbourhoods. Sites like the Tubman museum and Douglass Theatre pay tribute to Macon's strong African-American heritage.

Macon has a great music legacy as a cradle of soul and southern rock. The Georgia Music Hall of Fame pays tribute to local boys Little Richard and Otis Redding, and others who launched their careers here. Later, Mama Louise's soul food *(see panel, right)* kept the Allman Brothers Band going when they were still struggling musicians. In Macon, a little soul food and music is all the southern comfort you need.

Macon Festivals

Macon hosts several lively festivals throughout the year. Among the highlights are:
International Cherry Blossom Festival The town is painted pink for this 10-day festival, held in mid-March when the blossom is at its peak. It features concerts, events, exhibitions, food fairs, parades and hot-air balloons.
Tubman Pan Africa Festival African music and dancers, Caribbean steel bands, masquerades and cultural demonstrations foster peace, love, hope and unity at this April celebration.
Georgia State Fair Also in April, the oldest state fair in the Southeast offers amusement park rides, agricultural exhibits and entertainment.
Ocmulgee Indian Celebration Indian nations of the Southeast gather at the Ocmulgee Monument in September to celebrate their heritage through storytelling, dancing, music and art.

Above A thousand-year-old earth lodge of the Mississippi Native Indian culture

The Best Places to Eat Soul Food

H & H Restaurant inexpensive

Soul food and music go hand in hand at H & H Restaurant in downtown Macon. It was founded in 1959 by the late Inez Hill and her goddaughter and cousin, Louise Hudson, and "Mama Louise" is still cooking up a storm and welcoming customers with her warm smile. The restaurant is situated in an unassuming red-brick building with a small sign. Inside are simple tables with red-checked tablecloths, and walls covered with autographed photos of the Allman Brothers. Mama Louise fed the penniless band in their early days in Macon, and when they became famous they took her on tour with them. Otis Redding and other Macon musicians also feature on the jukebox.

The "meat-and-three" menu, which changes daily, offers main dishes such as fried chicken, roast beef, fried fish or baked ham, accompanied by collard greens, okra, black-eyed peas, corn and green beans. Leave room for the potato pie and other desserts. Breakfast is also served, with grits, of course, and homemade "biscuits" – like a British teatime scone, but designed to be dunked in gravy, any time of day.
807 Forsyth St, Macon; open 6:30am–4pm Mon–Sat; http://mamalouise.com

Also in Macon

Jeneane's at Pinebrook *(www.jeneanes.com; inexpensive)* is another Macon restaurant where you can choose from a daily menu of tasty meats, fish and soul-food side dishes: greens and creamed corn, rutabaga (swede), mashed potato and gravy and cheese grits. The pecan and chocolate pies are highly rated.

Also in the South

Mama Dip's Kitchen in Chapel Hill, North Carolina *(www.mamadips.com; inexpensive)*, features traditional country cooking in a pleasant, airy dining room with a wrap-around porch. House specialities include chicken-fried steak, pan-fried pork chops smothered in gravy and chicken and dumplings. **Swett's** *(www. swettsrestaurant.com; inexpensive)* in Nashville, Tennessee, is for anyone who loves southern cooking. Family-owned since 1954, it may feature pig's feet or pork shoulder alongside such daily favourites as fried chicken, meatloaf, turnip greens and fried cornbread.

In New York

Located in New York's Harlem, **Sylvia's** *(www.sylviasrestaurant.com; moderate)* is one of the most famous soul food restaurants in America, run by fabled southern matriarch Sylvia Woods and her family. Main dishes include Southern classics like smothered chicken and pork chops, oxtail, gumbo, chitterlings, fried catfish and short beef ribs. The Sunday Gospel lunch with live music is legendary.

Above An adobe building decorated Southwestern style with a turquoise-mosaic steer skull and *ristras* – bunches of dried chillies

Above Fiery red salsa is often served with blue corn tortilla chips, made from a variety of maize that is unique to New Mexico

A Day in Santa Fe

Santa Fe is brimming with art and history, and its world-class galleries form the second-largest art market in the country (after New York). It has a feast of striking architecture and several fascinating museums.

MORNING Start at the Plaza to browse the **Indian Market** outside the Palace of the Governors, then step inside to visit the **New Mexico History Museum**. For more art, choose from the nearby **Fine Arts Museum** and the **Georgia O'Keeffe Museum**, then stroll along the **Old Santa Fe Trail** to see the miraculous staircase in **Loretto Chapel** and the 17th-century **San Miguel** mission chapel.

AFTERNOON Go gallery-hopping along **Canyon Road**, or head to **Museum Hill** to visit the outstanding **Museum of International Folk Art** and the **Museum of Indian Arts and Culture**.

EVENING Return to the Plaza for souvenir shopping and admire the façade of **St Francis Cathedral** glowing in the setting sun. Take a patio table at one of the lively restaurant bars and relax with a margarita before dinner, soaking up the Southwestern atmosphere.

Essentials

GETTING THERE
Santa Fe is in New Mexico, USA. There is limited commercial service to **Santa Fe Municipal Airport**, so most visitors fly to **Albuquerque International Sunport** and make the hour's drive to Santa Fe by **rental car** or **shuttle service**.

WHERE TO STAY
Santa Fe Sage Inn (inexpensive) has small but comfortable rooms in an adobe motel near downtown. www.santafesageinn.com
Hotel Santa Fe (moderate) is Native American-owned and features beautiful artworks. www.hotelsantafe.com
Inn on the Alameda (expensive) has stylish adobe buildings and *casitas* (little houses). www.innonthealameda.com

TOURIST INFORMATION
201 W Marcy Street; www.santafe.org

SANTA FE USA

Fiery Chillies in Santa Fe

In the soft, clear light of a Santa Fe morning, Native American artisans spread their jewellery-laden blankets before the Palace of the Governors, built by Spanish settlers 400 years ago, while Anglo-American tourists stroll in the plaza below. This mix of cultures has given the city some wondrous arts and architecture, and a cuisine that calls on over 100 varieties of chilli pepper.

Set high against the backdrop of the Sangre de Cristo mountains, Santa Fe is the capital of New Mexico, the oldest state capital in North America, established when Spanish conquistadors from Mexico founded a colony here in 1610. Its mix of cultural history and contemporary Southwestern style offers plenty for everyone to explore. At its heart lies the Plaza, lined on three sides by storefronts – a shopper's delight for Southwestern clothes, jewellery, arts and crafts. The surrounding streets are as likely to lead to the earthy curves of old adobe houses as they are to hotels and public buildings sporting Spanish Colonial or Pueblo Revival styles, their soft pink and beige façades gleaming against a brilliant blue sky.

Old mission churches, sanctuaries and a magnificent cathedral evoke the city's colonial roots. There are excellent museums highlighting Native American traditions, culture and contemporary arts, and a wealth of fine arts galleries and museums. Artists have long come to northern New Mexico for its clear light and spectacular hues. But in the restaurants of Santa Fe, only two colours matter: red and green, the colours of piquant chilli peppers.

The local foods of the Native Americans have always used corn, beans, and above all, chilli peppers, and these form the basis of the cuisine of New Mexico. It's the spicy chilli that sets these dishes apart from Mexican cuisine found elsewhere in the USA. Instead of the standard tomato-based salsas, here you'll find fresh sauces of puréed green chilli or ground dried red chilli, lightly seasoned with garlic, salt or herbs to let the smoky, pungent flavours of the chillies shine through. Great with burritos or enchiladas, you can try both the red and green salsas by asking for "Christmas".

As well as forming the base for the zesty sauces of burritos, enchiladas and meat entrées, chillies are also used in mouthwatering dishes such as crispy deep-fried *chile rellenos* (stuffed chillies) and *carne adovada* (marinated pork). Other exotic local ingredients, such as blue corn, *nopales* (prickly pear cactus) and *chayote* (vegetable pear), also tickle the taste buds; Southwestern cuisine offers plenty for everyone to explore.

Above *Luminarias* light up the 300-year-old adobe buildings in Santa Fe

Cookery Classes

Whether you want to roast a green chilli or stuff one for a *chile relleno*, the **Santa Fe School of Cooking** (www.santafeschoolofcooking.com) is the best place to learn the secrets of New Mexican cuisine. Courses at this internationally renowned culinary academy are taught by some of the city's best chefs, but are geared towards recreational cooks as well as budding professionals. Courses range from morning or afternoon classes on a single topic or dish to the three-day **Southwest Culinary Boot Camp**, which covers everything from the history of the region's foods to in-depth cooking techniques. Demonstration and hands-on classes are on offer. There are also classes on New Mexican cheeses and wines, as well as restaurant walking tours. Participants can stock up on regional ingredients at the adjoining market.

The Best Places to Eat New Mexico Cuisine

The Shed moderate

Some of the best New Mexico cuisine in Santa Fe comes with loads of atmosphere at The Shed. Just east of the Plaza, a wooden gateway leads to a sunny, flower-filled patio and the old adobe hacienda, which dates from 1692. Its nine cosy, adjoining rooms are charmingly decorated with folk art, its niches and doorways are brightly painted, and there is alfresco dining on the patio in summer.

Family-owned for three generations, The Shed's menu features time-tested recipes such as the smoky-flavoured green chilli chicken enchiladas, and red chilli enchiladas topped with a fried egg, a local favourite. All of The Shed's chilli peppers are grown to order on local farms and ground daily in their own mill, making the food some of the freshest and tastiest around. It's also very spicy. Traditional entrées are served with blue corn tortillas, and may be accompanied by *posole* (a hominy stew), *calabacitas* (a squash dish) and pinto beans. Reservations are advised for dinner. The always-busy lunch time operates on a first-come, first-served basis.

113¹/₂ East Palace Avenue, Santa Fe; open 11am–2:30pm & 5:30–9pm Mon–Sat; www.sfshed.com

Also in Santa Fe

Several Santa Fe restaurants deserve a place on the "must try" list. **La Choza** *(+1 505 982 0909; inexpensive)*, The Shed's little sister near Railyard Park, is less busy, but serves the same great food. **Maria's New Mexican Kitchen** *(www.marias-santafe.com; moderate)* is famous for its margaritas but the menu is fantastic too; *carne adovada* (marinated pork) is a speciality here. **Tomasita's** *(+1 505 983 5721; moderate)* is another local favourite, with delicious *chile rellenos*.

Also in New Mexico

New Mexican food tends to be low to moderately priced, though dishes often feature in pricier Southwestern restaurants such as **Doc Martin's** in the historic **Taos Inn** *(www. taosinn.com; expensive)*, Taos. **Orlando's New Mexican Cafe** *(http://orlandostaos.com; inexpensive)*, also in Taos, serves superb dishes in hearty portions. In Albuquerque, head for the **Church Street Cafe** *(www.churchstreetcafe. com; moderate)* in the Old Town.

Around the World

It's hard to find authentic New Mexican cuisine outside the state of New Mexico, but **Little Anita's** *(www.littleanitas.com; moderate)* has several locations in Denver, USA. In Seattle, head for **Santa Fe Cafe** *(www.santafecafeseattle.com; moderate)* for blue corn tacos and chillies sourced from Hatch, New Mexico.

NEW ORLEANS USA

Jambalaya in the Big Easy

The mellow notes of a saxophone drift on the warm Gulf breeze through New Orleans' French Quarter, past elaborate wrought-iron balconies towards the jazz bars of Bourbon Street, mingling with the spicy scent of jambalaya wafting from restaurant windows. Welcome to the Big Easy – an extraordinary cultural and culinary melting pot where the good times roll.

New Orleans – nicknamed the Big Easy – is a sultry city that drawls its way through the daytime heat but snaps into life after dark, when the laughter, liquor and music flow in the bars of the French Quarter. Set along the Mississippi river, it is also a vibrant port, known around the world for its music and its exuberant Mardi Gras festival.

New Orleans is a city of districts, each with its own character. Uptown – home to two universities – has a young vibe, while the Warehouse District offers art lovers the Contemporary Arts Center and Ogden Museum of Southern Art. The Garden District, with its grand antebellum houses, was created by Americans after the 1803 Louisiana Purchase. Its sobriety is a stark contrast to the frenetic French Quarter, where you can see the city's historic Creole townhouses decked with ornate wrought-ironwork, visit antiques shops and enjoy plentiful entertainment.

At night, it's time to explore the city's musical heritage: New Orleans is the home of Dixieland jazz, but you'll also hear big band, jazz fusion, Delta blues, zydeco, funk and rock music bursting through the doorways on Bourbon Street in the French Quarter.

Jambalaya is the dish that perfectly embodies the city's history. Founded by the French in 1718, New Orleans remained culturally French through subsequent years of Spanish rule, and long after it became an American territory in 1803. The descendants of the French and Spanish settlers – the Creoles – lived alongside African slaves and Haitian refugees, as well as Cajuns: French-speaking exiles from Acadia (present-day Nova Scotia).

Acquiring its name from the Provençal word for "mixture", jambalaya was born in the French Quarter when Spanish settlers tried to re-create their favourite rice dish, paella, using ripe tomatoes instead of saffron. Caribbean spices such as cayenne enhanced the trinity of peppers, onions and celery cooked with chicken, peppery *andouille* sausage and fresh seafood. The result was Creole, or red, jambalaya. Cajun-style brown jambalaya is an earthier version of the dish that gains its colour from meat drippings browned in a cast-iron pot. It can contain such wild game foods as crawfish (crayfish), alligator, duck or venison. But whether juicy red or smoky brown, the best jambalaya is simmered slowly for an hour or more, allowing the rice to absorb the pungent blend of meat, seafood and spices that makes it so delicious. The result is a dish both hearty and exotic, much like New Orleans itself.

A Day in New Orleans

With its many museums, plentiful live music, the Audubon Zoo and Aquarium, New Orleans has plenty to offer visiting families, but it is best known as a party city, with festivals throughout the year. The partying reaches frenetic levels during Mardi Gras, or "Fat Tuesday" – a season of carnivals, parades and masked balls centred around the day before Ash Wednesday.

MORNING See the highlights of the **French Quarter**, including the **Presbytère** and **Cabildo**, **St Louis Cathedral**, the **French Market** and **Madame John's Legacy**. There are quirkier attractions too, such as **Lafitte's Blacksmith Shop** and the **Historic Voodoo Museum**.

AFTERNOON Head to the riverfront in the **Warehouse District** for Blaire Kern's **Mardi Gras World** at Kern Studios. It's the next-best way to experience New Orleans' biggest street party if you can't be there in person.

EVENING Return to the French Quarter and party the night away on **Bourbon Street**.

Essentials

GETTING THERE
Major airlines operate from **Louis Armstrong New Orleans International Airport**, 24 km (15 miles) west of the city.

WHERE TO STAY
Bon Maison Guest House (inexpensive) is a good budget choice at the quiet end of Bourbon Street. www.bonmaison.com
Claiborne Mansion (moderate) has an air of elegance. www.claibornemansion.com
Hotel Monteleone (expensive) is the pick of the French Quarter. www.hotelmonteleone.com

TOURIST INFORMATION
2020 St Charles Avenue; +1 800 672 6124

Above New Orleans hosts a renowned spring jazz festival, but live music energizes the city throughout the year

Left Tall, three-storey Creole houses, with shallow wrought-iron balconies, are typical of the French Quarter of New Orleans

Above Like its name, which fuses French and African influences, jambalaya brings together ingredients as diverse as seafood and game

What Else to Eat

Gumbo is the Creole answer to bouillabaisse and may be seasoned with *file*, a Native American spice made from dried, ground sassafras leaves and served over white rice. **Etouffée** is a thicker stew typically made of crawfish, though shrimp, crab or chicken can also be used, cooked in a roux with vegetables and spices. **Red beans and rice** is a typical New Orleans dish that may be served with grilled fish "blackened" with a coating of spices. **Po'boy** sandwiches of fried seafood or meat on foot-long baguettes are classic New Orleans street food, as are **beignets**, square doughnuts covered in powdered sugar.

The Best Places to Eat Jambalaya

K-Paul's Louisiana Kitchen
expensive

Chef Paul Prudhomme is a Louisiana legend, the first chef to make New Orleans food respectable to the modern gourmet diner. His Louisiana Kitchen is now a city landmark, and though the atmosphere is casual café-style, the food is upmarket, the quality superb and booking is essential. The restaurant building dates from 1834, with dining rooms on both floors, and alfresco tables in the atmospheric courtyard or on the balcony in season. Prudhomme uses only fresh ingredients, so the menu changes daily. Starters might include a cup of his chicken and *andouille* gumbo, made with his own *andouille* sausages; turtle soup, or his own inimitable version of Cajun jambalaya, simmered for hours in a rich stock with just the right amount of rice. The main-course temptations might feature another classic, crawfish *étouffée* – a stew simmered with the lid on, or "smothered" – or an aubergine pirogue (the name for a Cajun canoe) deep-fried and filled with Bay scallops, Louisiana shrimp and crawfish.

416 Chartres Street, French Quarter, New Orleans; open 11am–2pm Thu–Sat, 5:30pm–10pm Mon–Sat; www.kpauls.com

Also in New Orleans

You can sample the Creole version of jambalaya at **Mr B's Bistro** (*www.mrbsbistro.com; expensive*), where dishes like gumbo ya-ya, seafood gumbo and Gulf shrimp with grits offer more tastes of the Creole south. Come for the Sunday Jazz Brunch, when a jazz trio lends a festive air. **The Gumbo Shop** *(www. gumboshop.com; inexpensive)* offers an atmospheric taste of old New Orleans, from its faded decor to the long menu of Creole and Cajun favourites.

Also in the USA

For authentic New Orleans food and atmosphere in southern Florida, head to **Jambalaya Jeb's** *(http://jambalayajebs.com; inexpensive)* in Bonita Springs. This simple place in the Flamingo Island Flea Market is run by a family from Louisiana. They love the home-cooking they grew up with and make their jambalaya, gumbo and other dishes fresh each day and serve tasty New Orleans-style beignets.

Around the World

In the southern hemisphere, **South Restaurant** (*www.south-restaurant.com; moderate*) brings Creole cuisine to Sydney, Australia. Dishes include Creole jambalaya, gumbo, crawfish *étouffée* and the traditional New Orleans muffaletta sandwich – a round loaf filled with salami, cheese, ham and garlic, topped with an olive salad – which owes its origins to Sicilian immigrants to New Orleans.

Above Colourful *trajineras* (gondolas) offer a unique way to tour Xochimilco, an Aztec site just outside Mexico City

Above Soft tacos – tortillas stuffed with spicy meat, beans, fresh vegetables and jalapeño peppers – make a great picnic on the run

A Day in Mexico City

One day is precious little time in a city as large and interesting as Mexico City, but with careful planning and taco-fuelled stamina, it's surprising how much can be enjoyed and achieved.

MORNING Start the day in the cultural heart of the **Centro Historico**. In the huge main square (the **Zócalo**), take a guided tour of the ruined Aztec **Templo Mayor** and then drop into the **National Palace** to admire the Diego Rivera murals of revolutionary scenes.

AFTERNOON Take Line 2 of the metro as far south as it goes and change on to a Tren Ligero (light train) to explore the floating gardens of **Xochimilco**. It's best on a Sunday, when it's usually thronging with families and gaudily decorated barges. Join a punting trip and drift past lamb barbecues, mariachi musicians and endless stalls.

EVENING Begin with alfresco drinks in **Plaza Garibaldi**. Then choose between a top-flight restaurant or a simple eatery, before hopping into a taxi to **Zona Rosa** for late-night clubbing; or head for home, stopping off for *churros (see pp70–71)* and chocolate on the way.

Essentials

GETTING THERE
Benito Juarez **international airport** is 16 km (10 miles) east of the city, around 30 minutes by authorized **taxi** or the **metro** (Line 5). Get around the city on the excellent metro or use the iconic VW Beetle "bug" taxis.

WHERE TO STAY
Casa de la Condesa (inexpensive) is a modern, clean and comfortable hotel in Roma Norte. All rooms have kitchens. *www.casadelacondesa.net*
Hotel Casa Vieja (moderate) is a boutique gem in Polanco that offers luxurious suites and roof-terrace dining. *www.casavieja.com*
Condesa DF (expensive): minimalist design hotel in upmarket Condesa with a noted Japanese-fusion restaurant. *www.condesadf.com*

TOURIST INFORMATION
www.visitmexico.com

MEXICO CITY

MEXICO CITY MEXICO

Tackling the Taco in Mexico

Informal, exuberant, fast yet satisfying, tacos are perfectly in tune with Mexico City. It was the powerhouse of pre-Hispanic America and still burns brightly today, mixing ancient traditions with high-tech, urban sophistication. Whether you're in arty Roma, the *centro histórico* or well-heeled Polanco, pick your *taqueria* and enjoy a taco or two alongside the 25 million locals.

Without setting foot outside the massive metropolis of Mexico City, travellers can experience cultures nearly 700 years apart, all in the midst of teeming humanity, streaming traffic and – more often than not – the unmistakeable sound of an approaching mariachi band. Mexico's vast capital city is full of urban energy. Made up of a series of neighbourhoods, each has a very distinct character and many warrant exploration. It's almost impossible to miss the historic centre, which includes the huge Zócalo (the central square) and the ruins of the Aztec Templo Mayor (the Great Temple). The best hotels are found in the elegant Polanco district, which sits alongside the vast green space of Chapultepec Park, near the renowned Anthropology Museum. Just outside the city, the Pyramids of the Sun and the Moon rise up in ancient Teotihuacán.

In such heady surroundings, the tasty, speedy taco could have been invented with the regular and robust refuelling of Mexico City's overwhelmed visitors in mind. In fact, however, its origins may well date back as far as the Mayans and Aztecs. It makes use of that most traditional of Mexican foodstuffs – the corn tortilla – and the ubiquitous taco is a mainstay of the national diet. The name "taco" is a generic way to describe some kind of filling wrapped inside a tortilla, so it's essentially a Mexican-style sandwich. Many of the country's indigenous crops feature as fillings, such as chillies, tomatoes, avocados and beans, usually accompanied by some type of meat or fish.

Most common at lunch time, tacos make ideal late-night snacks too, with recipes and ingredients varying according to family traditions and regional influences. The *taco al pastor*, or shepherd-style taco, is a favourite; this usually contains pork, sliced directly and showily from the rotisserie into the tortilla, although it can also be made with chicken or shredded steak. Fishy versions commonly consist of grilled or fried fish or shrimps along with lettuce or cabbage. The trick is to pile two or three of your choice on to a gaudy plastic plate, then retire to the condiments counter for lime, onion, coriander and guacamole, topped off with fiery salsa. Roll, fold and devour – no cutlery required.

The Best Places to Eat Tacos

El Califa inexpensive

There are four El Califa *taquerias* in Mexico City, but the Condesa branch is the easiest to find and it buzzes with a healthy mix of visitors and locals. This canteen-style restaurant is sufficiently stark and industrial to feel "authentic", but the quality of its food and hygiene make it a perfect entry to the world of the *taqueria* – start here, and head for the street stalls when you and your palate are ready!

Vegetarians will struggle here, but carnivores can choose from various cuts of beef steak, rib or chop, and chicken or pork. El Califa's speciality is to serve the meat griddle-roasted and in whole pieces, rather than minced. Tortillas come to you fresh from the oven, liberally laden with melted Oaxaca cheese, golden from the grill. Choose an *al pastor* (pork in guajillo chilli salsa and grilled pineapple) and your marinated meat will be shaved off the spit in front of you. The *gaonera* (a slice of tender beef fillet with raw tomatillo sauce in a thick, handmade tortilla) is delicious. Take care when ordering from the salsa menu – they're all hot, despite what the menu says.

Altata 22, Condesa; open from 1pm "until the early hours"; www.elcalifa.com.mx/califa.html

Also in Mexico City

El Borrego Viudo ("the widowed sheep") *(Avenida Revolución Tacubaya; inexpensive)* is certainly authentic and well worth a late-night pilgrimage to this less-than-glamorous spot alongside the viaduct. Armies of servers clad in chef's whites bustle around the cavernous feeding house, taking tacos out to drive-through clients in the huge car park. Open 24 hours a day, it specializes in tacos *al pastor*.

Also in Mexico

Around six hours' drive southeast of Mexico City, Oaxaca is one of Mexico's most beautiful colonial cities. Follow the billowing smoke from **Mercado 20 de Noviembre**, an atmospheric and inexpensive food market, to find sizzling tacos. The stalls are mostly frequented by local people, and best at lunch time; pick the stall with the largest queue.

Around the World

Serving from a small gazebo with the menu propped up against it on a blackboard, **Buen Provecho** *(inexpensive)* is a one-man band consisting of Arturo Ortega Rodriguez, who serves up what must surely be London's most authentic Mexican food. He's in Waterloo (Lower Marsh) lunch time market during the week and Elephant and Castle market on Sundays. Tacos come with a choice of marinated meat fillings, and the salsa is for sale, should you want to reproduce the experience at home.

What Else to Eat

European and North American chain restaurants churning out "Mexican" dishes do no justice to a varied and imaginative national cuisine that makes full use of fresh indigenous produce. When you've had all the tacos you can take, be sure to try **tamales**, tasty and inexpensive snacks often sold from baskets by street sellers and once eaten by pre-Colombians. A *tamal* is a steamed parcel of corn dough with a sweet or savoury filling, wrapped within a corn husk or banana leaf. Alternatively, seek out a **torta** (sandwich) or tortilla containing **nopal**: chopped, de-spined prickly pear cactus "paddles", or leaf pads, which look and taste a little like avocado. Although Mexico City is inland, the fish dishes on offer are superb; tuck into shrimps in tangy sauces from Veracruz or whole fish fresh from the market, accompanied by hot, fresh salsa.

Above A *taqueria* (taco restaurant) often has a *maestro taquero*, a master-taco maker

Right Meaty Atlantic quahog clams are still harvested with wound-wire rakes and baskets

Below Clam chowder, which is thought to have developed from a 16th-century French fish stew, *la chaudrée*

A Day in Boston

Boston often seems more European than American, perhaps because it is a compact, walkable city where the streets meander pleasingly and buildings are mostly at human scale.

MORNING Begin a spin through Boston history at **Faneuil Hall**, the 18th-century meeting house where brewer and political agitator Samuel Adams demanded independence from Great Britain. Adjacent are the long granite buildings of **Quincy Market**, built in the 1820s and now a lively centre of shops and restaurants. Head to the waterfront to visit the fish, penguins and seals of the **New England Aquarium**.

AFTERNOON Book a **harbour cruise** at Long Wharf to admire Boston from its seaward side. Disembark in **Charlestown** to visit the world's oldest commissioned warship, the 1797 wooden frigate USS *Constitution*, known affectionately as "Old Ironsides".

EVENING Check listings for a drama or comedy in the restored early-20th-century playhouses of the lively **Theatre District**.

Essentials

GETTING THERE
Domestic and international airlines fly into Boston's **Logan International Airport**. Boston is also served by Amtrak **train** from New York. The city has a combined **public transport system** of subway, trolleys and buses known as the "T".

WHERE TO STAY
Constitution Inn (inexpensive) offers bargain accommodation near "Old Ironsides" at Charlestown. *www.constitutioninn.org*
Harborside Inn (moderate) occupies a former spice warehouse, just steps from Faneuil Hall marketplace. *www.harborsideinnboston.com*
Boston Harbor Hotel (expensive) is a showpiece of the revived waterfront. *www.bhh.com*

TOURIST INFORMATION
148 Tremont Street; *www.bostonusa.com*

BOSTON USA

Creamy Chowder in Boston

Bankers, brokers and tourists bustle down the Boston streets once trod by British soldiers and colonial revolutionaries. In this vibrant modern city, preservation is the watchword for historic buildings and gastronomy alike. No-one has truly experienced Boston without tasting its dearest culinary legacy: the rich, creamy, buttery broth known as New England clam chowder.

For all its modernity, Boston revels in its early history. Founded in 1630 as "a city on a hill", Boston was the epicentre of American foment against British rule and the cradle of the American Revolution. On the Freedom Trail, the redbrick path that snakes 4 km (2½ miles) through the city linking its historic sites, 12 of the 16 buildings predate the Revolution and some stand cheek-by-jowl with glass skyscrapers. Visitors can enter the hall where patriots rallied for liberty and can even board the world's most venerable active warship, USS *Constitution*, which bobs at anchor near the shipyard where she was constructed. In Boston's theatre district, new dramas unfold in the ornate interiors of some of America's oldest active playhouses.

Although the first English settlers of New England dismissed clams as "the meanest of God's blessings",

by the 18th century clam chowder had become a mainstay of the region's cuisine and a gastronomic benchmark for authentic Yankee cooking. Probably an offshoot of New England fish chowders – so-named because they were made in large iron cauldrons, or *chaudières*, as French-speaking Newfoundland fishermen called them – clam chowder is a felicitous marriage of clams, onions, butter and milk. Devotees disagree over whether the onion should be sautéed with salt pork or butter, and whether the chowder should be thickened with potato or ship's crackers. Even with such minor variations and controversies, creamy clam chowder is ubiquitous in Boston establishments, from hip new bistros to some of the oldest restaurants in the United States.

Clam chowder remains New England's favourite comfort food – a savoury, slightly salty and perfectly silken antidote to a chill November day or a restorative pick-me-up after an afternoon cruising Boston harbour. In the perfect chowder, each little clam explodes with flavour against the rich backdrop of the broth. Made from simple ingredients, it is one of the most democratic of luxuries. Historian Joseph C Lincoln even deemed clam chowder "as American as the Stars and Stripes, as patriotic as the national anthem. It is 'Yankee Doodle' in a kettle."

Chowder Variants

In Boston, even the trendiest chef knows better than to mess with New England clam chowder, perhaps daring only to add a sprig of chervil or parsley to provide a spot of colour in the milky sea of the bowl. But there are certain variants that appear in southern New England and elsewhere in the USA. The rarest is the clear Rhode Island clam chowder – little more than clams and their steaming juices, butter, onion and celery. The soup that most offends purists, however, is Manhattan clam chowder: a tomato-based vegetable soup to which clams are added, often served with cream to make a thick pink slurry. Scoffed one New England travel writer in 1940: "Tomatoes and clams have no more affinity than ice cream and horseradish."

Left Sailing boats add old-world charm to Boston's modern waterfront

The Best Places to Eat Clam Chowder

Union Oyster House moderate

Opening in 1826 as Atwood and Bacon Oyster House, this venerable establishment is the oldest restaurant in Boston and the oldest eatery in continuous operation in the United States. Its semicircular oyster bar on the ground floor has been a favourite of Boston society since the days when famed orator and politician Daniel Webster (1782–1852) daily drank a brandy-and-water with every half-dozen raw oysters (he usually ate six plates). John F Kennedy's favourite wooden booth on the upper level is marked with a commemorative plaque.

Although the Union Oyster House is most celebrated for its raw seafood bar of clams and oysters, the chefs make a meaty clam chowder dotted with small, juicy cherrystone clams – a young hard-shell clam indigenous to the Massachusetts coast – in a perfect broth, neither too thick nor too thin. A frequent winner of various chowder contests, it is served both as an appetizer and a main dish. Departing from tradition, the restaurant serves its chowder with corncakes instead of crackers.
41 Union Street, Boston; open 11am–9:30pm Sun–Thu, 11am–10pm Fri & Sat; www.unionoysterhouse.com

Also in Boston

Diners still eat at communal tables at **Durgin-Park** (*www.arkrestaurants.com; moderate*), in the Faneuil Hall Marketplace, which opened to feed the hungry traders of the 19th-century Quincy Market. Its clam chowder is a bastion of Yankee taste. More modern but equal as a Boston gastronomic icon, **Legal Sea Foods** (*www.legalseafoods.com; moderate*) evolved from a fishmonger into a celebrated chain of restaurants. Its several Boston branches include one located near the Aquarium on State Street.

Also in New England

Captain Parker's Pub in West Yarmouth, Massachusetts (*www.captainparkers.com; moderate*) is famed for making Cape Cod's finest clam chowder. Set in Rhode Island's fishing port of Galilee, **Champlin's Seafood Restaurant** (*www.champlins.com; moderate*) makes both creamy New England chowder and the clear-broth Rhode Island variant. In South Norwalk, Connecticut, **Sono Seaport Seafood** (*www.sonoseaportseafood.com; moderate*) is like Champlin's both a fishmonger and a restaurant, and offers creamy New England and tomato-based Manhattan clam chowders.

Around the USA

Bistro Boudin (*+1 415 351 5561; moderate*), a restaurant on Fisherman's Wharf in San Francisco, California, merges two culinary icons by serving New England clam chowder in a loaf "bowl" of San Francisco sourdough bread.

MEMPHIS USA

Barbecue and Blues in Memphis

The old cotton capital of Memphis, Tennessee, rises on a bluff overlooking a wide, lazy stretch of the Mississippi river. During the long, sultry summer afternoons, its residents lie low to escape the humid heat. But after dark, in the back-alley rib shacks and the blues clubs of Beale Street, the River City comes alive with what made it world-famous – music and barbecue.

Memphis is the home of the blues. From the 1920s onwards, black musicians from the Mississippi Delta made a beeline for Beale Street, where WC Handy, Howlin' Wolf, Muddy Waters and B B King jammed in its legendary "juke joints". In 1954, Memphis became the birthplace of rock 'n' roll when, in the tiny Sun Studio, local boy Elvis Presley recorded a blues number, "That's All Right", but with a daring new sound that set the world on fire. Then, in the 1960s, the artists at Stax Records – including Otis Redding, Isaac Hayes and Sam & Dave – turned Memphis into "Soulsville USA".

Memphis is also home to one of the oldest and most popular styles of Southern barbecue. This down-home food is a perfect complement to the raw, earthy music that sprang from the city's streets. In Memphis, home of the World Champion Barbecue Contest each May, barbecue means baby-back pork ribs. They come "wet" – cooked and served with a tangy sauce made from tomato, vinegar and spices – or "dry" – seasoned with a rub of dried spices, primarily paprika, which gives the meat a lusty red

colour. Dry ribs are lightly mopped with just enough spiced vinegar during cooking to keep them juicy.

What makes Memphis barbecue so delicious is the cooking. The ribs are smoked "low and slow" over a hickory wood fire, giving them plenty of time to absorb the smoky scent and coating them with a dark crispy crust while remaining succulent and tender inside, with all the flavour of the meat shining through. The result is hot, melting and sweet – just like Memphis music.

A passion for music still pulsates through Memphis today, whether you come to tour its music museums, pay homage to the King, buried at his Graceland mansion, or soak up some electric blues or R&B, moody jazz or a boogie beat in the neon-lit nightclubs on Beale Street. But there's a more sober side to Memphis too: in 1968, Martin Luther King was assassinated here, on the balcony of his room at the Lorraine Motel. The National Civil Rights Museum now located at this tragic spot is one of the most inspirational destinations in the USA, and it surely has a fitting home in this city, where music brought all races and classes together.

A Day in Memphis

Most of the top sights in downtown Memphis are a short walk or taxi ride from Beale Street. Many can also be reached by bus or the vintage downtown trolley cars. Further out are Soulsville: the Stax Museum of American Soul Music, and Graceland, Elvis Presley's former home. The city has many non-music attractions too, from botanic gardens and riverboat rides to film festivals and galleries, but on a one-day itinerary, it's almost inevitable that music-lovers are going to set the pace.

MORNING Get an early start at **Graceland** to see Elvis's sumptuous home and treasures, and pay your respects at his grave. Then head back downtown to the **Memphis Rock 'n' Soul Museum** for a fascinating look at the city's music history.

AFTERNOON Let your musical tastes decide whether to visit **Sun Studio** for an entertaining tour of the little studio that first recorded Elvis, Jerry Lee Lewis and Johnny Cash, or head to the **Stax Museum** to hear the phenomenal story of the label that launched American soul music and ogle Isaac Hayes's gold-trimmed blue Cadillac.

EVENING After a monster meal of Memphis barbecue, lick your fingers and head for **Beale Street** and a night of Memphis blues.

Essentials

GETTING THERE
Memphis International Airport is only 15 minutes by taxi or shuttle from the city centre. A **hire car** is useful for visiting Graceland.

WHERE TO STAY
Doubletree Hotel Memphis Downtown (inexpensive) has comfortable rooms just two blocks from Beale Street. *www.doubletree.com*
Memphis Marriott Downtown (moderate) is the city's largest hotel, right on the trolley line. *www.memphismarriottdowntown.com*
The Peabody Hotel (expensive): *the* place to stay in Memphis. *www.peabodymemphis.com*

TOURIST INFORMATION
Memphis Visitor Center, 3205 Elvis Presley Boulevard; *www.memphistravel.com*

Left Hail to the King: Elvis Presley's Graceland home welcomes more than half-a-million visitors each year

Above Sizzling "wet" pork ribs are brushed with a sauce made from tomatoes, vinegar and spices

Top Follow the "Brass Note Walk of Fame" on legendary Beale Street, home of the blues

Above The Museum of Modern Art (MoMA) is a modernist building that houses one of the largest collections of contemporary art in the world

Above New York street food is an intriguing mix of fast foods from around the world, often all for sale in one place

Three Days in New York City

New York has it all: iconic skyscrapers, lush parks, world-class museums, dazzling Times Square and glitzy Broadway shows.

DAY ONE Go to the top of the **Empire State Building** for jaw-dropping 360° views, to get a better idea of the city you'll be exploring. Spend the afternoon being wowed by art at the **Museum of Modern Art**.

DAY TWO Head to **Central Park** in the morning, focusing your explorations on the area between 59th and 79th streets, where you can saunter along shaded paths from the wooded **Ramble** to the elegant **Bethesda Terrace**. Then up the cultural stakes by admiring the Picasso masterpieces and the Roman Temple of Dendur at the **Metropolitan Museum of Art**.

DAY THREE Start the day with a brisk walk across the **Brooklyn Bridge**, the largest suspension bridge in the world when it was built in 1883. Afterwards, head to **SoHo** to shop in exquisite designer boutiques, and then cap off the day with a visit to neon-lit **Times Square** and a **Broadway** show in the nearby theatre district.

Essentials

GETTING THERE
New York City, USA, is served by three airports: **JFK, LaGuardia** and **Newark**. All share one website: *www.panynj.gov*. Travel into town by **subway, bus** or **taxi**.

WHERE TO STAY
Off SoHo Suites Hotel (inexpensive) features simple but clean rooms. *www.offsoho.com*
Hotel Chelsea (moderate) has large, well-maintained rooms, and sits in the middle of hip Chelsea. *www.hotelchelsea.com*
Enjoy Midtown luxury at the well-known **Waldorf Astoria** (expensive), with its sumptuous lobby and spacious rooms. *www.waldorfnewyork.com*

TOURIST INFORMATION
Times Square Visitor Center is the most central tourist office, at 1560 Broadway; +1 212 768 1560; www.nyc.gov

NEW YORK USA

New York's Urban Fuel

There's good reason for the famous phrase "in a New York minute". It's another way of saying fast, and it sums up the furious pace of New York life, which has given rise to the city's wildly popular "street food". This urban fuel for a city on the go reflects all of New York's diverse cultures, as food trucks offer everything from spicy Middle Eastern falafel or Jamaican jerk chicken to Belgian waffles.

Spend a day in New York, and you'll understand why it's one of the most popular destinations on Earth. The "city that never sleeps" features looming skyscrapers, elegant bridges, the vast Central Park, world-class museums and intriguing bohemian neighbourhoods lined with vintage boutiques. Equally diverse are New York's international cultures – and attendant cuisines – which you can sample at street carts across the city.

New York has a long history of street food, perhaps best exemplified by the basic hot dog. In 1936, Oscar Mayer rolled out the first portable hot dog cart – called the Wienermobile – and hot dogs have been sold on the streets of New York ever since. You'll spy vendors everywhere, from Battery Park to Times Square, and at a dollar and 50 cents for a hot dog slathered in condiments, it's one of the best deals in New York. For a taste of old New York, track down Nathan's Famous Hot Dogs, which began as a nickel counter in Coney Island in 1916, and is still the best place to sample a dog slathered in sauerkraut and relish.

If America is a melting pot, New York's culinary variety is one of its finest manifestations. You could find your way around New York on the scent from street carts alone, wafting the delicious smells of Italian pizza, Chinese crackling duck, Middle Eastern lamb kebabs, and freshly baked bagels smeared with cream cheese, first introduced by Jewish immigrants.

The street carts of Washington Square Park and nearby Bleecker Street specialize in spicy Asian fare, served up in a lively performance space jostling with buskers, chess players and skateboarders. The historic neighborhood of SoHo offers the chance to sightsee 19th-century architecture and quaintly cobblestoned streets, while eating from street carts selling everything from luscious chopped steak in maize tacos with salsa to brightly coloured cupcakes. Midtown is the quintessential Manhattan neighbourhood: skyscrapers glint in the noonday sun, spilling out office workers who continually appear to be in a mad dash. Not surprisingly, this area is a happy hunting ground for street carts, which cater to those on the hunt for a fast, hot lunch, whether they're workers or tourists.

Above The Empire State Building, Manhattan, has been a landmark since 1930

Classic New York Bars

Munching on street food builds up a thirst, which is easily assuaged by turning to New York's famous beer bars. Drink in history along with the beer at the oldest pub in New York City, **McSorley's Old Ale House** (www.mcsorleysnewyork.com). This landmark bar opened in 1854, and its clientele has included both US president Abraham Lincoln and ex-Beatle John Lennon. It serves only one drink: its own ale, available in light or dark. The bustling **P.J. Clarke's**, in Midtown (www.pjclarkes.com), is one of the city's most famous alehouses, with a superb line-up of international and domestic beers. Wrap up the night at the **Ear Inn** (www.earinn.com), a historic pub built in 1817 near the Hudson River that functioned as a speakeasy during Prohibition. It features a good mix of beers on tap and serves hearty American bar snacks.

The Best Places to Eat Street Food

Super Tacos inexpensive

As the sun sets on weekdays, dinner rolls into town for the Upper West Side. Teetering stacks of corn tortillas are unwrapped, gas grills fired up, and the Super Tacos' Sobre Ruedas ("On Wheels") truck at 96th and Broadway slides open its windows for business. The tacos are a study in simplicity: grilled meats are heaped on to corn tortillas and sprinkled with chopped onions and coriander. Eating them is simple too: the warm, foldable tacos are wolfed down at the dented, stainless steel bar that's lit by a buzzing fluorescent light. The roast pork and *barbacoa* chicken tacos are the runaway winners, tender and juicy; and the supple slivers of boiled tongue are tenderly robust.

Southwest corner of 96th St and Broadway, New York City; open 6pm–2am Mon–Thu, 6pm–3am Fri, noon–2am Sat–Sun; +1 917 837 0866

Also in New York

NY Dosa (+1 212 431 1733; inexpensive), on the southern edge of Washington Square Park, serves spicy South Indian vegan food. For tasty burritos, tacos and creamy guacamole on the run, try SoHo's **Calexico** (www.calexicocart.com; inexpensive). The company won the hard-contested Vendy Award (also known as "the street food Oscars") in 2008. In 2010 the award was won by Middle Eastern food vendor **King of Falafel & Shawarma** (www.thekingfalafel.com; inexpensive), normally found parked up at 30th Street and Broadway serving unbeatable falafel and chicken rice platters. **Jamaican Dutchy** (www.thejamaicandutchy.net; inexpensive) specializes in juicy jerk chicken. Satisfy your sweet tooth with warm waffles at **Wafels and Dinges** (www.wafelsanddinges.com; inexpensive), a company with trucks at various locations around Manhattan, including a permanent one on Fulton and Front streets.

Also in the USA

Los Angeles matches New York for superb food trucks. Abbot Kinney Boulevard in Venice features a range of street eats, including **Slammin' Sliders** (www.slamminsliders.com; inexpensive), with juicy Kobe-Wagyu beef sliders (small burgers); and **Che Che's Argentinian Cuisine** (twitter.com/chetruck; inexpensive), with tasty chicken *empanadas*.

Around the World

In the rest of the world, street carts offer one of the most memorable ways to sample local cuisine, from spicy soups in Southeast Asia to crepes in Paris. The pushcarts of Istanbul are outstanding, particularly those on the Galata Bridge waterfront on the European side of the Bosphorus. These are laden with treats including juicy kebabs, skewers of sausage, grilled corn on the cob and silky pastries stuffed with feta.

JAMAICA CARIBBEAN

Fiery Jerk Chicken in Jamaica

Jamaica is renowned for its vivid colours, from the alabaster beaches and indigo-hued mountain peaks to rainforests filled with tropical blooms. Old traditions are upheld with pride in the fishing villages and colonial-era towns, from bygone culinary secrets to riotous folkloric festivals and rhythmic dance. But reggae and food – Bob Marley and jerk chicken – remain Jamaica's lifeblood.

From swish coastal resorts and handsome colonial towns to neon-lit nightlife, Jamaica offers a variety of historic and cultural attractions. Lively Negril and Montego Bay, Jamaica's two main tourist areas, boast a mix of plush bars and rustic reggae-and-rum shacks together with long stretches of soft sands, popular restaurants and world-class golf. Montego Bay, known colloquially as Mo' Bay, upholds its reputation as a party town with great gusto with after-dark haunts that run from funky lounge bars and pumping discos to steel-pan gigs on the beach. Sleepy villages hug the 1,000 km (620 miles) of coastline, offering the quieter natural attractions of scenic Treasure Beach, Port Antonio and Oracabessa. Fertile farmlands and meadows form a colourful patchwork between mountainous ridges and forested ravines in a setting of palm-flanked azure seas, where fishing boats drag their nets ashore and sell their haul at tables on the sand.

In historic central Kingston the hypnotic, pulsating rhythm of languid reggae is a laid-back beat in Jamaica's otherwise fast-paced metropolis. Snack vendors vie for attention over tooting horns, blaring car stereos and the cries of street hawkers; housewives swap gossip over plates of ackee and saltfish as the aromas of slow-cooked seafood stews, seasoned chicken and fire-roasted meats hang in the air. No local snack is more commonly sought out than the full-flavoured "jerk": a uniquely Jamaican way of preserving and cooking meats and poultry.

Believed to have derived from the ancient hot-stone cooking practices of the indigenous Arawak people, jerk fuses smoky Jamaican pimento with the fiery, hot blood-red chillies originally brought here from South American shores by 16th-century mariners. Salt is added as part of the marinade and then the meat is roasted much as it was in times gone by, when escaped slaves, known as "maroons", spent years living in the Blue Mountains battling attempts at recapture by the British troops. Today, the deep, intense and complex jerk flavour is synonymous with Jamaican kitchens and a true test of culinary prowess. Every home has its own "secret" recipe, handed down through generations. Pride runs high among jerk cooks in Jamaica – each of whom considers "their" jerk the best.

Above Rick's Café sits beside a favourite jumping-off point, and its position on the West End Cliffs of Negril makes it a great place to enjoy sunsets with a cold beer

Food Markets

Few experiences in Jamaica excite the senses quite like a stroll around the island's many colourful food markets. Flower stalls stacked with a rainbow of scented blooms sit among food stands selling Blue Mountain coffee, freshly cut coconut and sugary cakes still warm to the touch. Housewives haggle over breadfruit, pimentos, codfish, plantain, avocados and callaloo, near red-hot grills that sizzle with skewers of seasoned pork, beef and chicken wedged between juicy green peppers. Choose from rice and peas, jerk chicken, beef patties or freshly cooked johnny cakes (fried dough biscuits) or banana fritters in Kingston's chaotic Coronation Market, Linstead Market in charming St Catherine, Brownstown Market in St Anne or the Savanna-la-mar Market in Westmoreland.

Three Days in Jamaica

Jamaica's extraordinary natural beauty runs through its mountain, beach and rainforest regions. Its villages and colonial settlements have enthralling histories and central Kingston has an irrepressibly vibrant nightlife.

DAY ONE Stroll around the historic streets of Kingston's **Spanish Town** in the relative cool of the morning to marvel at the magnificent homes, plaza and monuments. After lunch, visit the city's harbour museum, **Port Royal**, a memorial to the ancient capital city that was submerged following an earthquake in 1692. Then head to Hope Road to the **Bob Marley Museum** to revel in his writings.

DAY TWO Pack a picnic to hike through the bird-filled vegetation and coffee plantations around the **Blue Mountains**, perpetually cloaked in blue-tinged mists.

DAY THREE Spend a morning chilling out on ultra-hip **Doctor's Cave Beach** in **Montego Bay** to enjoy beautiful white sands and sparkling spring-fed waters. After lunch, explore a rainbow of underwater gardens in Mo' Bay's outlying shallow spurs from a glass-bottomed tour boat, a snorkel boat or in a group dive; an old anchor from a Spanish galleon begs discovery on the marine park's western side.

Essentials

GETTING THERE
Montego Bay International Airport is 3 km (2 miles) north of Kingston and there are **shuttle buses** into town.

WHERE TO STAY
Klem's Homestay (inexpensive) is a charming place to experience typical Jamaican hospitality. *www.klemshomestay.hostel.com*
Rockhouse Hotel (moderate) is an affordable boutique hotel set on secluded cliffs in Negril with an infinity pool. *www.rockhousehotel.com*
Ritz Carlton Rose Hall (expensive) offers beach-fronted luxury with a golf course, spa and five restaurants. *www.ritzcarlton.com*

TOURIST INFORMATION
www.visitjamaica.com

The Best Places to Eat Jerk Chicken

The Pork Pit inexpensive

You'll find plenty of food options among the character-packed beach restaurants, bars and rum-and-seafood shacks of Montego Bay. But for those who seek the very best in jerk chicken, there is only one place to go – the Pork Pit, near Walter Fletcher Beach. A favourite haunt with beach-goers, who descend on its outdoor tables en masse at noon, the Pork Pit serves a large lunch of melt-in-the-mouth jerk meat (not just pork but poultry and seafood as well), corn cobs and baked yam at shoestring prices. Delightfully informal with a seemingly unlimited supply of bottled Red Stripe beer, the Pork Pit favours plastic cutlery and throwaway plates over fancy tableware and simply lets the food speak for itself. Marvel at the guys in neon-yellow Pork Pit T-shirts as they carve up the jerk with gusto on to old iron griddles amid considerable smoke and sizzle.

27 Gloucester Avenue, Montego Bay; open 11am–11pm daily; +1 876 940 3008

In Kingston

Head to the **Chelsea Jerk Centre** (+1 876 926 6322; inexpensive) on Kingston's Chelsea Avenue for an urban take on this Jamaican food favourite. Jerk chicken, pork and seafood come with old-style corn fritters. True jerk aficionados also rave about **Our Place** (+1 876 927 7886; inexpensive) on Hope Road, where locals trade tales over a sweet-smelling jerk pit with an after-work beer. Unmarked and tucked away among the billboards of the commercial district, this secret hideaway boasts blissful anonymity away from the jostle of the fast-paced city.

Also in Jamaica

The most relaxed place to try piquant jerk ribs is **Ocho Rios Jerk Centre** (+1 876 974 2549; inexpensive) on Da Costa Drive, Ocho Rios. This delightfully rustic open-air jerk joint is one of Kingston's finest. Daily specials are posted on a chalkboard menu. Beers are frosted, the rum is strong and the exotic array of fresh fruit juices are thirst-quenchingly good.

Around the World

In the UK, British-Jamaican reggae musician, chef, entrepreneur and record producer Levi Roots brings plenty of spicy passion to his restaurant **Papine Jerk Centre** (www.100acres.com/papinejerk; inexpensive) in Wandsworth, South London. Using lip-smacking, zingy marinades to spice up chicken, fish and simple cuts of meat, Roots – the man behind "Reggae Reggae Sauce" – creates authentic mouthwatering West Indian cuisine. You can't miss the restaurant, as it is decked out in the bright Jamaican colours of yellow, red and green. Drop in, swap gossip and eat great-tasting jerk.

Above Jerk chicken is usually served with char-grilled sweetcorn or *tostones* (fried green plantains) and rice mixed with beans

Left Some of the best jerk chicken in Jamaica comes from street sellers at the roadside or in "jerk shacks" around the island

Above One of the largest museums in the USA, the Philadelphia Museum of Art (foreground) sits beside the Schuylkill river

Above Cheesecake straddles the line between dessert and cheese, especially when topped with a heaping of fruit in syrup

A Day in Philadelphia

Philadelphia is an easy city to navigate. To get your bearings, remember that the enormous City Hall sits on a square at the intersection of the two main thoroughfares, Market Street and Broad Street.

MORNING Explore the cobbled alleys of **Independence National Historical Park**. Don't miss the **Liberty Bell** on Market Street, or **Independence Hall** where the Declaration of Independence was signed. There are some fascinating exhibits in **Franklin Court**, a museum devoted to Benjamin Franklin. Nearby is elegant **Christ Church** and tiny **Elfreth's Alley** with its early colonial houses.

AFTERNOON Grab a snack at **Reading Terminal Market**. Then immerse yourself in the impressive collections at the **Philadelphia Museum of Art** or the **Rodin Museum**, which holds the largest collection of the sculptor's work outside France.

EVENING Catch a Broadway show or a performance by the Philadelphia Orchestra, Opera Company or the Pennsylvania Ballet at the **Kimmel Center for the Performing Arts**.

Essentials

GETTING THERE
The **Airport Rail Line** is the quickest and cheapest way into the city centre from **Philadelphia International Airport**. There are **subways**, **trains** and **buses** in the city.

WHERE TO STAY
The Gables (inexpensive) is an award-winning B&B in an 1889 mansion; it has comfortable rooms in Victorian decor. *www.gablesbb.com*
Penn's View Hotel (moderate) is a traditional hotel in the Old City, close to most main attractions. *www.pennsviewhotel.com*
Four Seasons Philadelphia (expensive) is an award-winning 5-star hotel whose Fountain Restaurant is one of the city's best. *www.fourseasons.com/philadelphia*

TOURIST INFORMATION
6th and Market Streets; *www.visitphilly.com*

PHILADELPHIA

PHILADELPHIA USA

Cheesecake in Philadelphia

In the leafy grounds of Philadelphia's Independence National Historical Park, visitors admire some of the most venerable buildings in America. Shoppers fill the bustling Market Street shopping district, while culture-seekers browse the city's fine art museums. When they need to recharge their batteries, only one thing will do: a cup of coffee and a slice of creamy Philadelphia cheesecake.

Philadelphia is one of the oldest cities in the United States. Its Quaker founder William Penn named it after a Greek word meaning "brotherly love", and from 1682 it became a refuge for those seeking religious and political freedom. Less than a century later, Thomas Jefferson wrote the Declaration of Independence here.

From Chinatown to Little Italy, Philadelphia's neighbourhood enclaves have given America some of its favourite foods, but creamy, dreamy Philadelphia cheesecake is the dish most likely to induce a feeling of brotherly love. Like the city's name, cheesecake has Greek origins, and it was baked for athletes at the first Olympic Games in 776 BC. Centuries later, Europeans brought their recipes to America, and it was here that cream cheese first became a key ingredient.

William Lawrence, a dairyman in New York's Hudson Valley, developed the process for making cream cheese by accident in 1872 while trying to make Neufchâtel, a soft French cheese. As his new cheese grew in popularity, he started selling it under the name

of "Philadelphia", trading on the city's reputation for quality food. He later sold it to a larger company, and the cheese became a global phenomenon.

Philadelphia-style cheesecake has a rich, creamy texture but is lighter than other variations. More cheese than cake, its basic ingredients are simple – cream cheese, sugar and eggs – but from there the sky's the limit. Chefs may add sweet almonds, tangy key lime, luscious chocolate or syrupy liqueurs to the batter, which is poured over a crunchy crust made of vanilla wafers or gingersnap biscuits, possibly mixed with nuts. A simple cheesecake is heavenly on its own, but a topping of fat juicy cherries, fresh blueberries or other seasonal fruits turns it into a work of art.

Fortunately Philadelphia is a perfect city to build up your appetite for cheesecake. Its historic neighbourhoods are packed with attractions – from the Liberty Bell to the renowned Philadelphia Museum of Art – and refreshed by sweeping green spaces. There's much to admire in the home of the Declaration that so famously stated a person's inalienable right to life, liberty and the pursuit of happiness.

The Best Places to Eat Cheesecake

Darling's Café and Famous Cheesecakes moderate

Darling's Café is the home of the original Philly cheesecake and makes the best cheesecakes in the city. It now has two branches, and both are unpretentious, charming little cafés with candles on the tables and some courtyard seating. They serve simple but hearty breakfasts such as bagels, oatmeal or French toast, and lunches including a range of salads and Philadelphia sandwiches. But it's the cheesecakes, of course, that keep people coming back for more, and there's a range of tasty choices. There are usually about ten cheesecakes on offer at any one time, at a modest few dollars a slice. You might want to start with the Philly Classic before going on to indulgences like the Perfect Pumpkin, the Peanut Butter Silk, the Key Lime Pie, the wicked Belgium Chocolate or even a Grand Marnier Cheesecake.

2100 Spring Street and 404 South 20th; open 7am–7pm Mon–Fri, 8am–7pm Sat, 9am–5pm Sun; www.darlingscheesecake.com

Also in Philadelphia

You might not think of going to a Mexican restaurant to sample Philly cheesecake, but local aficionados rate the pecan cheesecake at **Lolita** *(www.lolitabyob.com; expensive)* as one of the best desserts in the city. It's served with a goat's-milk caramel sauce and has a crust of dark chocolate with a hint of ancho chilli, adding some decidedly different flavours.

Also in the USA

New York takes its own cheesecakes every bit as seriously as Philadelphia, and a recent panel of food experts voted the cheesecakes at the **Mona Lisa Pastry Shoppe and Café** *(www.monalisabakery.com; inexpensive)* in Brooklyn the best in the city. Their "marble swirl" cheesecake, using chocolate imported from Switzerland, is especially heavenly. You can dine at pavement tables or take a slice of cheesecake away, and even order online if you live in the USA.

Around the World

A Dublin café run by two sisters who trained as pastry chefs in New York has received all kinds of accolades, from the *Dubliner* magazine to the *New York Times*. The **Queen of Tarts** *(www.queenoftarts.ie; inexpensive)* has an old-world charm and serves a delicious New-York-style cheesecake along with other exceptional desserts, Irish treats and pastries such as chocolate scones.

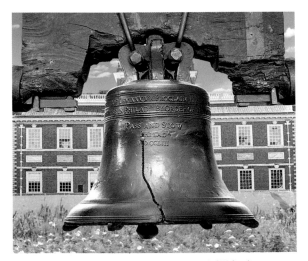

Above The Liberty Bell, cast in 1751, is a traditional symbol of US freedom

New York Cheesecake

Thick, smooth New York cheesecake is one of the most popular styles of cheesecake in the United States. While it is also made with cream cheese, it is denser and richer due to the addition of egg yolks in the recipe, and sometimes lemon or cottage cheese is used to give it a sharper taste. New York cheesecake is baked in a pan standing 13–15 cm (5–6 inches) high, so its slices stand impressively tall. Although some chefs dribble a dash of strawberry or chocolate sauce into the batter, New York cheesecake is traditionally served plain without any toppings. Arnold Reuben, a German immigrant and creator of the Reuben sandwich (a delicious mix of cheese, beef and sauerkraut on rye), is also credited with developing the first New York cheesecake in 1929. He served it at his Turf Restaurant on Broadway, where it became an instant hit.

Above A fruit vendor adds the finishing touches to his mouthwatering display in the Municipal Market, São Paolo, Brazil

South America

The Flavours of

South America

Few continents have been blessed with as varied a culinary heritage as South America, and this heritage is gaining wider international acclaim as more travellers start exploring the many different aspects of these nations. Rich stews and soups dominate the cooler mountain regions, while the long coastlines offer up fresh fish cured and cooked in unusual ways. Simply delicious beef is on the menu almost everywhere, but nowhere better than from the pampas of Argentina.

The indigenous peoples of South America, the conquering Spaniards and Portuguese and a large influx of African slaves have all contributed their distinct cooking traditions and ingredients to the culinary mix in the continent. And as if these weren't enough, Chinese, Japanese, Jewish, Indian, Lebanese, German, French, Italian and British gastronomical influences have followed in their wake, making South America a true foodie melting pot.

Many of the most popular foods enjoyed worldwide: potatoes, chillies and other peppers, peanuts, corn (maize) and – the one with the highest "yummy factor" of all – chocolate, hail from South America. In an unofficial exchange, Europeans introduced chicken, pork, beef (along with dairy products), wheat, sugar, citrus trees, onions and garlic, as well as certain herbs and spices such as oregano, parsley and cloves to South America, and also passed on their wine-making techniques, all of which changed the food culture forever.

> *The gastronomical centres of Lima, Buenos Aires and Rio de Janeiro now boast world-class restaurants.*

Today's cuisine has come a long way from its humble beginnings of often corn-based dishes, and the gastronomical centres of Lima, Buenos Aires and Rio de Janeiro now boast world-class restaurants. Food festivals, such as Lima's Mistura and Medellín's Otro Sabor, also attract visitors from near and far. What's influenced South American cuisine more than any other feature is also what has inspired many a traveller – its wonderful variety of landscapes: desolate high plateaux, deep-cut ravines, snow-capped *cordilleras* (mountain ranges), endless rolling pasturelands and the sheer immensity of the Amazon basin.

Coast-to-Coast Cuisines

In South America, food is often regional, rather than national, in character: warming stews and soups in the Andean region, good fish and seafood along the lengthy coastlines and mighty rivers, and superb beef in the cattle and farming areas. Peru's famous *ceviche* (lime-cured seafood with salt and perhaps a sprinkling of chilli pepper) is popular along many parts of the Pacific and Caribbean coasts. In Colombia and Venezuela, as well as northern

Right One of the many vibrant street markets in Cusco, Peru
Below Harvesting coffee at a plantation near Cuidad Bolivar, Colombia

Brazil, the African influence remains strong, particularly in coastal communities. The Brazilian state of Bahia specializes in seafood dishes of African origin, such as *acarajé*. Brazil is blessed with a wide variety of culinary trends and with a coastline of some 7,500 km (4,660 miles), it's no wonder fish and seafood feature heavily. The *moqueca capixaba*, a hearty fish stew flavoured with annatto seeds, hot chillies and coriander looks as well as tastes fantastic, the annatto colouring the dish a bright orange.

South American Feasting

From the crashing waves of the vast Atlantic, it's a short hop to the evergreen, huge grassy plains of the Argentinian pampa, home of the gauchos, Argentina's own cowboys. These hardy lads, most often found on horseback, have the enviable responsibility of taking care of the country's most prized asset – its cattle. Argentine meat is legendary and there is nothing quite like a *parrillada* – a meat feast where all the best cuts, masterfully grilled and lightly seasoned, are served until diners can eat no more, all washed down with a fine local red wine.

In neighbouring Chile, on the island of Chiloé, slow food is taken to dizzying heights in *curanto*, another form of feast, but one that's traditionally left to steam-cook in a hole in the ground. This far south in the Andean region, food goes with the climate and tends to be not just heart-warming, but body-warming as well.

Ecuador's *locro de papa* takes full advantage of the local ingredient *par excellence* – the potato. With 3,000 varieties found in the Andean countries alone, there's no shortage of choice and the humble potato has rarely tasted better than in this creamy soup, with nothing but a sliver of garlic, some chopped onion and a slice of bright green avocado to top it off.

The Andes climb further north into Colombia and Venezuela, where they have devised different ways of keeping warm and well-nourished, choosing the one meat that is otherwise somewhat underrepresented elsewhere in South America – the homely pig. In Colombia the *bandeja paisa*, originally from the centre of the country but now found everywhere, is a celebration of all things porky. Ground pork, sausages, crackling and pork cuts all jostle for space in this dish, colourfully accompanied by rice, beans, salad, avocado and fried potatoes, and topped off with a fried egg. Not for the cholesterol conscious. Venezuela's *chicharrónes*, or pork crackling, seem positively restrained by comparison. All across the continent there are vastly varied culinary adventures waiting to be enjoyed, with a mix of influences as unique as the continent itself.

> With 3,000 varieties found in the Andean countries alone... the humble potato has rarely tasted better.

Left Fresh fish landed from small fishing boats in Dalcahue Port, Chiloé island, Chile
Below Cooking ribs and meat on an open fire, Buenos Aires, Argentina

A Day in Salvador

Salvador offers so much in a relatively small space – vibrant culture, fascinating history and a string of lovely ocean and bay beaches.

MORNING Begin a wander through Salvador history on the **Terreiro de Jesus**, a square in the heart of the old city surrounded by a cluster of the best Baroque buildings in Brazil. These include the **Igreja e Convento do Sao Francisco**, whose interior is covered in almost a ton of gold. Afterwards pay a visit to **MAfro**, the African museum also on the square, then lunch in **Axego**.

AFTERNOON Wander downhill from Axego past the pastel-painted houses to **Pelourinho** for the best pictures of the colonial centre. Visit the old African church of **Nossa Senhora do Rosário dos Pretos** at the foot of the main square, built by slaves in their precious free time during the late 18th century. Then take a taxi to the **Mercado Modelo,** a big open market crammed with souvenirs.

EVENING Take a taxi along the beaches, stopping off at **Barra** for a juice and finishing in **Rio Vermelho** for *acarajé* and local nightlife.

Essentials

GETTING THERE
Domestic and international airlines fly into Bahia's Salvador **airport;** there are **buses** and **taxis** to the historic centre.

WHERE TO STAY
Albergue Hostel São Jorge (inexpensive) has backpacker bargain rooms in the heart of the historic centre. *www.saojorgehostel.com*
Pousada do Boqueirão (moderate) offers boutique comfort in a renovated colonial building with wonderful views over the Bay of All Saints. *www.pousadaboqueirao.com.br*
Pestana Convento do Carmo (expensive) is Salvador's grandest hotel, housed in a converted Baroque convent in the picturesque district of Pelourinho. *www.pestana.com*

TOURIST INFORMATION
www.bahiatursa.ba.gov.br

Right A *baiana de acarajé* in traditional white clothing, with a necklace in the colours of her personal *orixa* (deity)
Below The main square in Pelourinho, the 16th-century heart of Salvador

SALVADOR BRAZIL

Crispy Acarajé in Salvador

Salvador's steep, sun-baked streets are lined with glorious Baroque churches and brightly painted 18th-century mansions. Music bursts from every other doorway and in the coconut-palm-shaded squares, African Brazilians spin and swirl to the beats and claps of *capoeira*, a musical form of martial art. At street stalls, women dressed in flowing white cook *acarajé*, a piquant patty.

Salvador feels like a rich slice of tropical Africa cut from a coconut coast and transposed to Brazil. It is a city of pearly beaches, lush tropical trees and deep yellow light; of cobbled colonial streets lined with magnificent UNESCO heritage buildings, vibrant with rhythm and ritual. Pounding drum orchestras that parade at carnival troop through the narrow, Baroque building-lined streets of the old centre once a week. *Terreiros* – sacred temple grounds devoted to African-Brazilian Yorubá deities – dot the city, from the fervid *favelas* (shanty towns) to the affluent apartment blocks on the caramel-coloured cliffs above the aquamarine Atlantic.

Under the European slave trade more Africans were transported to Salvador and its state, Bahia, than to any other location in the Americas. They were mainly from the Yorubá nation (now Nigeria and the Republic of Benin) and, against all the odds, they largely kept their homeland culture – and its cooking. *Comida bahiana*, the food of Bahia, is celebrated throughout Brazil today for its full flavours, spiciness and sauces.

The most famous dish is *acarajé*, a spicy, stuffed falafel-like fritter that has been sacred for centuries. West African Yorubá legend has it that the warrior goddess Iansã (also known as Oya) journeyed to find a potion that would enable her to spit fire; she is the goddess of lightning, winds, fire and magic. Historically, the Yorubá people remembered her story through a fire-eating ritual in which they swallowed flaming balls of cotton soaked in *dendê* palm oil, which were called *àkàrà*. *Acarajé* means "to eat *àkàrà*" in Yorubá and the food – also covered in *dendê* oil – is still strongly associated with the ritual.

The best *acarajé* is prepared by *baianas*, local women dressed in ritual white robes who can be found all over the city, but in greatest numbers in Rio Vermelho, a neighbourhood of higgledy-piggledy streets near the ocean. The *baianas* carefully mash black-eyed beans and spring onion, sprinkle the mix with salt and chilli pepper and deep-fry it in a pan of sizzling *dendê* palm oil. The resulting patty is split and stuffed with salad and *vatapá*, a chilli-laden prawn, ginger and peanut sauce. Truly the food of the gods.

The Best Places to Eat Acarajé

Casa da Dinha inexpensive

The legendary Dinha has been making glorious Bahian food for over 20 years from what was originally her home kitchen in the bohemian district of Rio Vermelho. Her simple restaurant seats around 50 people over two floors, and serves the *acarajé* for which she became famous. They're rich and full of flavour, served with sumptuous *vatapá* and a host of other sauces (including *caruru*, made from okra and shrimp paste). The restaurant also offers a full menu of traditional Bahian dishes, a huge variety of delicious *moquecas* (see pp312–13) and the best fruit juices in Salvador. Be sure to try Dinha's *suco de pitanga* (cherry juice), whose tangy flavour perfectly complements *acarajé*.
Rua João Gomes 25, Largo de Santana, Salvador; open noon–4pm & 6pm–midnight Tue–Sat; www.casadadinhadoacaraje.com.br

Also in Salvador

Visitors have to clamber up steep stairs from the cobbled street of Rua João de Deus to find the delightful airy dining room of **Axego** (+55 71 3242 7481; moderate) in the heart of the historical centre, Pelourinho. The *acarajé* is possibly the best in any establishment in central Salvador, but the restaurant is equally famous for its huge *moquecas* – such as *moqueca de peixe* (Bahian fish and coconut stew) – which serve at least two people.

Acarajé on the Street

Baianas sell *acarajé* throughout the city of Salvador. The most reliable stalls are on and around the wide plaza of the **Terreiro de Jesus** in the old centre of Pelourinho (which has good crafts fairs at the weekend too), on the waterfront in **Rio Vermelho** and around the **Mercado Vermelho**, the market in Largo da Mariquita in Rio Vermelho.

Also in Brazil

Chef Ana Luisa Trajano spent several years travelling throughout Brazil, from the backwaters of the Amazon to the hinterlands of the northeastern desert, collecting recipes from local people. When she returned to São Paulo she opened **Brasil A Gosto** (*www.brasilagosto.com.br; expensive*), a cosy, bright restaurant on a quiet, leafy street in the upmarket neighbourhood of Jardins. It serves gourmet versions of authentic, traditional Brazilian dishes, including excellent *acarajé*. In Rio de Janeiro's bohemian neighbourhood of Santa Teresa, Bahian emigré Teresa Cristina Machado has been selling the city's finest *acarajé* for so long that she's become an institution. Try her perfect fritters at **Nega Teresa** (www.negateresa.com; inexpensive), and visit early, before the crowds get huge.

What to Drink

You'll need to wash down your spicy *acarajé* with plenty of liquid, and there's no need for canned fizzy drinks in Salvador. The city has a wealth of tropical juices *(sucos)*, most of which are completely unknown outside Brazil and are brought to Bahia from all over the country – from the temperate south to the rainforests of the Amazon. Choose any fresh juice – you won't be disappointed. For something energy-inducing opt for purple **açaí**, which packs a powerful pick-up punch. For a healthy option buy a **camu-camu** – a half-litre (one-pint) glass has almost a gram of Vitamin C. For simple thirst quenching you can't beat **umbu**, made from the milky pulp of a medicinal semi-desert fruit. **Caja**, a small fruit that tastes like a mixture of mango and peach, grows in Bahia and contains an amazing number of nutrients, including iron.

Above *Acarajé* stuffed with *camarão* – bright pink sun-dried shrimps – and *vatapá*

QUITO ECUADOR

Hearty Soup High in the Andes

Beneath towering snow-capped mountains, the highland Ecuadorians, living at some 3,000 m (10,000 ft) above sea level, have long cherished the restorative powers of their native crop, the potato. Amid the lower fertile valleys, herds of grazing cows provide fresh cheese and milk for the rich, creamy dish *locro de papa*, guaranteed to get you up and over the next hilltop.

The Ecuadorian Andes favour early risers. As the day warms, moisture condenses and gathers in the air and by afternoon, more often than not, clouds have obscured the peaks of the world's longest mountain chain. But at dawn the full glory of what 19th-century Prussian explorer Alexander von Humboldt named the "Avenue of the Volcanoes" is revealed, glacier-topped peaks puncturing the lush green, mountainous landscape.

The Andes run longitudinally through Ecuador, dividing the country into three separate realms. The rivers to the west feed the sweltering seaboard of the Pacific Ocean; those to the east forge their way to the great headwaters of the Amazon river, some 3,200 km (2,000 miles) distant. Down the centre, the mountain chain is like a Titan's stepladder laid flat north to south, with the higher ground as the ladder's rungs and the populated valleys as the spaces inbetween.

These valleys and their surrounding hillsides are painstakingly cultivated by Andean families on their smallholdings, maintaining their close bond with their land and with Pachamama, the Earth Mother. Rising at dawn, they till and toil beneath the piercing rays of the equatorial sun and the constant gaze of their *apus*, local mountains personified as deities. Days are long. At lunch, there's no better dish to restore their energy than *locro de papa*, a thick, creamy soup made with the Andes' most important bequest to the world, the potato, combined with milk and fresh, crumbly white cheese and usually topped with slices of avocado.

The Incas, who came as conquerors from Peru and occupied these lands for around 50 years, were particularly fond of potatoes. They even used the time it took a certain variety to cook as a measurement of time – rather like a boiled egg. They were right to sing its praises: we now know that this tuber supplies every vital nutrient except calcium, vitamin A and vitamin D. It grows fast, on very little land, almost anywhere.

And there are lots of varieties: wander through an Ecuadorian highland market and the colour, shape and size of the potatoes on sale is astonishing. In fact, the variety of all market produce here is amazing. Ecuador's varying altitudes and its position, right on the equator, allow it to produce just about every crop imaginable. On any one stall, you'll find blackberries next to bananas, avocados atop tree tomatoes, and corn cobs tumbling over sacks of rice. This cornucopia, crowned by the precious potato, is one of the delights of discovering this engaging, hardworking country.

Three Days in the Ecuadorian Highlands

The Ecuadorian highlands around the capital, Quito, are a tale of winding highways between valleys and mountains, rewarding the traveller with breathtaking scenery.

DAY ONE Head to **Quito's Old Town**, regarded as the largest, least-altered and best-restored in the Americas. A World Heritage site since 1978, its colonial grid of streets is dominated by churches, chapels, convents and monasteries, with enough museums and curiosities to keep enquiring minds happy for days.

DAY TWO Travel north to **Imbabura Province**, famed for flower-growing, haciendas-turned-inns, strong indigenous culture and a daily handicraft market in **Otavalo**, which on Saturdays also features early-morning livestock trading and a fruit-and-veg market.

DAY THREE Hop on the restored railway from Quito to chug south to **Cotopaxi Province**, overshadowed by the **Cotopaxi volcano** and a host of other craggy peaks. This is dairy and cowboy country *par excellence*, with comfortable haciendas making fine bases for hiking, mountain biking or horseback riding.

Essentials

GETTING THERE
Quito **airport** has fair international connections. Due to the state of the roads and erratic driving, it's best to hire a **guide and driver** for touring.

WHERE TO STAY
Volcanoland (inexpensive) is well-located by the Cotopaxi volcano. *www.volcanoland.com*
Hacienda Cusín (moderate) north of Quito has airy, pretty rooms. *www.haciendacusin.com*
Casona de San Miguel (expensive) is a converted colonial mansion in Quito. *www.casonasanmiguel.com*

TOURIST INFORMATION
Quito Visitors' Bureau; *www.quito.com.ec*

Above *Locro de papa* – literally, "potato stew" – may be served smooth or with potato chunks. *Achiote* (annatto) seeds impart a golden glow

Left The volcanic peak of Mount Cayambe looms over Quito, the world's second-highest capital city

Above A stallholder dishes up fried potatoes at the Thursday Saquisili market in Cotopaxi, south of Quito, one of the largest and busiest in Ecuador

What Else to Eat

A revelation for many, **hornado** might well change the way you regard roast pork. Slow-cooked, succulent and tender, served with **ají hot sauce** or chopped red onions, potato patties and fried corn, it's a must. The Plaza Grande Hotel in Quito serves a superb suckling pig version. A meal is not a meal in the highlands without a soup starter. Look out for those with **quinoa** grain, another Andean wonder-ingredient. Hacienda Zuleta (*www.zuleta.com*) serves delicious soups made from organic ingredients. To warm the cockles on a cold Andean night, a swig of **canelazo** hits the spot. It's a hot toddy, usually made with naranjilla fruit, a local liquor and spiced with cinnamon.

The Best Places to Eat Locro de Papa

Hacienda San Agustín de Callo
expensive

There's no better place to enjoy smooth and delicious, warming *locro de papa* than in the Inca-walled dining room of Hacienda San Agustín, in the shadow of the picture-postcard Cotopaxi volcano. The hacienda's walls are thought to have been part of an Incan temple, but even without them, this would be a fine place to dine. Its style is country-home-turned-inn, with individually painted rooms with quirky touches ringing a flower-filled central courtyard and fireplaces keeping the chill at bay at night. Service is personalized and, if you're staying here too, the living room with its comfy sofas and books soon feels like it could be your own.

The *locro* is rich and cheesy, topped with perfectly ripe avocadoes and with fresh, piquant *ají* sauce on the side for those who like a little zip in their soup. Also on the menu are quinoa soup and croquettes, *llapingachos* (potato cakes) with guacamole and *fritada* of fried pork in cumin, and all the vegetables are harvested from its own gardens. Desserts are a treat too – guaranteed to have you waddling off to a nearby sofa or hammock for a well-deserved siesta.

Lasso, Cotopaxi Province; open 1–3pm daily (booking advisable); www.incahacienda.com

In Quito

The list of establishments serving *locro* is as long as the list of its variants, but in Quito, **La Choza** in the La Floresta neighbourhood (*www.lachozaec.com; moderate*) is regarded by many as the best. It serves lots more fine, traditional Ecuadorian dishes as well, such as *hornado* roast pork (*see* What Else to Eat, *left*), goat stew, soups and ceviche.

Also in the Ecuadorian Andes

In the north, **Hacienda Zuleta** (*www.zuleta.com; expensive*) serves delicious soups made from organic ingredients; **Hacienda Cusín** (*see* Where to Stay) and historic **Hacienda Pinsaquí** (*www.haciendapinsaqui.com; expensive*) near Otavalo are also good options. South of Quito, **Estrella de Chimborazo** (*www.expediciones-andinas.com; inexpensive*) is a high-altitude mountain lodge with a spectacular setting beneath the Chimborazo volcano, while **Hostería Abraspungo** near Riobamba (*www.haciendaabraspungo.com; moderate*) has a nice rustic feel. In the southern highlands, try the **Posada Ingapirca** (*www.grupo-santaana.net; moderate*) close to the Inca ruins of the same name. In Ecuador's third-largest city, pretty Cuenca, **Hotel Santa Lucía** (*www.santaluciahotel.com; expensive*), **Mansión Alcázar** (*www.mansionalcazar.com; expensive*) and the cheerful **Raymipampa** (*+593 7 283 4159; inexpensive*) shouldn't disappoint.

LIMA PERU

Spicy Ceviche in the City of Kings

Lima may not have the immediate allure of other Latin cities, but this coastal capital isn't lacking in culture, history or cuisine. It boasts pre-Inca sites and colonial mansions, and some real gastronomic delights. An amazing assortment of ingredients alights in Lima from the Andes and the Amazon, but it's the fresh Pacific fish that everyone wants, transformed into *ceviche*.

More than 100 years ago culinary revolutionary Auguste Escoffier ranked Peruvian cuisine third-best in the world, behind only French and Chinese. Some might scoff at the claim, but Peru has a rich cooking tradition and the proof is in the pudding, or in this case, the fish.

Ask a Peruvian what their national dish is and more often than not the answer will be *ceviche*, small pieces of raw fish marinated, or "cooked", in lime juice mingled with sliced hot chillies (*ají limo*) and red onions. It's served up as soon as the fish has become firm and opaque on the outside (about five minutes), with a wedge of cooked sweet potato, a chunk of fresh-cooked corn cob and a frill of lettuce. The spicy juice from the *ceviche* marinade, called *leche de tigre* (tiger's milk), is, locals say, the best hangover cure around.

The secret to a good *ceviche* is the combination of Peruvian lime, which has an unusually high acid content, with the freshest of fish. *Limeños* (the inhabitants of the city) insist, in fact, that *ceviche* be eaten only at lunch time, when the fish is guaranteed to have come straight off the morning's boats.

There is a long tradition of eating marinated fish in Peru. The Incas were fond of fish steeped in home-made corn beer and fruit juices, and cultures before them marinated fish with a fruit known as "tumbo", a type of passion fruit. Later, the Spanish brought limes, lemons and onions to the table, and Japanese immigrants introduced the sashimi sensibility. And it all comes together on the plate in Lima, the coastal city created by conquistadors in 1535.

Lima was the capital of the Spanish dominion in Latin America for almost 200 years. Remnants of this cultural boom-time remain in the centuries-old streets and buildings of the centre, especially around Plaza Mayor, where it is obvious in the lavish carvings of enclosed wooden balconies, the ornate doorways and the tranquil inner courtyards of the city's mansions. Further afield, buzzing Barranco is dotted with the holiday villas of wealthy 19th-century Europeans, who flocked to the beaches here in summer. Peruvians have long had a love affair with the waters of the Pacific Ocean, and tourists can witness this both in the friezes of antique ruins and in the restaurants, where *ceviche* still reigns supreme.

Above The Cathedral commands the view over Plaza Mayor, where the city was founded in 1535, and down the pedestrian-friendly Passage Santa Rosa (above)

What Else to Eat

Lima's cuisine and restaurants are gaining a worldwide reputation for freshness and creativity, embracing Chinese, Italian, Japanese, African and Andean influences. This is especially evident in **lomo saltado**, a stir-fry with a distinct Peruvian twist: alongside strips of beef, onion, tomatoes, chillies and garlic come fried potatoes and rice. Try it at José Antonio (*www.joseantonio. com.pe*). Another favourite is **causa**: cool, yellow mashed potato mixed with lime juice and chilli paste and layered with avocado, mayonnaise, and tuna; Astrid & Gaston (*www.astridygaston. com*) does a good one. **Papas rellenas**, potato croquettes stuffed with minced meat, hard-boiled egg and olives are a Creole favourite. Brujas de Cachiche (*www.brujasdecachiche.com.pe*) serves them with a tangy, lime-infused *salsa criolla*.

A Day in Lima

Lima is a cosmopolitan city that has embraced its varied past with gusto. Andean and Spanish influences abound in city neighbourhoods, peppered with traces of Africa and Asia, all united by an unmistakeable Peruvian vibe.

MORNING Take a jaunt around the city's colonial centre, visiting **San Francisco Monastery** with its religious art collection and bone-packed crypt. Loiter in front of the **Presidential Palace** around 11:45am to see the changing of the guard, then walk down Jirón de la Unión to French-influenced **Plaza Saint Martín.**

AFTERNOON Hightail it to **Miraflores** to walk the clifftop parks, past the black-and-white lighthouse to the **Parque del Amor** ("Love Park"), which has sinuous mosaic walls inlaid with love adages and a colossal sculpture of a couple kissing. Finish up in smart-bohemian **Barranco** at the showy **Museo Pedro de Osma**.

EVENING Catch a taxi down to **Cala**, the beachfront lounge bar-restaurant below the Barranco cliffs, and order a pisco sour – a cocktail of Peruvian brandy, lemon juice, egg white and sugar syrup – and a *ceviche* scallop roll, then sit back and watch the Pacific waves ebb and flow.

Essentials

GETTING THERE
Lima's **Jorge Chavez International Airport** lies 16 km (10 miles) northwest of the city. Take an official, registered taxi from the airport to the city.

WHERE TO STAY
Hostal El Patio (inexpensive) is a basic but comfortable hotel in central Miraflores with a cool, leafy courtyard. *www.hostalelpatio.net*
Second Home Peru (moderate) is the Barranco home of Peruvian sculptor Victor Delfin, and now a stylish guesthouse with sea views and five airy bedrooms. *www.secondhomeperu.com*
Hotel Country Club (expensive) in upmarket San Isidro is a deluxe 1920s hacienda-style hotel. *www.hotelcountry.com*

FURTHER INFORMATION
www.peru.info

The Best Places to Eat Ceviche

La Mar (moderate)

Part of the expanding empire of restaurants run by Peru's culinary ambassador and cordon-bleu-trained chef Gastón Acurio, La Mar is a lunch-only, seafood-focused destination, a *cebicheria peruano* (Peruvian *ceviche* restaurant). The restaurant doesn't take bookings and the best way to secure a table is to arrive around noon, otherwise you're likely to have a lengthy wait at the bar. Not that this is a bad thing, as they produce a great version of the pisco sour cocktail – fluffy, icy and just that little bit addictive – as well as tempting snacks while you wait. There's a whole list of *ceviche* on the menu, from *clásico* with hot chilli, tiger's milk and fresh fish, to *tumbes* – black scallops from the north of Peru, with octopus, mussels, calamari and clams. Try the *degustación*: a selection of five *ceviche* to share, including *clásico*, *tumbes*, *nikei* (tuna), *elegante* (mixed fish) and *mistura* (shellfish, salmon and fiercely hot green *rocoto* chilli). There's also *tiradito*, which is like a cross between carpaccio and sashimi: paper-fine slices of raw fish dressed with lime and chilli.

Avenida La Mar 770, Miraflores, Lima; open noon–5pm Mon–Thu, noon–5:30pm Fri, 11:45am–5:30pm Sat–Sun; www.lamarcebicheria.com

Also in Lima

Just down the road from La Mar, **Pescados Capitales** *(www.pescadoscapitales.com; moderate)* is another lunch-only seafood destination. The name is a pun on *pescados* (fish) and *pecados* (sins) and the menu plays up the "deadly fins" theme: *ceviche* comes under the heading *pecado original* (original sin), while main courses carry names such as "vanity", "envy" and "infidelity". *Ceviche* at the restaurant features *lenguado* (sole), octopus, mixed fish and shellfish and deep-sea cachema fish.

Also in Peru

The improbably named **Big Ben** *(www. bigbenhuanchaco.com; inexpensive)* is the oldest restaurant in the beach resort-fishing village of Huanchaco on Peru's northern coast. Pick a table on the umbrella-covered terrace upstairs with a view over the ocean and order a fresh-off-the-boat *ceviche*.

Around the World

Not content with conquering Mexico, Chile, Brazil, Panama, Colombia and Peru, chef Gastón Acurio has opened a **La Mar** *(www. lamarcebicheria.com; expensive)* in San Francisco. Located at the Embarcadero waterfront, it serves up *ceviche* with a local flavour: mahi-mahi, calamari and octopus with coriander and yellow chilli marinade; Californian halibut in a classic marinade; and ahi tuna with Japanese cucumber, daikon and avocado in tamarind-flavoured tiger's milk.

Above The Parque del Amor in Miraflores is lined with long, undulating mosaic benches covered in quotes from Peruvian poets

Left The fresh white fish meat of *ceviche* is "cooked" by being steeped briefly in a marinade of lime juice and chilli

BUENOS AIRES

BUENOS AIRES ARGENTINA

Beefsteaks in Buenos Aires

Adorned with colourful plazas, *belle époque* palaces and grand boulevards, Buenos Aires is the "Paris" of South America. Its hinterlands are lush alfalfa grasslands that roll out towards the Andes mountains, providing rich grazing for Argentina's prized beef cattle. Steak has long been the succulent staple of the gaucho and the centrepiece of the *asado*, an Argentinian barbecue feast.

From its location at the mouth of the River Plate, Buenos Aires rose to prominence at the end of the 19th century, when it became an important commercial capital and one of the world's richest cities. It embarked on a decadent Golden Age, modelling itself on Europe's great capitals, erecting palaces and monuments that recalled the splendours of Paris. Today, Buenos Aires is synonymous with the passions of tango and a thrilling restaurant scene, led by the city's fantastic steakhouses.

Echoes of Europe abound in Argentina's great capital. Walking south from Plaza de Mayo, its central plaza, visitors soon reach the city's romantic old quarters, where Spanish churches, sepia cafés and colonial façades front cobbled lanes. North of the plaza, the glories of the *belle époque* unfold along broad, French-styled avenues decorated with patriotic statuary and Parisian mansions adorned with cupolas and lavishly latticed balconies.

Visitors to Buenos Aires in the 21st century will discover these vintage architectural glories, but a new sense of style as well. The modern city buzzes with tourists and locals – *Porteños* – busily walking, talking, shopping and café-hopping. At night, visitors to the city are in search of two things: the tango and the eating ritual known as the *asado*. An ongoing barbecue of incredible meats, it is said to have developed from the rough-and-ready eating habits of the legendary gaucho, the Argentinian cowboy, who first roamed the pampas in the 17th century and is said to have slaughtered landowners' cows before roasting their carcasses over open fires.

In celebration of the gaucho, steakhouses today perform their own versions of this centuries-old ritual. Great slabs of red meat are thrown on to charcoal grills or hung from cross-poles over glowing pits of burning embers on the restaurant floor. Juicy beef cuts – sirloin, rib-eye, tenderloin and more – are left to sizzle and smoke for hours until, beautifully tender, they are carved by an *asador* using long, glistening knives. A spectacle of dancing fires, bloody red meat and razor-sharp blades, the Argentinian *asado* is a ritual steeped in masculinity and atavism. Delicious delicacies – tongue, sweetbreads, intestines and blood sausages – wash the palate in rich, fatty flavours before the huge steaks arrive at table. The eating of every part of the animal is homage to the heroic gaucho, who left nothing of his kill for the vultures.

A Day in Buenos Aires

This city's historic central square, the Plaza de Mayo, is dominated by the Casa Rosada (Pink House), from whose balcony Eva Perón regaled the masses. This is the perfect place to start: *belle époque* wonders lie to the north, and colonial charms to the south.

MORNING From the **Plaza de Mayo**, go down Avenida de Mayo and have coffee at glorious **Café Tortoni**, the city's oldest café. Turn on to Avenida 9 de Julio, the city's greatest, patriotic thoroughfare, and admire the **Obelisco** and the **Teatro Colón** opera house. Take a taxi to the **Recoleta Cemetery**, where Eva Perón lies buried.

AFTERNOON Head back to **Plaza de Mayo** and walk south, into the old quarter. Stroll cobbled streets with colonial façades in **San Telmo**; enjoy an alfresco lunch in cobbled **Plaza Dorrego**; and go to **La Boca**, the colourful port district. Visit **La Bombonera**, the iconic stadium of Boca Juniors, Argentina's greatest football team.

EVENING Return to **San Telmo** for sizzling beefsteaks and a tango show at **El Viejo Alamcén**, one of the oldest buildings in the city.

Essentials

GETTING THERE
International flights land at **Ezeiza Airport**, 22 km (35 miles) from the city centre; use the official **taxi** service or a **shuttle bus**.

WHERE TO STAY
Abode Buenos Aires (inexpensive) is a modern B&B in Palermo. *www.abodebuenosaires.com*
Home Hotel (moderate) offers boutique rooms and apartments with spa, garden and pool facilities. *www.homebuenosaires.com*
Sofitel Buenos Aires (expensive) is pure luxury in a 1929 Art Deco building. *www.sofitel.com*

TOURIST INFORMATION
www.turismo.gov.ar

Above Street dancers perform the tango in La Boca, the colourful port district that is the birthplace of the famous dance

Left Tending the barbecue for an *asado* – an astonishing and seemingly never-ending array of tender grilled meats

Below The grassy plains, or pampas, around Buenos Aires provide grazing for beef cattle under the watchful eyes of the gauchos

Right Humpbacks and other species can be seen on whale-watching trips off the Bahia coast from July to October

Below The creamy fish stew of *moqueca* includes tangy lime-marinated fish and fresh tomatoes

Three Days in Espírito Santo and Bahia

The pretty, unspoiled towns and villages of these regions sit against a backdrop of Atlantic coastal rainforests and border some of the finest beaches in Brazil.

DAY ONE Visit the rainforests of the **Monte Pascoal National Park**, which shroud the peak first sighted by the Portuguese and hide jaguars among the trees. Continue to **Alcobaça**, the region's festival capital, whose streets are lined with crumbling 19th-century houses.

DAY TWO Take a boat trip from **Caravelas** to whale-watch and snorkel in the **Abrolhos Archipelago**. These waters are home to some of the most extensive coral reefs in the South Atlantic and are one of the best places in the world to see humpback whales, who calf here between July and December. Stay the night in Caravelas.

DAY THREE Drive south to the relaxing little fishing resort of **Itaúnas**, which sits nestled in dunes behind a string of magnificent beaches visited by three species of marine turtle.

Essentials

GETTING THERE
The state's main international hub is Salvador-Deputado Luís Eduardo Magalhães **airport**; domestic airlines fly into the smaller **Porto Seguro airport**; both have **car rental** facilities.

WHERE TO STAY
Vila Morena (inexpensive) in Itaúnas offers colourful and friendly bargain accommodation a stroll from the sea. *www.vilamorena.com.br*
Brisa dos Abrolhos (moderate) in Alcobaça is great for families. *+55 73 3293 2022*
Marina Porto Abrolhos (expensive) in Caravelas is the best hotel in the region, right on the beach. *www.marinaportoabrolhos.com.br*

TOURIST INFORMATION
Bahia: *www.bahiatursa.ba.gov.br;*
Espírito Santo: *www.setur.es.gov.br*

ESPIRITO SANTO AND BAHIA BRAZIL

Moqueca on the Brazilian Coast

ESPÍRITO SANTO
AND BAHIA

The coastline of the Espírito Santo and Bahia states is dotted with tiny fishing villages and glorious bays, where turtles nest in warm white sands and whales calf around the coral islands offshore. It was here that Europeans first set foot in Brazil, 500 years ago, and were doubtless offered a form of *moqueca*, a creamy seafood stew that is still the regional dish today.

Like Columbus before him, the Portuguese explorer Pedro Alvares Cabral was on his way to India in search of spices when he stumbled on Brazil on Easter Day in 1500. His coxswain sighted the spectacular verdant peak of Monte Pascoal, shrouded in rainforest and fringed with coral sand beaches. Instead of spices, Cabral found tantalizing tropical fruits and brilliantly coloured berries, both of which were used in the rich cooking of the local Tupi-speaking peoples. The first Portuguese person to write about Tupi cooking was Padre Luís de Grã, who commented on the delicious way the locals prepared their meat and fish – *carne* and *peixe* – as a *moquecada*, where the meat or fish is wrapped in a leaf or placed in a clay pot with Brazilian herbs, chilli and root vegetables, then cooked over red-hot embers.

The dish was transformed by the Portuguese, who added European fruits and spices to the pot and served the dish with rice and green vegetables. Renamed *moqueca*, it quickly became one of the most popular dishes in the country. But in the 20th century it sparked a bitter rivalry between the two coastline states of Bahia and Espírito Santo, first sighted by Cabral – as both claimed the dish as their own.

The Bahian *moqueca* is certainly the most Brazilian, though it is a blend of Portuguese, Tupi and African influences – the prawns are cooked in *dendê* palm oil and creamy coconut (both introduced to Brazil from Africa). The people of Espírito Santo curl their lip; their *moqueca* – known as *moqueca capixaba* – is, they insist, far closer to the original. It is also preferred by cooking connoisseurs. Juicy prawns or snook fish are marinated in lime juice and then pan-fried in olive oil in a clay pot. The chef then adds tomatoes, coriander leaf and the blood-red juice of *urucum* (annatto) berries, before leaving to simmer for an hour or so. The dish is served piping hot with a sprinkle of fresh parsley.

Regardless of who's right, it's hard to quarrel in such a peaceful region. The tiny, tranquil villages, forested mountains and wildly beautiful coastline induce feelings of both awe and contentment, surely echoing Cabral's first impressions, 500 years ago.

What Else to Eat

Nowhere has a richer local cuisine than Espírito Santo, where pre-Columbian indigenous methods of cooking in clay pots have been spiced up with European and African influences and ingredients. **Muma de siri** is a spicy prawn and crab dish simmered in a clay pot over a wood-fired stove and served with rice and *farofa* (roasted or pan-fried manioc flour). **Torta capixaba** is a seafood tart that's crammed with oyster-like *sururus*, soft-shell crabs, prawns and salted codfish. Fruits are myriad and many are unknown outside Brazil. Most make wonderful juices, such as **acerola**, a tart tropical cherry; **umbu**, a berry that's pulped to make a milky liquid; piquant **pitanga** (the Brazilian cherry) and juicy **seriguela**.

Left A view over the Abrolhos Marine National Park, Bahia

The Best Places to Eat Moqueca

Restaurante Céu-Mar inexpensive

This brightly painted little restaurant overlooking the lush banks of the Itaúnas river has been a favourite with visiting Brazilians in the know for well over a decade. They come for the delicious seafood, which is as fresh as it gets – the restaurant's chef plucks the choicest catches of the day from local boats every evening. The menu is broad but pride of place goes to the seafood and prawn *moquecas capixabas*, which are served bubbling with bright red *urucum* berry juice in traditional clay pots. Portions are big enough for two and come with white rice and a green salad.

Av Bento Daher, Itaúnas, Espírito Santo; open 11:30am–midnight; +55 27 3762 5081

Also on the Coast

Maresia's (*+55 73 3293 2471; inexpensive*) is a modest, family-run restaurant on Avenida Atlântica, overlooking Alcobaça's beautiful beach. This is where the local Bahian people come for a great *moqueca*. The prawns and snook fish are so fresh they are almost wriggling, and the huge Bahian *moquecas*, cooked in coconut and *dendê* palm oil, come in a simmering earthenware pot. Be sure to wash them down with a glass of tangy *mangaba* juice, made with fruits plucked from the trees that grow along the nearby river.

Also in Brazil

Bahian chef Neide Santos has created a mini-Bahia in Rio at **Yoruba** (*+55 21 2541 9387; moderate*), a colourful little restaurant on Rua Arnaldo Quintela, near the Sugar Loaf mountain. The dining room is decorated with brightly coloured Bahian ribbons and drapes and the menu consists almost entirely of Bahian dishes, including huge fish or prawn *moquecas* big enough for two.

Around the World

Made in Brasil (*www.made-in-brasil-bar. co.uk; moderate*) in Camden, London, aims to re-create the relaxed feeling of a Brazilian beach café with its tables of unfinished driftwood, shuttered windows and Latin American music. Its Brazilian chefs produce several types of *moqueca* including the classic Bahian *moqueca de peixe*, as well as other Brazilian dishes such as *feijoada* (see pp320–21) and *bobo de camarao* (tiger prawns in a creamy cassava and palm oil sauce).

In Massachusetts, USA, the Brazilian-owned and run **Muqueca Restaurant** (*www. muquecarestaurant.com; moderate*) serves seven types of *moqueca*, including a plantain and tofu version for vegetarians. Dishes come accompanied by a range of uniquely Brazilian super-fruit juices, including açaí (see p303), tart Amazonian *cupuaçú* and acerola, a vitamin-C super-fruit.

CHILOE CHILE

A Fine Feast in Southern Chile

An enchanted island archipelago, Chiloé is a bewitching place of silent forests and craggy peaks that tumble down to fishing villages and mist-shrouded bays. Once believed to be a place of demonic and benevolent spirits, its fishermen still look out for a beautiful mermaid, La Pincoya, who is said to ensure a bountiful catch – and fresh ingredients for *curanto,* an ancient feast.

Separated from mainland Chile by the narrow Chacao Channel, the Chiloé archipelago comprises one large island, Isla Grande, and several smaller ones. A magical, mystical world of emerald woods and silent fjords, its indigenous people, the Mapuche, lived here undiscovered for millennia until Spanish conquistadors arrived in the 1500s. Spain steered Chiloé on a historical course quite distinct from the mainland: the archipelago evolved its own culture, a unique cuisine and a distinctive mythology rooted in Spanish Catholicism and Mapuche legend, with mythological figures like La Pincoya. In the 1600s, Jesuit missionaries built wooden churches across Chiloé to evangelize the Mapuche and colourful towns grew around them.

On Isla Grande, Chiloé's capital city, Castro, is the archipelago's cultural heart. A small city of hilly lanes and fishermen's houses built on wooden stilts on the waters of the Castro Fjord, it was the beachhead for attempts to conquer the Mapuche. Nowadays, it is a springboard for inspirational road and ferry trips that travel through haunting waters, forest-cloaked mountains and spooky fishermen's villages full of ghostly churches and tales of witchcraft.

Traditional customs still abound, and the steamy feast known as *curanto* seems to have sprung from the old fishermen's habit of adding fresh fish to long-life foods such as cured meats, which they kept on board in case the weather forced them to stay at sea for weeks at a time. *Curanto* still blends shellfish and fish with meats such as pork and chicken in a kind of ancient "clambake" that's unique to this southern archipelago.

Traditionally, islanders cook *curanto* by digging a wide pit in the earth in which they build a fire beneath smooth, round stones. Once these are hot, the flames are doused, and a blanketing layer of the huge native *nalca* leaves is spread over the stones. Layers of food are then piled on – fresh seafood, including baby mussels, clams and fish, then meat and vegetables, including pork, chicken, potatoes, dumpling-like *chapaleles* and *milacos*, a mix of fried raw potato, butter and crackling. The food is covered with more *nalca* leaves, and then stones or chunks of turf to trap the heat, and the food is left to cook slowly over several hours. Today, restaurants prepare *curanto* *"a la olla"* – in huge cauldron-like pots, from which they serve small mountains of its many meats and vegetables. It's a magical concoction that's strangely perfect in these mystical islands.

Three Days on Chiloé

Frequent bus and ferry services connect the islands in the archipelago, but you'll need to rent a car to really explore the back-country roads and village life.

DAY ONE Visit **Castro**, Chiloé's capital. Tour **Iglesia San Francisco**, a UNESCO-protected Jesuit church; then descend hilly lanes to the **Castro Fjord**. Stroll along the waterfront, past the stilted, wooden fishermen's homes in the water. Go to the **Museo de Arte Moderno Chiloé**, where modern art examines Chiloé's island identity.

DAY TWO Hire a car and explore **Isla Grande**. Head north to **Ancud**, a historic fort settlement; then drive south to **Chonchi**, a village built into a vertiginous cliff overlooking a scenic bay. Visit **Iglesia de Chonchi**, a Jesuit church whose vanilla-and-powder-blue façade hides a vaulted interior painted with a thousand tiny white stars.

DAY THREE Hop on a ferry to small **Isla de Quinchao**, to walk the beaches and the gravel streets of old fishing village **Curaco de Vélez**. Back in **Castro**, round out your stay with a visit to a waterside restaurant for a dinner of steamy *curanto*.

Essentials

GETTING THERE
Fly to Santiago **international airport,** then take a **domestic flight** to the southern mainland city, Puerto Montt, where **ferries** cross to Chiloé.

WHERE TO STAY
Hotel Huildin (inexpensive) has garden cabins and rooms in Chonchi. *www.hotelhuildin.cl*
Hotel Unicornio Azul (moderate) is a restored 1910 building set on the Castro waterfront. *www.hotelgaleonazul.cl*
Hostería Ancud (expensive) overlooks the ocean and Ancud's historic fort. *+56 65 622 340*

TOURIST INFORMATION
www.visit-chile.org

Above A heaped bowl of *curanto*, demonstrating quite what a feast this is – slow-baked seafoods, meats, vegetables and dumplings are piled high

Left The seemingly precarious but longstanding *palafitos*, or stilt houses, rise up from the water all over Chiloé, but most impressively in Castro

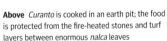

Above *Curanto* is cooked in an earth pit; the food is protected from the fire-heated stones and turf layers between enormous *nalca* leaves

Festival Costumbrista

The Festival Costumbrista Chilote is Chiloé's biggest annual festival and a vibrant celebration of its island culture. It takes place at locations across the archipelago in January and February. Festival-goers take part in island activities including cooking *curanto* in traditional earthen pits (visitors take a hand in creating the pit and its food), as well as weaving, sheep-shearing, driving oxen and making jams. Food stalls serve *curanto* and archipelago staples such as shellfish *empanadas* (savoury pastry turnovers), *licor de oro* (a fermented cow-milk liqueur) and ulmo honey – a sweet honey made from the native ulmo tree.

The Best Places to Eat Curanto

Restaurant Octavio moderate

The setting for this restaurant is an old fisherman's house overlooking the glassy waters of the Castro Fjord. Built from native island wood, the house stands on tall stilts in the fjord's frigid waters and has an exterior painted in bright primary colours. On the inside, it is total rusticity and warmth. A wooden entrance door creaks inwards, floorboards groan underfoot and, at the heart of the restaurant floor, an open fire crackles and roars. Choose a window table for its magical views across the Castro Fjord to mist-shrouded, forest-swathed mountains on the opposite shore.

The menu at Octavio brims with Chiloé specialities. Choose the *cochayuyo* (seaweed) soup appetizer and *curanto* main course. Prepared *a la olla*, in a witch's like cauldron, your *curanto* arrives steaming with clams and mussels plucked from the ocean at daybreak, and piled high with sausages and more. Servings are huge – you'll probably only need one portion between two. Round off your meal with Octavio's celestial papaya-fruit-and-cream dessert.

Avenida Pedro Montt 261, Castro; open noon–midnight daily; +56 65 632 855

Also in Chiloé

In Ancud, **Restaurant Kuranton** *(+56 65 623 090; moderate)* faces the sea and serves an inspired *curanto*. It has a snug ambience, with low ceilings and tangerine walls that are hung with carvings and aged artwork. All across the archipelago, colourful, family-run restaurants at fishermen's markets serve first-rate, and very cheap, *curanto*. **Ballena Sur** *(+56 99 414 354; inexpensive)*, over the waterfront and inside the market at Chonchi, is one of the very best, with beautiful views of Chonchi Bay. In Curaco de Vélez, on Isla de Quichao, **Restaurant Los Troncos** *(no telephone; inexpensive)* is a delight. A rustic garden restaurant with ocean vistas, it serves *curanto*, fresh salmon and the house speciality: salty oysters, eaten raw with a hunk of lemon.

Also in Chile

On the mainland, Chiloé's gateway city, Puerto Montt, shares the *curanto* tradition. At its raucous Angelmó Fish Market, climb wooden stairs to **La Estrella de Angelmó** *(no telephone; inexpensive)*, which serves the dish amidst a mind-boggling variety of ultra-fresh seafood specials, from stewed crabs to sea urchins. In the capital city, Santiago, **Restaurant El Galeón** *(www.elgaleon.cl; moderate)* is a seafood restaurant located within the capital's atmospheric Mercado Central (Central Market). It has dished up a fantastic *curanto* since 1935.

Above Angel Falls – the highest waterfall in the world – cascades over Mount Auyantepui in the Parque Nacional Canaima

Three Days in and around Caracas

The road from Caracas to Mérida in the Andean Mountains weaves between two mountain chains. To reach the grassy savannas of Los Llanos, you'll journey along roads hemmed by knots of ferns, palms and vines before delving into the domain of the Venezuelan cowboy.

DAY ONE Take a **city tour** of Caracas's challenging contemporary architecture, handsome ranchos, historic houses and extensive slums of tin huts and cardboard boxes, all overlooked by Mount Avila, which rises from the beautiful **Parque Nacional El Avila**.

DAY TWO Explore the sparsely populated **Los Llanos** countryside by driving across its picturesque rolling plains, punctuated by cattle farms and thousand-strong beef herds. Cook around an open fire on the banks of the **Orinoco**, South America's second-longest river.

DAY THREE Trek the scenic, leafy trails that loop the Andean town of **Mérida**, nestled in a verdant valley close to the **Mucuy National Park** and its crystal-clear rivers. Mérida also boasts the longest cable-car ride in the world, to the top of **Bolívar Mountain**.

Essentials

GETTING THERE
Simón Bolívar International Airport in Maiquetia is 20 km (13 miles) from Caracas city centre. There are **car rental** firms at the airport.

WHERE TO STAY
El Fundo de Pedernales (inexpensive) is a friendly lodge in the stunning Los Llanos plains offering guided tours. *+58 256 514 5070*
Hotel Plaza Mérida (moderate) is a charming 46-room hotel nestled in the mountain foothills that's packed with local art and crafts. *www.hotelplazamerida.com*
Embassy Suites by Hilton (expensive), in the business district of El Rosal, Caracas, has an outdoor swimming pool, gym and business suites. *http://embassysuites1.hilton.com*

TOURIST INFORMATION
www.inatur.gob.ve

Above Caracas sits at the foot of the slopes of the vast Mount Avila

CARACAS VENEZUELA

Chicharrones in Venezuela

Venezuela is a dream road-trip destination. Drivers navigate against a dramatic backdrop of snow-capped Andean peaks and white-sand Caribbean beaches as they cruise through the lush Orinoco Basin, the skyscrapers of Caracas or the grassy savannas of Los Llanos. The savanna roads are lined with gaily painted food stalls selling *chicharrones*, the nation's favourite travel snack.

Venezuela so inspired an awestruck Christopher Columbus during his third New World voyage that he described it as "paradise on earth". Today, its Angel Falls – the world's highest waterfall – still inspires plenty of hyperbole among travellers, as do the mighty Orinoco river and vast Lake Maracaibo. Elegant colonial towns steeped in whimsical nostalgia, such as the mountain settlement of Colonia Tovar, are easily reached by car from the valley-capital of Caracas via the rolling forests of the Cordillera de la Costa. Scenic shore-side roads reveal a palm-scattered, semitropical coast; the warm sands of the western coast roll out before emerald rainforest and resplendent cloud-topped mountain peaks.

Venezuela's maximum speed limit restricts every driver to a genteel 55 mph (80 kph), so even hotheads settle into a relaxed, steady pace on the road. The motorways have well-maintained surfaces that stretch out like asphalt tentacles to bird-filled rainforests, flooded meadows and rustic mud-and-thatch villages, extending further into ragged rural roadways, from dusty gravel to dirt tracks with potholes the size of minivans. Drivers need to keep their wits about them – all manner of farm animals and some extraordinary wildlife are prone to exploring Venezuelan roads too.

No road trip is complete without *chicharrones*, crunchy, deep-fried chunks of seasoned pork rind. Believed to have originated in Spain, they are plied by *buhoneros* (vendors) at virtually every street corner, road junction and layby of Venezuela's provinces and its bustling capital, Caracas. Some rinds are heavily salted, slightly greasy and slow-cooked to melt away the fat; others are peppered, fatty and chewy. Cooked to a deep russet red, many still have bristles poking up through the golden rind. Some are spicy and highly crinkled, while others are shiny, dry and smooth. All are frazzled until the rind puffs up into irregular curls and squiggles, some in great slabs, others in tiny popcorn-sized nibbles. There are dozens of *chicharrón* sellers in the capital's tree-lined Parque Central, each touting their own style of *chicharrones*, roasted to a special recipe handed down through the generations that invariably still tastes good today.

What Else to Eat

In Venezuela's cool, crisp mountain region, age-old Andean cuisine dates back to ancient pre-Hispanic cultures when warming, high-protein foods were cooked over glowing embers. Dishes were filling and calorific, using root vegetables, grains, nuts and plants together with meat from **guinea pig** *(cuy)* and llama. Several types of edible clay, such as **pasa**, were used as a gloopy sauce. **Quinoa** remains an all-important Andean food staple in stews and soups. Meat and fish are still preserved by drying and salting. In Los Llanos, culinary traditions centre on the region's grass-reared herds of cattle, with numerous recipes that celebrate a simple slab of **beef**. Steaks are man-sized, cut generously thick and hung over a smoky open fire for several hours. In Cowboy Country, very few green vegetables are consumed.

Above *Chicharrones*, roasted pork-skin snacks, are often eaten with coffee or aged rum

The Best Places to Eat Chicharrones

Sabana Grande Boulevard
inexpensive

Outdoor cooking on an open fire using the hottest fat helps to give *chicharrones* their salty, bacon-like flavour and irresistible crunch. The best places to savour the flavours of Caracas's ultra-crunchy style of pork are the side streets of Sabana Grande Boulevard, where you can enjoy them sitting between groups of elderly chess and domino players hunched over wooden tables, amid the food and clothes-strewn market stalls. Though different parts of the pig can be used, the skin of the belly strip is commonly the basis of Venezuelan pork rinds sold by sidewalk food stalls in Caracas. Often touted by the owners of the carts that sell *arepas* (fried cornbread patties), *chicharrones* are offered as an alternative to the normal patty stuffings, such as *carne mechada* (shredded beef), *caraotas negras* (black beans), *pollo guisado* (stewed chicken) and *queso rallado* (grated cheese).

Sabana Grande Boulevard, Caracas; hours vary (stalls operate virtually 24 hours a day, daily)

Also in Caracas

Both Sabana Grande Boulevard and Parque Central can be hectic; for a change of pace, venture into the city's atmospheric Spanish quarter of **La Candelaria** to find *chicharrón* sellers among its old cobblestone alleyways and handsome colonial plazas.

Also in Venezuela

You'll also find *chicharrones* along the road that crosses the Andes from Mérida to Barinas at the western edge of the Los Llanos region. At these welcome pit stops, rosy-cheeked women in colourful aprons cut belly pork into ribbons on jagged rocks, chickens pecking greedily on the scraps, while black cauldrons of fat spit and pop. Car-weary travellers satisfy their rumbling stomachs, dipping into paper cones for chunks of the salt-encrusted crackling, washed down by fizzy drinks hawked by the local children.

Around the World

In New York, richly flavoured home-made Venezuelan dishes are served up with considerable pride at the **Cocotero Restaurant** *(www.cocotero-restaurant.com; inexpensive)* on West 18th Street in Chelsea. An imaginative menu proves to NY gastronomes that Venezuelan fare extends well beyond griddle-cooked *arepas* without foregoing authentic simple recipes and homegrown produce. Yet it is the hole-in-the-wall joint **La Reina del Chicharrón** *(+1 212 304 1070; inexpensive)* that is the food temple in which fried pork scratchings are truly worshipped. Chef Elsa's *chicharrones* are crispy, crunchy and served in a bag solo or in a dish of mashed plantains. It's strictly cash only.

Right The laid-back little town of Salento is a great base for exploring coffee country

Below Colombia's unofficial national dish, *bandeja paisa* is part mixed grill, part tortilla, and extremely filling

Three Days in Coffee Country

Good roads connect the cities with the smaller towns and rural attractions beyond. Though earthquakes have destroyed many historic areas and left the rebuilt cities with a modern face, you can still find old colonial buildings and cathedrals in this area.

DAY ONE Spend the day on a **coffee farm** such as Villa Nora *(see Where to Stay, right)*, touring the fields and processing sites and enjoying the beautiful rural scenery.

DAY TWO Visit the **Parque Nacional del Café** (National Coffee Park), just west of Armenia, offering a coffee museum, guided walks, cultural shows, a children's theme park and an aerial cableway. Or visit **Panaca** in Quimbaya, an agricultural family attraction with farm animals, horseback riding and an impressive stunt-riding show.

DAY THREE From the charming town of **Salento**, with its traditional central plaza, hike into the **Cocora valley** with its lush vegetation and towering wax palms, or visit the **Acaime Natural Reserve** beyond.

Essentials

GETTING THERE
There are daily flights to Pereira's **Matecaña airport** from Bogotá and other cities. **Taxis** are inexpensive and you can use them to tour the region if you don't want to hire a car.

WHERE TO STAY
Villa Nora (inexpensive) in Quimbaya has simple rooms and beautiful views on a working coffee farm. *+57 6 321 4424*
El Eden Country Inn (moderate), just outside Armenia, has spacious, well-furnished rooms with a pool, restaurant and bar. *+57 6 749 5531*
El Delirio (expensive), near the National Coffee Park, has eight lovely rooms in a beautifully restored *finca*. *+57 6 745 0405*

TOURIST INFORMATION
www.turismocafeyquindio.com

ZONA CAFETERA COLOMBIA

Country Cooking in Colombia

Butting up against the rugged peaks of Colombia's Cordillera Central are rounded mountains in a dozen shades of green, their lush, forested slopes interspersed with wax palms, banana trees and bamboo, and acre upon rolling acre of plantations. This is coffee country – perfect for touring, hiking and all manner of outdoor recreation, with robust, rustic Andean cuisine to sustain you.

Colombia's Coffee Triangle, the Zona Cafetera, lies west of the capital Bogotá and south of Medellín. Apart from its spectacular natural beauty, it is a fascinating region to explore. Scenic roads between the three main cities – Pereira, Armenia and Manizales – are lined with coffee fields and with flowers, from swathes of carnations grown for export to exotic heliconias. Bustling small towns such as Salento, which overlooks the beautiful Cocora valley, offer glimpses of local life, from women cooking *arepas* (a kind of corn tortilla) on pavement grills to corner stands piled high with fruits and coconuts. National parks, hot springs and nature reserves offer a variety of ways to enjoy the magnificent scenery, and adventure sports are popular here too: you can go riding, rafting or "canopying" through the treetops on aerial cables.

But the coffee plantations themselves have the greatest appeal. Not only can you tour the farms and watch workers in broad-brimmed straw hats harvesting coffee beans by hand; many also offer simple but charming guest rooms in the brightly painted old haciendas and *fincas* (farmhouses), filled with antique furnishings and ringed with balconies on which to enjoy the views.

This is also the best place to eat a traditional *bandeja paisa*, the typical dish of Colombia's Andean region. *Paisa* is the name for the people of this region, while *bandeja* is the Spanish word for "platter" – and it takes an oversized plate to hold all 13 components of the dish. It includes minced beef, fried pork belly, spicy chorizo with lemon and red kidney beans cooked with pork in an aromatic soup, as well as black pudding and a fried egg. Balancing the dish with colour and texture are white rice, avocado and crispy fried plantain. Last but not least are large, flat *arepas*, topped with *hogao*, a spicy sauce made with onions, tomatoes and garlic.

Bandeja paisa is essentially a peasant dish, with enough protein and calories to keep the workers going through long days in the fields and treks over the mountains. An authentic *paisa* platter is a hearty, tasty, sizzling South American fry-up – one that has spread from the family kitchens of Colombia's coffee country to restaurant tables across the country.

Left Coffee bushes blanket the slopes of the rolling Zona Cafetera

What Else to Eat

Colombia has many other delicious regional dishes. In Bogotá and the surrounding Andean region, the most famous dish is **ajiaco**, a thick, tasty soup made with three kinds of potato, chicken, corn and guasca, a fragrant local herb. It is served with dishes of cream, capers and avocado, which you add to taste. On the north coast, another traditional soup is **sancocho**, made with various meats to which yucca, plantain, corn, potato and spices are added. **Tolimenses** are a kind of corn tamale from the Tolima region, made with *lechona* (roast pig stuffed with rice and vegetables) wrapped in plantain leaves and boiled for several hours. **Ternera llanera**, a dish from the eastern Llanos cattle ranchlands, is veal spit-roasted over an open fire.

The Best Places to Eat Bandeja Paisa

Mama Flor moderate

Ask someone in the coffee region where to eat *bandeja paisa* and the first answer is always an enthusiastic one – Mama Flor! Located in a high-class residential area in one of Pereira's oldest neighbourhoods, the restaurant is surrounded by green zones and has fine views of the city from its small balcony. It was founded by two local businessmen and named after one of the partners' mothers.

Built in the typical style of the coffee region from wood and *guadua* (the native bamboo), the restaurant has an airy, open dining room and rustic decor, which attracts international tourists as well as locals who come for the delicious grilled meats and traditional dishes. You can get a great *bandeja paisa*, known here as "bandeja Mama Flor". Other special dishes to try include Mama Flor pork (the haunch tip), *chunchurria* (pork belly) and Mama Flor soup, a traditional plantain recipe. The restaurant also offers some fish dishes, such as trout and sea bass.

Calle 11 No. 15–12, Los Alpes, Pereira; open noon–11pm Mon–Sat, noon–5pm Sun; +57 6 325 1713

Also in the Zona Cafetera

Another place in Pereira to try *bandeja paisa* is **La Piazzolla**, on Av 30 de Agosto (*+57 6 326 5433; inexpensive*). In Armenia, **La Fogata** (*+57 6 749 5980; moderate*) is a popular restaurant serving steaks and pork chops as well as typical *paisa* dishes.

Also in Colombia

In Medellín, **Hato Viejo** (*+57 4 268 6811; expensive*) is a beautiful hacienda with a flower-filled courtyard and fine views of the city. The Plato Montañero is their *bandeja paisa*; those with smaller appetites can order a half-portion. Another Medellín favourite is **El Rancherito** (*www.elrancherito.com.co; moderate*), with a large airy dining room and open grill. In Bogotá, enjoy the best of traditional Colombian cuisine at **El Portal de La Antigua** (*www.portaldelaantigua.com; expensive*), a smart restaurant with live music.

Around the World

In the USA, Houston in Texas has several Colombian restaurants; one of the best for *bandeja paisa* is **Gran Colombia** (*www.grancolombiarestaurante.com; inexpensive*). The favourite place for London's Colombian community to enjoy *bandeja paisa* is **La Bodeguita** (*www.labodeguita.co.uk; inexpensive*), tucked away in the rather ugly Elephant and Castle shopping centre on the south side of the River Thames.

RIO DE JANEIRO

RIO DE JANEIRO BRAZIL

Feijoada in Rio de Janeiro

There is nothing that the people of Rio de Janeiro enjoy more than the beach. Unless it's a *feijoada*. Brazil's national dish is not so much food as the centre of social celebration. After a swim off Ipanema beach, a walk through Tijuca national park or a spot of shopping, families get together on Sunday lunch times over this hearty bean and meat stew to catch up and chew the fat.

Ipanema is the most famous beach in Brazil. This stunning sweep of pearly sand is sandwiched between towering headlands that twinkle with lights in the lilac dusk. A towering statue of Christ watches over it all, perched high on the rocky, rainforest-covered mountain of Corcovado. The Atlantic Ocean is bottle-green and the weather eternally sunny.

Ipanema is also Rio's most fashionable neighbour-hood, packed with chic shops, swish restaurants and cafés, and frequented by Brazil's beautiful people. Not far away, vast slum cities sprawl up the surrounding hillsides. The communities are a world apart, but united by the love of a few key things: samba, football, the beach and the national dish, *feijoada*.

Feijoada is a black bean, pork and sausage stew that is simmered for hours in a clay pot and served with rice, spring greens, *farofa* (pan-fried manioc flour), slices of orange and strong *cachaça* rum. The dish is almost as old as Brazil itself: legend has it that *feijoada* evolved from stews cooked by Brazilian and African slaves on the sugar plantations in northeast

Brazil, from leftovers given to them by the Portuguese and meagre amounts of homegrown food. There was little time for preparation, but meat offcuts and beans could be quickly thrown in a pot to simmer over hot embers all day as the slaves worked the fields.

Like samba music, the dish spread from Brazil's poor communities to the rest of the country over the centuries. In the 19th century, a French traveller to Brazil, Augustin Saint-Hilaire, noted that black bean stew was as common at a rich man's table as it was in the wattle-and-daub houses of his slaves, and by 1833 a dish called *feijoada à la Brazilian* (beans Brazilian-style) was being served in high society restaurants.

By the 20th century, eating *feijoada* every Friday had become a country-wide ritual to mark the end of the working week. Nowadays most Brazilians, rich or poor, get together for a Sunday *feijoada* lunch with family and friends. Visitors can enjoy the dish in a similar way – in good company and over several lunch-time hours – in one of Rio's traditional *feijoada* restaurants. The best *(see facing page)* sits just behind the beach in Ipanema, strategically positioned for diners to work up an appetite with a swim.

Above The statue of *Christ the Redeemer* overlooks Rio from the Corcovado mountain in the Tijuca National Park; it can be reached by cable car

---

Rio's Restaurant Street

Rua Dias Ferreira, a five-minute taxi ride from Ipanema, is one of South America's top foodie destinations. This 500-m (550-yd) street is lined with restaurants on both sides – from swanky São Paulo fusion establishments to nouvelle cuisine sushi, Brazilian Thai and, of course, the inevitable spit-roast meat restaurants. This is the place for a leisurely stroll on a balmy evening, when you're in search of a restaurant. The most famous are **Carlota** (www.carlota.com.br), serving Brazilian food with an Asian and French twist, **Zuka** (www.zuka.com.br), with its fabulous beef; **Sushi Leblon** (www.sushileblon.com), where you can try slivers of fish with *pâté de foie gras*; and **Sawasdee** (www.sawasdee.com.br), with a Brazilian take on Southeast Asian cooking that is full on flavour and low on spice.

A Day in Rio de Janeiro

With breathtaking views at every turn, mountains covered in rainforest and a myriad marvellous beaches, Rio de Janeiro is resolutely an outdoor city. *Cariocas*, as the locals are called, meet, greet and eat outdoors.

MORNING Spend the morning on **Ipanema beach** – leave your valuables in the hotel and take nothing more than a *kanga* (shawl) and a *tanga* (bikini) or *sunga* (swimming briefs) with you to the beach. In the late morning, wander Ipanema's streets in search of a café or juice bar for lunch.

AFTERNOON Take a helicopter flight over the **Christ at Corcovado** for possibly the world's most unforgettable urban views. Land on the summit of the **Morro de Urca** mountain and spend the day walking around the forests here and the neighbouring **Sugar Loaf** mountain (reachable by cable car).

EVENING Swing and sway to the samba beat in a bar, club or just on the streets in **Lapa**, Rio's liveliest nightlife neighbourhood, which is heaving with party crowds at the weekend. Or opt for a more elegant evening spent sipping a cocktail in the super-chic 1920s **Copacabana Palace** or the Philippe Starck **Fasano** hotel.

Essentials

GETTING THERE
Domestic and international airlines fly into Rio's Tom Jobim international **airport**. The city can be reached by **bus** from all over Brazil. The best way to get around Rio is by **subway** or **taxi**.

WHERE TO STAY
Cama e Café (inexpensive) offers bargain homestays and the chance of *feijoada* with a local family. www.camaecafe.com.br
Arpoador Inn (moderate) sits in a modest block in a superb location overlooking the Atlantic. www.arpoadorinn.com.br
Fasano (expensive) is the most luxurious hotel in the city, situated right on the beach in Ipanema. www.fasano.com.br

TOURIST INFORMATION
www.rioguiaoficial.com.br

The Best Places to Eat Feijoada

A Casa da Feijoada moderate

This traditional restaurant, just a stroll away from the beach in Ipanema, has been serving *feijoada* to local families for decades. It's best to come with a very empty stomach for a full feast, which begins with a little bowl of rose coco (borlotti) bean soup. This is followed by a steaming tureen of *feijoada* (with extra bowls of meat so relentless carnivores can add to the stew at whim), and traditional accompaniments of spring greens pan-fried in garlic, fried manioc, rice, *farofa* (toasted manioc flour) and slices of succulent orange. Portions are large enough for two. Unlike most Rio restaurants, this one serves *feijoada* every day. Crowds get large on a Sunday, so be sure to book in advance.

Prudente de Morais 10, Ipanema, Rio de Janeiro; open noon–11pm daily; +55 21 2247 2776

Also in Rio

The Casa da Feijoada vies with another fashionable alfresco restaurant and bar in nearby chic Leblon – **Academia da Cachaça** *(+55 21 2529 2680; expensive)*. Like its rival, the Academia serves a traditional *feijoada* daily (with downsized portions for kids on request). A meal here wouldn't be complete without a glass or two of fine Minas Gerais *cachaça* rum, from the most extensive *cachaça* menu in Rio.

Also in Brazil

In a poll conducted by São Paulo's prestigious *Folha* newspaper, **Veloso** *(+55 11 5572 0254; moderate)* was voted the best place in the city for *feijoada*. The lively bar and restaurant serves the classic stew with traditional trimmings. Drink it with a caipirinha cocktail (*cachaça* and lashings of lime) – barman Souza is said to serve one of the best in Brazil.

Around the World

The uber-trendy, arty Shoreditch bar and restaurant **Favela Chic** *(www.favelachic. com; moderate)* in London was inspired by the colourful bric-a-brac of a Rio *favela* slum and is famed for its exuberant atmosphere. Its daytime menu includes *feijoada* and the bar serves caipirinha cocktails, *cachaça* rum and Portuguese Sagres beer. There's a branch of the restaurant in Paris too.

New Yorkers dine from a varied menu of Brazilian favourites at **Ipanema** (*www. ipanemanyc.com; moderate)*, a mid-West Side restaurant in the heart of a cluster of streets that have become known collectively as "Little Brazil". Prices are great value for Manhattan and the choice includes a huge *feijoada* big enough for at least two people.

Above Rio's Ipanema beach stretches for 3 km (2 miles); two mountains, the Dois Irmãos ("two brothers"), mark its western end

Left Traditionally made using pork offcuts, *feijoada* can encompass a range of different meats, from pork *choriço* to salted, cured beef

Food Festivals Around the World

No celebration is complete without good food and drink, but sometimes the food or drink itself is the reason for a party. It may be to welcome the coming of spring, or harvest time; to rejoice in the arrival of seasonal produce; to pay tribute to a traditional local skill; or simply to celebrate a feast day handed down through the generations. Whatever the reason, the next eight pages give just a taster of the tens of thousands of food festivals that take place each year around the world – the best, the oldest, the most rustic and the quirkiest. To take part in any one of them is to get a real sense of the place and the people, and is an opportunity not to be missed.

JANUARY

EUROPE

St Antoni Abat, Andorra
Perched high in the Pyrenees between France and Spain, Andorra keeps out the cold on St Anthony's Day with huge vats of its national dish, *escudilla*, a meaty stew cooked on an open fire and served in the terracotta dish of the same name. Everyone is welcome to join in the feast.

St-Vincent Tournante, Burgundy, France
At the end of January, when the vines are bare and snow is often on the ground, the villages of the Burgundy region take it in turn to laud the patron saint of winemakers with colourful processions, solemn ceremony – and a great deal of conviviality and fine wine. *www.st-vincent-tournante.fr*

Burns Night, Scotland
The birthday of Scotland's national poet, Robert Burns, on 25 January is enthusiastically celebrated across the country with readings of his verse, dishes of haggis *(see pp22–3)*, "neeps and tatties" (mashed swede and potato) and, most importantly, a few drams of fine Scottish whisky. *www.robertburns.org/suppers*

ASIA AND AUSTRALASIA

Auckland Seafood Festival, New Zealand
Auckland honours its fishing heritage with the biggest seafood festival in New Zealand. After a ceremonial blessing of the fleet, the harbour becomes a licensed market where visitors can sample the freshest seafood, matched with local wines and beers. *www.aucklandseafoodfestival.co.nz*

Blues, Brews and BBQs, Mount Maunganui, Hastings and Blenheim, New Zealand
Celebrate the Kiwi summer in style at this community-oriented festival, held over three Saturdays in different towns. Top New Zealand blues bands entertain the ear, locally brewed beers, ciders and wines amuse the palate and gourmet chefs prepare barbecue to satisfy every taste. *www.bluesbrews.co.nz*

NORTH AMERICA

Niagara Icewine Festival, Canada
Over three weekends in January, Canada's vine-growing region celebrates its famous Ontario Icewine (produced from grapes left to freeze on the vine) with vineyard tours, tastings at alfresco ice bars, warming chestnut roasts and Cellar Room dinners that pair award-winning wines with mouthwatering dishes and fine local cheeses. *www.niagarawinefestival.com*

Cayman Cookout, Grand Cayman, Cayman Islands
Not as rustic as it sounds, this festival of food and wine in the idyllic setting of the Cayman Islands is an exercise in contrasts – for example, when a "beach barbecue" is hosted by a world-renowned chef. A once-in-a-lifetime experience – heavenly cuisine in a tropical paradise. *www.caymanislands.ky*

Mendocino County Crab & Wine Days, California, USA
It's the height of the Dungeness crab season on Mendocino County's coastline, and these seven seafood-filled days feature everything from an all-you-can-eat Crab Feed to a Crab Cake Cookoff, with tastings to help match local wines to the food. *www.mendocino.com*

SOUTH AMERICA

Fiesta Nacional de Chivo, Mendoza, Argentina
The Feast of the Goat is Argentina's biggest food festival. Over 1,000 kid goats are roasted *asado*-style over open fires in a week-long extravaganza of meat, fire and folk music. At daily gaucho shows, Argentinian cowboys display remarkable feats of horsemanship.

Costumbrista Chilote, Chiloé, Chile
On this misty, magical archipelago, legend and ceremony come together in the traditional dish *curanto (see pp314–5)*, and never more so than during Chiloé's annual celebration of island life and culture. The earth-oven-baked meat and fish sustained islanders against the lure of mermaids and trolls – folklore performances recount the tales.

FEBRUARY

EUROPE

Fête du Citron, Menton, France
After the Carnival of Nice, the biggest event on the Riviera is the spectacular Menton Citrus Festival. Over 150 tons of lemons, limes and oranges are displayed as magnificent creations – from smiling Buddhas to marauding dinosaurs – on parades of gargantuan floats. *www.feteducitron.com*

Rye Bay Scallop Week, East Sussex, UK
The Cinque Port of Rye yields some of the finest scallops in the country and this festival combines award-winning wines with music and eight days of events, from scallop-cutting, preparing, cooking and tasting to the wheelbarrow-pushing "What a Load of Scallops" race. *www.ryebayscallops.co.uk*

Fiera del Cioccolato, Florence, Italy
The premier artisan chocolatiers of Tuscany come together once a year in Florence's historic and beautiful Piazza della Croce to display their skills and their wares. Visitors can watch these masters of their art at work and, of course, sample some of the finest chocolate creations in the world.

Brez'n Angeln, Oberammergau, Germany
Oberammergau is famed for spiritual sustenance in its Passion Play, but for food of a more earthly kind, it goes "Pretzel Fishing". Townsfolk in traditional dress, accompanied by a marching band, tour the town in a horse-drawn cart from which fresh-baked pretzels are dangled on rods and lines. Everyone has to jump like fishes to snatch a savoury treat.

THE MIDDLE EAST AND AFRICA

Prickly Pear Festival, Port Elizabeth, South Africa
Strangely, on South Africa's famous Garden Route, they make a big fuss about a little fruit once considered an "alien undesirable". So much so that 16 tons of prickly pears are processed for the festival – into preserves, chutneys, sweets and *witblits*, a fiery spirit that is only legally distilled right here.

ASIA AND AUSTRALASIA

Setsubun, Japan

On the last day of winter, people flock to Buddhist temples and Shinto shrines to throw roasted soybeans and chant "Demons out, happiness in". It's considered lucky to catch and eat as many beans as your age. These events are supported by entertainers, celebrities and sumo wrestlers.

Marlborough Wine Festival, New Zealand

The lovely Marlborough wine region of South Island is the largest in New Zealand, and was pivotal in introducing New World Sauvignon Blanc to a grateful Old World. Enjoy tastings and tutorials amid the vines of beautiful Brancott Estate. *www.wine-marlborough-festival.co.nz*

NORTH AMERICA

Feria del Alegría y el Olivo, Santiago Tulyehualco, Mexico City, Mexico

The sacred Aztec amaranth grain and the Spanish-introduced olive sit side by side in a festival that blends ancient culture with modern ideas. Visitors flock to this historic quarter of the city to taste olives and their oils, munch amaranth cakes and cookies, and watch displays of traditional dance and music.

Portland Seafood and Wine Festival, Oregon, USA

The finest Oregon seafood can be found at this family-oriented event, including lobster, crayfish and the famous Dungeness crab. There's also an Oyster Shuck & Swallow Contest, a Celebrity Crab Cracking Contest, cooking demonstrations and live music. Adults can sample from 50 local wines while the kids enjoy puppet shows and building sandcastles. *www.pdxseafoodandwinefestival.com*

SOUTH AMERICA

Pisco Sour Day, Lima, Peru

Some say that the pisco sour is as Peruvian as Machu Picchu. Those inclined to agree will lift a glass in Lima on the first Saturday in February and join in the celebrations for this pisco brandy, lime, egg white and sugar cocktail, with bartender contests, music and feasts of traditional Peruvian cuisine.

MARCH

EUROPE

Carnevale di Ivrea, Piedmont, Italy

Imagine thousands of brightly costumed combatants pelting each other with oranges, some in horse-drawn carts, others milling around them in the streets, up to their shins in citrus pulp. Or go to Ivrea on Shrove Tuesday and join in the fun. Huge pots of beans and sausages, cod and polenta are all served free. Magnificent.

Beer Day, Reykjavík, Iceland

Prohibition in the USA lasted 13 years; in Hungary it was only 133 days; but in Iceland beer was banned for 74 years, until 1 March 1989. Not surprisingly, that day became National Beer Day and is celebrated in style in pubs, clubs and restaurants across the party town of Reykjavík.

Maslenitsa, Russia

Maslenitsa is a lively week-long festival that blends the pagan farewell to winter with the Orthodox preparation for Lent. The focus of the feast is the blini, a Russian pancake, round and golden like the sun, topped with soured cream, smoked salmon, honey or caviar and washed down with vodka.

THE MIDDLE EAST AND AFRICA

Lamberts Bay Kreeffees, South Africa

Kreeffees is Afrikaans for "crayfish feast", and crayfish are in abundance at this festival in beautiful Lamberts Bay in the Western Cape. Match your tastings with a glass of Graça, South Africa's best-selling seafood wine, while watching stunning aerial displays and listening to live music. For the more energetic there is bungy-jumping and even a half-marathon. *www.kreeffees.com*

ASIA AND AUSTRALASIA

Melbourne Food & Wine Festival, Australia

Possibly the largest extravaganza of its kind, this event boasts more than 250 gastronomic and wine events over ten days, including "The World's Longest Lunch" and masterclasses from international chefs with more Michelin stars than you can shake a stick at. *www.melbournefoodandwine.com.au*

Wildfoods Festival, Hokitika, New Zealand

Judging by the crowds that flock here every year, it seems that everyone wants to try such delicacies as wasp larvae ice cream, huhu grubs and beer-battered beetles. There's whitebait, venison sausages and the like for the less adventurous, and a wide range of entertainment. Fancy dress is positively encouraged. *www.wildfoods.co.nz*

NORTH AMERICA

Vermont Maple Open House, USA

"Sugar-on-Snow" – the pouring of boiling maple syrup on to a fresh snowfall to make taffy – is just the icing on the cake of this special weekend, when the region's "sugarhouses" open their doors for demonstrations, events and tastings. *www.vermontmaple.org/events.php*

Yuma Lettuce Days, Arizona, USA

Yuma is the "Winter Lettuce Capital of the World", so it's no surprise that folks here make a bit of a song and dance about all things green and good, with culinary classes, food tastings, microbrew beers and local wines, and fun events such as ice carving and tractor-trailer rides. *www.yumalettucedays.com*

SOUTH AMERICA

Fiesta de la Vendimia, Mendoza, Argentina

As befits the wine capital of Argentina, Mendoza hosts the biggest and most spectacular grape-harvest festival in the land, drawing tens of thousands to the party. They come for horseback gaucho parades, music-and-light shows, firework displays and, of course, delicious, robust local red wine.

From left to right Piping in the haggis at a Burns Night dinner in Edinburgh, Scotland; children throwing beans during Setsubun in Tokyo, Japan; an impressive reconstruction of the Taj Mahal using citrus fruits at the Fête du Citron, Menton, France; the "World's Longest Lunch" at the Melbourne Food & Wine Festival

APRIL

EUROPE

Eel Day, Ely, UK
Ellie the Eel, a giant replica of the slippery fish that gave this Fenland city its name, leads a colourful procession from the 7th-century cathedral to the Jubilee Gardens, where everyone joins in the eel-tasting, beer-swilling, hog-roasting and medieval jollity. There's even an eel-throwing contest – though these days they use socks!

Fiestas del Bollo, Avilés, Spain
On Easter Monday, Avilés' historic town centre pulsates with traditional music, decorated floats, folk dancers and throngs of people in vivid costumes. Rows of tables, hundreds of place-settings long, are covered with a communal feast of mouthwatering Asturian dishes, the focus of which is the *bollo*, a multi-tiered, star-shaped extravaganza of an iced bun.

Fête de la Coquille, Côtes d'Armor, France
Three ancient fishing ports on the Côtes d'Armor take turns to host this celebration of the scallop. Up to 80,000 seafood-lovers come to see the boats unload their day's catch, watch the waterside auctions and sample Brittany's legendary *coquilles St Jacques* against a background of Celtic music.

THE MIDDLE EAST AND AFRICA

Ikeji, Arondizuogu, Nigeria
Ikeji isn't just a yam festival, it's a centuries-old veneration of the Aro tribal culture. The yam isn't just a vegetable either: it is revered as the very essence of the Aro economy and way of life. As revellers enjoy a sumptuous feast, masked gods dance amongst them, dispelling evil spirits to the delirious rhythms of traditional drums, bells and flutes.

Prince Albert Olive Festival, South Africa
High in the Swartbergs in the Western Cape, on the edge of the Great Karoo, the climate is perfect for growing olives. Village farms offer tastings of fresh and marinated olives and their oils, Karoo lamb stews, award-winning cheeses and delicious local wines. Fire-dancers, folk music, fun runs, stargazing, ghost walks and even a pit-spitting contest make this a great family experience. *www.patourism.co.za*

ASIA AND AUSTRALASIA

Hanshi, Xiamen, China
This festival dates back 2,500 years when, once a year, cooking fires were extinguished and allowed to rest before relighting with new-season firewood. The custom is honoured with cold food feasts of rice porridge, pickled vegetables, fish paste, bamboo shoots, tofu, date cakes and preserved eggs.

World Gourmet Summit, Singapore
Singapore is always a gastronomic paradise, but never more so than in April, when some of the world's most renowned chefs come together to share their secrets with eager gourmets. Events include culinary masterclasses, intimate Chef's Table dinners, tutored tastings and in-depth workshops. Every serious foodie should make the pilgrimage at least once. *www.worldgourmetsummit.com*

NORTH AMERICA

World Grits Festival, St George, South Carolina, USA
It's over 25 years since St George discovered it was the world's biggest consumer of grits – a dish made of coarsely ground corn – and the town hasn't stopped celebrating yet. Tens of thousands join in the fun and games – tossing corn cobs, rolling in vats of gooey grits and chowing down in an all-you-can-eat contest.

Oistins Fish Festival, Barbados
Beautiful Barbados honours its fishermen and celebrates the spectacular harvest of its waters at this Easter event. Visitors can choose from a vast array of seafood and dine in the sunshine or under the stars to a calypso beat. If that's too laid-back, games and competitions include a fish-boning challenge and even a greasy pole contest.

Le Pince d'Or, Grand'Rivière, near Fort-de-France, Martinique
The tiny fishing village of Grand'Rivière brings together the island's French and Caribbean flavours in its Pince d'Or (Golden Pincer) competition, held each Easter Sunday. The aim is to cook the best *matoutou*, a rich crab stew flavoured with lime, cinnamon, chilli and garlic. Join the locals along the palm-fringed riverside for a day of feasting and music.

MAY

EUROPE

Spargelfest, Schwetzingen, Germany
Historic Schwetzingen is Europe's white asparagus capital. At the spring harvest festival this "Royal Vegetable" is sold in the castle square, fresh or cooked in many different recipes. A favourite is with hollandaise sauce and smoked ham, but there's even asparagus ice cream. There are colourful parades, banquets and the triumphant crowning of the festival's Asparagus King or Queen.

Fête des Fromages, Rocamadour, France
One of the most beautiful villages in France hosts the largest cheese festival in the south. It begins with a blessing of the herds of sheep and goats, which are then paraded through the streets, and continues with an outdoor festive lunch, a farmers' market and performances of traditional regional music. Be sure to try Rocamadour's own esteemed Cabécou goat's cheese. *http://fromages.rocamadour.free.fr*

Watercress Festival, Alresford, UK
Mineral-rich spring water is the secret behind Alresford's success as the UK's largest producer of this versatile and delectable superfood. The Watercress King and Queen lead a parade of jazz bands and morris dancers, handing out the new season's watercress to thousands of revellers. There's a huge street market, cooking demonstrations from celebrity chefs and the World Watercress Eating Championship. *www.watercressfestival.org*

European Beer Festival, Copenhagen, Denmark
Probably the best beer festival in the world? Who knows, but brewing giant Carlsberg opens its historic cellars and stables to host this intoxicating extravaganza that offers visitors the opportunity to taste hundreds of Danish and international beers, ales and lagers. The festival is hosted in various venues across the city. Book events early to avoid disappointment.

THE MIDDLE EAST AND AFRICA

South African Cheese Festival, Stellenbosch

This is South Africa's biggest cheese festival, with over 200 palate-tingling varieties and a veritable cornucopia of accompaniments. Meander through the story of milk from the udder to the plate while the kids try their hand at milking, then relax by the waterfront with a tasting plate and unforgettable views of a Table Mountain sunset. www.cheesefestival.co.za

Taam Hair (A Taste of Tel Aviv), Israel

Indulge all of your senses at this explosion of sounds, sights, smells and superb samplings from top Israeli chefs and vintners. Tour the culinary booths and take your pick of the tastes, eat while strolling through Hayarkon Park or sitting on the grass, or simply dance with thousands of partygoers.

ASIA AND AUSTRALASIA

Cheung Chau Bun Festival, Hong Kong

In one of the world's most exciting festivals, residents of Cheung Chau dress in colourful costumes and parade through the streets to commemorate the sea god Pak Tai. At midnight on the last day, teams race up 18-m (60-ft) towers to collect buns, which are then handed out to revellers.

NORTH AMERICA

Castroville Artichoke Festival, Monterey County, California, USA

In 1948, Marilyn Monroe was crowned Castroville's first Artichoke Queen – what finer pedigree could a festival have than that? Try this delicious edible bud fried, pickled, marinated, sautéed, griddled or creamed and sip silky California wines, all in this quaint little town at the heart of artichoke country. www.artichoke-festival.org

Maui Onion Festival, Lahaina, Hawaii, USA

Sweet, juicy Maui onions are prized by chefs and they're the star of the show here at Whaler's Village in a full day and evening of events, including chef demonstrations, a Best Onion Recipe contest, a Raw Onion Eating challenge, island music and fine dining. www.whalersvillage.com/onionfestival.htm

Toledo Cacao-Fest, Belize

True chocoholics should make a pilgrimage to the land where cocoa ripens in the tropical sun, to see it being grown, harvested and processed the traditional, hand-made way into the food of the (Mayan) gods. It's all possible in this idyllic reef-and-rainforest setting, along with a gourmet Wine and Chocolate dinner, cultural events and a spectacular festival finale of music and fireworks.

JUNE

EUROPE

Vlaggetjesdag, Scheveningen, Netherlands

"Flag Day" is named for the bright pennants that flutter from the rigging of the herring boats as they race the first of the new season's catch back to Scheveningen to be auctioned. Thousands line the quay to watch them arrive, listen to sea shanties and, most importantly, eat herrings – pickled, smoked or even raw. www.vlaggetjesdag.com

La Grande Bufala, Eboli, Italy

Everyone agrees that buffalo-milk mozzarella is the best, and Eboli believes its Mozzarella di Bufala Campagna is the best of all. Leafy Piazza della Repubblica is the showcase for everything to do with this unctuously soft and milky cheese, offering tastings, workshops and other events lauding all things deliciously Mediterranean.

Batalla del Vino, Haro, Spain

Every 29 June, the normally sedate town of Haro, in La Rioja, goes wine crazy. Revellers armed with buckets, bottles and even water pistols full of wine launch into pitched battles during which everyone ends up soaking wet and purple from head to toe. It's all good-natured and ends with uproarious feasting and a lot more wine – quaffed, rather than thrown.

THE MIDDLE EAST AND AFRICA

V&A Waterfront Wine Affair, Cape Town, South Africa

Over 70 of the Western Cape's top wineries come together in this gorgeous water's-edge setting. Gourmet food is on hand as well, so visitors can match the perfect Pinotage to charcuterie or grilled ostrich fillet, or sip Sauvignon Blanc with ocean-fresh oysters. No need to fret over which wine route to drive – you can tour them all here in one place.

Feria Oramena, Taolagnaro, Madagascar

Beautiful Fort-Dauphin Bay is the backdrop to this culinary carnival in honour of the delicious and abundant seafood of Madagascar – notably the spiny lobster (oramena), which is the heart of the banquet. Enjoy the best of the fun down on the Esplanade by the Town Hall.

Fête des Goyaviers, La Plaine des Palmistes, Réunion

Perched high on Réunion's lush slopes, La Plaine des Palmistes may be the smallest community but it has the biggest presence during this island-wide celebration of the fragrant and versatile guava. It's a lively time of tastings, music, dance and stories, and it's almost impossible to come away without at least one pot of delicious guava jam.

ASIA AND AUSTRALASIA

Chanthaburi Fruit Festival, Thailand

An exotic and mouthwatering celebration of "the fruit bowl of Thailand". Pluck rambutan, mangosteen and longan fresh from the trees. Taste the ripest mangos, zalaccas and custard apples and savour the "king of fruits", the soft and creamy durian. Parades of multicoloured fruit floats, regional music and beauty pageants are all part of the experience.

A Taste of Manly, Sydney, Australia

Manly was once described as "seven miles from Sydney and a thousand miles from care". With stalls serving high-quality Australian, Indian, Malaysian, Thai, African and Mediterranean cuisine, supported by popular New South Wales wines, this seaside festival attracts over 30,000 visitors, with world music, jazz, street performers and beach games for all the family.

NORTH AMERICA

Taste of Chicago, Illinois, USA

Lovely lakeside Grant Park is the venue for the "World's Biggest Food Festival", a ten-day event that takes place in the run-up to Independence Day. All the city's top restaurants are represented, offering "taster" plates so that the 3-million-plus visitors can try as many dishes as possible, from classic Chicago deep-pan pizza to iconic Eli's cheesecake.

Arcata Main Street Oyster Festival, California, USA

Arcata Bay, a stunning, almost landlocked circle of blue water in northwest California, provides 70 percent of the state's oysters. The citizens of Arcata are proud of their tasty molluscs and love to show them off at this friendly festival, when local chefs serve them every which way, from raw to barbecued, and fearless gourmets compete in the "Shuck and Swallow" contest. www.oysterfestival.net

From left to right Crowds armed with "wine-pistols" at La Batalla del Vino in Haro, Spain; contestants scramble for buns up an 18-m (60-ft) tower at the Cheung Chau Bun Festival in Hong Kong; pavements are taken over by hundreds of food stalls at the Taste of Chicago food festival; bunting decorates stalls preparing and selling herring during Vlaggetjesdag in the Netherlands

OCTOBER

EUROPE

Fiera del Tartufo, Alba, Italy

Historic Alba's White Truffle Festival is an unforgettable experience for lovers of the "white diamond", with its truffle fair, market and (for top chefs and gourmet millionaires only) auction. Many of Alba's restaurants have special menus, or will simply shave the truffle over risotto or pasta – perfect with a glass or two of delicious Barolo wine. *www.fieradeltartufo.org*

Fiesta de Exaltación del Marisco, O Grove, Spain

Over ten days of seafood heaven, the small fishing community of O Grove becomes an aromatic market teeming with mussels, oysters, scallops, crabs, clams, octopus, hake, sea bass, turbot and sole. Sample them, fresh or cooked, with a glass of the local Rías Baixas wine, while enjoying Galician-Portuguese folk dancing and Celtic *gaita* bagpipes.

Fête des Vendanges de Montmartre, Paris, France

In 1933, the citizens of Montmartre resurrected a tiny vineyard only streets away from Sacré-Coeur. Ever since, they've rejoiced in the harvest and auctioned the wine off for charity. The festival is now so popular that hundreds of thousands of celebrants fill the streets to revel in the vintners' parades, live music, theatre and poetry, and buy wines from all over France.

Salone del Gusto, Turin, Italy

Showcase of the Slow Food Movement, the biennial Salon of Taste attracts exhibitors from around the world. Seasonality, locale and quality are essential criteria for the cured meats, fish, vegetables, cheeses, fruits and breads on display here. *www.salonedelgusto.it*

THE MIDDLE EAST AND AFRICA

Fête des Dattes, Erfoud, Morocco

With nearly a million date palms to harvest, it's not surprising that the people of Erfoud celebrate the year's harvest with such zeal. For three days they feast and dance to traditional music; then comes the climax, a thrilling camel race into the dunes of the Sahara. A definite date for the diary.

ASIA AND AUSTRALASIA

Crave Sydney, Australia

With a whole month of over 600 diverse gastronomic events across the city, Sydney is the place to be in October, with gourmet dinners, night noodle markets, pop-up barbecues and bush tucker experiences. But the showpiece is Breakfast on the Bridge, when the traffic stops and the Harbour Bridge is grassed over for a grand picnic. *www.cravesydney.com*

Phuket Vegetarian Festival, Thailand

In this extraordinary but energetic and colourful festival, participants abstain from meat and other stimulants to expunge evil spirits and bring good luck. Vegetarian dishes are eaten but not everyone will have the stomach for the fire-walking and outlandish body piercing displays by entranced Ma Song devotees. *www.phuketvegetarian.com*

NORTH AMERICA

American Royal Barbecue, Kansas City, USA

Claiming to be the largest barbecue competition in the world, the American Royal attracts hundreds of tongs-bearing, apron-wearing, grill-firing teams from across the USA. To the rhythms of live bands they cook brisket, pork ribs, pork and chicken for the title, with a sauce competition as a bonus. Most important, though, it's all tasteable. *www.arbbq.com*

World Championship Gumbo Cook-Off, New Iberia, Louisiana, USA

On the banks of the Bayou Teche, picturesque Bouligny Plaza is filled with makeshift kitchens and tantalizing aromas waft into the sultry air. Saturday begins with traditional jambalaya, *étouffée*, boudin and fried fish, then on Sunday the great Cook-Off gets under way. Around 5,500 kg (12,000 lb) of chicken and sausage, seafood, game and even alligator gumbo make this a truly jumbo event.

New York City Wine and Food Festival, USA

To get an idea of the pace, excitement and ground covered in this crammed foodie weekend, think "New York Marathon meets Woodstock meets Iron Chef". From meatballs to masterchefs, fizzy drinks to finest New World wines, Blumenthal to Bourdain, there is something for everyone of every age. Book early. *www.nycwineandfoodfestival.com*

SOUTH AMERICA

Oktoberfest, Blumenau, Brazil

Founded in 1850 by Herman Otto Blumenau, his namesake city is a mini-Germany in the south of Brazil, but there's nothing small about their Oktoberfest. Over two weeks, a million party-lovers crowd the streets for the brightly costumed parades, marching bands, folk dancing, authentic German cuisine and, of course, the local brews.

NOVEMBER

EUROPE

Les Trois Glorieuses, Beaune, France

It's been called "the greatest eating and drinking experience on the face of the planet", and certainly the Three Glorious Days, centred on Burgundy's famed charity wine auction, live up to their name. Tickets for Monday's eight-hour lunch at Château Meursault are beyond the reach of most, but everyone can enjoy the open-house tastings and the festive atmosphere that pervades noble Beaune and its vineyard villages.

Olioliva, Imperia, Liguria, Italy

Liguria's tiny purple Taggiasca olive is said to produce the finest olive oil in the world – mellow, woody, peppery and utterly delicious. Imperia welcomes the new season's oil with a huge street market, and visitors from all over northern Italy and nearby Provence come to sample and buy – not just oils but Liguria's famed pesto, focaccia and Cinque Terre wines too.

Ziebel Märit, Bern, Switzerland

Bern's medieval Onion Market begins as you would expect. Hundreds of stalls are laden with every kind of allium – plaited, bouqueted, decorated and turned into all sorts of tasty onion-flavoured produce, as well as lots of other hearty

winter food. Later, though, the carnival kicks off, with jesters, singers, onion-costumed locals and wild confetti battles long into the winter's night.

ASIA AND AUSTRALASIA

Guangzhou International Food Festival, China

Guangzhou is rightly proud of being said to have the best food in all of China. People flock from nearby Hong Kong and Macau to dine here, and never more so than during this annual exhibition of its culinary prowess. Lots of different cuisines are on display, but don't miss the Cantonese delicacies on offer.

Nabanna, Dhaka, Bangladesh

The name Nabanna means "new food" and, in the Bangladeshi countryside, it's one of the most important events of the year. The rice harvest is celebrated with symbolic foods such as *payesh* (rice pudding) and *pitha* (rice flour cakes), as well as traditional music and dances, and offerings to the Hindu goddess of wealth, Lakshmi.

NORTH AMERICA

Kona Coffee Festival, Big Island, Hawaii, USA

Wake up and smell the coffee at Hawaii's oldest food festival. It's the rich volcanic soil that's said to give this pure arabica its rare depth of flavour and aroma, prized by connoisseurs the world over. No wonder the people of the Kona district choose to honour it with pageants, parades, competitions, cultural events and plantation tastings. *www.konacoffeefest.com*

Chitlin' Strut, Salley, South Carolina, USA

Some say that, for a true taste of the south, nothing quite beats a chitlin'. Others prefer the fried chicken or barbecued ribs to deep-fried pig's intestines, but everyone's in agreement that a great time is to be had at the Salley Chitlin' Strut, with parades, a pancake breakfast, carnival rides, dancing and the great Hawg Call competition. *www.chitlinstrut.com*

Festival Gourmet International, Puerto Vallarta, Riviera Nayarit, Mexico

Drawing culinary superstars from around the world to host events such as Chef's Table and Winemaker's Night dinners, Gourmet Safaris and even a Chefs' Hell Raising Party, it's not difficult to see why this festival on Mexico's Pacific Riviera has made its mark. *www.festivalgourmet.com*

Cornucopia, Whistler, British Columbia, Canada

With snow already thick on the slopes, it's hard to imagine anyone is in town for anything else. But now's the time that serious foodies make a pilgrimage to Whistler for one of the most exciting and informative gastronomic events of the year – this is a wining and dining experience to beat any off-piste adventure. *www.whistlercornucopia.com*

DECEMBER

EUROPE

Les Glorieuses de Bresse, France

With its red comb, white body and blue legs, the Bresse chicken is the *tricouleur* emblem of France – and rightly so, since it is often judged the finest poultry in the land. Four towns in this Burgundian region each host a day of this fête in its honour, with gourmet markets, tastings, culinary demonstrations and dinners at which the *coq* is king. *www.glorieusesdebresse.com*

Sagra del Singhiale, Suvereto, Italy

The narrow streets, squares and cloisters of this ancient Tuscan town take on a medieval flavour for the Wild Boar Festival. Pageants, archery, fencing, jesters and even human chess games all contribute to the magical atmosphere. The focus of the feasting is, of course, roast wild boar, served with grilled polenta and wild mushrooms and plenty of local wine.

Christkindlesmarkt, Nuremberg, Germany

The Christmas Angel opens Nuremberg's magical olde-worlde market, when the city square sparkles and the air is filled with the delicious aromas of mulled wine, hot chestnuts, roast sausages, gingerbread, fruit loaves and marzipan sweets. Hundreds of decorated stalls form a "Little Town of Wood and Cloth". *www.christkindlesmarkt.de*

Fiera dia Castagna, Bocognano, Corsica, France

Corsicans call the chestnut the "tree of life" and its flour is used in bread, polenta, cakes and even beer. Chestnut jam, honey and liqueurs are highly prized, as is charcuterie from the local boar that feed on the nuts. As the island's most important crop it truly deserves this annual celebration, which involves competitions, demonstrations and market stalls piled high with chestnut produce.

THE MIDDLE EAST AND AFRICA

Franschhoek Cap Classique and Champagne Festival, South Africa

With a French heritage going back over 300 years, Franschhoek is understandably proud of its reputation as the gourmet capital of South Africa. Set in "the most beautiful wine valley in the world", it celebrates its good fortune, presenting its own Cap Classique bubbly alongside the great names of Champagne. Mouthwatering French delicacies are served to complement the wine. *www.franschhoek.org.za*

ASIA AND AUSTRALASIA

Taste Festival, Hobart, Tasmania, Australia

Charming Sullivan's Cove, in Tasmania's capital city, plays host to ten days of feasts and fun, culminating on New Year's Eve with a grand firework display over the tranquil harbour waters. Circus acts, buskers, stilt-walkers and street theatre entertain the kids, while the grown-ups can enjoy artisan beers, fine Tasmanian wines and Tasting Tours of local gourmet cuisine.

NORTH AMERICA

Night of the Radishes, Oaxaca, Mexico

Leave radishes in the ground for months until they grow up to two feet long. Then dig them up and carve them into fantastic sculptures of Nativity scenes, dancers, warriors, folk heroes, trees and buildings. Sounds crazy, but that's what happens at this extraordinary one-of-a-kind Christmas festival in Oaxaca.

Inn-to-Inn Cookie and Candy Tour, White Mountains, New Hampshire, USA

What better way to get into the holiday spirit than to make a snowy tour around the quaint inns of New Hampshire, all decked out in their Christmas finery? Visitors are welcomed with handmade cookies, candy canes and other festive treats, and can vote on stunning gingerbread sculptures, collect family recipes and depart with visions of sugarplums to last a lifetime.

SOUTH AMERICA

Santuranticuy, Cusco, Peru

Plaza del Armas becomes a vast, illuminated Nativity scene in the days before Christmas Eve's breathtaking Santuranticuy ("saints for sale") market. Country people flock into town with ceramic manger figures to sell, including the Andean baby Jesus, El Niño Manuelito. There's sweet rum punch, roast corn and *panetón* cake for those who can afford it, while hot chocolate and fruited biscuits are given to the poor.

From left to right Blessing food at the Phuket Vegetarian Festival in October; stalls lit up at night during Christkindlesmarkt, in Nuremburg's central square; singers and dancers perform in traditional dress at the Fête des Dattes in Erfoud, Morocco; a craftsman displays figures carved from radishes during Mexico's Night of the Radishes celebrations in December

Acknowledgments

The publishers would like to thank the following for their text contributions:

Rudolf Abraham (pp40–1, 164–5, 178–9); **Joshua Armstrong** (pp212–5, 238–9); **Brett Atkinson** (pp240–3); **Maryanne Blacker** (pp 14–15, 34–5, 48–9, 58–9, 72–3, 88–9, 98–101, 114–5, 128–9, 142–3, 154–5, 216–7, 306–7); **Michael Booth** (pp196–7, 208–9, 218–9, 234–5, 246–7); **Jonathan Bousfield** (pp56–7, 108–9); **James Brennan** (pp172–3, 176–7); **Philip Briggs** (pp 166–7, 170–1, 182–3); **Jules Brown** (pp12–13, 42–3, 46–7, 84–7, 104–5, 126–7); **Joe Cummings** (pp244–5, 252–3); **Donna Dailey** (pp260–1, 272–283, 288–91, 296–7, 318–9); **Nick Edwards** (pp192–3, 210–1, 228–231, 250–1); **Anna Maria Espsäter** (The Flavours of South America; pp106–7, 116–7, 152–3); **Steve Fallon** (pp120–1); **Fay Franklin** (pp 322–9); **Mike Gerrard** (pp134–5, 150–1, 174–5); **Frances Linzee Gordon** (The Flavours of the Middle East and Africa; pp28–9, 50–3, 110–13, 162–3, 168–9, 180–1, 184–5); **Dominic Hamilton** (pp304–5); **Patricia Harris** and **David Lyon** (The Flavours of Europe; The Flavours of North America; pp18–21, 60–1, 68–71, 82–3, 102–3, 118–9, 136–7, 258–9, 286–7); **Rachel Howard** (pp32–3, 62–3, 140–1); **David Leffman** (The Flavours of Asia and Australasia; pp190–1, 198–9, 200–7, 220–3, 248–9); **Sarina Lewis** (pp194–5, 232–3); **Gail Mangold-Vine** (pp 44–5, 138–9); **Anthony Mason** (pp78–9, 96–7, 144–5); **Declan McGarvey** (pp 308–11, 314–5); **Norman Miller** (pp22–3, 124–5); **Jenny Myddleton** (pp262–3, 284–5); **Gillian Price** (pp16–17, 30–1, 54–5, 66–7, 80–81, 90–91, 122–3, 146–9, 156–7); **Dan Richardson** (pp74–5, 94–5); **Alex Robinson** (pp302–3, 312–3, 320–1); **Annelise Sorensen** (pp264–9, 292–3); **Christian Williams** (pp26–7, 36–9, 64–5, 76–7, 93–3, 130–3); **Dan White** (pp224–5, 236–7); **Matt Willis** (pp24–5); **Sarah Woods** (pp270–1, 294–5, 316–7) and **Martin Zatko** (pp226–7).

General introduction by **Patricia Harris** and **David Lyon**: www.hungrytravelers.com

Dorling Kindersley would also like to thank Douglas Amrine, Georgina Small, Alexandra Whittleton, Louise Dick, Shahid Mahmood, Chloe Roberts, Rose-Innes Designs and Kevin Gould for their part in the making of this book.

Cobaltid would like to thank Ellen Root and Marta Bescos for assistance with picture research, Hilary Bird for the index and Kati Dye for proofreading.

Picture Credits

The publishers would like to thank the following for their kind permission to reproduce their photographs:

(Key: a–above; b–below/bottom; c–centre; f–far; l–left; r–right; t–top)

Rudolf Abraham: 41tr, 165br.
Alamy Images: AA World Travel Library 120br; Hank Abernathy 258t; AllOver photography 56t; B.A.E. Inc. 1c; Pat Behnke 96t; Jeffrey Blackler 6b; Sam Bloomberg–Rissman 69br; Bluemagenta 272br; Bohi 196–197t; Bon Appetit 51br, 53t, 72tr, 95tr, 127bl, 142tr, 148c, 262bl, 280bl, 305tr; Terry Bruce 165tr; JS Callahan/Tropicalpix 327br; Franck Camhi 312t; Wendy Connett 189r, 212–213t, 226t, 246b; Dennis Cox 290br; CuboImages srl 111tr; Yaacov Dagan 310b; Jean–Dominique Dallet 112b; DBimages 112t, 118bl, 179tr, 266b, 270–271c; DC Premiumstock 65br; Danita Delimont 66t, 66cl; Gary Doak 322bl; Peter Eastland 18–19c; Susie M. Eising 16bl; EuroCreon Co.Ltd. 227br; Eye Ubiquitous 300r; F1online Digitale Bildagentur GmbH 73b; Kevin Foy 7b; Stephen French 133b; Gastromedia 27bl, 83bl, 105bl; Simon Hadley 42tl; David Hancock 241tr; Glenn Harper 58bl; Gavin Hellier 254–255c, 286–287b; Tim Hill 118tr, 167br, 182cl, 224l, 275tl; Hornbil Images 210–211c; Peter Horree 51tr; Ilianski 24br; Imagebroker 38t, 252–253t, 262t; IMAGEMORE Co. Ltd. 191br; Islemount Images 193br; Itanistock 177bl; Jan Smith Photography 135cr; Graham Jepson 275bl; John Warburton–Lee Photography 249br; Jon Arnold Images Ltd 15t, 29tr, 29cr, 288–289b; Tarek el Juan 31br; Paul Kingsley 52b, 328bl; Oliver Knight 78bl; Yadid Levy 20bl, 175tr, 175br, 303br; Lightworks Media 214c; Lonely Planet Images 33tr; David Lyons 84–85c, 277br; Marka 317br; Martin Thomas Photography 36–37clb; Iain Masterton 132b; Tony McNicol 209bl; Mikecranephotography.com 208–209t; Bildarchiv Monheim GmbH 92–93b; Eric Nathan 86b; Michael Neelon 286t; Niceartphoto 323bl; David Parker 200–201b, 218tr; Patrick/Sagaphoto.com 68–69bc; PCL 199b; Pegaz 120–121tc; PjrTravel 77br, 137br; Plinthpics 325br; Vova Pomortzeff 27br; Prisma Bildagentur AG 117b; Simon Reddy 47br, 113t, 139bl, 229br, 238tr, 253bl; Robert Harding Picture Library Ltd 329bl; Robert Preston Photography 178–179c; Roger Cracknell 01/Classic 22br; Pep Roig 230tr; Margaret S 182t; Pere Sanz 34–35c; Andre Seale 312–313b; Alex Segre 20tr; Neil Setchfield 75crb, 204r; Slick Shoots 87c; Michael Sparrow 315cr; Stock Italia 91bl; Stockfood Ltd 106cl, 170tr, 216cl; Jochen Tack 83br; Terry Harris Just Greece Photo Library 141tr; Domenico Tondini 184bl; Mikael Utterström 116t; Vario Images 306–307t; Michael Ventura 290tr; David Wall 242c; Graham Watts 70tr; Maximilian Weinzierl 146cr; Ken Welsh 19br, 106t; George Wilson 326bl; Gregory Wrona 21bl, 25l; Brian Yarvin 279br.
Antica Focacceria San Francesco: 149b.
Bettys of Harrogate: 85tr, 85br, 86t.
Blue Pepper Restaurant: 125br.
Austin Bush: 212–213bl.
Choco–Story: 145tr.
Corbis: Peter Adams 10l, 167bl, 281bl; Piyal Adhikary 231bl; Alan Schein Photography 293bl; Abel Alonso 324bl; H.Amiard/Photocuisine 146–147cb; Arcaid 292bl; Art Bank 209br; Yann Arthus–Bertrand 32–33c; Astock 326br; Atlantide Phototravel 11r, 12–13t, 122b, 188l; Olga Rosario Avendano 329br; Youssef Badawi/epa 161r; Denis Balibouse 44tr; Morton Beebe 129tr; Neil Beer 71cl; Yannis Behrakis 141cr; Remi Benali 198bl; Bilic 48l; Blend Images/Inti St Clair 7b; Christophe Boisvieux 35crb; Massimo Borchi 16t; J Boyer 48tr, 78t ; Demetrio Carrasco 30bc; Roderick Chen 168l; Li Xu Cheng 207br; Romain Cintract 60b; David Clapp 82–83c; Jerry Cooke 101t; Pablo Corral V 304–305c; Creativ Studio Heinemann 74l, 107tl, 117tl, 239tl, 284bl; Richard Cummins 272–273t; Fridmar Damm 76b; Pascal Deloche/Godong 214t; P.Desgrieux 203bl; Nacho Doce 105br; Nacho Doce/Reuters 13bl, 13br; M.Duffas 155br; Envision 278–279t, 289br; Robert Essel 234–235t; Macduff Everton 244br, 315tr; Neil Farrin/JAI 241br; Fleurent 283br; Owen Franken 10r, 54crb, 81cr, 100b, 115br, 243b, 310c; Stuart Freedman/In Pictures 146–147tc; Franz–Marc Frei 101b, 131br; Marc Garanger 95br; J.Garcia 80l; J.Garcia/Photocuisine 181tl; Bertrand Gardel 102tr; Sean Gardner 283tr; Hen Gongzheng/XinHua/Xinhua Press 185b; Philip Gould 74–75c, 256r; Tim Graham 100c, 216t; Darren Greenwood 274tr; Justin Guariglia 215b; Gyro Photography 235br; Paul Hardy 58t; Blaine Harrington III 6–7b; 196r, 246t; Martin Harvey 12l, 229tr; Chris Helgren 123br; Gavin Hellier 98–99c, 99br, 176–177tc, 180t; Jon Hicks 129br, 231tl, 232t, 232–233b, 235bl, 250b; Olivier Hoslet 128–129c; Dave G. Houser 4t, 131tr, 267b; Xie Guang Hui/Redlink 190–191t; Image Source 245tr; Janet Jarman 285bl; Wolfgang Kaehler 271tr, 280t, 305cr; Layne Kennedy 295bl; Kham/Reuters 239br; Reinhard Krause 206tr; Bob Krist 38b, 39t, 161l, 166–167tc, 296t; Kamil Krzaczynski 325bl; Zurab Kurtsikidze 41br; Last Refuge 316t; Last Refuge/Robert Harding World Imagery 134–135c; Graham Lawrence/Robert Harding World Imagery 94–95c; Lester Lefkowitz 297bl; Danny Lehman 257l, 298–299c, 302b, 320–321t, 321br; Jean–Pierre Lescourret 142b; Leser/SoFood 89br; Yadid Levy 52t; Barry Lewis/In Pictures 11l; James Leynse 292t; Lisa Linder 204tr; Xiaoyang Liu 220–221b; Eduardo Longoni 308–309c; Steve Lupton 220l, 266c; Lo Mak/Redlink 226bl; Mascarucci 148b; René Mattes 274cr; Stephanie Maze 291bl; Colin McPherson 23bl; A.Muriot 102br; Michael Nicholson 172–173tc; Morteza Nikoubazl 179br; Kazuyoshi Nomachi 164–165c; Richard T. Nowitz 197l; Ocean 23tl, 109tr, 260tr, 270l, 306l; Pilar Olivares 307br; Othk 200–201tc; Owaki/Kulla 282–283c; Douglas Pearson 22t, 39b, 152tl, 294–295t; Clay Perry 279bl; Photolibrary 126b; Radius Images 163br, 195b; Jose Fuste Raga 17bl, 138–139t, 216–217b, 236t, 327bl; Steve Raymer/National Geographic Society 263bl; Redlink 220t; Carmen Redondo 67br; Michael Reynolds 191bl; Jose Manuel Ribeiro 126tr; Riou 307bl; J.Riou 71tl; Riou/photocuisine 45br; Riou/SoFood 34l, 321bl; Riviere 169cr; Robert Holmes 269bl; Martin Roe/Retna Ltd. 266t; Rosenfeld 97l; Guenter Rossenbach 62–63c, 64b; Hans Georg Roth 56–57b; Roulier/Turiot 19tr, 35cra; Pablo Sanchez 61br; Michel Setboun 309tr; Hugh Sitton 309br; SoFood 81tr, 281l; Sylvain Sonnet 55cl, 72b; Brigitte Sporrer 122tr; Sprint 108l; Inti St Clair/Blend Images 7b; Klaus Stemmler 174l; Hans Strand 14–15c; Studio Eye 88l, 202tr; Keren Su 124–125tc; Jim Sugar 181br; David Sutherland 184t; Murat Taner 50–51c, 261br; Luca Tettoni 244t, 245br, 247br; Nico Tondini 312l; Onne van der Wal 314–315c; Niels van Gijn 170b; Jose Manuel VidaLepa 119br; Steven Vidler/Eurasia Press 2–3c; Westend61 130l; Nik Wheeler 155tr, 202br; Peter M. Wilson 46–47c, 284t; Michael S. Yamashita 301r; Bobby Yip 248–249t; Bo Zaunders 63tr, 256l.
Dorling Kindersley: 17tl, 28l, 32l, 33cr, 59l, 61l, 62l, 84l, 98l, 114l, 119l, 134tl, 150l, 153l, 162tl, 173br, 222l, 225tl, 259l, 261l, 287t, 293l, 313tl, 314l; Roger Dixon 18l, 40l, 54l, 127l, 278l, 282l, 308l, 319l; Philip Dowell 46l, 82l, 143l, 185tl, 248l; Andrew Downes 243t; Ben Fink 128l; John Freeman 317tl; Jill Fromer/iStock Exclusive © Getty 164l; Will Heap 93tl, 94l, 204l, 277l, 320l; John Heseltine 67tl; Dinesh Khanna 210l; Dave King 14l, 49l, 73tl, 166l, 178l, 183tl, 240l, 297l; David Murray 137l, 157cr, 247tl; David Murray and Jules Selmes 138l; Ian O'Leary 31tl, 77tl, 90l, 102l, 124l, 146tl, 195tl, 207l, 217tl, 221l, 227tl, 234l, 294l; Roger Phillips 303tl; Rob Reichenfeld 202cr; Tim Ridley 43tl; Russell Sadur 110l; Helena Smith 242t; Simon Smith 140l, 193tr; Clive Streeter 63cr, 196l, 199t; Lorenzo Vecchia 171tl, 208l, 228l, 263tl, 285l, 304tl; Chris Villano 50l, 172l; Colin Walton 163tl; Linda Whitwam 140–141c.
Getty Images: 28–29c, 68–69c, 108–109c, 242b, 318t, 324br, 328br; A485 290cr; Peter Adams 110–111c, 162b, 228–229c, 240–241c; AFP 54–55t, 113b, 177br, 189l, 206b, 223br, 300l, 322br, 323br; Sang An 76tl; Bill Arce 53b; Klaus Arras 223bl, 232c; James Baigrie 125bl; Scott E Barbour 103l; Santiago Barrio 60tr; Meike Bergmann 269br; J Boyer 143br; Austin Bush 215t; Rosemary Calvert 68l; Car Culture 257r; Stephen Caraccio 42l; Clive Champion – Champion Photography Ltd 21tl; Michael Coyne 5r; Creativ Studio Heinemann 65tl, 154l; Creative Crop 24l; Sebastian D'Souza/Stringer 192b; De Agostini 40–41c, 79bl; Bruno De Hogues 238b; Dea/M. Borchi 152b; Stuart Dee 59bl; Karen Desjardin 154–155c; Joseph Devenney 5l; Digital Vision 13br; Allison Dinner 180br; Dinodia Photos 211br; Jessica Dixon 274br; Shaun Egan 144–145c; Luzia Ellert 26l; Anel Fernandez 136br; Dennis Flaherty 268–269t; Foodcollection 30tr, 38c, 57tl, 157br, 212l, 296bl, 311b; FoodPhotography Eising 258l; Foodpicto 56cl; Franz Marc Frei 130–131c; Lee Frost 171br; Eric Futran 310t; Gentl and Hyers 15c; Dennis Gottlieb 249bl; Tim Graham 87t; Sylvain Grandadam 198t; Jorg Greuel 36–37t; Andrew Gunners 301l; Gyro Photography/amanaimagesRF 200l; Tim Hall 224t; Martin Harvey 5c; Will Heap 237tl; Katja Heinemann 271cr; Gavin Hellier 111br, 158–159c; Peter Hendrie 222–223tc; Chris Hepburn 169tr; Jon Hicks 188r; Hiroshi Higuchi 92t; Andrew Holt 150–151c; Enamul Hoque 251tl; Simeone Huber 114–115c; Hisham Ibrahim 316br; Image Source 47tr, 115tr; IMAGEMORE Co, Ltd. 219tl; Images of Africa 291tl; Spencer Jones 268l; Jupiterimages 87b, 192tr, 230bl, 318l; Ray Kachatorian 91br; Wolfgang Kaehler 173bl; Jonathan Kantor 288l; Kaveh Kazemi 160r; Wilfried Krecichwost 92cl; Kroeger/Gross 104l; Thomas Larsen 21l; Brian Lawrence 88–89c; Siegfried Layda 70br, 121cl; Brian Leatart 295br; Emma Lee/Life File 44b; Justin Lightley 194bl; Vincenzo Lombardo 147br; Sabine Lubenow 37br; Robin MacDougall 149t; MIB Pictures 52c; Alison Miksch 276tr; MIXA 219br; Camille Moirenc 89tr; Gareth Morgans 151tr; Ippei Naoi 218b; Neo Vision 100t; Karl Newedel 64tr, 231cl; NY Daily News 311t; Panoramic Images 42–43bl, 182–183b; PhotoAlto/Laurence Mouton 252l; Photosindia 250tr; Andrea Pistolesi 112c, 214b; Nicholas Pitt 205l; Paul Poplis 109br; James Randklev 273br; Peter Richardson 139br; Anne Rippy 260b; Lew Robertson 272l; Michael Rosenfeld 233tl; Jeff Rotman 160l; Michael Runkel 213br; Joern Rynio 75tc; Tom Schierlitz 79l; Ralf Schultheiss 132c; Sandro Sciacca 123tl; Paule Seux 211tr; Pankaj Shah 251br; Martin Shields 66bl; Vladimir Shulevsky 120l; Camilla Sjodin 116bl; Slow Images 90–91t, 104–105c; Otto Stadler 224–225b, 253br, 267t; Stefano Stefani 80–81c; Armstrong Studios 286c; Keren Su 174–175c; Jean–Daniel Sudres 99tr; Jane Sweeney 318–319b; Tai Power Seeff 302tr; Murat Taner 48–49b; Tetra Images 288–289t; Teubner 36l, 153br; Tom Till 106–107b; Travelpix Ltd 136t, 203tl; Luca Trovato 156bl; Ellen van Bodegom 156t; Heinrich van den Berg 133t; Guy Vanderelst 96–97b; VisionsofAmerica/Joe Sohm 258–259b; Matthew Wakem 236br; Anna Watson 148t; Brian Yarvin 71bl; H. & D. Zielske 26–27tc.
Glenn Grossman Photography: 276b.
© Le Gruyère AOC: 45tl.
David Hogan Junior: 237br.
Antony Mason: 96l.
Photodisc: felipedupouy.com 190l.
Photolibrary: Fabian von Poser 168–169c.
Rules Restaurant: 151br.
Vasse Felix Vineyard: 194t.
Marek Walisiewicz: 24tr, 135tr.
Zum Wenigemarkt 13: 132t.

Jacket images:
Front: **Alamy Images**: Robert Harding Picture Library Ltd/Michael DeFreitas bl; **Corbis**: National Geographic Society/Karen Kasmauski bc; **Lonely Planet Images**: Anders Blomqvist br; **Photolibrary**: The Travel Library/Paul Hill t.
Back: **Corbis**: Jon Hicks r, Jean–Pierre Lescourret l.
Spine: **Dorling Kindersley**: Suzanne Porter t.

All other images © Dorling Kindersley
For further information see: www.dkimages.com

Ultimate Food Journeys:
Dishes Around Europe

NORWAY

SWEDE

Bergen
Gravadlax
p152

Bohuslan
Smorgasbord
p116

NORTH SEA

DENMARK

Copenhagen
Smørrebred
p106

Edinburgh
Haggis
p22

Whitby
Fish & chips
p42

York
Afternoon tea
p84

REPUBLIC OF IRELAND

North Norfolk
Gastropub food
p134

NETHERLANDS

Amsterdam
Rijsttafel
p124

Berlin
Eisbein
p26

UNITED KINGDOM

Bruges
Chocolate
p144

Brussels
Moules-frites
p78

GERMANY

London
Roast beef
p150

Ghent
Waterzooi
p96

Aachen
Sauerbraten
p92

BELGIUM

LUXEMBOURG

CZECH REPU

Nuremberg
Bratwurst
p130

Paris
Macarons
p58

Strasbourg
Choucroute garnie
p154

Ulm
Spätzle
p76

Munich
Knodel
p64

Brittany
Crêpes
p34

ATLANTIC OCEAN

Loire Valley
Tarte Tatin
p114

Alsace
Tarte Flambée
p72

Zurich
Rösti
p138

Salzburg
Torten
p36

AUSTRIA

Beaune
Boeuf Bourguignon
p14

SWITZERLAND

Gruyères
Cheese fondue
p44

Treviso
Tiramisu
p90

SLOVENIA

FRANCE

Lyon
Lyonnais bouchons
p48

Savoie
Cheese
p98

Milan
Risotto
p30

Kvarner C
Scampi
p66

Liguria
Pesto
p156

Tortellini
Bologna
p146

Nice
Salade Niçoise
p88

Umbria
Truffles
p80

Toulouse
Cassoulet
p142

San Sebastian
Modern Spanish cuisine
p60

Marseille
Bouillabaisse
p128

Rome
Carciofi
p54

ITALY

Porto
Bacalhau
p46

SPAIN

Barcelona
Zarzuela
p102

Naples
Pizza
p16

Capri
Insalata Caprese
p122

PORTUGAL

Madrid
Churros, p68
Cocido, p136

Valencia
Paella
p82

Lisbon
Pasteis de Nata
p12

Evora
Porco à Alentejana
p126

Alicante
Tapas
p18

Algarve
Cataplana
p104

Seville
Gazpacho
p118

Noto
Gelati
p66

ALGERIA

TUNISIA

MEDITER

MOROCCO